KNOWLEDGE ENCYCLOPEDIA

ANIMAL!

DK | Penguin Random House

DK UK:
Senior Editor Jenny Sich
Senior Art Editor Stefan Podhorodecki
Editors Scarlett O'Hara, Rona Skene
Editorial Assistant Vicky Richards
Jacket Design Development Manager Sophia MTT
Jacket Editor Claire Gell
Producer (Pre-Production) Dragana Puvacic
Producer Nancy-Jane Maun
Managing Editor Francesca Baines
Managing Art Editor Philip Letsu
Publisher Andrew Macintyre
Associate Publishing Director Liz Wheeler
Art Director Karen Self
Design Director Philip Ormerod
Publishing Director Jonathan Metcalf

DK India:
Senior Editor Rupa Rao
Senior Art Editor Anjana Nair
Art Editors Amit Varma, Alpana Aditya, Tanvi Sahu
Assistant Editor Charvi Arora
Senior DTP Designers Shanker Prasad, Vishal Bhatia, Harish Aggarwal
DTP Designer Ashok Kumar
Senior Picture Researcher Sumedha Chopra
Illustrator Arun Pottirayil
Jacket Designer Dhirendra Singh
Managing Jackets Editor Saloni Singh
Pre-Production Manager Balwant Singh
Production Manager Pankaj Sharma
Picture Research Manager Taiyaba Khatoon
Managing Editor Kingshuk Ghoshal
Managing Art Editor Govind Mittal

***Animal Science* chapter written by** Tom Jackson, Tim Harris

First published in Great Britain in 2016
by Dorling Kindersley Limited,
80 Strand, London WC2R 0RL

A Penguin Random House Company

10 9 8 7 6
022 – 282998 – October/2016

A CIP catalogue record for this book is available from the British Library.

ISBN: 978-0-2412-2841-8

Printed and bound in China

A WORLD OF IDEAS:
SEE ALL THERE IS TO KNOW

www.dk.com

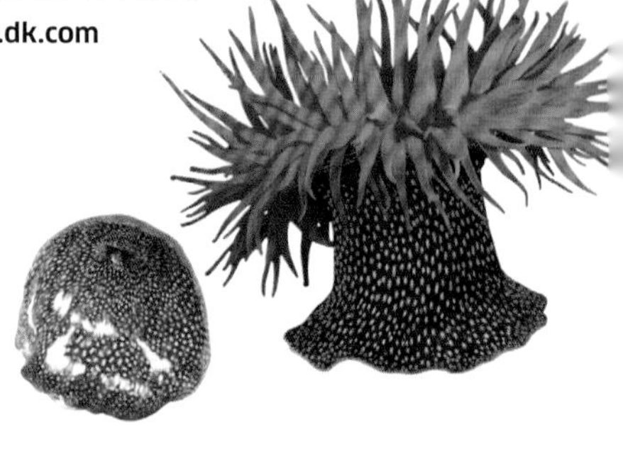

KNOWLEDGE ENCYCLOPEDIA

ANIMAL!

Written by John Woodward
Consultant Dr Kim Dennis-Bryan

Illustrators Val @ Advocate-Art, Andrew Beckett @ Illustration Ltd, Adam Benton, Peter Bull, Dynamo Ltd, Andrew Kerr, Jon @ KJA, Arran Lewis, Peter Minister, Stuart Jackson-Carter – SJC Illustration

CONTENTS

BIRDS

MAMMALS

Scales and sizes
The sizes given in this book are **average maximums**. For scale, animals are shown next to an average-height adult man, an adult human hand, or half a thumb. Where the length of an animal is given, this refers to: for fish, amphibians, and reptiles, the measurement from head to tail; for birds, the measurement from beak to tail; for mammals, the head-body length (excluding tail).

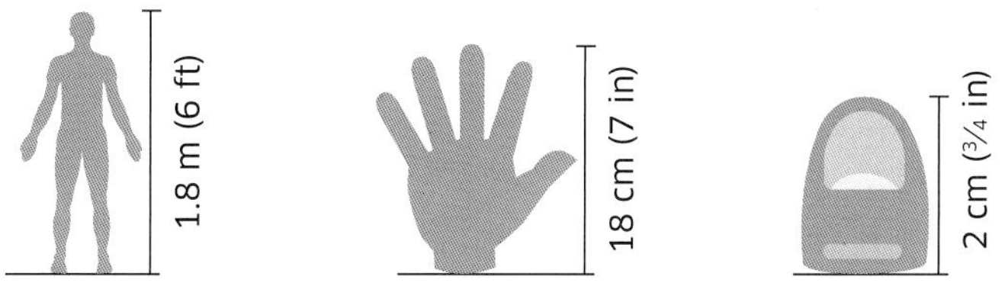

What is an animal?

Animal life encompasses an astonishing diversity of form and behaviour. Many animals seem familiar to us, because we are animals too. We instinctively understand the needs of an animal such as a cat, for example, and how it responds to its environment. But some animals have ways of life that are harder to comprehend, and creatures such as corals may seem to behave more like plants. What is it that links corals with the cat, and with us? Why are they animals, and not some other form of life?

SEVEN KINGDOMS OF LIFE

Scientists currently divide life on Earth into seven "kingdoms". Four of these – the archaea, bacteria, algae, and protozoans – are mainly made up of microscopic organisms, and we are not often aware of them, even though other life could not exist without them. The other three are plants, fungi, and animals. Plants make their food using light energy, but fungi and animals consume their food. Fungi mainly absorb decomposing materials, while most animals move around to eat other organisms.

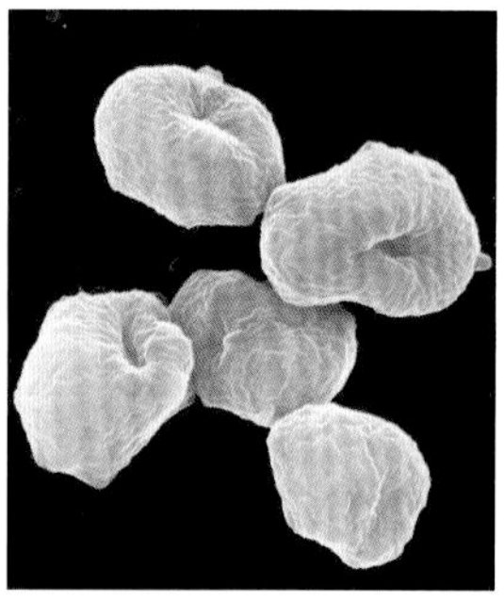

Archaea
Many of these single-celled organisms live in harsh habitats, such as hot acidic pools or even inside animals.

SIX KEY ANIMAL FEATURES

Ranging from microscopic worms to colossal whales, animals are amazingly diverse in shape, size, and anatomy. Despite this they all share some key features, including the most basic structure of their bodies, the way they fuel their growth and reproduction, their ability to sense their environment, and their mobility.

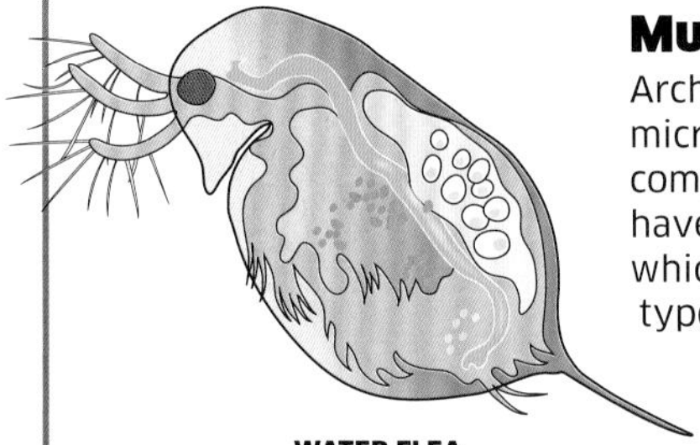

WATER FLEA

Multicellular bodies

Archaea, bacteria, and most protists consist of microscopic single cells containing the complex chemicals needed for life. All animals have bodies built up from many of these cells, which are typically organized into different types of tissue and organs. Even this water flea (a type of freshwater crustacean) has specialized organs, though it is only up to 5 mm (¼ in) long.

Energy and food

Living things need energy to function. Plants use the energy of sunlight to make tissues that store the energy. Animals eat these tissues, or those of other living things, and process them to release the energy and essential chemicals they need to fuel and build their own bodies.

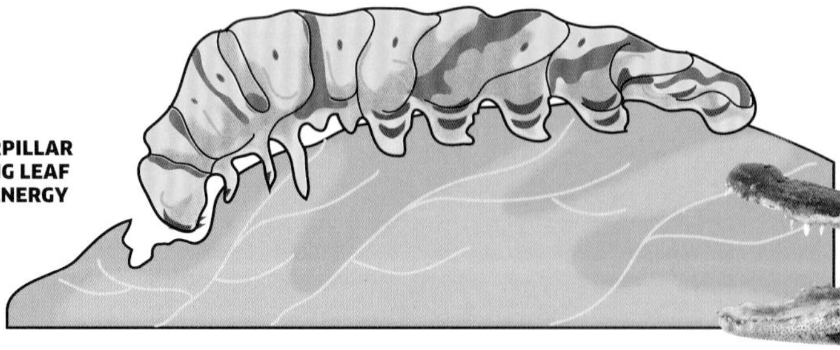

CATERPILLAR EATING LEAF FOR ENERGY

BASKING SHARK FILTERS FOOD FROM WATER

Finding food

All animals eat living organisms, or the remains of dead ones. Most have ways of processing them in digestive organs that break down the tissues, turning them into nutrients. Some aquatic animals filter food particles from the water, but most have mouths that they use to seize and swallow food. Animals have acute senses and most are mobile. Both these traits help them to find food and, if necessary, catch it.

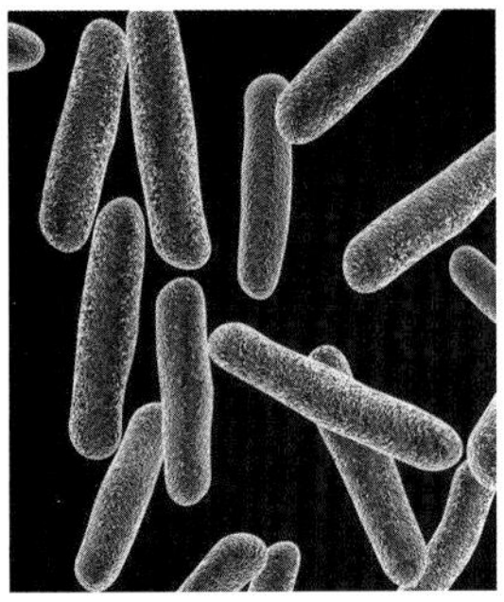

Bacteria
Single-celled bacteria are abundant. Many help to keep other things alive by recycling nutrients, but some cause disease.

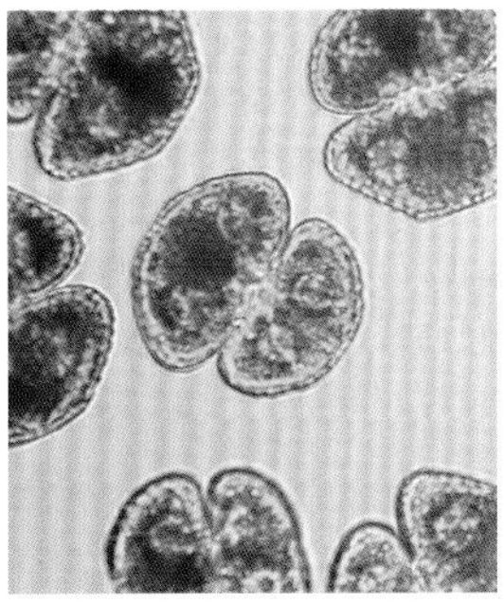

Algae
Much like plants, algae make food using the sun's energy. They have a simple structure and mostly live in water.

Plants
Made up of many cells, plants are typically land-based and use solar energy to fuel their growth.

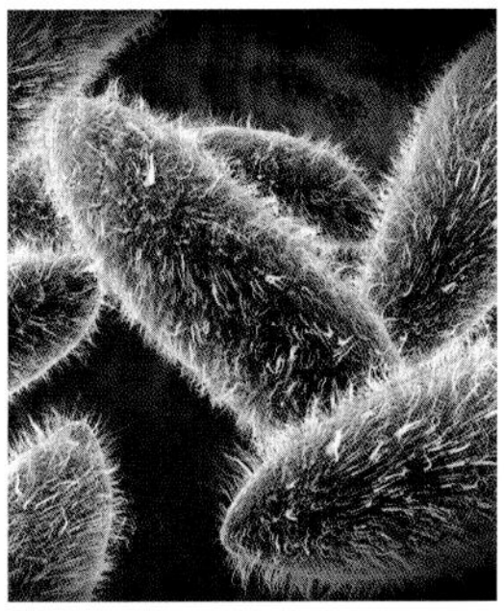

Protozoans
More complex than single-celled bacteria, most protozoans move around and feed like microscopic animals.

Fungi
Single-celled or multi-celled fungi typically obtain energy by feeding on dead plant and animal material.

Animals
Virtually all animals are multi-celled. Most have muscles and nerves that help them move and react to get their food.

Gas exchange
Animals need oxygen to release energy from food, in a process that produces carbon dioxide. The bodies of insects contain tubes that pipe air to their muscles and organs, which absorb the vital oxygen from the air and release waste carbon dioxide. In most other animals this exchange of gases takes place in the gills or lungs, which have a rich blood supply to carry the gases to and from all parts of their bodies.

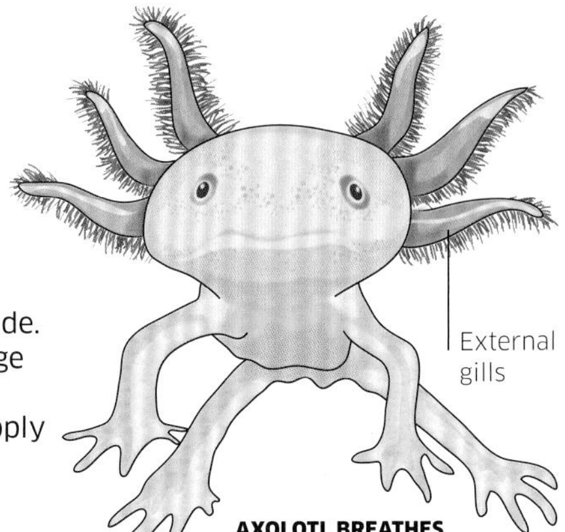

AXOLOTL BREATHES THROUGH GILLS

BALD EAGLE HAS EXCELLENT EYESIGHT

Sensory systems
Nearly all animals have networks of nerve cells in their skin that respond to touch. More advanced animals have specialized sense organs that detect light, heat, scent, taste, sound, pressure, and even electrical activity. Their brains can memorize the patterns of these stimuli, enabling the animals to learn by experience and identify them again. Most of the sense organs of a typical animal, such as this eagle, are concentrated on its head, near its mouth and brain.

Getting around
The most obvious feature of animals is their mobility. Some animals such as mussels and barnacles spend their adult lives attached to rocks and may not move visibly. But they do open and close their shells, and may pump water through their bodies. Most other animals are able to crawl, swim, walk, run, and even fly. This enables them to find food, escape enemies, and seek out breeding partners.

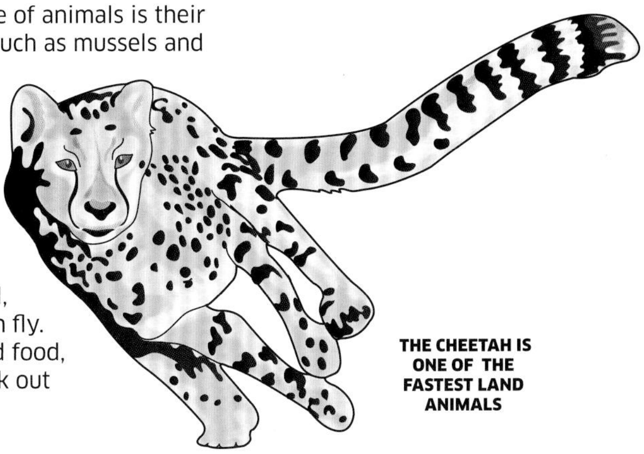

THE CHEETAH IS ONE OF THE FASTEST LAND ANIMALS

Evolution and extinction

The rich diversity of animal life is the result of a continuous process of evolution – the change in living things over time as they adapt to their environment. As the world changes, animals that are best equipped for survival – the "fittest" – prosper and multiply, while others become extinct, vanishing for ever.

INDIVIDUAL VARIATION

When animals breed, the offspring inherit their parents' features. For example, some individuals may have the same colouring as their mother and others the same as their father, or a shade in between the two. If an unexpected colour arises as a result of a mutation (change), it may give that individual an advantage, such as better camouflage.

NATURAL SELECTION

Natural selection is the process by which the fittest organisms survive and produce more offspring. Over time it means that animals with a helpful adaptation become more numerous than those without, so the species gradually evolves. For example, in 19th-century Britain a rare dark form of the peppered moth became common in places where trees were blackened by industrial pollution, because it was better camouflaged and less visible to hungry birds.

DARK FORM OF PEPPERED MOTH

PALE FORM OF PEPPERED MOTH

LOST ANCESTORS

Life on Earth is changing all the time as new species appear and others become extinct. Because fossil evidence is very incomplete, it is impossible to know which animal is ancestral to another, and the further back in time you look the more difficult it becomes. Scientists look for similarities between animals but this does not always mean they are closely related.

MORE THAN 90 PER CENT OF ALL THE SPECIES THAT HAVE EVER EXISTED ARE NOW EXTINCT.

Branching family tree
The ancient animals shown here are not the direct ancestors of the modern elephant. However, they are all thought to be descended from a common ancestor, making them members of the same branching family tree.

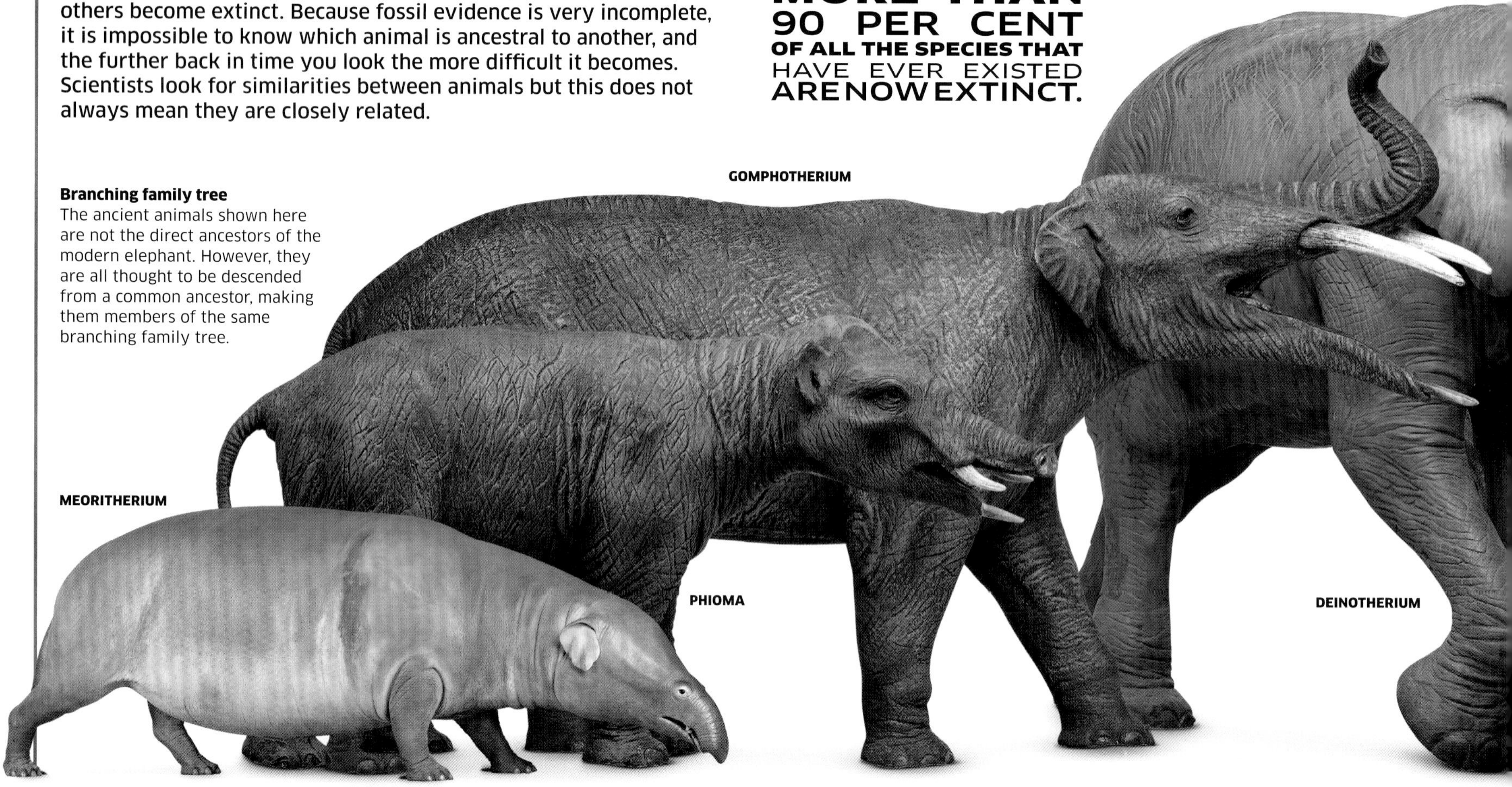

NEW CHALLENGES

Animals that move into new habitats face new problems, and features that were once useful may lose their value. If birds start living on islands where there are no predators, they have no need to fly to escape them. Flying uses a lot of energy, so birds that cannot fly may thrive. Over time this can result in a flightless species, like this Galápagos flightless cormorant.

FLIGHTLESS CORMORANT

CHANGING WORLD

Living things may be perfectly adapted to their environment, but then the environment itself changes. This is happening to the polar bear, which lives for part of the year on Arctic sea ice. Climate change is making the ice melt, and the polar bear is so specialized for life on the ice that it cannot adapt. As a result it may become extinct.

MASS EXTINCTION

Sometimes a cataclysmic event changes the world so radically that very few animals survive it. About 66 million years ago, an asteroid or comet is thought to have crashed on Earth, causing the mass extinction of the giant dinosaurs and flying pterosaurs. The survivors included the ancestors of modern mammals and birds.

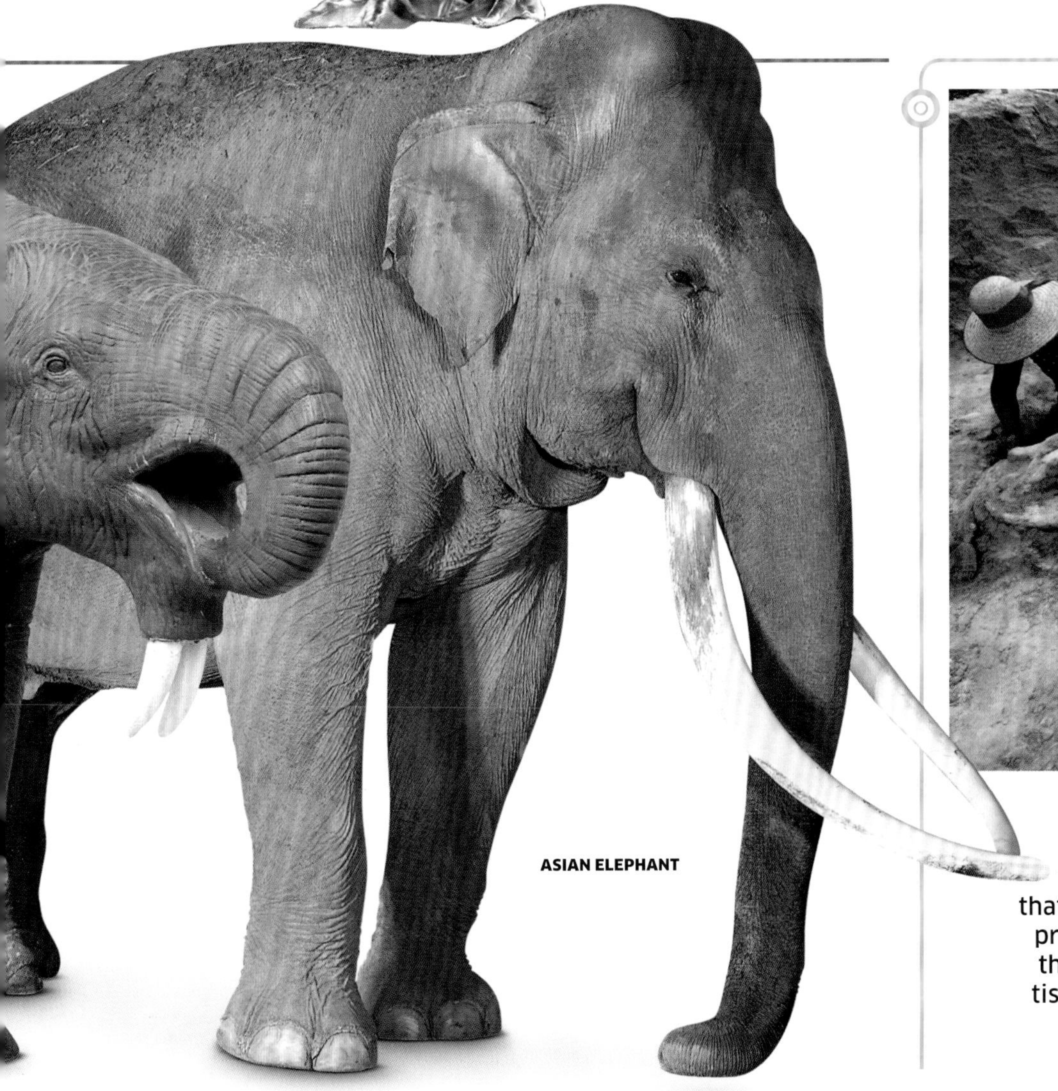

ASIAN ELEPHANT

FOSSIL EVIDENCE

Everything that we know about extinct animals is deduced from fossils – the remains or traces of long-dead organisms that have survived the normal processes of decay. Most fossils preserve shells and bones, which were buried in mud or sand that turned to rock. Minerals in the rock then turn the animal tissue to stone. Other types of fossils preserve impressions of soft-bodied animals, or soft tissues such as feathers.

Animal history

For most of Earth's 4.6-billion-year history, the only living things on the planet were microscopic organisms such as bacteria. Then 600 million years ago a different form of life appeared – the first simple animals. They originated in the oceans, because ocean water contains all the chemicals needed to make the complex substances vital to life. But some 430 million years ago the earliest land animals appeared, and since then animals have managed to colonize almost every habitat on Earth.

Geological time

Scientists divide the history of Earth into eras, which are then further divided into smaller time spans called periods. This is the basis of the timeline shown here, measured in millions of years ago (MYA). During this immense span of time the processes of evolution and extinction have created and destroyed an astonishing diversity of animal life.

Key

- Early Earth
- Palaeozoic Era
- Mesozoic Era
- Cenozoic Era

PRECAMBRIAN

4.6 billion to 541 MYA
Throughout much of this vast stretch of time the only life forms were single-celled organisms. Eventually these began forming colonies, and about 600 million years ago some colonies evolved into the first multi-celled animals.

Volcanic seas
Water vapour erupting from ancient volcanoes created the oceans where life first evolved.

Dickinsonia
These early animals resemble jellyfish or worms, with no hard parts, which is why their fossils are so rare.

DEVONIAN

419–358 MYA
Many new types of sea fish evolved during the Devonian, and some 375 MYA a group of animals with four bony limbs started living partly on land. These were the first amphibians – the ancestors of all land vertebrates.

Rolfosteus
This late Devonian fish used its broad jaws to crush shellfish.

CARBONIFEROUS

358–298 MYA
During the Carboniferous, life on land expanded rapidly, with primitive tree-like plants forming large areas of forest. Insects and spiders flourished, and were hunted by large amphibians.

Ichthyostega
One of the earliest four-legged animals, *Ichthyostega* retained some fish-like features such as its tail fin and small, fish-like scales.

Archaeopteryx
Towards the end of the Jurassic Period a group of feathered dinosaurs developed wings that enabled them to fly. This species is one of the earliest we know of.

CRETACEOUS

145–66 MYA
The Cretaceous Period saw the evolution of some of the biggest, most spectacular dinosaurs. But it ended with a mass extinction that wiped out all the giant dinosaurs.

Tyrannosaurus
The most famous dinosaur, *T. rex* lived at the end of the Cretaceous.

Liaoxiornis
Early flying dinosaurs had teeth and long, bony tails. But by the Cretaceous the first true birds had evolved.

PALEOGENE

66–23 MYA
Some small mammals survived the catastrophe that destroyed the giant dinosaurs. They gave rise to larger plant-eaters and hunters that took the place of the extinct giants.

Uintatherium
A heavily built herbivore, *Uintatherium* was the size of a modern rhinoceros.

NEOGENE

23–2 MYA
During the Neogene Period many modern types of mammal appeared, including some fearsome carnivores adapted for hunting the big plant-eaters.

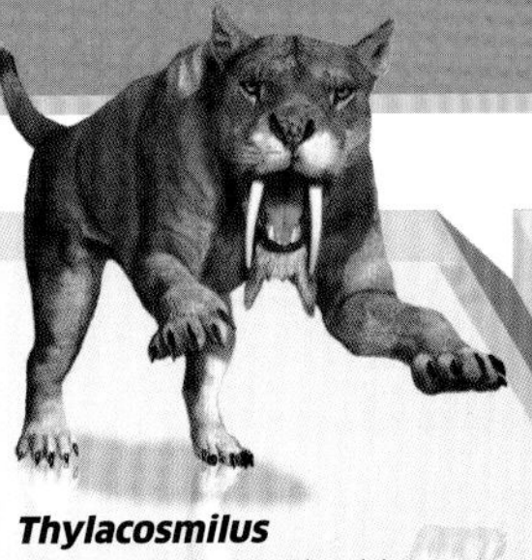

Thylacosmilus
This sabre-toothed hunter lived in South America some 3 million years ago.

QUATERNARY

2 MYA to the present
This period has included long ice ages separated by warmer phases, such as the one we live in today. The dominance of humans has driven many types of animals to extinction.

Woolly mammoth
Most closely related to the modern Asian elephant, this was adapted for life in icy climates. It died out 3,700 years ago.

JURASSIC

201–145 MYA
Dinosaurs dominated animal life in this period. They included huge plant-eaters and powerful predators, but also smaller, feathered types that gave rise to the birds.

Morganucodon
This mouse-sized, furry insect-eater was typical of the first mammals, which appeared about 225 million years ago.

Isanosaurus
A plant-eater that walked on all four feet, this dinosaur could also rear up to feed in tall trees.

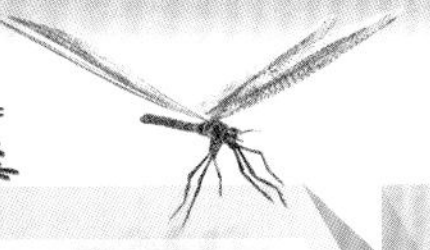

Meganeura
This dragonfly-like insect had a 75-cm (29-in) wingspan.

Lepidodendron
Plants such as this grew to 30 m (100 ft) tall, providing food and habitats for animals.

PERMIAN

298–252 MYA
By the Permian, the amphibians had given rise to scaly-skinned reptiles that could live in all warm land habitats.

Dimetrodon
This sail-backed animal was related to the ancestors of mammals.

TRIASSIC

252–201 MYA
The Permian Period ended with a catastrophic mass extinction. But by the end of the Triassic Period that followed, the first dinosaurs had evolved, along with the flying pterosaurs and the earliest true mammals.

Cooksonia
This was one of the first plants to have stems. Such plants provided food for the earliest land animals – invertebrates that resembled scorpions and centipedes.

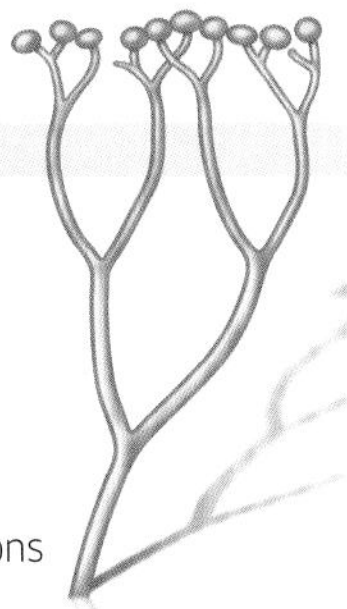

SILURIAN

443–419 MYA
Bony fish with movable jaws evolved during the Silurian. By this time life had spread from the seas on to land, in the form of the earliest green plants.

Sacabambaspis
The earliest fish lacked hinged, bony jaws, as do modern lampreys. They also had no pectoral or pelvic fins, so were probably not very strong swimmers.

The oldest-known land animal is a tiny millipede that lived around 428 million years ago.

CAMBRIAN

541–485 MYA
Near the beginning of this period there was an increase in the diversity of animal life. Many had hard shells, so they were more likely to form fossils than the soft-bodied animals that existed before.

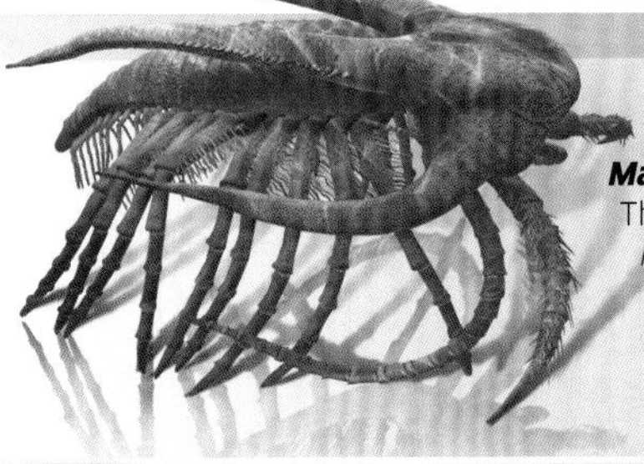

Marrella
The spiny, hard-shelled *Marrella* lived on the sea bed about 500 million years ago. It had jointed legs like a crab, and was less than 2 cm (¾ in) long.

ORDOVICIAN

485–443 MYA
Early fish – the first vertebrates – appeared in the oceans during the Ordovician Period, and lived alongside other animals, such as trilobites. However, many of these animals were wiped out by a mass extinction event at the end of this period.

ANIMAL KINGDOM

The animal kingdom

Almost 1.4 million species of living animals have been scientifically described and named, and more are found and classified every day. They belong to 35 major groups, each known as a phylum. Just one of these phyla, the chordates, includes all the vertebrates – the fish, amphibians, reptiles, birds, and mammals. All the rest are invertebrates – animals with no internal skeleton. One phylum, the arthropods, contains more species than all the others put together.

INVERTEBRATES

Invertebrates
The term invertebrates is not a scientific classification, it merely describes all animals that lack internal jointed skeletons. There are more than 30 separate invertebrate phyla in the animal kingdom. This chart shows some of the main groups.

SPONGES
PHYLUM

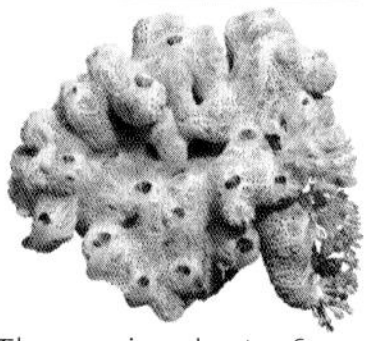

These simplest of all animals have no specialized organs and are just a mass of similar cells.

CNIDARIANS
PHYLUM

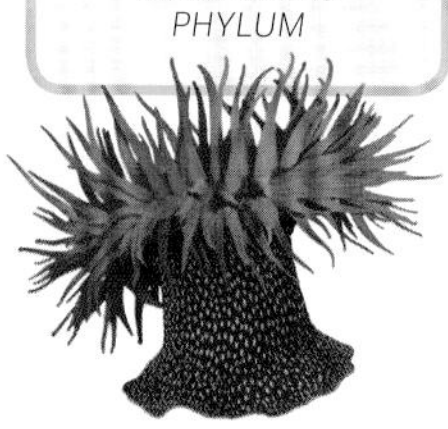

Jellyfish, corals, hydras, and sea anemones are all aquatic animals with stinging tentacles.

ECHINODERMS
PHYLUM

This group includes the sea urchins, starfish, sea cucumbers, and brittle stars.

ARTHROPODS
PHYLUM

MYRIAPODS
SUPERCLASS

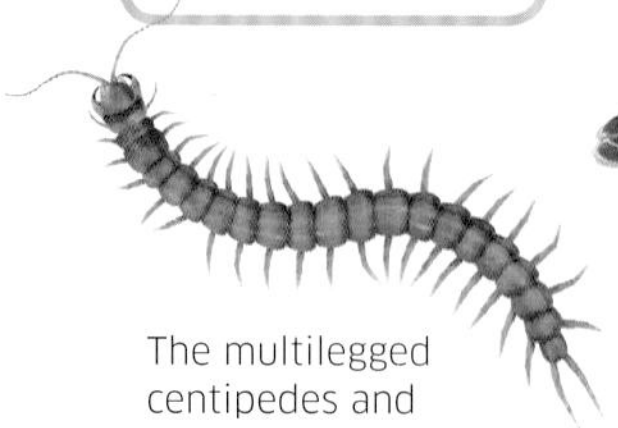

The multilegged centipedes and millipedes all live on land, mainly in damp places.

CRUSTACEANS
SUPERCLASS

Apart from woodlice, these are all aquatic. There are many types, including crabs and lobsters.

ARACHNIDS
CLASS

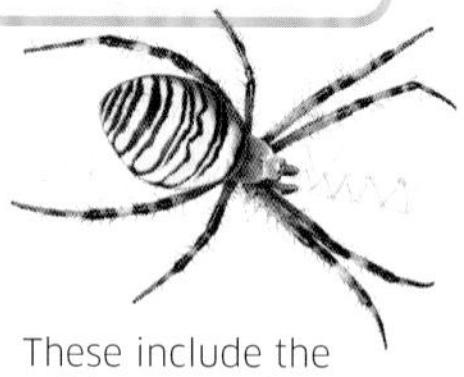

These include the spiders, scorpions, and ticks – all with four pairs of legs. Many are venomous.

INSECTS
CLASS

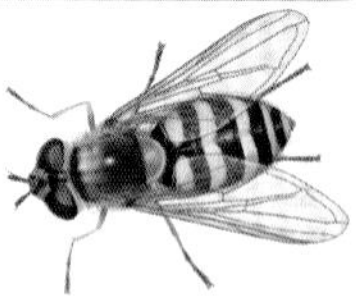

Insects have three pairs of legs, and most have wings. They are the largest animal group.

BRYOZOANS
PHYLUM

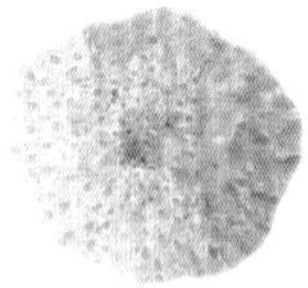

These aquatic “moss animals” live in colonies on hard surfaces, and filter food from the water.

ROUNDWORMS
PHYLUM

Also known as nematodes, these slender worms live in many habitats, including inside other animals.

FLATWORMS
PHYLUM

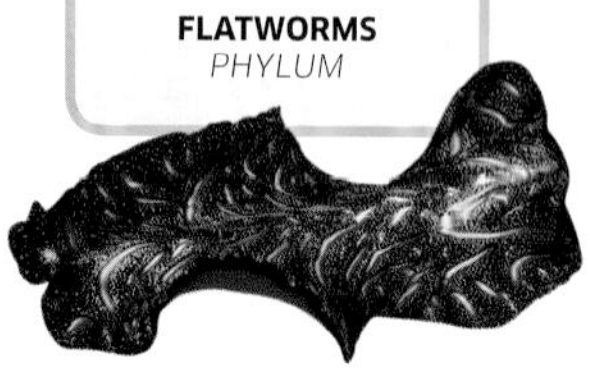

These very simple ribbon-shaped animals absorb food through their skin.

MOLLUSCS
PHYLUM

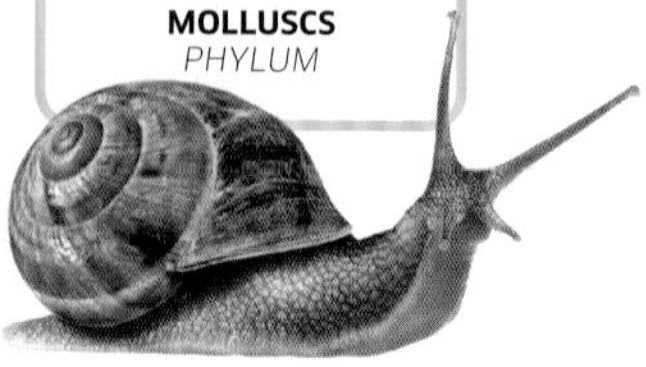

Mainly marine, these include the snails, clams, and octopuses and their relatives.

SEGMENTED WORMS
PHYLUM

Also known as the annelid worms, these include earthworms and marine worms.

It is thought that of all the animal species on Earth, **fewer than 20 per cent** have been scientifically described and classified.

Animal relationships

Different types of animals are classified in various groups depending on the features they share. Some groups are clearly related to others, enabling scientists to arrange them in a "family tree" of the animal kingdom. This shows how the groups are linked by their last common ancestor, although the details are always being revised in the light of new discoveries.

CHORDATES
PHYLUM

Chordates

The chordates are animals that have either a backbone or a pliable rod running the length of the body. They include all the vertebrates, and also the aquatic tunicates (sea squirts and salps) and lancelets.

JAWLESS FISH
CLASS

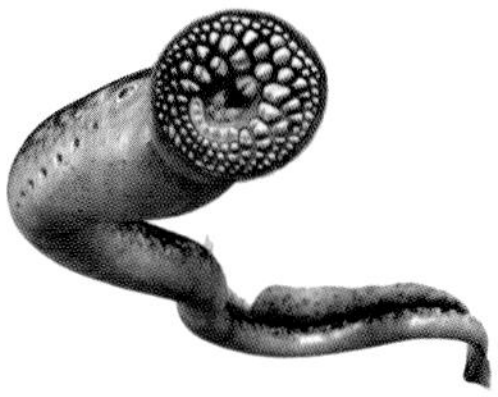

This group is made up of the lampreys, and may also include their distant relations the hagfish.

CARTILAGINOUS FISH
CLASS

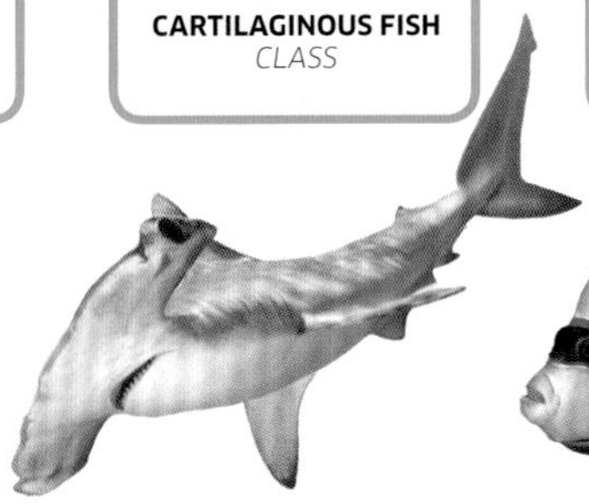

The sharks, rays, and chimaeras all have skeletons made of gristly cartilage instead of bone.

BONY FISH
CLASS

This includes typical ray-finned fish and the lobe-finned fish related to the first four-legged animals.

AMPHIBIANS
CLASS

These are the frogs, toads, newts, and relatives which live on land but mainly breed in water.

MAMMALS
CLASS

These typically furry vertebrates include humans and all the biggest living animals.

BIRDS
CLASS

Defined by their feathers, the birds are the main group of flying vertebrates.

REPTILES
CLASS

Cold-blooded and mainly scaly, this group includes the lizards and snakes.

CLASSIFICATION

All living things that have been scientifically described are classified in a multilevel system of groups. Each group of closely related organisms is part of a larger group, and each type of group has its own name.

Kingdom
All animals belong to the animal kingdom. The other kingdoms are plants, fungi, and three types of mainly microscopic organisms.

Phylum
The animal kingdom is divided into phyla – the main groups of animals. A phylum may be split into two or more subphyla.

Class
Each phylum usually consists of several classes. Some of these classes are grouped together to form superclasses.

Order
Every class contains many orders. For example, the class Mammalia (mammals) contains the order Carnivora (carnivores).

Family
An order such as the Carnivora consists of several families. One family of carnivores is the Felidae, which includes all cats.

Genus
The family is divided into smaller groups, each called a genus. The genus *Panthera* contains the big cats.

Species
A genus is a group of individual species. Each species has a two-part scientific name such as *Panthera uncia*, the snow leopard.

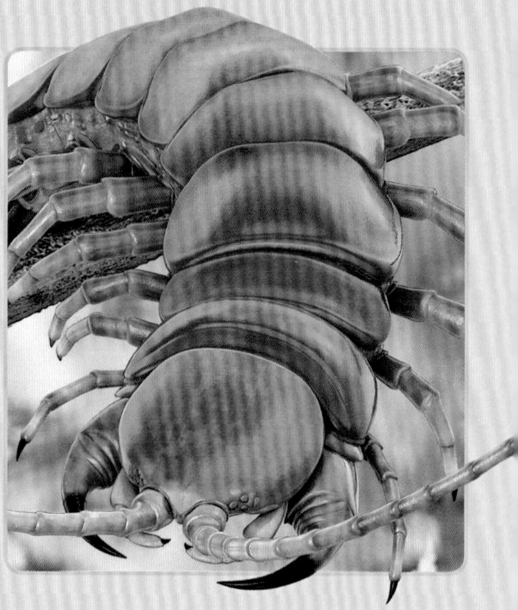

INVERTEBRATES

Most of the animals on Earth are not furry mammals, scaly reptiles, or feathery birds. They are invertebrates – animals that do not have an internal jointed skeleton. Many live in the oceans, but many more live on land. They include the most numerous, successful animals of all – the insects.

WHAT IS AN INVERTEBRATE?

An invertebrate is any animal that does not have an internal jointed skeleton. The term includes a wide diversity of animals, ranging from microscopic worms to giant squid, with little in common except the lack of a vertebrate skeleton. Some have soft bodies and many others have protective shells. But the most abundant are the amazing variety of crustaceans, insects, spiders, and similar animals that have hard, jointed external skeletons – the arthropods.

Outnumbered

Altogether, the invertebrates make up at least 97 per cent of all the animal species on Earth. The vertebrates include most of the biggest animals, but they are hugely outnumbered.

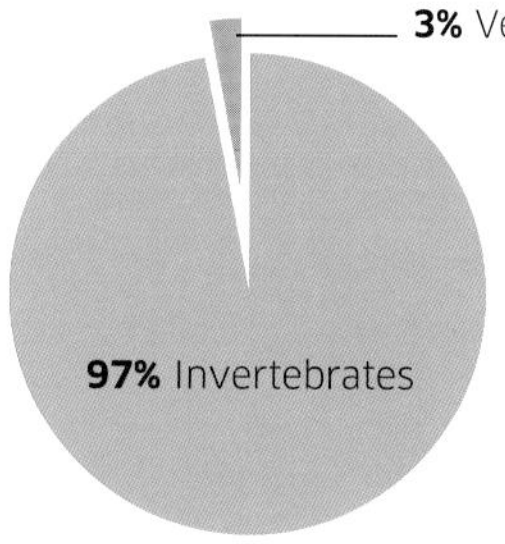

TYPES OF INVERTEBRATE

There are 35 major groups of species in the animal kingdom, each called a phylum. The vertebrates form part of just one phylum; all the other 34 phylae are made up of invertebrates. Shown below are some of these.

Sponges
These aquatic organisms are the simplest animals. They consist of many cells, but do not have specialized organs. They gather food by filtering it from the water.

Segmented worms
Also known as annelid worms, these include the earthworm and many marine species. Their bodies are made up of many identical, soft-skinned segments.

Molluscs
This large phylum consists of the snails and clams, as well as octopuses and similar animals. Most live in the sea, and many have chalky, protective shells.

Echinoderms
The word echinoderm means "spiny skin" – an apt name for a phylum that includes the spiny sea urchins. It also includes the starfish and sea cucumbers.

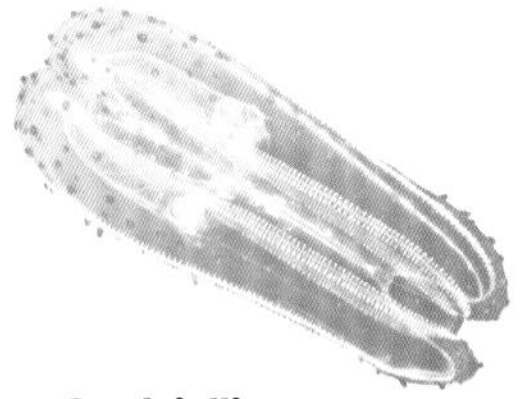

Comb jellies
These ocean drifters snare other animals and draw them into their transparent bodies. They swim by beating rows of comb-like structures on their skin.

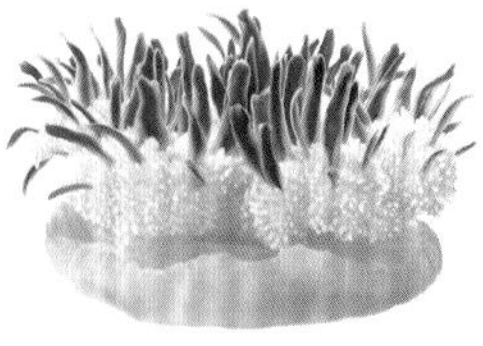

Cnidarians
These include the sea anemones, corals, and jellyfish. They all live in the water where they extend their stinging tentacles to catch small animals.

Arthropods
The largest phylum consists of animals that have tough external skeletons with jointed legs. Their strong skeletons allow them to live on land as well as in water.

ARTHROPODS

More than 80 per cent of all known animal species are arthropods, and most of them are insects. They also include crustaceans, millipedes and other myriapods, and arachnids such as scorpions and spiders.

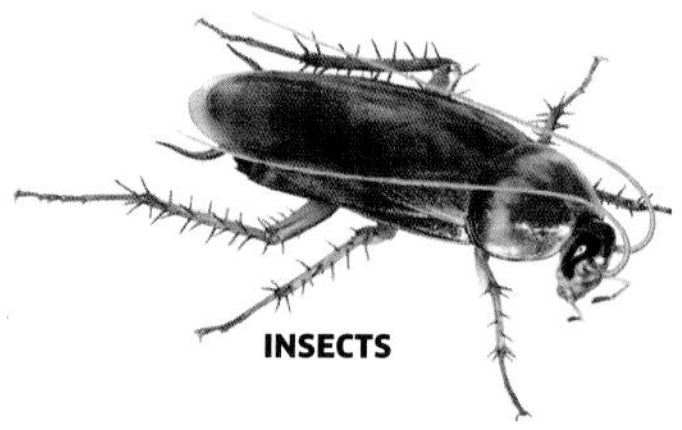

INSECTS

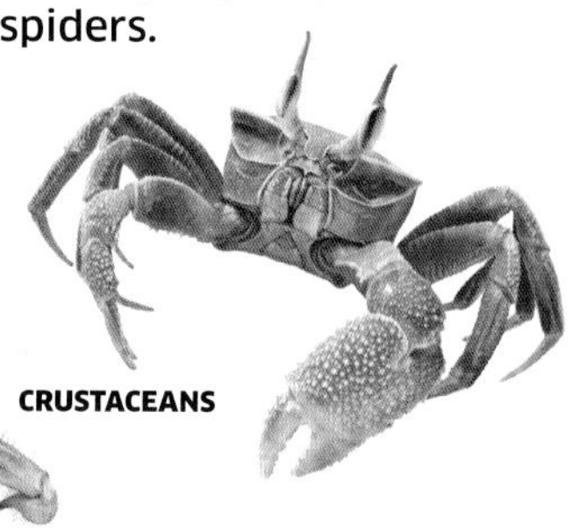

CRUSTACEANS

MYRIAPODS

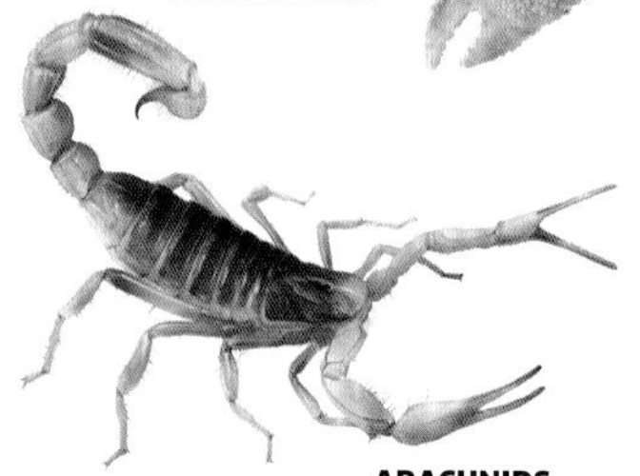

ARACHNIDS

Inside an arthropod

An arthropod has many body segments, each supported by tough skin that acts as a skeleton. The skin may be thickened or reinforced with chalky minerals to form protective armour. Thin, flexible skin between the segments allows movement.

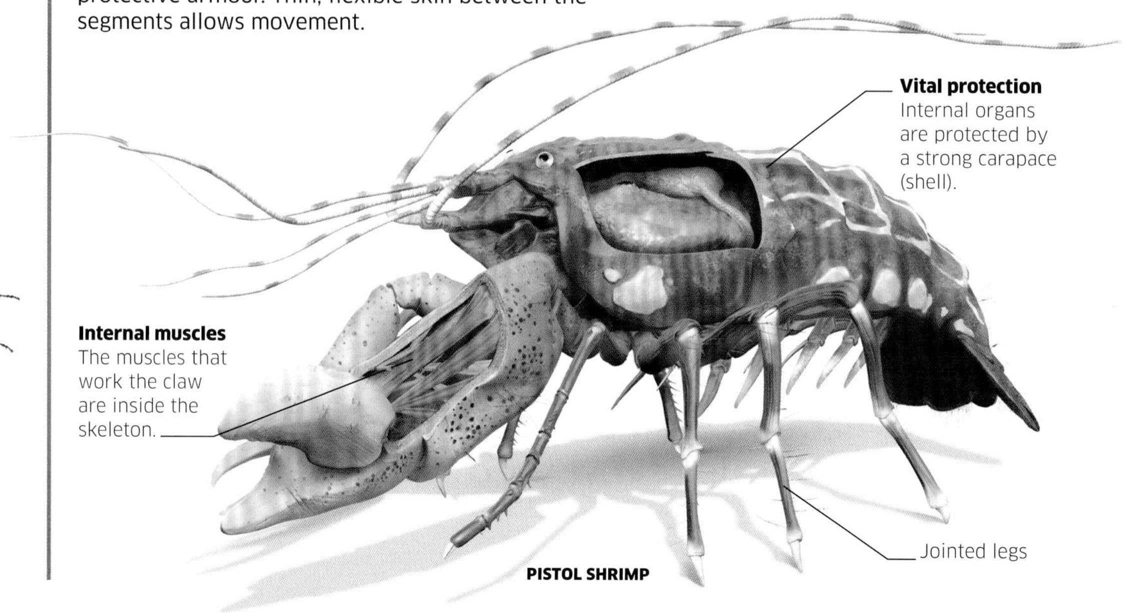

PISTOL SHRIMP

HEADS AND TAILS

Invertebrates display a huge variety of body shapes. Many have the familiar body plan of a head, containing a brain and well-developed sense organs, a body equipped with legs, and a tail end. These animals often display bilateral symmetry, in which the right and left sides of the body are mirror images. But many other invertebrates either have a very different type of symmetry, while sponges have none at all.

Insect
This ladybird has bilateral symmetry. It has a distinct head, and a body made up of a thorax, bearing three pairs of legs, and an abdomen.

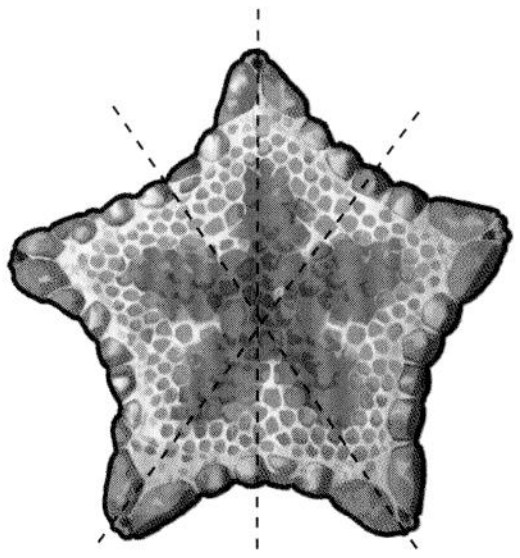

Sea star
Starfish and related animals have radial symmetry. Their bodies are arranged around a central point.

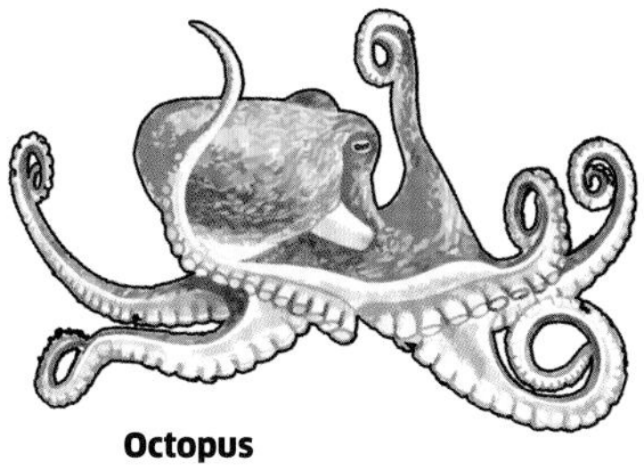

Octopus
Squid, octopuses, and their relatives have a strange body plan. The tentacles are attached directly to the head and their organs are contained in the bag-shaped mantle.

Clam
Inside its shell, a clam or similar bivalve mollusc has no clear body plan. It has no head, no brain, and only very basic sense organs.

BODIES AND SHELLS

Many invertebrates have soft bodies and do not need supportive skeletons. They maintain their shape using their muscles and body fluids. But soft bodies are vulnerable, so some have protective shells. The tough exoskeletons of arthropods provide both support and protection.

Soft body
This earthworm's body is supported by the soil, so it does not need a strong skeleton. The bodies of many aquatic invertebrates are supported by water in a similar way. The worm can move by stretching its head end forwards, then contracting to pull its tail forward too.

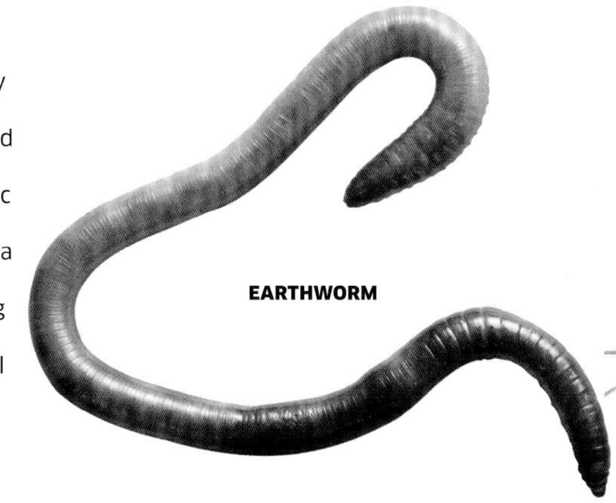

EARTHWORM

GARDEN SNAIL

Protective shell
A land snail has a soft body, but it also has a strong shell. If it feels threatened, it can draw its entire body into the shell. This also helps it survive dry weather, because the shell stops it losing body moisture.

Hard exoskeleton
The external skeleton of this spider supports its body, and also forms its venomous fangs. But the skeleton stops the spider growing, so at intervals it has to be shed and replaced. The soft new skeleton takes time to harden, leaving the spider very vulnerable.

GOLDENROD CRAB SPIDER

AQUATIC INVERTEBRATES

Many invertebrates live in the oceans. The water supports their bodies and gives them a steady supply of food. Land animals must search for things to eat, but aquatic invertebrates can wait for food to come to them.

SNAKELOCK'S ANEMONE

Rich pickings
Coastal seas are so rich in food that huge numbers of invertebrates can live in colonies on the rocks. These mussels feed by filtering the water through their bodies to gather edible particles. There is plenty for all.

BLUE MUSSELS

Rooted to the spot
This sea anemone spends most of its life attached to a rock. It does not need to move around, because water flowing around it carries small animals that it can catch with its long tentacles.

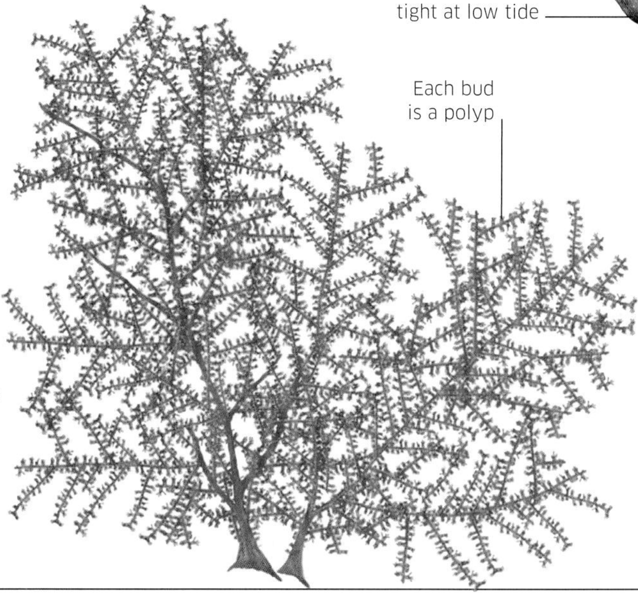

ORANGE TREE GORGONIAN

Linked colonies
Many colonies of invertebrates are made up of separate animals. But others consist of animals that are linked together like buds on the branches of a tree. This sea fan is made up of many tiny feeding polyps that all share the same skeleton.

Sea nettles cannot see images, but they sense light and dark using organs called ocelli.

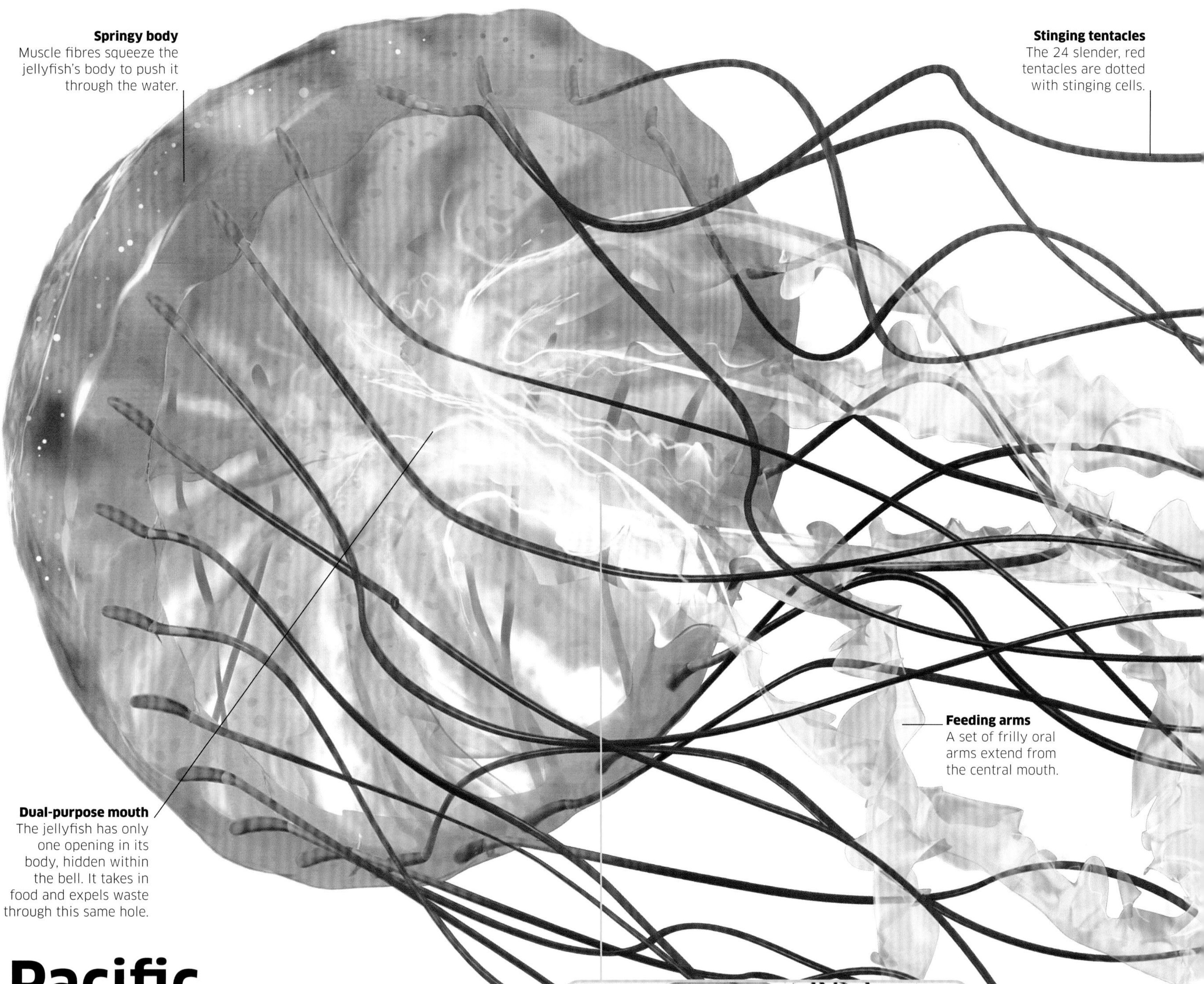

Pacific sea nettle

Drifting through the north Pacific Ocean, this huge colourful jellyfish lives by snaring small animals in its long, stinging tentacles, then reeling them into its body cavity to digest them. It can swim slowly by contracting its bell-shaped body, but it mostly drifts with the ocean currents.

Jellyfish are among the simplest animals. They have few senses, no brain to process and store information, and only the most basic digestive system. But they have a complex lifecycle, and their long, trailing tentacles, armed with fearsomely effective venomous stinging cells, make them highly efficient predators.

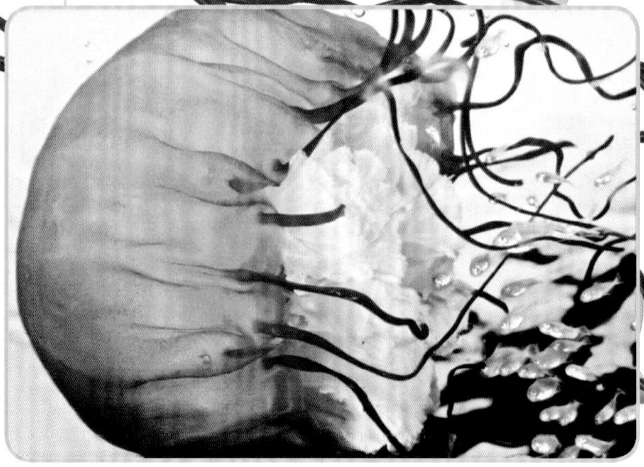

Poison protection
The sea nettle's venom can be deadly, but some small fish such as the Pacific butterfish are not affected by it. A thick layer of slimy mucus stops the stinging cells penetrating their skin. The fish shelter from their enemies among the jellyfish's trailing tentacles.

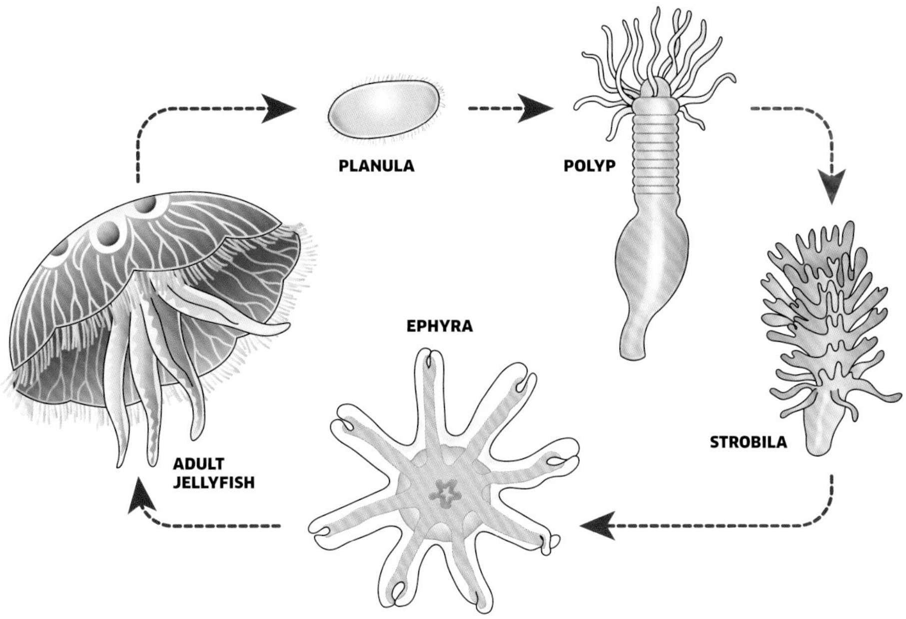

Complex lifecycle

An adult jellyfish produces small larvae called planulae. These grow into flower-shaped polyps that attach to a solid surface. Each one eventually becomes a strobila – a stack of miniature jellyfish called ephyrae that split off and drift away to grow into mature jellyfish.

Venomous cells

The tentacles and arms of stinging jellyfish are covered with microscopic cells called cnidoblasts. Each cell is a barbed hollow thread with a sharp, venomous tip, stored inside-out inside a capsule. If prey brushes against the trigger, the capsule lid flips open. The thread shoots out and injects a dose of venom into the victim.

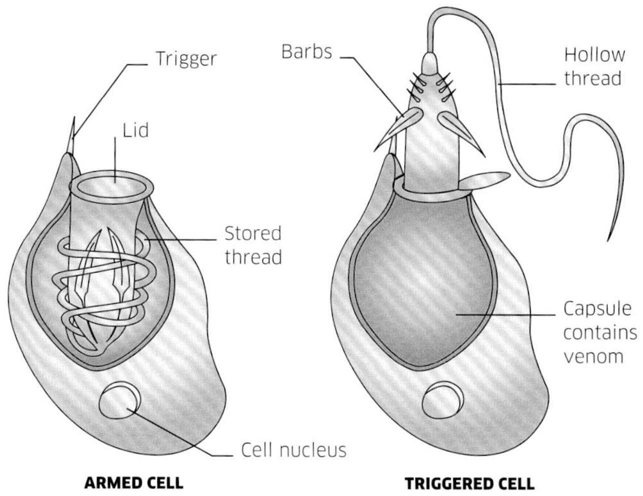

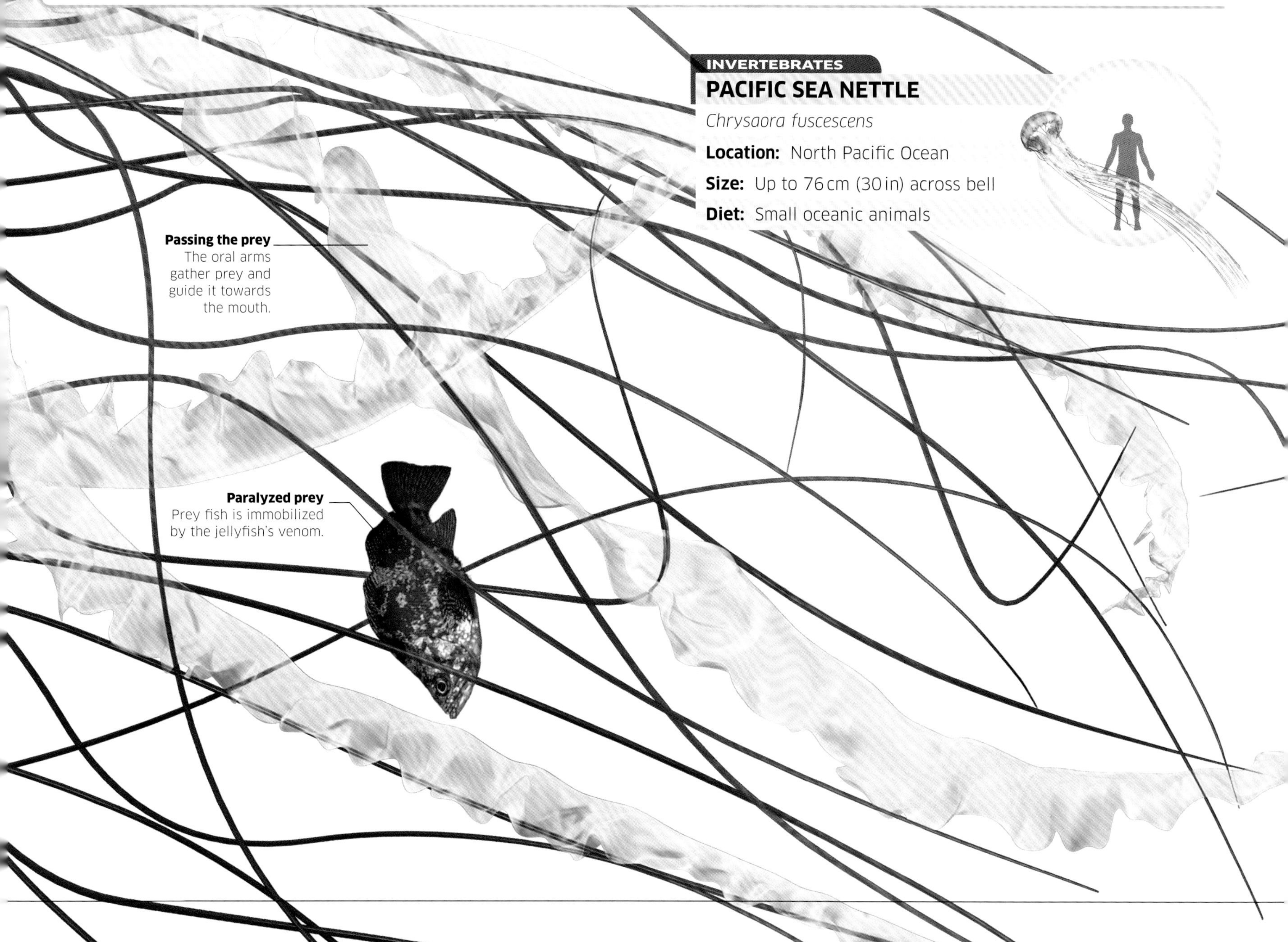

INVERTEBRATES

PACIFIC SEA NETTLE

Chrysaora fuscescens

Location: North Pacific Ocean

Size: Up to 76 cm (30 in) across bell

Diet: Small oceanic animals

A **Portuguese man o' war** can give **serious stings** even when washed up **dead on a beach.**

24 The number of **eyes** a **box jellyfish** has.

Cnidarians

Jellyfish, corals, sea anemones, and their relatives are all cnidarians – aquatic animals with soft bodies that are usually armed with stinging cells for catching prey. Many are very beautiful, but a few can be deadly.

A typical cnidarian has a body made of jelly enclosed by two layers of cells – one on the outside, and the other forming the animal's stomach lining. It may also have a crown of mobile tentacles. Some cnidarians are free-drifting medusae, or jellyfish, but many are polyps (hollow cylinders surrounded by tentacles) that spend their lives attached to rocks or the sea bed. Many corals and sea anemones form colonies of interconnected polyps that share nutrients they gather from the water.

SNAKELOCKS ANEMONE

Anemonia viridis

Location: Mediterranean, Atlantic

Size: Up to 7 cm (2¾ in) across

Often seen in coastal tide pools, the snakelocks anemone has long stinging tentacles that it uses to catch tiny animals. The green colour is caused by microscopic algae that live in the tentacles; these use the energy from sunlight to make sugar, which helps feed the anemone.

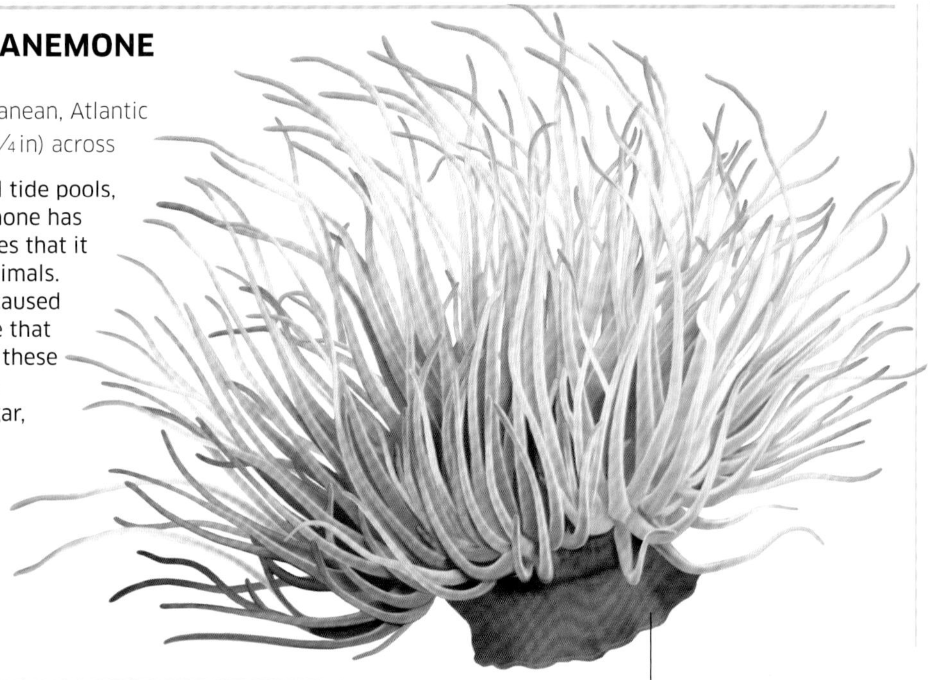

STRAWBERRY ANEMONE

Actinia fragacea

Location: N.E. Atlantic Ocean

Size: Up to 10 cm (4 in) across

Like several other sea anemones, this lives on rocky shores where the falling tide leaves it exposed out of water twice a day. It survives by retracting its tentacles into its body cavity, where they stay moist until the tide rises again and they can extend back out to catch food.

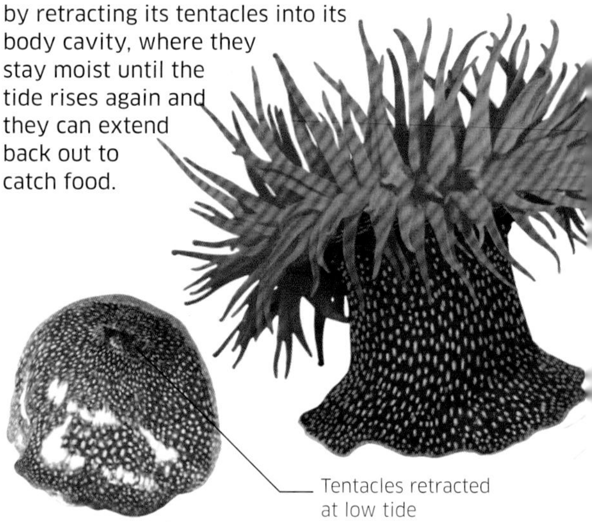

MUSHROOM CORAL

Ctenactis echinata

Location: Indo-Pacific region

Size: Up to 25 cm (9¾ in) across

Solitary corals are similar to sea anemones, with cylindrical or oval bodies crowned by small tentacles surrounding a central mouth. This species is one of the stony, reef-building corals, with a limestone skeleton made from minerals absorbed from the seawater that it lives in.

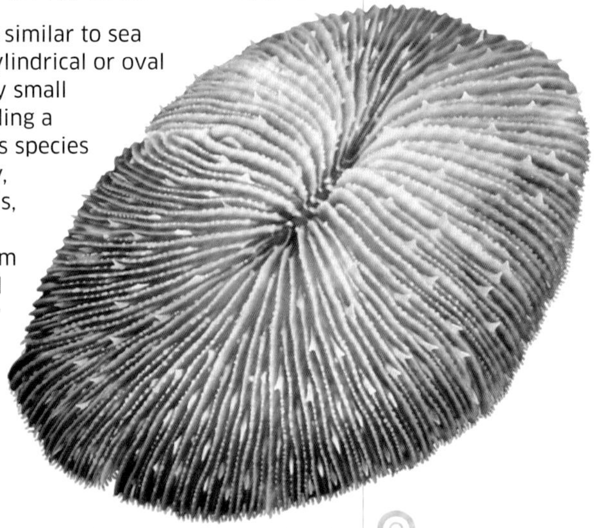

BRAIN CORAL

Diploria labyrinthiformis

Location: Caribbean Sea

Size: Up to 2 m (6½ ft) across

Looking like a human brain, this is a colonial stony coral, formed from thousands of interconnected coral polyps. While each one has its own array of food-gathering tentacles, the polyps also benefit from microscopic algae in their tissues that use solar energy to make food.

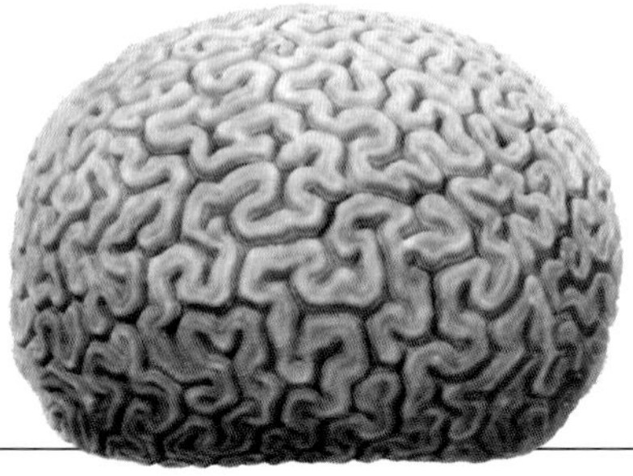

ORANGE TREE GORGONIAN

Swiftia exserta

Location: W. Atlantic Ocean

Height: Up to 2 m (6½ ft)

Also known as a sea fan, this is a colonial coral with many linked polyps attached to a skeleton of horny, flexible material. The colony grows in a flat, branching form, and gathers food from ocean currents that flow through the branches.

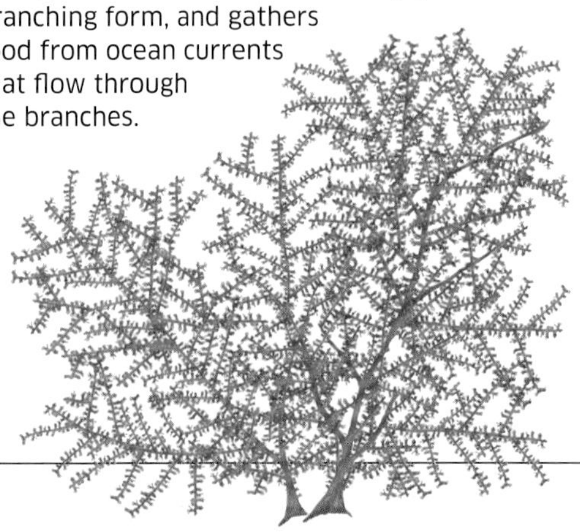

PURPLE SEA PEN

Virgularia sp.

Location: N. E. Atlantic, Mediterranean

Height: Up to 50 cm (19¾ in)

Made up of many feeding polyps attached to a much bigger central polyp that forms a stalk, sea pens gather food from the water in the same way as sea fans. The name comes from the way their feathery shape resembles a quill pen.

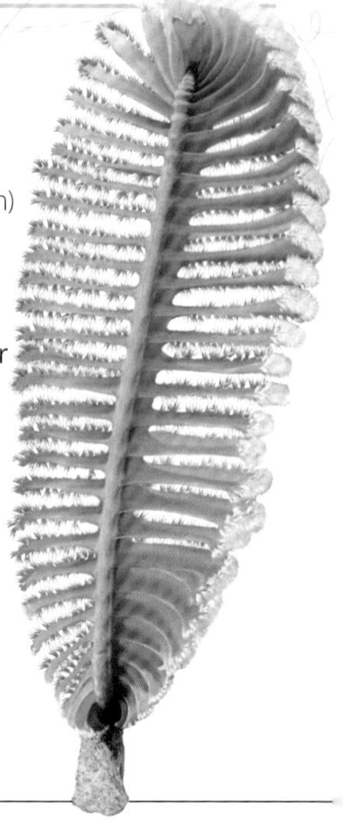

GREEN HYDRA

Hydra viridissima

Location: Northern temperate regions

Height: Up to 3 cm (1¼ in)

Hydras are among the few cnidarians that live in freshwater. They gather tiny, drifting animals with their tentacles, but the green hydra also contains green algae that use light energy to make food. Buds that form on its body develop into new hydras.

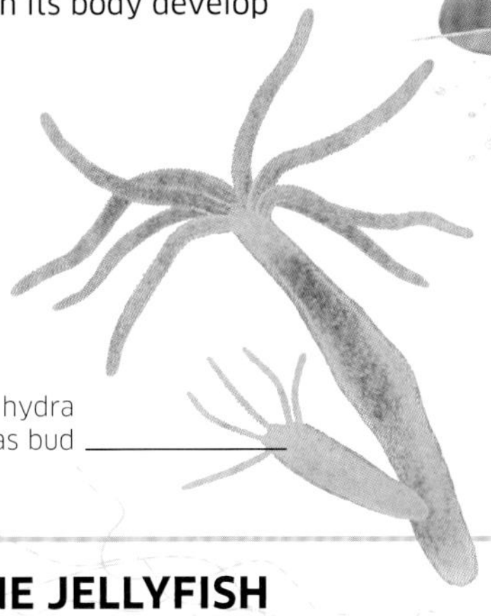

PORTUGUESE MAN O' WAR

Physalia physalis

Location: Tropical and temperate seas worldwide

Size: Float up to 30 cm (11¾ in) across

This extraordinary organism is not a single animal, but a colony of polyps, each with a special role. One polyp forms a float that drifts on the ocean, supporting other polyps that gather food, digest it, or produce new polyps. The long, trailing tentacles deliver a dangerous sting.

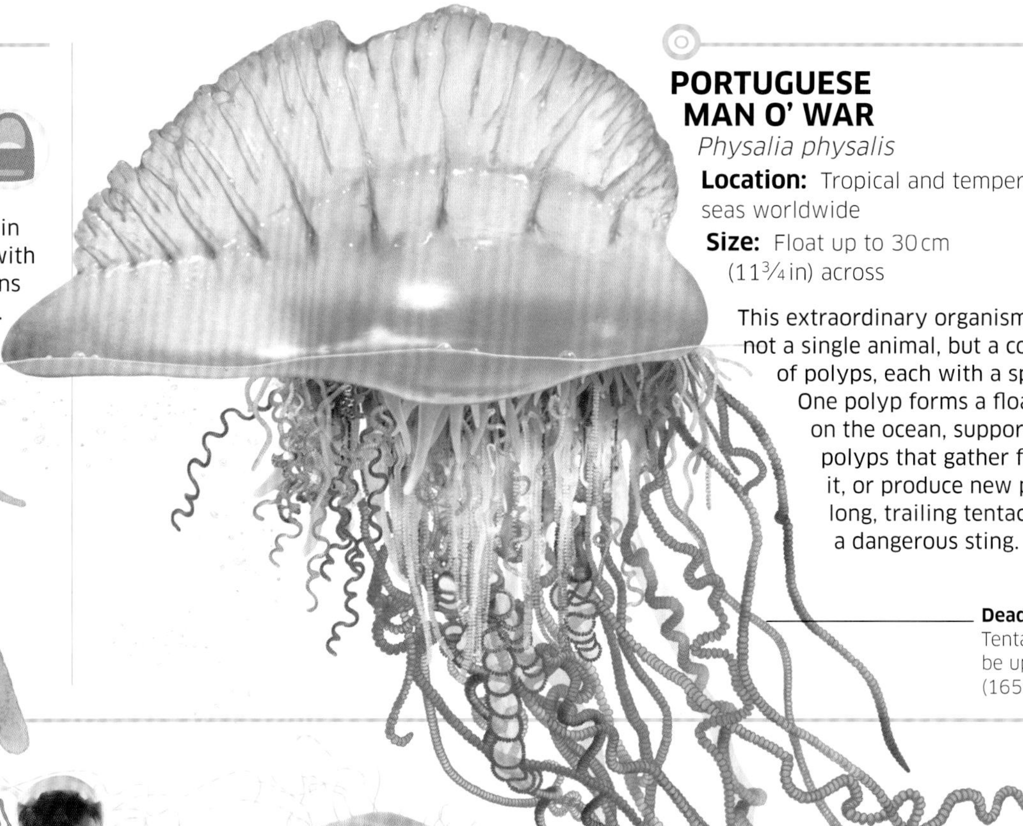

LION'S MANE JELLYFISH

Cyanea capillata

Location: Arctic Ocean

Size: Up to 2 m (6½ ft) across

One of the biggest of the true jellyfish, this ocean giant can swim slowly by contracting its broad, bell-shaped body, but normally drifts with the currents. It preys on fish, squid, and any other animals that it can trap in its long, stinging tentacles.

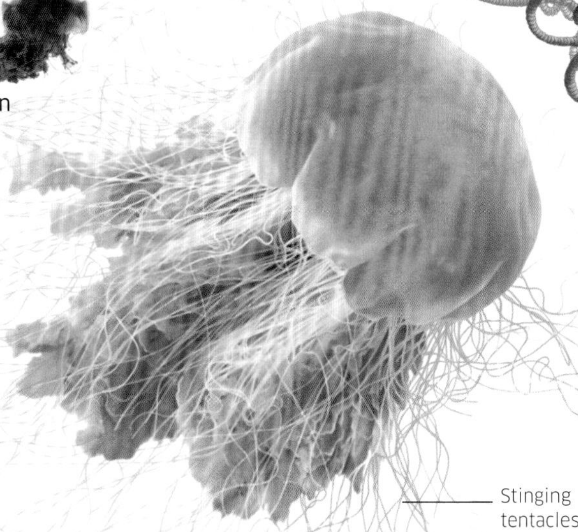

UPSIDE-DOWN JELLYFISH

Cassiopea andromeda

Location: Gulf of Mexico, Caribbean

Size: Up to 30 cm (11¾ in) across

Most jellyfish swim or drift in open water, but this unusual species lies upside down on the sea bed with its stinging tentacles extending upwards. This enables it to feed like a sea anemone, trapping animals carried past by the current.

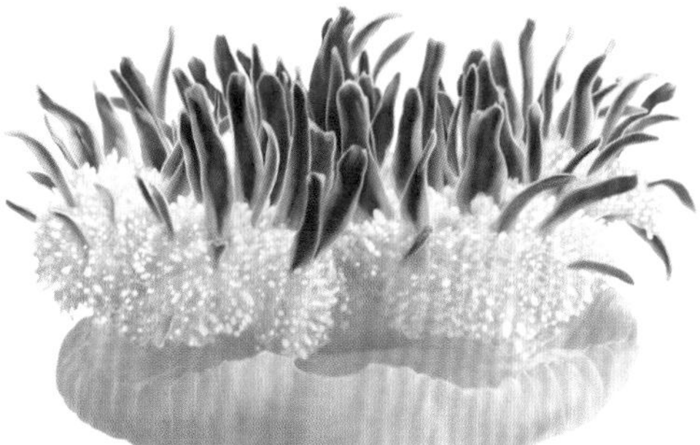

STALKED JELLYFISH

Haliclystus antarcticus

Location: Southern Ocean

Size: Up to 4 cm (1½ in) across

Recently discovered in shallow, near-freezing waters near Antarctica, this jellyfish has a central stalk and eight arms, each with a cluster of stinging tentacles. It clings to rocks and traps prey drifting in the cold but food-rich currents.

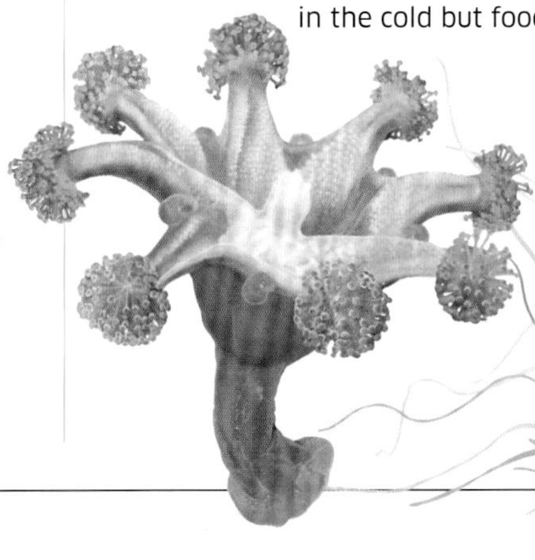

BOX JELLYFISH

Chironex fleckeri

Location: Indo-Pacific region

Size: Up to 25 cm (10 in) across

One of the most dangerous sea creatures, the box jellyfish is also known as the sea wasp because of its lethal sting. Each of its 60 long tentacles is armed with stinging cells that can cause serious and even fatal injuries to human swimmers.

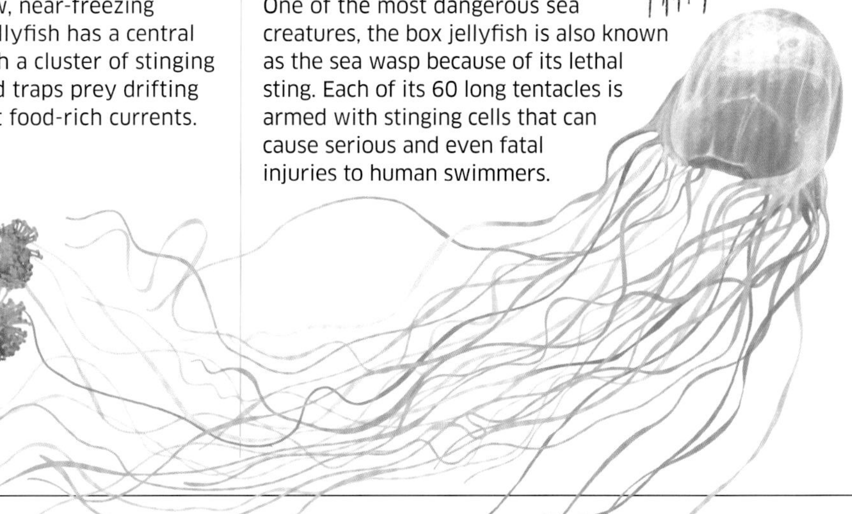

In some countries, the clam's adductor muscle is considered a delicacy. Giant clams are **becoming rarer every year** due to **overharvesting**.

INVERTEBRATES

GIANT CLAM

Tridacna gigas

Location: S. Pacific and Indian oceans

Size: Shell up to 1.4 m (4½ ft) across

Diet: Plankton

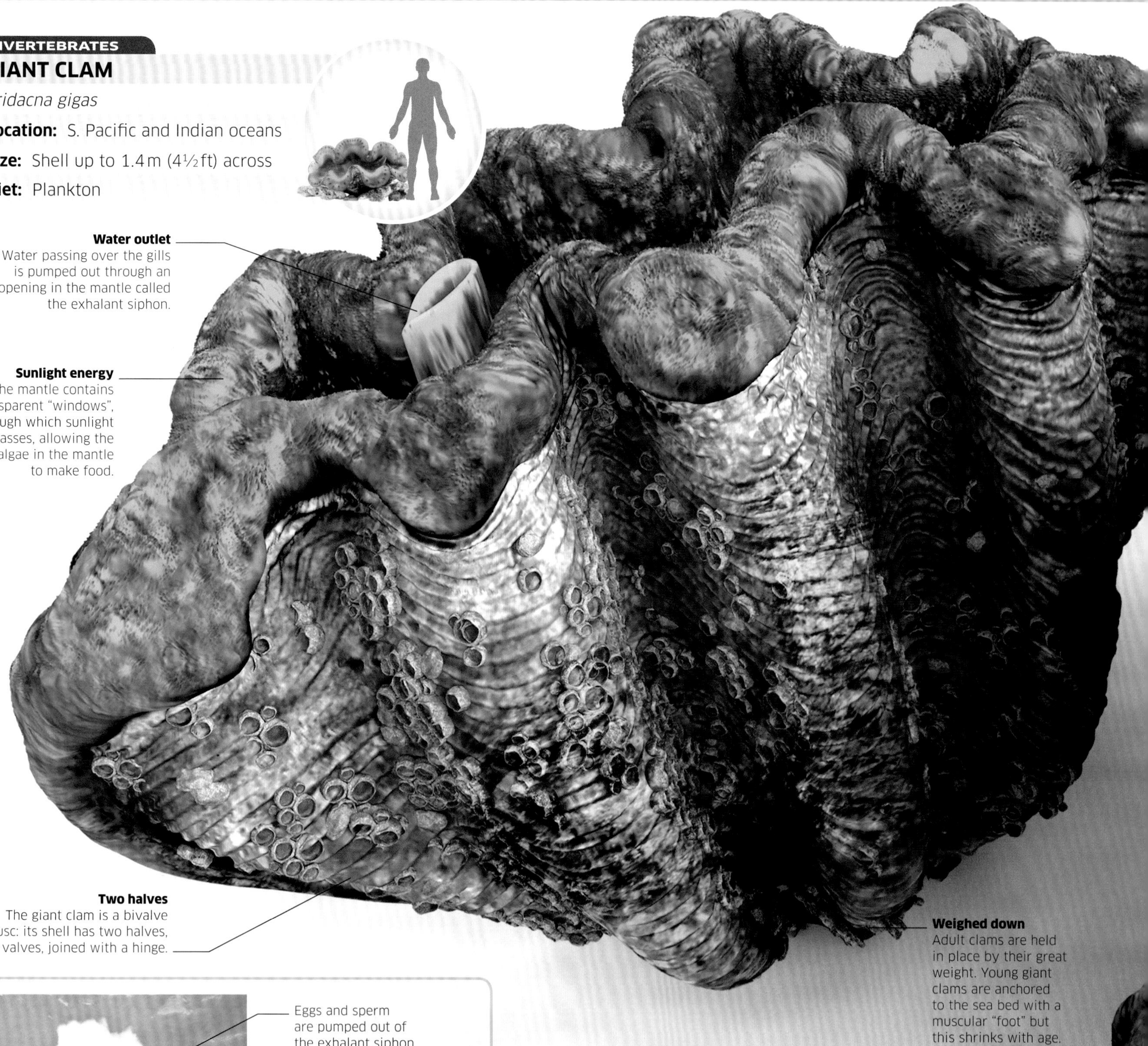

Water outlet
Water passing over the gills is pumped out through an opening in the mantle called the exhalant siphon.

Sunlight energy
The mantle contains transparent "windows", through which sunlight passes, allowing the algae in the mantle to make food.

Two halves
The giant clam is a bivalve mollusc: its shell has two halves, or valves, joined with a hinge.

Weighed down
Adult clams are held in place by their great weight. Young giant clams are anchored to the sea bed with a muscular "foot" but this shrinks with age.

Eggs and sperm are pumped out of the exhalant siphon

Spawning

Giant clams cannot move around, so they reproduce by all spawning at the same time. Each clam can produce both eggs and sperm, and it releases them into the water where they can be fertilized by those of a nearby clam. The sperm is released first to reduce the risk of self-fertilization. Fertilized eggs hatch into larvae that drift away in the current.

Giant clam

The magnificent giant clam is the heaviest living mollusc – a colossal relative of cockles, mussels, and oysters. It typically spends its life rooted in the sand of a tropical coral reef, growing bigger each year.

A giant clam spends its first few days of life as a free-drifting larva, without a shell, in the tropical Indo-Pacific Ocean. But it soon turns into a tiny replica of its parents, and settles on a coral reef. It feeds on plankton strained from water pumped through its body, but up to two-thirds of the nutrients it needs are supplied by millions of microscopic, plant-like algae that live in its soft mantle tissue using the energy of sunlight to make food.

Like many **bivalve molluscs**, the giant clam can **produce pearls** inside its shell.

100 years – the **age** a giant clam **can reach**.

6 billion The number of **eggs** an adult giant clam can **release during its lifetime**.

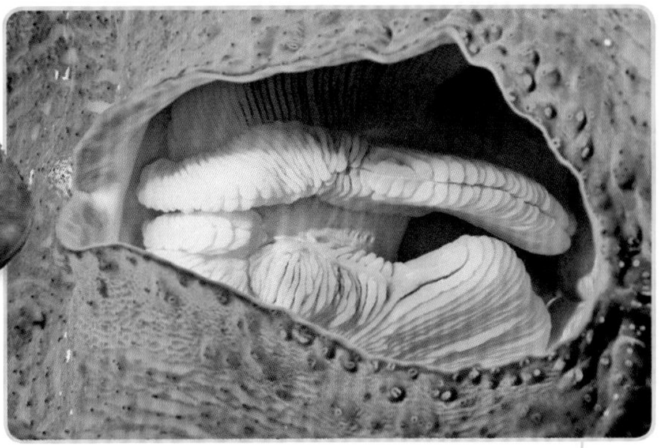

Filter-feeding
Water enters the clam through the inhalant siphon, and passes over the white feathery gills, which absorb oxygen from the seawater. The gills also filter the water for tiny planktonic animals and other food particles, which provide essential protein. Some of the digested protein helps support the algae that keep the clam supplied with sugary carbohydrate food.

Food detector
Chemoreceptors on the inhalant siphon can "taste" the water to detect the presence of plankton.

Shell gap
A fully grown giant clam cannot completely close its shell.

Soft mantle
The clam's mantle secretes calcium carbonate – the hard substance that forms the shell – and encloses the mantle cavity, a water-filled space inside the clam that contains the gills and vital organs.

Iridescent shade
The microscopic algae living in the clam's soft tissue give the fleshy mantle its vivid colours. Each clam has its own unique coloration.

Open up
The two halves of the shell are connected by a muscle called the adductor, which contracts to close the shell. When the muscle is relaxed the shell opens up.

Massive shell
The heavy shell has four or five vertical folds, and many horizontal ridges indicating its growth. The more ridges it has the older it is.

The largest giant clam ever found weighed in at a hefty 300 kg (660 lb).

A giant squid's eyes are up to 27 cm (10½ in) across – bigger than footballs.

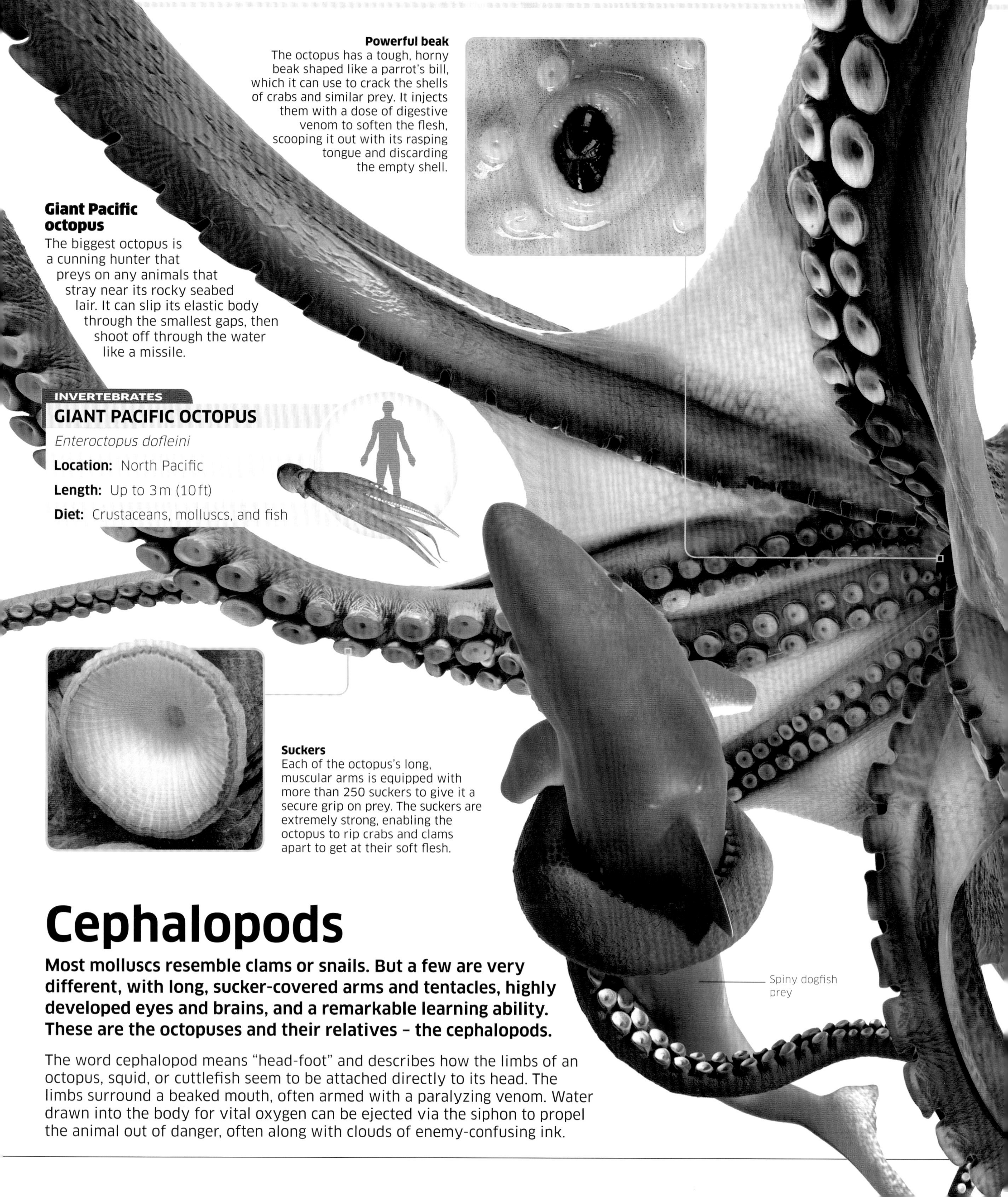

Powerful beak
The octopus has a tough, horny beak shaped like a parrot's bill, which it can use to crack the shells of crabs and similar prey. It injects them with a dose of digestive venom to soften the flesh, scooping it out with its rasping tongue and discarding the empty shell.

Giant Pacific octopus
The biggest octopus is a cunning hunter that preys on any animals that stray near its rocky seabed lair. It can slip its elastic body through the smallest gaps, then shoot off through the water like a missile.

INVERTEBRATES

GIANT PACIFIC OCTOPUS

Enteroctopus dofleini

Location: North Pacific

Length: Up to 3 m (10 ft)

Diet: Crustaceans, molluscs, and fish

Suckers
Each of the octopus's long, muscular arms is equipped with more than 250 suckers to give it a secure grip on prey. The suckers are extremely strong, enabling the octopus to rip crabs and clams apart to get at their soft flesh.

Cephalopods

Most molluscs resemble clams or snails. But a few are very different, with long, sucker-covered arms and tentacles, highly developed eyes and brains, and a remarkable learning ability. These are the octopuses and their relatives – the cephalopods.

The word cephalopod means "head-foot" and describes how the limbs of an octopus, squid, or cuttlefish seem to be attached directly to its head. The limbs surround a beaked mouth, often armed with a paralyzing venom. Water drawn into the body for vital oxygen can be ejected via the siphon to propel the animal out of danger, often along with clouds of enemy-confusing ink.

A vampire squid's body is covered in light-producing organs that glow in the dark.

The venom of the blue-ringed octopus contains a neurotoxin 1,200 times more toxic than cyanide.

CHAMBERED NAUTILUS

Nautilus pompilius

Location: Western Pacific

Length: Up to 20 cm (7¾ in) across shell

Distinguished by its coiled, multi-chambered shell, the nautilus floats in mid-water where it regulates its buoyancy by adjusting the amount of gas in the shell chambers. It has 90 small tentacles, and pinhole eyes with no lenses.

COMMON CUTTLEFISH

Sepia officinalis

Location: Eastern Atlantic

Length: Up to 45 cm (17¾ in)

A cuttlefish is adapted for hunting on shallow sea beds, swimming slowly and seizing prey with two extendible tentacles. Its skin is peppered with nerve-controlled colour cells that can expand or contract to change its pattern, to express its mood, to hide, or to startle predators.

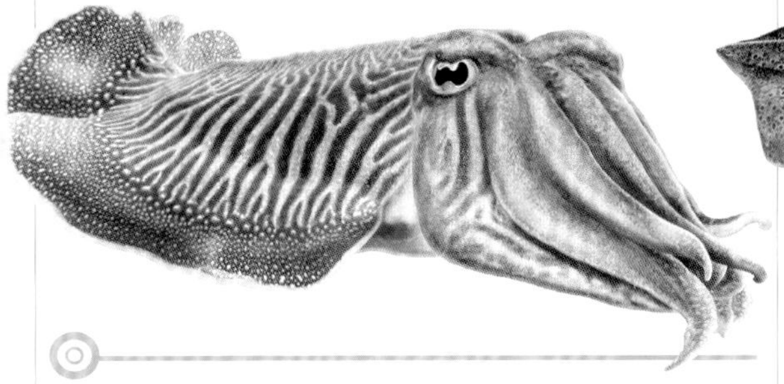

OPALESCENT INSHORE SQUID

Doryteuthis opalescens

Location: Eastern Pacific

Length: Up to 30 cm (11¾ in)

Similar to cuttlefish, squid have the same feeding technique and colour-changing abilities. But they are adapted for speed, shooting through the water by jet propulsion. This Pacific species preys on fish, crabs, and even other cephalopods.

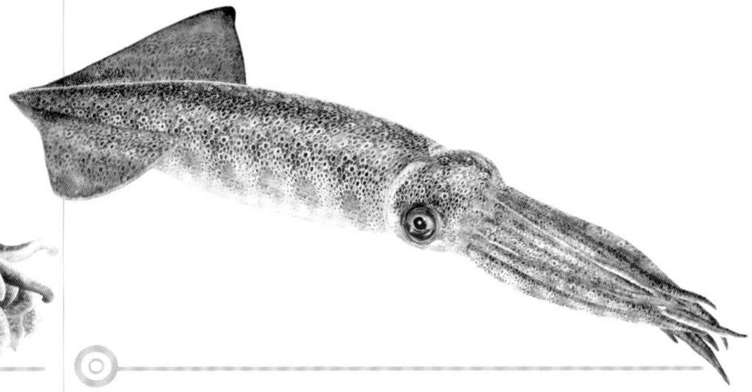

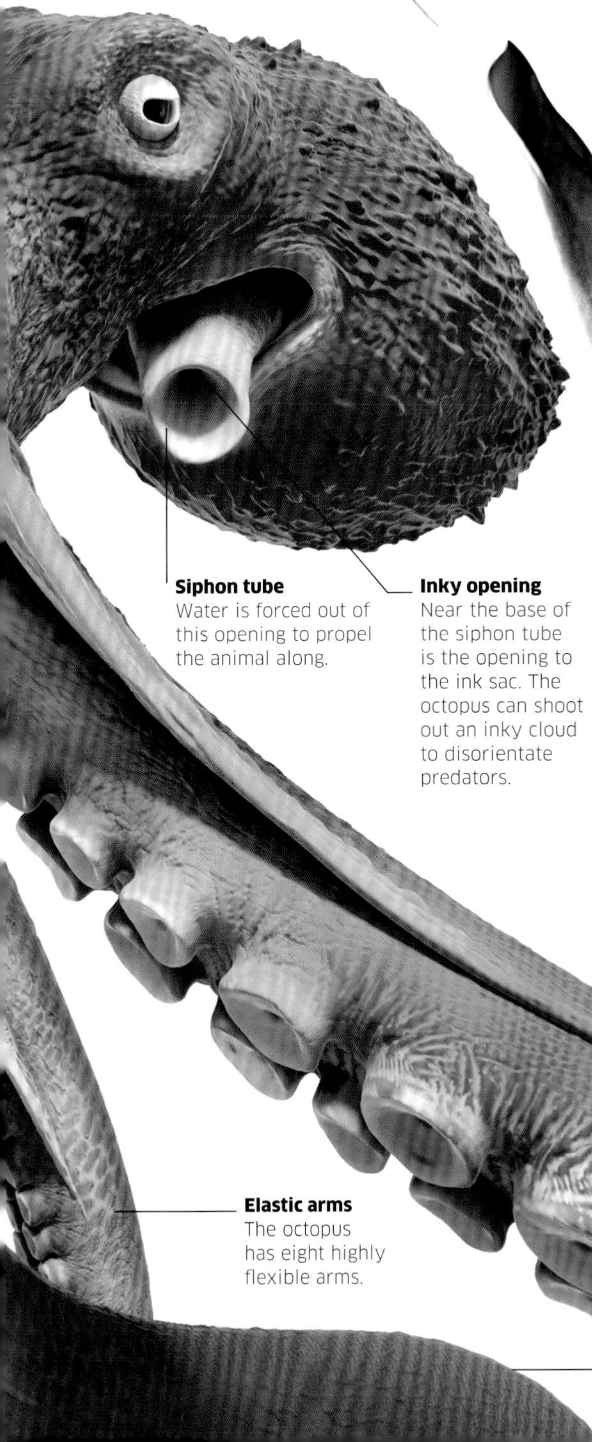

GIANT SQUID

Architeuthis dux

Location: Deep Atlantic

Length: Up to 13 m (42½ ft)

This gigantic, elusive deep-ocean cephalopod is rarely seen alive, but has occasionally been found stranded on sea shores. It has the largest eyes of any animal, which it uses to target prey in the gloom of the oceanic twilight zone.

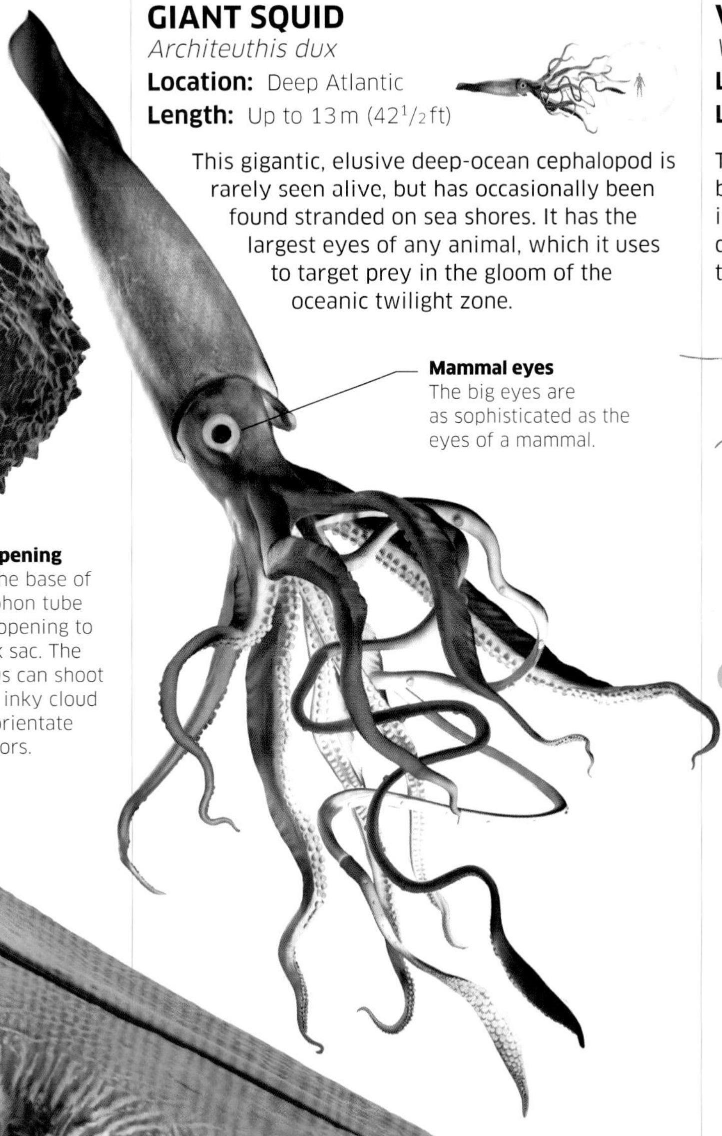

VAMPIRE SQUID

Vampyroteuthis infernalis

Location: Deep oceans worldwide

Length: Up to 28 cm (11 in)

The umbrella-like vampire squid is named for its blood-red coloration rather than its habits. It drifts in the dark zone of the deep ocean, eating edible debris and other invertebrates that it catches with the suckered tips of its arms.

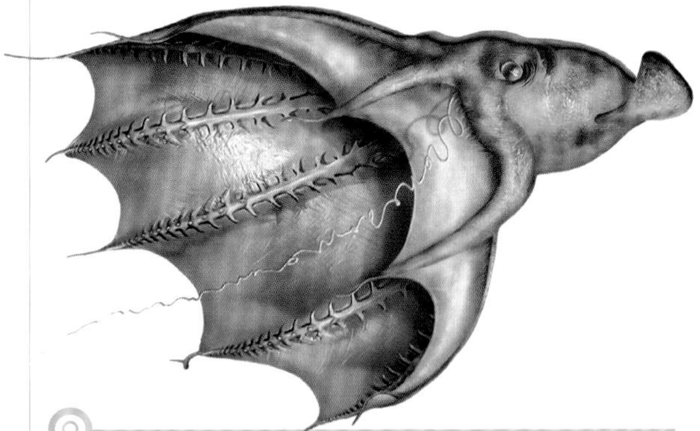

GREATER BLUE-RINGED OCTOPUS

Hapalochlaena lunulata

Location: Indo-Pacific coral reefs

Length: Up to 10 cm (4 in)

Like other octopuses this small, colourful species has a venomous bite for immobilizing small crabs, fish, and other prey. Its venom is incredibly toxic, making it one of the most deadly animals on Earth.

80 per cent of molluscs are **gastropods** – snails, slugs, and their relatives.

LINED CHITON
Tonicella lineata
Location: North Pacific coasts
Length: Up to 5 cm (2 in)

Forming a group of their own, chitons crawl over rocks on a slimy foot, like snails do. Their shells are divided into eight interlocking plates. They have no eyes or tentacles but contain cells in their shells that react to light. This species feeds on marine algae.

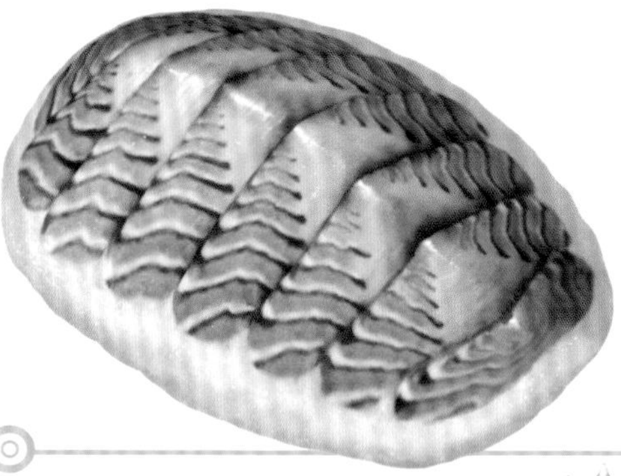

GARDEN SNAIL
Helix aspersa
Location: Worldwide
Shell length: Up to 4.5 cm ($1\frac{3}{4}$ in)

Familiar in gardens throughout Europe and many other parts of the world, this typical snail glides over the ground or plants on its muscular foot, leaving a trail of slimy mucus. In dry weather it retreats into its coiled shell.

RED RAMSHORN SNAIL
Planorbis rubrum
Location: Europe, North Africa
Shell length: Up to 2 cm ($\frac{3}{4}$ in)

Many snails live in ponds, lakes, and rivers. This species is one of the most colourful ramshorn snails – aquatic air-breathers that forage for food underwater, and return to the surface to breathe.

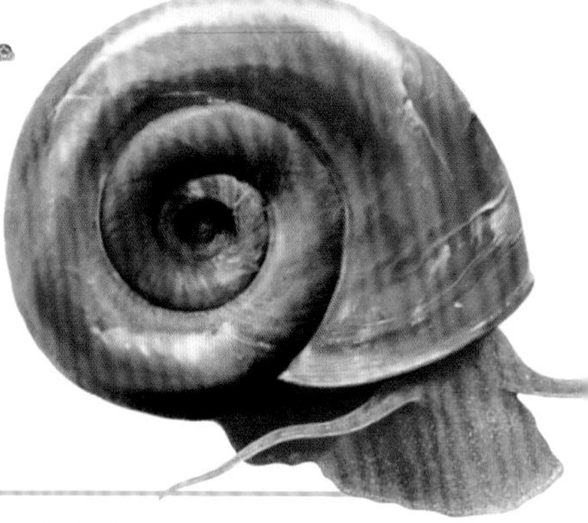

QUEEN CONCH
Lobatus gigas
Location: Caribbean Sea
Shell length: Up to 35 cm ($13\frac{3}{4}$ in)

The queen conch is a giant marine snail that feeds on seagrasses and seaweeds in tropical seas. It is well known for its big, pinkish-tinged shell.

SPANISH SHAWL NUDIBRANCH
Flabellina iodinea
Location: Pacific Ocean
Length: Up to 7 cm ($2\frac{3}{4}$ in)

A nudibranch is a type of sea slug – a gastropod with no shell. Many, including this Pacific species, prey on stinging animals and store the stinging cells in their tentacles for their own defence.

BLUE SEA SLUG
Glaucus atlanticus
Location: Pacific, Atlantic, and Indian oceans
Length: Up to 3 cm ($1\frac{1}{4}$ in)

This sea slug floats upside down on the ocean surface, where it preys on other drifting animals – including venomous jellyfish.

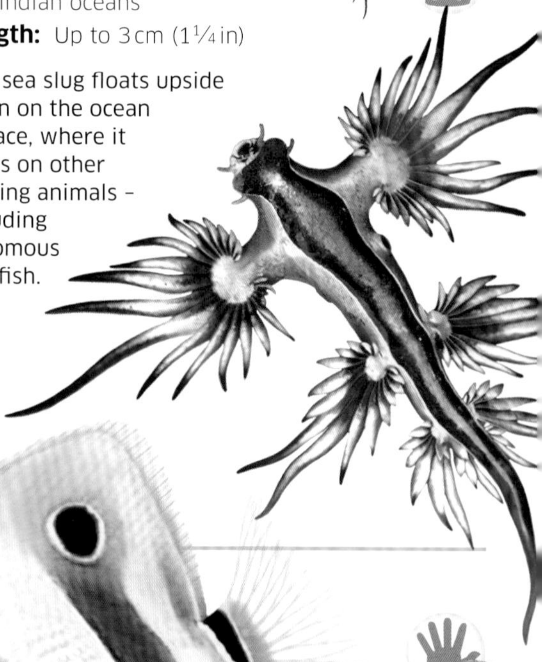

TEXTILE CONE SHELL
Conus textile
Location: Indo-Pacific region
Shell length: Up to 15 cm (6 in)

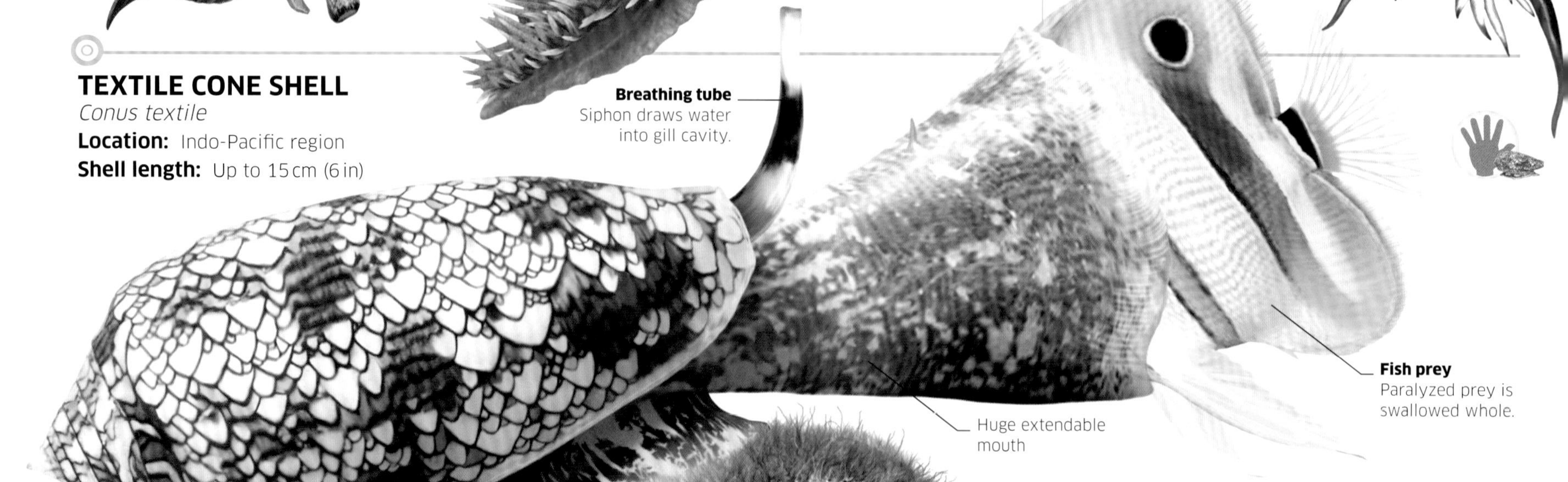

The beautifully marked shell of this tropical sea snail conceals a deadly weapon – a tiny harpoon that injects a potent nerve poison. The cone shell uses it to paralyze its prey, but the venom is powerful enough to kill a human.

507 The **age** of a type of **edible clam** found in the **North Atlantic** in 2006. It was the **oldest-known living animal**.

110,000 living **species of molluscs** have been **scientifically described and named**.

Molluscs

These mainly marine animals include some of the most colourful and diverse of all invertebrates. Many have elaborate shells that protect their soft bodies, allowing some to survive exposure to the air on tidal shores.

Molluscs consist of three main groups. Cephalopods (see pp.24–25) include the octopuses and their relatives. Gastropods – snails and slugs – are mainly mobile animals that crawl on a muscular foot; many are hunters that track down and kill their prey. The two-shelled bivalves mostly live in burrows or attached to rocks, and filter the water for food.

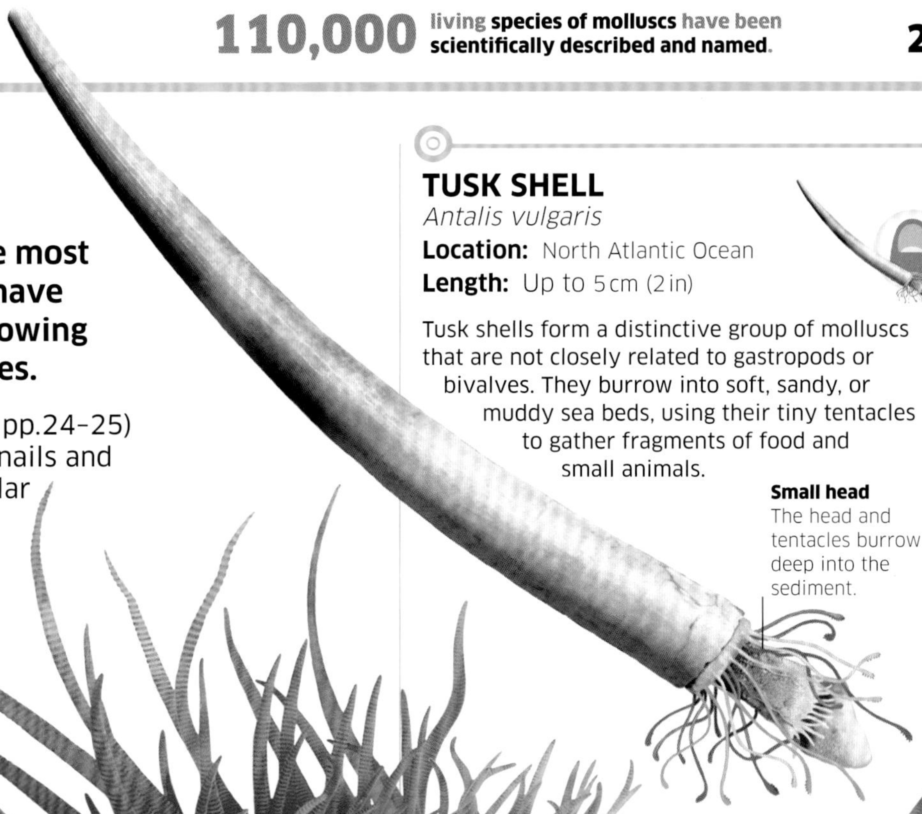

TUSK SHELL

Antalis vulgaris

Location: North Atlantic Ocean

Length: Up to 5 cm (2 in)

Tusk shells form a distinctive group of molluscs that are not closely related to gastropods or bivalves. They burrow into soft, sandy, or muddy sea beds, using their tiny tentacles to gather fragments of food and small animals.

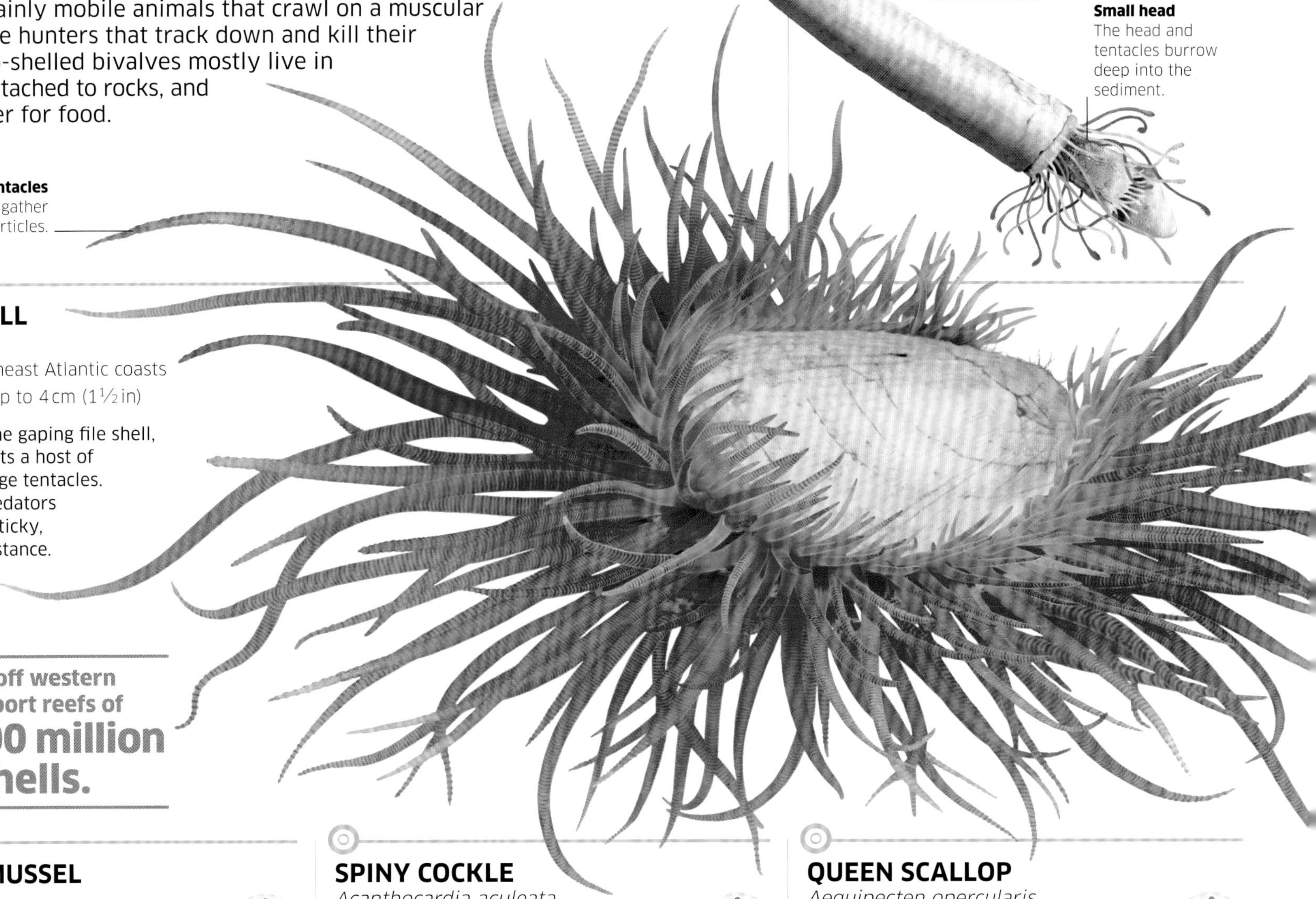

FLAME SHELL

Limaria hians

Location: Northeast Atlantic coasts

Shell length: Up to 4 cm ($1\frac{1}{2}$ in)

Also known as the gaping file shell, this bivalve sports a host of flamboyant orange tentacles. These put off predators by producing a sticky, sour-tasting substance.

Shallow seas off western Scotland support reefs of up to 100 million flame shells.

COMMON MUSSEL

Mytilus edulis

Location: Atlantic and Pacific oceans

Shell length: Up to 10 cm (4 in)

Harvested and farmed in vast numbers for food, this bivalve mollusc attaches itself to rocks on tidal shores with strong, silk-like threads. It feeds by filtering the water for edible particles.

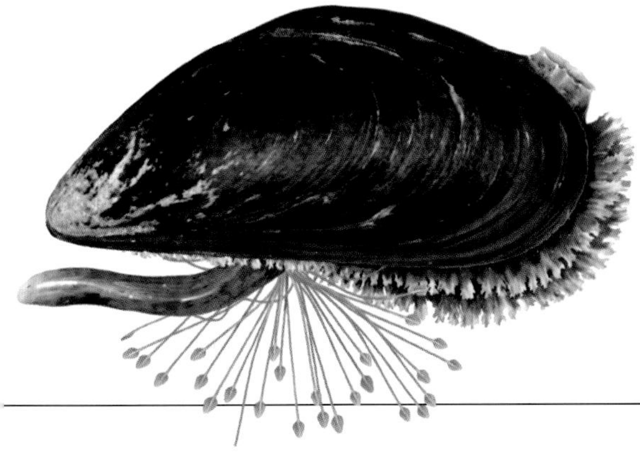

SPINY COCKLE

Acanthocardia aculeata

Location: Mediterranean Sea

Shell length: Up to 10.2 cm (4 in)

Like many bivalve molluscs, this small clam spends its life buried in soft sand. It draws water though its body to gather oxygen and filter out food particles. Its two hinged shells can be tightly closed for protection.

QUEEN SCALLOP

Aequipecten opercularis

Location: North Atlantic Ocean

Shell length: Up to 11 cm ($4\frac{1}{4}$ in)

Scallops are unusual bivalves because they can swim. By clapping its hinged shells together to force water out, the scallop shoots backwards out of danger.

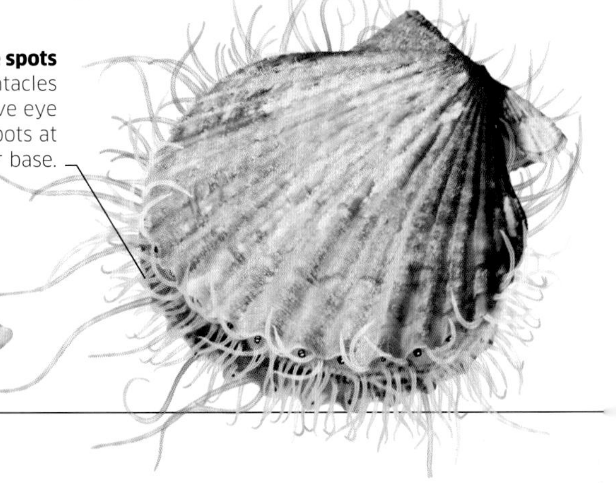

Common lobsters are **blue when alive**. They only turn the familiar **bright red-orange** colour when they are **cooked**.

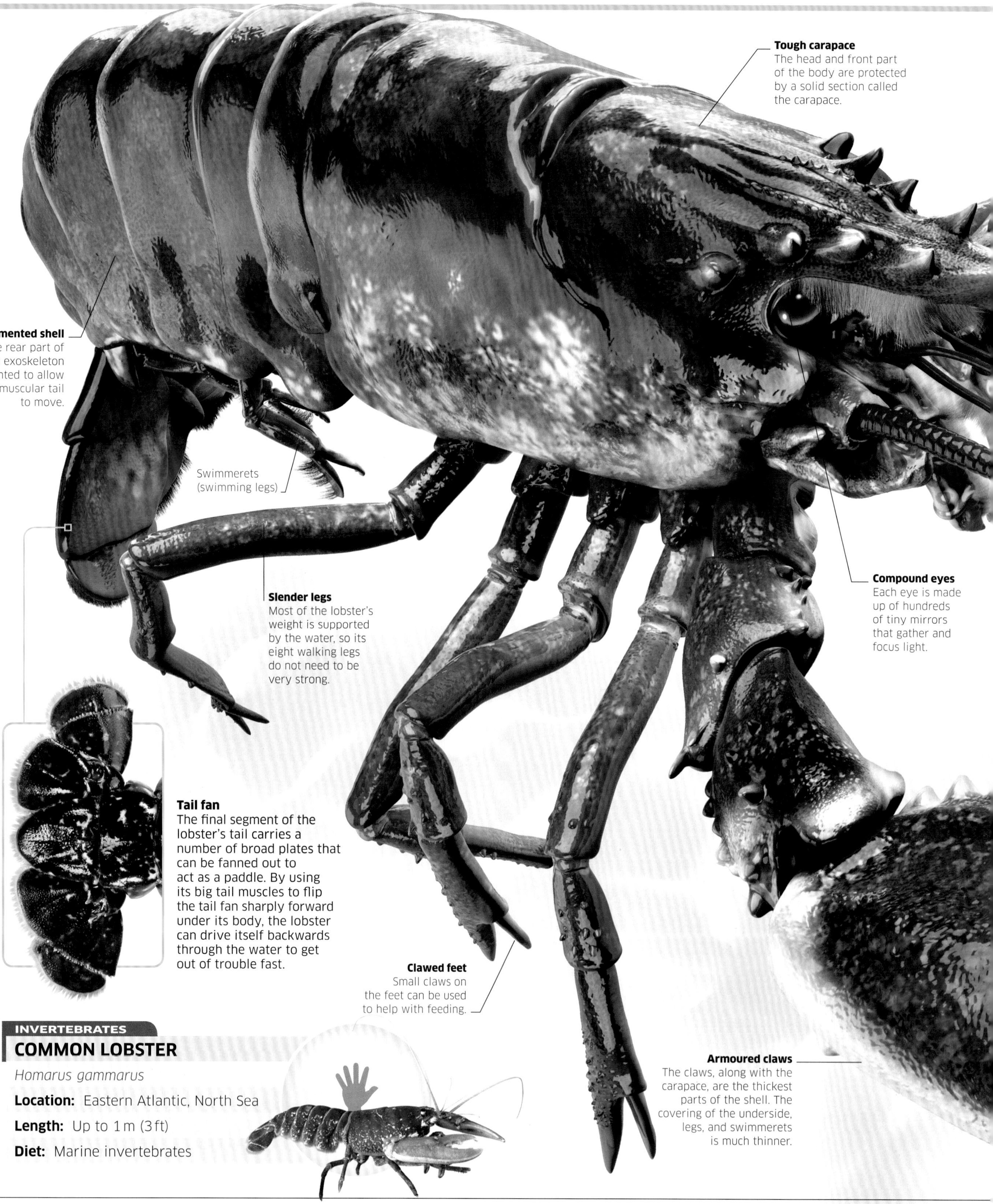

Tough carapace
The head and front part of the body are protected by a solid section called the carapace.

Segmented shell
The rear part of the exoskeleton is jointed to allow the muscular tail to move.

Swimmerets (swimming legs)

Slender legs
Most of the lobster's weight is supported by the water, so its eight walking legs do not need to be very strong.

Compound eyes
Each eye is made up of hundreds of tiny mirrors that gather and focus light.

Tail fan
The final segment of the lobster's tail carries a number of broad plates that can be fanned out to act as a paddle. By using its big tail muscles to flip the tail fan sharply forward under its body, the lobster can drive itself backwards through the water to get out of trouble fast.

Clawed feet
Small claws on the feet can be used to help with feeding.

Armoured claws
The claws, along with the carapace, are the thickest parts of the shell. The covering of the underside, legs, and swimmerets is much thinner.

INVERTEBRATES

COMMON LOBSTER

Homarus gammarus

Location: Eastern Atlantic, North Sea

Length: Up to 1 m (3 ft)

Diet: Marine invertebrates

9.3 kg (20 lbs 8 oz) – the **weight** of the **largest** common lobster **ever caught**.

The largest lobsters can **live** for **more than 70 years**.

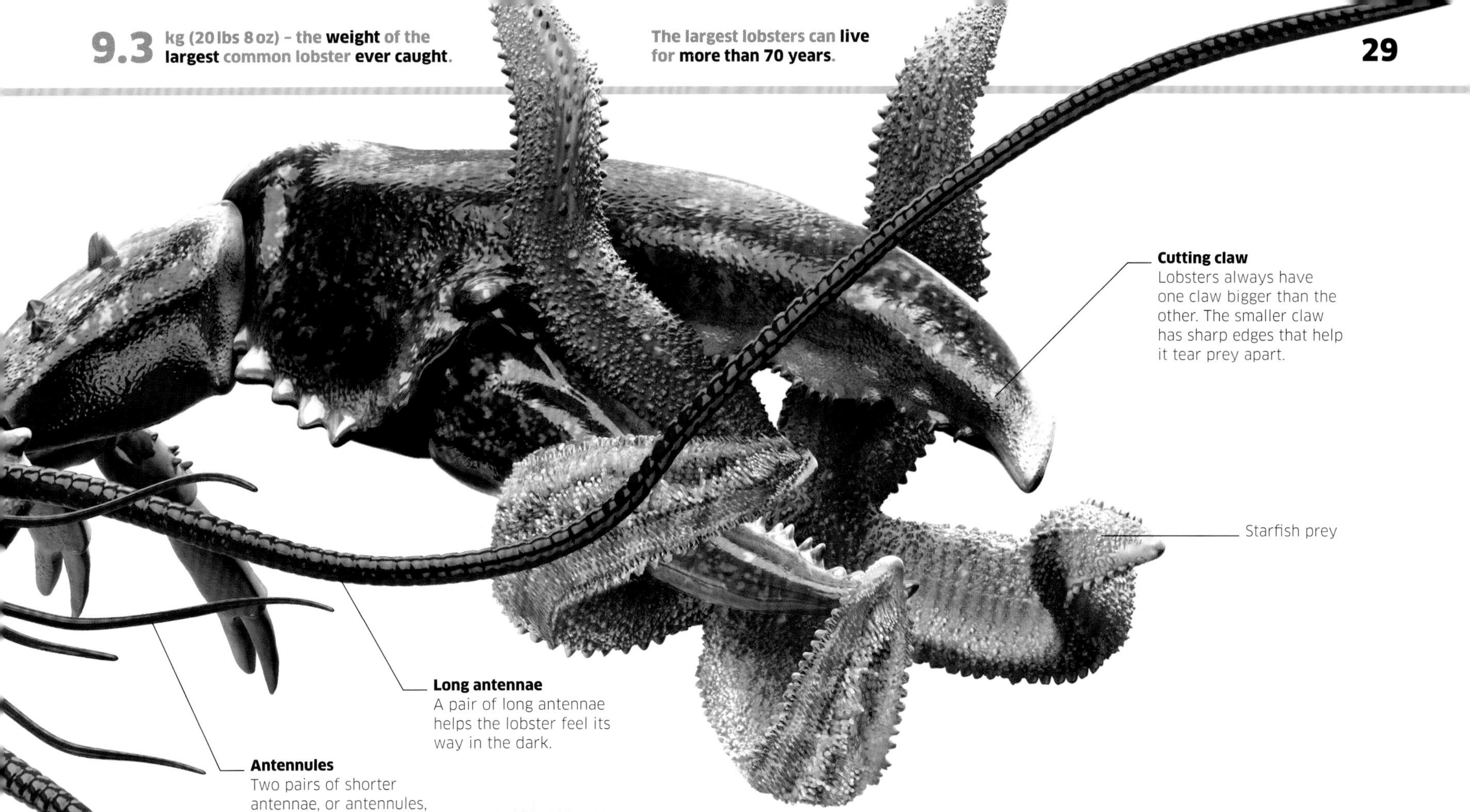

If a lobster loses **a claw, a leg, or an antenna,** it can grow another one.

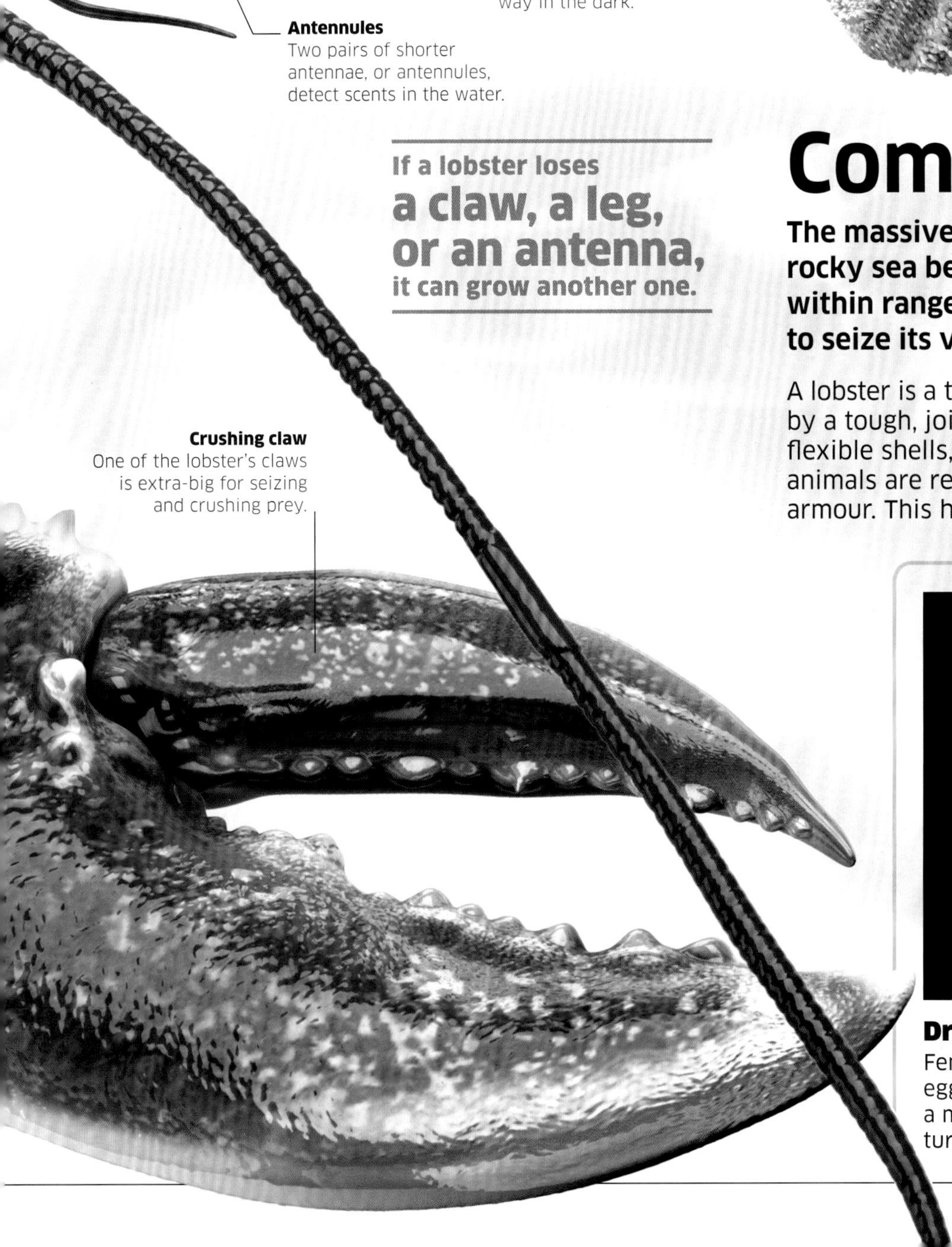

Common lobster

The massively armoured lobster lurks in crevices on the rocky sea bed, watching and waiting for prey to wander within range of its lair. Despite its weight it can move fast to seize its victims with its immensely powerful claws.

A lobster is a type of crustacean – an animal with a body supported by a tough, jointed shell, or exoskeleton. Many crustaceans have flexible shells, but the thicker shells of lobsters, crabs, and similar animals are reinforced with chalky minerals to form a very hard armour. This helps to protect them from fish and other enemies.

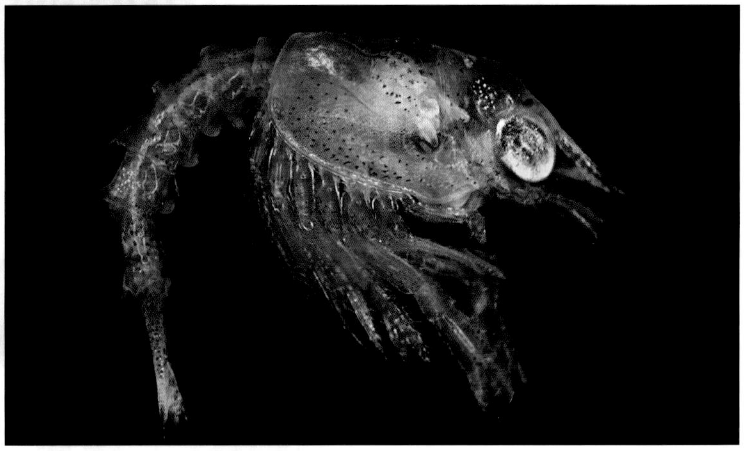

Drifting larvae

Female lobsters release thousands of eggs into the water. The eggs hatch as tiny larvae that drift with the currents for about a month, feeding on other small animals. Eventually each larva turns into a miniature lobster that sinks to the sea bed.

450 sq km (174 sq miles) – the **area** covered by the **largest-known swarm** of **Antarctic krill**.

WATER FLEA

Daphnia magna

Location: North America

Length: Up to 5 mm (¼ in)

Tiny water fleas swarm in ponds and streams, where they are an important food for fish. Each water flea's body is enclosed by a protective carapace that is usually transparent, so its internal organs are visible.

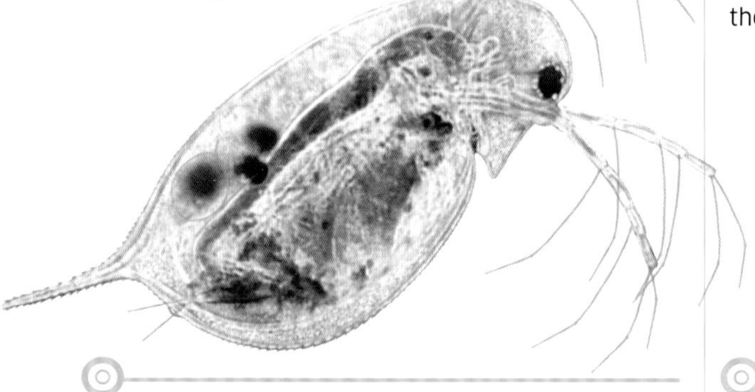

ACORN BARNACLE

Balanus glandula

Location: North Atlantic coastlines

Length: Up to 2.2 cm (¾ in)

Although they look like molluscs, barnacles are relatives of shrimps. When mature they settle on rocks, grow shells, and gather food with their feathery limbs.

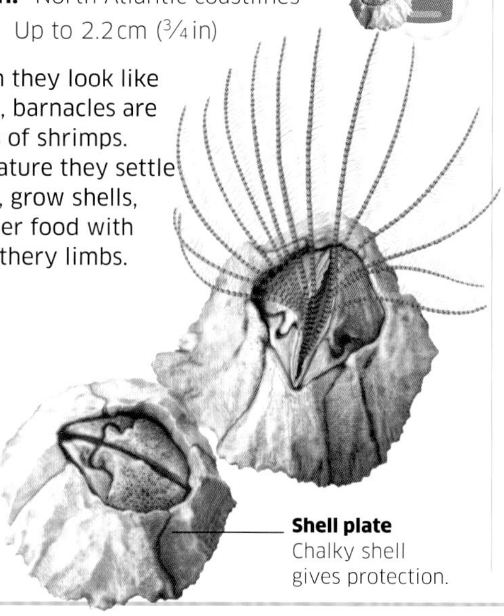

FISH LOUSE

Argulus foliaceus

Location: Europe, Asia, America

Length: Up to 7 mm (¼ in)

Fish lice are parasites – creatures that prey on other living animals. This one uses its two suction cups to cling to a fish, piercing the scaly skin with its sharp mouthparts and sucking the blood. It can also swim if it needs to find a new victim.

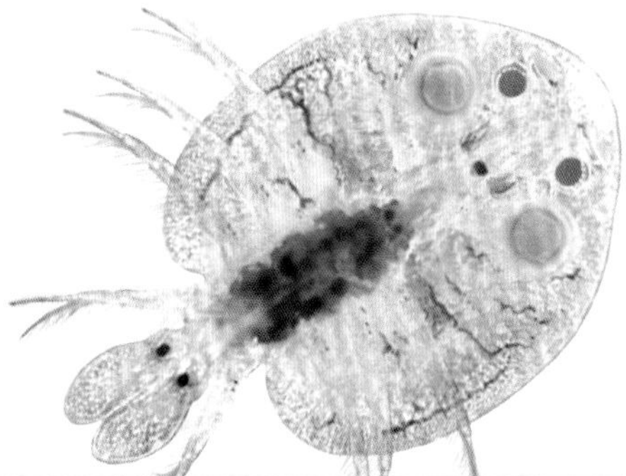

COPEPOD

Calanus glacialis

Location: Arctic waters

Length: Up to 5.2 mm (¼ in)

Billions of tiny copepods live in the oceans, where they feed on microscopic drifting algae. This species builds up thick reserves of fat to combat the cold, making it a vital food source for Arctic fish, seabirds, and even giant whales.

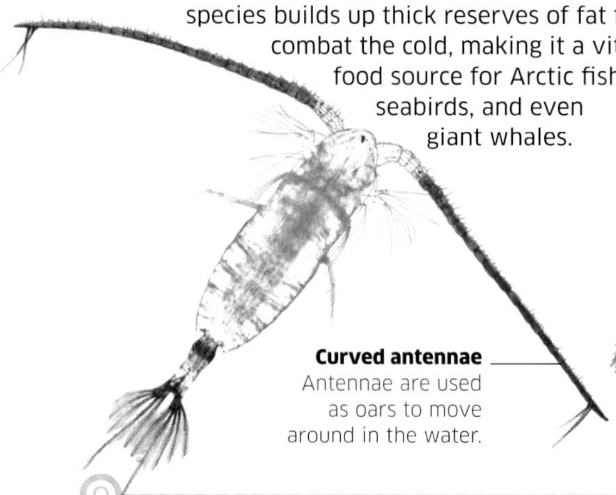

PEACOCK MANTIS SHRIMP

Odontodactylus scyllarus

Location: Indo-Pacific region

Length: Up to 18 cm (7 in)

Mantis shrimps are formidable predators. Some have claws with sharp, barbed tips for spearing passing fish. This one has club-like claws that it uses to punch its prey – hitting them so hard that they are killed instantly.

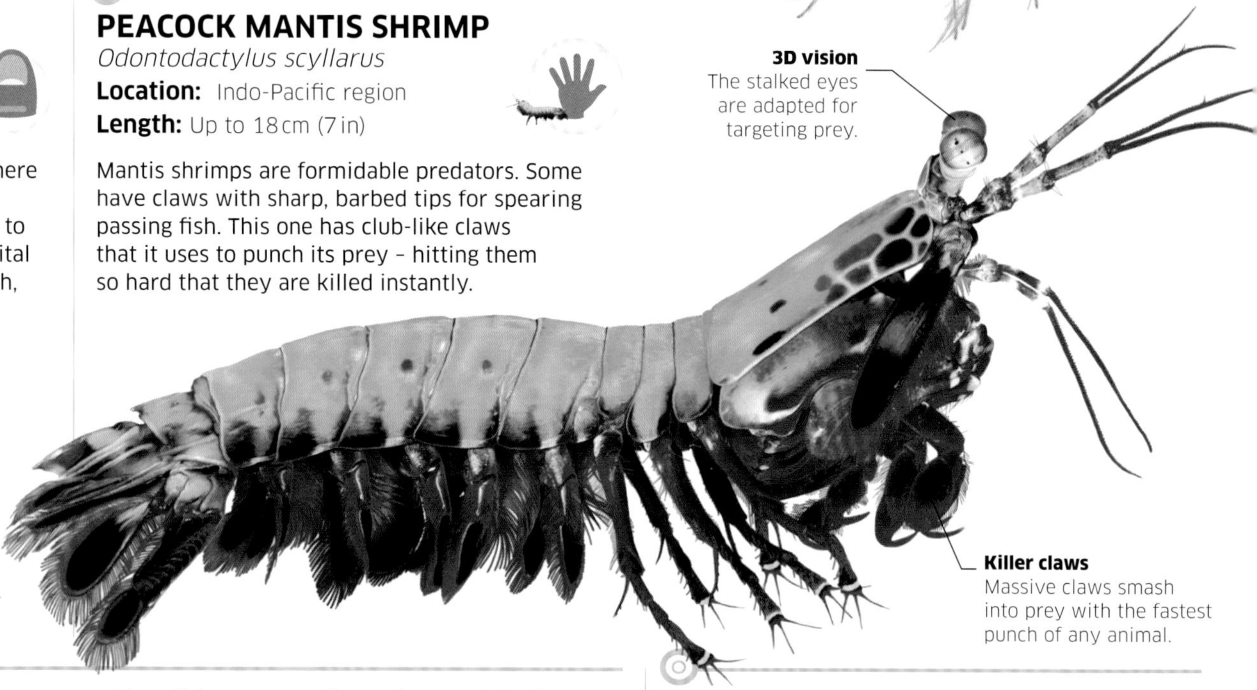

PILL-BUG

Armadillidium vulgare

Location: Eurasia, North America

Length: Up to 18 mm (¾ in)

The pill-bug, or woodlouse, is one of the few crustaceans that lives on land. Its segmented armour helps retain vital body moisture, but despite this it cannot survive in very dry places, and retreats to damp crevices on hot days. It eats decaying plant material.

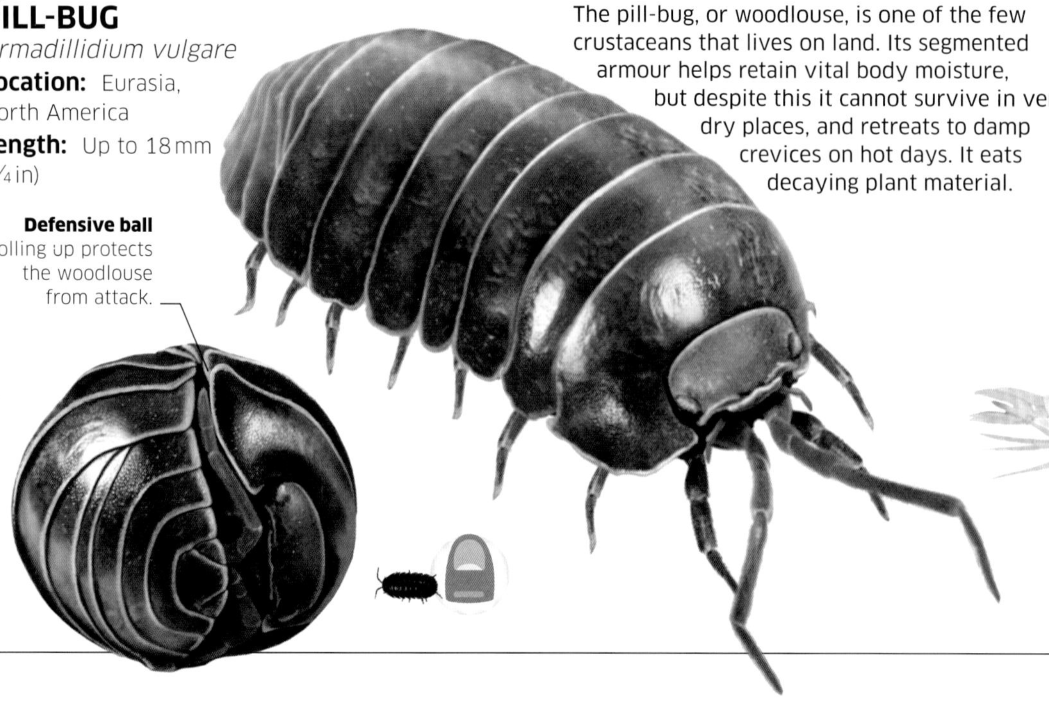

DEEP-SEA AMPHIPOD

Eurythenes gryllus

Location: Southern Ocean

Length: Up to 15 cm (6 in)

Amphipods are relatives of shrimps, found in all seas and fresh waters. This one lives in the permanently dark, cold world of the deep oceans, where it scavenges the remains of dead animals that have settled on the ocean floor.

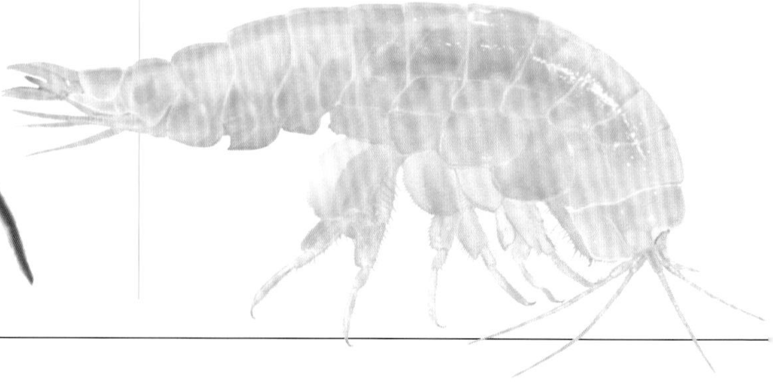

70,000 The approximate number of **crustacean species.**

The **largest-known crustacean** is the **Japanese spider crab.** Its **claws** can span up to **4 m (13 ft).**

ANTARCTIC KRILL

Euphausia superba

Location: Southern Ocean

Length: Up to 6 cm (2¼ in)

Shrimp-like krill live in vast swarms, drifting with the ocean currents and feeding on microscopic plankton. The Antarctic krill is the most abundant species, and is the main food of most Antarctic penguins, seals, and whales – including the largest of all animals, the colossal blue whale.

BANDED CORAL SHRIMP

Stenopus hispidus

Location: Indo-Pacific region

Length: Up to 6 cm (2¼ in)

The extraordinary cleaner shrimp feeds by picking parasites and flakes of dead skin from the bodies of fish. The fish could easily eat the shrimp, but they value its services too highly to do it any harm.

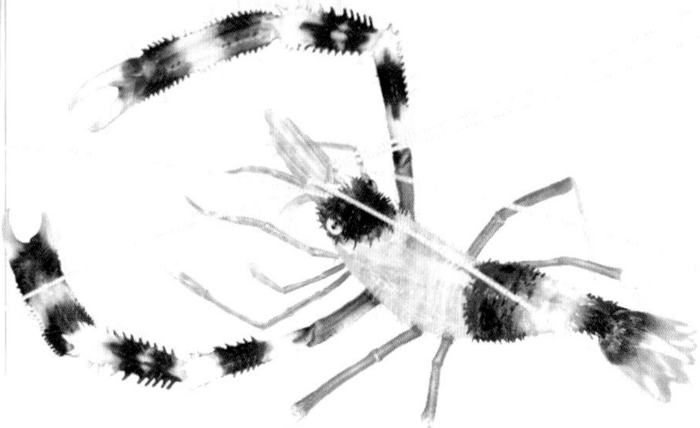

SIGNAL CRAYFISH

Pacifastacus leniusculus

Location: North America

Length: Up to 18 cm (7 in)

This lobster-like crustacean lives in rivers and lakes, where it eats any animal and plant material it can find. Native to North America, it has been introduced to Europe where it is now widespread, and considered a pest.

Crustaceans

Crabs, prawns, and lobsters are some of the most familiar crustaceans – invertebrates with armoured bodies and jointed limbs. Most of them live in the sea, but a few are adapted for life on land.

The crustaceans are part of the huge group of animals known as arthropods. Their boneless bodies are protected and supported by hardened skins that act as external skeletons. The rigid sections are linked by flexible joints that allow them to move.

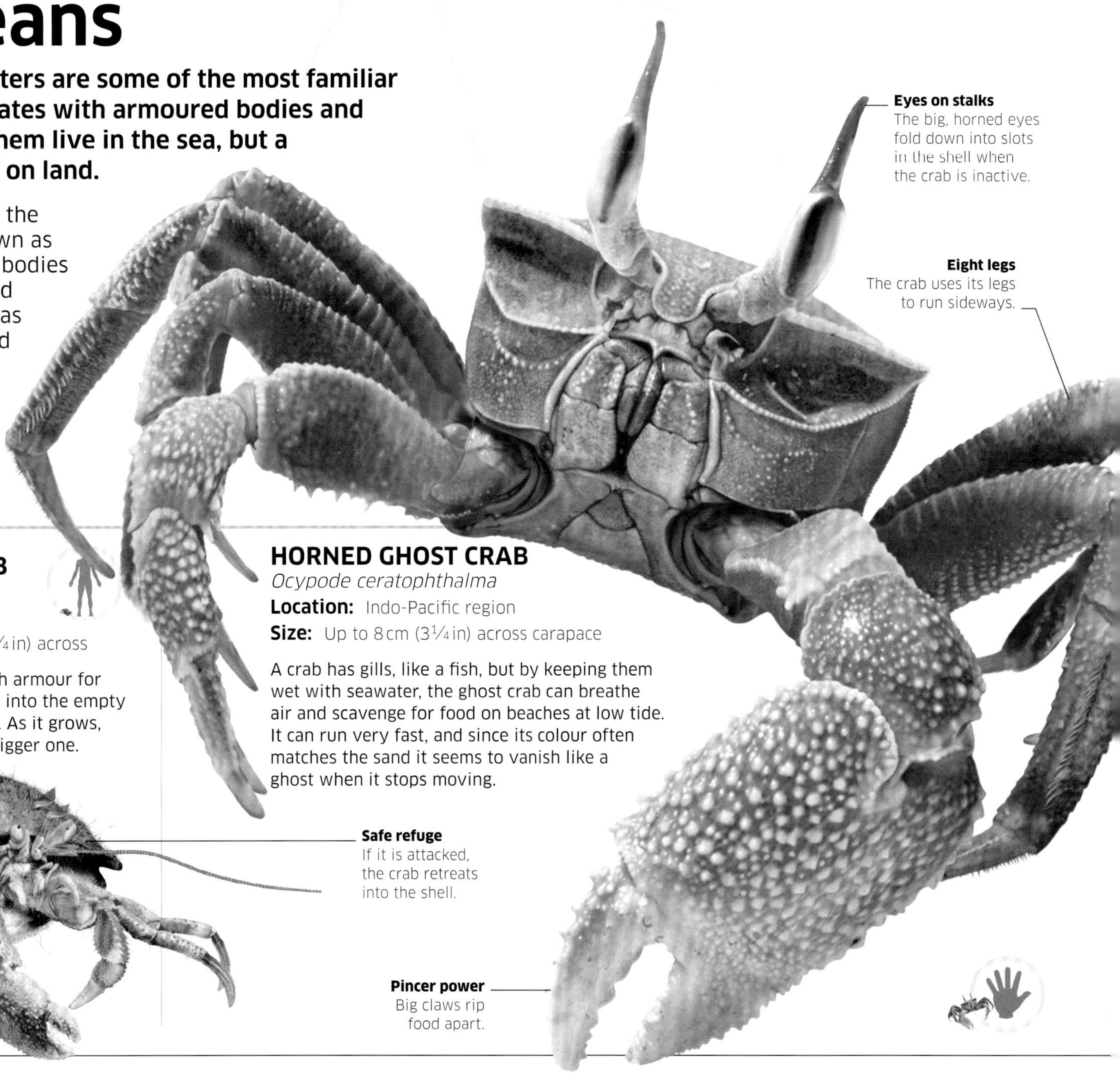

COMMON HERMIT CRAB

Pagurus bernhardus

Location: N. W. Europe

Size: Host shell up to 35 cm (13¾ in) across

Instead of relying on its own tough armour for protection, the hermit crab moves into the empty shell of a mollusc such as a whelk. As it grows, it keeps swapping the shell for a bigger one.

HORNED GHOST CRAB

Ocypode ceratophthalma

Location: Indo-Pacific region

Size: Up to 8 cm (3¼ in) across carapace

A crab has gills, like a fish, but by keeping them wet with seawater, the ghost crab can breathe air and scavenge for food on beaches at low tide. It can run very fast, and since its colour often matches the sand it seems to vanish like a ghost when it stops moving.

Desert locust

Although it is notorious for flying in huge, hungry swarms that destroy every green leaf and edible plant they encounter, the desert locust may spend its entire life in a solitary and harmless state.

Desert locusts are a type of grasshopper and like other grasshoppers they normally feed quietly on grass and similar plants. But if food gets scarce and the locusts are forced to crowd together, their behaviour and their colour change and they turn into a ravenous army, eventually taking off in a gigantic swarm in search of any food they can find.

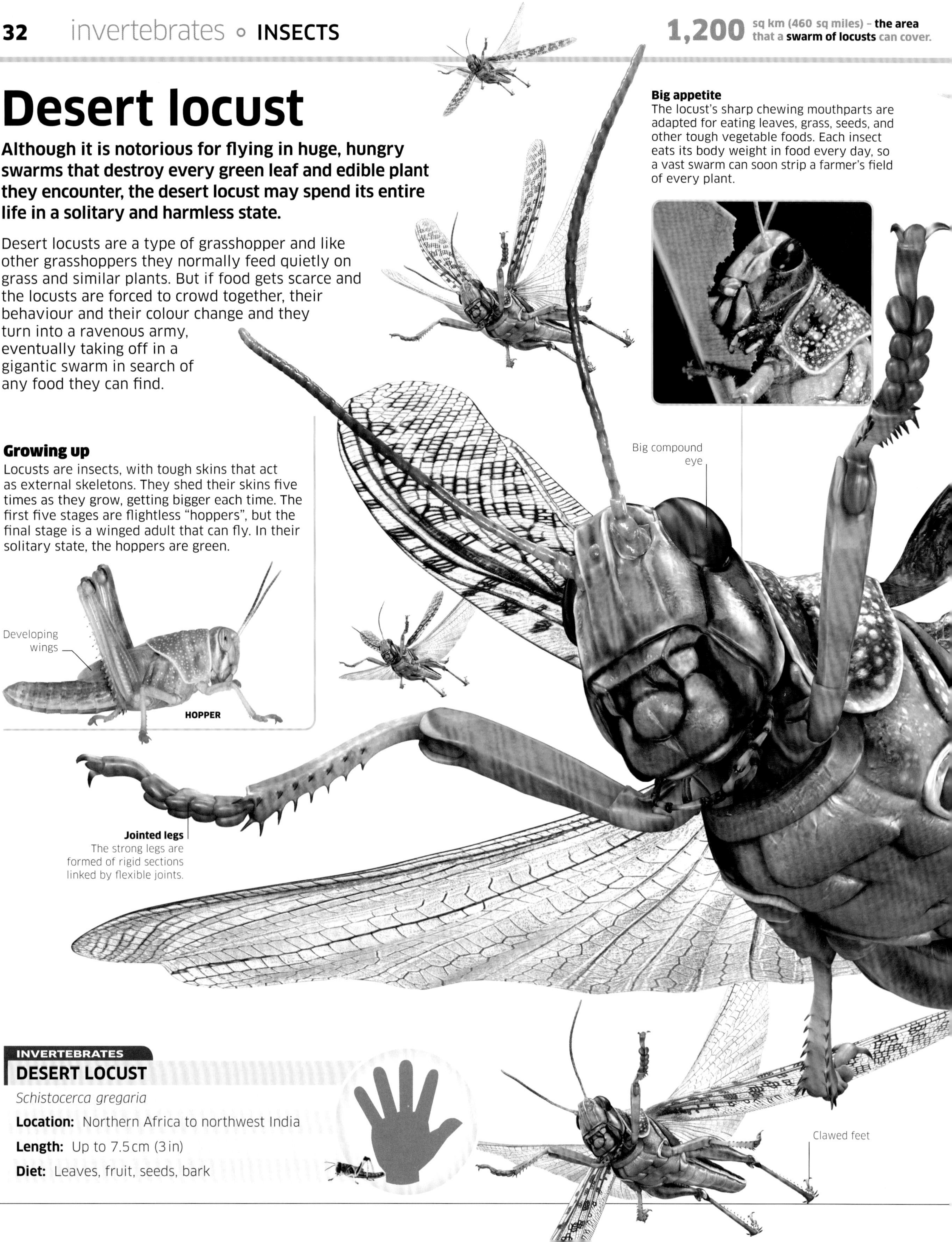

Big appetite
The locust's sharp chewing mouthparts are adapted for eating leaves, grass, seeds, and other tough vegetable foods. Each insect eats its body weight in food every day, so a vast swarm can soon strip a farmer's field of every plant.

Growing up

Locusts are insects, with tough skins that act as external skeletons. They shed their skins five times as they grow, getting bigger each time. The first five stages are flightless "hoppers", but the final stage is a winged adult that can fly. In their solitary state, the hoppers are green.

Jointed legs
The strong legs are formed of rigid sections linked by flexible joints.

INVERTEBRATES
DESERT LOCUST

Schistocerca gregaria

Location: Northern Africa to northwest India

Length: Up to 7.5 cm (3 in)

Diet: Leaves, fruit, seeds, bark

A single swarm of locusts may contain more than **40 billion hungry insects**.

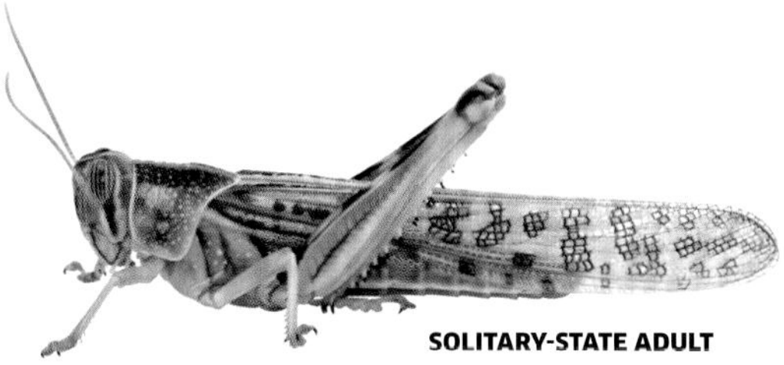

SOLITARY-STATE ADULT

Harmless locust

A locust may live as a solitary insect, feeding on vegetation but not being particularly destructive. In this state, the adult locusts are a sandy-brown colour, camouflaged from hungry birds. If food remains plentiful it will always live like this. But if too many locusts start competing for scarce food, this causes them to start swarming.

Swarming

When locusts crowd onto the same food plants, it triggers a change. They change colour and start swarming. Flightless hoppers turn black-and-yellow and flood over the ground, and winged adults take to the sky. They fly downwind towards areas where rain may have fallen, fuelling the growth of plants that they can eat.

30,000 The number of **lenses** in a **dragonfly's eye.**

Dragonflies have **existed on Earth** for at least **325 million years.**

Emperor dragonfly

Vividly coloured, amazingly fast, and spectacularly agile in the air, the emperor dragonfly is one of the most spellbinding of all insects. It is a deadly enemy of small flies such as mosquitoes, snatching them out of the air and even eating them on the wing.

Dragonflies, and their similar-looking relatives the damselflies, have long bodies and big eyes. The emperor dragonfly is one of the hawker or darner dragonflies – big, powerful insects that specialize in patrolling the air for prey rather than ambushing it from a perch. It usually hunts over ponds, lakes, and slow-flowing rivers, flying over the surface in search of airborne prey that it can seize in its specially adapted legs.

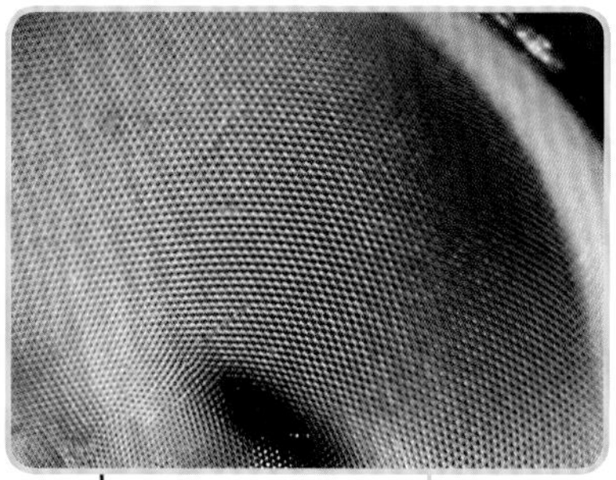

Huge eyes
A dragonfly has huge compound eyes, each made up of thousands of microscopic lenses. They are wrapped around its head like a helmet, giving it a virtually 360-degree view, so it can spot prey anywhere and is very difficult to take by surprise.

On the wing
Unlike other insects, dragonflies have two pairs of wings that beat independently. This is a feature of some of the earliest flying insects and it gives the emperor exceptional flexibility in the air. It can fly forwards at amazing speeds, hover on the spot, and even fly backwards or sideways.

Get a grip
A pair of sharp, curved claws at the end of each leg helps to grip prey.

INVERTEBRATES

EMPEROR DRAGONFLY

Anax imperator

Location: Europe, central Asia, north Africa

Length: Up to 7.8 cm (3¼ in)

Diet: Flying insects

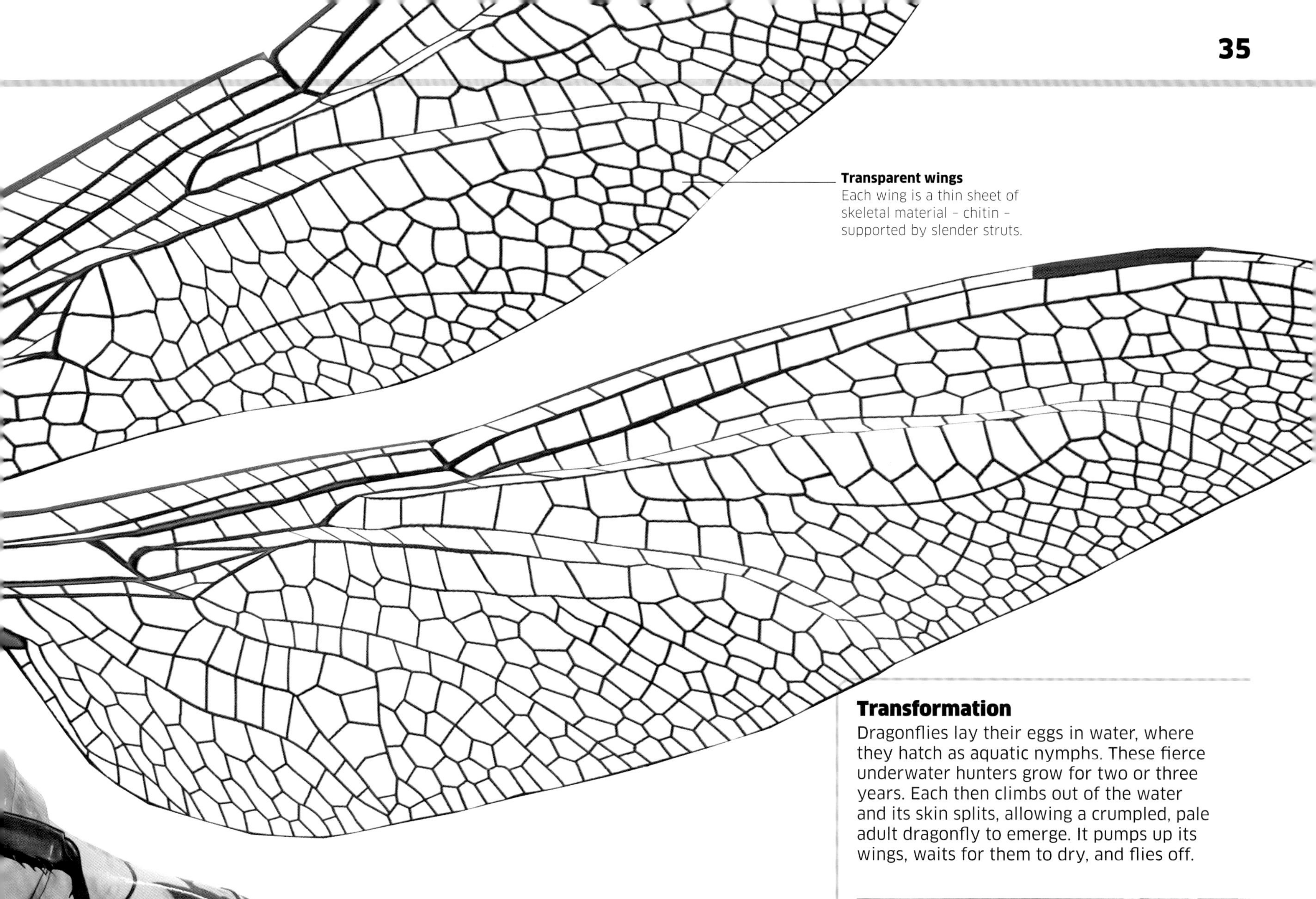

Transparent wings
Each wing is a thin sheet of skeletal material – chitin – supported by slender struts.

Sky blue
A male's abdomen is bright blue with black markings. A female's is greener.

Prey snare
The dragonfly's spiny legs are so specialized for seizing prey that it cannot walk.

Secure grip
The male has claspers on the tip of his abdomen for gripping females.

Transformation

Dragonflies lay their eggs in water, where they hatch as aquatic nymphs. These fierce underwater hunters grow for two or three years. Each then climbs out of the water and its skin splits, allowing a crumpled, pale adult dragonfly to emerge. It pumps up its wings, waits for them to dry, and flies off.

Aerial attack

As it darts over the water at speed, the emperor watches for any hint of an airborne victim. Swerving into the attack, it thrusts its bristly legs forwards to scoop its prey out of the air. If the victim is small enough the emperor will eat it in flight, but it carries larger prey to a perch before mashing it up with its powerful, serrated jaws.

Beetles

Almost a quarter of all known animal species are beetles. This makes them the most successful animals on the planet. Most of them are instantly recognizable by their tough, shiny wing cases.

Known to scientists as elytra, the wing cases are modified, hardened forewings, which cover and protect the beetle's delicate, folded hindwings when they are not needed. This allows many beetles to scramble through dense plant foliage, burrow underground, or even swim underwater without putting their flying ability at risk. As a result, they can live in an amazingly wide variety of habitats, where they eat all kinds of food ranging from flower nectar to the remains of dead animals.

Reflex bleeding
If attacked, the ladybird oozes a noxious yellow fluid from its body joints – a tactic known as reflex bleeding. The vivid pattern on its wing cases warns birds and other enemies that it tastes bad.

Sharp claws
Curved claws on each foot give the beetle a good grip on smooth plant stems.

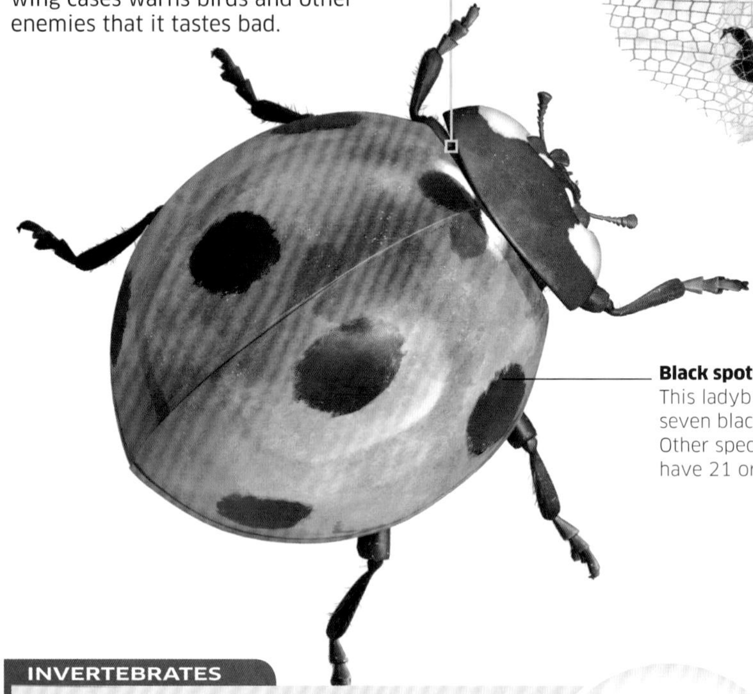

Open wide
The wing cases hinge open for flight, and may help by providing extra lift.

Black spots
This ladybird has seven black spots. Other species may have 21 or more.

Folded wings
Long, delicate wings have to be quickly unfurled for flight.

An adult ladybird can eat as many as 75 aphids in just one day.

INVERTEBRATES

SEVEN-SPOT LADYBIRD

Coccinella septempunctata

Location: Europe, North America

Length: Up to 1 cm (½ in)

Diet: Aphids

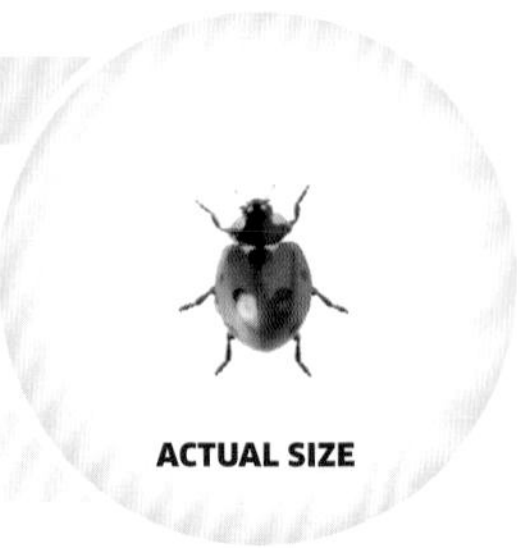

ACTUAL SIZE

Seven-spot ladybird

This small, colourful beetle lives in grassland and woodland where it is a voracious predator. Both the adult beetle and its wingless young hunt small, soft-bodied insects, especially sap-sucking aphids such as greenfly.

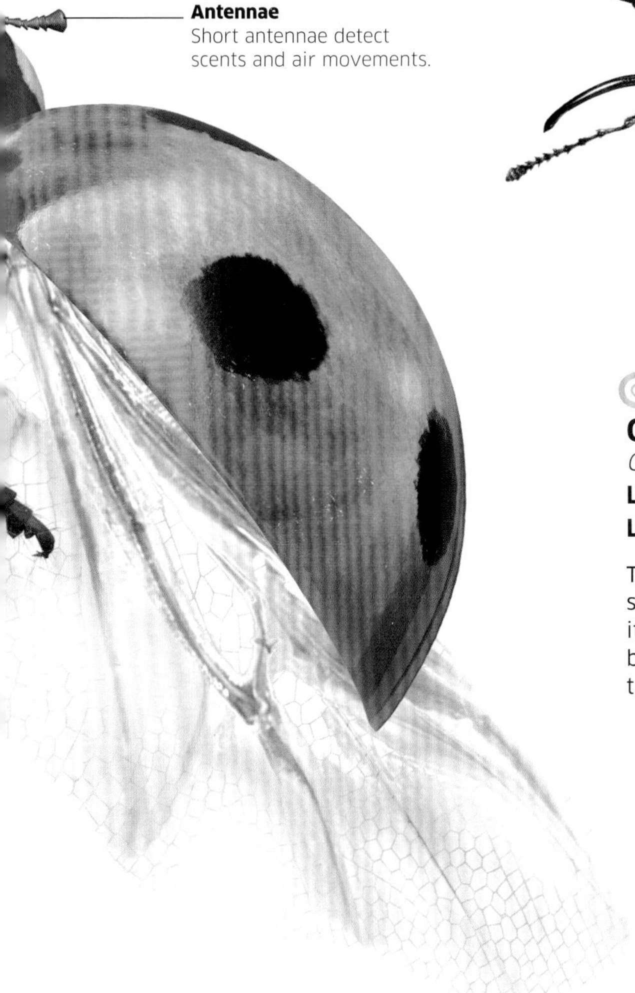

NUT WEEVIL

Curculio nucum

Location: Europe

Length: Up to 9 mm (¼ in)

The nut weevil's amazingly long snout has a pair of tiny jaws at the tip. The female uses them to drill into a hazel nut, where she lays an egg. When it hatches, the weevil grub eats the nut.

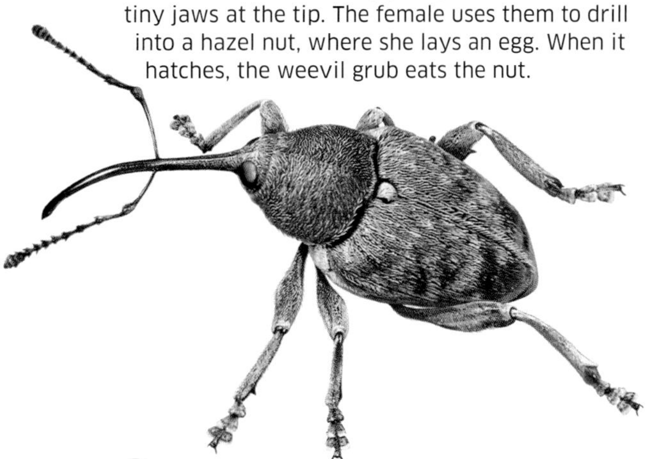

SIX-SPOTTED TIGER BEETLE

Cicindela sexguttata

Location: North America

Length: Up to 1.4 cm (½ in)

Relative to its size, this ferocious hunter runs faster than any other animal. It can cover 125 times its own body length in a second as it chases after insect prey in the broad-leaved woodland where it lives.

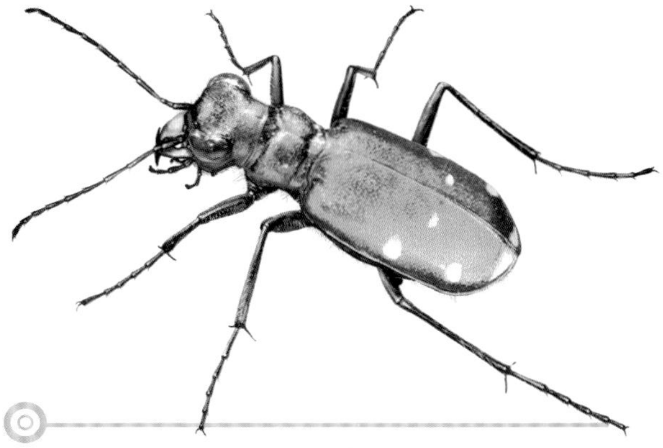

GOLDEN CHAFER

Chrysina resplendens

Location: Central America

Length: Up to 2 cm (¾ in)

The armoured body of this tropical American scarab beetle reflects light in a way that makes it look metallic. Also called the golden scarab beetle, it inhabits tropical rainforest.

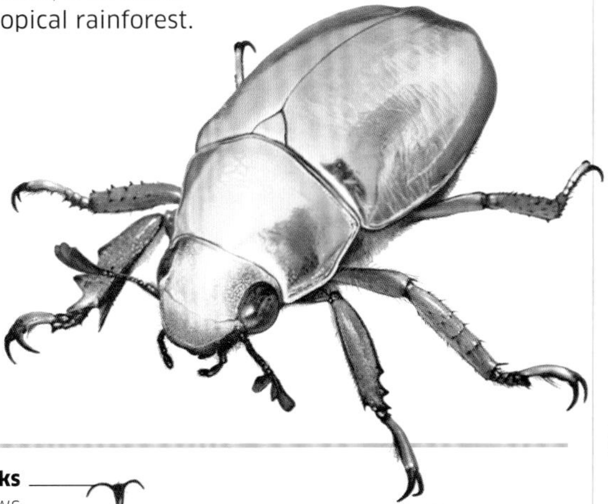

AMERICAN BURYING BEETLE

Nicrophorus americanus

Location: USA

Length: Up to 3.8 cm (1½ in)

This is one of many similar beetles that seek out the dead bodies of larger animals, in grassland or scrubland, and bury them by digging away the ground below. The female then lays her eggs on the carcass, and helps her young feed when they hatch.

STAG BEETLE

Lucanus cervus

Location: Europe

Length: Up to 7.5 cm (3 in)

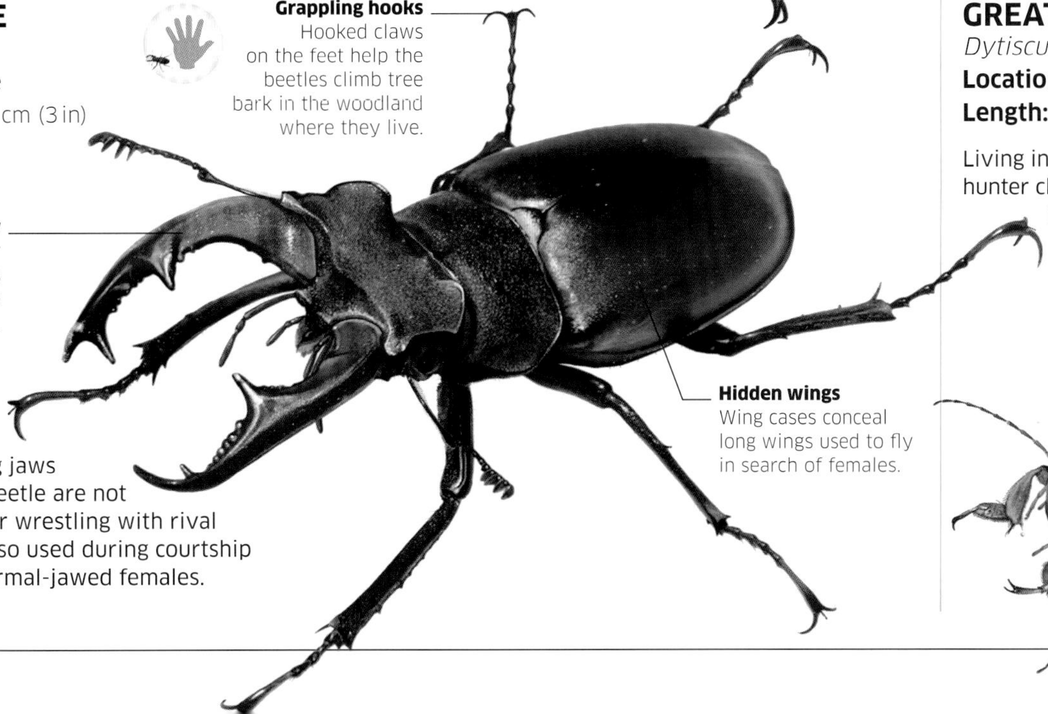

The alarmingly big jaws of the male stag beetle are not for hunting, but for wrestling with rival males. They are also used during courtship displays to the normal-jawed females.

GREAT DIVING BEETLE

Dytiscus marginalis

Location: Europe, Northern Asia

Length: Up to 3.5 cm (1½ in)

Living in ponds, lakes, and rivers, this underwater hunter chases small fish and other prey by driving itself along with its hair-fringed legs. It carries an air supply of bubbles beneath its wing cases so it can breathe.

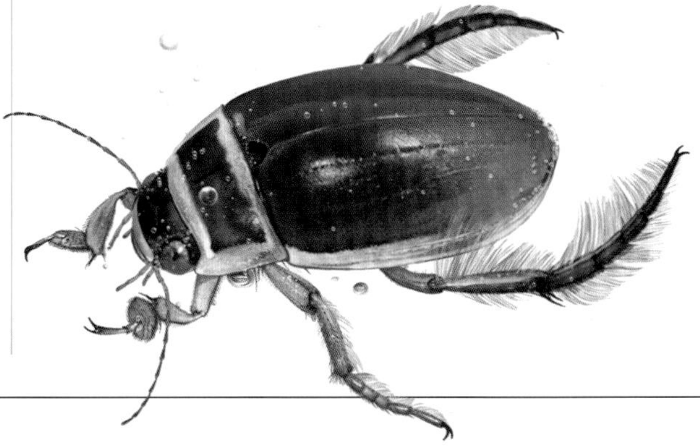

Malaria mosquito

The most deadly animal on Earth is not a killer shark or a venomous snake, but a small fly with a bloodsucking bite – the malaria mosquito. The parasites that it carries in its body are responsible for at least a million human deaths every year.

Mosquitoes are slender two-winged flies with an irritating habit. The females suck the blood of larger animals to get the nutrients they need to make their eggs. Mosquitoes are found all over the world and most are nothing more than a nuisance. But certain tropical species in the genus *Anopheles* can pass on some serious diseases, the most deadly of which is malaria. The malarial parasite infects a victim's red blood cells, causing a fever that can be fatal.

Bloodsucker

The female flies mainly by night, and finds her victims by detecting their breath and body heat. She can often land and bite without being detected, allowing her to drink her fill of a victim's blood. After a blood meal the abdomen fills with eggs over two to three days. The eggs are then laid in water.

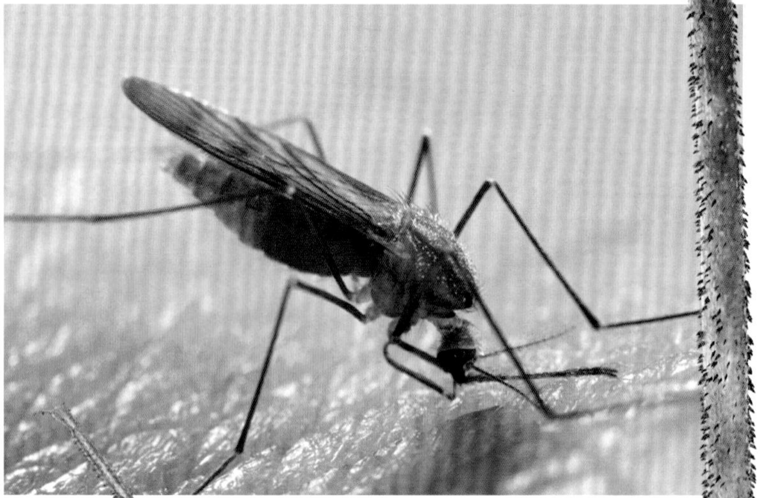

INVERTEBRATES

MALARIA MOSQUITO

Anopheles gambiae

Location: Africa

Length: Up to 8 mm ($^1/_4$ in)

Diet: Nectar and blood

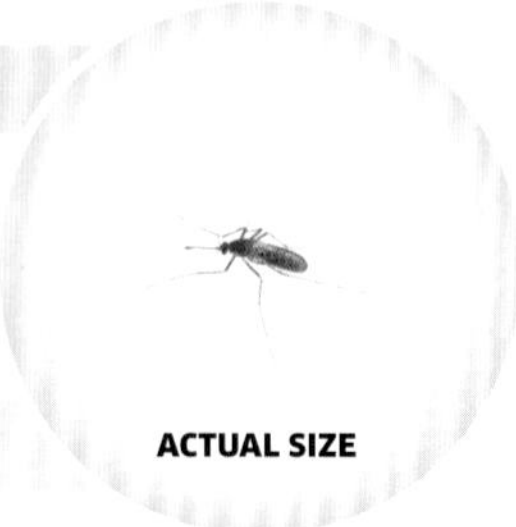

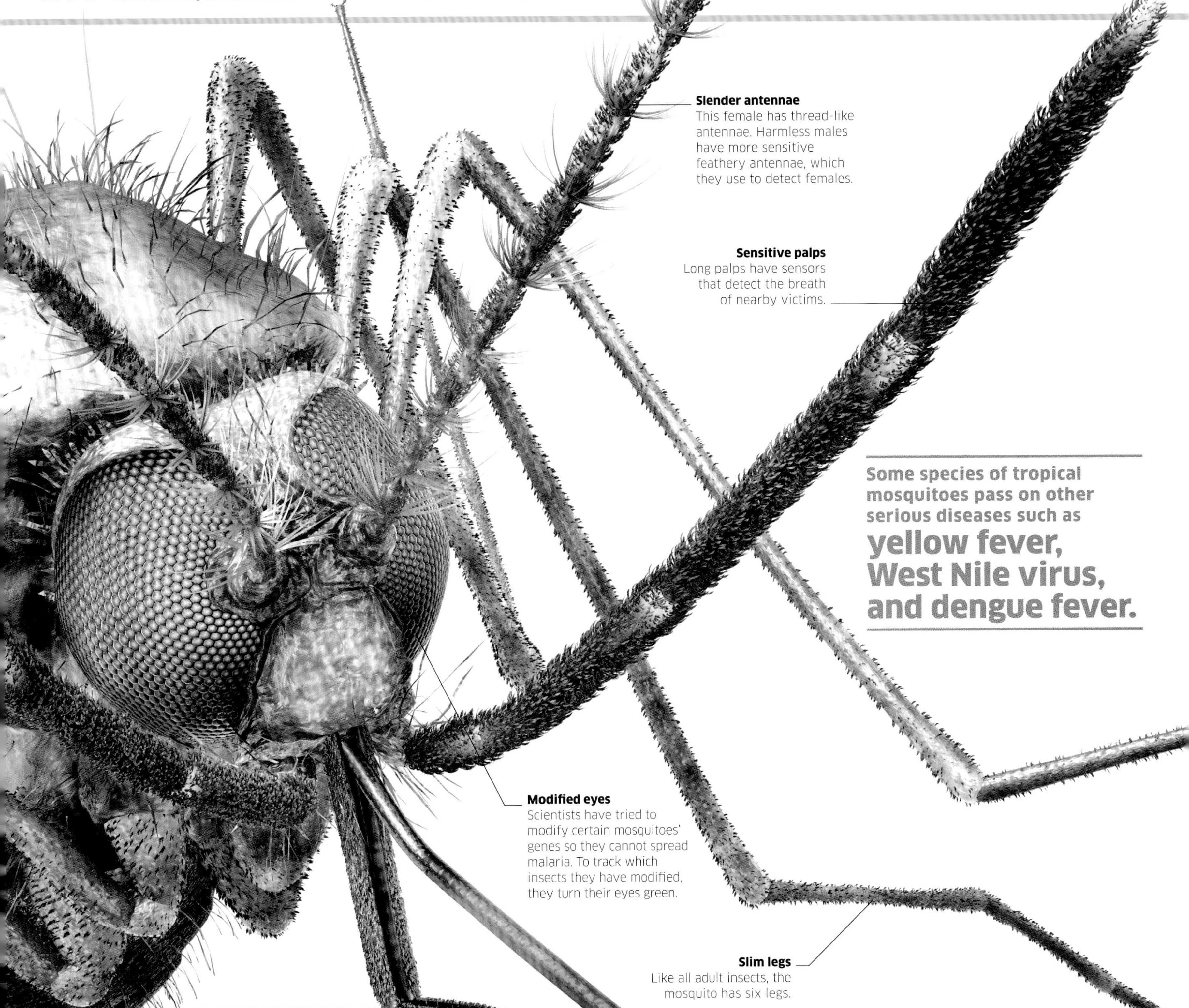

Slender antennae
This female has thread-like antennae. Harmless males have more sensitive feathery antennae, which they use to detect females.

Sensitive palps
Long palps have sensors that detect the breath of nearby victims.

Some species of tropical mosquitoes pass on other serious diseases such as **yellow fever, West Nile virus, and dengue fever.**

Modified eyes
Scientists have tried to modify certain mosquitoes' genes so they cannot spread malaria. To track which insects they have modified, they turn their eyes green.

Slim legs
Like all adult insects, the mosquito has six legs.

Protective sheath
When the mosquito pierces a host's skin to feed, the sheath bends back out of the way.

Long proboscis
A mosquito's straw-like mouthparts are used to suck up blood, or the sugary nectar of flowers.

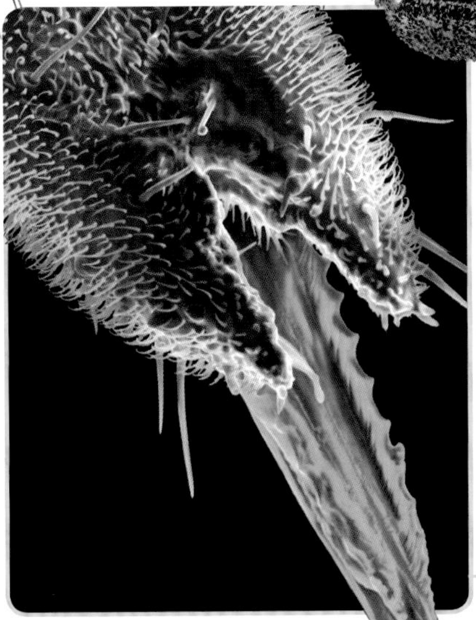

Precision tool
This false-colour image reveals the cluster of sharp stylets (probes) at the tip of the mosquito's long proboscis, emerging from their protective sheath. The sensitive tip of the sheath can detect a vein beneath the victim's skin.

The **largest butterfly**, Queen Alexandra's birdwing, has a **wingspan** of up to 27.3 cm (10¾ in).

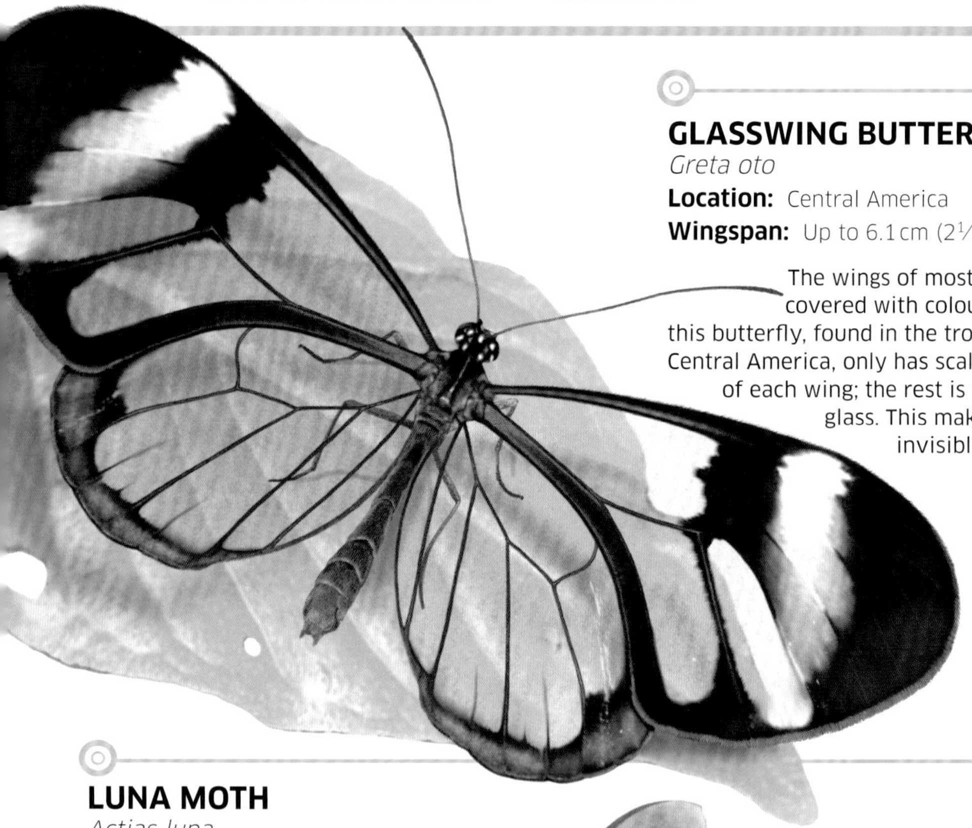

GLASSWING BUTTERFLY

Greta oto

Location: Central America

Wingspan: Up to 6.1 cm (2½ in)

The wings of most butterflies are covered with coloured scales. But this butterfly, found in the tropical rainforest of Central America, only has scales on the edges of each wing; the rest is transparent, like glass. This makes it almost invisible to its predators.

MONARCH BUTTERFLY

Danaus plexippus

Location: Europe, Americas, Australasia

Wingspan: Up to 11 cm (4¼ in)

The big, powerful monarch is renowned for its long migration flights. In North America, the butterflies gradually work their way northeast across the continent in summer, then fly all the way back to California and Mexico, where they spend the winter.

LUNA MOTH

Actias luna

Location: North America

Wingspan: Up to 11.5 cm (4½ in)

Like several other butterflies and moths, the luna moth has an amazingly brief adult lifespan. It spends most of its time as a caterpillar, and the beautiful, winged adult lives for only a week – just long enough to mate and lay eggs. It does not eat but lives on the nutrients it took in as a caterpillar.

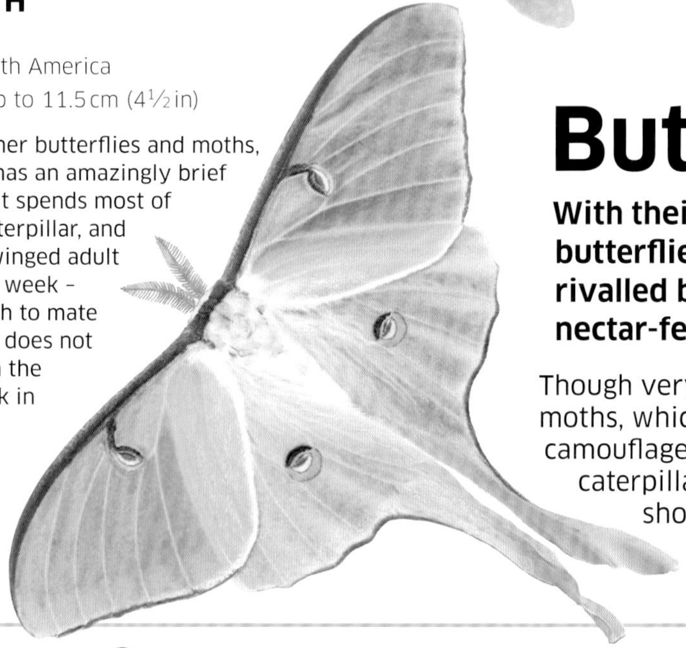

Butterflies and moths

With their big, often brightly coloured wings and dancing flight, butterflies are among the most attractive insects. But they are rivalled by some moths – close relatives that share the same nectar-feeding lifestyle of most butterflies.

Though very similar, butterflies are active by day, unlike typical moths, which fly by night and spend the day concealed by their camouflage from hungry birds. They all start life as soft-bodied caterpillars that eat voraciously before turning into short-lived, winged adults.

HUMMINGBIRD HAWKMOTH

Macroglossum stellatarum

Location: Eurasia, North America

Wingspan: Up to 4.5 cm (1¾ in)

The hummingbird hawkmoth lives in woodland and grassland and is unusual because it flies by day. Its name refers to the way it hovers on whirring wings to sip sweet nectar, just like a tropical hummingbird. It is a powerful flier, making long journeys to find food.

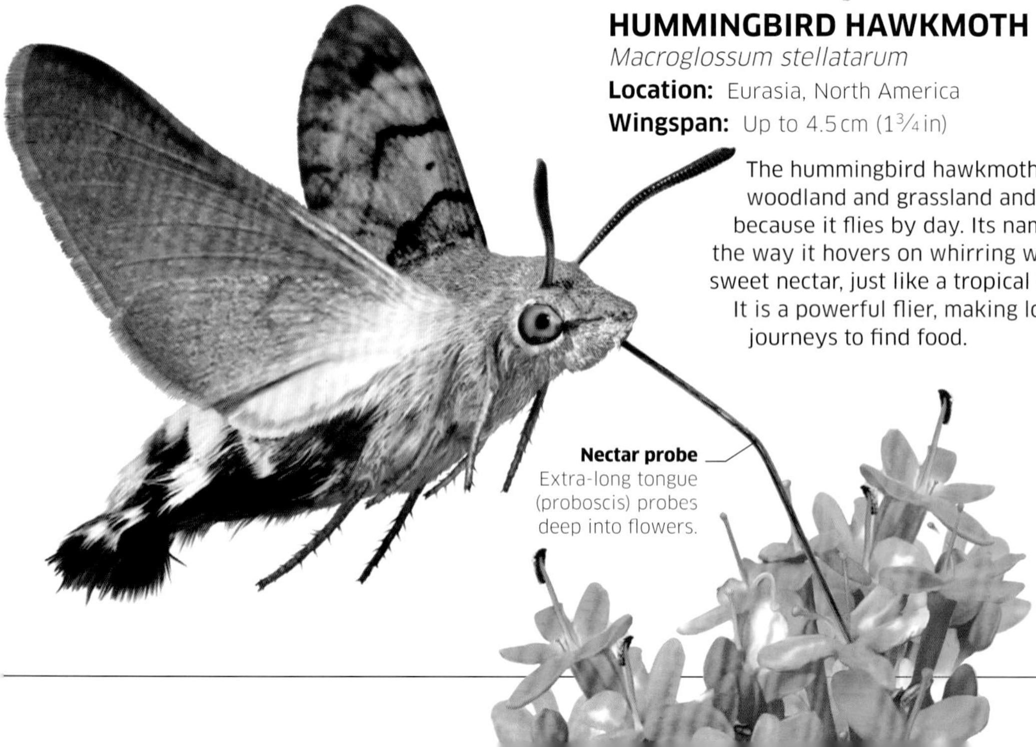

RED UNDERWING

Catocala nupta

Location: Europe

Wingspan: Up to 8 cm (3¼ in)

Most moths fly at night, and are camouflaged by day. This moth is the same, but when it flies it reveals red hindwings. These may confuse birds, which cannot find the moth when its red wings are hidden again.

CAIRNS BIRDWING

Ornithoptera euphorion

Location: Australasia

Wingspan: Up to 15 cm (6 in)

The tropical birdwings are the biggest of all butterflies, with very long wings; they even fly rather like birds. They are a spectacular, frequent visitor to gardens in tropical northeastern Australia, where they often sip nectar from hibiscus flowers.

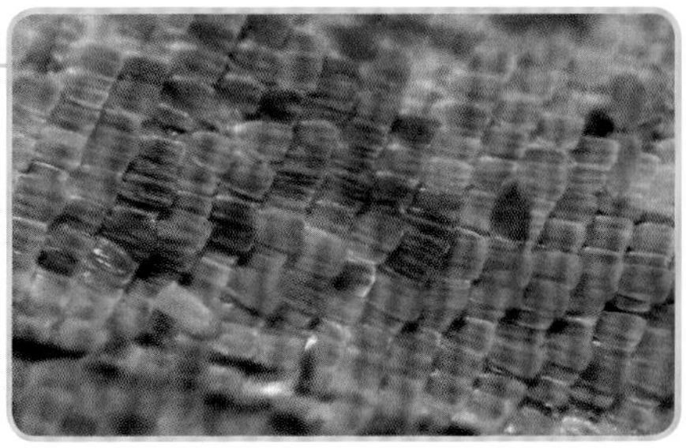

Wing scales
The patterns on the painted lady's wings are made up of very small, coloured scales that overlap like tiles on a roof. Over time the scales fall away, so the longer the butterfly lives, the less colourful it becomes. All butterflies and moths have wing scales of this type.

Clubbed antennae
Like most butterflies the painted lady has long, club-ended antennae.

Wing speed
Butterflies beat their wings steadily when they fly. Moths, in comparison, move their wings so fast that they are a blur.

Nectar feeding
The butterfly uses a long, hollow proboscis to sip sugary, energy-rich nectar from flowers, coiling it up like a spring when it is not needed.

Painted lady

Many butterflies have a very restricted range, but the painted lady is widespread in dry, open areas. It can also fly long distances, making mass migrations in search of good breeding grounds. The butterfly has six legs, but keeps the front pair tightly folded against its body.

INVERTEBRATES

PAINTED LADY

Vanessa cardui

Location: Europe, Asia, N. America, Africa

Wingspan: Up to 7.5 cm (3 in)

Diet: Adult drinks nectar

Honeybee

Named for the way they use sweet flower nectar to make fragrant honey, honeybees also provide a vital service by carrying pollen from plant to plant in order for cross-pollination to occur. Without bees, some plants might struggle to survive.

Bees are vegetarian wasps. Instead of hunting other insects, they gather sugary nectar and protein-rich pollen, which they take back and store in the hive. Many live solitary lives, but honeybees form big colonies centred on a single breeding queen. She is the mother of thousands of worker bees that build the nest, gather nectar and pollen, and make honey from regurgitated nectar to feed the colony during the winter.

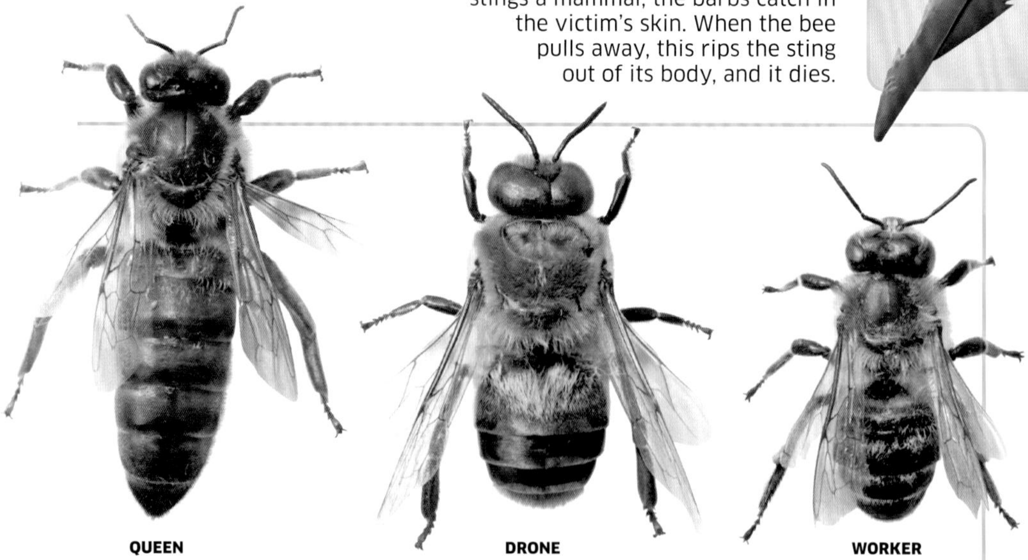

Bee colony

Although the queen is not much bigger than the other bees, she may lay thousands of eggs in a day. Each egg is placed into a honeycomb cell where it hatches as a legless larva. Some of these larvae develop into new queens or male "drones", but most become sterile female workers. The function of the drone is to mate with the queen from another colony.

INVERTEBRATES

HONEYBEE

Apis mellifera

Location: Worldwide

Length: Up to 1.5 cm (½ in) (worker)

Diet: Nectar and pollen

ACTUAL SIZE

Compound eyes
Made up of many tiny lenses, compound eyes see colour well to help the bee find nectar-rich flowers.

Sensitive antennae
Each antenna has thousands of scent detectors for finding fragrant flowers.

Hair trap
Hairs all over the bee's body pick up pollen from flowers.

Proboscis
When a honeybee lands on a flower it unrolls a long, tubular proboscis that acts like a drinking straw. The bee uses it to suck sugar-rich nectar into a part of its digestive system called the crop. When its crop is full it returns to the colony, where it passes the nectar to other bees. These then turn it into honey.

Wings
In flight, the two pairs of wings are joined by tiny hooks so they beat as one.

Bristly legs
The legs have bristly combs for brushing pollen off the bee's body and into the pollen sacs.

400 million years – the approximate length of time insects have existed on Earth.

There are more than a million known species of insects.

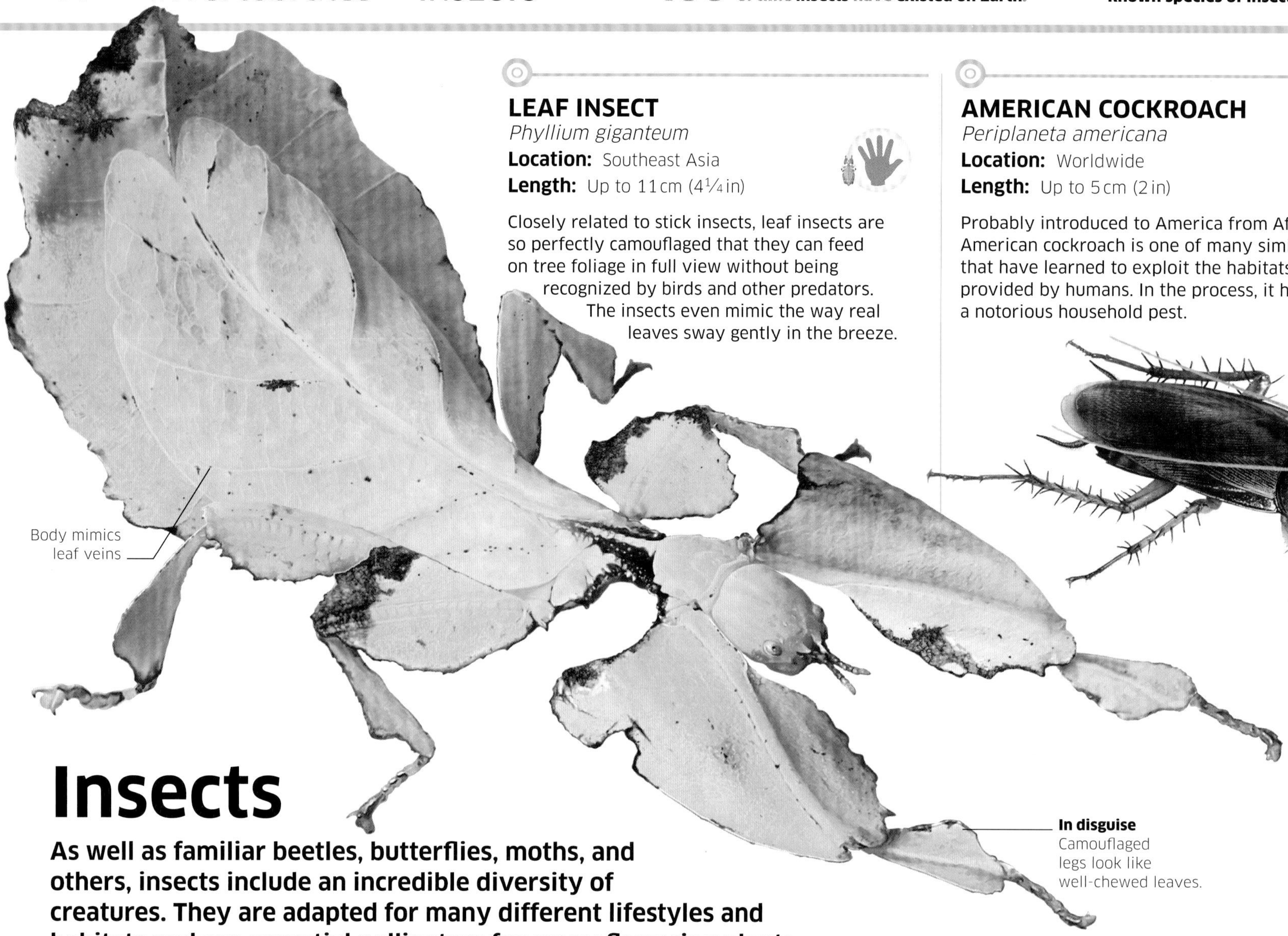

LEAF INSECT

Phyllium giganteum
Location: Southeast Asia
Length: Up to 11 cm ($4\frac{1}{4}$ in)

Closely related to stick insects, leaf insects are so perfectly camouflaged that they can feed on tree foliage in full view without being recognized by birds and other predators. The insects even mimic the way real leaves sway gently in the breeze.

AMERICAN COCKROACH

Periplaneta americana
Location: Worldwide
Length: Up to 5 cm (2 in)

Probably introduced to America from Africa, the American cockroach is one of many similar insects that have learned to exploit the habitats and food provided by humans. In the process, it has become a notorious household pest.

Insects

As well as familiar beetles, butterflies, moths, and others, insects include an incredible diversity of creatures. They are adapted for many different lifestyles and habitats and are essential pollinators for many flowering plants.

All adult insects share the same basic three-part body structure of head, thorax, and abdomen, with three pairs of legs and, typically, two pairs of wings. Many insects also have multi-stage life cycles, hatching as wingless, caterpillar-like larvae that eventually turn into breeding adults, although some simply grow to adult size by moulting several times.

More than half of all known species of living things are insects.

RED WOOD ANT

Formica rufa
Location: Europe
Length: Up to 1 cm ($\frac{1}{2}$ in)

The red wood ant builds large mound nests in woodlands, with each colony containing up to 400,000 ants. Worker wood ants spray formic acid from their tail ends at any animal that threatens the colony.

SABRE WASP

Rhyssa persuasoria
Location: Northern hemisphere
Length: Up to 4 cm ($1\frac{1}{2}$ in)

This is one of the biggest ichneumon wasps, a family of wasps that lays its eggs on the larvae of other insects. The female drills into timber with her sharp egg-laying tube to lay an egg on a larva. When the wasp larva hatches from the egg, it eats the host larva alive.

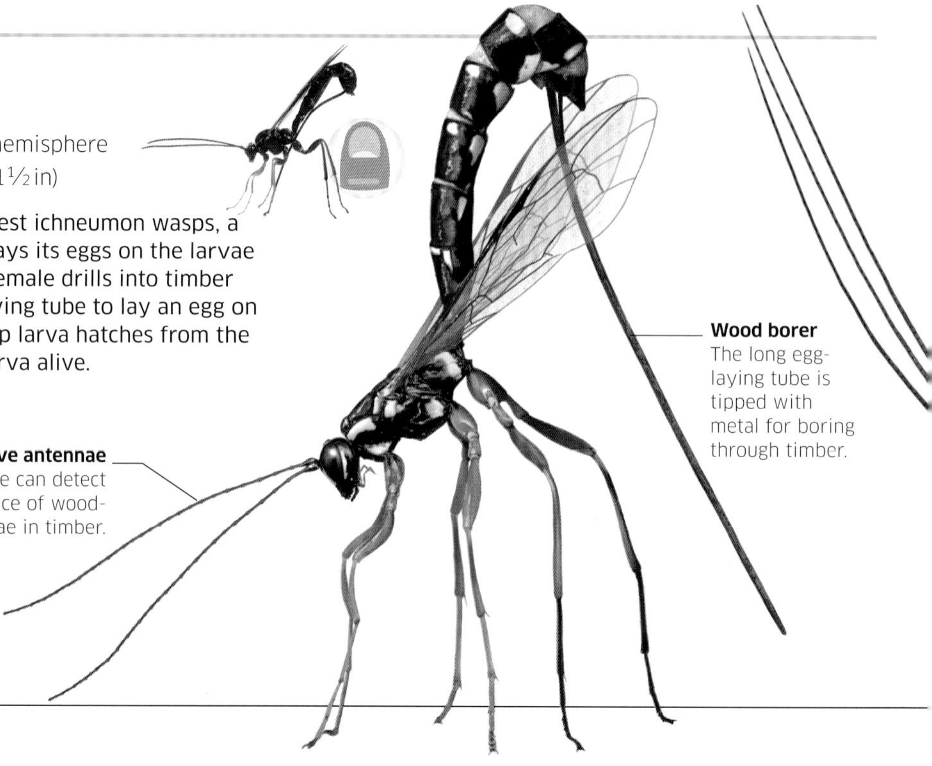

Insects were the **first animals to fly**. The oldest-known flying insect lived **300 million years ago**.

Although **insects** live in **every type** of land and freshwater habitat, **very few** live in **seas and oceans**.

RABBIT FLEA

Spilopsyllus cuniculi

Location: Northern hemisphere

Length: Up to 1 mm ($^1/_{16}$ in)

Fleas are parasites that feed on the blood of other animals. Some species are adapted for attacking a particular host, and this one favours rabbits. It has powerful hind legs for leaping onto its victims, and sharp mouthparts for piercing their skin.

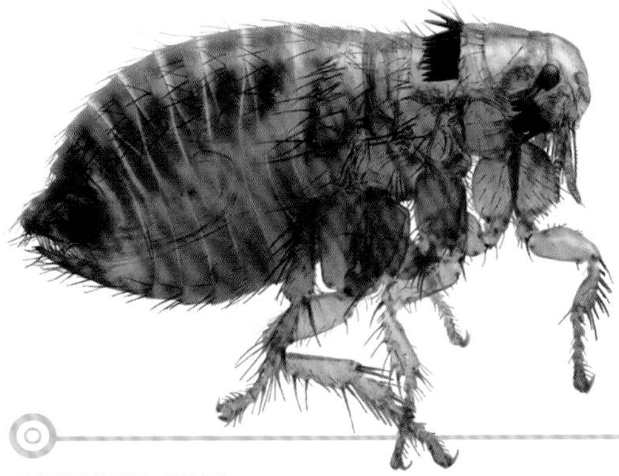

SPECKLED BUSH CRICKET

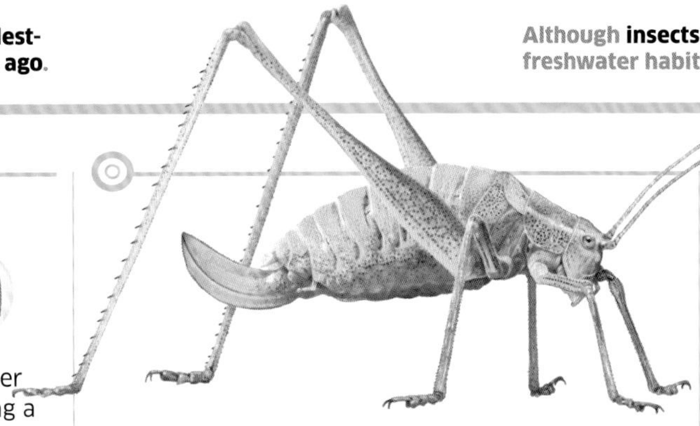

Leptophyes punctatissima

Location: Europe

Length: Up to 3 cm ($1\frac{1}{4}$ in)

Also known as katydids, the bush crickets are relatives of grasshoppers. They have long hind legs for leaping, but rarely do so, preferring to climb slowly through bushes looking for food. This species cannot fly. The female, seen here, has a curved, blade-like, egg-laying organ.

AFRICAN TERMITE

Macrotermes bellicosus

Location: Africa

Length: Soldier up to 2.5 cm (1 in)

This termite lives in vast colonies, each centred on a single breeding queen. It builds tall, tower-like nests of mud, defended by big-jawed soldiers. The smaller workers gather grass and use it as compost for growing edible fungus inside the nest.

HOVER FLY

Syrphus ribesii

Location: Europe

Length: Up to 1.3 cm ($^1/_2$ in)

One of many hover fly species, this skilled flier can dart forwards or back in the air, fly sideways, or hover on the spot. It is a harmless nectar-feeder, but has warning stripes that mimic those of wasps to deter birds and other predators.

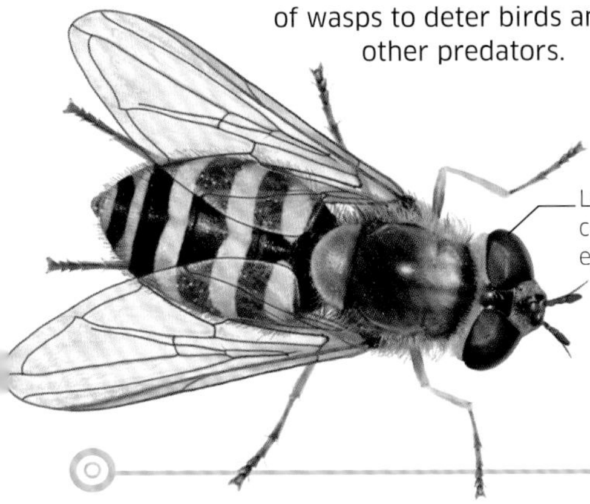

GREEN LACEWING

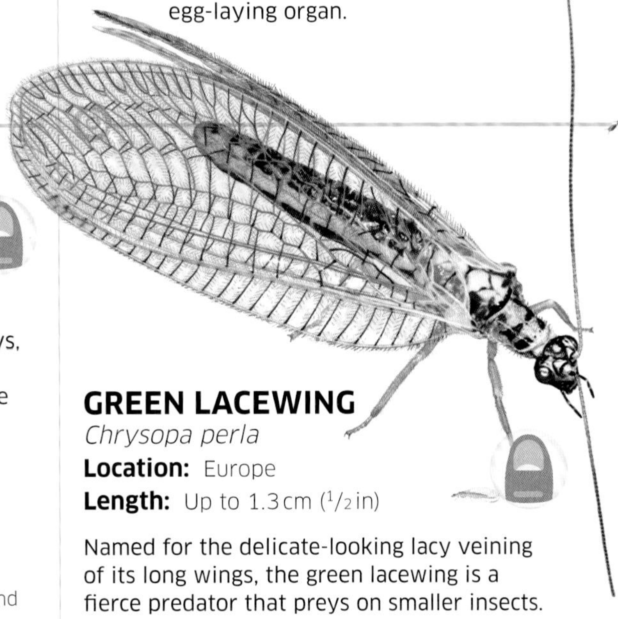

Chrysopa perla

Location: Europe

Length: Up to 1.3 cm ($^1/_2$ in)

Named for the delicate-looking lacy veining of its long wings, the green lacewing is a fierce predator that preys on smaller insects. Its caterpillar-like larvae do the same, and are important controllers of plant pests such as sap-sucking aphids.

PERIODICAL CICADA

Magicicada septendecim

Location: USA

Length: Up to 4 cm ($1\frac{1}{2}$ in)

Cicadas spend most of their lives as burrowing nymphs, then emerge briefly as winged adults to breed. Most cicadas do this each year, but American periodical cicadas emerge every 13 or 17 years, then vanish until the next mass emergence.

MAYFLY

Ephemera danica

Location: Europe

Length: Up to 2.5 cm (1 in)

Mayflies are famous for their short adult lifespans. This species survives for only a few days – just long enough to find a mate and breed. However, it has a much longer life as a larva, feeding underwater for up to three years before it takes to the air.

PRAYING MANTIS

Mantis religiosa

Location: Central and Southern Europe

Length: Up to 7.4 cm (3 in)

The most well known of many similar mantids, this fearsome predator seizes other insects with its powerful, spiny forelegs, bites off their heads, and eats them. It perches motionless waiting for prey to come within range, then ambushes its victim with a split-second strike.

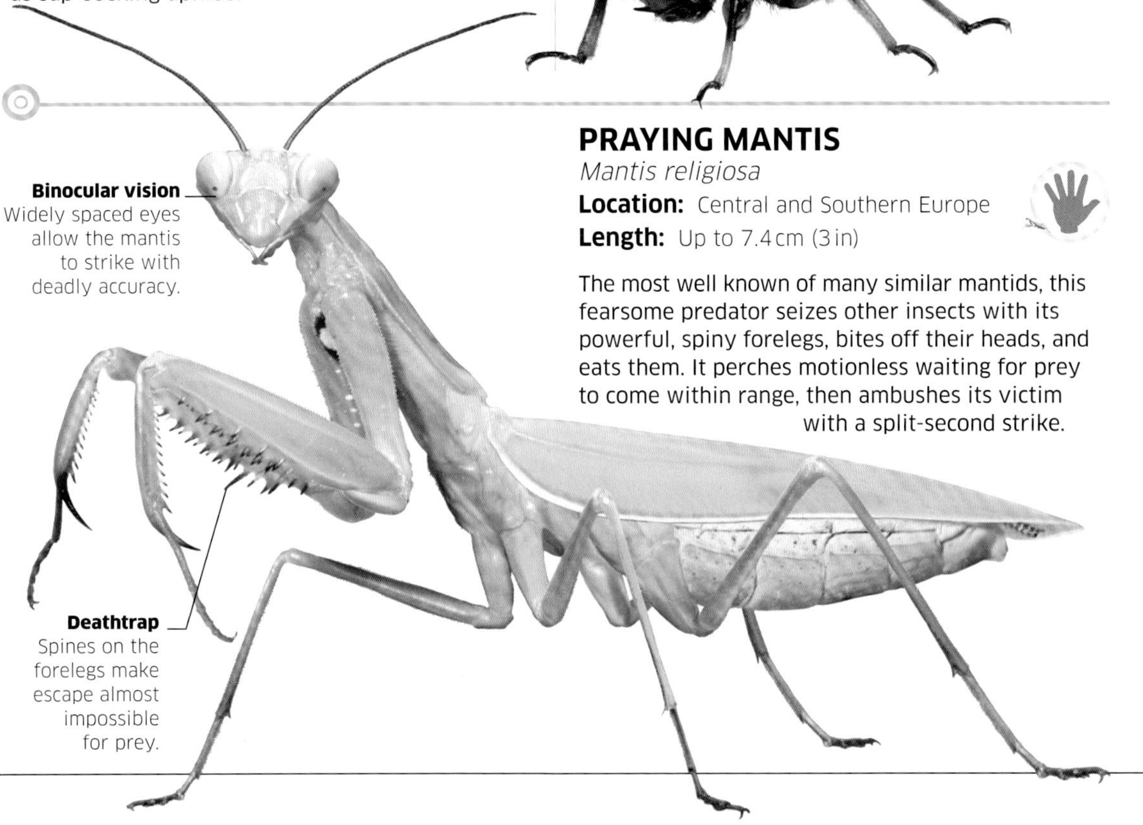

The **giant centipede** can dangle from a cave ceiling to **snatch passing bats**.

The mother centipede **coils around her eggs** to **protect them** from predators.

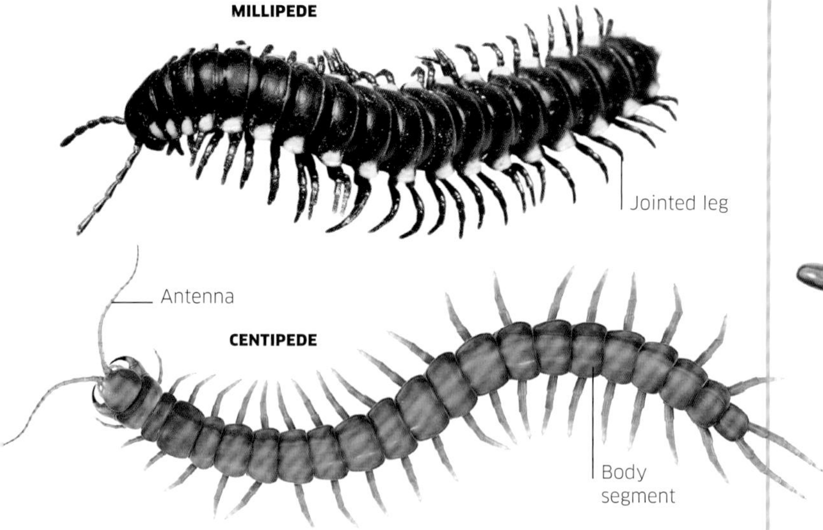

Multi-legged myriapods

Centipedes belong to a group of invertebrates called myriapods, which also includes millipedes. Their bodies consist of many segments that form a long, flexible chain. Each body segment of a centipede bears a pair of jointed legs, while each segment of a millipede bears two pairs. One species of millipede has up to 750 legs, but the giant centipede usually has just 46.

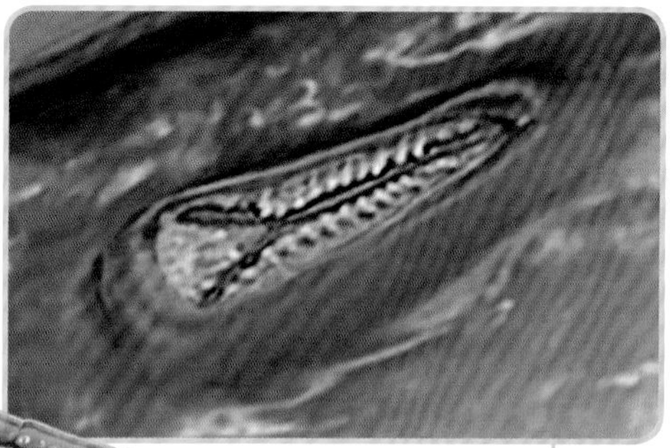

Vital ventilation
Long, triangular openings, or spiracles, in the sides of the centipede's body allow air into a system of tubes called tracheae. The airflow through the tracheae supplies oxygen to the muscles and vital organs, and carries away waste carbon dioxide. Insects breathe in the same way.

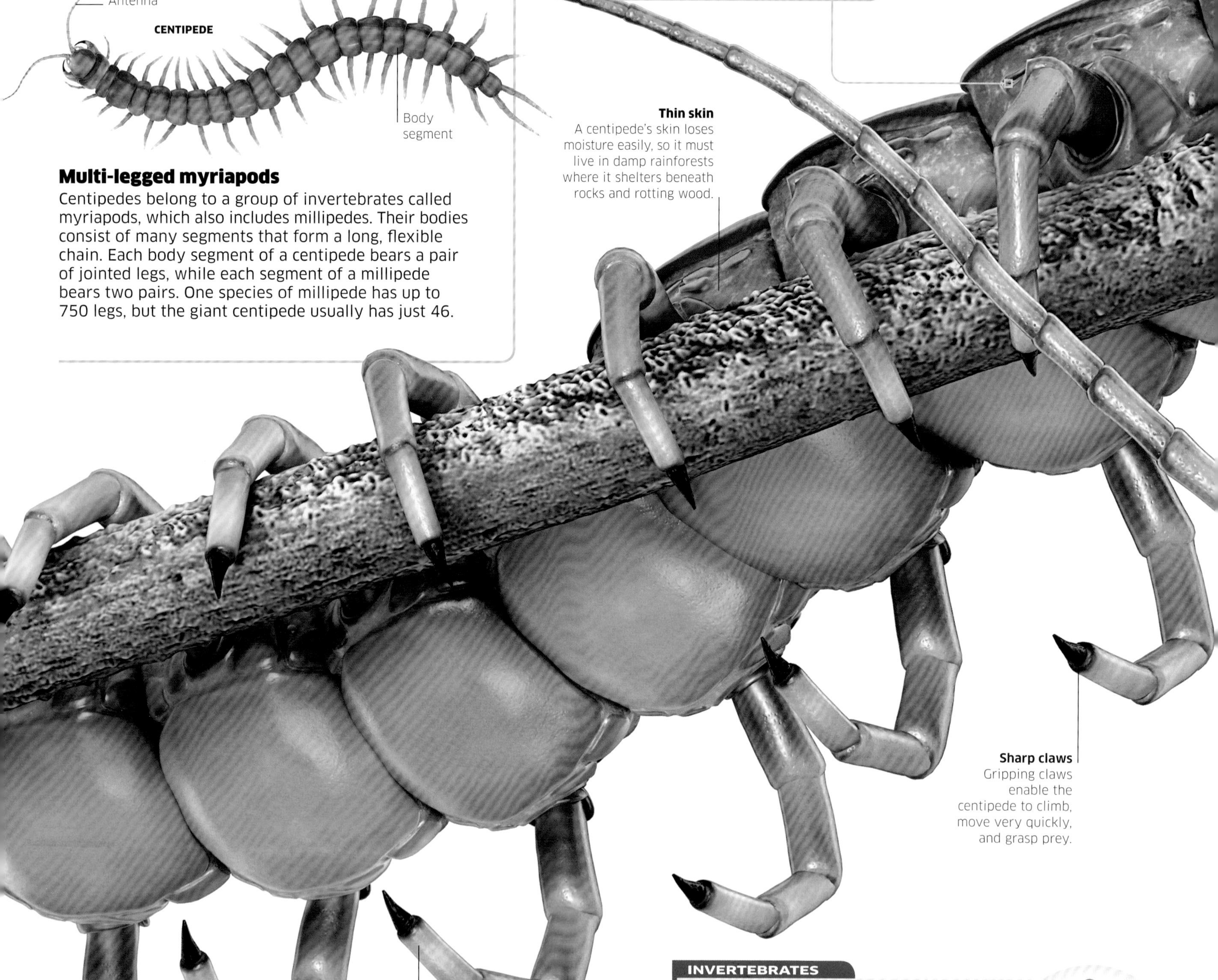

Thin skin
A centipede's skin loses moisture easily, so it must live in damp rainforests where it shelters beneath rocks and rotting wood.

Sharp claws
Gripping claws enable the centipede to climb, move very quickly, and grasp prey.

Rippling legs
The legs move in waves that ripple down the body from head to tail.

INVERTEBRATES
GIANT CENTIPEDE
Scolopendra gigantea

Location: South America

Length: Up to 30 cm (11¾ in)

Diet: Small animals

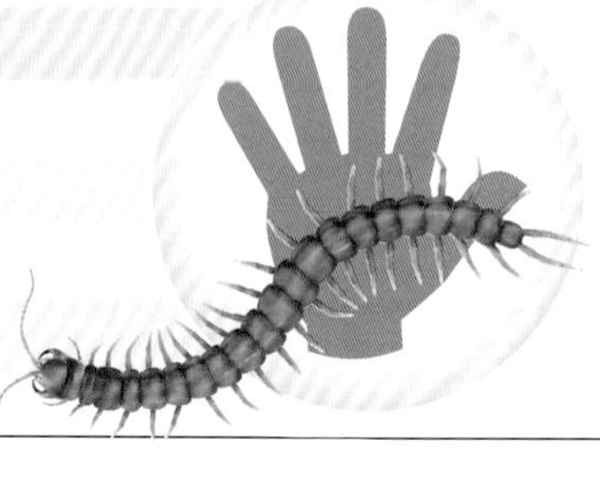

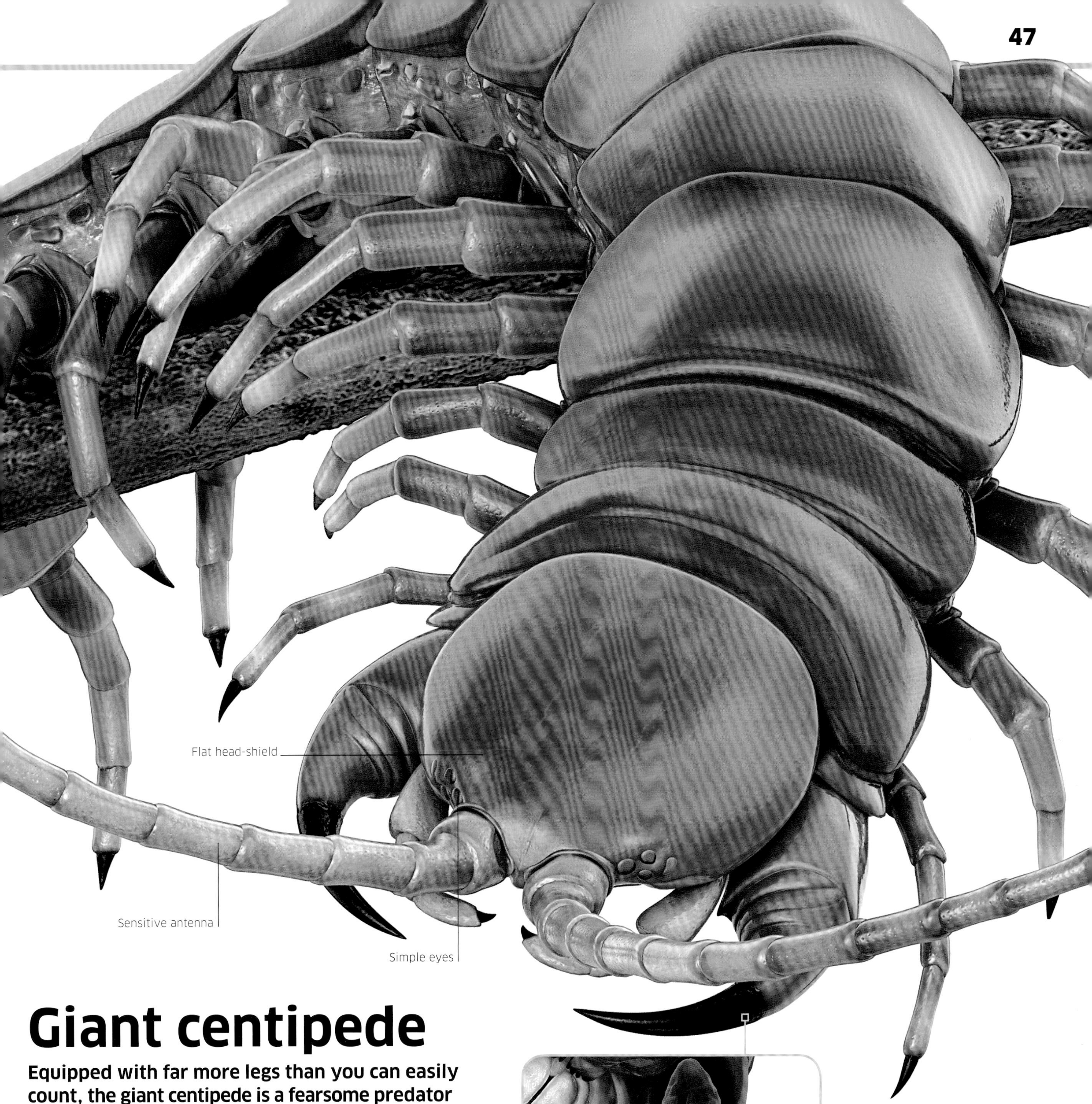

Giant centipede

Equipped with far more legs than you can easily count, the giant centipede is a fearsome predator of tropical forest floors that can overpower and eat a tarantula.

Although the centipede has a cluster of small, simple eyes on each side of its head, it cannot see well and relies on its long, sensitive antennae to detect the scent and feel of prey. It will attack any small animal it runs into, and has even been known to kill bats returning to roost in caves. Its main weapon is its pair of modified, claw-like legs, or forcipules, which inject a potent venom.

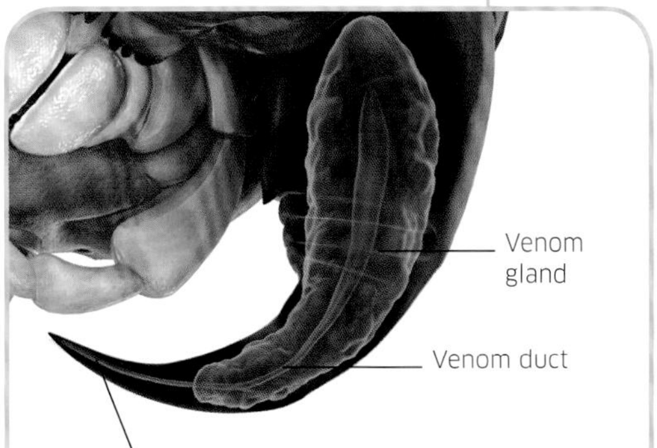

Venomous bite
The claw-like forcipules contain glands that produce a powerful venom. When the centipede seizes its prey, muscles squeeze venom through the sharp tips into the victim's body, paralyzing or even killing it. The centipede then pulls it apart and eats it.

Tarantulas sometimes spin a line of silk across the entrance to their burrows. The line acts as a tripwire, alerting them to approaching prey.

Mexican red-kneed tarantula

One of the biggest spiders, the red-kneed tarantula is an ambush hunter that pounces on small animals wandering near its burrow at night. Darting out, the spider seizes its victim and injects a paralyzing venom with its fangs.

Tarantulas are spiders with big, hairy bodies, which typically prey on large insects. Like all spiders, a tarantula has eight legs attached to the front part of its body, and mouthparts tipped with a pair of sharp fangs. But instead of pinching together, as in most spiders, a tarantula's fangs stab downwards.

Threat display
Rearing up on hind legs with its front legs raised, the tarantula is displaying its fangs to warn off enemies.

INVERTEBRATES

MEXICAN RED-KNEED TARANTULA

Brachypelma smithi

Location: Southwestern Mexico

Length: Body up to 10 cm (4 in)

Diet: Small animals

Jointed legs
Each long leg is made up of seven rigid segments linked by flexible, red-orange joints that give the spider its name.

Bulbous body
The body has two main sections, joined by a narrow waist. The bulbous rear part is called the abdomen. The front part, or prosoma, combines the head and thorax.

Sensitive feet
The spider's main sense organs are on its feet. A pad on the end segment of each leg is sensitive to scents and tastes, and fine hairs detect air movements and vibrations passing through the ground. At the end of each leg, two sharp claws are used for grip as the tarantula walks.

Young Mexican red-kneed tarantulas **moult every two weeks** for the first four months of their lives.

30 The number of years a female red-kneed tarantula can live. Males have much shorter lives.

The tarantula's bite is venomous, but its effect on humans is no worse than a bee sting.

Spider silk

All spiders make silk, which some use to spin prey-trapping webs. A red-kneed tarantula uses silk to line its burrow. The female uses it to make a silk mat where she lays her eggs. She then bundles the mat into a ball to protect the eggs and her newly hatched young.

Barbed defence

Most spiders bite to defend themselves, but this tarantula has a better tactic. Its abdomen is covered with barbed, very fine hairs that the tarantula can kick into an attacker's face. The hairs embed themselves in the eyes and nose and cause intense irritation.

8 years – the **length of time** an emperor scorpion **may live in captivity.**

Hitching a ride

Scorpions give birth to live young that are like tiny, pale-skinned replicas of their parents, complete with stings. As they are born, they crawl up their mother's pincers and legs onto her back. She carries them around until they can fend for themselves.

Strange glow

The hard cuticle, or exoskeleton, of a scorpion contains fluorescent chemicals that make it glow a bright green-blue under ultraviolet light. No one really knows the reason for this, but it helps scientists to locate them in the dark.

The emperor scorpion's sting is no worse than a bee's, but the sting of some other scorpions can be **deadly to humans**.

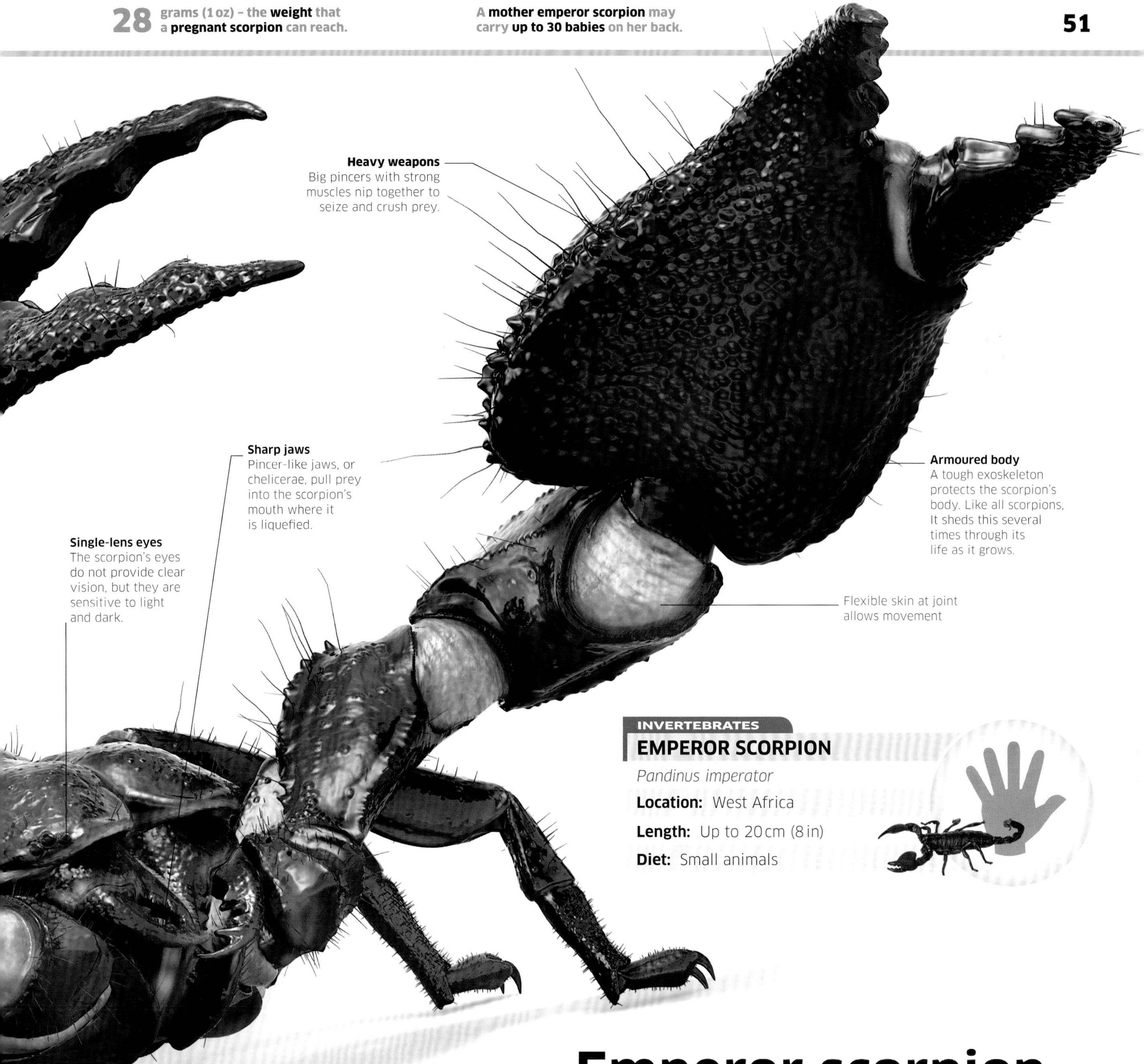

INVERTEBRATES

EMPEROR SCORPION

Pandinus imperator

Location: West Africa

Length: Up to 20 cm (8 in)

Diet: Small animals

Emperor scorpion

Armed with an enormous pair of pincers and a sting in its tail, the emperor scorpion prowls the forest floor at night in search of prey. One of the biggest scorpions, it hunts almost entirely by touch, sensing the movement of prey by detecting vibrations in the ground.

A scorpion might look like a lobster, but it is actually an arachnid – a relative of spiders. Instead of venomous fangs it has a stinging tail, which it can arch over the top of its head to stab prey held in its pincers. But the emperor is strong enough to simply tear its victims apart, and rarely needs its sting.

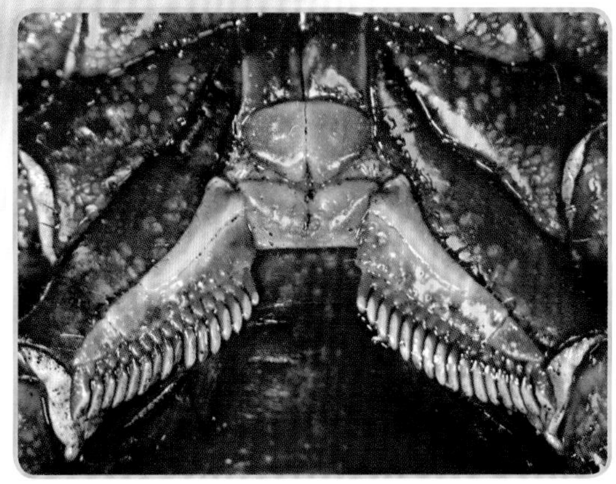

Vibration detectors
Beneath its body, the scorpion has a pair of comb-like sensory organs called pectines. When it presses these to the ground, it can pick up the faint tremors caused by small animals moving nearby in the dark.

The **fastest spider** is the **giant house spider**, which is able to **run** at speeds of **50 cm (20 in) per second**.

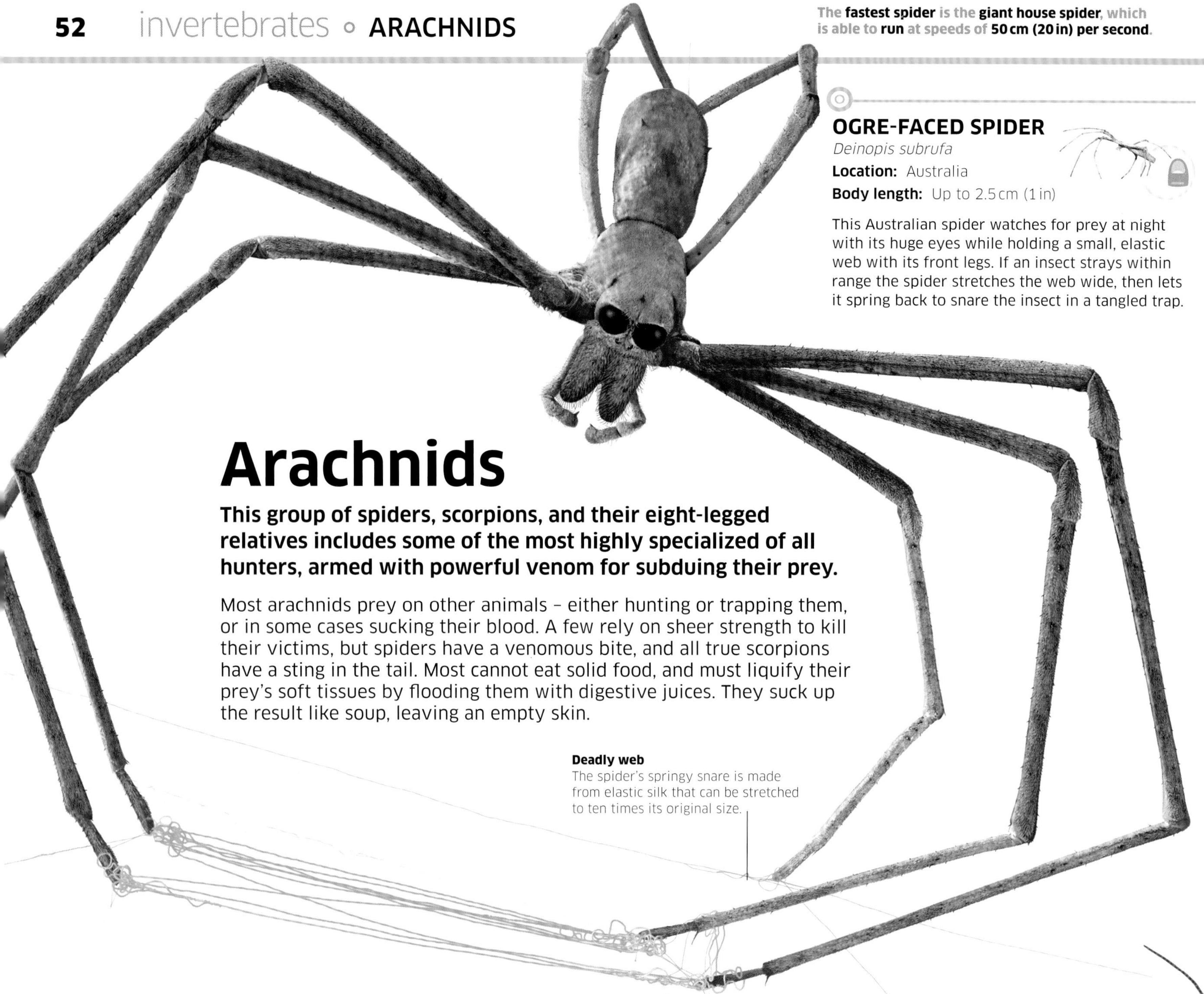

Arachnids

This group of spiders, scorpions, and their eight-legged relatives includes some of the most highly specialized of all hunters, armed with powerful venom for subduing their prey.

Most arachnids prey on other animals – either hunting or trapping them, or in some cases sucking their blood. A few rely on sheer strength to kill their victims, but spiders have a venomous bite, and all true scorpions have a sting in the tail. Most cannot eat solid food, and must liquify their prey's soft tissues by flooding them with digestive juices. They suck up the result like soup, leaving an empty skin.

Deadly web
The spider's springy snare is made from elastic silk that can be stretched to ten times its original size.

OGRE-FACED SPIDER

Deinopis subrufa
Location: Australia
Body length: Up to 2.5 cm (1 in)

This Australian spider watches for prey at night with its huge eyes while holding a small, elastic web with its front legs. If an insect strays within range the spider stretches the web wide, then lets it spring back to snare the insect in a tangled trap.

ORB WEAVER

Argiope bruennichi
Location: Europe
Body length: Up to 1.8 cm (¾ in)

Many spiders trap insect prey in spiral orb webs. Also known as the wasp spider, this arachnid weaves its web low in the grass, where it is ideally placed to catch leaping grasshoppers.

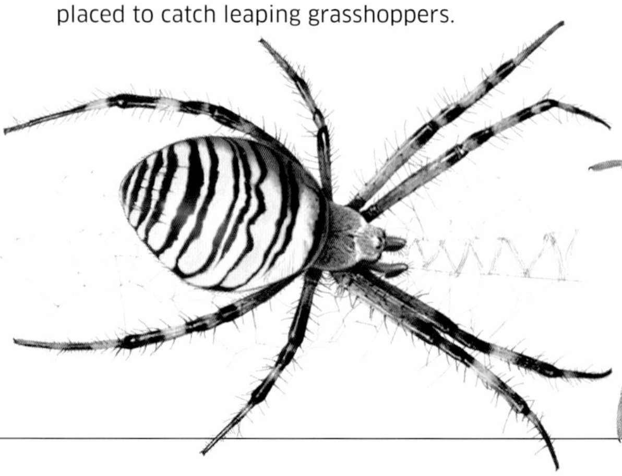

GOLDENROD CRAB SPIDER

ACTUAL SIZE

Misumena vatia
Location: North America, Europe
Body length: Up to 1.1 cm (½ in)

Instead of making a web, the goldenrod crab spider lurks among flower petals to ambush insects that visit the flower. Ornamented with pink stripes, it can change its colour from white to yellow to match the flower it is hiding in.

RAFT SPIDER

Dolomedes fimbriatus
Location: Europe
Body length: Up to 2.2 cm (¾ in)

A raft spider hunts on the water, with its weight supported by the surface film. It detects prey by sensing ripples in the water, and skates across the surface to seize it.

DIVING BELL SPIDER

Argyroneta aquatica

Location: Europe, Central Asia

Body length: Up to 1.5 cm (½ in)

This is the only spider that lives underwater. But it must breathe air, which it gathers at the surface and carries in a silvery bubble around its body. It weaves a bell-shaped web underwater, which it fills with transported air and uses as a nursery for its young.

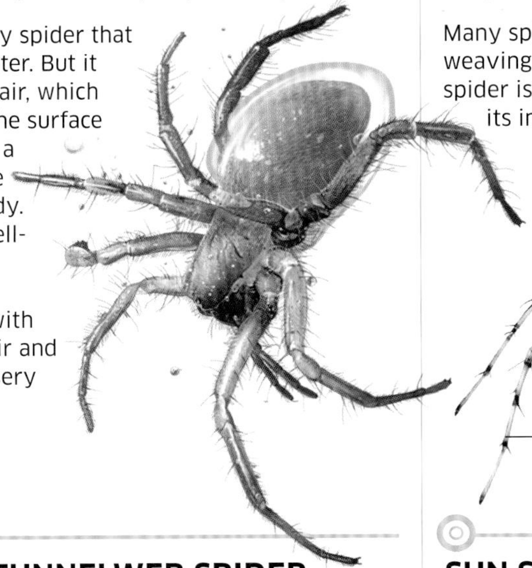

GREEN LYNX SPIDER

Peucetia viridans

Location: North America

Body length: Up to 2.2 cm (¾ in)

Many spiders roam in search of prey, instead of weaving webs to trap a victim. This American spider is a fast-moving hunter that pounces on its insect victims like a cat.

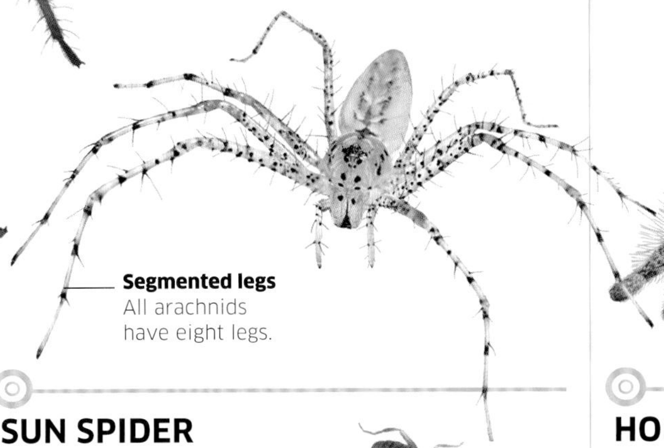

REGAL JUMPING SPIDER

Phidippus regius

Location: S. E. North America

Body length: Up to 2.2 cm (¾ in)

Jumping spiders target prey with their huge eyes, judge their moment, then leap on the prey to deliver a lethal bite. They are mostly small, with short legs; this species is one of the biggest.

SYDNEY FUNNELWEB SPIDER

Atrax robustus

Location: Australia

Body length: Up to 5 cm (2 in)

Notoriously dangerous, this bulky Australian spider is armed with a potent venom that can kill an adult human. When alarmed it rears up to threaten enemies with its huge, deadly fangs.

SUN SPIDER

Metasolpuga picta

Location: S. W. Africa

Body length: Up to 5 cm (2 in)

Despite its name and appearance this arachnid is not a true spider, and it does not have venomous fangs. It hunts insects on the dunes of the Namib Desert, seizing and cutting them up to devour with its powerful jaws.

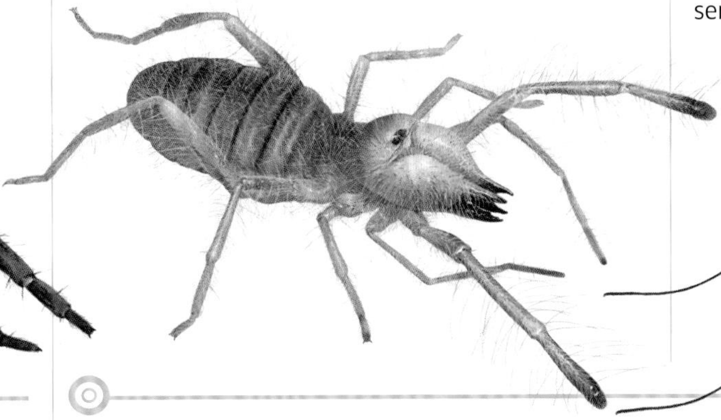

HORNED HARVESTMAN

Phalangium opilio

Location: Northern hemisphere

Body length: Up to 9 mm (¼ in)

Although similar to a spider, a harvestman has a one-piece body that looks like a bean, supported by eight very long, slender legs. It has small pincer-like jaws that it uses to eat a wide variety of foods, detecting them with its extra-long, very sensitive second pair of legs.

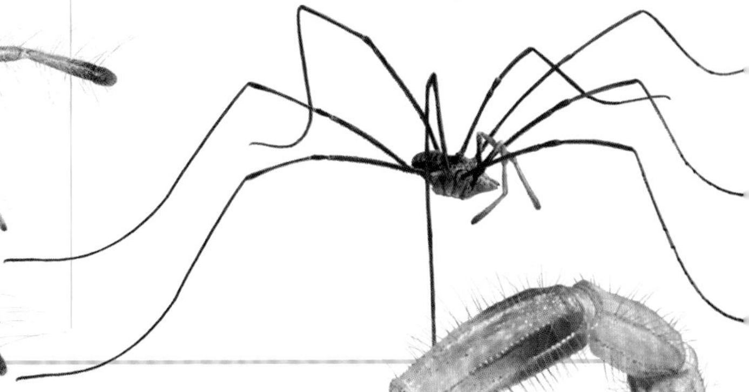

WHIP SCORPION

Mastigoproctus giganteus

Location: S. North America

Body length: Up to 6 cm (2¼ in)

This American species is also known as the giant vinegaroon because of the way it defends itself by spraying vinegary acid from its whip-like tail. It has no sting.

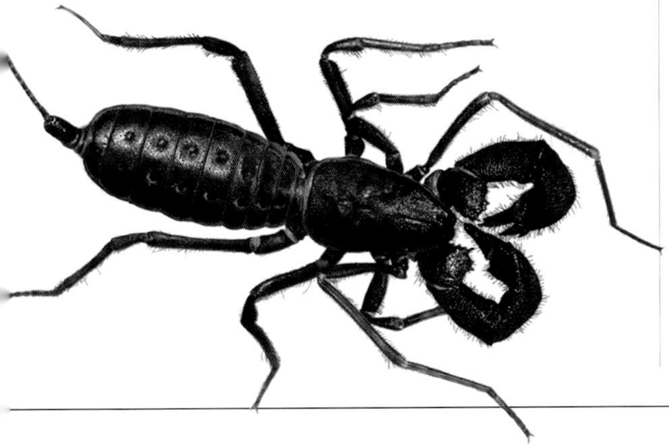

YELLOW SCORPION

Leiurus quinquestriatus

Location: Widespread

Length: Up to 11 cm (4¼ in), including tail

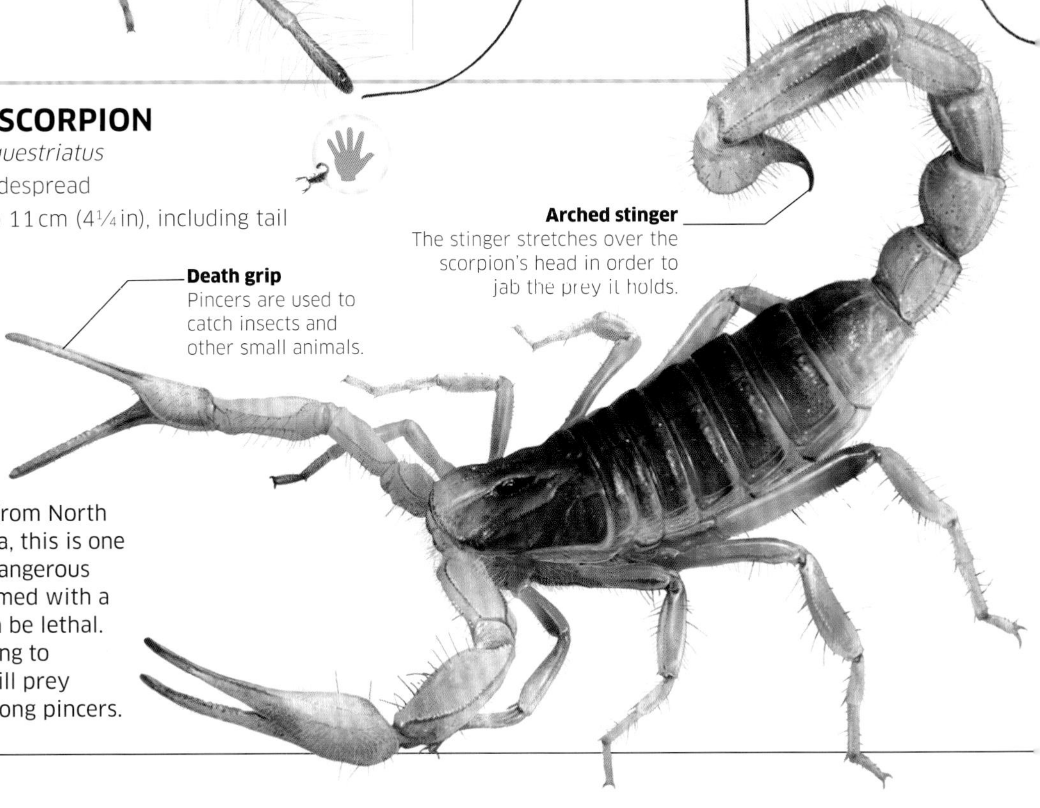

Widespread from North Africa to India, this is one of the most dangerous scorpions, armed with a sting that can be lethal. It uses the sting to paralyze or kill prey held in its strong pincers.

10 years – the **maximum lifespan** of a common starfish.

Common starfish

Gliding over the sea bed towards a clam, on hundreds of flexible feet, the common starfish creeps up on its victim and launches an attack. It pulls the clam's shell apart so it can consume the soft flesh within.

A starfish may not look like a hunter, but to other marine animals it is a voracious predator, prepared to eat anything – even other starfish – that cannot escape its clutches. It hunts by scent, following the chemical trail until its victim is within reach. Gripping the prey animal with the suckers of its tiny tube feet, the starfish forces out part of its stomach lining through its central mouth and smothers the soft parts of its victim with digestive juices. The juices break down the prey's soft tissues, so the starfish can suck them into its body.

When spawning, a female common starfish releases up to **2.5 million eggs**.

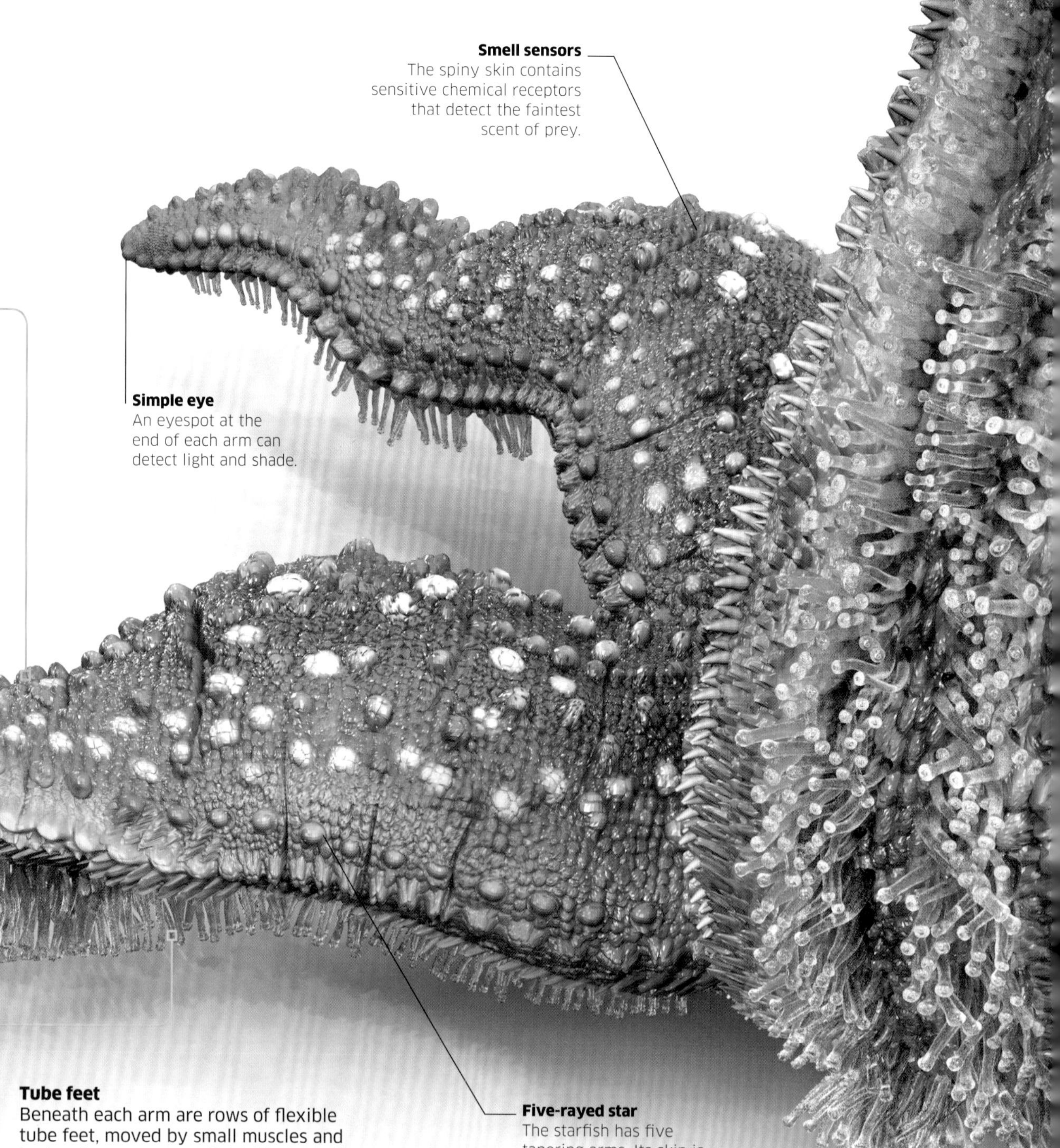

Smell sensors
The spiny skin contains sensitive chemical receptors that detect the faintest scent of prey.

Simple eye
An eyespot at the end of each arm can detect light and shade.

Five-rayed star
The starfish has five tapering arms. Its skin is usually orange but can be shades of purple or brown.

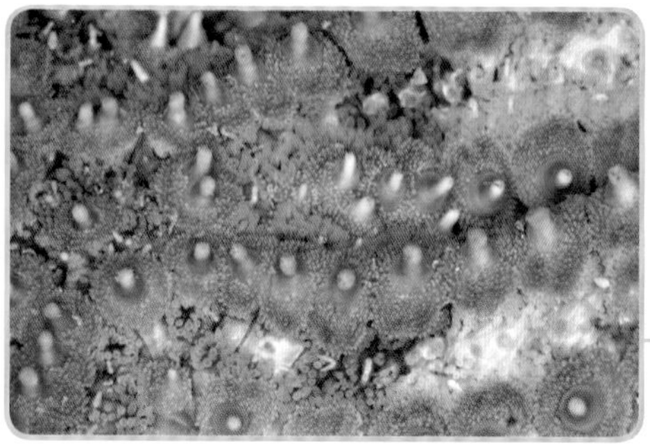

Spiny skin
Rows of short white spines are flanked by bumpy skin. Soft structures called papulae (orange in this image) protrude through gaps in the skin. These act in the same way as gills, absorbing oxygen from the water and releasing carbon dioxide.

Tube feet
Beneath each arm are rows of flexible tube feet, moved by small muscles and hydraulic pressure, as fluid-filled sacs in the arms squeeze water into the tube feet to make them move. Each foot ends in a sucker that can grip the sea bed, so the starfish can crawl around.

The **surface of a starfish** is dotted with **hundreds of minuscule pincers** that keep it **free of dirt** and **stop other animals settling on its skin**.

INVERTEBRATES

COMMON STARFISH

Asterias rubens

Location: North Atlantic

Size: Up to 50 cm (19 3/4 in) across

Diet: Immobile animals and carrion

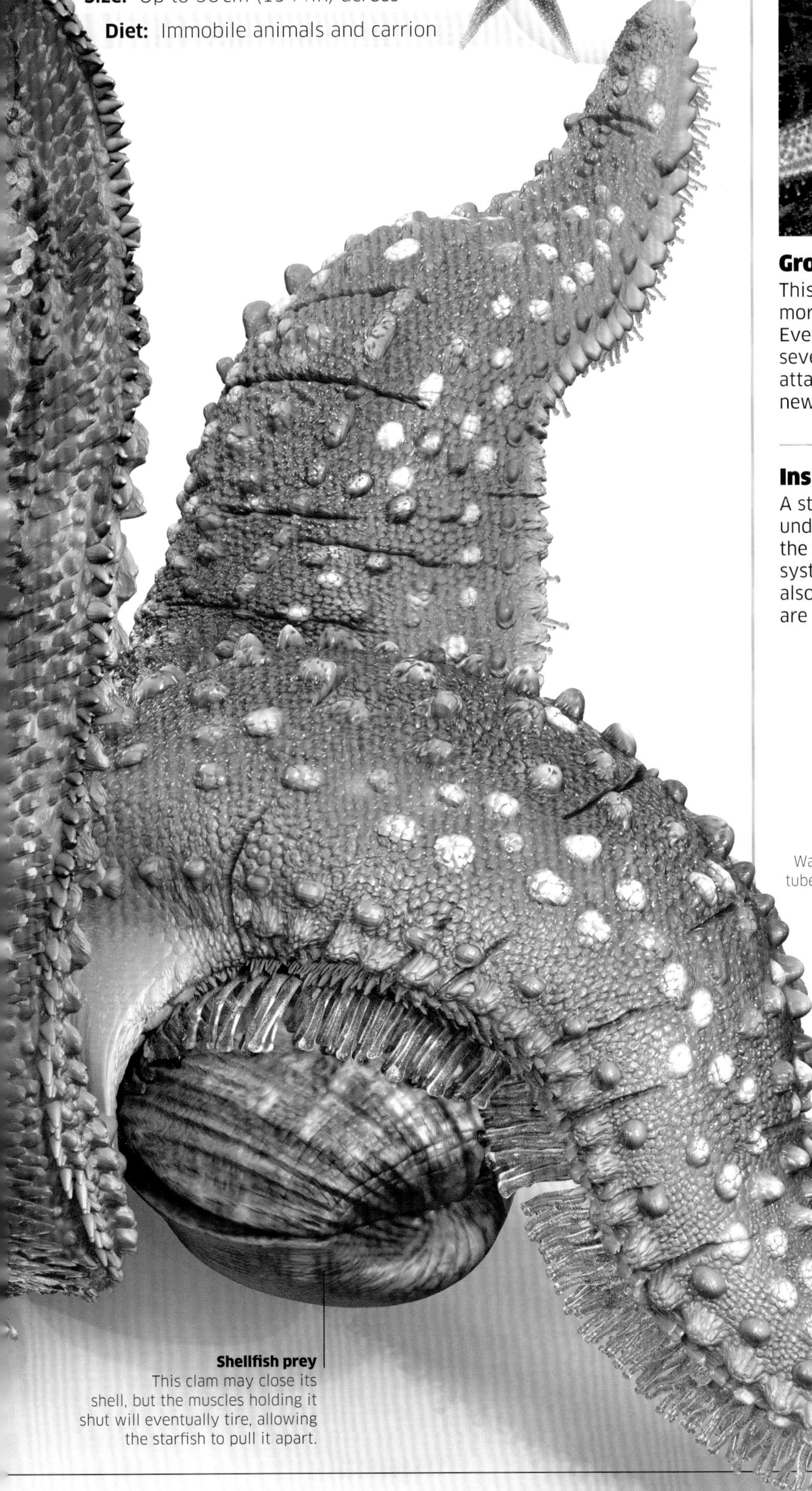

Shellfish prey
This clam may close its shell, but the muscles holding it shut will eventually tire, allowing the starfish to pull it apart.

Spotted with spines
The spines are outgrowths of hard plates called ossicles that lie beneath the skin.

Growing new limbs

This starfish has lost two of its arms, but it will simply grow two more. The arms start as small buds, but eventually reach full size. Even more amazingly, an entire starfish can grow from a single severed arm, provided part of the original central disc is still attached. If a starfish is sliced in two, each part can become two new starfish.

Inside a starfish

A starfish's stomach is in its central disc, and opens to the mouth underneath and the anus on its upper surface. The five arms each have the same anatomy and functions, containing branches of the digestive system and the water-filled sacs that move the tube feet. Each arm also contains reproductive organs, which produce eggs or sperm. These are released from pores at the base of the arms during spawning.

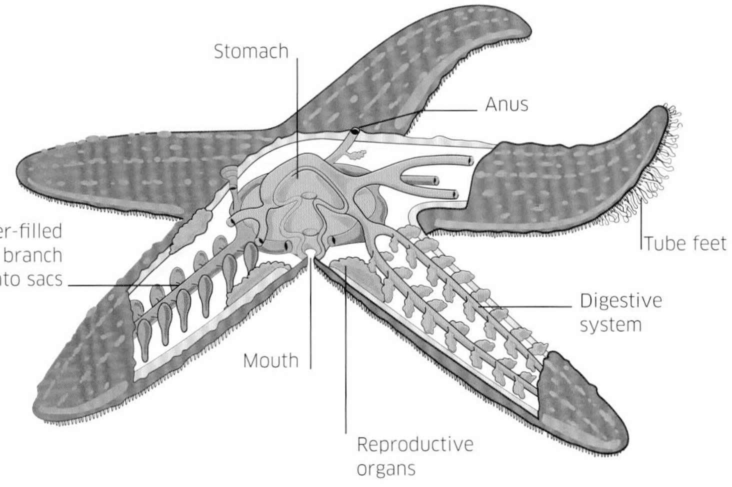

Echinoderms are among the few animals that **do not have heads.**

Some **sea urchins** can use their spines to **burrow into solid rock.**

Echinoderms

Starfish, sea urchins, and their relatives are known as echinoderms, which means "spiny-skinned". The spines are very obvious on some sea urchins, which are the prickliest creatures on the planet.

Other echinoderms are studded with hard plates, or have flexible but tough skins. All sea-dwelling creatures, they have bodies that are built on a radial plan, with a mouth and stomach in the centre and segments extending outwards like a flower.

CROWN-OF-THORNS STARFISH

Acanthaster planci

Location: Indo-Pacific region

Width: Up to 35 cm (13¾ in)

One of the biggest, spiniest sea stars, this is a notorious predator of reef-building corals. Armies of them swarm over the reefs, and devour the coral by smothering it with digestive juices and soaking up the result, leaving a skeleton of bare rock.

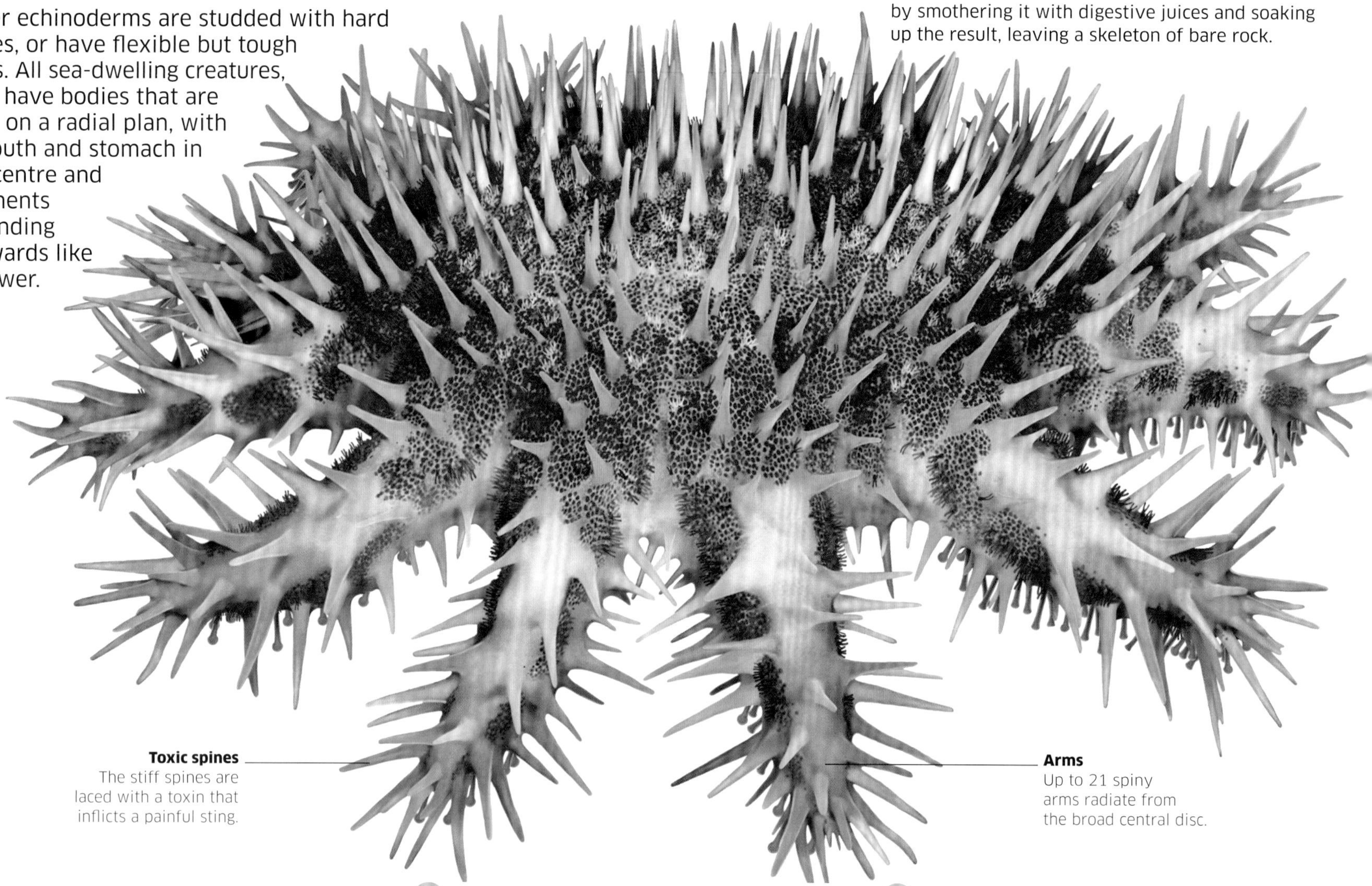

Toxic spines The stiff spines are laced with a toxin that inflicts a painful sting.

Arms Up to 21 spiny arms radiate from the broad central disc.

BLUE STARFISH

Linckia laevigata

Location: Indo-Pacific region

Width: Up to 30 cm (11¾ in)

One of the most colourful echinoderms, this tropical starfish grazes on algae or the encrusting animals that cling to rocks and reefs. It has five arms but, like all starfish, has the ability to grow new ones if it loses any.

BISCUIT STAR

Tosia australis

Location: South Australian coastline

Width: Up to 10 cm (4 in)

Starfish come in many shapes and sizes. This south Australian biscuit star has a typical five-sided form, but very short arms. Like all starfish it creeps over the sea bed on many small, tube feet with suckers at the tips.

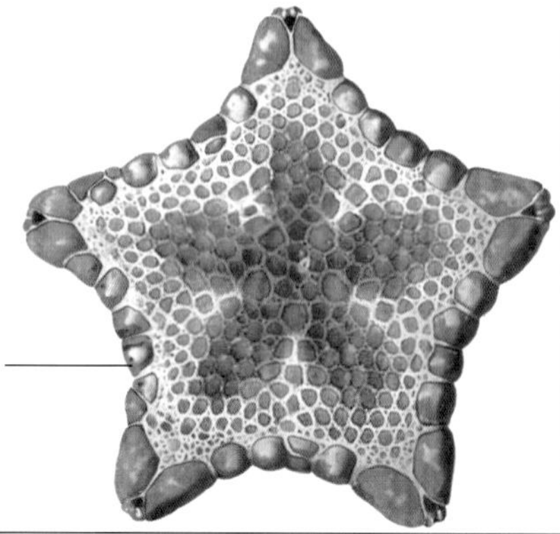

Plate armour Body is fringed with tough plates.

CELTIC FEATHER STAR

Leptometra celtica

Location: Coasts of N. W. Europe

Width: Up to 30 cm (11¾ in)

Feather stars are built like starfish, but live upside down attached to rocks, and filter food from the water with their feathery arms. Their bodies are mostly made up of hard, chalky plates and spines.

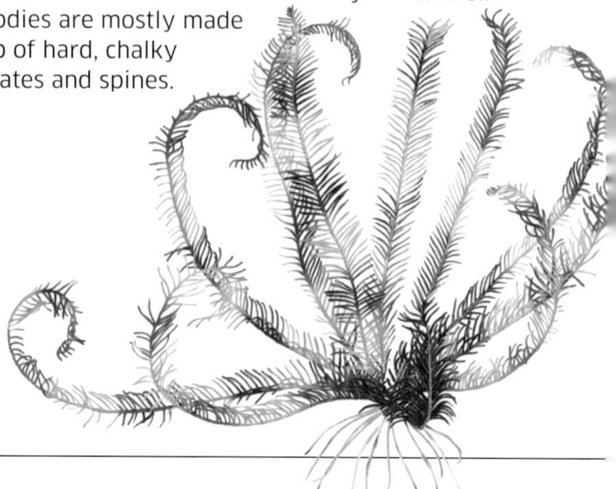

PURPLE URCHIN

Strongylocentrotus purpuratus

Location: North American coastline

Width: Up to 10 cm (4 in), excluding spines

A sea urchin body's is made up of five "radial segments", a bit like the segments of an orange, enclosed in a spiny skeleton. This species feeds on giant kelp seaweed in the coastal Pacific.

THORNY SEA URCHIN

Goniocidaris tubaria

Location: Australian coastline

Width: Up to 4.5 cm (1¾ in), excluding spines

Typical sea urchins have slender, sharp-tipped spines, but this south Australian species has very stout spines armed with thorns. Like other sea urchins it has a set of central jaws that it uses to eat a wide variety of foods.

LONG-SPINED SEA URCHIN

Diadema antillarum

Location: Western Atlantic Ocean

Width: Up to 10 cm (4 in), excluding spines

The extremely long spines of this tropical urchin make it a prickly mouthful for predators, but despite this it is still eaten by some fish. It feeds at night on algae and coral, retreating to dark crevices by day.

Sharp spines The sharp, brittle black spines can be up to 30 cm (12 in) long.

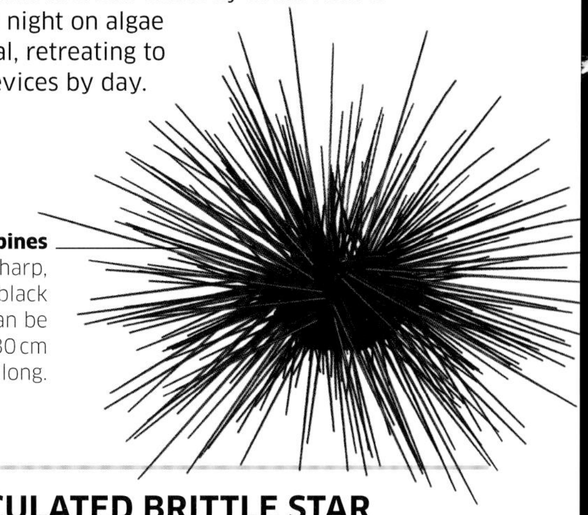

WESTERN SAND DOLLAR

Dendraster excentricus

Location: Pacific North American coast

Width: Up to 7.5 cm (3 in)

Some urchins are adapted for burrowing in sand. They are covered in tiny bristly spines, and often have distinct front and back ends. This American species has an unusually flattened body.

Petal-shaped structure on surface

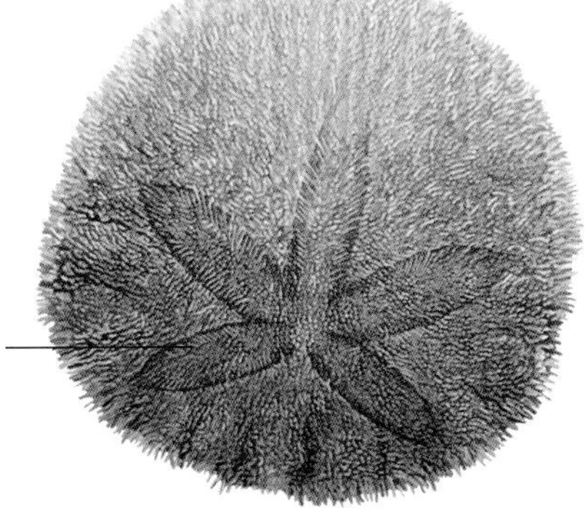

BASKET STAR

Astroboa nuda

Location: Indo-Pacific region

Width: Up to 1 m (3¼ ft)

Similar to feather stars, basket stars cling to rocks or corals in places with strong currents, and use their multi-branched arms to gather food from the water. They are closely related to brittle stars, with the same bony, yet flexible structure.

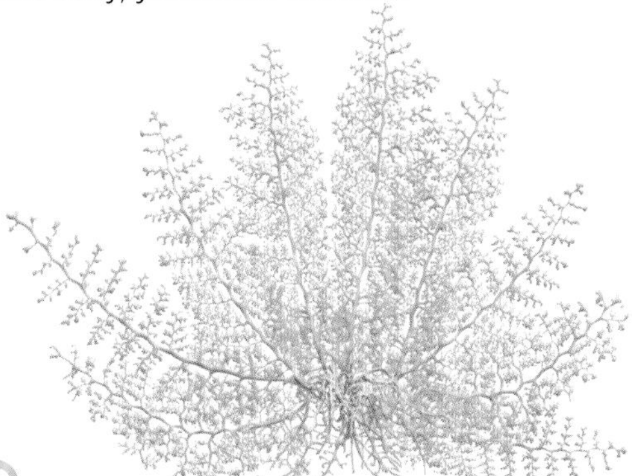

RETICULATED BRITTLE STAR

Ophionereis reticulata

Location: N. and S. American coastline

Width: Up to 25 cm (9¾ in)

A brittle star has a small central disc and five slender, very mobile arms, each supported by a flexible chain of bony plates. It uses its arms to cling to corals and rocks, or crawl across the sea bed in search of edible debris.

Spiny arms Each flexible arm is fringed with rows of spines.

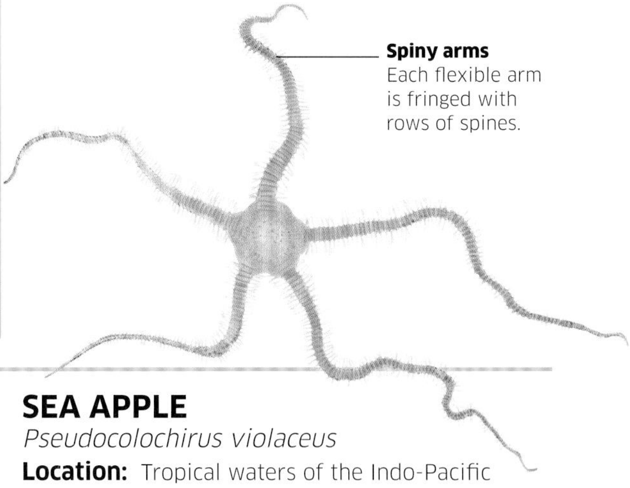

FLORIDA SEA CUCUMBER

Holothuria floridana

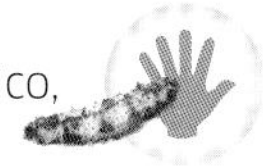

Location: Caribbean Sea, Gulf of Mexico, Florida coast

Length: Up to 20 cm (8 in)

The body of a sea cucumber is formed of five radial segments like a typical sea urchin, but elongated. The animal's mouth is at one end, surrounded by a ring of tentacles used for gathering particles of food.

Knobbly skin Leathery skin is dotted with conical studs.

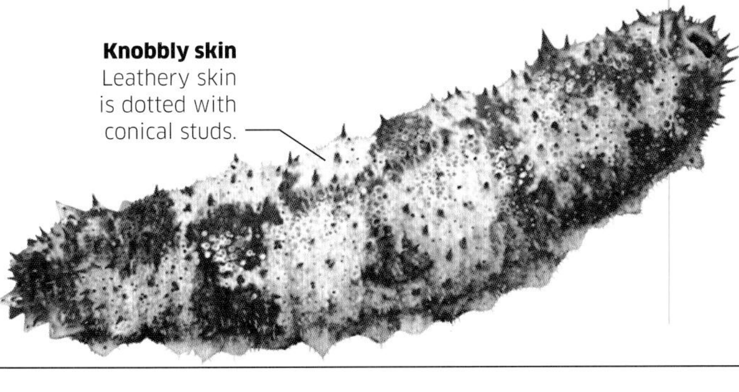

SEA APPLE

Pseudocolochirus violaceus

Location: Tropical waters of the Indo-Pacific

Length: Up to 18 cm (7 in)

Unlike most sea cucumbers, which roam over the sea bed in search of food, a sea apple stays in one place and uses its tentacles to filter edible plankton from the water. This coral reef species is particularly colourful.

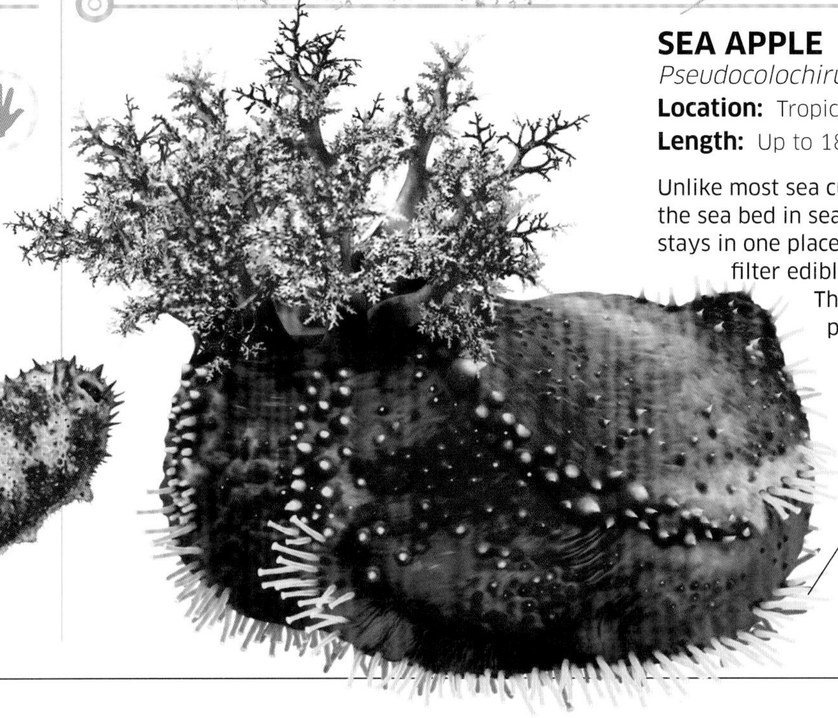

Tube feet Hydraulic tube feet with suckers on the end allow the sea apple to attach itself to rocks.

FISH

Fish were the first animals to have bony internal skeletons, and therefore the first vertebrates. Since their appearance in the seas and oceans more than 500 million years ago, they have evolved into a dazzling diversity of forms, ranging from delicate seahorses to huge, powerful, predatory sharks.

WHAT IS A FISH?

Fish are easy to recognize, but harder to define. They include three distinct groups of animals, most of which breathe through gills but are otherwise quite different. But a typical fish is a streamlined swimmer that propels itself through the water using strong muscles anchored to a flexible backbone.

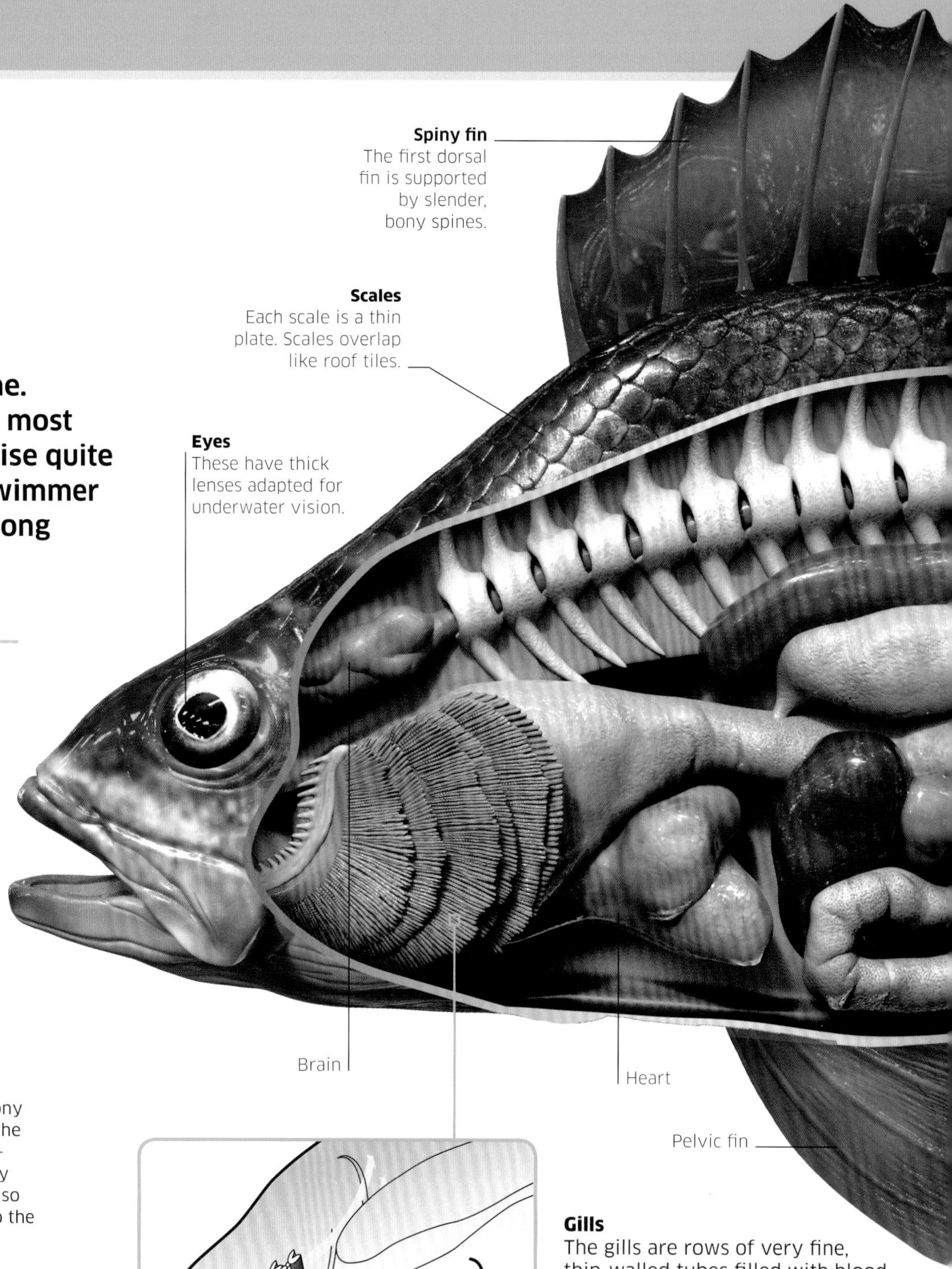

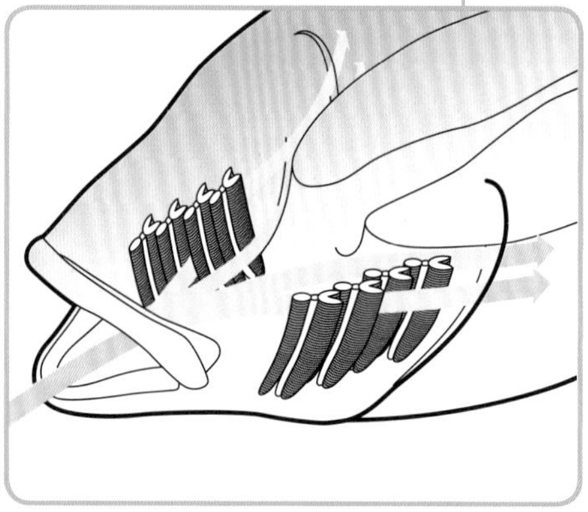

Gills
The gills are rows of very fine, thin-walled tubes filled with blood that is pumped around the body. The blood contains waste carbon dioxide produced by muscles and organs. Water flowing into the fish's mouth and through the gills carries away the carbon dioxide, replacing it with oxygen absorbed from the water. The fish uses this oxygen to turn its food into energy.

TYPES OF FISH

The first fish to evolve were jawless fish, which flourished in the distant past but have now been reduced to a few species. The cartilaginous sharks and rays are more numerous, but the vast majority of fish belong to the large group of bony fish.

SEA LAMPREY

Jawless fish
As their name indicates, the jawless fish do not have hinged jaws. The group consists of fewer than 40 species of eel-like lampreys, and may also include the slimy hagfishes.

EUROPEAN ANCHOVY

Bony fish
With some 32,000 species, the bony fish make up most of the fish on the planet. Nearly all of them are ray-finned fish (with fins supported by bony struts or spines), but they also include lobe-finned fish related to the ancestors of all land vertebrates.

SCALLOPED HAMMERHEAD SHARK

Cartilaginous fish
The sharks, rays, and their relatives have skeletons made from gristly, pliable cartilage instead of bone. There are about 1,200 species, which include the largest, most powerful fish in the sea.

KEY FEATURES

All fish share a number of key features, although the nature of those features varies. They are all vertebrates, with internal skeletons based on spinal vertebrae. Their skin is usually protected by scales, and almost all have gills that gather oxygen from the water. Mainly cold-blooded, they all live primarily in the water of oceans, seas, lakes, and rivers.

Vertebrates
A typical fish's skeleton consists of the spine, skull and jaws, ribs, and fin supports.

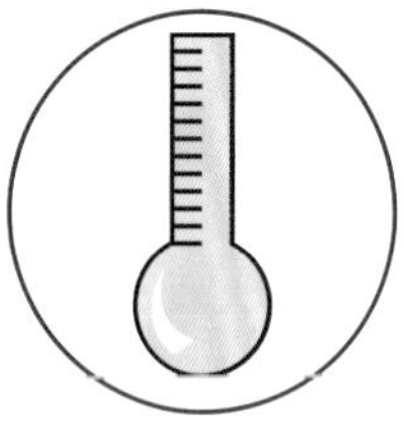

Cold-blooded
The body of a typical fish is the same temperature as the water in which it lives.

Breathe with gills
Blood in the gills absorbs oxygen from the water, but a few fish can breathe air.

Live in water
All fish live in either fresh water or salty seawater. A few can move between the two.

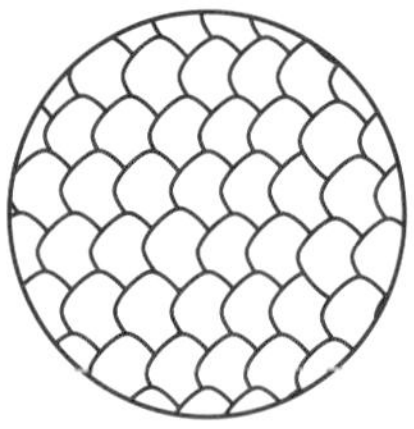

Scaly skin
Tough, overlapping scales cover the skin of most fish, but some types have no scales.

Inside a fish

The streamlined body of this European perch is supported by the water, and the main function of its flexible, bony skeleton is to anchor the big muscles that the fish uses for swimming.

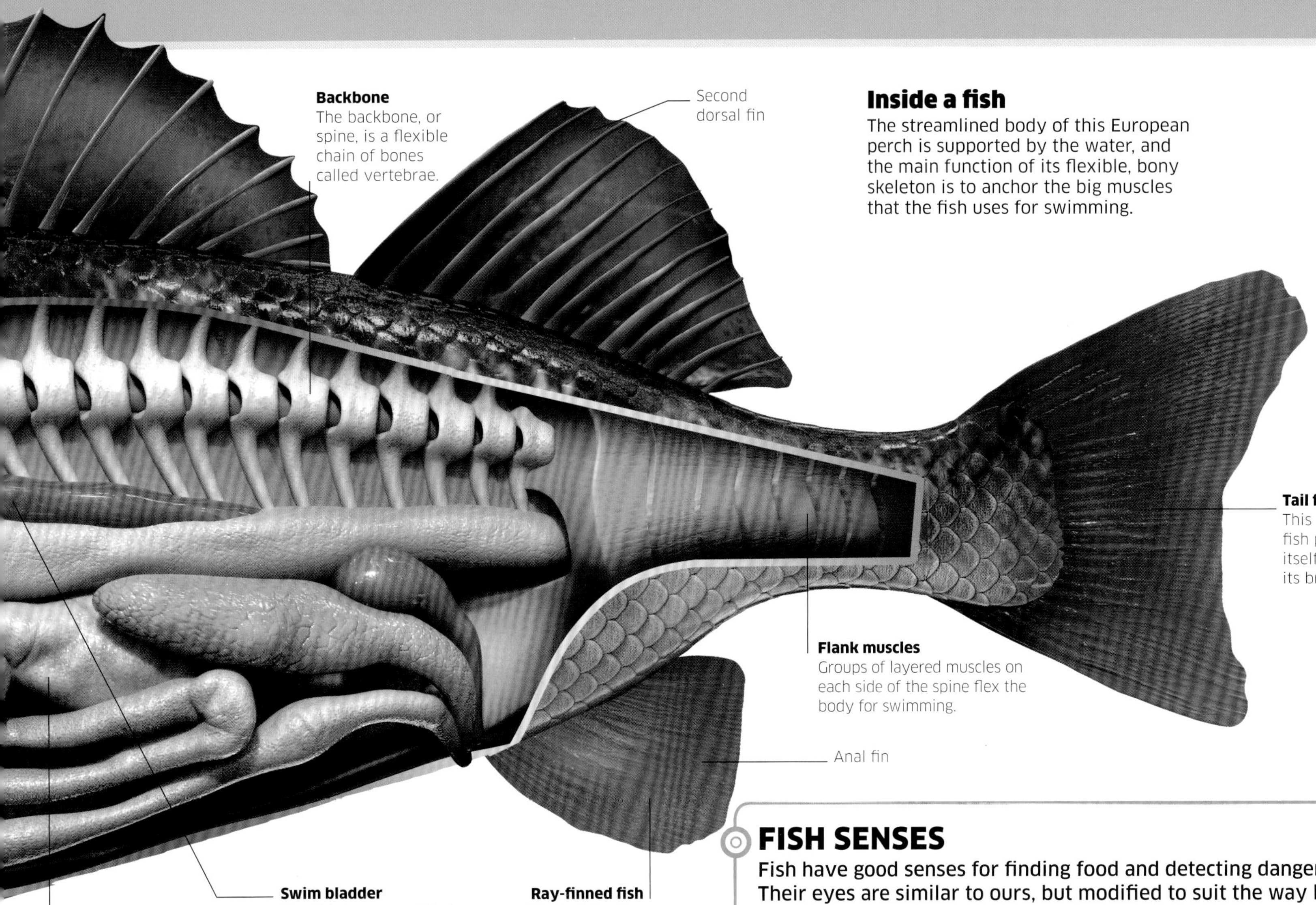

SWIMMING LIKE A FISH

Eels swim by flexing their bodies like snakes, creating rippling waves that push them through the water. Many other fish swim in a similar way, using the massive flank muscles on each side of their backbones, with the greatest movement at the tail. Some make greater movements of their bodies than others. The fastest fish – which include tuna, some sharks, and the sailfish – hold their bodies straight and use their flank muscles to flick their tail fins from side to side.

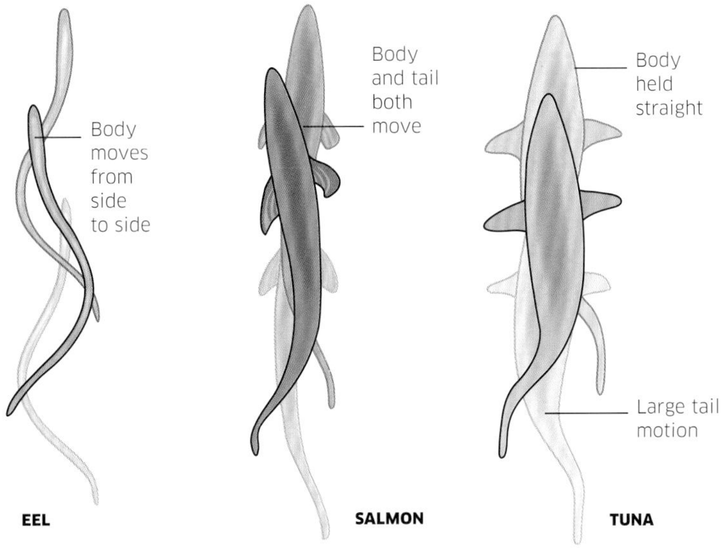

FISH SENSES

Fish have good senses for finding food and detecting danger. Their eyes are similar to ours, but modified to suit the way light passes through water. They have acute senses of smell and taste, and most can pick up sound waves. More importantly they detect pressure changes using a network of sensors called the lateral line. These sensors alert the fish to nearby movements and allow them to swim in perfectly coordinated shoals.

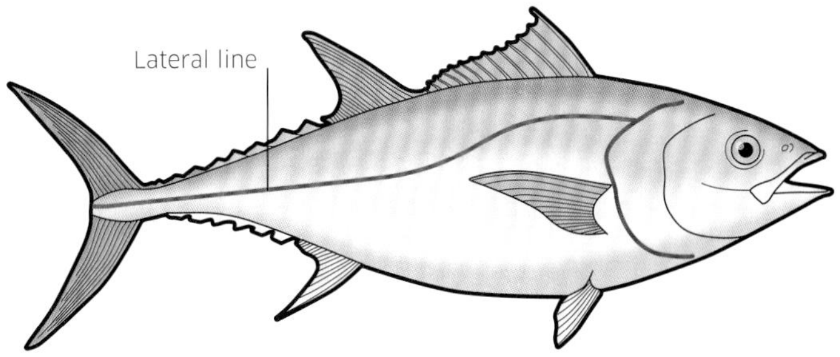

EGGS AND YOUNG

A female shark's eggs are fertilized internally, and many sharks bear live young that develop inside the mother. But most female fish produce large numbers of eggs and release them into the water to be fertilized by the male. The eggs usually drift in open water where most of them are eaten by other fish, but this mouth-brooding fish protects its eggs in its mouth.

Adult sea lampreys **live** for only about **20 months**.

100,000 The number of **eggs** a **female sea lamprey** can lay.

Vampire attack

When a fish is attacked by a sea lamprey, it has few defences. The lamprey clings tightly with its sucker, and is not easy to dislodge. As it bores into its victim's flesh, its saliva stops the blood clotting, so the lamprey can drink its fill. Its prey will be lucky to survive the attack.

Inside view

A lamprey's skull and skeleton are made of pliable cartilage, like those of a shark, but unlike a shark the lamprey does not have a hinged jaw. The mouth is surrounded by a disc of tough, flexible tissue studded with teeth made of keratin – the substance that forms our fingernails. The mouth and respiratory tube are separate, so the lamprey can draw water over its gills while its mouth is clamped to a victim.

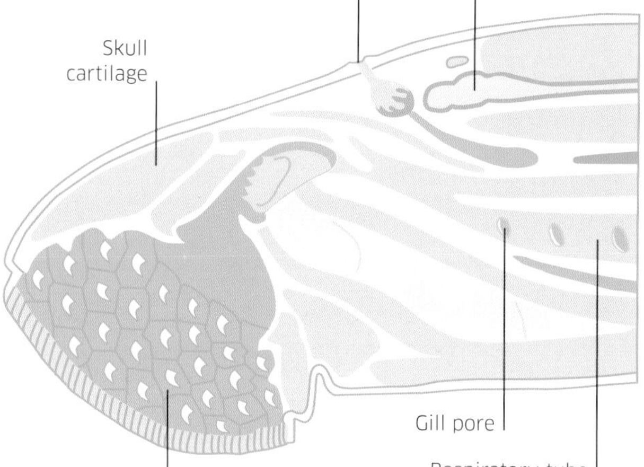

CROSS-SECTION OF A LAMPREY HEAD

FISH
SEA LAMPREY

Petromyzon marinus

Location: N. Atlantic, N. America, Europe

Length: Up to 1.2 m (4 ft)

Diet: Fish blood

The worm-like larval stage of a sea lamprey can live for **up to 17 years** buried in a river- or lake-bed.

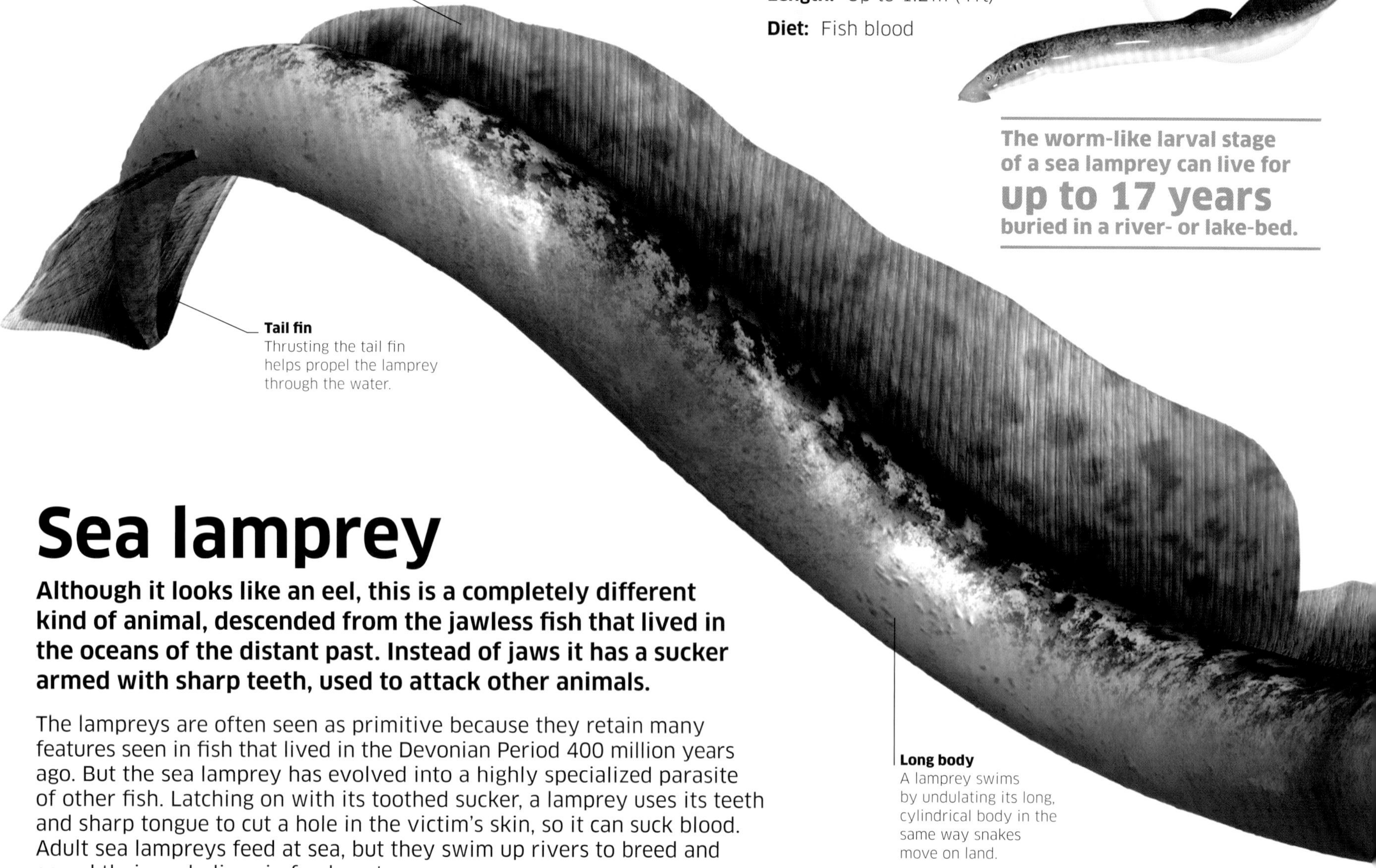

Sea lamprey

Although it looks like an eel, this is a completely different kind of animal, descended from the jawless fish that lived in the oceans of the distant past. Instead of jaws it has a sucker armed with sharp teeth, used to attack other animals.

The lampreys are often seen as primitive because they retain many features seen in fish that lived in the Devonian Period 400 million years ago. But the sea lamprey has evolved into a highly specialized parasite of other fish. Latching on with its toothed sucker, a lamprey uses its teeth and sharp tongue to cut a hole in the victim's skin, so it can suck blood. Adult sea lampreys feed at sea, but they swim up rivers to breed and spend their early lives in fresh water.

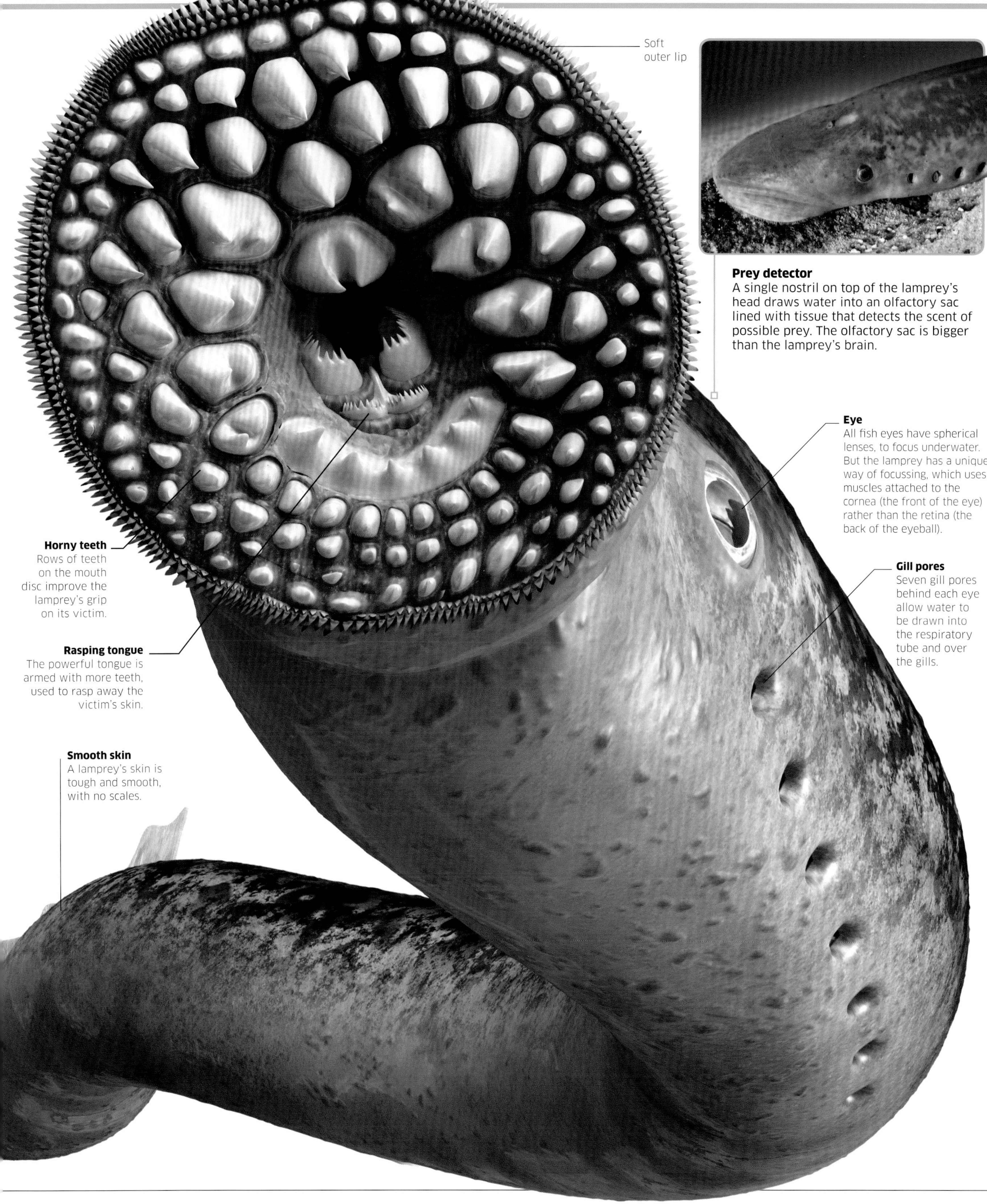

Prey detector
A single nostril on top of the lamprey's head draws water into an olfactory sac lined with tissue that detects the scent of possible prey. The olfactory sac is bigger than the lamprey's brain.

As a great white shark seizes its prey, its eyes roll back in their sockets to protect them.

Great white sharks may cooperate with each other to outwit prey.

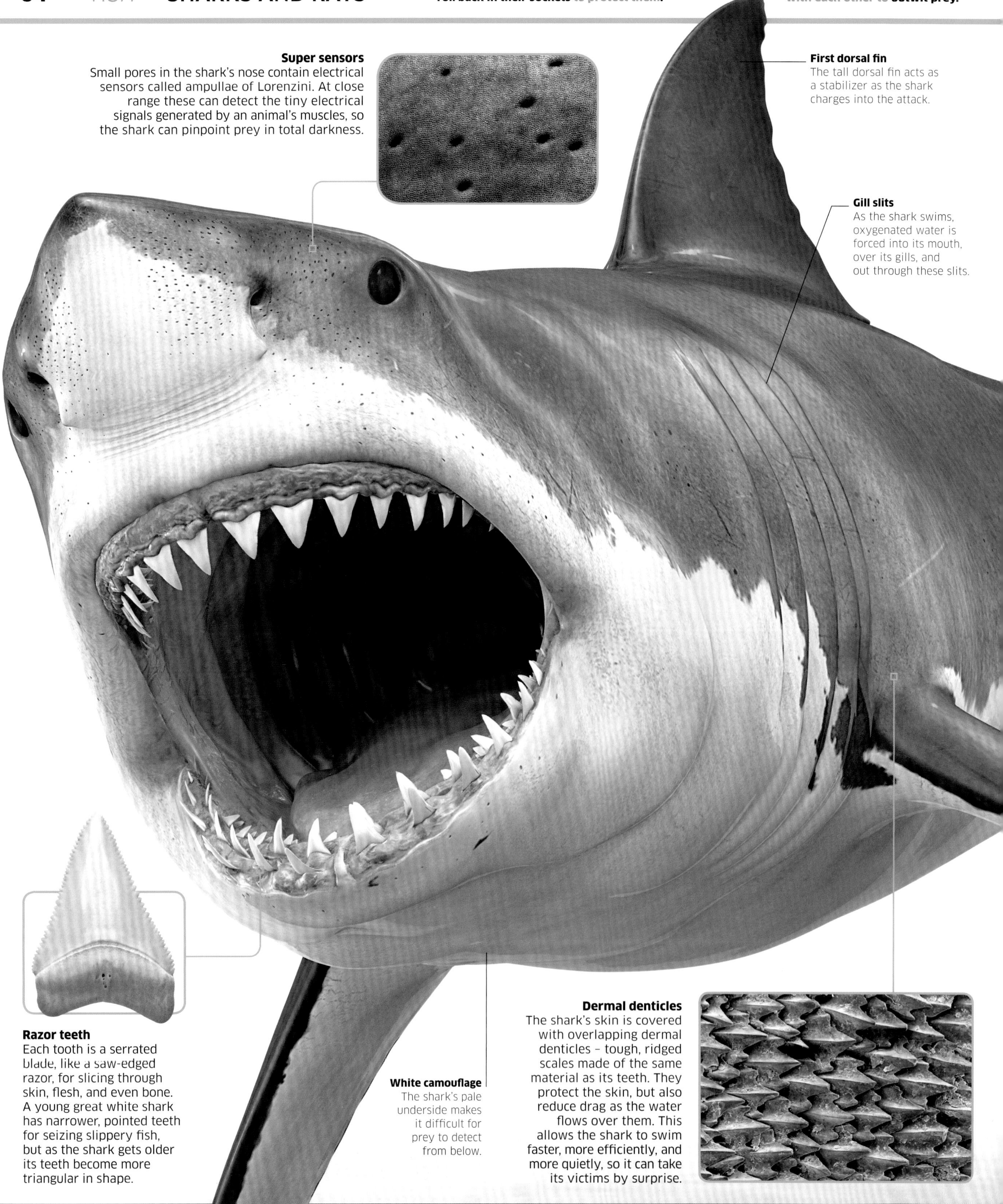

Super sensors
Small pores in the shark's nose contain electrical sensors called ampullae of Lorenzini. At close range these can detect the tiny electrical signals generated by an animal's muscles, so the shark can pinpoint prey in total darkness.

First dorsal fin
The tall dorsal fin acts as a stabilizer as the shark charges into the attack.

Gill slits
As the shark swims, oxygenated water is forced into its mouth, over its gills, and out through these slits.

Razor teeth
Each tooth is a serrated blade, like a saw-edged razor, for slicing through skin, flesh, and even bone. A young great white shark has narrower, pointed teeth for seizing slippery fish, but as the shark gets older its teeth become more triangular in shape.

White camouflage
The shark's pale underside makes it difficult for prey to detect from below.

Dermal denticles
The shark's skin is covered with overlapping dermal denticles – tough, ridged scales made of the same material as its teeth. They protect the skin, but also reduce drag as the water flows over them. This allows the shark to swim faster, more efficiently, and more quietly, so it can take its victims by surprise.

Great white shark

Notorious as the most deadly of all sharks, the great white is specialized for hunting big, warm-blooded animals such as seals, dolphins, and even whales.

Few creatures have such a murderous reputation as the great white shark. Hugely powerful and fast, it is equipped with a devastatingly efficient array of senses for detecting its prey, and a set of ripsaw teeth that can slice its victims in half with a single bite. Capable of killing and eating almost anything it runs into – including people – its only enemies are orcas and human hunters.

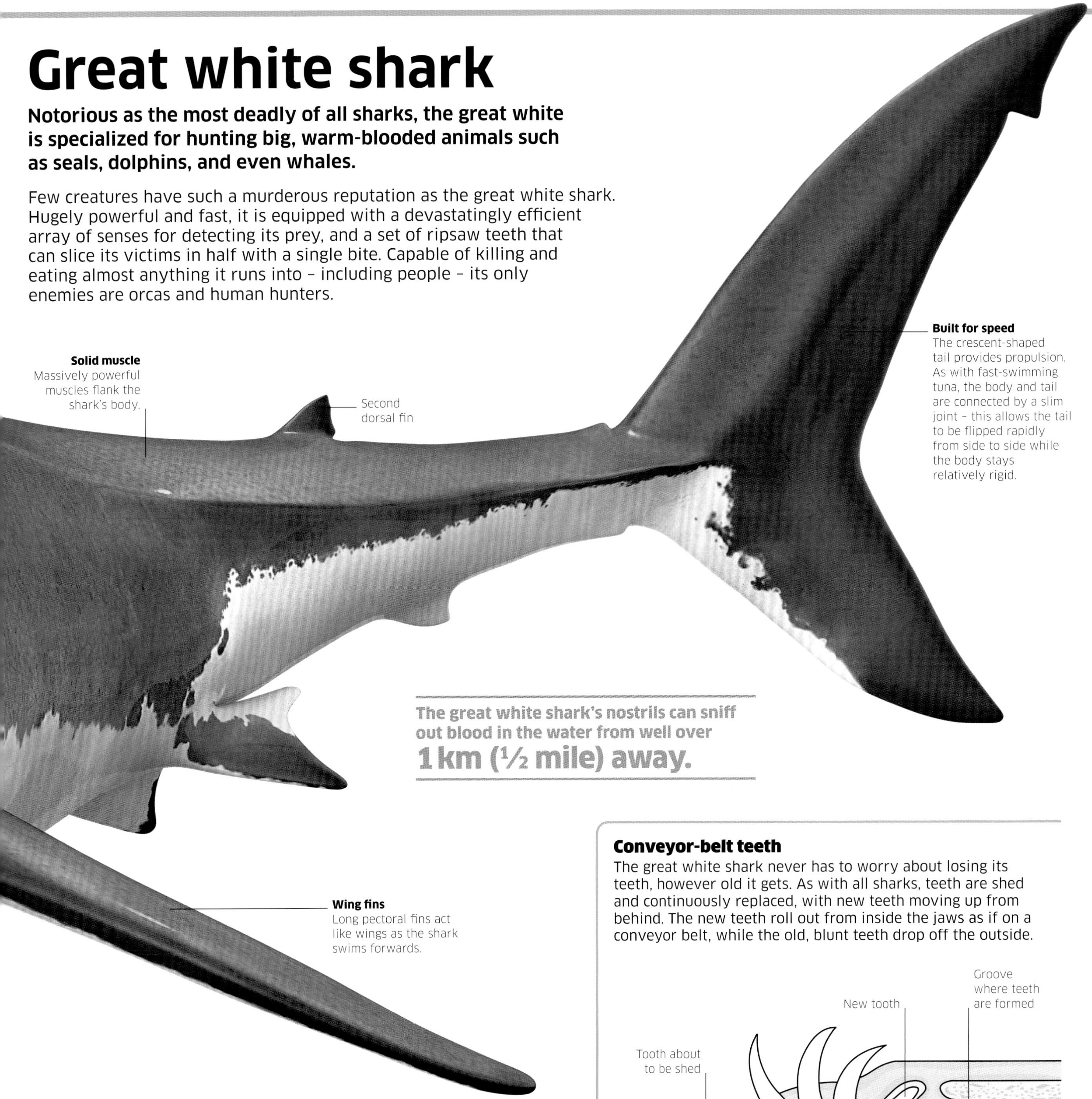

The great white shark's nostrils can sniff out blood in the water from well over 1 km (½ mile) away.

Conveyor-belt teeth

The great white shark never has to worry about losing its teeth, however old it gets. As with all sharks, teeth are shed and continuously replaced, with new teeth moving up from behind. The new teeth roll out from inside the jaws as if on a conveyor belt, while the old, blunt teeth drop off the outside.

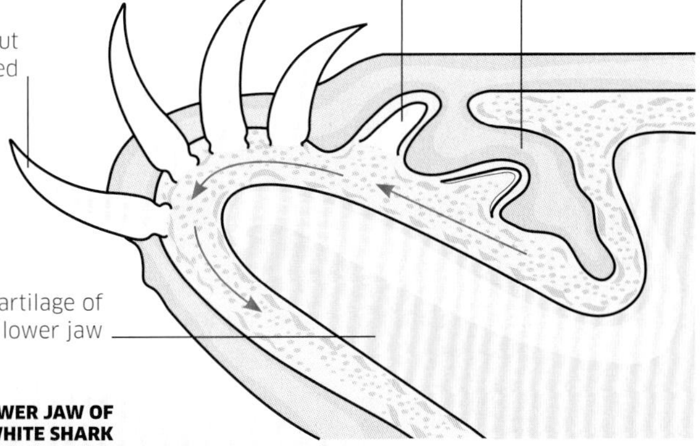

LOWER JAW OF GREAT WHITE SHARK

FISH

GREAT WHITE SHARK

Carcharodon carcharias

Location: All warm oceans

Length: Up to 7.2 m (24 ft)

Diet: Fish, seals, and cetaceans

The **sting** of this stingray **can inflict incredibly painful injuries**, but it is **used only in defence**.

The **mouth** has two **shell-crushing plates** made up of **15–24 rows of teeth**.

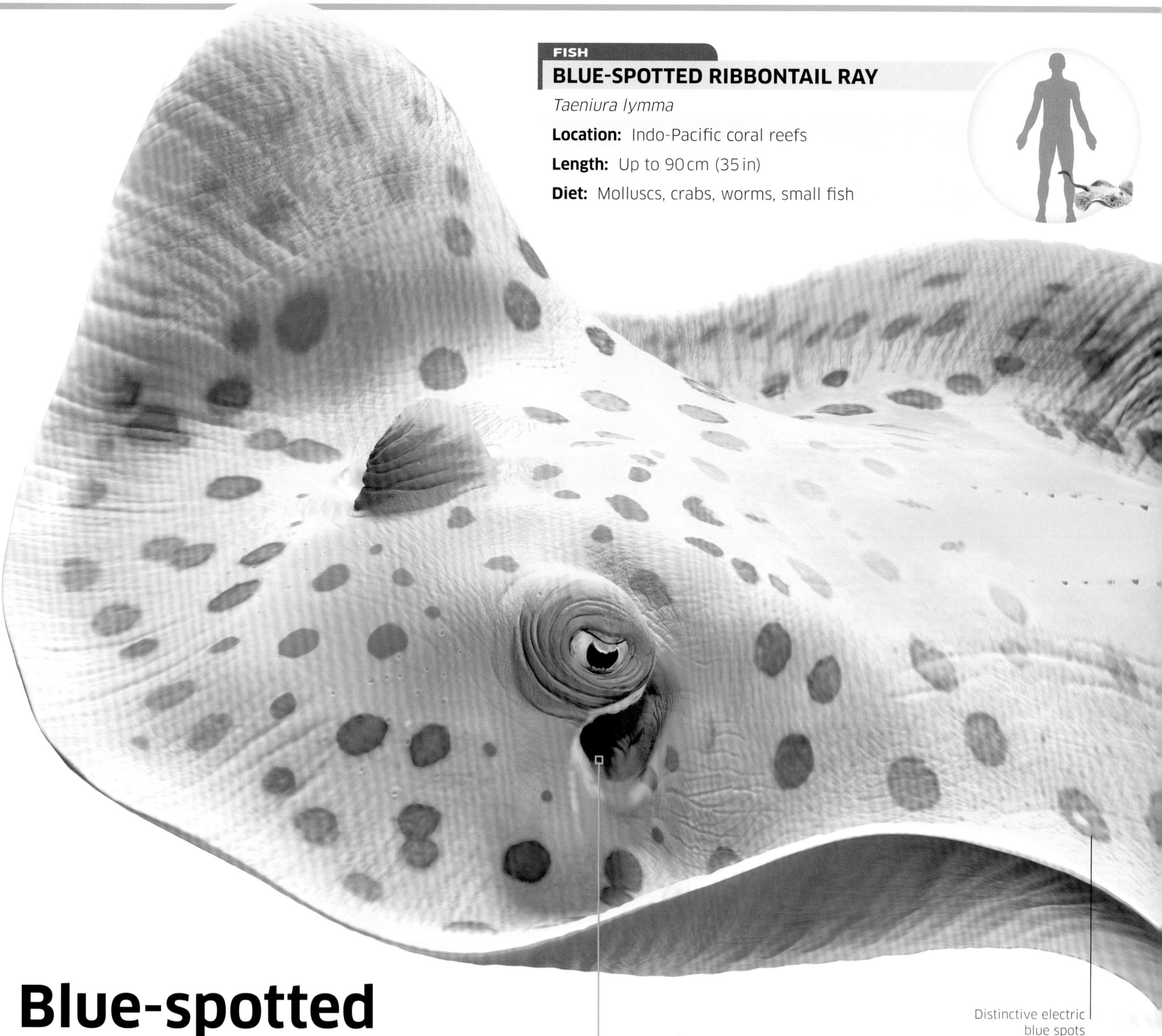

FISH

BLUE-SPOTTED RIBBONTAIL RAY

Taeniura lymma

Location: Indo-Pacific coral reefs

Length: Up to 90 cm (35 in)

Diet: Molluscs, crabs, worms, small fish

Blue-spotted ribbontail ray

Armed with a barbed sting that can inject an extremely painful venom, this colourful stingray is well defended from sharks and other predators as it searches the sandy beds of tropical coral seas for food.

Relatives of the sharks, most skates and rays are adapted for life on the sea bed. Their bodies are flattened, and often well camouflaged so they can lie on the bottom undetected, but this coral reef stingray is unusually colourful. Like most rays it eats a variety of worms, clams, crabs, and other shellfish, crushing their shells with a battery of broad, flattened teeth that are constantly replaced before they are worn out.

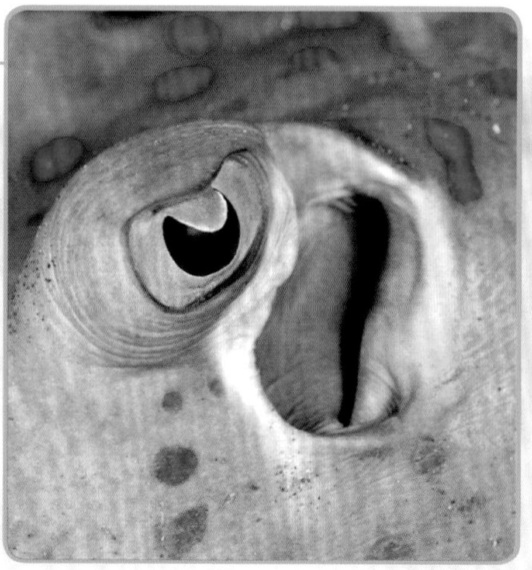

Spiracle
Behind each of the ray's eyes is a large opening, called a spiracle. It is used to draw in oxygenated water from above the ray's body when it is lying with its mouth flat on the sea bed. After passing through the ray's gills, the water is pumped out though the gill slits on its underside.

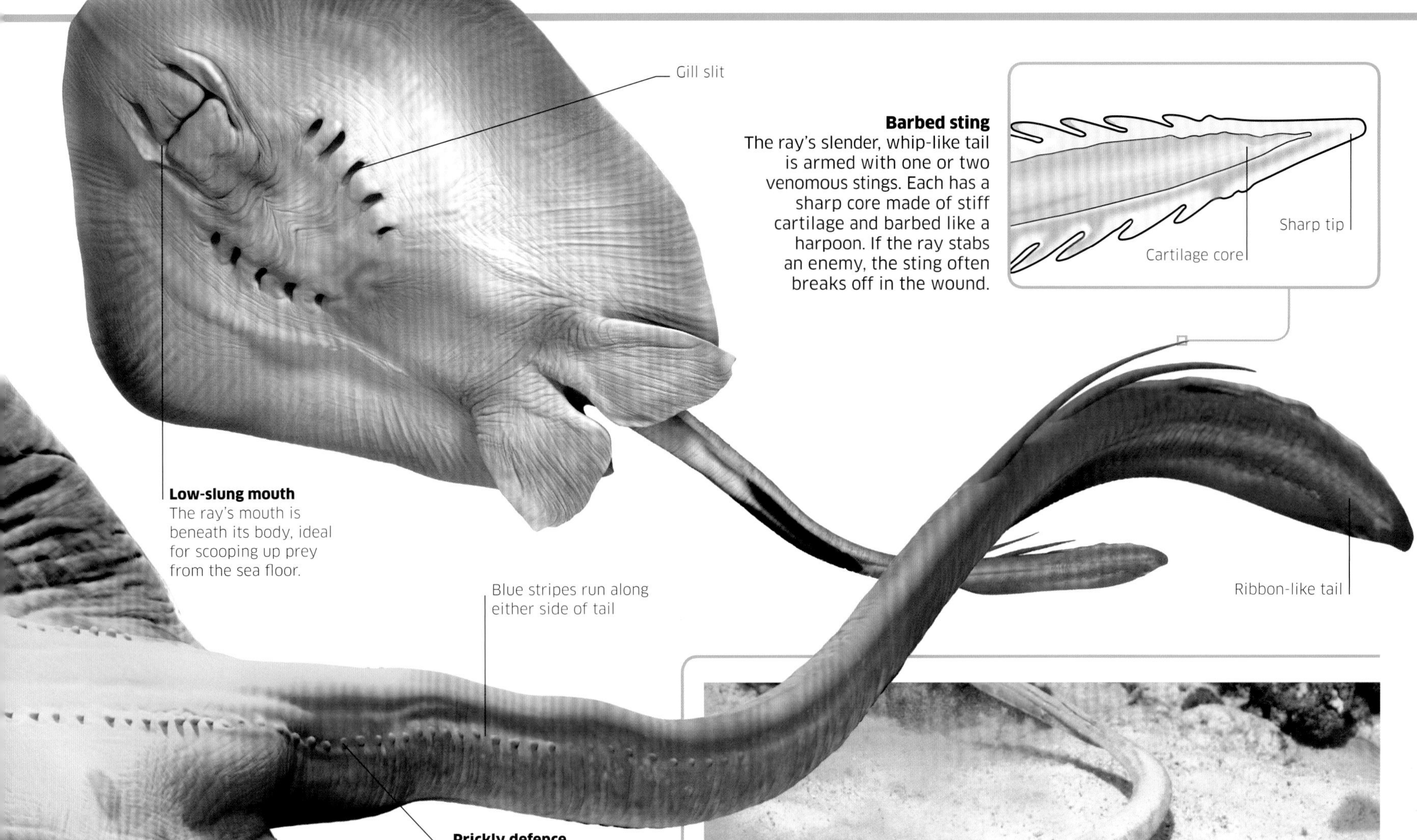

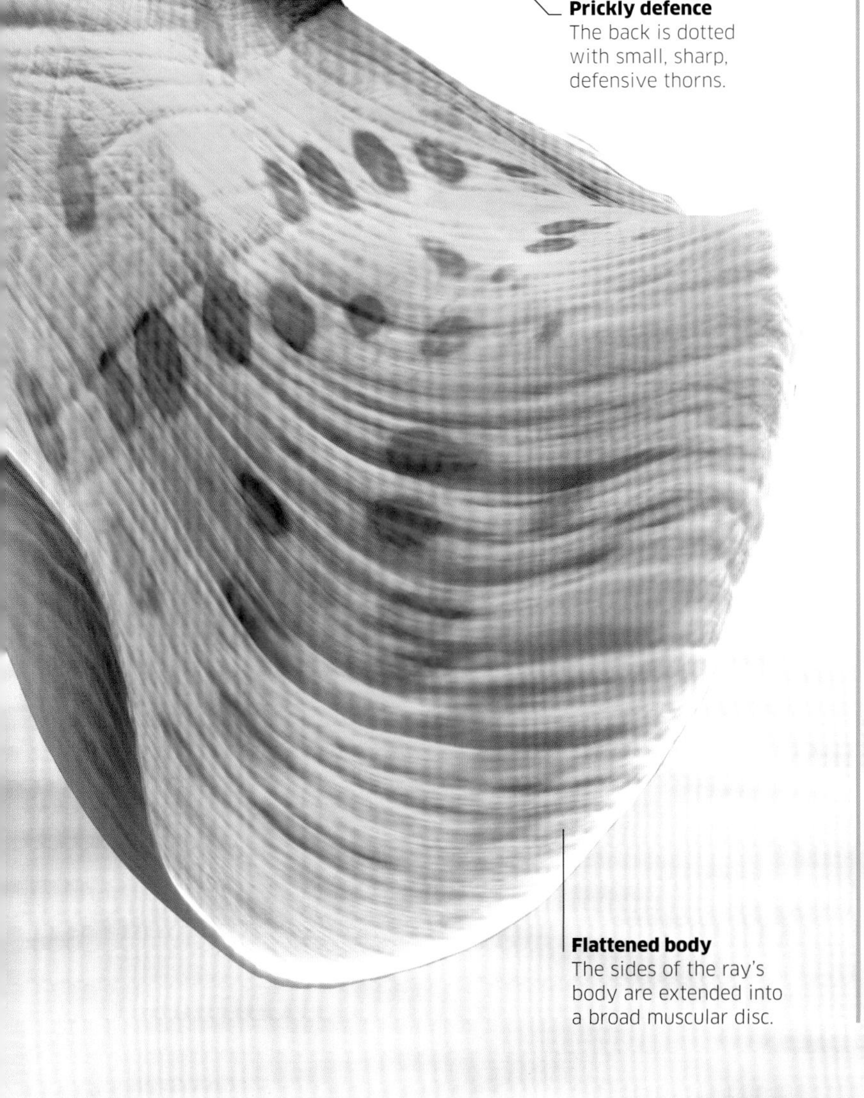

Barbed sting
The ray's slender, whip-like tail is armed with one or two venomous stings. Each has a sharp core made of stiff cartilage and barbed like a harpoon. If the ray stabs an enemy, the sting often breaks off in the wound.

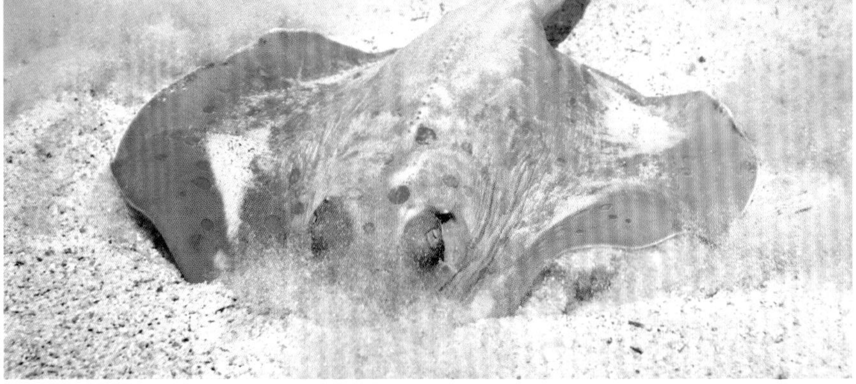

Night hunter

The ray hunts at night in the reef shallows. It searches for prey in the sand using its sharp sense of smell and its electro-receptors, which can detect the electrical activity of an animal's nervous system. By day it lurks among the coral further offshore, hiding from enemies such as hammerhead sharks.

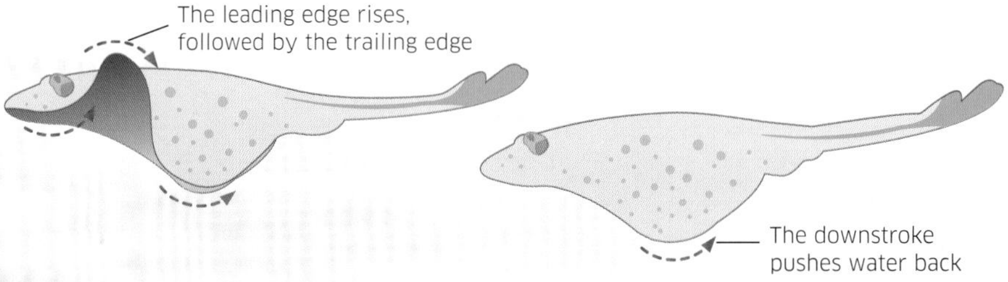

Underwater flight

Unlike most fish, rays do not use their tails to propel themselves when swimming. Instead, they move by "flying" through the water, using their muscular pectoral fins like wings. The fins ripple in "S" waves that push the water back, driving the ray forward.

The **earliest-known** sharks **lived** more than **420 million years** ago.

Some rays **stun or kill** their prey by **electrocuting** them.

Sharks and rays

Sharks have a fearsome reputation, but they are not all powerful predators like the notorious great white. Many prey on fish, and the very biggest sharks eat only tiny marine animals. Most rays feed on shellfish on the sea bed.

The sharks and rays are cartilaginous fish, with skeletons made of gristly cartilage instead of bone. Cartilage is pliable, and usually not strong enough to support a large animal's body, but this is not a problem for a shark or ray because its body is supported by the water. This allows some species to grow to a colossal size.

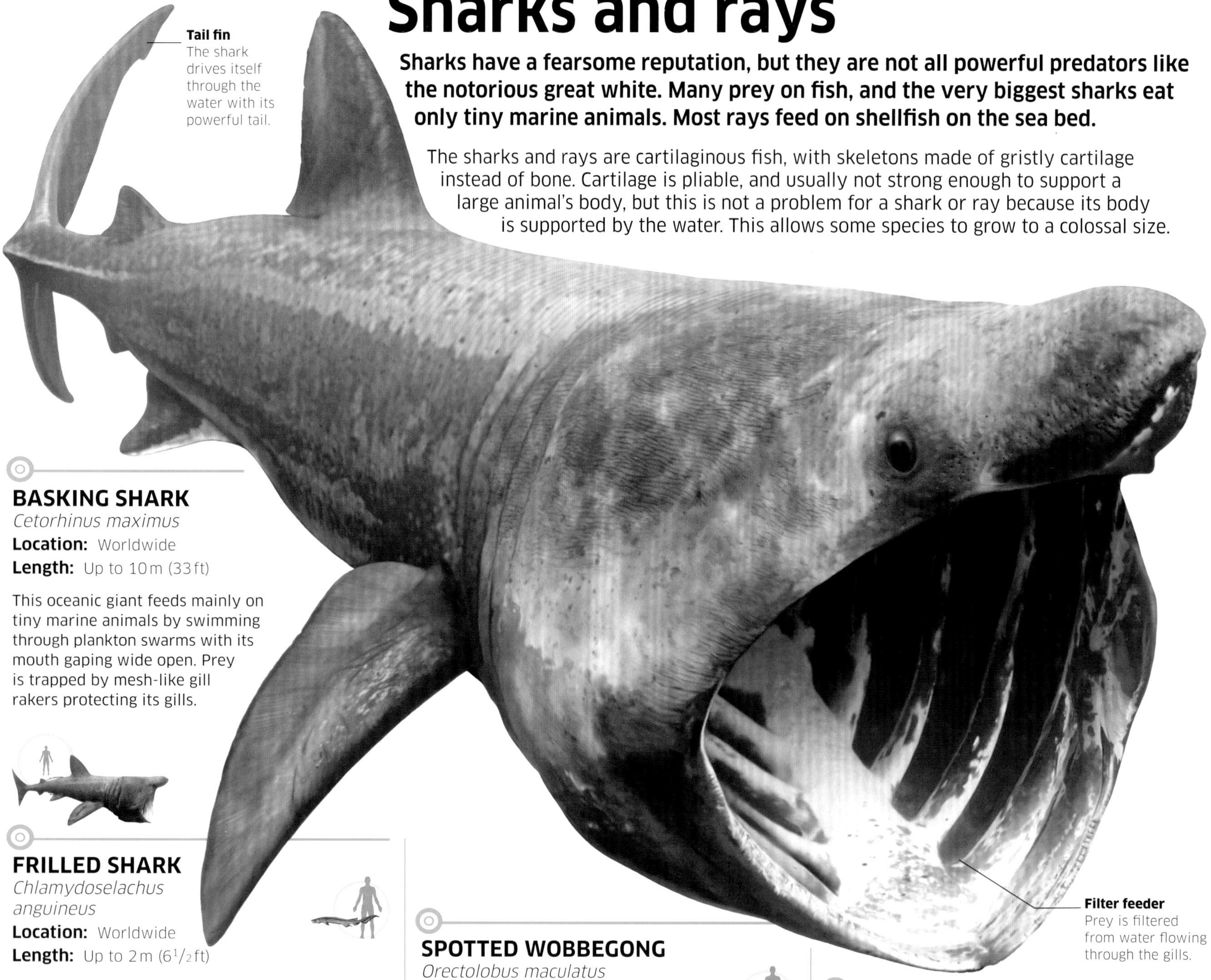

BASKING SHARK

Cetorhinus maximus

Location: Worldwide

Length: Up to 10 m (33 ft)

This oceanic giant feeds mainly on tiny marine animals by swimming through plankton swarms with its mouth gaping wide open. Prey is trapped by mesh-like gill rakers protecting its gills.

FRILLED SHARK

Chlamydoselachus anguineus

Location: Worldwide

Length: Up to 2 m ($6\frac{1}{2}$ ft)

This eel-like shark gets its name from the frilled appearance of the gill slits behind its head. Similar to many primitive, extinct sharks, it feeds mainly on squid.

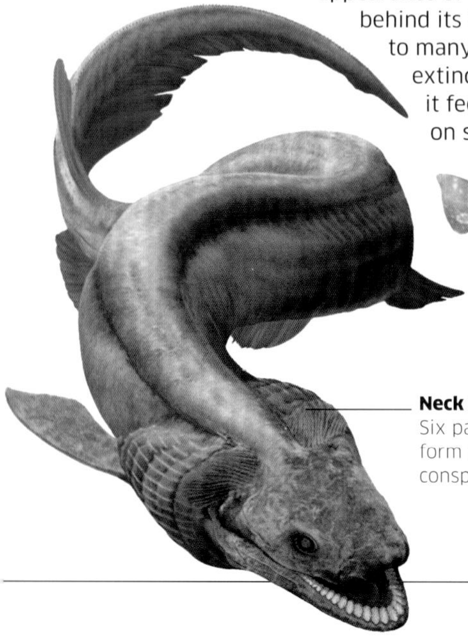

SPOTTED WOBBEGONG

Orectolobus maculatus

Location: South Australia

Length: Up to 3 m ($9\frac{3}{4}$ ft)

Many sharks are specialized for life on the sea bed. This superbly camouflaged ambush predator lies concealed from its prey by its skin patterns and the coral-like fringes around its snout. It is powerful enough to eat smaller sharks.

THRESHER SHARK

Alopias vulpinus

Location: Worldwide

Length: Up to 5.7 m ($18\frac{3}{4}$ ft)

A thresher shark has an extremely long upper tail lobe, which it uses like a whip to herd and attack shoaling fish and squid. Stunned by the blows, they make easy prey for the shark's needle-sharp teeth.

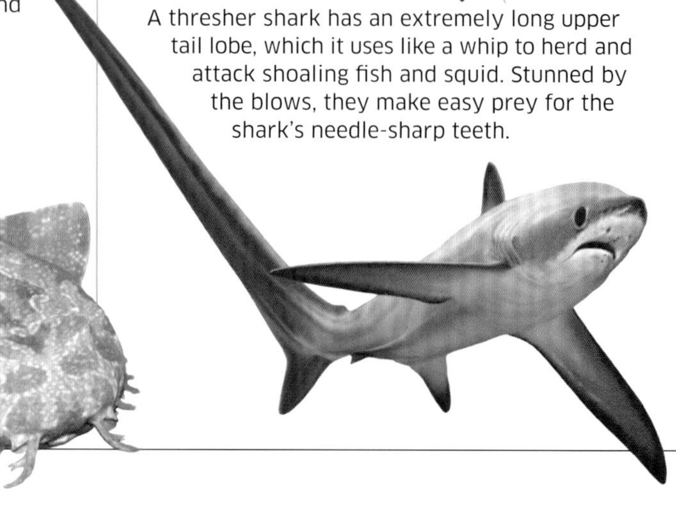

SANDTIGER SHARK

Carcharias taurus

Location: Coastal waters worldwide

Length: Up to 3.2 m (10½ ft)

The ferocious-looking sandtiger shark is specialized for catching fish. Its ragged, spiky teeth are ideally adapted for seizing and gripping slippery, struggling prey, which it then swallows whole or in large mouthfuls. It usually hunts by night, often near the sea bed.

BLUE SHARK

Prionace glauca

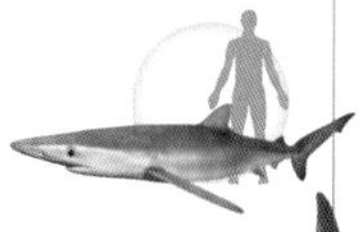

Location: Worldwide

Length: Up to 3.8 m (12½ ft)

Sleek and elegant, the blue shark gets its name from its metallic blue back. Its slender body and pointed snout make it superbly streamlined for cruising at speed in search of prey, which are mainly smaller fish and squid. It sometimes hunts in packs.

SCALLOPED HAMMERHEAD

Sphyrna lewini

Location: Worldwide

Length: Up to 4.2 m (13¾ ft)

A hammerhead shark has a bizarre plank-like head with its eyes and nostrils at each tip. This shape may help it make tight turns in the water, or it may provide space for extra electro-receptors for detecting hidden prey.

ANGEL SHARK

Squatina squatina

Location: Northern Atlantic Ocean, Mediterranean Sea, Black Sea

Length: Up to 2.4 m (7¾ ft)

The broad, flattened body of the angel shark is more like that of a ray than a typical shark. Its shape enables it to lie concealed on the sea bed, waiting for fish to swim within ambush range.

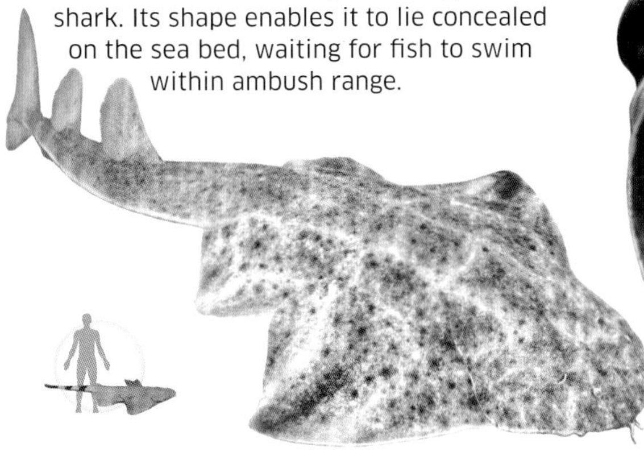

GIANT MANTA RAY

Manta birostris

Location: Worldwide

Length: Up to 7.6 m (25 ft)

The biggest of the rays, the giant manta is a filter-feeder like the basking shark. It cruises tropical oceans searching for swarms of planktonic animals, and feeds by straining the water through its gills to trap prey.

SPOTTED EAGLE RAY

Aetobatus narinari

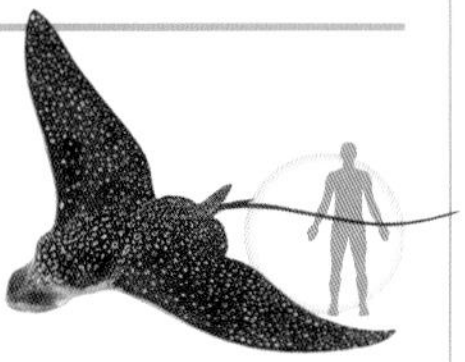

Location: Worldwide

Length: Up to 5 m (16½ ft)

This elegant ray often swims in open water, sometimes in groups of 10 or more. Despite this, it feeds mainly on the sea bed by digging into the sand with its shovel-shaped snout for clams, crabs, and other shellfish. It has very strong, flattened teeth for crushing shells.

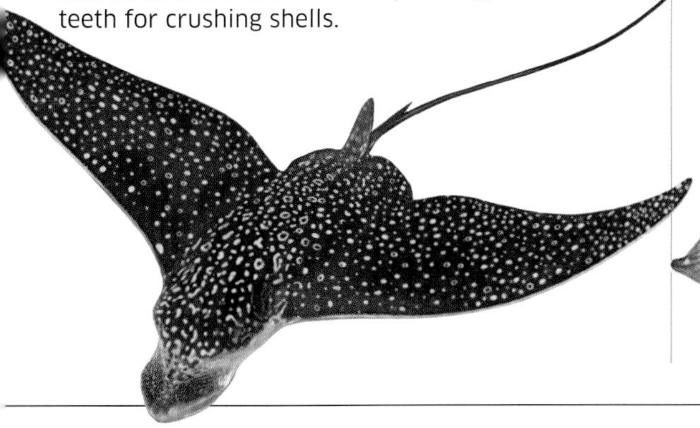

THORNBACK RAY

Raja clavata

Location: Eastern Atlantic, Mediterranean

Length: Up to 1 m (3¼ ft)

Although this ray has the kite-shaped body typical of many rays, its back is covered in sharp, thorny spines that extend down its long tail. Its mouth is beneath its head, so it can scoop buried prey off the sea bed.

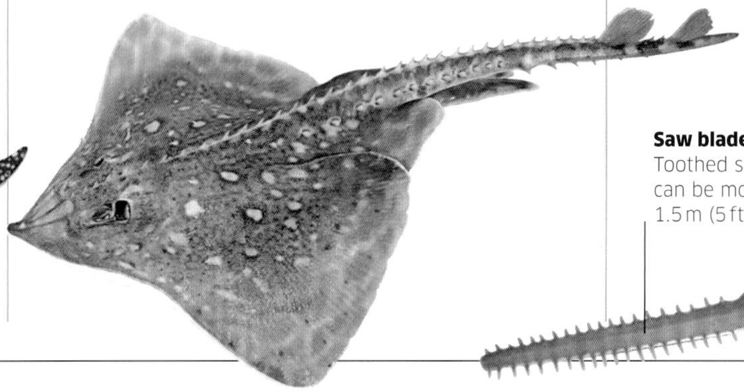

LONGCOMB SAWFISH

Pristis zijsron

Location: Indo-Pacific region

Length: Up to 4.3 m (14 ft)

The extraordinary snout of this sawfish is a long, slender blade fringed with rows of triangular teeth. The fish uses it to strike and stun fish prey, and to rake burrowing animals from the sea bed.

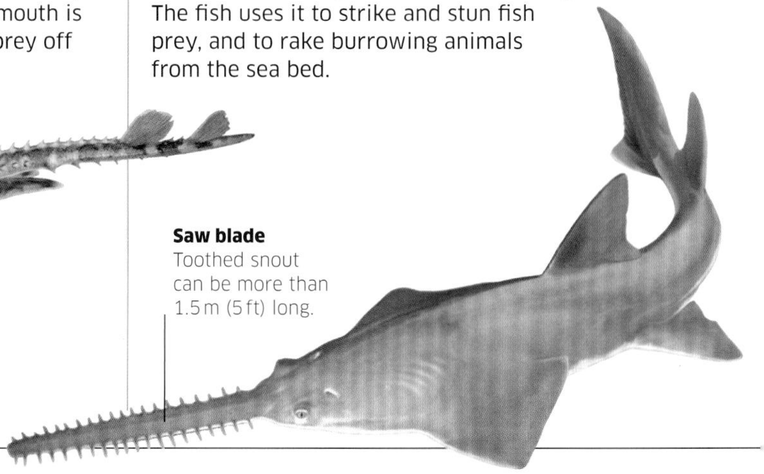

6 mm (¼ in) – **the length** of a spotted seahorse **at birth**.

Spotted seahorses **pair up for life**, renewing their bond each morning with a **courtship dance**.

Spotted seahorse

Named for their horse-like head shape, seahorses are highly specialized fish with a unique swimming technique and one of the most extraordinary breeding systems in the entire animal kingdom.

Widespread in the Indo-Pacific regions the spotted seahorse lives in shallow coastal waters where it feeds on small, drifting animals. It can swim slowly in a vertical position, propelled by its beating dorsal fin, but prefers to use its prehensile (grasping) tail to cling to corals, seagrasses, and seaweed and watch for prey. As with all seahorses, the female passes her eggs to the male, who holds them in a pouch on his belly, fertilizing and nurturing them until they become miniature seahorses.

Chameleon colour
The spotted seahorse is typically yellowish with darker spots and blotches. But like most seahorses it is able to change its skin colour, by making colour cells in its skin expand or contract. The seahorse can then blend with its surroundings for protective camouflage. It often turns very dark to conceal itself from both enemies and prey. But it may also glow a deep red, especially during its courtship displays.

Planktonic prey
The seahorse's prey are small shrimp-like animals that drift in open water and make up plankton. Watching intently with its big, mobile eyes, the seahorse targets a victim and swivels its snout towards it. Using its flexible neck, it lunges at the animal and sucks it into its toothless mouth, swallowing it whole.

FISH

SPOTTED SEAHORSE

Hippocampus kuda

Location: Indian and Pacific Oceans

Length: Up to 35 cm (13¾ in)

Diet: Small planktonic animals

The male spotted seahorse usually gives birth at night, when there is a full moon. The process takes several hours.

Mobile eyes
Unlike nearly all other fish, a seahorse has eyes that rotate in their sockets, like ours. The eyes also move independently, so the seahorse can look in two directions at once as it scans the surrounding water for prey while also watching for danger.

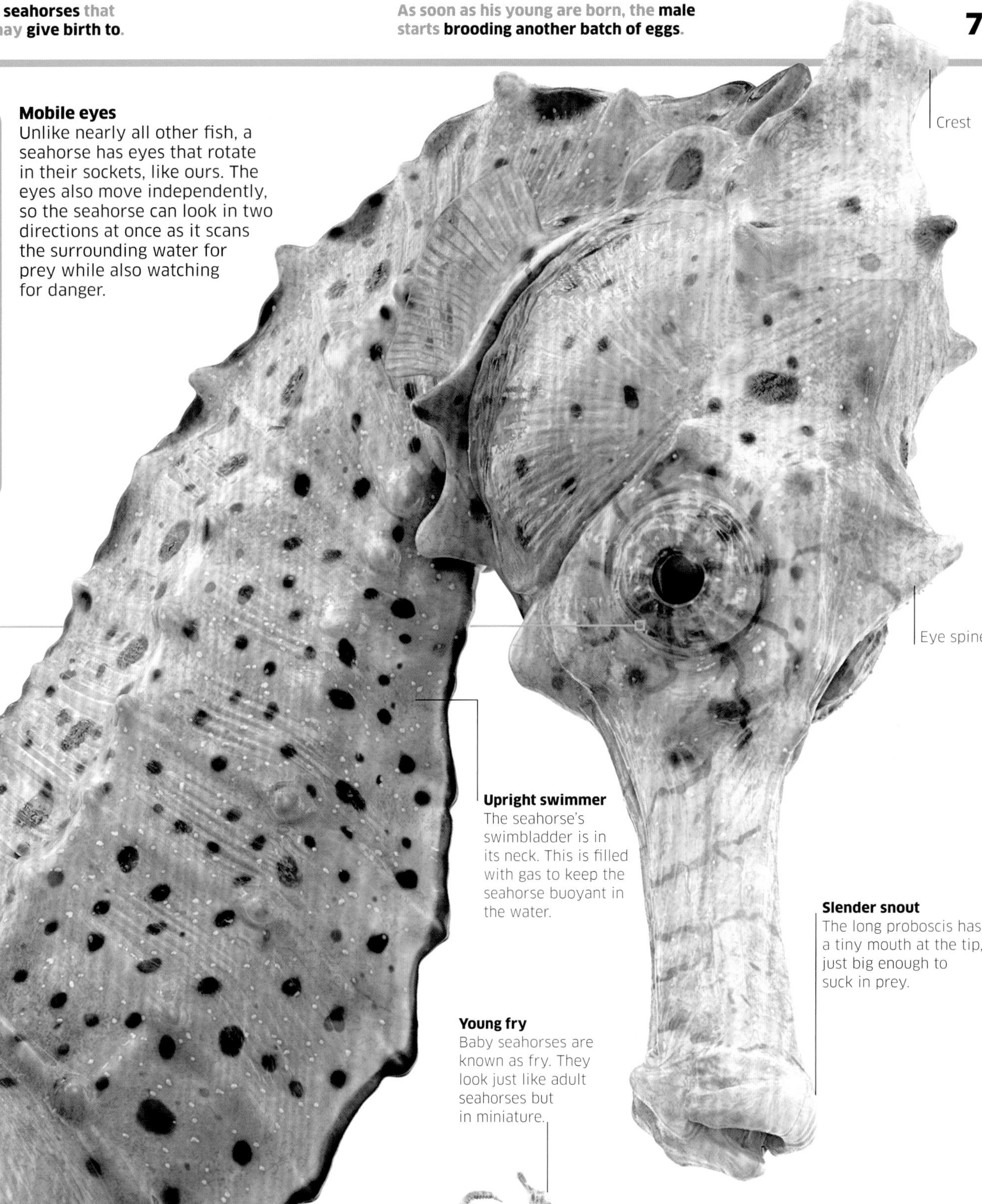

Crest

Eye spine

Dorsal fin
The seahorse's rippling dorsal fin pushes it through the water.

Upright swimmer
The seahorse's swimbladder is in its neck. This is filled with gas to keep the seahorse buoyant in the water.

Slender snout
The long proboscis has a tiny mouth at the tip, just big enough to suck in prey.

Young fry
Baby seahorses are known as fry. They look just like adult seahorses but in miniature.

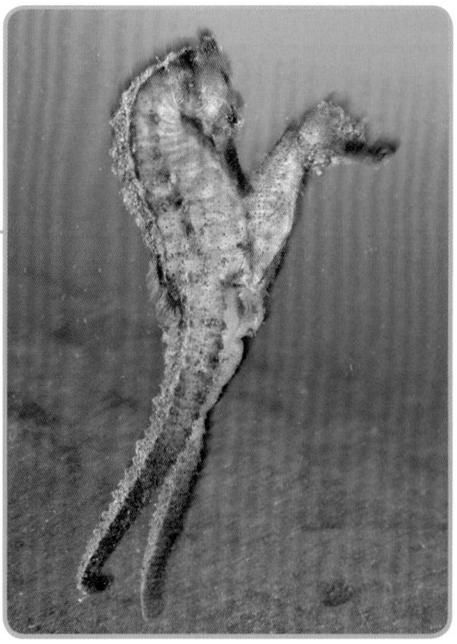

Brooding male
When spotted seahorses come together to breed, the female deposits hundreds of eggs in the male's brood pouch. Each egg is fertilized and attached to the pouch wall, which supplies it with vital nutrients. Three to four weeks later, the babies are fully developed and the male ejects them into the water.

Brood pouch
The male's pouch acts like a womb, protecting and feeding the young.

Native to the **Indo-Pacific**, red lionfish have been **introduced to the western Atlantic** where they are now considered a **serious pest**.

Red lionfish

This spectacular sea fish is a resident of tropical coral reefs, where it creeps up on smaller fish that it can seize and swallow whole. Venomous spines ensure that it rarely suffers the same fate itself.

The lionfish's candy-striped pattern and feathery fans of spiny finlets create a dazzling impression, designed to warn bigger fish that it is dangerous to eat. Its flamboyant fins slow it down, but this is not a problem for a fish that lives in the food-rich waters of the coral reef. Surrounded by prey, it uses its superb mobility to work its way into position for a lightning-fast strike, snapping up each victim before it has a chance to escape.

Head tentacles
A strange feature of the lionfish is the pair of tentacles that sprouts from its head. These vary in form across different populations: some are spiky (below) while others are feathery (left). They may help the fish win a mate, or might act as lures to attract inquisitive prey.

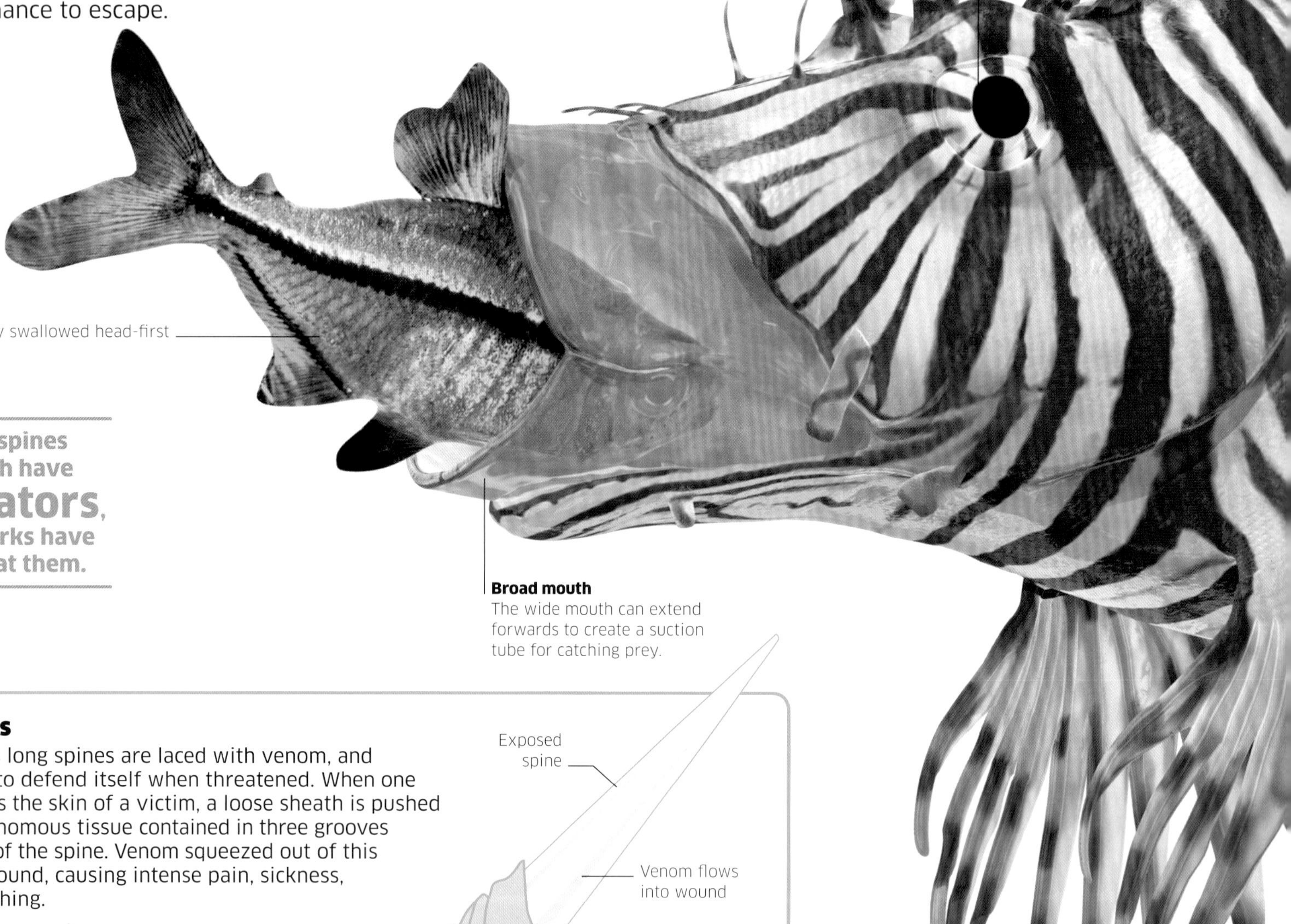

Outsized eyes
Large eyes, which maximize the amount of light captured, give the lionfish sharp vision.

Prey swallowed head-first

Broad mouth
The wide mouth can extend forwards to create a suction tube for catching prey.

Their venomous spines mean that lionfish have **few predators**, though some sharks have been known to eat them.

Defensive spines

Many of a lionfish's long spines are laced with venom, and the fish uses them to defend itself when threatened. When one of the spines pierces the skin of a victim, a loose sheath is pushed down to expose venomous tissue contained in three grooves running the length of the spine. Venom squeezed out of this tissue enters the wound, causing intense pain, sickness, and difficulty breathing.

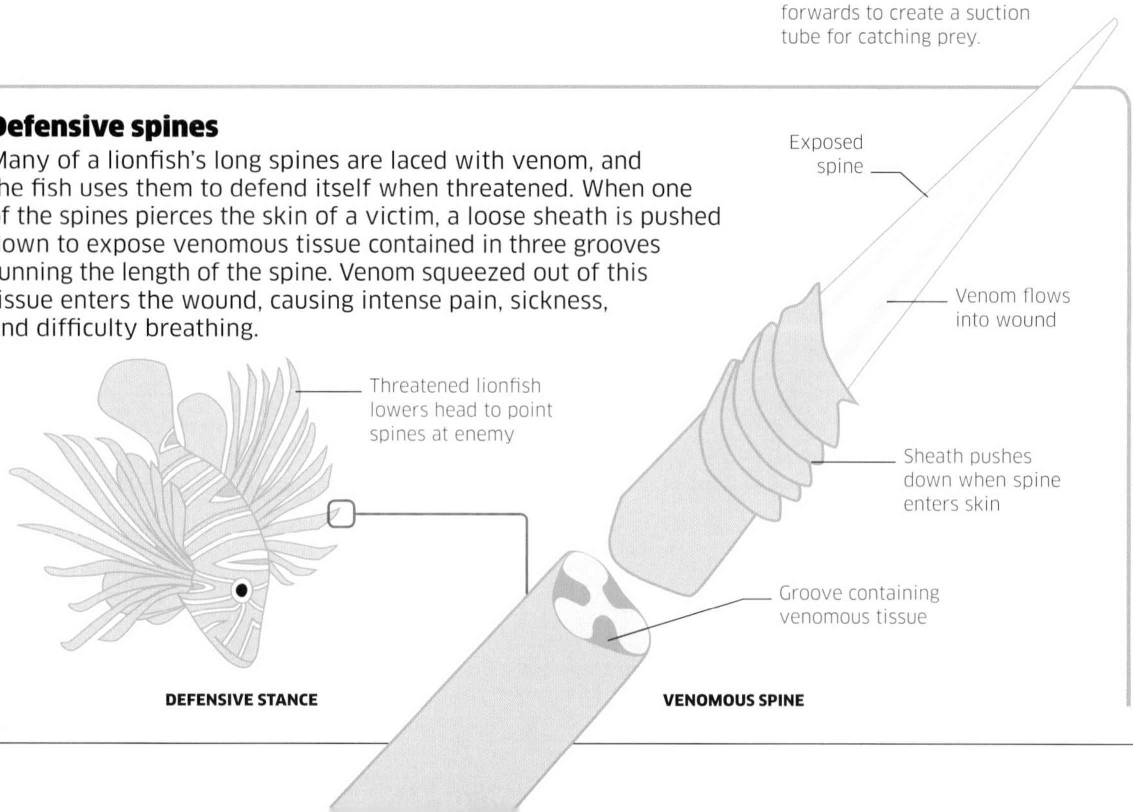

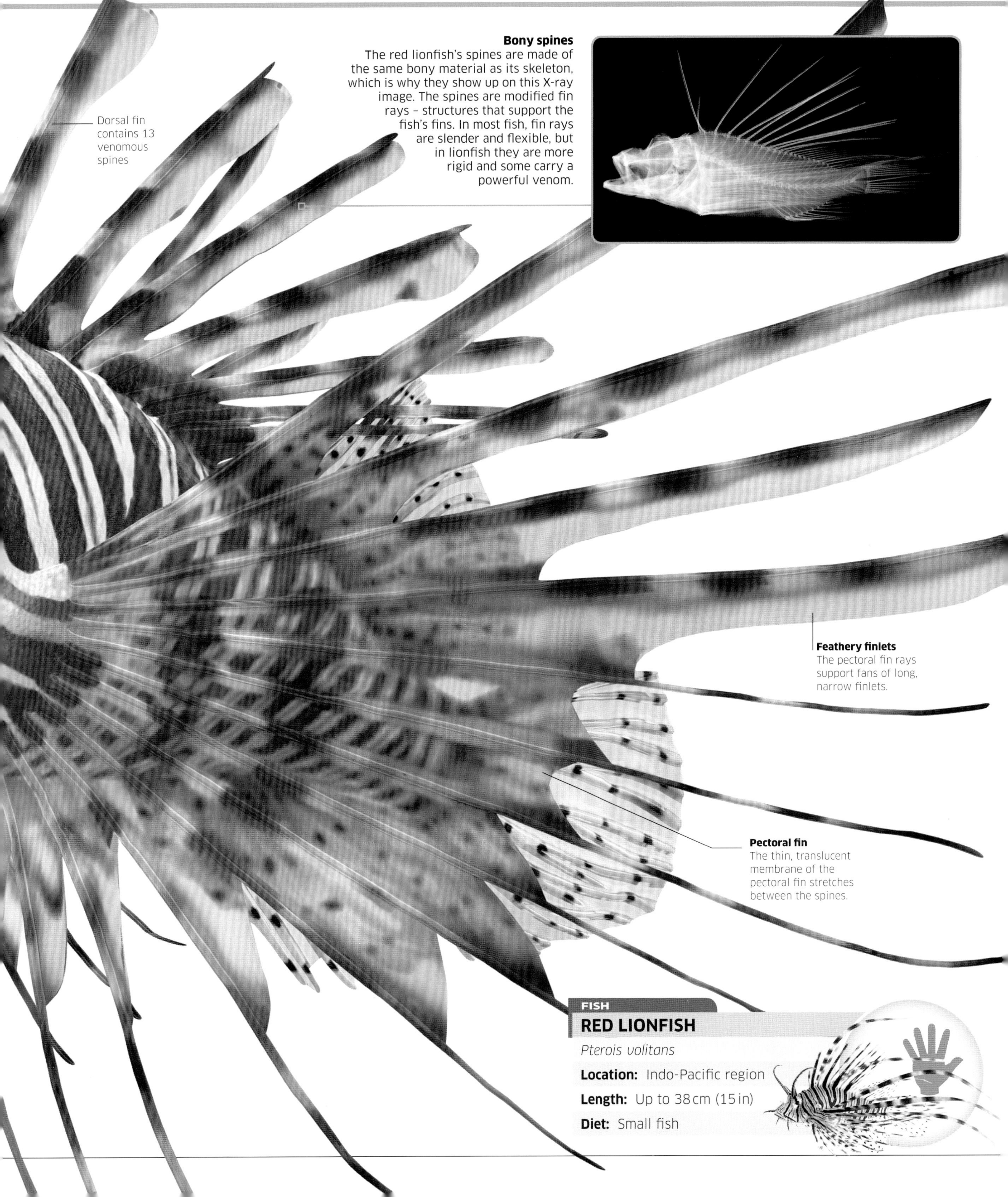

Dorsal fin contains 13 venomous spines

Bony spines
The red lionfish's spines are made of the same bony material as its skeleton, which is why they show up on this X-ray image. The spines are modified fin rays – structures that support the fish's fins. In most fish, fin rays are slender and flexible, but in lionfish they are more rigid and some carry a powerful venom.

Feathery finlets
The pectoral fin rays support fans of long, narrow finlets.

Pectoral fin
The thin, translucent membrane of the pectoral fin stretches between the spines.

FISH

RED LIONFISH

Pterois volitans

Location: Indo-Pacific region

Length: Up to 38 cm (15 in)

Diet: Small fish

Young sailfish may **swim together** in schools of **up to 30**. Adults swim in **smaller groups** or **on their own**.

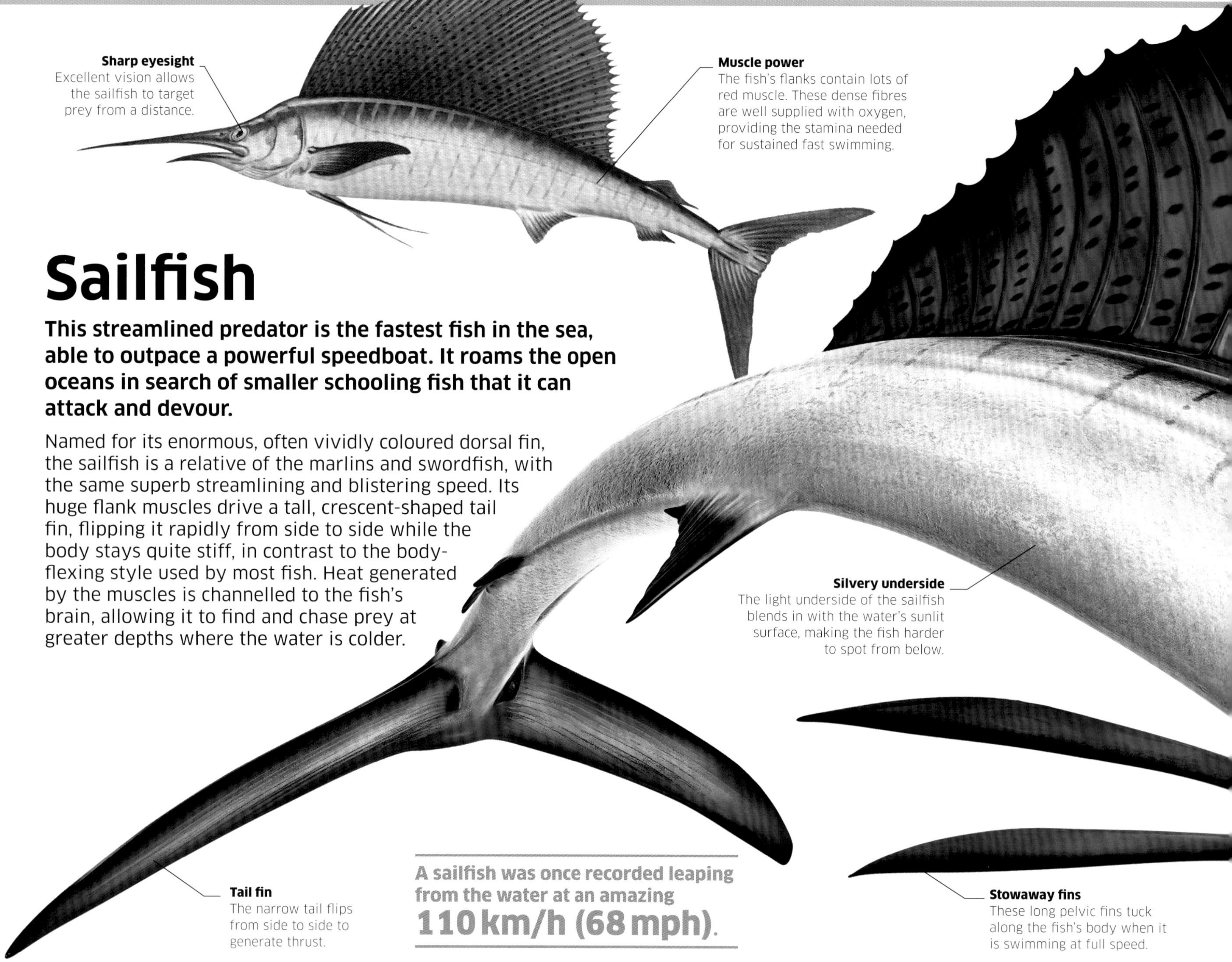

Sailfish

This streamlined predator is the fastest fish in the sea, able to outpace a powerful speedboat. It roams the open oceans in search of smaller schooling fish that it can attack and devour.

Named for its enormous, often vividly coloured dorsal fin, the sailfish is a relative of the marlins and swordfish, with the same superb streamlining and blistering speed. Its huge flank muscles drive a tall, crescent-shaped tail fin, flipping it rapidly from side to side while the body stays quite stiff, in contrast to the body-flexing style used by most fish. Heat generated by the muscles is channelled to the fish's brain, allowing it to find and chase prey at greater depths where the water is colder.

A sailfish was once recorded leaping from the water at an amazing 110 km/h (68 mph).

Baitball hunting

The main targets of hungry sailfish are small fish, such as sardines and anchovies, which swim in shoals and form tightly-packed "baitballs" if they feel threatened. Three or four sailfish may work together to herd the fish into a baitball, then dart through them to isolate small groups that the sailfish can attack more effectively. The sailfish slash their long bills from side to side, stunning or even crippling their prey to make the smaller fish easier to scoop up and swallow whole.

Sailfin
The dorsal fin is supported by stiff fin rays. The large surface area of the fin may help the fish lose excess heat after a burst of speed.

Dazzling colour

Although normally dark blue and silver, a sailfish can change colour in an instant. Different colour cells in its skin expand and contract to replace the blue with red, orange, or brown, highlighted with iridescent stripes and spots. These colours often appear when the sailfish is hunting, probably because it is excited by the chase.

Folding fin
When the sailfish is swimming fast, it folds the dorsal fin into a groove along its back, so its body is streamlined like a torpedo. The fish raises its huge, flamboyant dorsal fin when it is excited, and when it wants to make itself look bigger to scare or herd prey fish or to discourage enemies such as sharks.

Steering fins
Wing-like pectoral fins help the fish turn fast as it swoops into the attack.

Teeth
Small teeth in the upper jaw give a good grip on slippery prey.

Pointed bill
The elongated bill cuts through the water for better streamlining. It is also used to slash at prey.

FISH

SAILFISH

Istiophorus platypterus

Location: Indo-Pacific region

Length: Up to 3.5 m (11½ ft)

Diet: Fish, squid

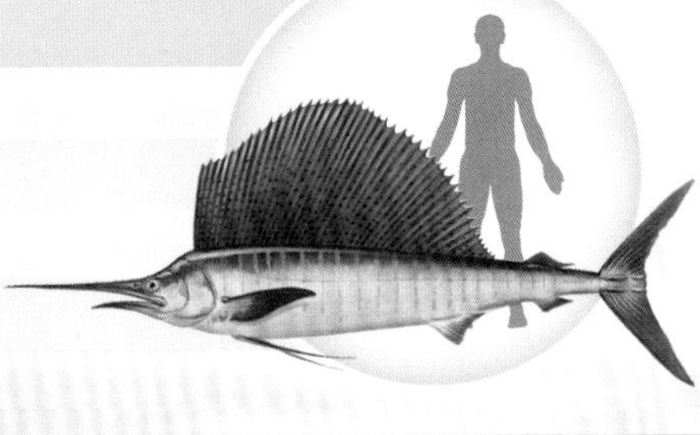

There are about **30 species** of piranha, all living in the **rivers of South America**.

Some piranha species are **herbivores**: they live entirely off **plant matter** and eat **no meat at all**.

Feeding frenzy
When piranhas start attacking their prey, the billowing blood in the water attracts even more piranhas, and sends the shoal into a feeding frenzy. The fish crowd together to grab a share of the feast, and may even kill and eat each other in their excitement.

Red-bellied piranha

Notorious for the way it can use its razor-sharp teeth to strip its prey to the bone within minutes, the piranha is the most feared of all freshwater fish. In reality it is mainly a scavenger, feeding on dead and dying animals, small fish, and invertebrates, but there is no doubt about the terrifying efficiency of its feeding technique.

Red-bellied piranhas live in the lowland rivers of tropical South America, where they often swim in shoals. When they find a meal they all start feeding at once, slicing off mouthfuls of flesh, and soon reduce their prey to a bare skeleton. On rare occasions they have done the same to human victims.

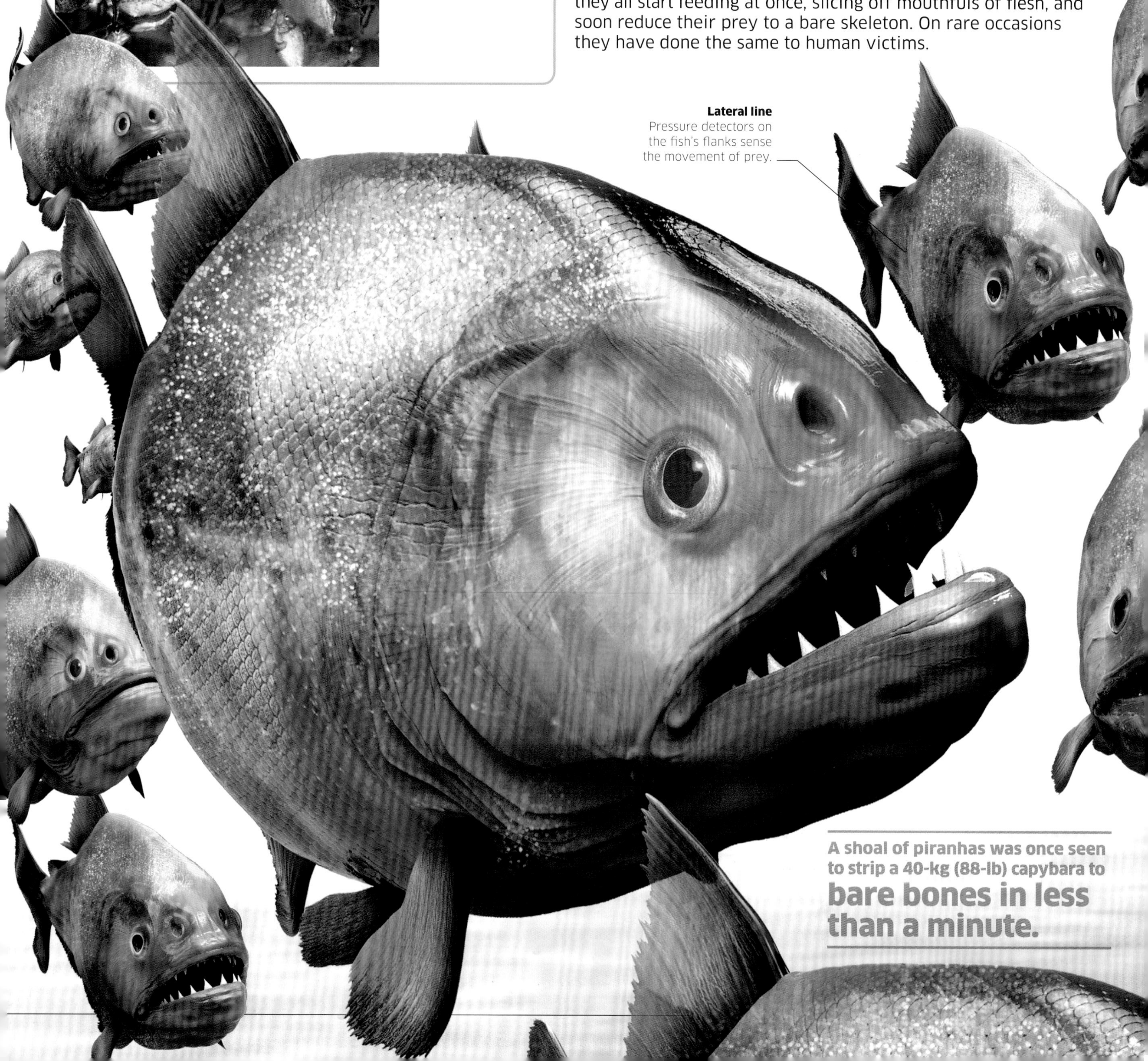

Lateral line
Pressure detectors on the fish's flanks sense the movement of prey.

A shoal of piranhas was once seen to strip a 40-kg (88-lb) capybara to **bare bones in less than a minute.**

Piranhas swim in shoals for protection from their enemies, not for hunting in packs.

A piranha can smell a drop of blood in 200 litres (422 pints) of water.

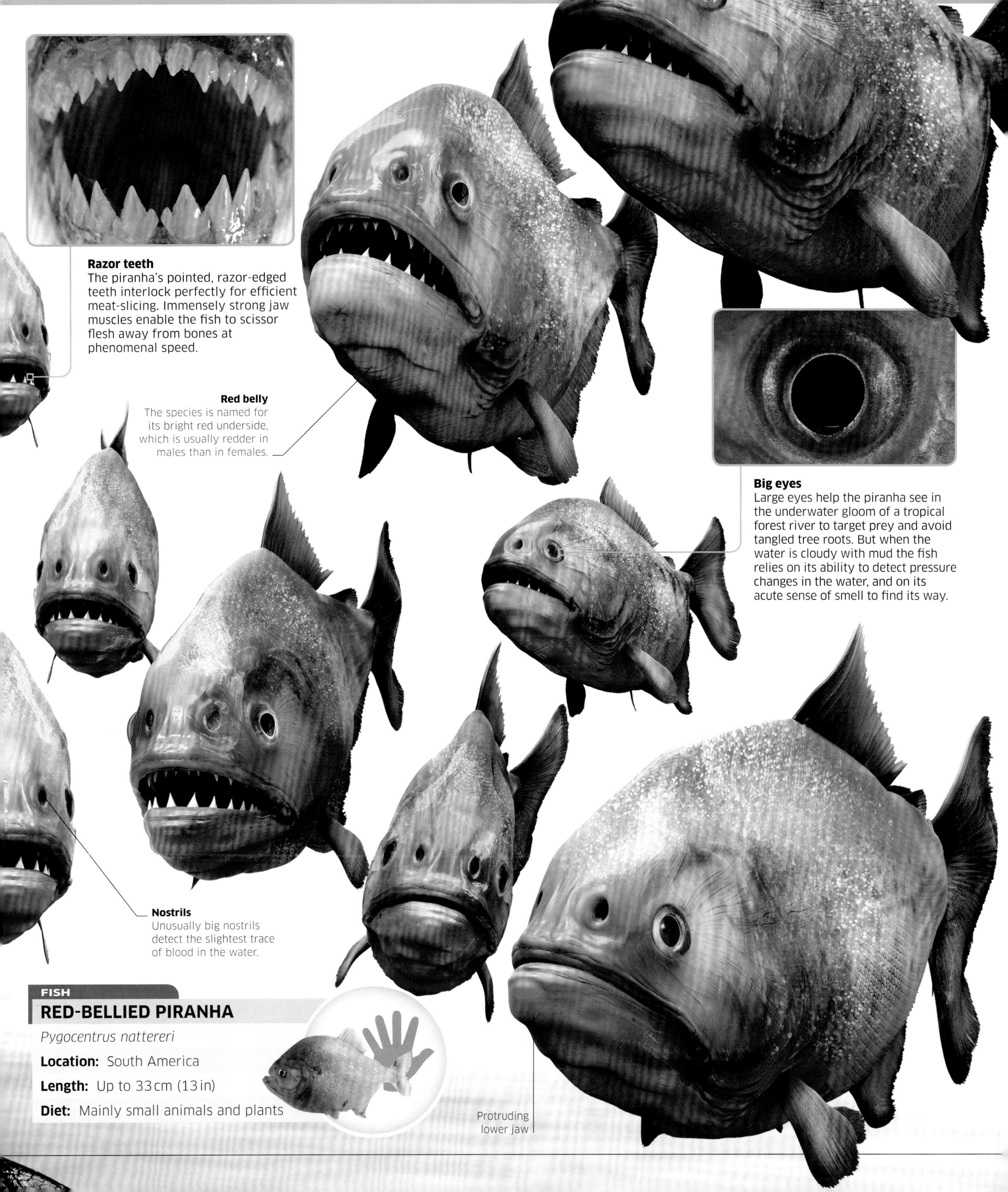

Razor teeth
The piranha's pointed, razor-edged teeth interlock perfectly for efficient meat-slicing. Immensely strong jaw muscles enable the fish to scissor flesh away from bones at phenomenal speed.

Red belly
The species is named for its bright red underside, which is usually redder in males than in females.

Big eyes
Large eyes help the piranha see in the underwater gloom of a tropical forest river to target prey and avoid tangled tree roots. But when the water is cloudy with mud the fish relies on its ability to detect pressure changes in the water, and on its acute sense of smell to find its way.

Nostrils
Unusually big nostrils detect the slightest trace of blood in the water.

Protruding lower jaw

FISH

RED-BELLIED PIRANHA

Pygocentrus nattereri

Location: South America

Length: Up to 33 cm (13 in)

Diet: Mainly small animals and plants

The **earliest-known bony fish lived about 420 million years ago.**

Bony fish

The seas, lakes, and rivers of the world are home to a dazzling diversity of bony fish, adapted for a wide variety of aquatic habitats and lifestyles.

Most bony fish belong to the ray-finned group, with fins supported by slender bony struts and spines. But a few – the coelacanths and lungfish – have two pairs of fleshy lobed fins on the lower body containing strong bones. Similar lobe-finned fish were the ancestors of all four-legged vertebrate animals.

GREEN MORAY

Gymnothorax funebris

Location: Western Atlantic Ocean

Length: Up to 2.5 m (8¼ ft)

Morays are fiercely predatory eels that lurk in the crevices of rocky reefs. They detect prey mainly by scent, darting out to seize fish and other animals in their sharp, hooked teeth. The moray's vibrant colour comes from the thick protective layer of mucus that covers its skin.

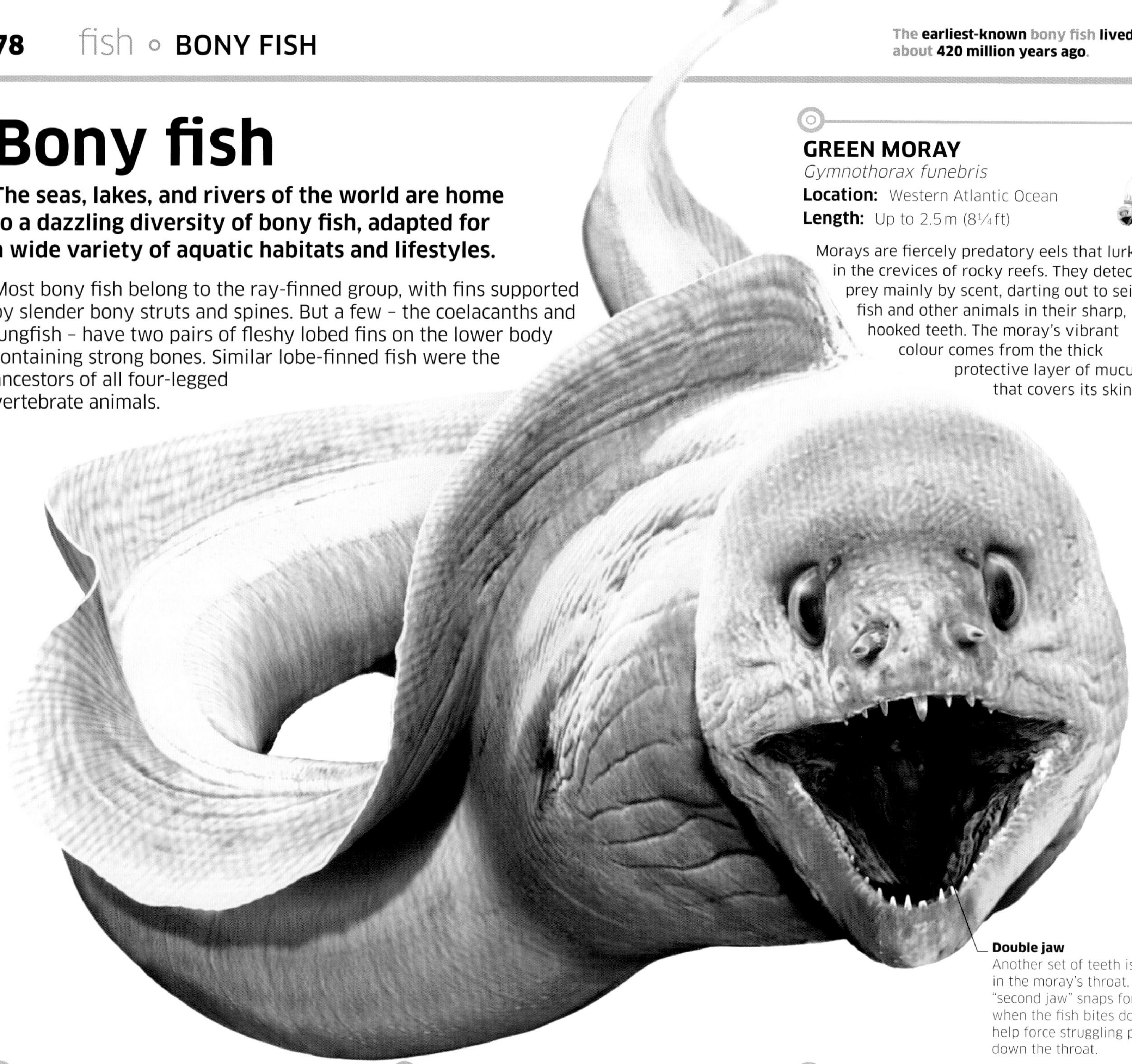

Double jaw
Another set of teeth is hidden in the moray's throat. This "second jaw" snaps forward when the fish bites down, to help force struggling prey down the throat.

MEDITERRANEAN FLYINGFISH

Cheilopogon heterurus

Location: Northeastern Atlantic

Length: Up to 40 cm (15¾ in)

These sleek fish swim near the ocean surface where they feed on small animals. They escape the attacks of bigger fish by shooting out of the water and gliding over the waves on their long, wing-like pectoral fins.

STARRY FLOUNDER

Platichthys stellatus

Location: North Pacific Ocean

Length: Up to 91 cm (35¾ in)

Flatfish, such as the starry flounder, start life looking like normal juvenile fish. As the fish grows, one eye moves to other side of its head, so both eyes are on the same side. It spends the rest of its life lying flat on its other side on the sea bed.

SOCKEYE SALMON

Oncorhynchus nerka

Location: North Pacific Ocean

Length: Up to 84 cm (33 in)

Like other salmon, this species spends most of its adult life at sea, but swims up rivers to spawn in fresh water. Breeding males have a bright red body with a green head and tail.

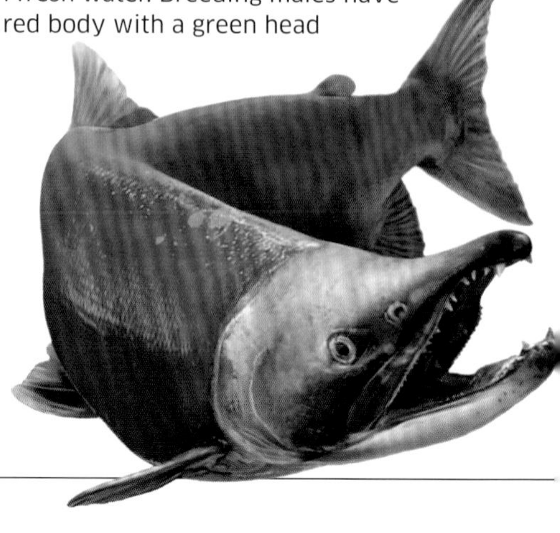

EUROPEAN ANCHOVY

Engraulis encrasicolus

Location: Eastern Atlantic Ocean

Length: Up to 20 cm (8 in)

Anchovies swim in huge schools, filtering water through their gills to trap tiny marine animals. Other schooling fish such as herring feed in the same way. The schools are preyed upon by oceanic hunters including tuna, sharks, seabirds, and even giant humpback whales.

EMPEROR ANGELFISH

Pomacanthus imperator

Location: Indo-Pacific region

Length: Up to 40 cm (15¾ in)

Tropical coral reefs glitter with colourful fish of many types, each with their own way of life. This angelfish lives in reef crevices, and the males defend patches of the reef as their own territories.

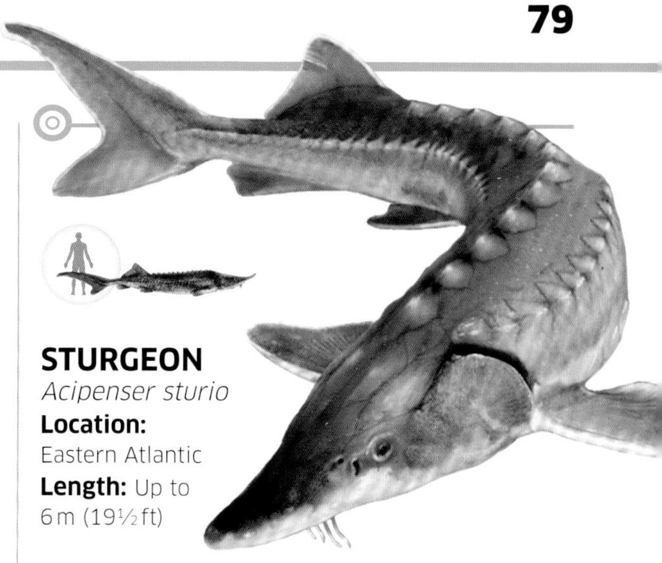

STURGEON

Acipenser sturio

Location: Eastern Atlantic

Length: Up to 6 m (19½ ft)

The sturgeons include some of the largest fish found in fresh water, and the longest-lived – this species may live for 100 years. It spends most of its life in coastal seas, where it feeds on molluscs, crabs, and similar animals on the sea bed, but swims upriver like a salmon to spawn.

COELACANTH

Latimeria chalumnae

Location: Indian Ocean

Length: Up to 2 m (6½ ft)

One of a group of lobe-finned fish once thought to have died out 65 million years ago, the coelacanth was discovered living in the Indian Ocean in 1938. It lives in deep tropical coastal waters, where it preys on fish and molluscs.

SLOANE'S VIPERFISH

Chauliodus sloani

Location: All temperate oceans

Length: Up to 35 cm (13¾ in)

This viperfish is one of many fearsome predators that prowl the dark depths of the oceans. Its huge teeth ensure that its prey has little hope of escape.

ATLANTIC COD

Gadus morhua

Location: N. Atlantic, Arctic

Length: Up to 2 m (6½ ft)

Familiar as a food fish, this big marine species is a predator that hunts near the sea bed for smaller fish and squid. It has been badly affected by overfishing, with some local populations declining by more than 95 per cent.

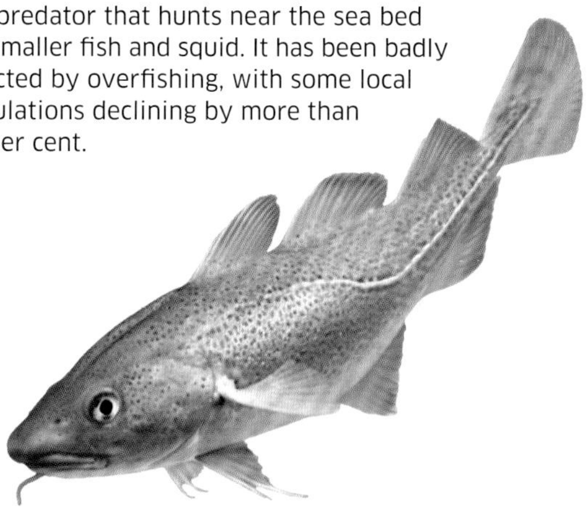

BLACK-BLOTCHED PORCUPINE FISH

Diodon liturosus

Location: Indo-Pacific, S. E. Atlantic

Length: Up to 65 cm (25½ in)

Closely related to the very poisonous pufferfish, this tropical reef fish defends itself from predators by gulping water to inflate itself into a spiny ball. This makes it almost impossible to swallow.

NORTHERN PIKE

Esox lucius

Location: N. America, Europe, Asia

Length: Up to 1.5 m (5 ft)

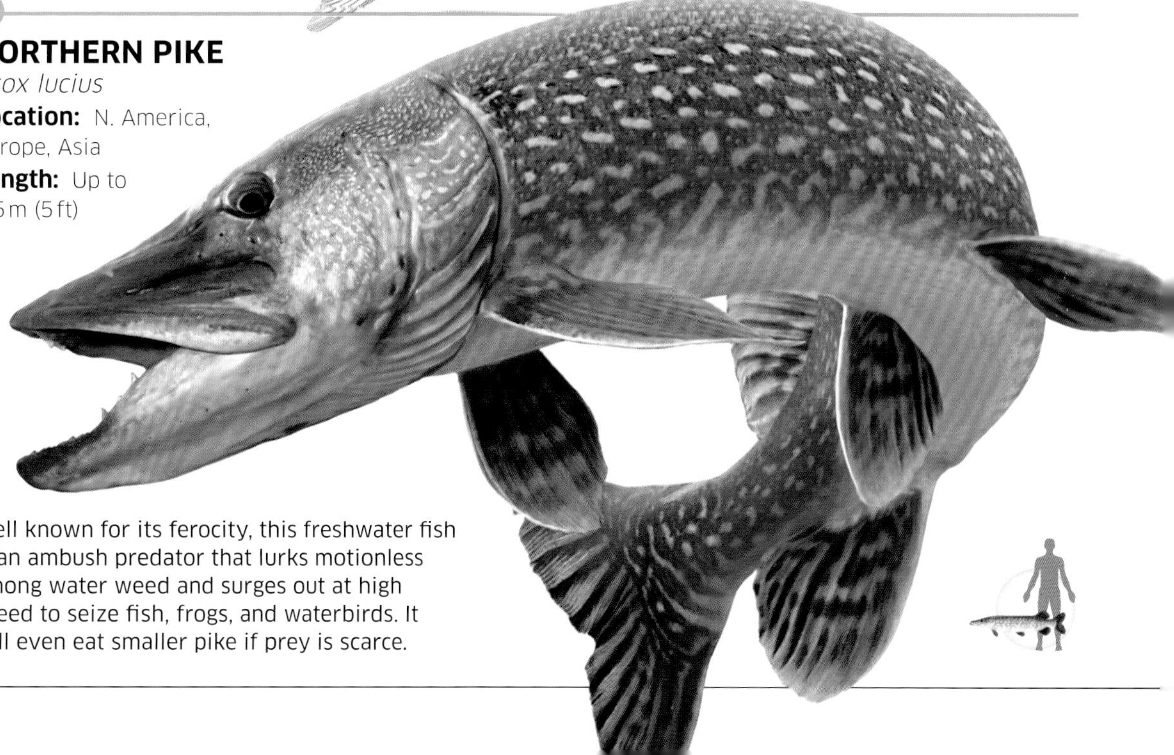

Well known for its ferocity, this freshwater fish is an ambush predator that lurks motionless among water weed and surges out at high speed to seize fish, frogs, and waterbirds. It will even eat smaller pike if prey is scarce.

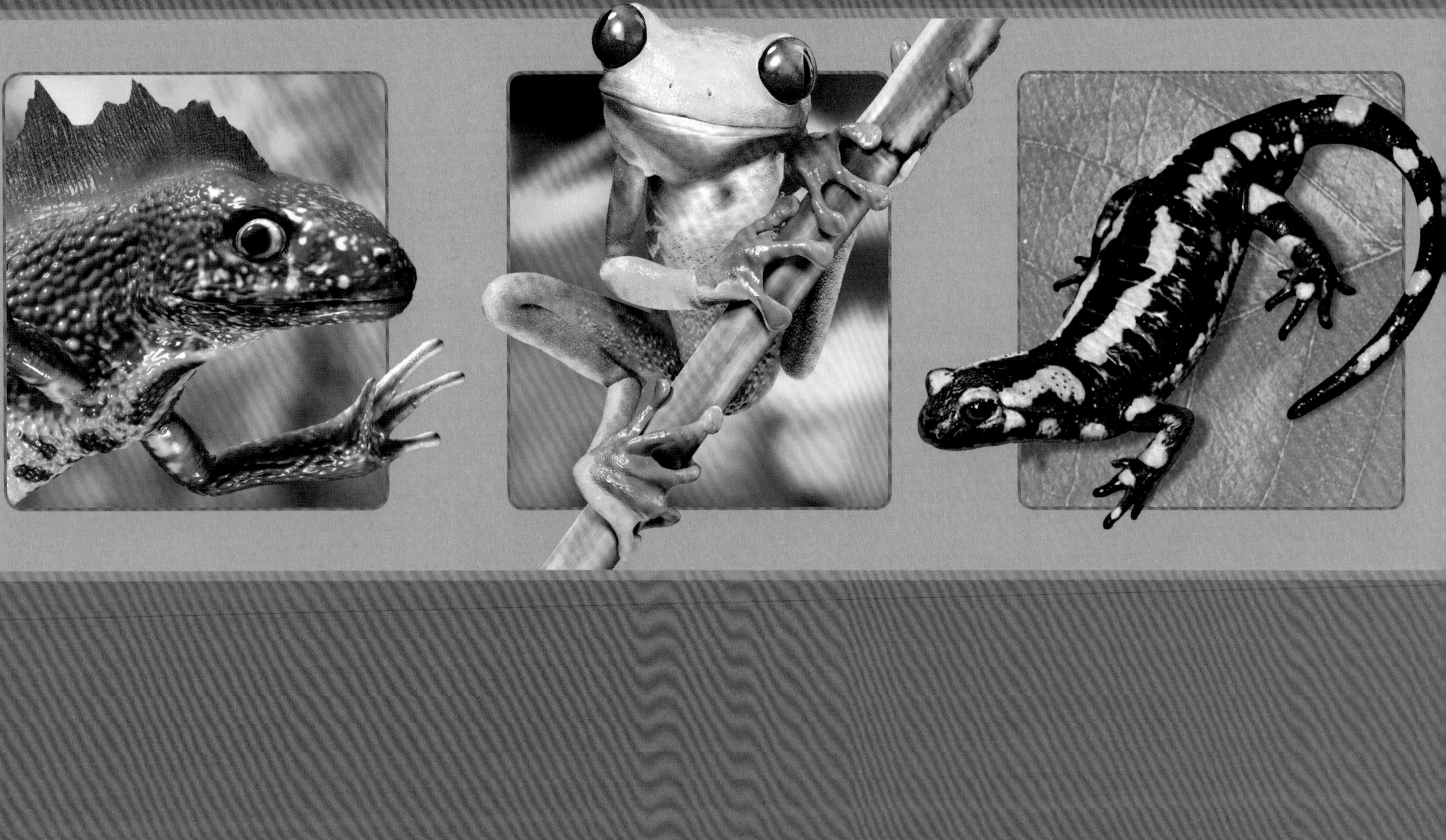

AMPHIBIANS

Named for the way they live both in the water and on land, amphibians are the most mysterious of the vertebrates. Many are very secretive, emerging only at night and slipping into dark, damp places by day. They have extraordinary lifecycles, and they include some of the most poisonous animals on Earth.

WHAT IS AN AMPHIBIAN?

The first amphibians evolved from fish that were able to breathe air, and crept out of the water on four limb-like fins to find prey on land. But the fish had to lay their eggs in water, and their amphibian descendants still have to breed in pools or damp places. They also have thin skins that lose body moisture easily, so they must take care not to dry out.

TYPES OF AMPHIBIAN

The most familiar amphibians are the frogs and toads, with their big heads and tailless bodies. The long-tailed salamanders and newts lead similar lives, but the worm-like tropical caecilians are secretive burrowers.

Frogs and toads
This is the largest group, with 6,641 species. There is no scientific difference between frogs and toads. They have the same basic form, but typical frogs have smoother skins.

FIRE-BELLIED TOAD

Salamanders and newts
As with frogs and toads, these are basically different names for the same type of animal. There are 683 species; some are wholly aquatic while others spend most of their lives on land.

FIRE SALAMANDER

Caecilians
The 205 species of caecilians have no limbs, and are almost blind. They live underground, using their reinforced heads to burrow in search of worms and insects.

CONGO CAECILIAN

Inside an amphibian

This European common frog has the four-limbed body plan that has been inherited by all land vertebrates, although some amphibians – and reptiles – have lost their legs during the course of evolution.

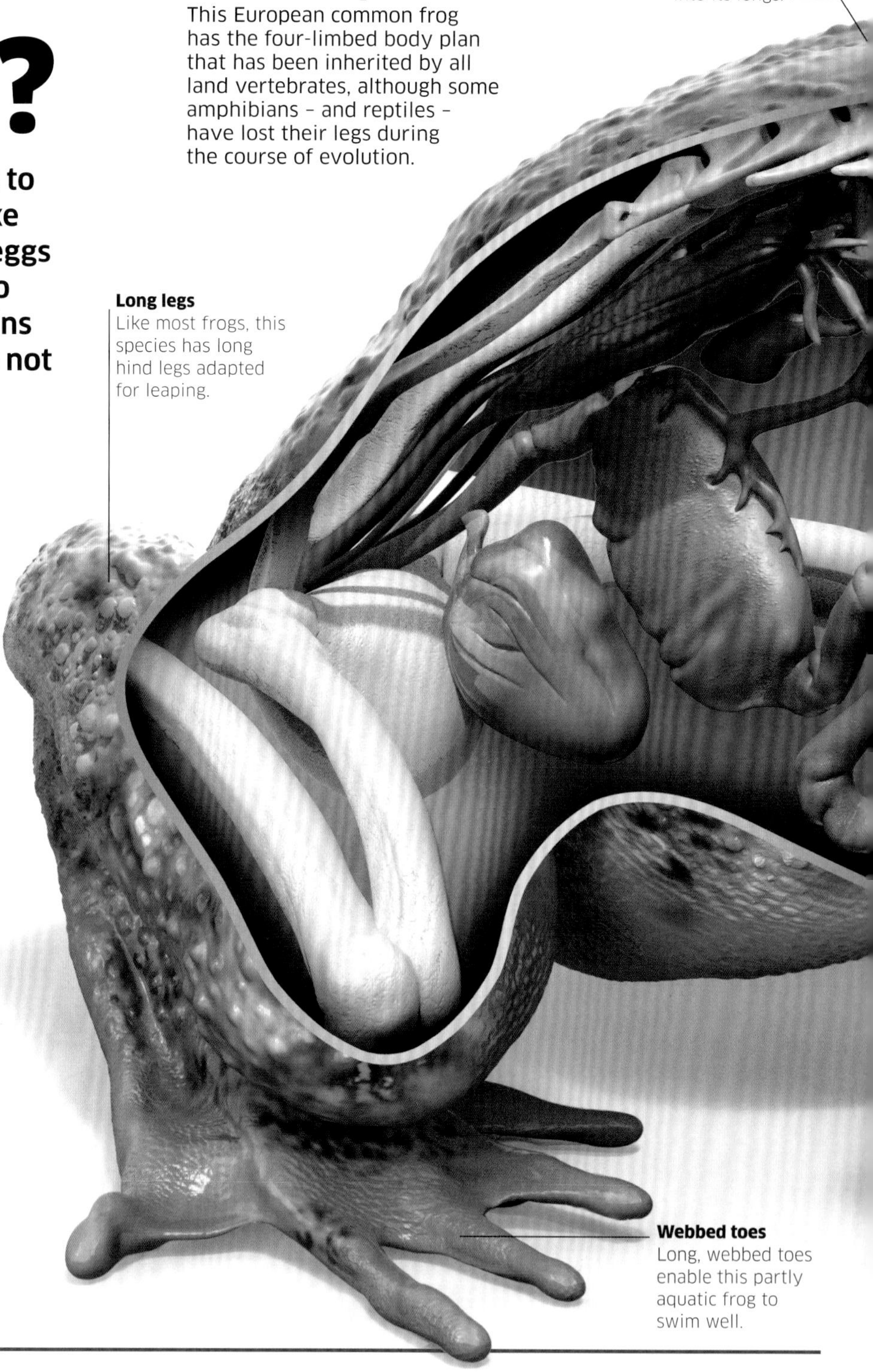

KEY FEATURES

There are only three types of amphibians, but they include animals with a remarkably wide variety of lifestyles and breeding systems. Despite this, most of them share certain key features. All amphibians are air-breathing, cold-blooded vertebrates, and they have thin skins that are not waterproof. Most lay eggs that must be kept moist, and many spend part of their lives in water.

Vertebrates
Like their bony fish ancestors, all amphibians have internal skeletons made of bone.

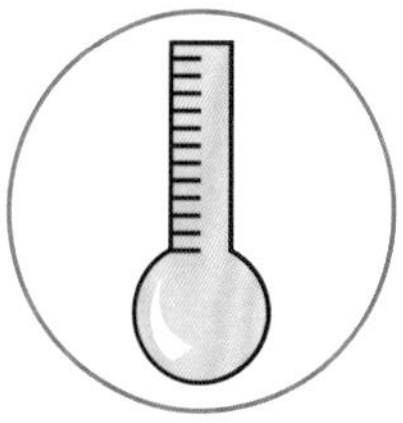

Cold-blooded
An amphibian's body temperature is the same as that of the air or water around it.

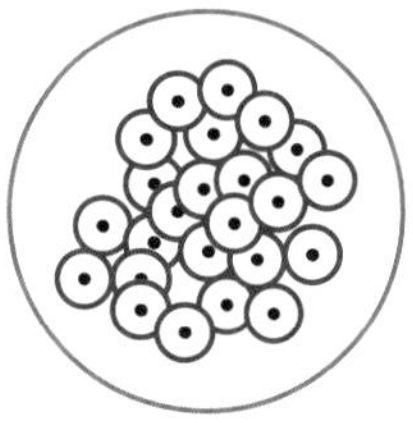

Most lay eggs
Caecilians bear live young, but most amphibians lay eggs with no hard shells.

Aquatic young
Typically the young hatch as aquatic tadpoles that eventually turn into adults.

Moist skin
An amphibian's thin, moist skin loses water easily, but can also absorb oxygen.

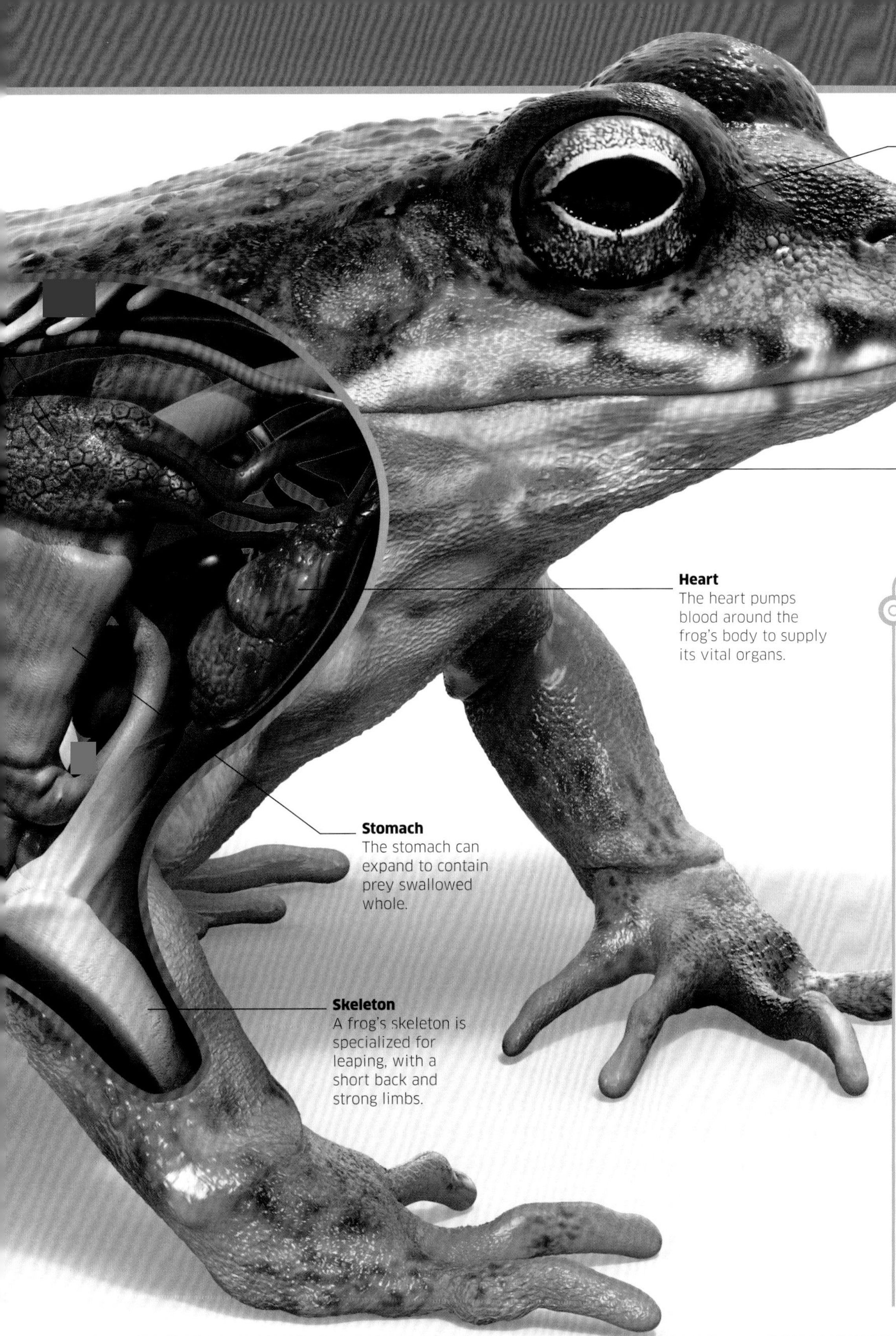

CHANGING SHAPE

Amphibians are the only vertebrates that change their form as they turn to adults – a process known as metamorphosis. A typical frog egg develops into a long-tailed tadpole that lives like a fish for several weeks. Over time it develops legs, and eventually turns into a tiny air-breathing froglet. Finally, its tail shrinks away and it hops onto land to begin its adult life.

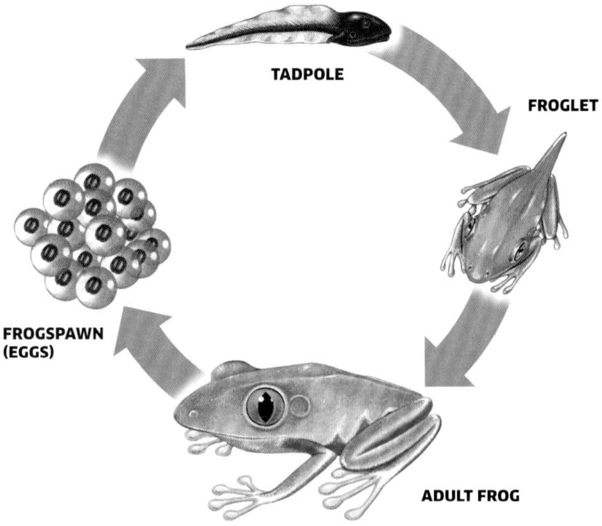

BREATHING SKIN

Many amphibians start life as aquatic tadpoles, with gills that absorb vital oxygen from the water. When they become adults they develop lungs and can breathe air. But their thin skins can also absorb oxygen from water or air, provided they stay moist, and this allows one group, the lungless salamanders, to survive without either lungs or gills.

LETHAL DEFENCE

The dramatic pattern of this tiny tropical American tree frog warns birds and other enemies that it is extremely dangerous to eat. Its skin oozes poisons made from chemicals in its insect prey, and these are so powerful that these frogs' secretions have been used to make poisoned arrows. Many other amphibians have similar toxic defences.

5 years – the **average lifespan** of a **red-eyed tree frog** in the wild.

Sharp eyes
Widely spaced eyes judge distance well for catching prey.

Startling defence
The frog's huge eyes can be covered by transparent lower eyelids marked with a network of gold lines. This conceals their vivid red while allowing the frog to watch for danger. If it is discovered, the frog suddenly opens its eyes wide to startle its enemy, giving the frog time to escape.

Slimy skin
The frog's skin oozes a slime that makes it distasteful to predators if eaten.

Red-eyed tree frog

Although it is an amphibian, which must live and breed in damp places, this slender, agile frog spends most of its time high in the trees. It thrives because it lives in the tropical rainforests of Central America, where the climate is always warm and wet.

Like all tree frogs, the red-eyed tree frog has long hind legs that enable it to leap from branch to branch as it searches for insect prey. It hunts at night, using its big eyes to spot insects in the dim light, scooping them up with its long, sticky tongue.

When males claim breeding territories on twigs, they **croak loudly and shake the leaves** with their hind legs to attract females.

Versatile feet
Suction-cup toes allow the frog to cling to leaves, but the feet are also semi-webbed in case it needs to swim.

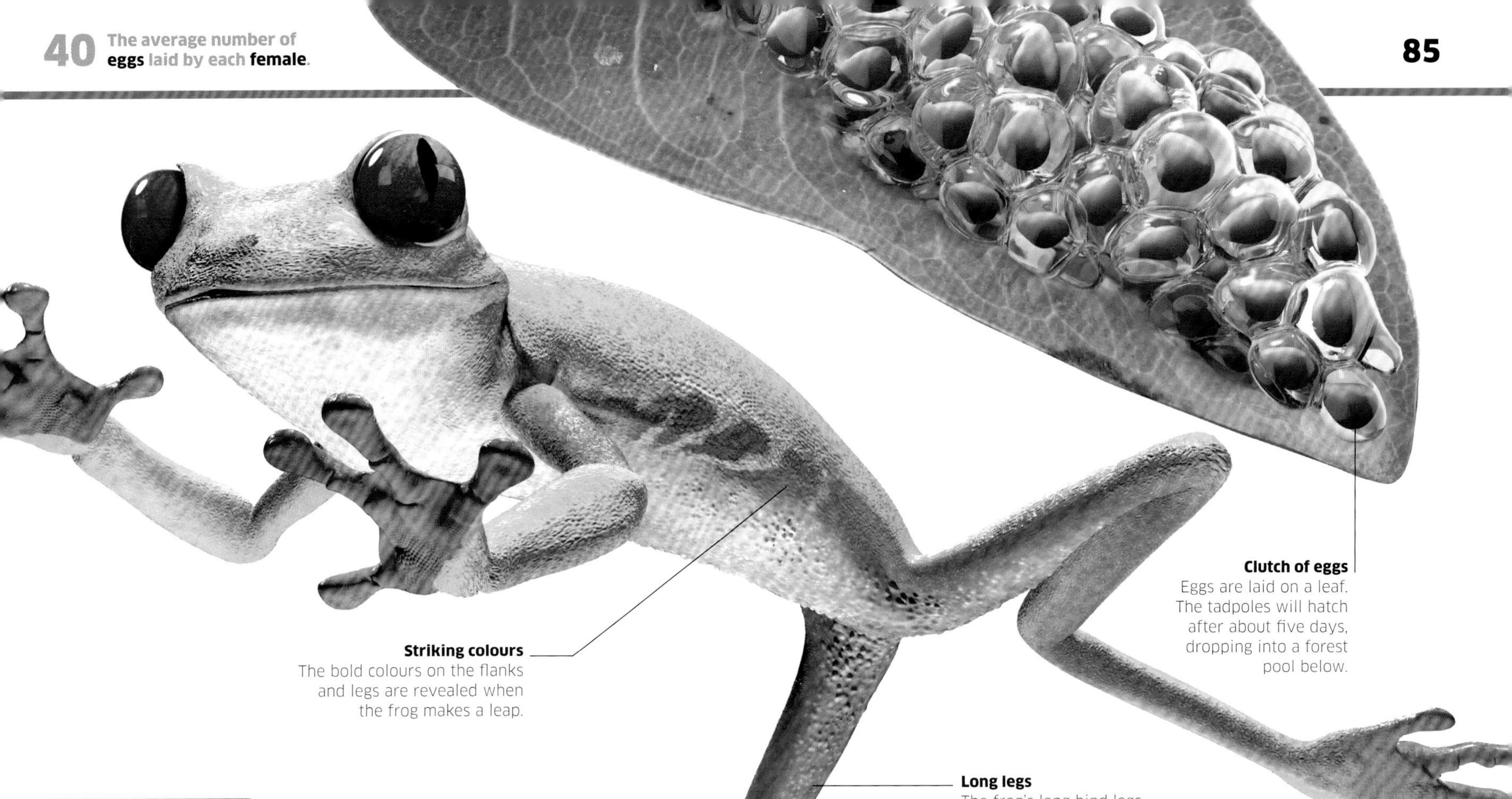

AMPHIBIANS

RED-EYED TREE FROG

Agalychnis callidryas

Location: Central America

Length: Up to 7.7 cm (3 in)

Diet: Mainly insects

Leafy nursery

Most frogs lay their eggs in water, but the red-eyed tree frog attaches them to a leaf overhanging a forest pool. When the tadpoles hatch they fall into the water, where they stay until they turn into miniature frogs. If the eggs are disturbed, for instance by a hungry snake, the tadpoles can react by hatching early and dropping off the leaf to escape.

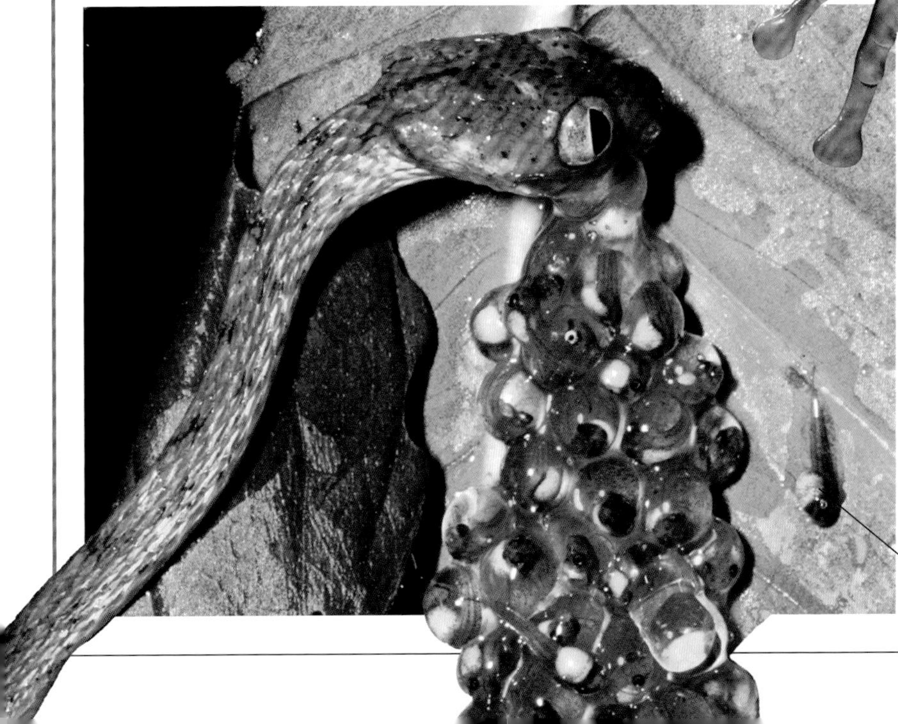

Escaping tadpole

Camouflage tactics

By day, a red-eyed tree frog hides from birds and other enemies by clinging to the underside of a leaf. Concealing its bright orange feet and blue legs beneath its green body, it closes its red eyes, and stays perfectly still. This makes it almost invisible against the green tropical foliage. It rarely stirs before dusk, when most hunting birds have retreated to their roosts.

50 years – the **known lifespan** of **common toads in captivity**.

Oozing poison
The bulging parotid gland behind each eye secretes a fluid containing a foul-tasting poison called bufotoxin. This is enough to put off many predators that might try to eat the toad – although some, such as the grass snake, seem unaffected by it.

AMPHIBIANS

COMMON TOAD

Bufo bufo

Location: Europe, N. Africa

Length: Up to 15 cm (6 in)

Diet: Small animals

Common toad

Slow-moving and incapable of leaping like a long-legged frog, the warty-skinned common toad does not behave like a hunter. But to insects and other small animals it is a deadly predator, able to seize and eat them with lightning speed.

Like many toads, the common toad lives entirely on land except when it is spawning in its breeding pools. It usually hides away by day, emerging at dusk to prey on insects, worms, slugs, and any other small creatures that catch its eye. Watching intently, it suddenly flicks out its long tongue, grabs its victim with the sticky tip, and swallows the prey whole.

Copper eyes
Big, copper-coloured eyes have horizontal pupils that dilate (open wide) in the dark.

Quick action
The tongue must flick out quickly to catch prey.

Sticky tip
The toad's sticky-tipped tongue is attached to the front of its mouth to give it extra-long reach.

Nuptial pads
At the beginning of the spring breeding season the male toad develops black pads on his first three fingers. These have a rough surface that helps him grip the wet, slippery skin of the female when she is laying her eggs in their breeding pool.

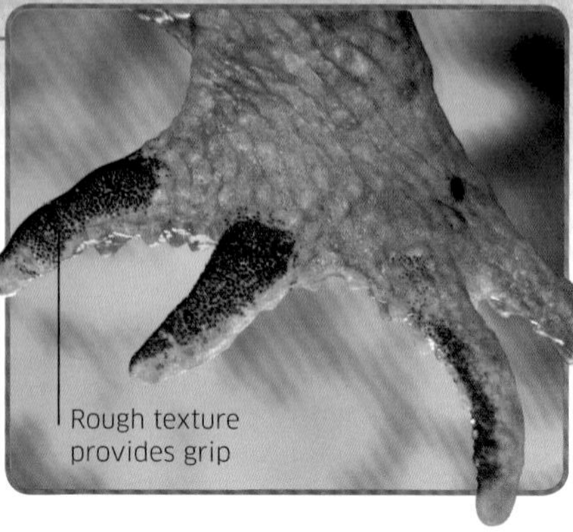

Rough texture provides grip

Toad tadpoles take **6 to 12 weeks** to develop into **tiny toadlets** and **leave the water**.

A big **common toad** is **capable of eating mice** and even **small snakes**.

Toads can travel up to
3 km (2 miles)
to breed, usually returning to the pond where they were born.

Inflatable defence

When threatened by a predator such as this grass snake, a common toad gulps in air and stands on tiptoe with its head lowered. This defensive stance makes it look bigger, more alarming, and a lot harder to swallow. If the toad is lucky, the snake will look for an easier meal.

A MATING PAIR

NEWLY FERTILIZED SPAWN

Spawning pairs

In spring, male toads return to traditional breeding pools and compete to mate with the females, who arrive a few days later. Females are the larger of the species and each male clings to one to fertilize her strings of eggs as she lays them. The eggs hatch as aquatic tadpoles that eventually turn into toadlets.

The **Australian striped rocket frog** can **leap 50 times** its own length.

Frogs and toads

Instantly recognizable by their big heads and mouths, short tailless bodies, and long hind legs, frogs and toads are the most successful and diverse of the amphibians.

There is no scientific distinction between frogs and toads. The sleeker, more aquatic species are usually called frogs, while the less elegant, land-living types are known as toads. But some toads live in fresh water, and several frogs spend their lives in trees. Many have evolved unusual breeding adaptations.

AFRICAN BULLFROG

Pyxicephalus adspersus

Location: Africa

Length: Up to 24.5cm (9½in)

This massively built frog lives in dry places where it spends most of its life buried in the ground to keep moist. During wet seasons it emerges to prey on small mammals, birds, reptiles, other frogs, and indeed anything it can catch. Its huge mouth enables it to swallow its prey whole.

A notorious cannibal, the African bullfrog will even sometimes eat its own young.

RETICULATED GLASS FROG

Hyalinobatrachium valerioi

Location: Central and South America

Length: Up to 2.6cm (1in)

The red, beating heart of this small, tropical tree frog can be seen through the transparent skin on its underside. The male attracts several females to lay eggs beneath a leaf, which he then guards until they hatch.

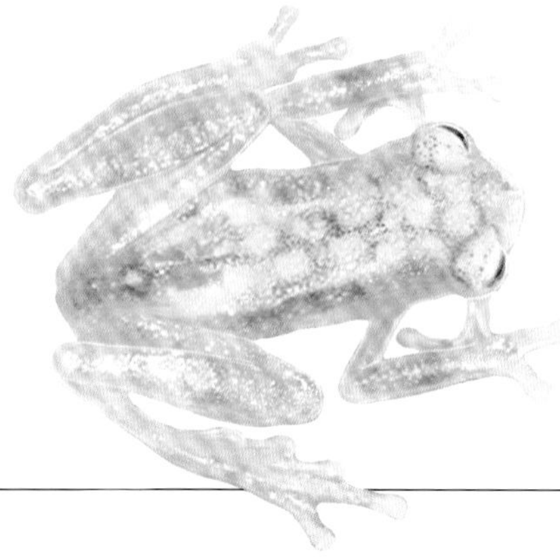

EUROPEAN COMMON FROG

Rana temporaria

Location: Europe, Asia

Length: Up to 9cm (3½in)

Like most amphibians, the common frog spends much of its life hunting insects, slugs, and other small animals on land, at night in damp places. It returns to ponds to breed, with the males arriving first and competing to attract females with croaking choruses.

WALLACE'S FLYING FROG

Rhacophorus nigropalmatus

Location: S. E. Asia

Length: Up to 10cm (4in)

The big, broad, webbed feet of this Malaysian tree frog act as parachutes when it leaps from tree to tree. They enable it to glide 15m (50ft) or more to land on another branch without coming down to ground level. Sticky pads on each toe help it cling to glossy leaves.

ORIENTAL FIRE-BELLIED TOAD

Bombina orientalis

Location: East and S. E. Asia

Length: Up to 8 cm (3¼ in)

Many frogs and toads are able to defend themselves with toxic skin secretions. This East Asian toad advertises its toxicity with a vivid red-and-black belly, sometimes even lying on its back to display it to enemies. It obtains the red coloration from pigments in the prey it consumes.

LONG-NOSED HORNED FROG

Megophrys nasuta

Location: S. E. Asia

Length: Up to 12 cm (4¾ in)

This frog is spectacularly well camouflaged. Its spiky, angled shape and coloration mimic the litter of dead leaves so well that the frog is almost invisible on the tropical forest floor. It uses this camouflage to ambush small animal prey.

GREAT PLAINS TOAD

Anaxyrus cognatus

Location: North and Central America

Length: Up to 11 cm (4¼ in)

During the breeding season, rival males compete for females with loud calls. This North American toad inflates a big vocal sac to amplify a metallic trill that can last for several minutes.

DYEING POISON-DART FROG

Dendrobates tincturius

Location: South America

Length: Up to 4.5 cm (1¾ in)

The bright colours of these tiny tropical South American poison frogs warn that they are some of the most toxic animals on the planet. Local hunters use them to make poisoned arrows.

DARWIN'S FROG

Rhinoderma darwinii

Location: South America

Length: Up to 3 cm (1¼ in)

Some frogs and toads have found novel ways of avoiding having to breed in water. The male Darwin's frog gathers up the hatching eggs in his mouth, and keeps the tadpoles in his vocal sac until they turn into tiny frogs.

STRIPED BURROWING FROG

Cyclorana alboguttata

Location: Australia

Length: Up to 7 cm (2¾ in)

This Australian frog is one of many that cope with droughts by burrowing underground, storing water in its body and sealing itself inside a cocoon of waterproof mucus. It may stay buried for years before rain enables it to emerge.

TOMATO FROG

Dyscophus antongilii

Location: Madagascar

Length: Up to 10.5 cm (4¼ in)

Found only on Madagascar, the tomato frog owes its name to its vivid colour – a warning to enemies that its skin oozes sticky toxins. It spends much of its time immobile, waiting for insects and other prey to come within striking range.

SURINAM TOAD

Pipa pipa

Location: South America

Length: Up to 18 cm (7 in)

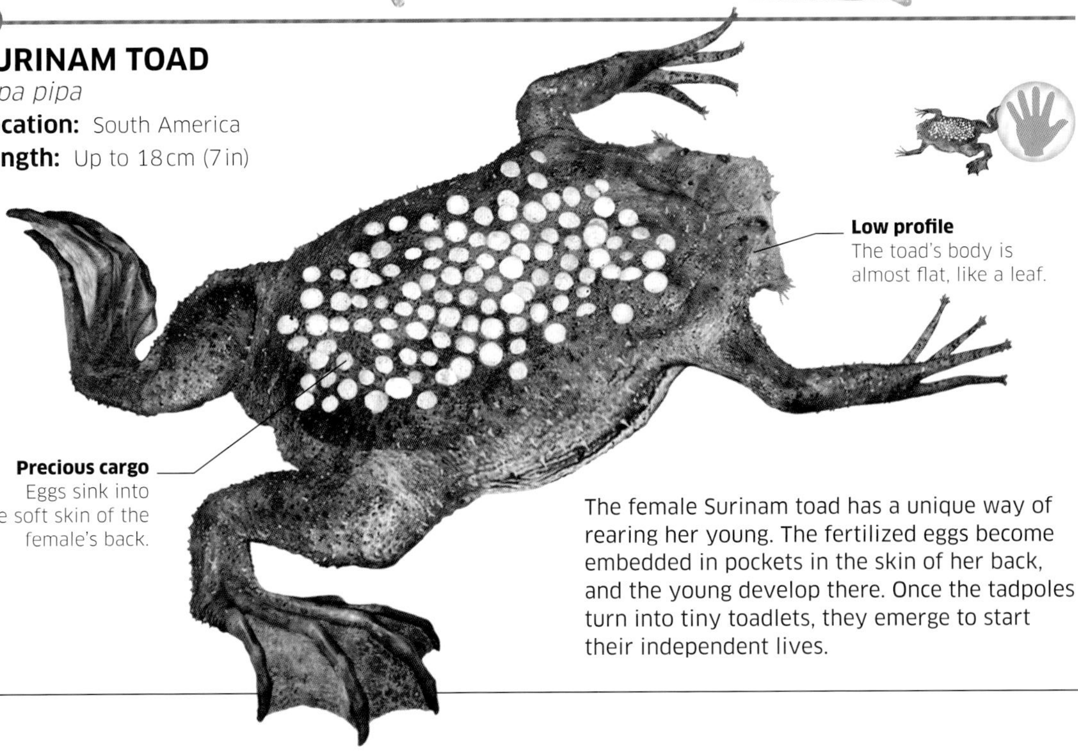

The female Surinam toad has a unique way of rearing her young. The fertilized eggs become embedded in pockets in the skin of her back, and the young develop there. Once the tadpoles turn into tiny toadlets, they emerge to start their independent lives.

Great crested newts are found only in **northern Europe**, from Britain to Ukraine.

AMPHIBIANS

GREAT CRESTED NEWT

Triturus cristatus

Location: Northern Europe

Size: Up to 16 cm (6¼ in)

Diet: Small animals

Great crested newt

At night in spring the male great crested newt performs an elaborate courtship before a female. He dances in the water, using his tail to fan enticing scents towards her.

Like most amphibians, great crested newts spend much of their lives hunting small animals on land. But in spring they return to ponds to breed, and each night the flamboyantly crested males perform their displays. They prefer large ponds with plenty of water weed where they can hide and where the females can lay their eggs.

Precious package

During mating, the female picks up a packet of sperm that the male has placed on the bed of the pond. This fertilizes her eggs, which she can then start laying. She carefully places one egg, or a chain of two or three, on a leaf, and uses her hind feet to wrap the leaf around it. A sticky substance covering the egg holds the folded leaf together.

Aquatic young

Tadpole-like larvae hatch from the eggs after about a month. They have yellow skin and feathery gills that gather oxygen from the water. The front legs grow first, then the back legs. Eventually their skin darkens, their gills disappear, and they climb out of the pond as air-breathing "efts".

A great crested newt can **live** for about **eight years**.

600 The highest **number of eggs** a **breeding female** can produce **each season**.

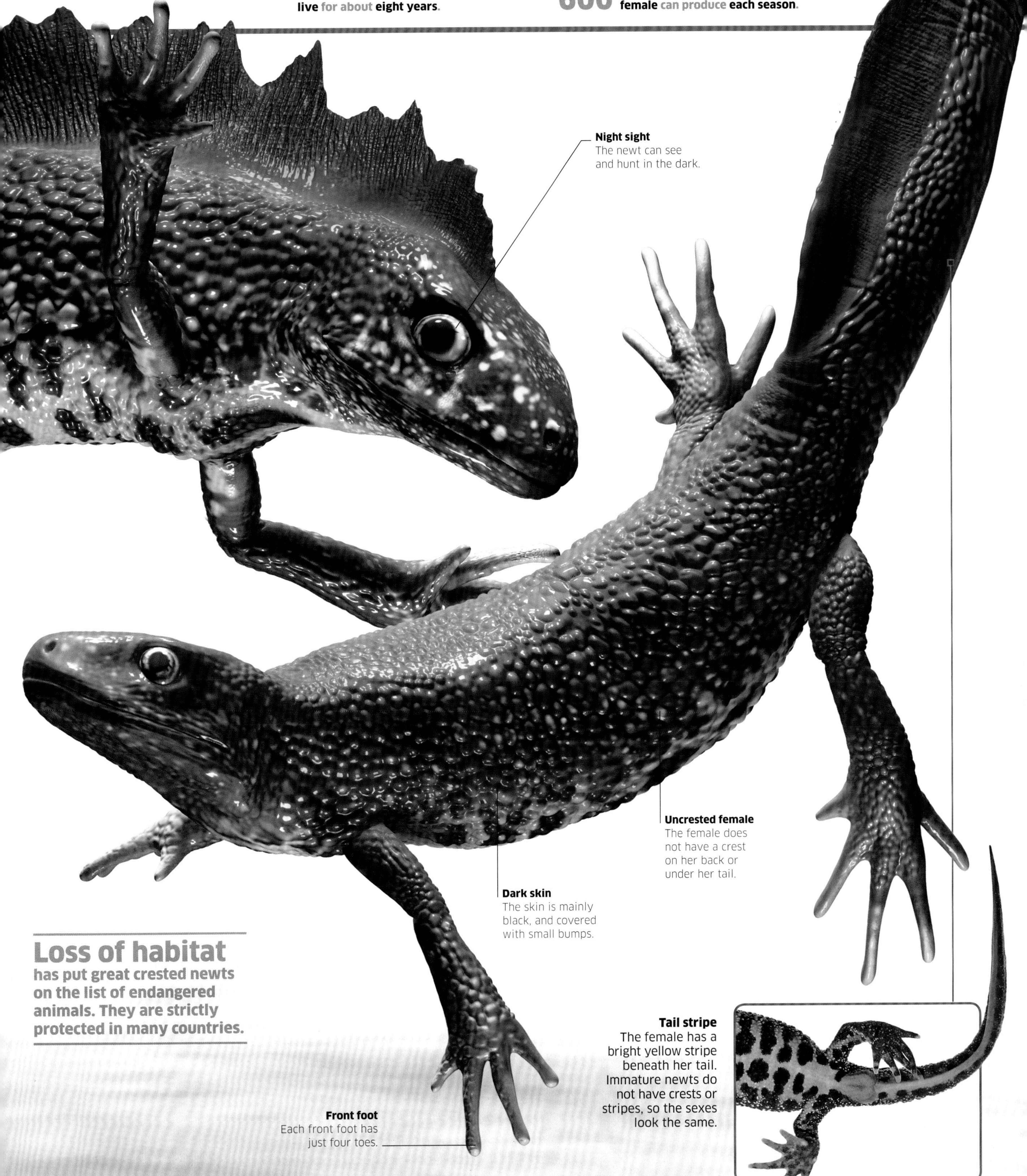

Loss of habitat

has put great crested newts on the list of endangered animals. They are strictly protected in many countries.

Salamanders were once thought to be **immune to fire**, and **able to crawl through flames** unharmed.

JAPANESE GIANT SALAMANDER

Andrias japonicus

Location: Japan

Length: Up to 1.4 m (4½ ft)

This super-sized salamander lives in cool mountain streams and never emerges onto land. Like most salamanders, it absorbs vital oxygen from the water through its thin, wrinkled, grey skin.

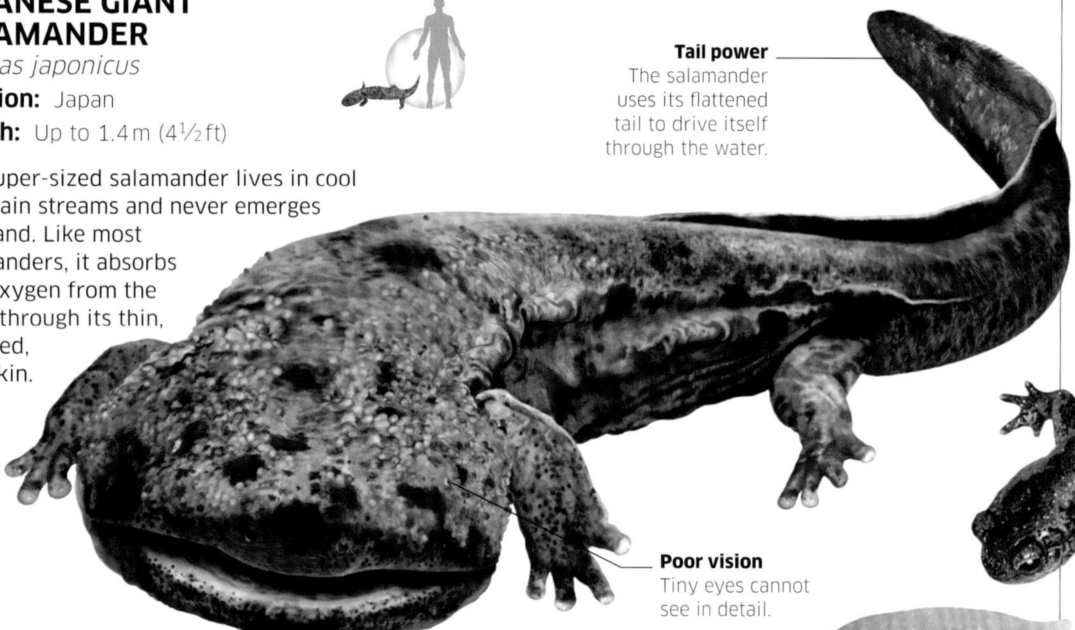

SIBERIAN NEWT

Salamandrella keyserlingii

Location: Northeast Asia

Length: Up to 15 cm (6 in)

Astonishingly this cold-blooded animal can live in regions where the temperature drops as low as −35°C (−31°F). It can survive being frozen solid for years, returning to its normal lifestyle when it thaws out.

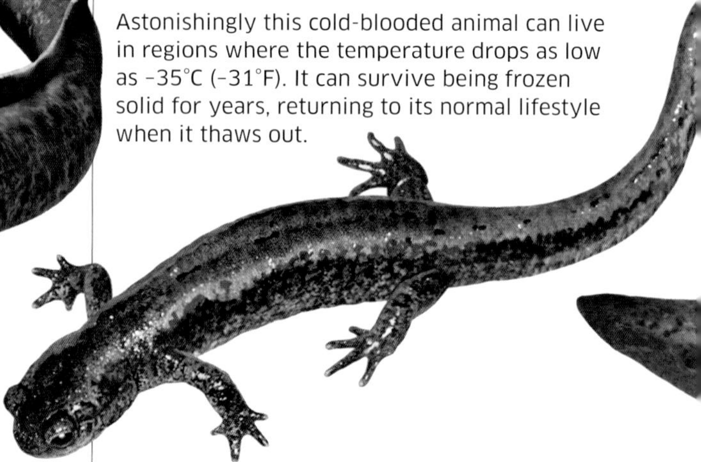

Salamanders and newts

Although they look like lizards, with their long tails and short legs, these animals are amphibians related to frogs and toads. They lose body moisture easily, so they cannot survive in dry places. Despite this, many spend their entire lives on land.

Newts are part of the same group of amphibians as salamanders, but tend to be more aquatic, returning to ponds each spring to breed. Most true salamanders lay their eggs in damp places on land. But some salamanders are even more aquatic than newts, and never leave the water.

GREATER SIREN

Siren lacertina

Location: Southeastern USA

Length: Up to 90 cm (35½ in)

Many salamanders have very short legs, but the sirens are a group that have lost their hind legs altogether. The greater siren is the biggest of these, and like the others it is aquatic, with feathery gills on each side of its neck for breathing underwater. It hunts at night for insects and other small animals.

FIRE SALAMANDER

Salamandra salamandra

Location: Central and southern Europe

Length: Up to 28 cm (11 in)

The vivid colour scheme of the fire salamander warns predators that its skin glands ooze dangerous poisons. The salamander can squirt this milky fluid from these openings on its back.

CALIFORNIA GIANT SALAMANDER

Dicamptodon ensatus

Location: Western North America

Length: Up to 30 cm (11¾ in)

Although not nearly as big as the Japanese giant salamander, this is a lot larger than most species. It spends its early life in the water, breathing through feathery gills, and typically lives on land as an adult. But some individuals remain aquatic and keep their gills as adults.

TWO-TOED AMPHIUMA

Amphiuma means

Location: Southeastern USA

Length: Up to 1.1 m (3½ ft)

This is the biggest of three species of amphiumas, a group of aquatic salamanders. It favours the still waters of swamps and ditches. Like many salamanders, its four legs are only vestigial, no longer having any function.

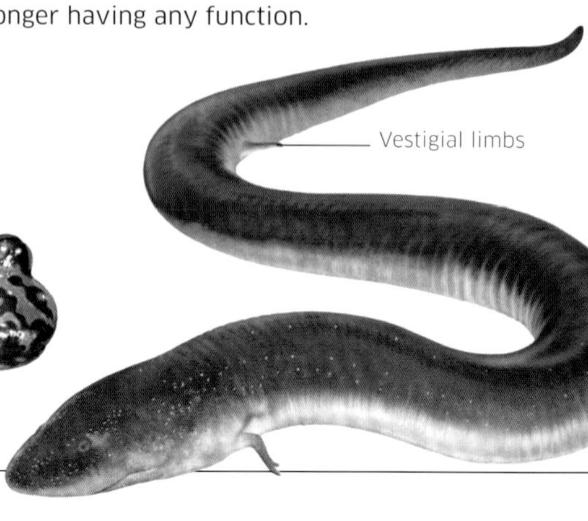

OLM
Proteus anguinus

Location: Southern Europe

Length: Up to 30 cm (11¾ in)

The strictly aquatic olm is a type of salamander that spends its entire life in the dark, in the waters that flow through limestone caves. It cannot see, hunting by scent, touch, and sound, and its body has lost all colour apart from the red blood that flows visibly through its feathery gills.

ANDERSON'S NEWT
Echinotriton andersoni

Location: Japan

Length: Up to 16 cm (6¼ in)

Elusive, endangered, and restricted to just a few Japanese islands, this newt has a unique way of defending itself. If it is seized by a predator, its sharp-tipped ribs protrude through wart-like poison glands in its skin, stabbing its enemy in the mouth and causing enough pain to make it release its grip.

MEXICAN AXOLOTL
Ambystoma mexicanum

Location: Mexico

Length: Up to 30 cm (11¾ in)

Most amphibians start life in water and breathe through external gills, which are lost as they mature. But the axolotl breeds while in its larval form and normally keeps its gills as an adult. It is now rare, as its habitats have been destroyed.

SALVIN'S MUSHROOMTONGUE
Bolitoglossa salvinii

Location: Central America

Length: Up to 12.5 cm (5 in)

Typical salamanders live on the ground or underwater. But this tropical forest species is adapted for climbing, with a prehensile tail it uses to cling to branches. It has a very long tongue with a sticky tip that it shoots out to catch insects.

SOUTHERN TORRENT SALAMANDER
Rhyacotriton variegatus

Location: Western USA

Length: Up to 11.5 cm (4½ in)

This is one of four species of torrent salamanders that live near rocky, fast-flowing streams in coastal conifer forests. It dries out easily, so although it hunts insects on the forest floor during heavy rain, it retreats to a stream as soon as the rain stops.

RED SALAMANDER
Pseudotriton ruber

Location: Eastern USA

Length: Up to 18 cm (7 in)

All amphibians can absorb oxygen through their thin, moist skin, but most have gills or lungs as well, except for lungless salamanders. This lungless salamander lives on land in summer, but is aquatic in winter.

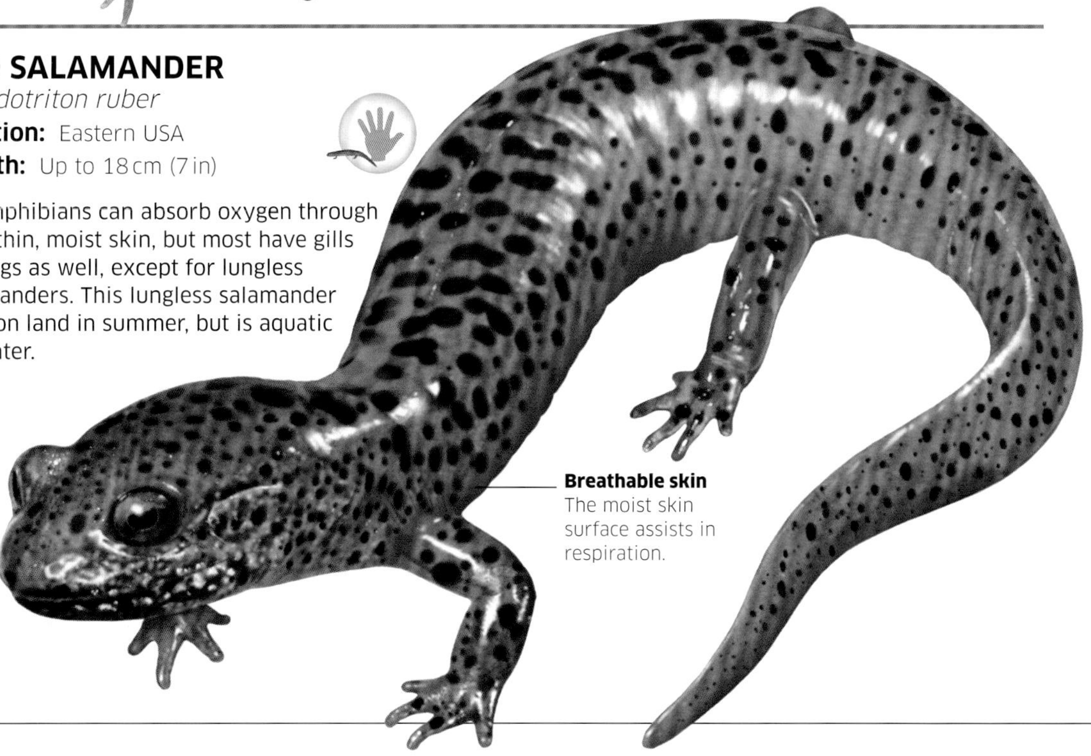

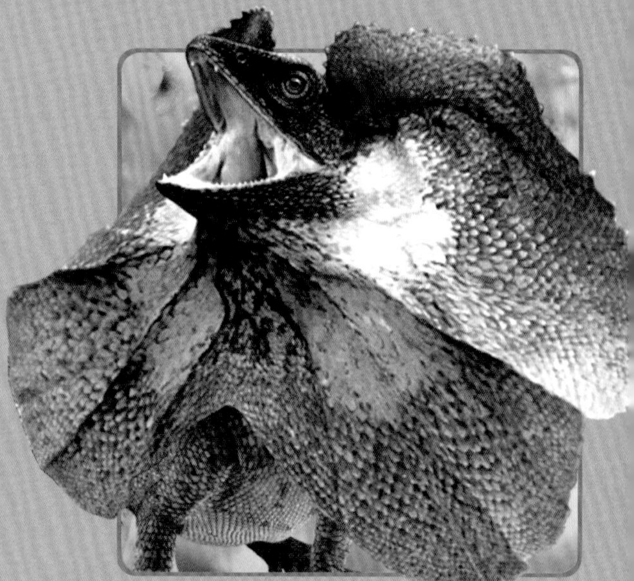

REPTILES

Scaly, cold-blooded, and even venomous, reptiles probably inspire more fear than admiration. But they are fascinating creatures, with many special adaptations that enable them to survive. From lumbering tortoises to unusual flying snakes, they include some of the world's most extraordinary animals.

WHAT IS A REPTILE?

Reptiles were the first vertebrates able to live entirely on land. They evolved scaly, waterproof skins that prevent them losing vital body moisture in hot, dry climates. Most reptiles lay eggs that have a tough outer covering for the same reason. As a result, reptiles flourish in all land habitats apart from the very coldest parts of the world.

TYPES OF REPTILE

There are four main orders of reptiles, but one of these contains just one surviving species – the tuatara. The others are the aquatic turtles and land-living tortoises, the crocodiles and alligators, and a single order that consists of the lizards, snakes, and the burrowing, worm-like amphisbaenians.

Turtles and tortoises
These are the most recognizable reptiles, with their domed shells that are fused to the spine and ribs. Tortoises live on land, while turtles live in oceans and fresh waters. There are 340 species.

DIAMONDBACK TERRAPIN

Tuatara
The tuatara is the sole survivor of a group of reptiles that flourished during the age of giant dinosaurs, but mostly died out 100 million years ago. It lives in New Zealand.

TUATARA

Lizards and snakes
Snakes and lizards belong to the largest reptile order, with 9,905 species. The burrowing, limbless amphisbaenians, or worm-lizards, also belong to this group, although there are only a few species.

CORAL SNAKE

Crocodilians
Crocodiles, alligators, and their relatives number only 25 species, but they include the biggest and most formidable of the reptiles. All crocodilians are primarily aquatic, although a few may sometimes hunt on land.

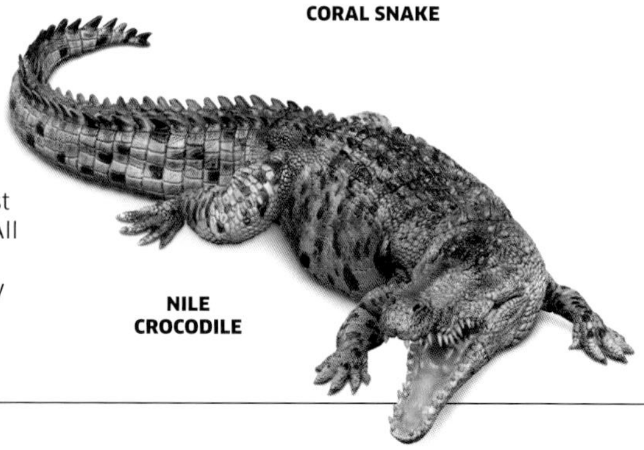

NILE CROCODILE

KEY FEATURES

Reptiles include an amazing diversity of animals adapted for a wide variety of habitats, ranging from oceans to deserts, but they share a number of key features. All living reptiles are cold-blooded vertebrates with tough, waterproof skins that allow them to survive in some of the driest places on Earth. Most reptiles lay eggs with leathery, waterproof shells, but a few give birth to live young.

Vertebrate
A reptile's body is supported by a bony skeleton.

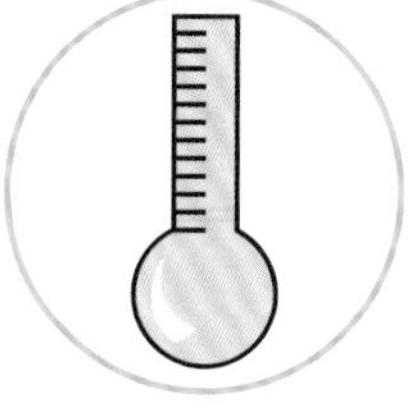

Cold-blooded
Body temperature depends on the environment.

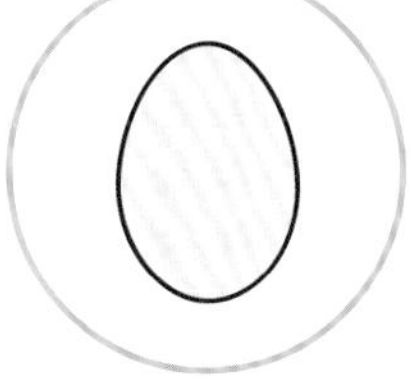

Lay eggs
Reptile eggs are enclosed by waterproof shells.

Inside a reptile

Fully equipped with a tough, waterproof, scaly skin for living on dry land, this Aldabra giant tortoise is also armoured with a strong, bony shell for protection from hungry enemies.

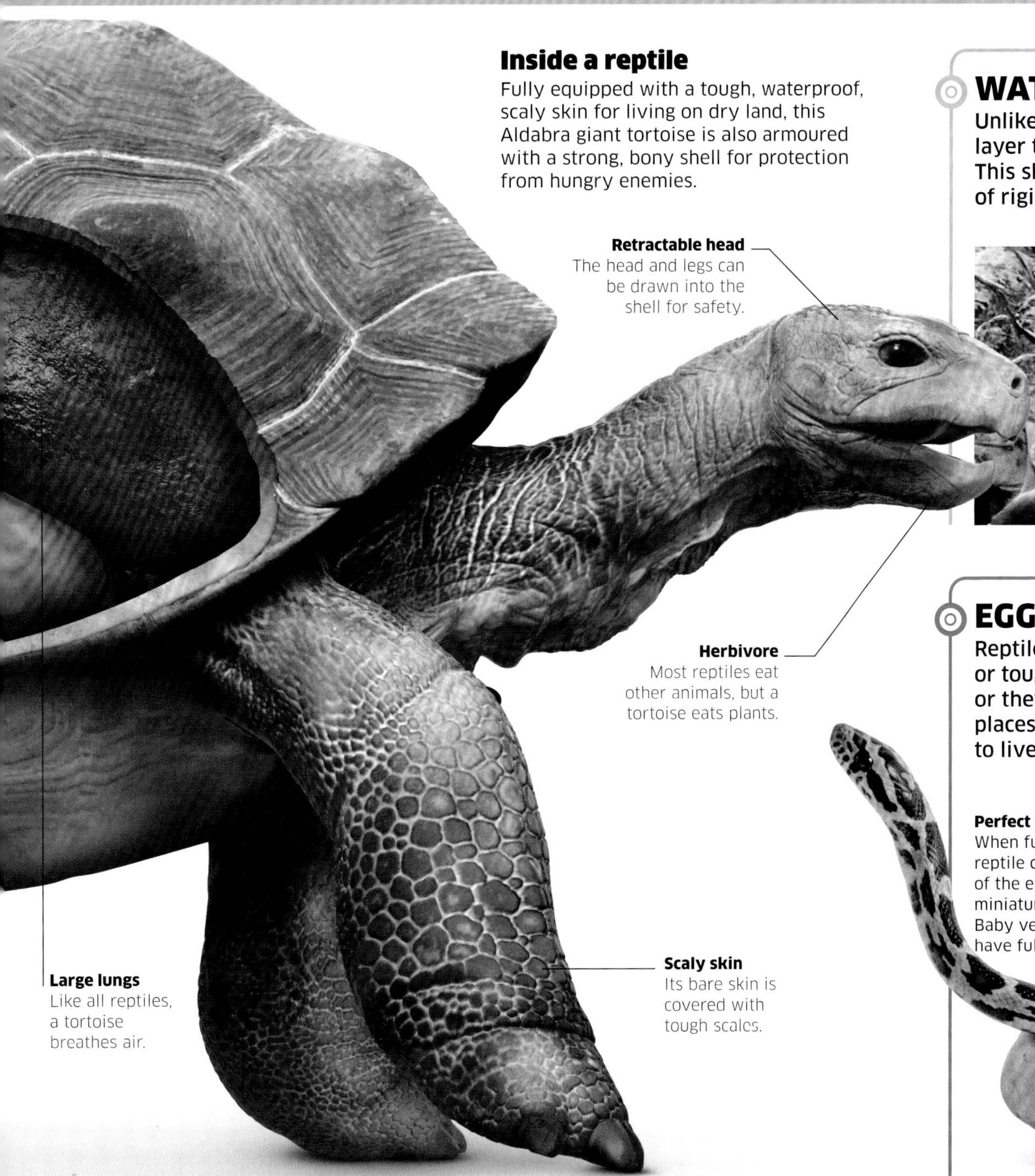

WATERPROOF SKIN

Unlike an amphibian, a reptile has a tough skin layer that stops moisture escaping from its body. This skin layer is protected by a flexible armour of rigid, often overlapping scales.

Rattlesnake scales
The root of each scale is attached to the outer skin layer. The snake sheds this layer at intervals throughout its life, and the scales are shed with it to reveal new scales that have formed underneath.

EGGS AND YOUNG

Reptile eggs may have hard shells, like birds' eggs, or tough but flexible shells. They must be kept warm or they will not hatch, so they are laid in warm places. In cool climates, some reptiles give birth to live young that do not need to be kept warm.

Perfect miniatures
When fully developed, a baby reptile cuts or chips its way out of the egg, and emerges as a miniature version of the adult. Baby venomous snakes even have fully working fangs.

CORN SNAKE

LEOPARD TORTOISE

IN THE DISTANT PAST, THE REPTILES ALSO INCLUDED THE GIANT **DINOSAURS** – THE BIGGEST LAND ANIMALS THAT **HAVE EVER LIVED.**

Scaly skins
The scales protect the skin and resist water loss.

Live young
Some snakes and lizards bear fully formed young.

ENERGY SAVERS

Although reptiles are described as cold-blooded, their bodies need to be warm to function properly. They rely on their environment to provide this warmth, so few reptiles live in regions with cold winters, and those that do are active only in summer. In tropical regions this is not a problem, and a reptile saves so much energy by not generating its own body heat that it can survive on far less food than a warm-blooded animal of similar size.

GREEN IGUANA

Temperature control
A reptile such as this green iguana controls its body temperature by its behaviour. When it needs to warm up it basks in the warm sunshine, and if it gets too hot and needs to cool off it slips into the shade.

150 cm (59 in) – the **length** that the **shell** of a **Galápagos tortoise** can reach.

Galápagos tortoise

One Galápagos tortoise in captivity is thought to have lived to the **amazing age of 170.**

Galápagos tortoises are the largest tortoises on Earth, capable of growing to a colossal size and an immense age. They once lived in their thousands on at least seven of the volcanic Galápagos islands off Ecuador, and owed their success to the remoteness of their island homes, where they had no predators or competitors for food.

Isolation of different tortoise populations on the islands led to the evolution of 15 local subspecies, each with its own distinctive features. Today, the Galápagos tortoise is at risk from various introduced species, including rats that prey on young tortoises and goats that compete for food. The number of subspecies has dwindled to 10, with several classified as endangered.

Growth rings
When a baby Galápagos tortoise hatches from its egg it is no bigger than a mouse, but its shell already has the pattern of scutes (tough scales) that it will keep for life. As the tortoise grows, each scute grows too, adding a ring each year. But the oldest parts wear away over time, so counting the rings does not reveal the tortoise's true age.

Scaly legs
The skin of each leg is covered with strong, protective scales.

Defence tactic
The tortoise can pull its legs and head into its shell for protection.

Sensitive nostrils

Horny beak
The tortoise has no teeth. Instead, it gathers food with a sharp-edged horny beak. It eats a variety of plant food in the grassland and forest where it lives, including grass and the succulent stems of the prickly pear cactus. Some of the subspecies have specially shaped shells that allow them to reach high into bushes to gather leaves. The shell above the neck is raised in an arch to allow them to stretch up higher.

Bony carapace

Like all tortoises and turtles, the Galápagos tortoise has a domed, bony upper shell or carapace that is fused to its ribs, and a similar bony plastron (flat shell) beneath its body. The bone is covered with tough scutes (scales) made of horny keratin – the material that our hair and fingernails are made of.

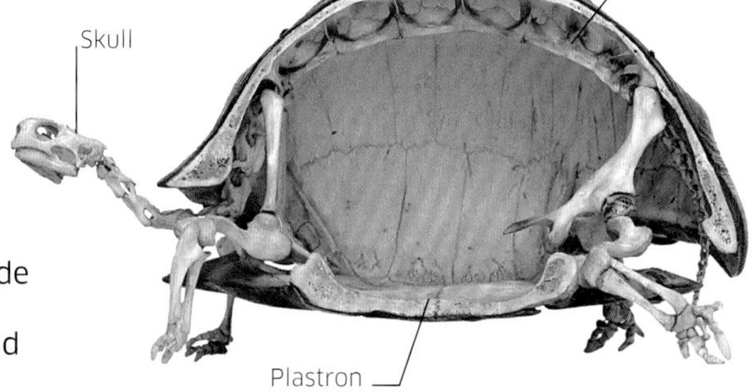

Rival males

When mature males come face to face in the mating season, they compete with each other in a ritual dominance display. Standing as tall as they can, they stretch their necks up and open their mouths wide. They may fight, but the shorter-necked tortoise usually backs off first.

Armour plate
The underside is protected by a lower shell, or plastron.

Stout claws
Each front foot has five broad claws. The hind feet have just four.

REPTILES

GALÁPAGOS TORTOISE

Chelonoidis nigra

Location: Galápagos Islands

Length: Up to 1.2 m (4 ft)

Diet: Leaves, cacti, berries, and lichens

188 The number of **years** one **radiated tortoise** is thought to have **lived** for – longer than any other land animal.

ALLIGATOR SNAPPING TURTLE

Macrochelys temminckii
Location: North America
Length: Up to 80 cm (2½ ft)

Named for its powerful bite, this freshwater turtle hunts by lying still with its mouth open to expose a pink, worm-like tongue. Animals attracted by the lure are soon snapped up.

Tempting bait
Few fish can resist the temptation of the turtle's wriggling, worm-like tongue.

PIG-NOSED TURTLE

Carettochelys insculpta
Location: New Guinea, Australia
Length: Up to 75 cm (29½ in)

Unlike other freshwater turtles, the pig-nosed turtle has flippers like those of a sea turtle instead of clawed feet. It owes its name to its fleshy snout, which has pig-like, forward-facing nostrils.

ASIAN NARROW-HEADED SOFTSHELL TURTLE

Chitra chitra
Location: South Asia, Indonesia
Length: Up to 1.6 m (5¼ ft)

Softshell turtles have hard shells or carapaces like other turtles, but with a covering of leathery skin instead of tough scutes. This species is one of the biggest, with males having longer, thicker tails than females.

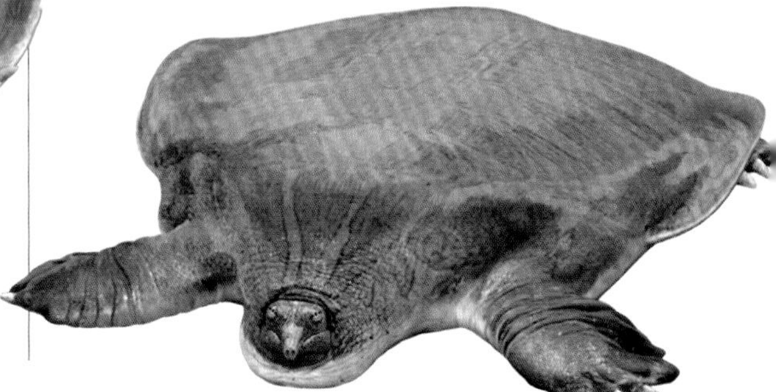

Turtles and tortoises

Instantly recognizable by their domed shells, turtles and tortoises come in many shapes and sizes and occupy a variety of habitats. Most of the 341 species are aquatic turtles. The land-dwelling tortoises number only 58 species and all belong to a single family.

These reptiles have a long history, dating back more than 220 million years to a time when the first dinosaurs were evolving. Their bony armour has served them well ever since, especially in the water where its weight is no problem. On land, it is one reason why tortoises are so famously slow.

Horny beak
The sharp-edged beak is ideal for cropping seagrasses.

GREEN SEA TURTLE

Chelonia mydas
Location: Worldwide
Length: Up to 1.5 m (5 ft)

An elegant, graceful swimmer, the green sea turtle is found in tropical oceans all over the world. Like other sea turtles it makes long migrations to favoured breeding beaches to lay its eggs, often returning to the same beach year after year. Most turtles are carnivorous but this one is a herbivore, feeding mainly on seagrasses and marine algae.

LEATHERBACK SEA TURTLE

Dermochelys coriacea
Location: Worldwide
Length: Up to 2.7 m (8¾ ft)

The biggest turtle by far, this oceanic giant has a carapace covered with leathery, oily skin. It eats jellyfish and other drifting, soft-bodied creatures.

Carapace
Streamlined, leathery carapace has seven ridges.

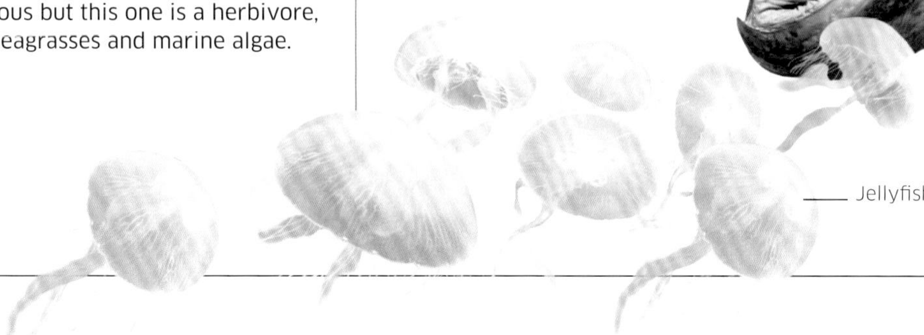

Jellyfish prey

DIAMONDBACK TERRAPIN

Malaclemys terrapin

Location: North America

Length: Up to 23 cm (9 in)

Widespread along the Atlantic coast of North America, this small turtle is adapted for life in tidal saltmarshes and mangrove swamps. It preys mainly on snails, clams, and other molluscs.

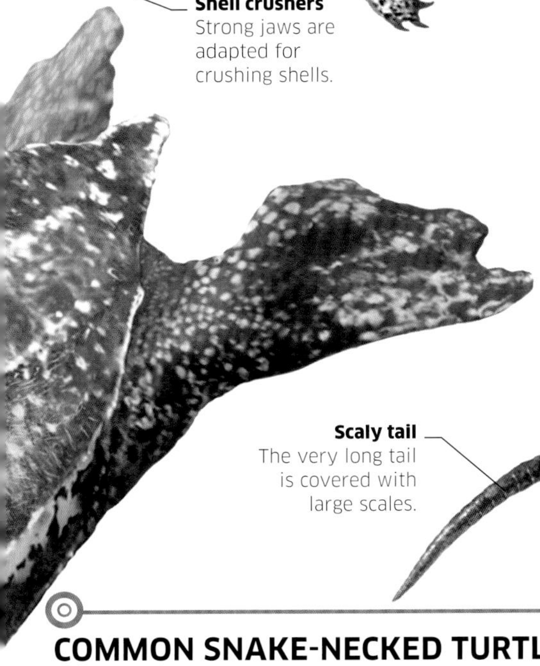

STINKPOT TURTLE

Sternotherus odoratus

Location: North America

Length: Up to 14 cm (5½ in)

When alarmed, this small, long-necked turtle releases a foul-smelling liquid from glands beneath its carapace. It eats a wide variety of foods, finding them by walking on the stream bed instead of swimming.

BIG-HEADED TURTLE

Platysternon megacephalum

Location: East Asia

Length: Up to 40 cm (15¾ in)

This freshwater turtle's head is so big that it cannot be pulled back into the animal's shell. The head has its own bony protective shield instead, and the turtle also has a powerful bite.

RADIATED TORTOISE

Astrochelys radiata

Location: Southern Madagascar

Length: Up to 40 cm (15¾ in)

Tortoises are essentially turtles adapted for life on land. This Madagascan species has an unusually ornate carapace. It resides in dry woodland and mainly eats grass, but will also eat fruit and succulent cactus flesh.

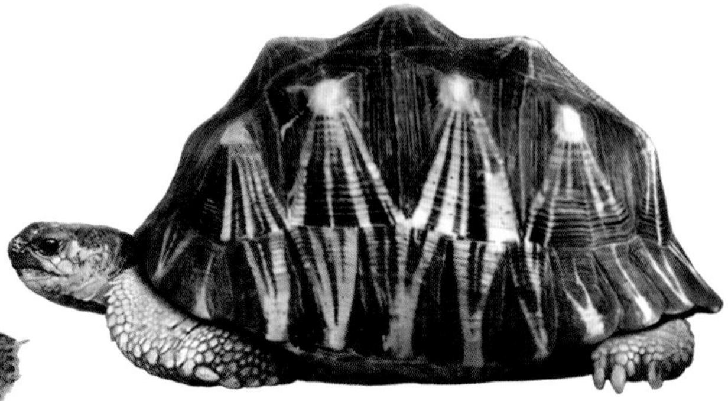

PANCAKE TORTOISE

Malacochersus tornieri

Location: East Africa

Length: Up to 20 cm (8 in)

Inhabiting rocky hills, the well-named pancake tortoise has a very flat, flexible shell that enables it to slip into narrow crevices. For a tortoise, it can move very fast, diving into the nearest refuge whenever it senses danger.

COMMON SNAKE-NECKED TURTLE

Chelodina longicollis

Location: Australia

Length: Up to 28 cm (11 in)

Unlike typical turtles, snake-necked turtles hide their heads in their shells by bending their long necks sideways. This species preys on small aquatic animals.

MATAMATA

Chelus fimbriatus

Habitat: South America

Length: Up to 70 cm (27½ in)

Relying on its superb camouflage to conceal it, the matamata lurks in ambush on the bottom of shallow streams and pools. When prey comes within range, the turtle suddenly gapes its mouth wide open so the water rushes in, sucking its victim in with it.

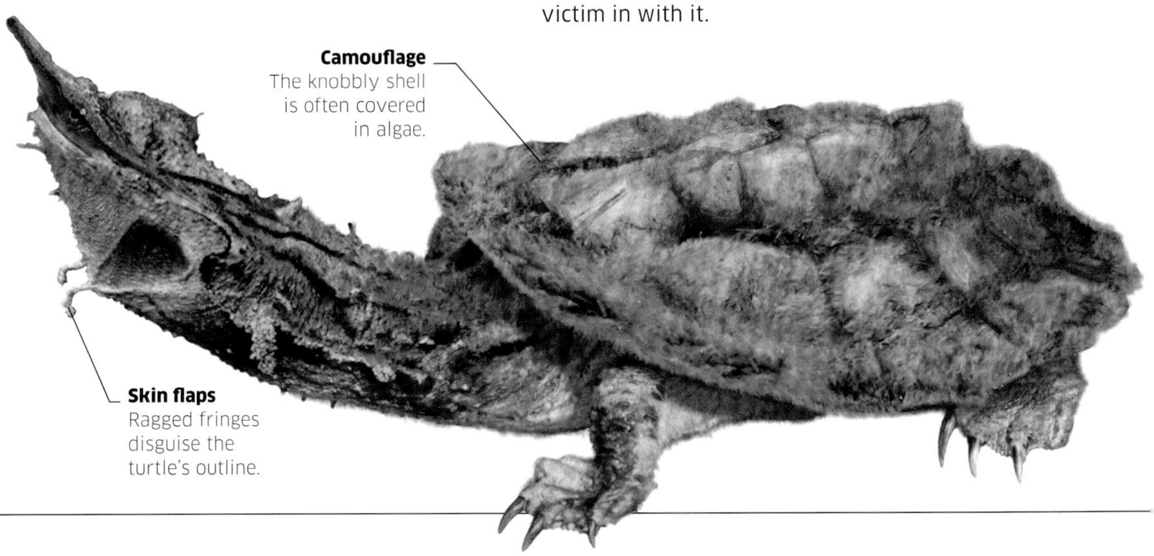

200 The minimum number of **known species of chameleon**. There are probably **many more** that have **not yet been discovered**.

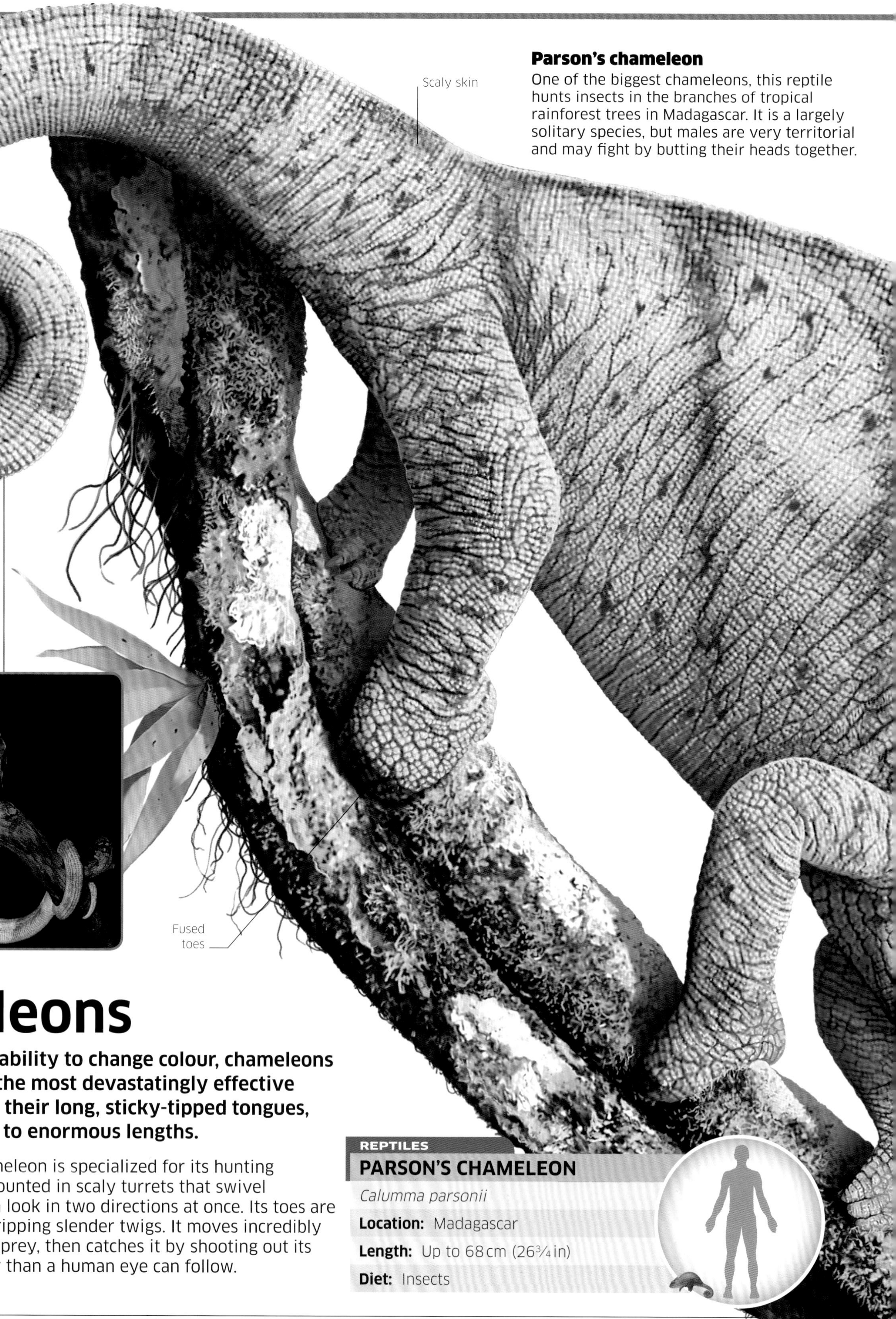

Parson's chameleon

One of the biggest chameleons, this reptile hunts insects in the branches of tropical rainforest trees in Madagascar. It is a largely solitary species, but males are very territorial and may fight by butting their heads together.

Prehensile tail
Normally coiled like a spring, the chameleon's muscular, mobile tail can be wrapped tightly around a perch for stability. This is particularly useful when targeting prey.

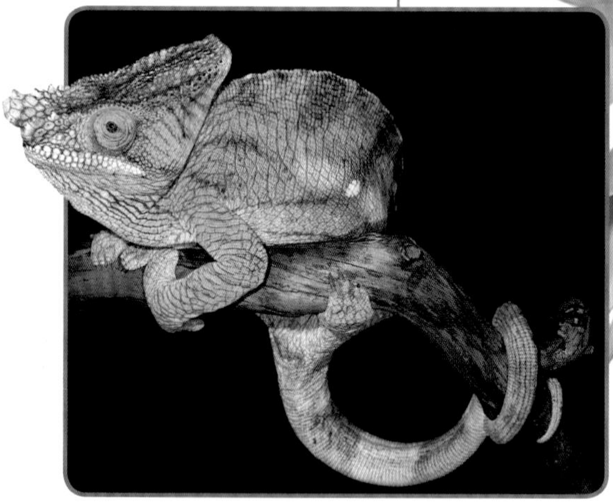

Chameleons

Renowned for their ability to change colour, chameleons also possess one of the most devastatingly effective weapons in nature – their long, sticky-tipped tongues, which can shoot out to enormous lengths.

Every feature of a chameleon is specialized for its hunting lifestyle. Its eyes are mounted in scaly turrets that swivel independently, so it can look in two directions at once. Its toes are fused into clamps for gripping slender twigs. It moves incredibly slowly to avoid scaring prey, then catches it by shooting out its incredible tongue faster than a human eye can follow.

REPTILES

PARSON'S CHAMELEON

Calumma parsonii

Location: Madagascar

Length: Up to 68 cm (26¾ in)

Diet: Insects

Changing colour
As with many chameleons, this species can undergo dramatic colour changes. Its pattern usually depends on its mood, but may provide camouflage. This one is displaying to a rival.

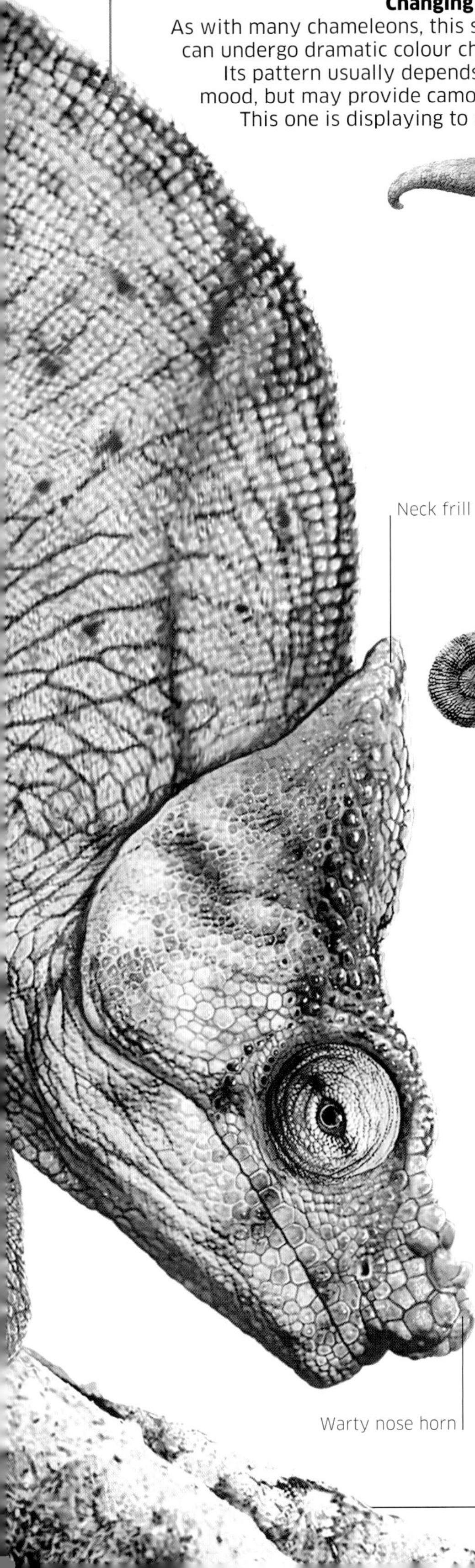

MADAGASCAN DWARF CHAMELEON

Brookesia micra

Location: Madagascar

Length: Up to 2.8 cm (1¼ in)

Discovered in 2012, this is the smallest chameleon and one of the smallest of all vertebrate animals. It sleeps in trees at night but hunts insects by day, foraging on the ground. Unlike most chameleons it is not able to change its colour, and is always brown.

NAMAQUA CHAMELEON

Chamaeleo namaquensis

Location: Southwest Africa

Length: Up to 25 cm (10 in)

Unlike most chameleons this desert species lives on the ground. It often turns black on cool mornings to absorb heat efficiently.

FISCHER'S CHAMELEON

Kinyongia fischeri

Location: East Africa

Length: Up to 30 cm (11¾ in)

Many chameleons live in remote regions, where they forage up in the trees. This species lives only in the forests of Tanzania, where it is rarely seen by humans, and little is known about its behaviour.

MEDITERRANEAN CHAMELEON

Chamaeleo chamaeleon

Location: S. Spain, N. Africa, Middle East, Mediterranean islands

Length: Up to 40 cm (15¾ in)

This chameleon is regularly seen on the Mediterranean islands of Crete and Cyprus. It is a solitary, stealthy hunter that creeps up on insects and captures them with a rapid flick of its telescopic tongue.

PANTHER CHAMELEON

Furcifer pardalis

Location: Madagascar

Length: Up to 50 cm (19¾ in)

Similar to Parson's chameleon, this species lives in dry forests where the males compete vigorously over territory. Rivals glow with vivid colour when they meet, but the loser rapidly fades to drab brown.

JACKSON'S CHAMELEON

Trioceros jacksonii

Location: East Africa

Length: Up to 38 cm (15 in)

As with many chameleons, the male of this species is more ornamented than the female, with three long horns on his snout, which are displayed in clashes over territory.

A Komodo dragon can **detect the smell of a dead animal** from 10 km (6 miles) away.

30 The approximate **number of years** a Komodo dragon **can live.**

Komodo dragon

The biggest of the lizards, the mighty Komodo dragon is a fearsome predator, powerful enough to ambush, kill, and devour a fully-grown water buffalo. It will even kill and eat its own kind.

The Komodo dragon lives on the island of Komodo and nearby islands and coasts near Java in southern Indonesia, where it preys on any animals it can catch. An adult Komodo dragon can knock a deer down with one blow of its tail, then hold its victim with its long claws while using its saw-edged teeth to kill the deer and then tear it apart. Rival males also use their strength to fight each other when competing for females or territory, rearing up on their hind legs to wrestle until one manages to force the other to the ground.

Armoured skin
The skin of a Komodo dragon is covered with scales that contain tiny bones called osteoderms. These form a tough but flexible armour, like the chain mail of linked steel rings worn by medieval soldiers. Similar armour defends other lizards against bigger predators, but in the case of Komodo dragons it protects them from each other.

Safe refuge

The only animals a Komodo dragon has to fear are bigger Komodo dragons, which are likely to kill and eat it if they get the chance. Young dragons take to the trees directly after hatching and do not begin to live on the ground until they have grown to around 1.2 m (4 ft) long. Even then, a smaller dragon has to give way to bigger dragons when feeding. It may even make itself smell disgusting by rolling in the gut contents of its prey, to put off any hungry cannibals.

An adult Komodo dragon may eat up to 80 per cent of its own body weight in a single meal.

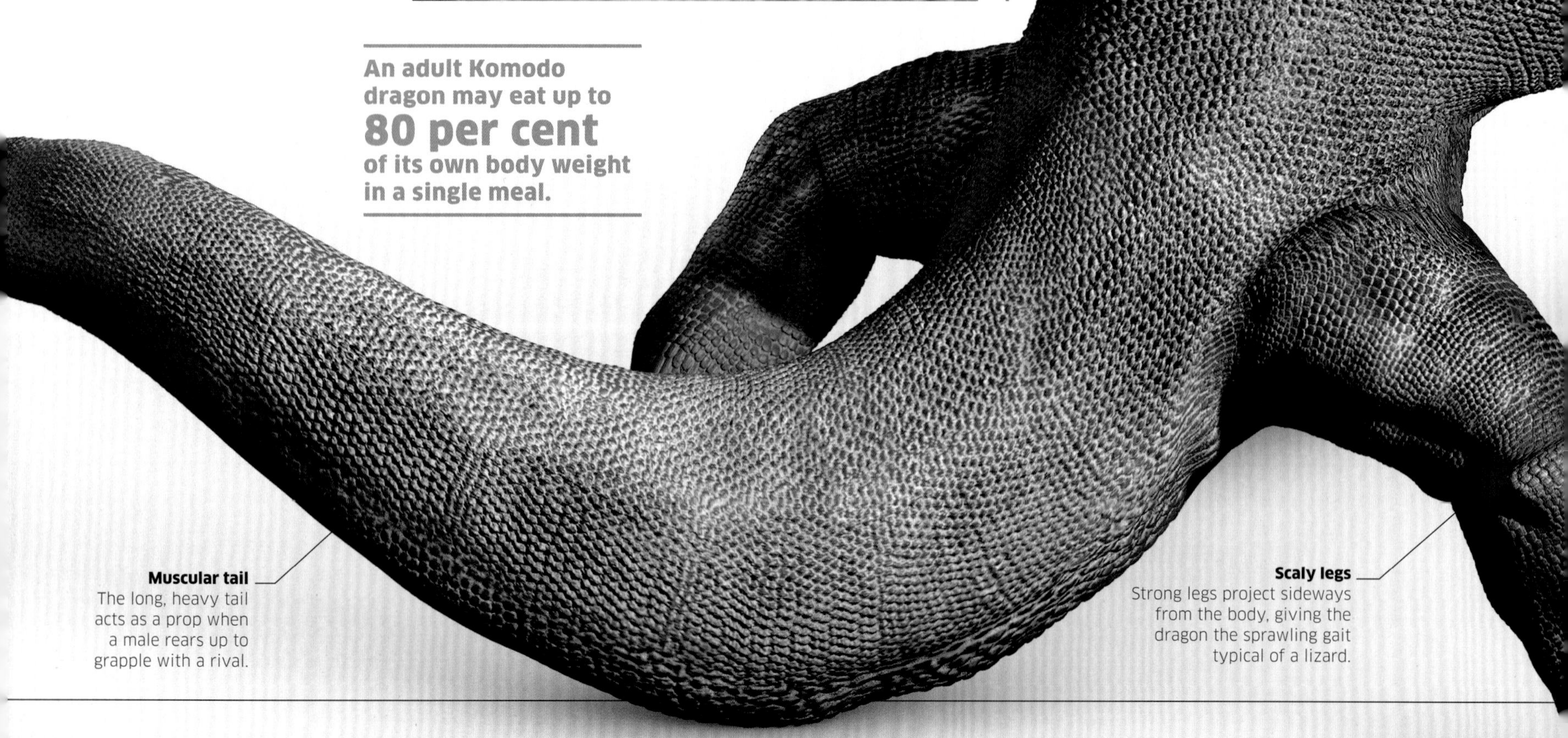

Big body
The bulky body can hold enough food to last the dragon for a month.

Muscular tail
The long, heavy tail acts as a prop when a male rears up to grapple with a rival.

Scaly legs
Strong legs project sideways from the body, giving the dragon the sprawling gait typical of a lizard.

12 The number of **big meals** an adult Komodo dragon can **survive** on in **a year**.

Komodos were **unknown** to **western science** until **1912**.

Forked tongue
The long tongue is forked like a snake's, and is flicked out to detect the scent of carcasses and follow scent trails.

Vision
The dragon can see in colour, but has poor night sight and relies on its sense of smell.

Slicing teeth
Up to 60 curved teeth, serrated like steak knives, allow the dragon to slice through the tough hide and flesh of prey.

Venomous bite
The drooling saliva of a Komodo dragon is laced with venom produced by glands in the lower jaw. The venom mixes with the lizard's saliva so it flows into the wounds inflicted by the blade-like teeth. It stops the victim's blood from clotting, and may also trigger internal bleeding. So even if an animal manages to escape the initial attack, it soon collapses from blood loss and shock, making easy prey for the dragon following its trail.

Long claws
Each foot has five massively powerful claws for seizing prey. Young dragons also use them for climbing.

REPTILES

KOMODO DRAGON

Varanus komodoensis

Location: Indonesia

Length: Up to 3.1 m (10¼ ft)

Diet: Carrion and live animals

300,000 The number of marine iguanas on the **Galápagos Islands**. They are found **nowhere else on Earth**.

Marine iguana

This extraordinary lizard survives on its remote island home by feeding on seaweed – marine algae – slicing it off the rocks of the shoreline with its sharp-edged teeth. Some marine iguanas even swim out to sea and dive below the surface to gather seaweed.

REPTILES

MARINE IGUANA

Amblyrhynchus cristatus

Location: Galápagos Islands

Length: Up to 1.5 m (5 ft)

Diet: Marine algae

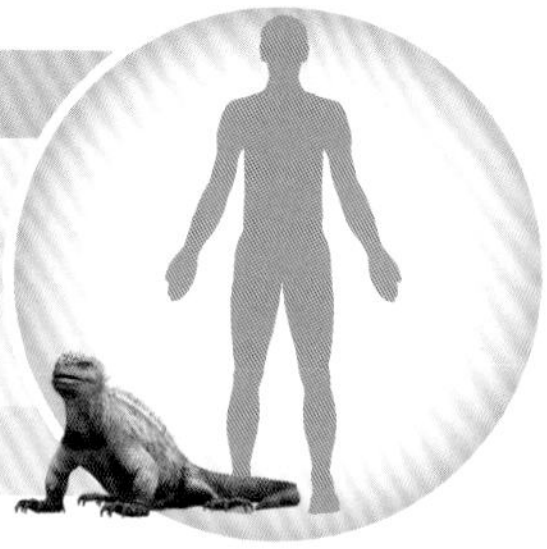

The marine iguana lives on the rocky coastlines of the Galápagos Islands in the eastern Pacific, where much of the land is bare volcanic rock with few plants. But seaweed is abundant, and over millions of years the marine iguana has evolved special ways of making the most of its unusual food source.

Spiky crest
A jagged crest of elongated, pointed scales extends down the back from head to tail.

Blunt snout
The iguana's blunt nose makes grazing on seaweed easier.

Chisel teeth
The iguana has small, flattened teeth, each with three branches, or cusps. The cusps have sharp chisel tips, perfect for shaving seaweed off hard rock. They never get blunt because they are continually renewed, with old teeth falling out and being replaced by new, sharp ones.

45 **minutes** – the length of time a marine iguana can **hold its breath**.

Female marine iguanas lay **six eggs**, at most, and then **bury them in the sand** or soft soil.

Powerful tail
The tail is flattened from side to side and helps drive the iguana through the water.

Breeding colours
Marine iguanas are usually black but during the breeding season some males flush vibrant shades of green and pink.

Protective scales
The skin is protected from damage by tough, horny scales.

Long claws
Unusually strong for a lizard, the iguana's limbs have long toes with extra-long, sharp claws for clinging to seaweed-covered rocks. This helps it keep a firm foothold on wave-battered shores, and also stops it being swept away by the ocean currents when feeding underwater.

Feeding underwater

Most marine iguanas feed at low tide, grazing seaweeds from the exposed rocks. Only a few iguanas – mainly the bigger males – gather seaweed underwater. They may graze for up to half an hour, but most stop sooner because they are chilled by the cold water of the Humboldt Current that flows around the Galápagos islands.

Sneezing salt

When a marine iguana emerges from the sea it must warm up before it can digest its food. It does this by basking on the hot shoreline rocks beneath the tropical sun. Meanwhile it gets rid of the excess salt it has eaten with the seaweed by sneezing frequently and ejecting a salty spray from special salt glands in its nostrils.

The biggest marine iguanas may dive **more than 10 m (33 ft)** below the waves to find a good meal.

6,145 The number of known species of lizards.

60 per cent of all reptile species are lizards.

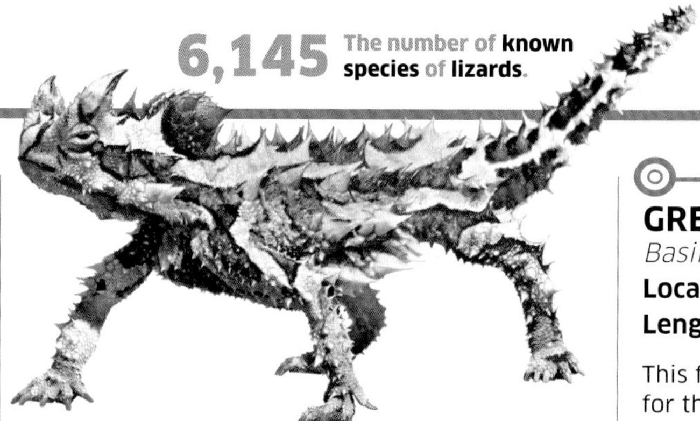

COMMON GREEN IGUANA
Iguana iguana
Location: Central and South America
Length: Up to 1.5 m (5 ft)

Unusually for a lizard, this large tropical species is a herbivore, which climbs trees and uses its sharp, blade-like teeth to feed on leaves and fruit. Its spiky crest helps protect it from hungry hawks and eagles. Despite its name, its skin can be orange, black, or blue.

THORNY DEVIL
Moloch horridus
Location: Australia
Length: Up to 20 cm (8 in)

Native to hot deserts, the thorny devil bristles with conical spines for defence against predators. Channels between the spines collect moisture from the air, which the lizard can drink. It preys almost exclusively on ants.

GREEN BASILISK
Basiliscus plumifrons
Location: Central America
Length: Up to 61 cm (24 in)

This flamboyantly crested lizard is famous for the way it can dash across the surface of deep water supported by the long, flattened toes of its hind feet. It usually does this to escape from enemies.

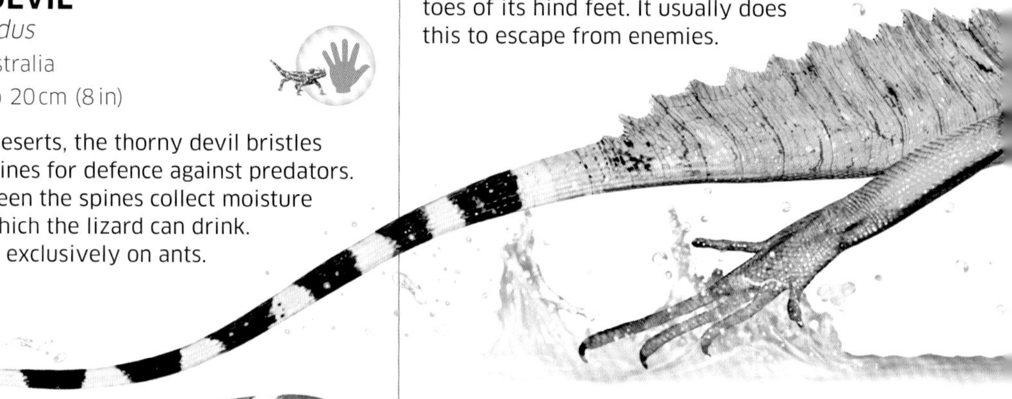

ARMADILLO GIRDLED LIZARD
Ouroborus cataphractus
Location: Southern Africa
Length: Up to 10 cm (4 in)

Armoured on its back with stout, spiny scales, this lizard defends itself by rolling up and gripping its tail in its mouth. The resulting ball makes a prickly mouthful for any predator. When unrolled, it feeds on insects, spiders, and other small animals, hunting them by day in rocky desert terrain.

BLUE-TONGUED SKINK
Tiliqua scincoides
Location: East Australia
Length: Up to 61 cm (24 in)

One of the biggest skinks – a large family of stumpy, short-legged lizards – this reptile has a bright blue tongue, which it flips out when faced by a predator. The sudden flash of vivid electric blue startles its enemy, giving the skink a chance to make its escape.

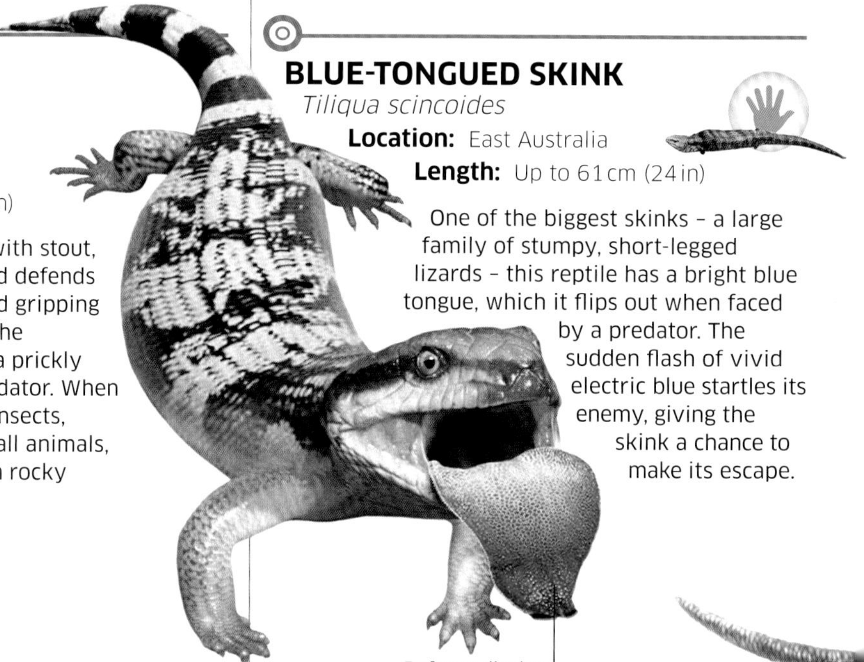

Defence display

SANDFISH SKINK
Scincus scincus
Location: North Africa
Length: Up to 20 cm (8 in)

This skink is adapted for moving swiftly through soft, dry sand by making swimming movements like a fish. Its body is superbly streamlined for slipping through the sand, with a wedge-shaped head and smooth, shiny scales. It catches insects by sensing their movements in the sand.

DWARF-PLATED LIZARD
Cordylosaurus subtessellatus
Location: Southern Africa
Length: Up to 15 cm (6 in)

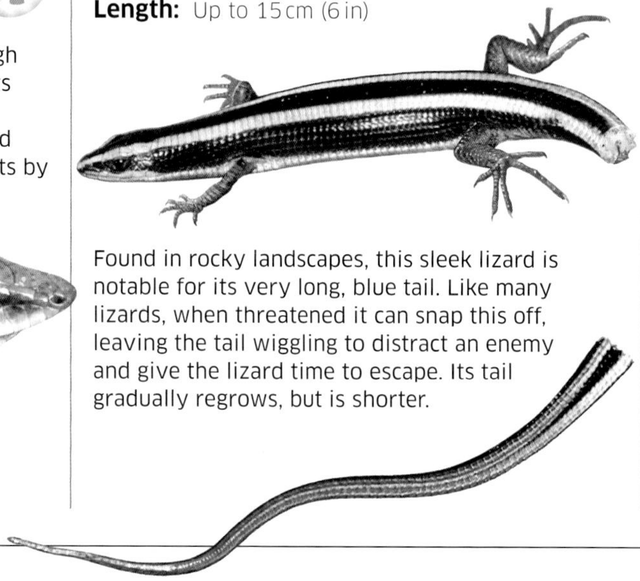

Found in rocky landscapes, this sleek lizard is notable for its very long, blue tail. Like many lizards, when threatened it can snap this off, leaving the tail wiggling to distract an enemy and give the lizard time to escape. Its tail gradually regrows, but is shorter.

VIVIPAROUS LIZARD
Zootoca vivipara
Location: Europe, Asia
Length: Up to 15 cm (6 in)

Most lizards lay eggs, relying on warm weather to incubate them. But a few, such as this widespread Eurasian species, give birth to live young. This allows it to live in cooler regions than other lizards, as far north as the Arctic. It is mainly an insect-eater.

Lizards appeared on Earth about 250 million years ago – earlier than the first dinosaurs.

SLOW WORM

Anguis fragilis

Location: Eurasia, N. W. Africa

Length: Up to 48 cm (19 in)

Neither a worm nor particularly slow, this is one of several species of legless lizard. It resembles a small snake, but unlike a snake, it can blink its eyes, and it cannot swallow large prey whole. It feeds on insects, slugs, and worms.

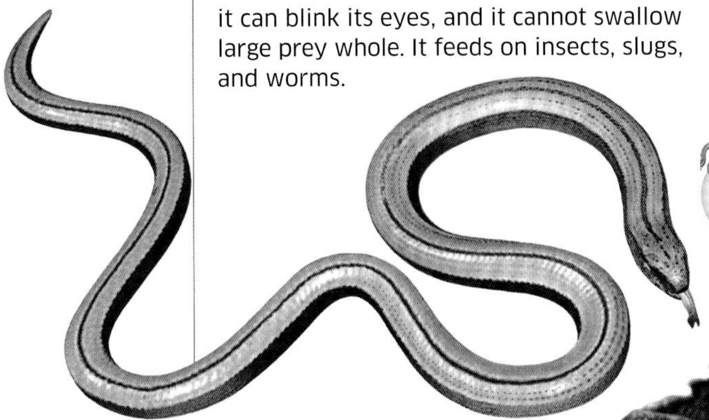

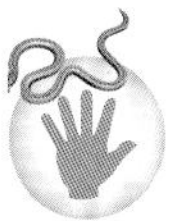

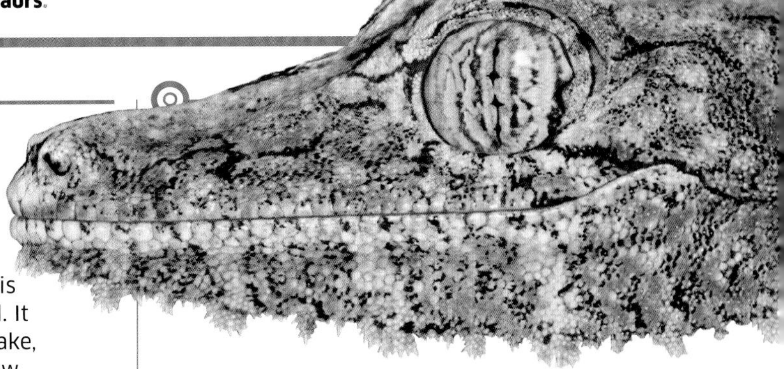

COMMON FLAT-TAILED GECKO

Uroplatus fimbriatus

Location: Madagascar

Length: Up to 33 cm (13 in)

Geckos are a distinctive group of lizards that are superbly adapted for climbing, with sticky structures under the tips of their toes that can cling to any surface. This species is exquisitely camouflaged, and invisible when crouched on tree bark. It has super-sensitive night vision for hunting insects.

Lizards

With more than 6,000 species worldwide, lizards are the largest and most diverse group of reptiles. They come in all shapes and sizes, ranging from tiny chameleons (see pp.102–103) to giant monitor lizards the size of crocodiles.

A typical lizard has a scaly skin, four legs, and a long tail. Its legs extend sideways from its body, giving it a sprawling stance with its belly close to the ground. Some lizards have very short legs or even none at all. A few species even have a venomous bite.

GILA MONSTER

Heloderma suspectum

Location: North America

Length: Up to 60 cm (23½ in)

Despite being closely related to snakes, very few lizards are venomous. This bulky hunter is one of the exceptions. The venom glands are in its lower jaw, and it uses its venom for defence – a tactic backed up by its bright warning coloration.

FRILL-NECKED LIZARD

Chlamydosaurus kingii

Location: New Guinea, Australia

Length: Up to 90 cm (35½ in)

The dramatic neck-frill of this Australasian lizard is usually kept folded against its body. But if the lizard is cornered by a predator, it spreads the frill and opens its mouth wide to reveal a brightly coloured lining. It uses the same display for courtship.

4 months or more – the length of time a boa can go without food.

20 The number of years an emerald tree boa may live for.

Emerald tree boa

Camouflaged among the tropical forest foliage by its green skin, the emerald tree boa drapes itself over a low branch watching for a victim to stray within striking range.

Like nearly all snakes the emerald tree boa is a hunter. It is mainly nocturnal and preys on the small mammals and birds that live in the lowland tropical forests of South America, using heat-sensitive organs on its lips to detect their warm bodies even in the dark. Unlike some snakes it is not venomous. Instead it seizes prey in its extra-long teeth and squeezes the animal to death in its powerful coils.

REPTILES

EMERALD TREE BOA

Corallus caninus

Location: South America

Length: Up to 1.8 m (6 ft)

Diet: Mainly small mammals

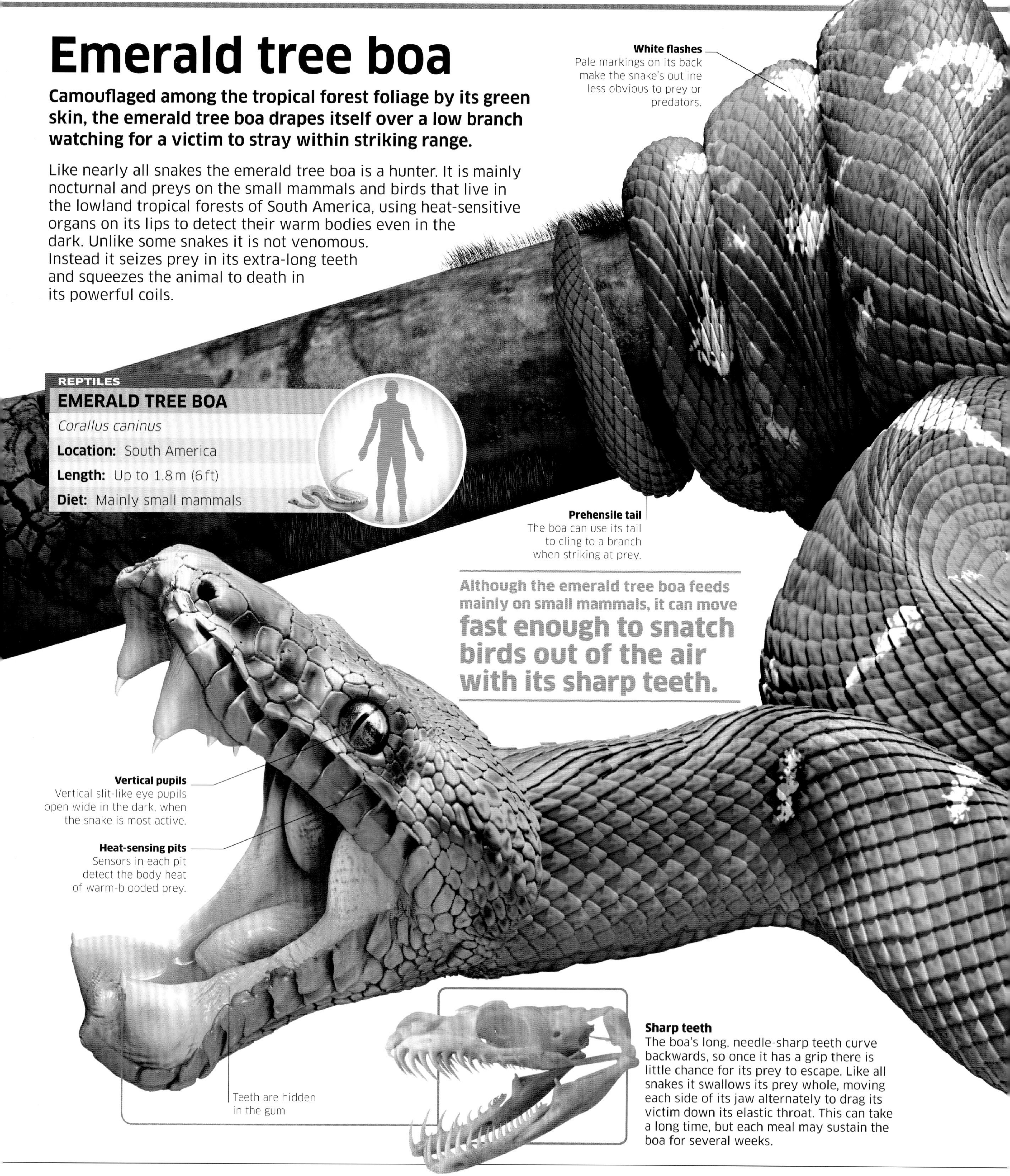

Although the emerald tree boa feeds mainly on small mammals, it can move **fast enough to snatch birds out of the air with its sharp teeth.**

Sharp teeth
The boa's long, needle-sharp teeth curve backwards, so once it has a grip there is little chance for its prey to escape. Like all snakes it swallows its prey whole, moving each side of its jaw alternately to drag its victim down its elastic throat. This can take a long time, but each meal may sustain the boa for several weeks.

Death grip

While still gripping a branch, a boa kills by constriction – throwing several coils around its prey and squeezing tighter every time the victim breathes out. This soon stops the animal breathing at all, and may also interrupt the vital blood flow to its heart and brain. Once its prey is dead, the snake swallows its meal head-first.

JUVENILE EMERALD TREE BOA

Colour change

Emerald tree boas may be born green like their parents, but they are often brick red, orange, or all three colours, turning green after 6 months to a year. This coloration may help the young snakes deter predators by mimicking the colours of venomous tree-living vipers.

A wild rattlesnake can survive for up to two years without food.

Warning rattle
The tail rattle is made up of loose, scaly rings that make a buzzing noise when shaken.

Fangs ready to strike

Big mouthful
When the snake senses a possible victim, it glides closer to investigate, picks its moment, and strikes. Darting its head forwards, it gapes its mouth wide open and stabs the animal with its fangs. The snake waits for the venom to take effect, then starts to swallow its prey whole, working it back into its throat with its very mobile, sharp-toothed jaws.

Diamondback
Blotches on the skin are outlined with diamond-shaped pale and dark lines.

This species is North America's **most dangerous rattlesnake,** responsible for the most human deaths by snakebite.

Overlapping scales

REPTILES

WESTERN DIAMONDBACK RATTLESNAKE

Crotalus atrox

Location: Mexico, southwest USA

Length: Up to 2.1 m (6¾ ft)

Diet: Small mammals

Western diamondback rattlesnake

Equipped with huge venomous fangs and a sixth sense for detecting its prey in the dark, the western diamondback rattlesnake is one of the world's most deadly predators.

Rattlesnakes are vipers – venomous snakes with long fangs at the front of the mouth that fold back to allow the mouth to close. The fangs inject a potent venom that destroys blood vessels and muscle, and which is powerful enough to kill a human adult. But the snake would rather save its venom for hunting, and uses its warning rattle to keep its enemies at bay.

Keeled scales
The scales on the rattlesnake's skin have distinct central ridges, or keels. These may scatter light in a way that stops the scales flashing in the sunshine, helping the snake avoid being seen by prey and enemies.

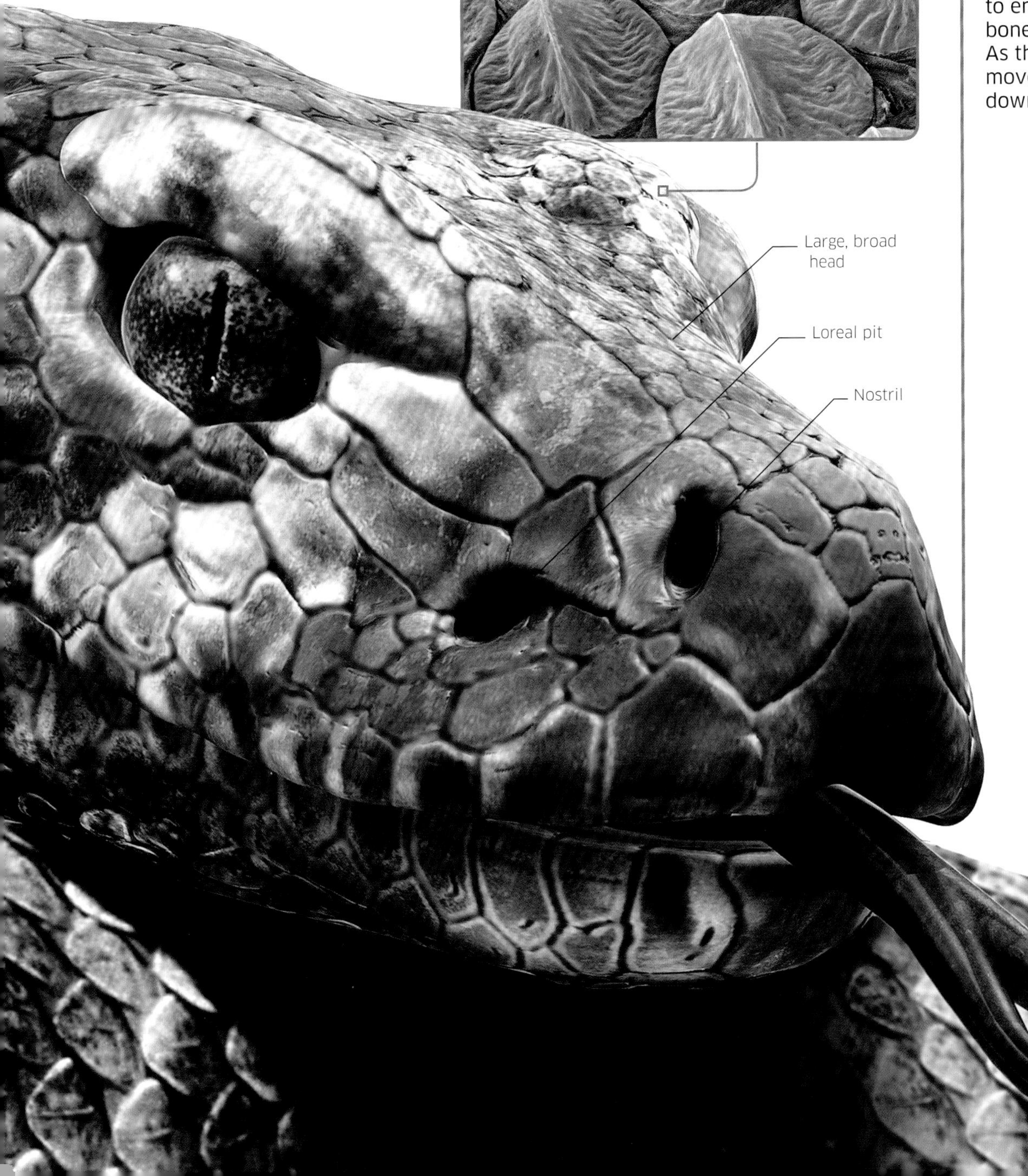

Forked tongue
The snake's flicking tongue picks up the scent of prey.

Hunting in the dark

A rattlesnake is a pit viper – a type of viper with heat-sensitive organs called loreal pits, one on either side of its head. These pits detect the body heat of warm-blooded prey, allowing the snake to "see" in the dark. To a rattlesnake, a mouse almost glows in the dark, making it an unmissable target.

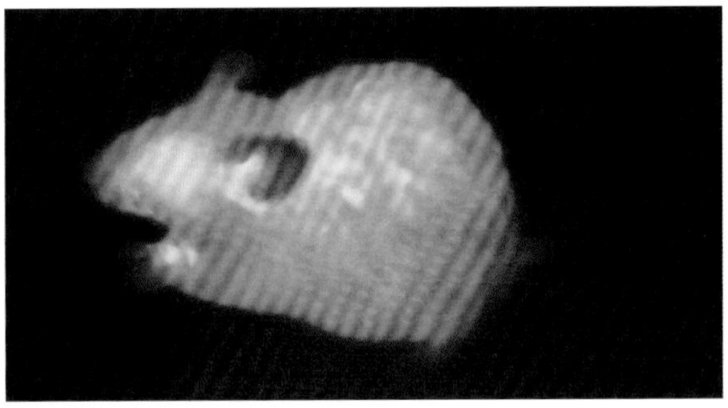

Hinged fangs

A rattlesnake can open its mouth incredibly wide to engulf prey, thanks to the way its lower jaw bones are attached to mobile quadrate bones. As the jaws open, the mobile upper jaw bones move forward, making the hinged fangs swing down ready to strike.

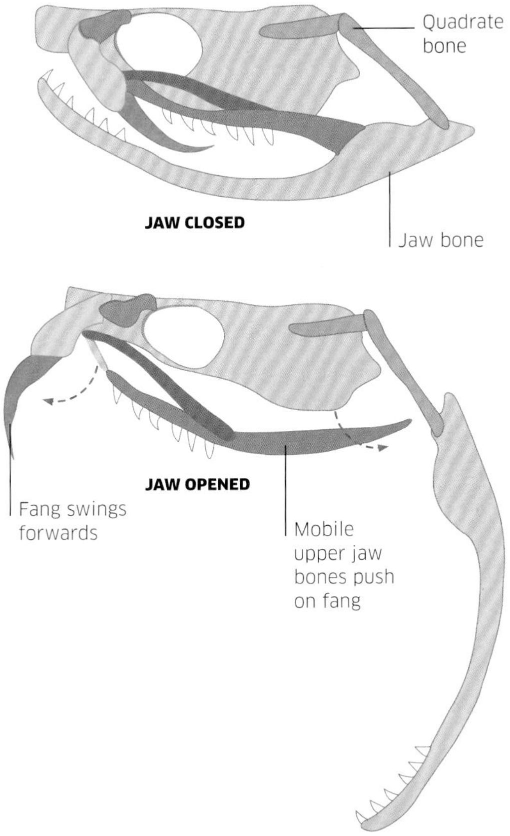

5 cm (2in) – the length a **gaboon viper's fangs** can grow to.

A **golden flying snake** can **glide** for distances of up to **100m (330ft)**.

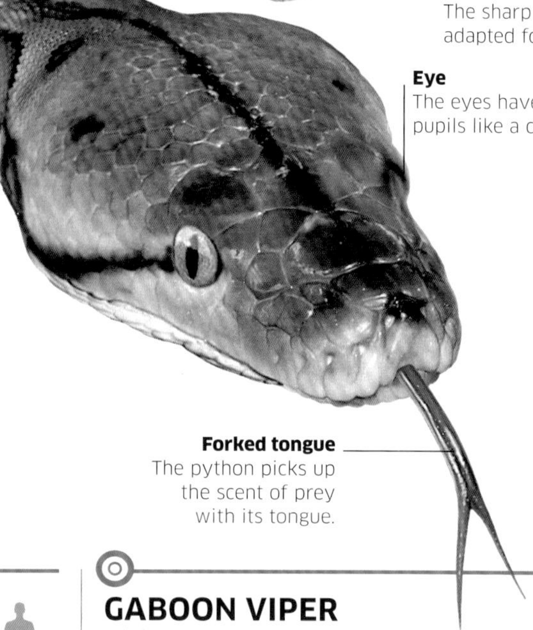

RETICULATED PYTHON

Malayopython reticulatus

Location: S. E. Asia

Length: Up to 10m (33ft)

The longest snake, and one of the heaviest, this tropical Asian giant is a constrictor that kills prey by coiling around it and squeezing it to death.

SCHLEGEL'S GIANT BLINDSNAKE

Afrotyphlops schlegelii

Location: Eastern and southern Africa

Length: Up to 1m (3¼ft)

Specialized for burrowing, and rarely seen above ground, this African snake does have eyes, but they are very small and covered by stout scales. It has a spade-like snout that it uses to tunnel in search of the termites that are its sole prey.

Snakes

Highly specialized for their predatory lifestyle, snakes are among the most efficient of all hunters. Their adaptations also make them some of the most dangerous animals on Earth.

Snakes are dedicated killers. With very few exceptions they hunt live prey, kill it, and swallow it whole. They have specialized senses for detecting their quarry, and they can move surprisingly quickly for animals with no legs. Their jaws and skulls are highly modified for swallowing animals bigger than their own heads, and some snakes are armed with deadly venom.

BOMBAY EARTH SNAKE

Uropeltis macrolepis

Location: South Asia

Length: Up to 30cm (11¾in)

This small, burrowing south Indian forest snake has a curiously wedge-shaped tail, armoured with unusually tough scales. It uses this as a shield to block the end of its burrow when it is tunnelling, and keep out hungry predators.

SIDEWINDER

Crotalus cerastes

Location: North America

Length: Up to 80cm (31½in)

One of the highly venomous rattlesnakes, the sidewinder is named for the way it crawls over hot, dry, wind-blown desert sand by looping its body sideways. It lives in the deserts of northern Mexico and the southwestern United States.

GABOON VIPER

Bitis gabonica

Location: West and central Africa

Length: 2m (6½ft)

The African gaboon viper is a massively built killer that uses its superb camouflage to ambush prey in its tropical forest habitat. It has the longest venomous fangs of any snake.

INDIAN COBRA

Naja naja

Location: South Asia

Length: Up to 2.4 m (7¾ ft)

One of the most dangerous snakes, the highly venomous Indian cobra is famous for its hooded threat display. Compared to a viper it has short fangs, but they deliver a potent venom containing paralyzing nerve toxins.

EASTERN CORAL SNAKE

Micrurus fulvius

Location: North America

Length: Up to 1.2 m (4 ft)

Bands of vivid colour spell danger for any animal tempted to attack this highly venomous snake. The warning is so effective that harmless species such as the scarlet kingsnake mimic the banded pattern for their own defence.

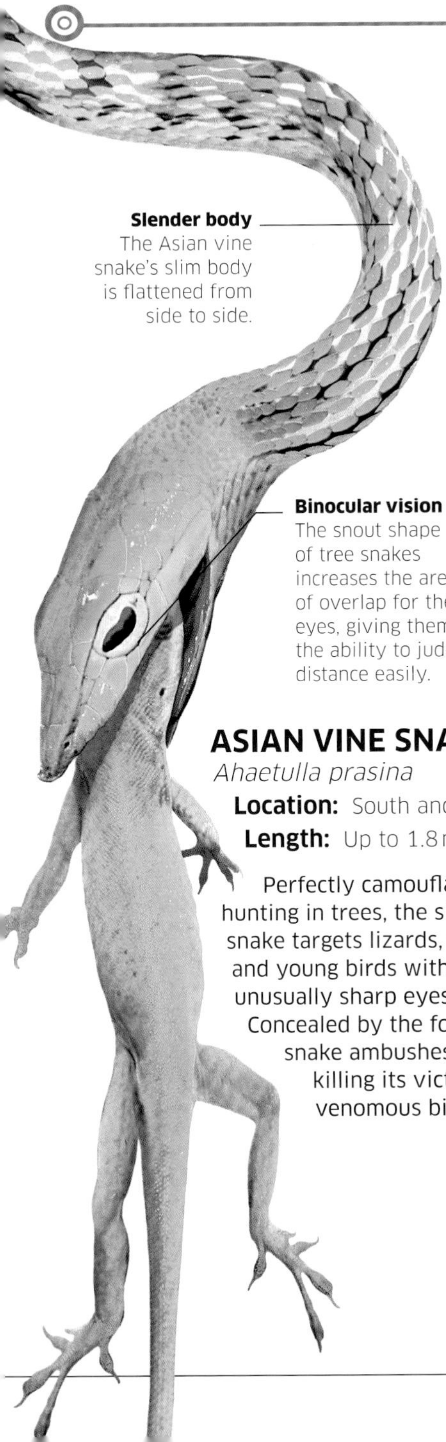

ASIAN VINE SNAKE

Ahaetulla prasina

Location: South and S.E. Asia

Length: Up to 1.8 m (6 ft)

Perfectly camouflaged for hunting in trees, the slender vine snake targets lizards, tree frogs, and young birds with its unusually sharp eyesight. Concealed by the foliage, the snake ambushes its prey, killing its victim with a venomous bite.

YELLOW-LIPPED SEA KRAIT

Laticauda colubrina

Location: Indo-Pacific region

Length: Up to 1.5 m (5 ft)

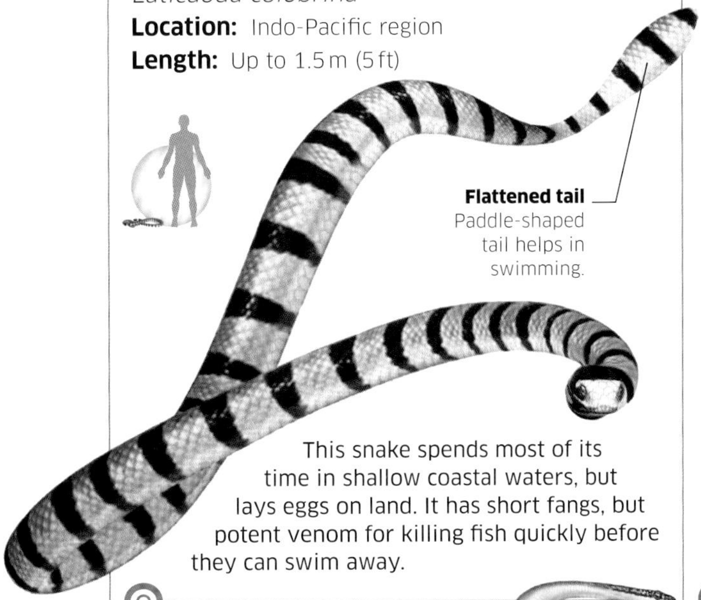

This snake spends most of its time in shallow coastal waters, but lays eggs on land. It has short fangs, but potent venom for killing fish quickly before they can swim away.

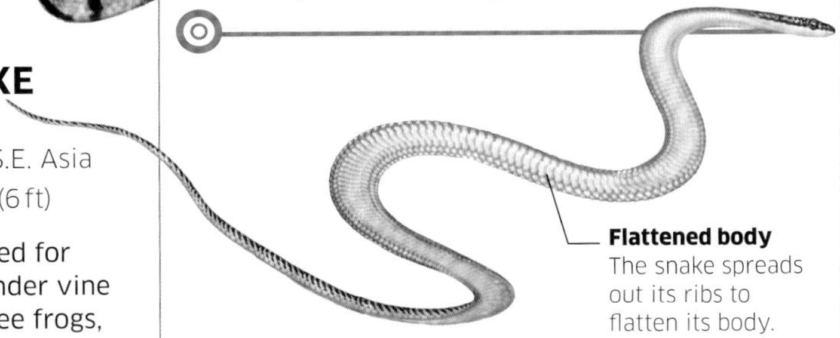

GOLDEN FLYING SNAKE

Chrysopelea ornata

Location: South and S. E. Asia

Length: Up to 1.3 m (4¼ ft)

This extraordinary south Asian snake hunts small animals in trees, and avoids coming down to ground level by hurling itself into the air and gliding from tree to tree. Once airborne it flattens its body into a big S-shape that floats on the air like a frisbee.

COMMON EGG-EATER

Dasypeltis scabra

Location: Africa, West Asia

Length: Up to 1.2 m (4 ft)

All snakes can eat huge meals, but the African egg-eater can take a whole egg in its mouth. The snake breaks it up with spiny projections of its neck vertebrae, then coughs up the crushed shell.

RING-NECKED SNAKE

Diadophis punctatus

Location: North America

Length: Up to 46 cm (18 in)

If threatened this small American snake coils its tail and flips it over to expose the vividly coloured underside. This may warn enemies that the snake can bite, although its venom is not very strong.

A Nile crocodile can **kill** a full-grown **African buffalo**.

100 years or more – the possible **lifespan** of a crocodilian.

Crocodilians

The biggest, most powerful reptiles, crocodilians are superbly equipped for their aquatic way of life, and are notorious for their fearsome jaws and their ability to kill and eat almost anything.

The crocodilians consist of three families – the gharials, the alligators and caimans, and the crocodiles. They are all dedicated meat-eaters with the same basic body shape, but their jaws vary in form depending on their diet. They propel themselves through the water with their long, muscular tails, and are able to stay concealed underwater without breathing for long periods as they wait to ambush prey.

REPTILES

NILE CROCODILE

Crocodylus niloticus

Location: Tropical Africa

Length: Up to 6.1 m (20 ft)

Diet: Fish, mammals, birds

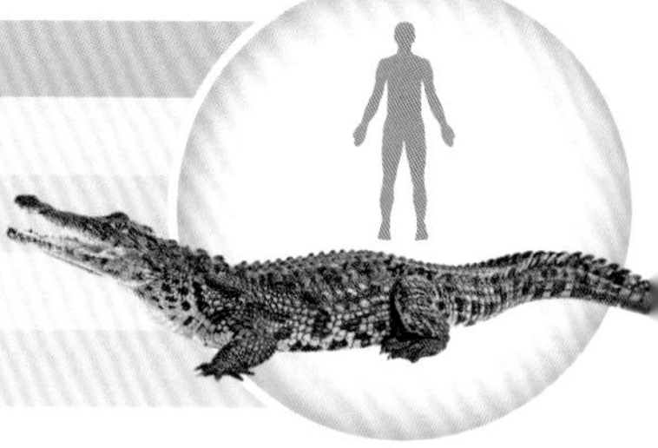

Armoured scutes
A crocodile's back is armoured with big, bony plates embedded in thick, oversized scales known as scutes. These protect it from bigger crocodiles, as well as the sharp hooves and horns of struggling prey.

Splayed legs
Short legs are used for steering underwater.

Flattened tail

Food processor
Highly acidic juices in the stomach digest everything, including hair, bones, hooves, and horns.

Strong, pointed teeth

Death grip
Powerful jaws can exert a colossal biting force for gripping and dismembering prey.

Renewable teeth
The crocodile has up to 68 teeth. Some are much bigger than others and, as in all true crocodiles, many of the teeth are visible when the jaws are closed. Each tooth is replaced by a new one as it wears out, so a crocodile always has a full set.

The **closest living relatives** of crocodilians are **birds**.

After a big meal, a crocodilian can go without food for **six months** or more.

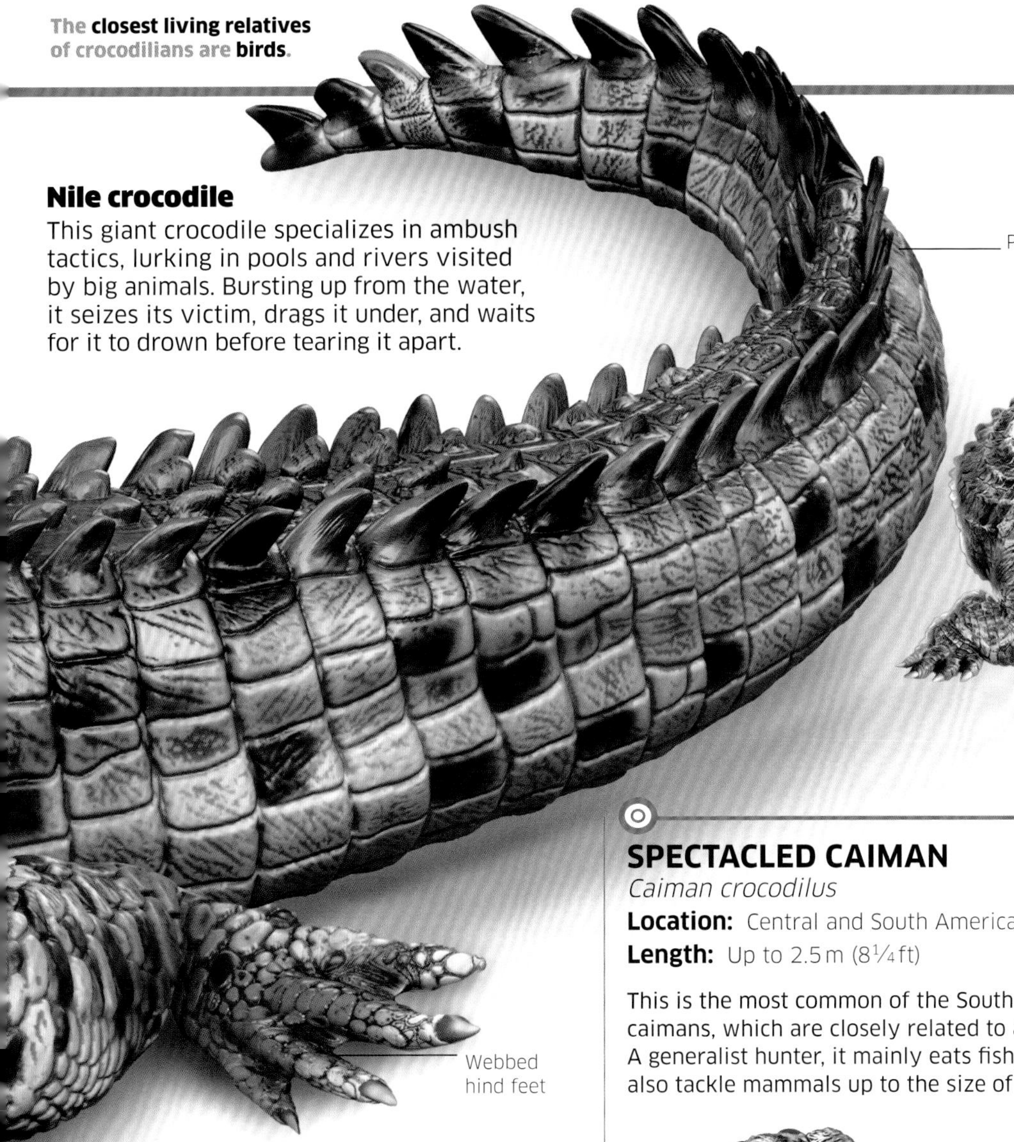

Nile crocodile
This giant crocodile specializes in ambush tactics, lurking in pools and rivers visited by big animals. Bursting up from the water, it seizes its victim, drags it under, and waits for it to drown before tearing it apart.

SALTWATER CROCODILE

Crocodylus porosus

Location: India to Australia

Length: Up to 7 m (23 ft)

Named for its habitat of coastal mangrove swamps and tidal estuaries, the saltwater crocodile regularly swims out to sea to reach other shores. The biggest crocodilian, it is capable of killing almost any animal that enters its territory.

SPECTACLED CAIMAN

Caiman crocodilus

Location: Central and South America

Length: Up to 2.5 m (8¼ ft)

This is the most common of the South American caimans, which are closely related to alligators. A generalist hunter, it mainly eats fish, but will also tackle mammals up to the size of wild pigs.

AMERICAN ALLIGATOR

Alligator mississippiensis

Location: Southern USA

Length: Up to 5 m (16½ ft)

Alligators have broad snouts, and their lower teeth are hidden when their jaws are closed. This species is the best known; ranging from Texas to Carolina, it lives in swamps and rivers, and preys on fish, turtles, mammals, and birds.

GHARIAL

Gavialis gangeticus

Location: India, Pakistan

Length: Up to 7 m (23 ft)

The very long, slim snout of the endangered gharial is an adaptation for catching fish. It has up to 110 sharp teeth, ideal for piercing and gripping the slippery bodies of its prey. A mature male has an unusual swelling, or boss, on the end of his snout, known as a ghara.

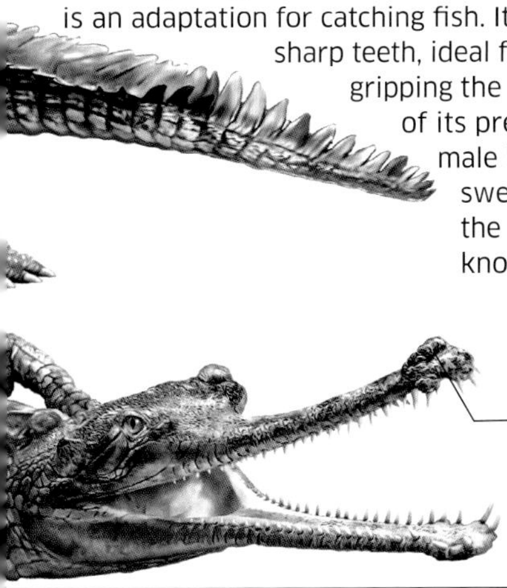

Male adornment The ghara may help the male to win a mate.

AFRICAN SLENDER-SNOUTED CROCODILE

Mecistops cataphractus

Location: Central and west Africa

Length: Up to 4 m (13 ft)

Like the gharial, this species is specialized for eating fish, using its slender snout to sweep through the water. But this crocodile also uses its snout to probe riverbank burrows or exposed tree roots for other prey.

DWARF CROCODILE

Osteolaemus tetraspis

Location: Central and west Africa

Length: Up to 2 m (6½ ft)

The smallest of the crocodiles, this shy, nocturnal reptile has a relatively short, blunt snout and is heavily armoured – possibly for protection from bigger crocodiles. It feeds mainly on fish, especially during the floods of the tropical rainy season, but also eats frogs and crustaceans.

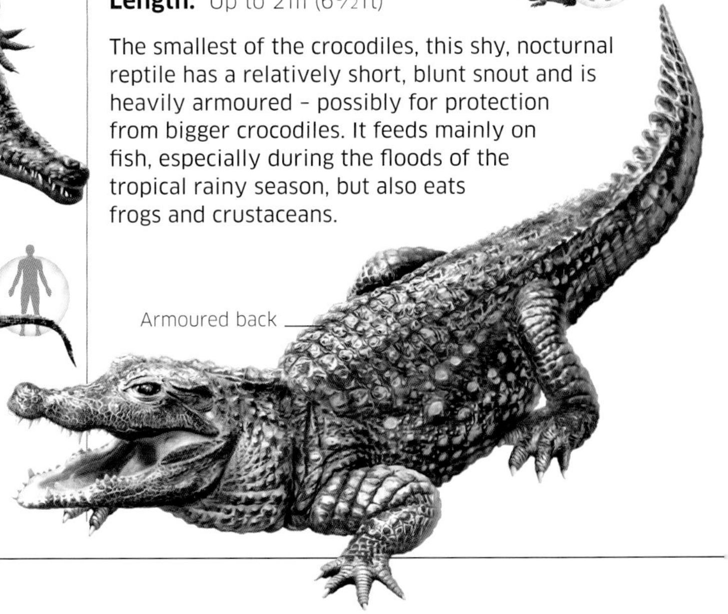

BIRDS

With their often dazzling plumage and mastery of the air, birds are the most instantly attractive animals. Many also sing, filling the air with music during the spring breeding season. Highly adapted for flight, they are among the most specialized vertebrates, but also some of the most successful.

WHAT IS A BIRD?

Since the 1990s, the discovery of many miraculously preserved fossils has proved beyond doubt that birds are feathered dinosaurs – relatives of two-legged hunters such as *Velociraptor*. Birds inherited their feathers from such animals, along with their warm blood and super-efficient lungs. These enabled the first primitive birds to take to the air more than 140 million years ago, and by 66 million years ago they had evolved into birds very like the ones that fly around us today.

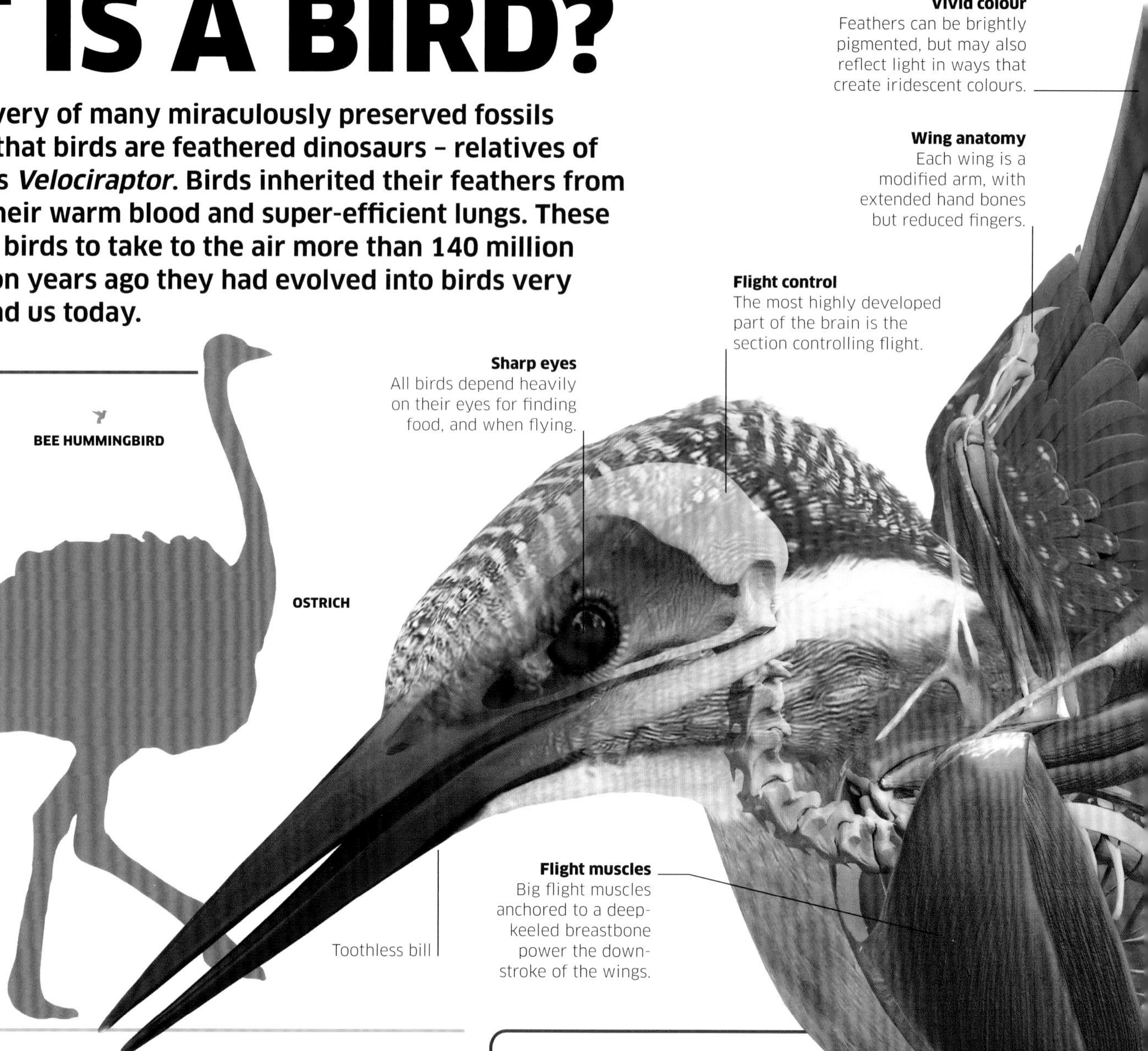

BIRD VARIETY

There are well over 10,000 species of birds, belonging to 28 major groups, or orders. One order, the perching birds, accounts for more than half of the species; other orders include distinctive birds such as owls, parrots, and birds of prey.

Biggest and smallest
The biggest bird is the flightless ostrich, which can weigh more than eight times as much as the heaviest flying bird. The smallest bird, the bee hummingbird, is little bigger than the ostrich's eye.

BILL SHAPES

Bird bills have evolved in different ways to deal with many types of food and ways of feeding, from sipping sweet flower nectar to tearing prey apart.

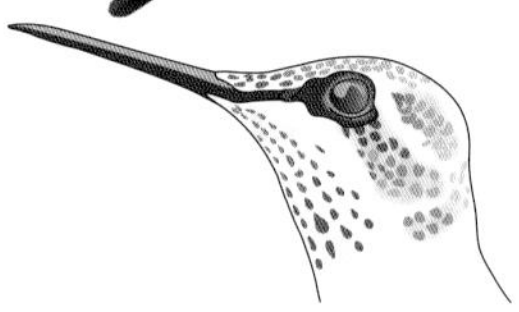

Nectar-gatherer
A hummingbird's bill is a precision tool, adapted for slipping into narrow, tubular flowers to extract sugary nectar.

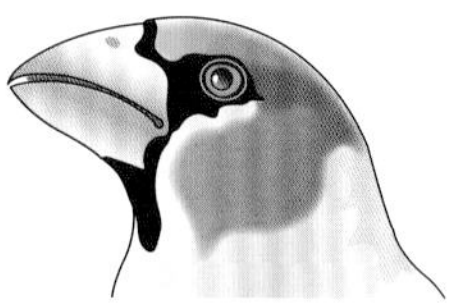

Nut-cracker
Seed-eaters have extra-strong bills. The powerful bill of the hawfinch can crack a cherry stone.

Butchery tool
The hooked bill of this white-tailed eagle is used for stripping meat from the bones of fish, birds, and mammals.

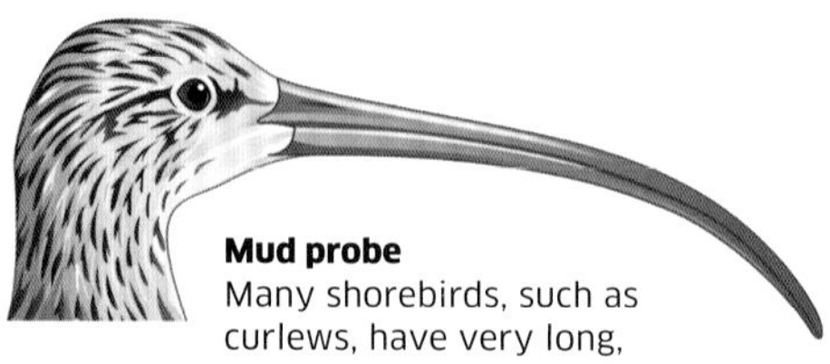

Mud probe
Many shorebirds, such as curlews, have very long, sensitive bills for probing deep into soft mud in search of prey.

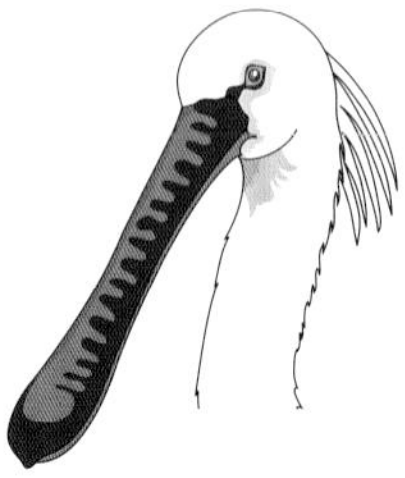

Water-sifter
The spoonbill sweeps its highly specialized bill from side to side through shallow water to sift out small animals.

AMAZING LUNGS

A bird's lungs are relatively rigid structures with air tubes passing right through them. The tubes lead to many balloon-like air sacs that pump air through the lung tissue. The system is far more efficient than mammal lungs, absorbing the extra oxygen essential for powering the flight muscles.

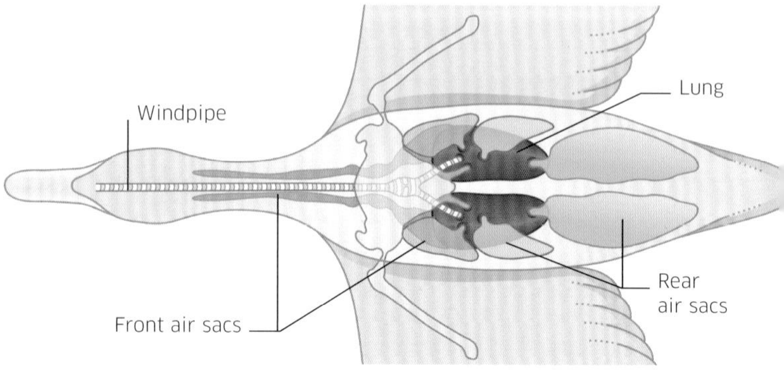

Inside a bird

The strong yet light skeleton, very powerful muscles, and lightweight feathers of this river kingfisher are all specialized for flight – the feature that has made birds masters of the air.

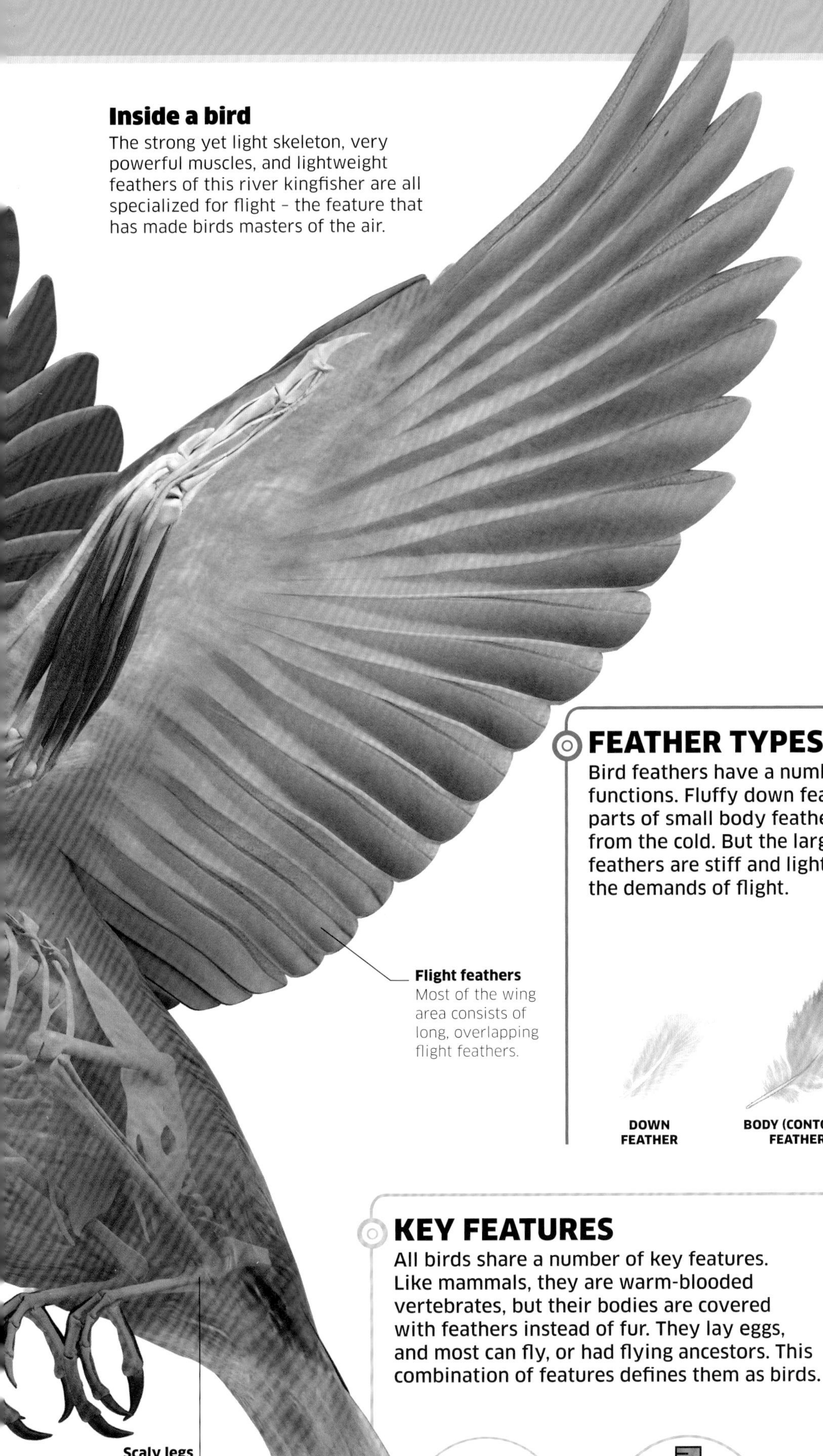

Flight feathers
Most of the wing area consists of long, overlapping flight feathers.

Scaly legs
The legs have scaly skin, and sharp-clawed feet for gripping and perching.

Tail
Like the wings, the tail is mostly made up of feathers. It is used for steering, and as an air brake.

NESTS AND EGGS

Most birds build nests where they can lay their eggs, keep them warm until they hatch, and then care for their young. Nests range from scrapes on the ground to elaborate constructions woven from a variety of materials. Some are hidden in holes, while others are built in trees or on ledges.

REED BUNTING NEST

FEATHER TYPES

Bird feathers have a number of different functions. Fluffy down feathers, and the downy parts of small body feathers provide insulation from the cold. But the larger wing and tail feathers are stiff and lightweight, ideal for the demands of flight.

DOWN FEATHER

BODY (CONTOUR) FEATHER

FLIGHT FEATHER

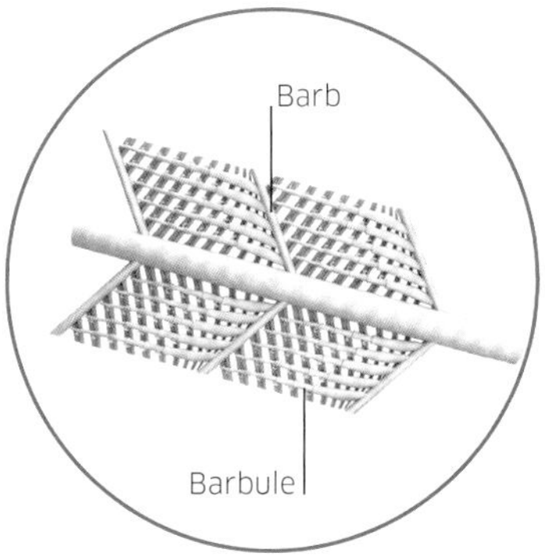

Feather structure
Each branching barb of a flight feather is fringed with hooked barbules that zip together to form a flat surface known as a vane.

KEY FEATURES

All birds share a number of key features. Like mammals, they are warm-blooded vertebrates, but their bodies are covered with feathers instead of fur. They lay eggs, and most can fly, or had flying ancestors. This combination of features defines them as birds.

WE OFTEN THINK OF BIRDS AS **FEATHER-BRAINED,** BUT IN FACT SOME CROWS AND PARROTS **ARE AS INTELLIGENT AS APES AND DOLPHINS.**

Vertebrates
A bird's body is supported by an internal skeleton.

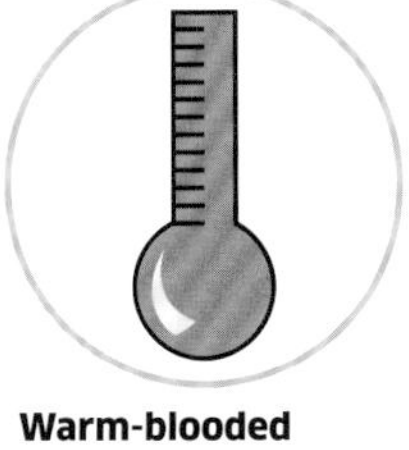

Warm-blooded
Birds generate their own body heat in all environments.

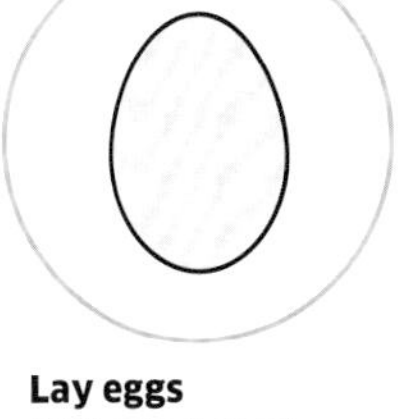

Lay eggs
All birds breed by laying eggs with hard shells.

Most fly
Some birds spend most of their lives in the air.

Feathered
Feathers retain heat and enable birds to fly.

1.4 kg (3 lb) – the **weight** of a single **ostrich egg**, heavier than at least **20 hen's eggs**.

Deadly enemy
The cheetah is one of the few hunters that can overtake an ostrich.

Sun shades
An ostrich uses its wings for dancing displays, and to shade its young.

BIRDS
OSTRICH
Struthio camelus
Location: Africa
Height: Up to 2.8 m (9 ft)
Diet: Small plants and animals

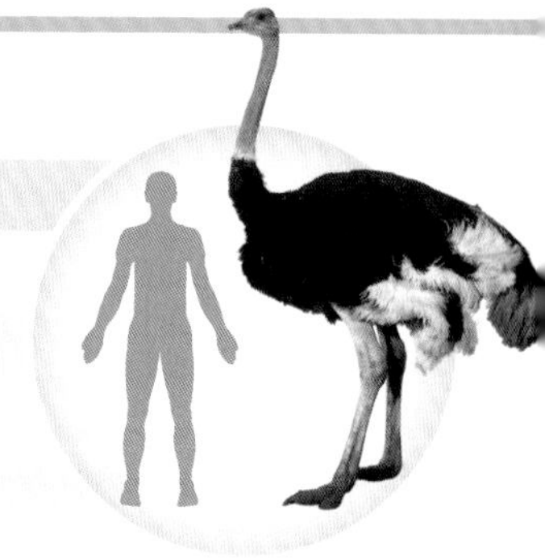

Ratites

The huge, spectacular ostrich is the biggest of the ratites – a group of flightless birds that rely on their running speed to escape predators. Some are also notorious for their ferocity when cornered.

Although ratites do have wings, they cannot fly because their wings have soft, fluffy, or hair-like feathers instead of stiff flight feathers. Their relatively weak wing muscles are attached to a flat breastbone instead of the deep-keeled breastbone found in other birds. They are thought to share a common ancestor with the tinamous – a group of ground-dwelling birds that are able to fly, although only over short distances.

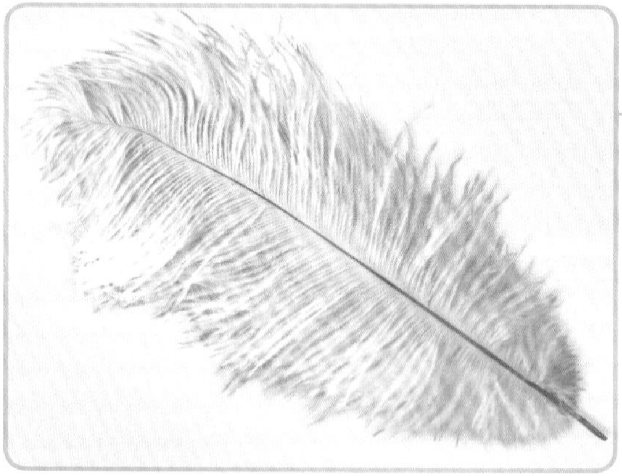

Fluffy feathers
Ostrich feathers are fluffy and soft, and resemble the insulating down feathers of other birds. They lack the rows of hooked barbules that zip together to form stiff vanes on flight feathers.

Powerful legs
Very long legs allow the ostrich to outrun most of its enemies.

Two toes
Each foot has two toes, with a big hoof-like nail on the large inner toe.

Ostrich
The largest of all birds, the ostrich is specialized for roaming the open grassland and deserts of tropical Africa in search of scarce food. The black-and-white males mate with up to seven browner females, which all lay their eggs in one communal nest. The male helps to incubate the eggs.

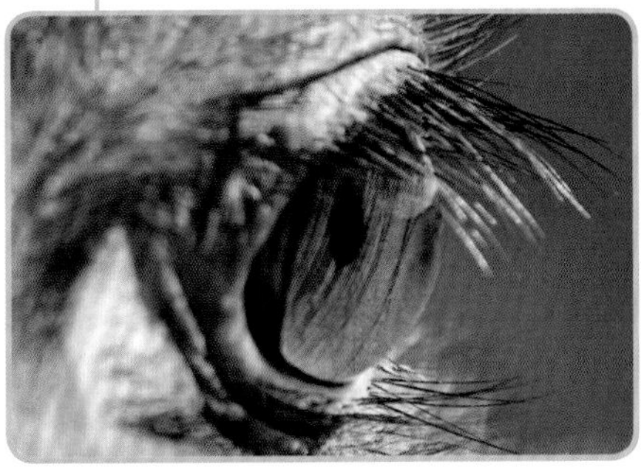

Huge eye
The eyes of an ostrich are enormous – each eyeball is up to 5 cm (2 in) wide. Like nearly all birds it relies on its acute sense of sight to locate food, detect danger, and find breeding partners.

Long neck
The ostrich has a good view of approaching danger thanks to the length of its neck.

An ostrich cannot chew, so it **swallows stones** to help its muscular gizzard grind up its food.

GREATER RHEA

Rhea americana

Location: South America

Height: Up to 1.5 m (5 ft)

This is the South American counterpart of the ostrich, with a similar way of life. It lives in flocks on open grassland and feeds on a variety of plant and animal foods.

SOUTHERN CASSOWARY

Casuarius casuarius

Location: Indonesia, New Guinea, Northern Australia

Height: Up to 1.8 m (5½ ft)

Living in tropical rainforest, the big, powerful cassowary has sharp, spear-like claws that can be dangerous to anyone who comes near them. The female is more colourful than the male, with a taller casque (helmet-like crest) on her bill.

EMU

Dromaius novaehollandiae

Location: Australia

Height: Up to 1.9 m (6¼ ft)

The Australian equivalent of the ostrich, the emu wanders nomadically over most of the continent. It prefers wooded country with plentiful food, but can survive for long periods without eating.

SOUTHERN BROWN KIWI

Apteryx australis

Location: South Island, New Zealand

Height: Up to 65 cm (25½ in)

Much smaller than other ratites, the kiwis of New Zealand have fur-like plumage. At night they use their long bills to probe the ground for invertebrates.

ELEGANT CRESTED TINAMOU

Eudromia elegans

Location: Southern Chile to Argentina

Height: Up to 41 cm (16 in)

The tinamous of South and Central America are now thought to be part of the ratite group of birds, even though they are able to fly. This species lives in flocks in the cold, dry scrublands of Patagonia.

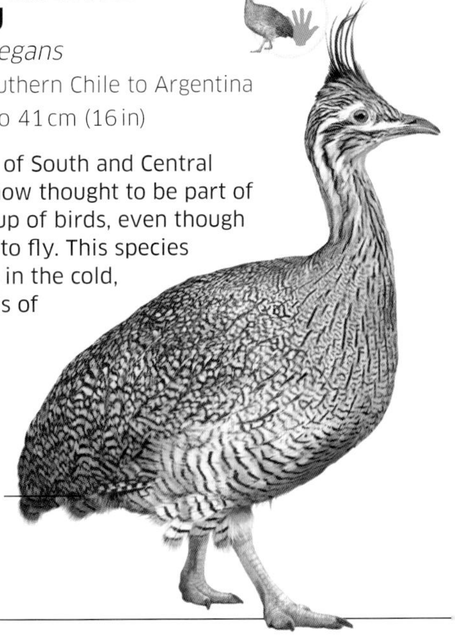

50 The **number of years** an emperor penguin **can live**.

A **breeding emperor penguin** often has to **walk 100 km (62 miles)** or more across the ice **to feed in open water**.

Emperor penguin

The emperor is a sleek hunter that dives under the Antarctic ice to catch fish and squid. Emperors breed on sea ice, the female laying a single egg then returning to open waters to feed. The male incubates the egg, waiting patiently for his mate to return before making the long journey across the ice to feed.

Emperors lay their eggs earlier than other penguins so that the chicks can develop all through spring and summer, before winter sets in again. Smaller penguins develop more quickly, so they can wait until after the spring thaw to breed and lay their eggs on rocky shores.

Excellent insulation
The emperor has adapted to withstand extreme cold, with an extra-thick layer of insulating fat, or blubber, beneath the skin. Its feathers are short and stiff, and overlap to form a waterproof covering that keeps out the cold.

An emperor penguin may dive to **500 m (1,640 ft)** or more to reach the sea bed.

Barbed tongue
An emperor penguin preys on a variety of small fish, squid, and shrimp-like krill, using its swimming speed to pursue and catch each animal individually. Its tongue bristles with rear-facing barbs that stop the prey escaping before the penguin can swallow it.

Flightless wings
The penguin's wings are adapted for swimming, acting as stiff flippers to propel the penguin through the water.

Downy chick
When it hatches, the chick is covered with a thick coat of silvery-grey down feathers.

First feathers
The downy feathers will be replaced after about three months by the chick's juvenile plumage.

BIRDS
EMPEROR PENGUIN
Aptenodytes forsteri
Location: Antarctica
Height: 1.2 m (4 ft)
Diet: Fish, squid, and krill

Standing tall
On land, the emperor walks upright with a highly energy-efficient, waddling gait.

Colourful bill
The lower mandible of the bill can be orange, pink, or lilac.

Streamlined body
The emperor's body is long and tapered at each end, forming a streamlined shape for underwater swimming.

Webbed feet
The scaly, webbed feet steer the penguin when it swims underwater.

Winter vigil

All winter, the male guards the egg. It sits on his feet, covered with a fold of skin to prevent it from freezing. While the male incubates the egg, he does not eat, losing up to half his body weight over two months.

In their element

Like all penguins, emperors are superb swimmers. They are fast, with a top speed of 24 km/h (15 mph), and can stay underwater for up to around 20 minutes.

Keeping out the cold

To survive the bitter Antarctic winter, male emperors form tight huddles of up to 5,000 birds. They constantly shuffle around so that each penguin takes a turn on the colder, windy side of the huddle.

The **nearest relatives of penguins** are the **albatrosses** and **shearwaters**.

22 The number of **minutes** a **diving penguin** can **hold its breath** underwater.

Penguins

Highly adapted for hunting underwater, penguins are the most specialized of ocean birds. Most live in the far south, in some of the coldest waters on Earth.

Penguins are built for swimming, with streamlined bodies, stiff flippers, and webbed feet at the very back of the body, a position ideal for underwater efficiency. But these adaptations make them awkward and vulnerable on land, so most species breed in colonies on remote shores where there are no land predators.

KING PENGUIN

Aptenodytes patagonicus

Location: Sub-Antarctic islands

Height: 95 cm (37½ in)

Very like the emperor penguin, but slightly smaller, the king penguin breeds in vast colonies on sub-Antarctic islands. It feeds mainly on fish and squid.

CHINSTRAP PENGUIN

Pygoscelis antarcticus

Location: Antarctic coasts and islands

Height: 68 cm (26¾ in)

Several million chinstrap penguins breed on Antarctic coasts and nearby islands. Some island colonies are on the slopes of active volcanoes, where the warm rock helps incubate their eggs.

GENTOO PENGUIN

Pygoscelis papua

Location: Sub-Antarctic islands

Height: 81 cm (32 in)

This is the third-largest species of penguin and has an unusually long tail. It breeds in small colonies on the islands around Antarctica, as far north as the Falklands.

ADÉLIE PENGUIN

Pygoscelis adeliae

Location: Antarctica

Height: 70 cm (27½ in)

This small penguin breeds further south than any other penguin except the emperor, forming large colonies on rocky Antarctic shores that become free of snow in spring and summer. It feeds mainly on krill, often resting on drifting ice floes and icebergs between hunting trips.

Some Adélie penguin colonies contain **more than 250,000** breeding pairs.

GALÁPAGOS PENGUIN

Spheniscus mendiculus

Location: Galápagos Islands

Height: 50 cm (19¾ in)

The Galápagos penguin is the only penguin that lives north of the equator. It nests in rocky crevices and feeds on small tropical fish. However, its species is endangered and fewer than 2,000 remain.

HUMBOLDT PENGUIN

Spheniscus humboldti

Location: South America

Height: 68 cm (26¾ in)

Like the Galápagos penguin, this species breeds on warm shores but hunts in the cold waters of ocean currents flowing north from Antarctica. It raises its young in burrows or coastal caves, to shelter from the tropical sunshine.

AFRICAN PENGUIN

Spheniscus demersus

Location: South Africa

Height: 70 cm (27½ in)

Also known as the jackass penguin because of its loud, braying call, this penguin hunts in the food-rich waters of the cold Benguela Current that flows along the west coast of Africa.

ROCKHOPPER PENGUIN

Eudyptes chrysocome

Location: Southern seas and islands

Height: 55 cm (21¾ in)

The rockhopper is named for its agility on rocky shores, where it often scales steep rock faces to reach its nesting sites. It is one of several related species that have flamboyant crests of yellow feathers above their eyes.

YELLOW-EYED PENGUIN

Megadyptes antipodes

Location: New Zealand

Height: 76 cm (30 in)

Found only on the southern shores and islands of New Zealand, this species is unusual, because it nests in isolated pairs in scrub or forest, instead of in coastal colonies. However, many of its breeding sites have been destroyed, and it is now very rare.

LITTLE PENGUIN

Eudyptula minor

Location: New Zealand, Australia

Height: 40 cm (15¾ in)

The smallest penguin, this species hunts in shallow coastal seas, returning to shore each night. It nests in burrows and caves – sometimes in pairs, but also in large colonies.

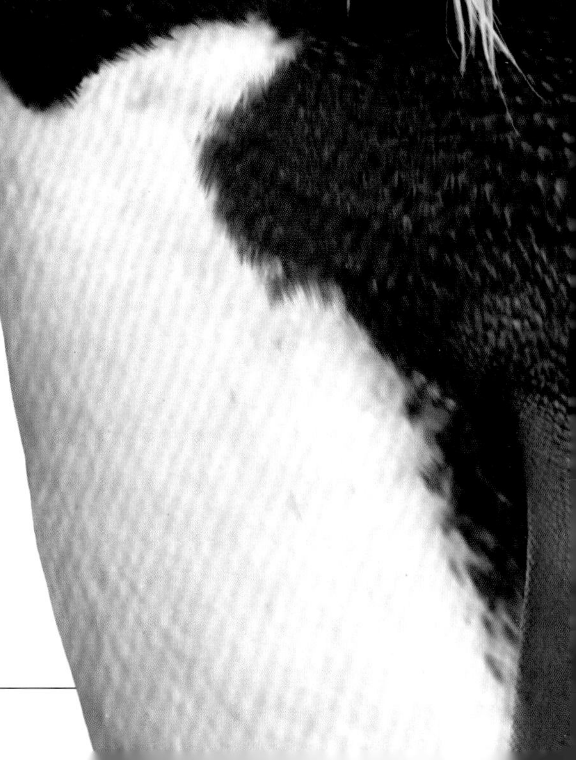

The **ancestors of chickens** were first **domesticated** more than **5,000 years ago**.

BIRDS

INDIAN PEAFOWL

Pavo cristatus

Location: India

Length: Up to 2.2 m (7¼ ft)

Diet: Seeds, fruit, insects

In flight
Their enormous fan of plumes is a slight hindrance, but peacocks can fly well enough to reach a safe perch in a tree to spend the night. In their native forests this is vital to their survival.

Glorious plumes
The "tail" is actually made up of elongated feathers growing from the male's back.

Subtle colouring
Female peafowl have far less dramatic plumage, and a shorter train of feathers.

Foraging tools
The bird uses its strong feet to scratch in the soil for insects and seeds.

Indian peafowl

The peafowl is a type of pheasant that has the most dazzling of courtship displays. The vividly coloured male, or peacock, woos the female by spreading a spectacular fan of iridescent feathers, dotted with big glowing "eyes". If the female is sufficiently impressed she may allow him to mate.

MALLEE FOWL

Leipoa ocellata

Location: Australia

Length: Up to 61 cm (24 in)

This is one of the megapodes – birds that build mounds of warm, decaying vegetation covered with soil to act as incubators for their eggs. The male regularly tests the temperature, and either ventilates the mound, or adds soil to retain heat.

GREAT CURASSOW

Crax rubra

Location: Central America

Length: Up to 92 cm (36¼ in)

The great curassow is a poor flier, spending much of its time foraging on the forest floor for fruit and small animals, but despite this it roosts high in the canopy. Destruction of its tropical forest habitat has now made it rare.

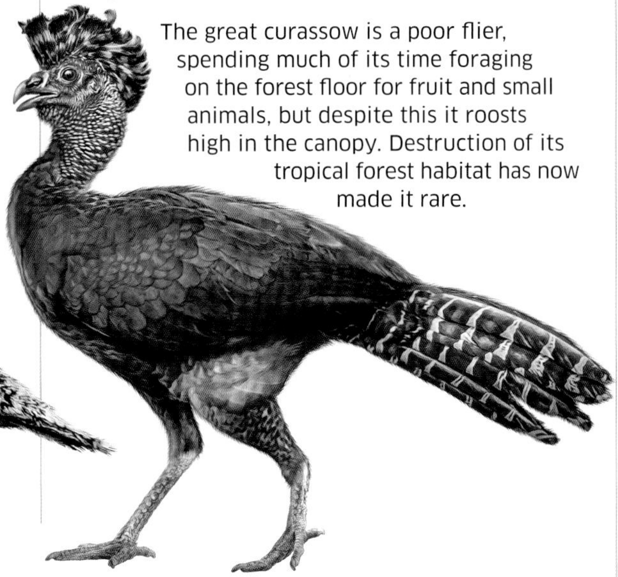

WILD TURKEY

Meleagris gallopavo

Location: North America

Length: Up to 1.2 m (4 ft)

Like the peacock, the male wild turkey is quite different from the female, and is a huge, highly ornamented bird that performs elaborate strutting displays accompanied by gobbling calls. It eats seeds, fruit, and insects.

GREATER PRAIRIE CHICKEN

Tympanuchus cupido

Location: North America

Length: Up to 47 cm (18½ in)

Gamebirds

Many of these plump, ground-feeding birds have been hunted for food for centuries, which is why they are called gamebirds. But some like the peafowl also have spectacularly beautiful plumage.

Pheasants, partridges, turkeys, grouse, and their relatives are mainly forest or woodland birds that live on the ground and rarely fly. Many have a polygamous breeding system, with each extravagantly ornamented male courting as many females as possible. In most species, females nest and raise their young alone, which is possible because the chicks can feed themselves almost as soon as they hatch.

Adapted for life on grasslands, this species of grouse has spectacular males that compete to mate with as many females as possible. Inflating their orange neck sacs, the males give booming cries while performing stamping dances.

GREY PARTRIDGE

Perdix perdix

Location: Europe

Length: Up to 31 cm (12¼ in)

Unlike many gamebirds, the grey partridge has just one mate during the breeding season, and the sexes look very similar. A bird of open country, it was once common on farmland. But it has been badly hit by the use of farm pesticides that kill the insects its chicks eat.

RED JUNGLEFOWL

Gallus gallus

Location: Southeast Asia

Length: Up to 78 cm (30¾ in)

This exotic-looking jungle pheasant is the ancestor of the domestic chicken. In the wild it forages for seeds and insects in bamboo forests, clearings, and nearby scrubland, often in flocks of up to 50. Each male courts and mates with several females.

Lethal weapons
Each of the male's legs is armed with a sharp spur, which is used in fights with rivals.

A golden eagle can live for up to 20 years in the wild, and more than 40 in captivity.

Eagle eyes
Relative to its head, the eagle's eyes are huge. They detect more colour, and can see up to five times more detail than the human eye. This enables the eagle to target prey from more than 3 km ($1\frac{3}{4}$ miles) away.

Golden crown
The eagle gets its name from the golden crown and neck feathers of the mature adult bird.

Lethal talons
The eagle's main weapons are its talons – big, powerful feet armed with very long, sharp claws. The eagle thrusts them forwards as it slams into its prey, then squeezes them together in a lethal grip. The victim is often killed outright when the claws pierce its body and vital organs.

Fanned tail
Just before impact with its prey, the eagle fans its long tail to slow down.

The golden eagle **rarely makes a sound,** just a **thin whistle** while it is in flight.

Female golden eagles are slightly **larger than the males.**

BIRDS

GOLDEN EAGLE

Aquila chrysaetos

Location: N. America, Europe, Asia, N. Africa

Length: Up to 90 cm (35½ in)

Diet: Small mammals and carrion

Flight feathers
When the wingtip feathers are spread out, they help to stop the bird from stalling at slow speeds.

Golden eagle

This magnificent bird is the most widespread of the eagles, and one of the biggest. Soaring over open country on broad wings, it scans the ground below for prey to seize in its powerful talons.

Eagles are the largest raptors – birds that live by killing and eating smaller birds, mammals, and other vertebrates. They catch and kill their prey with their clawed feet, and use their hooked bills to tear it apart. Some eagles specialize in catching fish, but the golden eagle usually hunts rabbits, hares, and big ground-feeding birds. It can soar for hours, circling on rising air currents with its wings held in a slight v-shape, before targeting prey and plunging into the attack.

A golden eagle pair will mate for life and return to the same nest year after year.

Moving target
Hares and rabbits are common prey, but the eagle will even take young deer.

Killer instinct

Golden eagles pair for life, and build nests on cliffs and trees. The female usually lays two eggs. The first to be laid hatches first, so one chick is older and usually stronger than the other. If food is short, the stronger chick kills the other one so it can eat its share, ensuring that at least one chick survives.

ANDEAN CONDOR

Vultur gryphus

Location: South America

Length: Up to 1.1 m (3½ ft)

The biggest vulture, and largest bird of prey, the magnificent Andean condor searches for food among the mountains by riding updraughts on huge outspread wings. It may soar for an hour or more without making a single wingbeat.

OSPREY

Pandion haliaetus

Location: Worldwide except Antarctica

Length: Up to 58 cm (22¾ in)

The osprey is a specialized fish hawk that plunges into rivers, lakes, and shallow seas to seize fish in its talons. Its feet have spiny soles that help the bird grip the slippery, struggling fish as it surges up from the water and carry its prey to a perch to eat.

SNAIL KITE

Rostrhamus sociabilis

Location: N., S., and C. America

Length: Up to 43 cm (17 in)

This slow-flying specialist feeds almost exclusively on freshwater snails, which it plucks from marshes and scissors out of their shells with its long-hooked bill. It lives mainly in Central and South American wetlands, but also in the Florida Everglades.

BALD EAGLE

Haliaeetus leucocephalus

Location: North America

Length: Up to 90 cm (35½ in)

Familiar as the "American eagle", the national symbol of the United States, this powerful hunter feeds mainly on fish but also takes other prey. Although it ranges as far south as Mexico, most bald eagles live in the far north, in Alaska and western Canada.

A bald eagle builds the **largest nest** of any bird. It can weigh over 2,700 kg (6,000 lbs) – more than a rhinoceros.

Hawks and eagles

Birds of prey are the top predators of the bird world – powerful fliers with sharp claws and hooked bills that attack and eat other animals. Most of them are active hunters, but a few are adapted for scavenging carcasses of dead remains.

Ranging from sparrow-sized falcons to gigantic condors, birds of prey (also known as raptors) are some of the most spectacular and exciting of all birds. They include powerful eagles that can rip monkeys out of trees, fast-flying falcons that pursue and kill other birds in flight, super-agile forest hawks, specialized fish hunters, owl-like harriers, and soaring, scavenging vultures.

A **diving peregrine falcon** can reach a speed of **322 km/h (200 mph)** or more.

The **secretary bird** sometimes kills snakes by **leaping on their backs and breaking their necks.**

An **Andean condor** may have a **wingspan** of **more than 3 m (9¾ ft)**.

PALM-NUT VULTURE

Gypohierax angolensis

Location: Tropical Africa

Length: Up to 60 cm (23½ in)

Technically a bird of prey and closely related to the scavenging vultures, this big, black-and-white bird feeds mainly on the fruit of oil palm trees. It uses its hooked bill to tear into the husk, which is rich in nutritious oil.

LAMMERGEIER

Gypaetus barbatus

Location: Eurasia, Africa

Length: Up to 1.1 m (3½ ft)

Sometimes called the bearded vulture because of the dark bristles flanking its bill, the lammergeier usually lives in rocky, mountainous habitats. It is well known for seizing large bones and dropping them onto rocks to break them open and expose the bone marrow inside.

NORTHERN HARRIER

Circus cyaneus

Location: Eurasia, N. and C. America

Length: Up to 51 cm (20 in)

Harriers are long-winged, slender birds that specialize in flying low over open ground, looking for small prey. The male northern harrier is a lovely dove-grey colour.

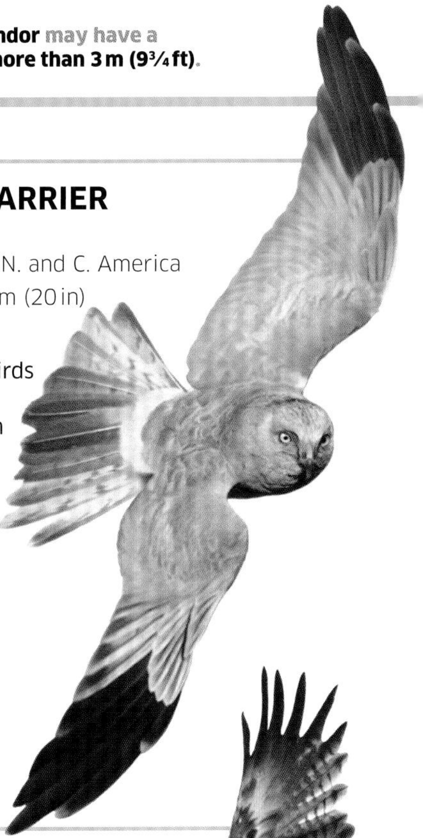

NORTHERN GOSHAWK

Accipiter gentilis

Location: North America, Eurasia

Length: Up to 66 cm (26 in)

This is one of the biggest forest hawks – relatively short-winged, long-tailed hunters adapted for fast, swerving flight through trees. It uses its flying skill to snatch squirrels and birds from their perches, and other prey such as pheasants from the ground.

HARPY EAGLE

Harpia harpyja

Location: Tropical America

Length: Up to 1.1 m (3½ ft)

One of the world's most powerful birds of prey, this huge tropical forest eagle uses its formidable talons to rip monkeys and sloths from their perches in the crowns of rainforest trees.

WEDGE-TAILED EAGLE

Aquila audax

Location: Australia, New Guinea

Length: Up to 1 m (3¼ ft)

Identifiable by its pointed tail, this is the biggest bird of prey in Australia. It hunts by soaring over the plains or watching from a perch, and is big enough to seize a small kangaroo.

SECRETARY BIRD

Sagittarius serpentarius

Location: Tropical Africa

Length: Up to 1.5 m (5 ft)

The secretary bird stalks the African savannas on very long legs, using its feet to catch and kill small mammals, insects, and snakes.

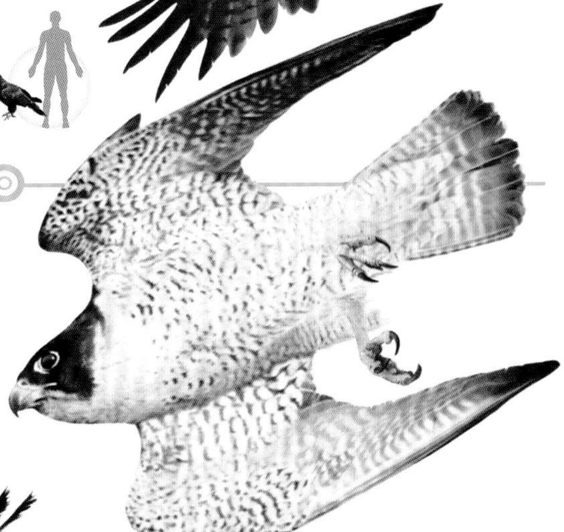

PEREGRINE FALCON

Falco peregrinus

Location: Almost worldwide

Length: Up to 48 cm (19 in)

Most falcons specialize in hunting airborne prey, including insects and bats. The peregrine attacks birds, plummeting from a height on half-folded wings to rip into its victims with its talons.

Some **African grey parrots** are **able to copy human speech** to ask for things they want.

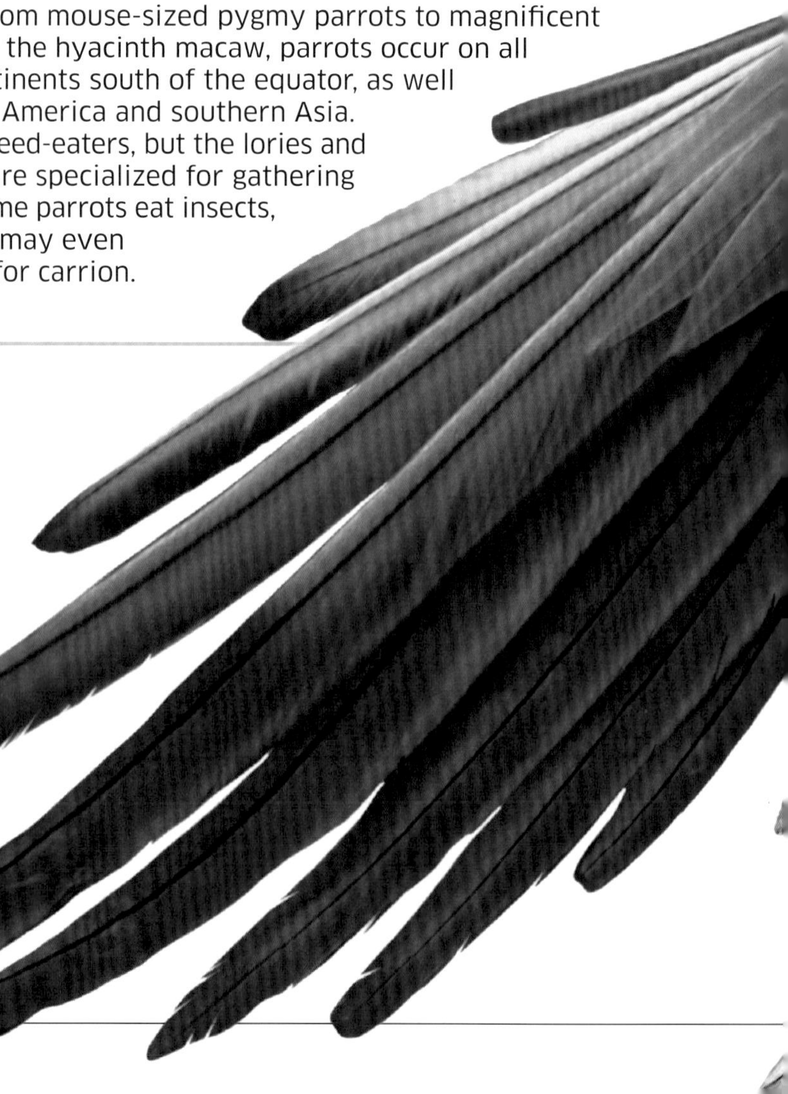

Parrots

Celebrated for their intelligence and ability to mimic human speech, parrots are colourful birds with powerful, hooked bills for cracking seeds and nuts. Most parrots live in tropical forests and grasslands, often in large flocks, but a few are now very rare.

Ranging from mouse-sized pygmy parrots to magnificent giants like the hyacinth macaw, parrots occur on all warm continents south of the equator, as well as Central America and southern Asia. Most are seed-eaters, but the lories and lorikeets are specialized for gathering nectar. Some parrots eat insects, and a few may even scavenge for carrion.

GALAH

Eolophus roseicapilla

Location: Australia

Length: Up to 36 cm (14 in)

Widespread in grassland and woodland across Australia, this is one of the crested parrots known as cockatoos. It feeds on small seeds and grain, including wheat. It forages in flocks, but forms lifelong breeding pairs that nest in holes in trees.

RAINBOW LORIKEET

Trichoglossus moluccanus

Location: Australia, New Guinea

Length: Up to 30 cm (11¾ in)

Screeching flocks of rainbow lorikeets forage together for food in the forests of Australia and New Guinea. A lorikeet's tongue has a brush-like tip for gathering nectar, but it will also eat fruit and insects. At dusk the birds gather in huge communal roosts to spend the night.

KAKAPO

Strigops habroptila

Location: New Zealand

Length: Up to 60 cm (23½ in)

The kakapo is a giant, flightless ground parrot that evolved in New Zealand at a time when there were no predators to threaten it. The introduction of stoats, rats, and cats led to its near-extinction, and it now survives in forest and scrubland on just a few remote islands.

BUDGERIGAR

Melopsittacus undulatus

Location: Australia

Length: Up to 18 cm (7 in)

Wild budgerigars live in big, nomadic flocks on the dry grasslands of Australia, moving from place to place in search of good crops of seeds. They breed in tree holes, whenever and wherever food is plentiful, and a pair may raise several broods of young in a good year.

Mobile tongue
The hyacinth macaw feeds mainly on palm nuts, cracking their tough shells with its stout bill and using its mobile tongue to extract the kernels. A parrot's tongue is strong and very sensitive, so the bird can use it to explore its environment in the same way that we use our fingers.

Hyacinth macaw
The spectacular hyacinth macaw is the longest and largest of the parrots, though the flightless kakapo is heavier. It lives in the tropical lowland forests of Brazil and nearby regions, where it forages for food in small flocks, and breeds in tree holes.

Agile foot
The feet are very mobile, with two toes pointing forwards, and two pointing back.

BIRDS

HYACINTH MACAW

Anodorhynchus hyacinthinus

Location: South America

Length: Up to 1 m ($3^{1}/_{4}$ ft)

Diet: Nuts, seeds, fruit

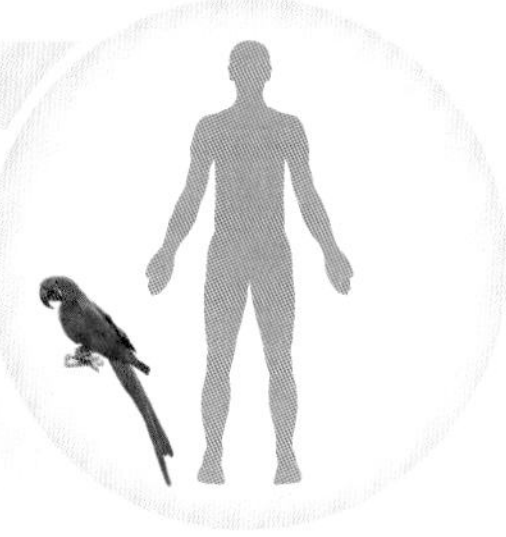

ECLECTUS PARROT

Eclectus roratus

Location: Australasia

Length: Up to 43 cm (17 in)

Male and female eclectus parrots are so different that they were once thought to be separate species. While the male is emerald green with patches of red and blue, the female is crimson with a blue belly. They live in the tropical forests of New Guinea and nearby regions.

CONGO AFRICAN GREY PARROT

Psittacus erithacus

Location: Africa

Length: Up to 33 cm (13 in)

This species is well known for its intelligence and vocal mimicry. In the wild the Congo African grey forages in small groups for food such as fruit and nuts, but roosts in large flocks. Like other parrots, it uses its bill as a climbing aid.

Wandering albatrosses **really do wander**; one bird was recorded travelling **6,000 km (3,730 miles)** in 12 days.

Dynamic soaring

To fly long distances over the ocean, the albatross angles its outspread wings into the powerful wind to gain lift and height, then turns and glides downwind to cover distance. By repeating this, the bird can stay in the air for days.

Lonely chick

Each pair of albatrosses builds a nest of mud and vegetation on a ridge near the shore. After their single egg hatches the parents take turns to brood the chick for six weeks. Then they both leave to hunt at sea, returning to feed the chick only at rare intervals.

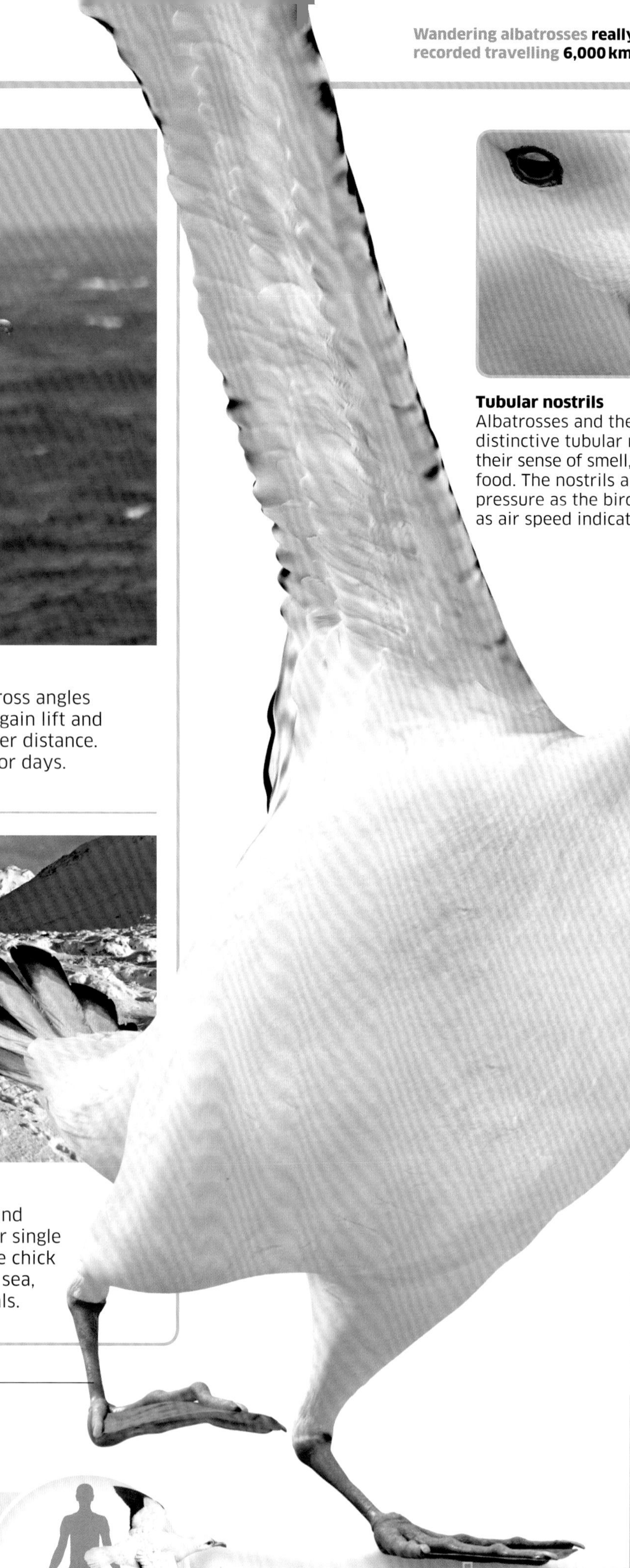

Sturdy legs
Strong legs and wide feet assist the albatross in landing and swimming.

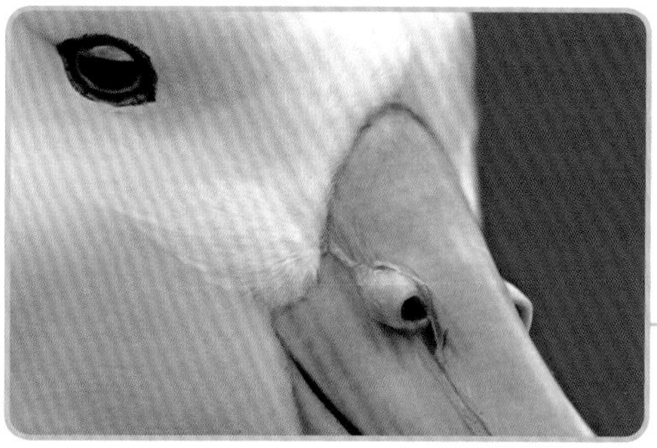

Tubular nostrils

Albatrosses and their close relatives have distinctive tubular nostrils that enhance their sense of smell, helping them find food. The nostrils also detect air pressure as the bird flies, acting as air speed indicators.

Webbed feet

Broad webbed feet allow the albatross to swim like a duck. It may even make shallow dives beneath the surface to seize particularly tempting prey.

BIRDS

WANDERING ALBATROSS

Diomedea exulans

Location: Southern Ocean

Length: Up to 1.3 m (4¼ ft)

Diet: Small marine animals

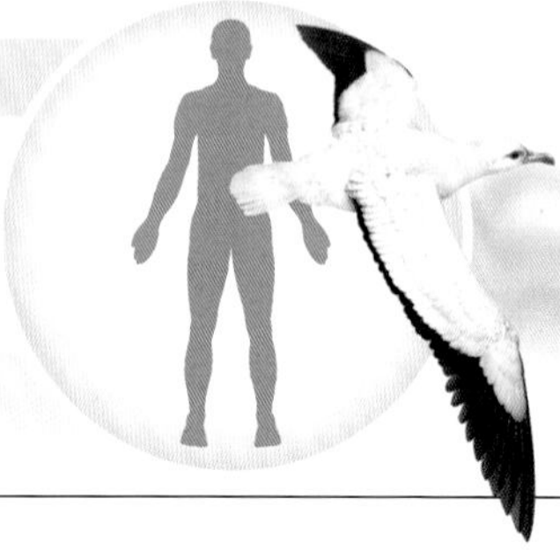

Wandering albatross

In summer, the bleak, windswept islands around Antarctica become theatres for the spectacular courtship dances of wandering albatrosses, as they return to the islands to breed.

Equipped with the longest wings of any bird, this seabird is specialized for life in the air, soaring for days on end over the vast, icy Southern Ocean. It flies low, watching for small fish, squid, and shrimp-like krill to snatch from the surface. The albatross may land on the sea to gather food, but its long wings are not built for easy take-off, and getting airborne again is hard work.

Waterbirds, seabirds, and shorebirds

A huge variety of birds are specialized for feeding in or near water. Some hunt at sea, while many more feed on tidal shores or in freshwater wetlands.

Some of these birds have webbed feet and other adaptations for efficient swimming. Others have long legs, for wading in deep water. Many have bills that are modified for special feeding techniques.

GREAT CRESTED GREBE

Podiceps cristatus

Location: Eurasia, Africa, Australia

Length: Up to 51 cm (20 in)

Grebes are highly adapted for diving after prey but their feet are so far back on their bodies that they struggle to walk on land. This species builds a floating nest for easy access from the water, and is famous for its elaborate, "dancing" courtship displays.

BROWN PELICAN

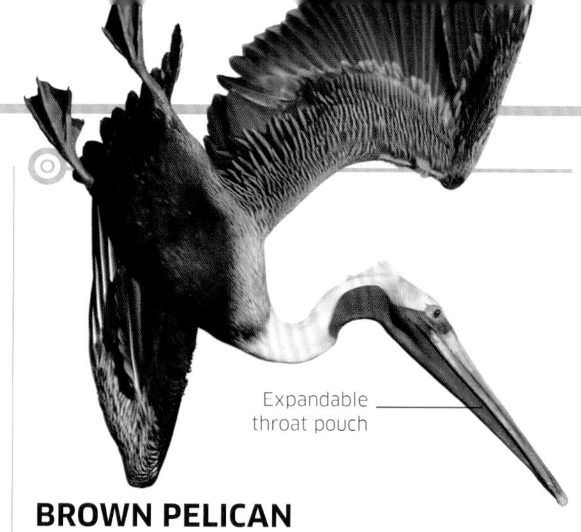

Expandable throat pouch

Pelecanus occidentalis

Location: Caribbean and the Americas

Length: Up to 1.4 m (4½ ft)

Pelicans have huge, expandable throat pouches, used for scooping up water teeming with small fish. Unlike other pelicans, this species hunts by plunge-diving into the sea from the air.

GREAT CORMORANT

Phalacrocorax carbo

Location: Worldwide except South America and Antarctica

Length: Up to 1 m (3¼ ft)

Widespread on coasts and fresh waters, this underwater hunter pursues fish by propelling itself with its big, webbed feet. Its plumage absorbs water, reducing the bird's buoyancy so that when it dives, it can stay submerged more easily.

MAGNIFICENT FRIGATEBIRD

Fregata magnificens

Location: Tropical American seas

Length: Up to 1.1 m (3½ ft)

The long-winged tropical frigatebird soars over the ocean, searching for prey or even stealing it in mid-air from other birds. Males have red throat pouches that they inflate for courtship displays.

PURPLE HERON

Ardea purpurea

Location: S. Eurasia, Africa

Length: Up to 90 cm (35½ in)

Herons mainly hunt in fresh water, standing motionless in the shallows, waiting for prey to approach. Like all herons, the purple heron has a "kink" in its neck. This acts like a hinge, allowing the bird to dart its head forward to seize prey with a quick stab of its spear-like bill.

Spreading the weight Extra-long toes help the heron to walk over floating vegetation.

GREATER FLAMINGO

Phoenicopterus roseus

Location: S. Eurasia, Africa, Central America

Length: Up to 1.5 m (5 ft)

Flamingos are extraordinary birds, specialized for filter-feeding on tiny aquatic organisms. Some eat microscopic algae, but the greater flamingo feeds on insects and shrimps. Holding its head upside down in the shallows, it pumps water through its specially adapted bill, which has rows of comb-like bristles to trap prey.

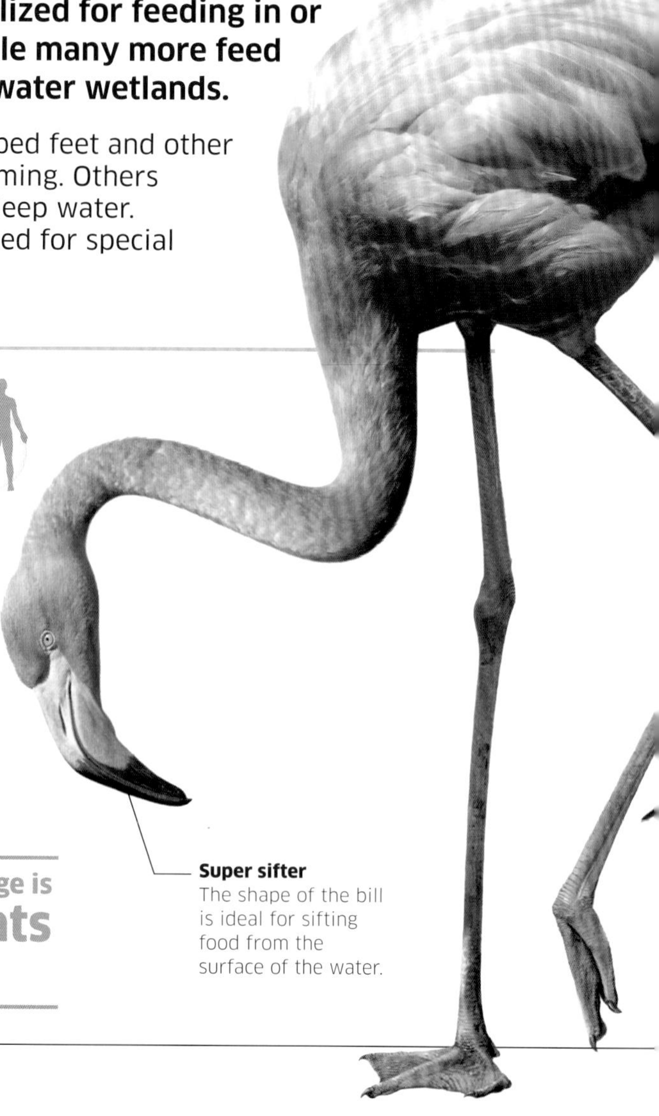

Super sifter The shape of the bill is ideal for sifting food from the surface of the water.

The flamingo's rosy pink plumage is caused by pigments in its food.

WHOOPER SWAN

Cygnus cygnus

Location: Eurasia

Length: Up to 1.6 m (5¼ ft)

The pure-white whooper swan breeds in the subarctic in summer and migrates south for the winter, gathering in large flocks on freshwater marshes and estuaries. Its name comes from its loud, whooping call.

WOOD DUCK

Aix sponsa

Location: North America

Length: Up to 51 cm (20 in)

The colourful male wood duck makes a striking contrast with the grey-brown female. The male's dazzling plumage is for courtship display, whereas the female's drab colouring keeps her safe while incubating her eggs. Unlike most ducks, the wood duck nests in tree holes.

WATER RAIL

Rallus aquaticus

Location: Eurasia, North Africa

Length: Up to 28 cm (11 in)

Rails are short-winged waterbirds that live in freshwater wetlands. The water rail is one of the shyest, with a narrow body ideal for slipping through dense reedbeds. It is more often heard than seen, uttering a variety of pig-like grunts and squeals.

Long toes
The toes spread the bird's weight when walking on soft mud.

EURASIAN CURLEW

Numenius arquata

Location: Eurasia, Africa

Length: Up to 60 cm (23½ in)

Long-legged and long-billed, the Eurasian curlew is one of the largest of the shorebirds or waders – birds adapted for gathering food from tidal shores and wetlands. Its extremely long, curved bill is specialized for probing deep into soft mud for worms, clams, crabs, and other animals.

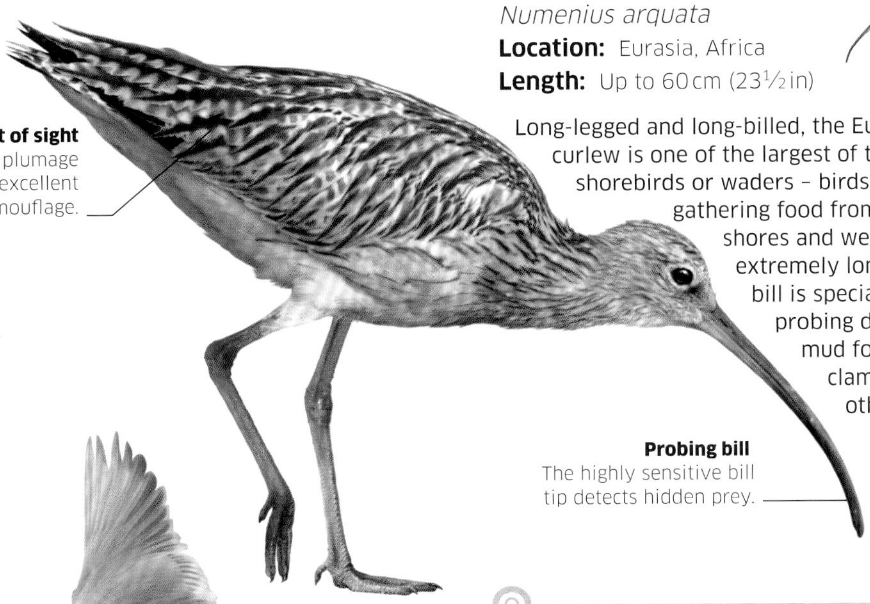

Out of sight
Mottled plumage provides excellent camouflage.

Probing bill
The highly sensitive bill tip detects hidden prey.

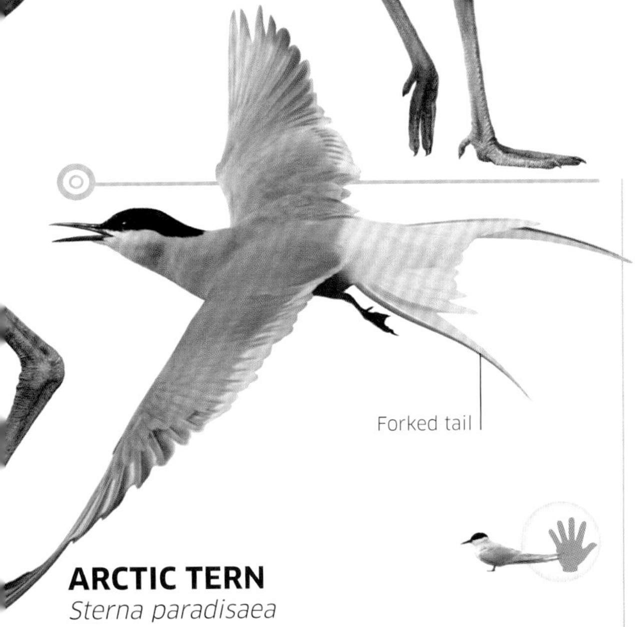

Forked tail

ARCTIC TERN

Sterna paradisaea

Location: Arctic and Antarctic regions

Length: Up to 35 cm (13¾ in)

The elegant, slender Arctic tern makes the longest migration of any bird. It breeds in the Arctic in the northern summer, then flies all the way to the Southern Ocean around Antarctica to feed during the northern winter.

ATLANTIC PUFFIN

Fratercula arctica

Location: North Atlantic, Arctic

Length: Up to 30 cm (11¾ in)

The Atlantic puffin is one of the auks – northern seabirds specialized for hunting underwater using their wings to drive them forwards, like penguins. It has a large, colourful bill, which is adapted for carrying many small fish at once.

Dual-purpose wings
Short wings act as flippers underwater, but are long enough for flight.

Seasonal colour
Both the bill and the bright orange feet become paler in winter.

The eagle owl **hunts** over a **territory** of up to **80 sq km (40 sq miles)**.

The male eagle owl's **deep, booming hoot** can be **heard** from more than 1 km (1/2 mile) away.

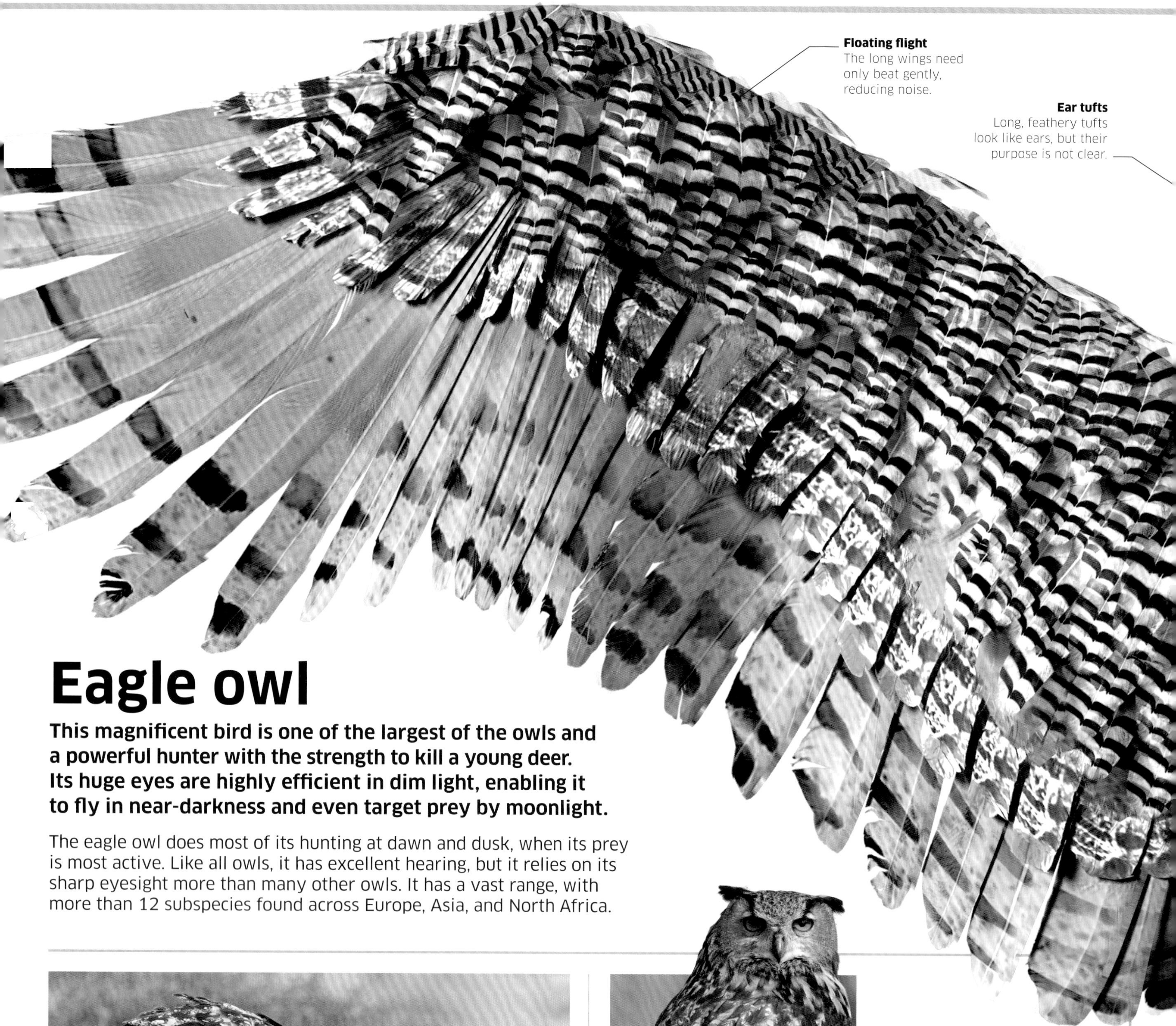

Floating flight
The long wings need only beat gently, reducing noise.

Ear tufts
Long, feathery tufts look like ears, but their purpose is not clear.

Eagle owl

This magnificent bird is one of the largest of the owls and a powerful hunter with the strength to kill a young deer. Its huge eyes are highly efficient in dim light, enabling it to fly in near-darkness and even target prey by moonlight.

The eagle owl does most of its hunting at dawn and dusk, when its prey is most active. Like all owls, it has excellent hearing, but it relies on its sharp eyesight more than many other owls. It has a vast range, with more than 12 subspecies found across Europe, Asia, and North Africa.

Eagle of the night
Most owls take prey that they can swallow whole, in one gulp. The eagle owl does hunt like this, but it will also sometimes attack and kill larger animals. It then tears the flesh into bite-sized mouthfuls with its hooked bill, like a true eagle.

Direct view
The owl's eyes are not spherical, like ours, but conical and fixed in place in the skull. An owl cannot simply roll its eyes to look at something, as we can, it has to turn its whole head. Luckily, an owl's flexible neck enables it to swivel its head up to 270°, which is three-quarters of a full turn.

1.8 m (6 ft) – the **maximum wingspan** of an eagle owl.

Night sight
Large eyes are up to three times more sensitive in the dark than human eyes.

Feathered feet
The legs and feet are covered with feathers for protection against sharp-toothed prey.

Deadly weapons
Powerful, black-clawed talons grip and kill the owl's prey.

Soft-edged feathers
The owl's flight feathers have special, comb-like leading edges that muffle the noise of air rushing over its wings. This allows the owl to fly silently, so it can listen for prey, then take the animal by surprise.

BIRDS

EAGLE OWL

Bubo bubo

Location: Eurasia, North Africa

Length: Up to 75 cm (29½ in)

Diet: Mainly small mammals

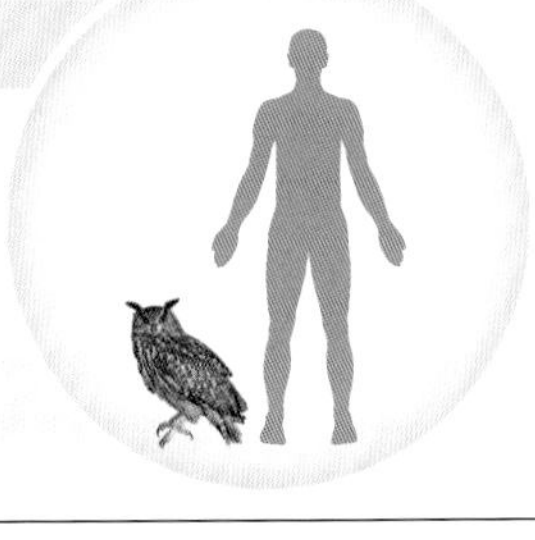

40 g (1½ oz) – the **average weight** of an adult **elf owl.**

Owls

Owls are the nocturnal equivalents of hawks and eagles, and use their acute hearing and sensitive eyesight to hunt at night for small animals, such as mice. But some owls also hunt by day, and a few are specialized for catching fish.

An owl is immediately recognizable by its big, forward-facing eyes, which look even bigger than they really are because they are surrounded by a disc of stiff feathers that channel sound to the owl's ears. Most owls have large wings that allow them to fly slowly and silently as they search the ground for prey.

Sharp talons
Long legs and sharp claws are adapted for seizing prey.

BARN OWL
Tyto alba

Location: Worldwide except Antarctica
Length: Up to 35 cm (13¾ in)

This pale-coloured owl has black eyes and a distinctive heart-shaped white facial disc. It is highly adapted for night hunting, and is one of the few owls that can hunt entirely by sound in total darkness. Despite this, it may also emerge to hunt by day, especially in spring when feeding its young.

GREAT HORNED OWL
Bubo virginianus

Location: Americas
Length: Up to 53 cm (21 in)

This big, powerful owl is the American equivalent of the eagle owl, with similar feathery tufts or "horns". It occurs in many different types of habitat, including forests, grasslands, and deserts, where it hunts a wide variety of prey. Unusually for an owl, it often takes large prey such as rabbits that it cannot swallow whole, and also picks birds off their roosting perches.

Threat display
If it is alarmed by an intruder, the great horned owl raises its wings as a threat.

SNOWY OWL
Bubo scandiacus

Location: Arctic regions
Length: Up to 66 cm (26 in)

Insulated from the cold by its thick feathers, the snowy owl is an Arctic hunter that targets voles, lemmings, and other small animals by listening for their movements under the snow. The females have plumage marked with stripes, as seen here, but males are almost pure white.

PEL'S FISHING OWL
Scotopelia peli

Location: Africa
Length: Up to 61 cm (24 in)

Most owls hunt animals on the ground, but this very large tropical forest owl is an expert at catching fish. It targets them at night by watching from a low perch in a tree overhanging a river or pool. When it detects telltale ripples in the water, it swoops down to seize its prey in its talons.

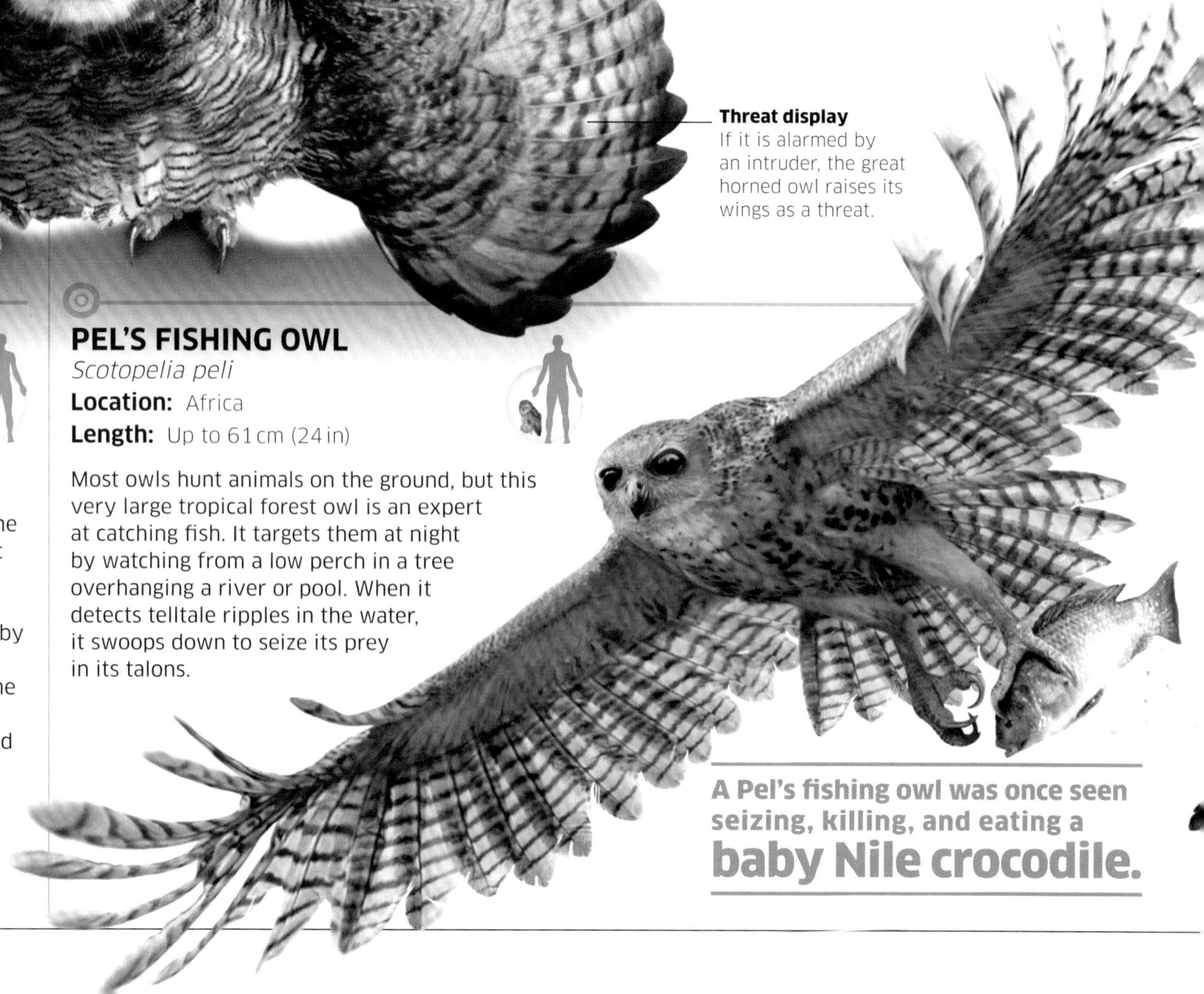

A Pel's fishing owl was once seen seizing, killing, and eating a baby Nile crocodile.

The soft plumage of an owl is not waterproof, so, unlike most birds, it cannot fly in wet weather.

Young burrowing owls scare predators out of their dark burrows by making a sound like the rattle of a rattlesnake.

TAWNY OWL

Strix aluco

Location: Europe, Asia, N. Africa

Length: Up to 38 cm (15 in)

The quavering hoot of the male tawny owl is a well-known sound of the night in most of Eurasia. Strictly nocturnal, the owl lives in woodland territories where it knows every vole run and burrow, enabling it to hunt at night very efficiently.

GREAT GREY OWL

Strix nebulosa

Location: Northern N. America, Eurasia

Length: Up to 69 cm ($27\frac{1}{4}$ in)

One of the biggest owls, this majestic bird lives in vast forests, where it hunts voles and mice. It is notoriously defensive of its nest site, attacking intruders and sometimes causing serious injuries.

CRESTED OWL

Lophostrix cristata

Location: Central and South America

Length: Up to 40 cm ($15\frac{3}{4}$ in)

Several owls have tufts of feathers that look like horns or ears, but none are quite as flamboyant as those of this tropical owl. A nocturnal hunter, it spends its days hidden on a perch in dense cover.

SPECTACLED OWL

Pulsatrix perspicillata

Location: Central and South America

Length: Up to 46 cm (18 in)

Most owls are well camouflaged so they can roost undisturbed by day. But this forest owl has a bold pattern of dark brown and white, with pale "spectacles" around its big yellow eyes. Juveniles are pale with brown faces.

ELF OWL

Micrathene whitneyi

Location: North America

Length: Up to 14 cm ($5\frac{1}{2}$ in)

The world's smallest owl, the elf owl lives in desert regions, where it hunts at night for insects, spiders, and scorpions. For its size, the owl is incredibly vocal, making a variety of loud calls. It nests in woodpecker holes, often in the stems of giant saguaro cacti.

Poised to strike
The elf owl often hunts from a perch, darting after insects to catch them in flight.

BURROWING OWL

Athene cunicularia

Location: America and Caribbean

Length: Up to 25 cm ($9\frac{3}{4}$ in)

This unique owl lives up to its name by nesting in burrows on treeless grassland. It can dig its own burrows, using its bill and long legs, but prefers to take over those of other animals. Unlike most owls, it is not nocturnal and can often be seen standing outside its burrows during the day.

BOOBOOK OWL

Ninox novaeseelandiae

Location: Australasia

Length: Up to 35 cm ($13\frac{3}{4}$ in)

The boobook owl takes its name from its two-part hooting call, which is often heard from trees in its native Australia and New Zealand. It feeds mainly on insects, and in urban areas it ambushes flying moths attracted by street lights.

SHORT-EARED OWL

Asio flammeus

Location: North America, South America, Europe, Asia, and Africa

Length: Up to 39 cm ($15\frac{1}{4}$ in)

This very widespread species is one of several owls that regularly hunt by day, flying low over marshes and rough grassland in search of small mammals. It has little fear of humans, often approaching to inspect them with its piercing yellow eyes.

BIRDS

TOCO TOUCAN

Ramphastos toco

Location: South America

Length: Up to 61 cm (24 in)

Diet: Fruit, eggs, and small animals

Toco toucan

The toco toucan is the largest of all the toucans. The function of its distinctive bill is not clear, although its length is useful for plucking fruit, and its bright colour may be used to impress other toucans. It is also used in courtship rituals, where a toucan will toss fruit to a potential mate to try and initiate a game of catch.

Short wings
The wings are short and rounded, and only employed for brief flights from tree to tree.

Blue patch of skin around eye

Lightweight structure
Despite its size, a toucan's bill weighs very little because a tough sheath of keratin encloses an airy, foam-like structure of slender bony struts with a hollow space in the middle. A network of blood vessels beneath the sheath may act as a radiator, helping the bird lose excess heat.

Flexible tail
Three of the toucan's tail vertebrae are fused together, allowing it to snap its tail forwards until it touches its head. It sleeps in this position.

Gripping feet
Feet are like those of a parrot, with two toes pointing forward and two backward.

Instead of calling to claim territories, many woodpeckers use their bills to drum rapidly on trees.

The seeds of some trees are distributed by toucans, as they pass right through the birds without being digested.

RED-BREASTED SAPSUCKER

Sphyrapicus ruber

Location: N. America

Length: Up to 19 cm (7 1/2 in)

Most woodpeckers are insect-eaters, but this small North American species gets most of its food by drilling small holes in tree bark laden with sugary sap. It makes a few test holes first, creating many more when it finds a good source. It then laps up the sap, as well as seizing any insects that may be attracted to the sap.

GREEN WOODPECKER

Picus viridis

Location: Europe

Length: Up to 30 cm (11 3/4 in)

Woodpeckers have extremely long tongues, which they use to extract timber-boring insects from trees. But this species feeds mainly on ants, searching out their nests by hopping over the ground in grassy pastures and meadows. It has a very loud, laughing call.

BLACK WOODPECKER

Dryocopus martius

Location: Europe, Asia

Length: Up to 45 cm (17 3/4 in)

Found in woodlands, the black woodpecker uses its powerful bill and strong neck muscles to hammer into trees to find beetle grubs, and to make nesting cavities. Stiff tail feathers support it as it works.

Toucans and woodpeckers

These closely related birds have found very different uses for their most striking feature – their bills. A woodpecker's bill is a tool, but a toucan's is largely for show.

Although both are mainly forest birds, toucans are restricted to the tropical forests of Central and South America while woodpeckers live almost worldwide. Toucans feed mainly on fruit, but they also catch small animals and steal the eggs and nestlings of other birds. Typical woodpeckers live up to their name by drilling into timber to find insect prey, and to excavate nest holes.

GUIANAN TOUCANET

Selenidera piperivora

Location: South America

Length: Up to 35 cm (13 3/4 in)

Unusually for toucans, the male and female Guianan toucanet have different plumage, although both have a distinctive yellow patch behind each eye. They often forage for food in pairs, searching the canopy for berries and insects.

COLLARED ARACARI

Pteroglossus torquatus

Location: Central and South America

Length: Up to 40 cm (15 3/4 in)

Aracaris are smaller and not as robustly built as typical toucans. This species is usually seen in small parties that work their way through the forest picking fruit, stealing eggs, and feeding on any insects and similar animals they find.

EMERALD TOUCANET

Aulacorhynchus prasinus

Location: Central and South America

Length: Up to 33 cm (13 in)

The vivid plumage of the emerald toucanet looks spectacular, but when perched among lush tropical foliage it can be almost invisible. However, it is a noisy species, which produces a variety of harsh, rattling, croaking calls. Like all toucans, it is an opportunist that eats a range of foods.

The same **display trees** may be used by the birds for **20 years** or more.

Local tribes have long **hunted** birds of paradise for their **glorious plumes**.

Rival males

Male Raggiana birds of paradise are polygamous – they compete to mate with as many females as possible. Gathering in traditional display trees, each tries to eclipse his rivals with the most impressive display. The winners, decided by the males, claim the most prominent perches, so a female simply targets a high-ranking male, who then treats her to his final, most entrancing display before they mate. As with all polygamous species, the male plays no part in raising the young.

TWO BIRD OF PARADISE SPECIES DISPLAYING IN THE SAME TREE

Raggiana bird of paradise

Many birds have fine plumage, but few are so breathtakingly beautiful as male birds of paradise. Their gorgeous colours and spectacular plumes are the result of intense competition for the chance to breed, which only the most eye-catching male can hope to win.

Widespread and common in the tropical forests of its native New Guinea, the Raggiana bird of paradise is one of the most flamboyant species. The female has relatively muted dark red-brown plumage, but the male is adorned with a glorious cascade of maroon or russet feathers. He displays these to full advantage when performing an elaborate bowing dance to beguile a potential mate.

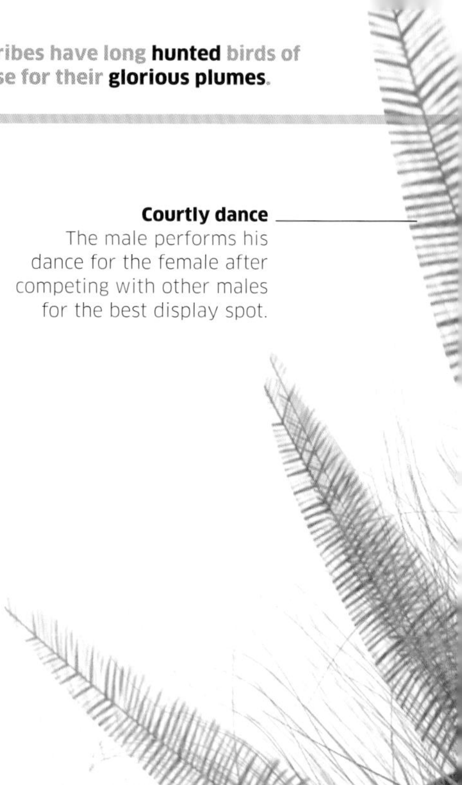

BIRDS

RAGGIANA BIRD OF PARADISE

Paradisaea raggiana

Location: New Guinea

Length: Up to 34 cm (13½ in)

Diet: Fruit, insects, spiders

Eurasian starling

One of the most widespread and adaptable of the perching birds, this noisy, very sociable starling has spread far beyond its native Eurasian range, partly through human introductions.

Some birds are specialized for a particular way of life, but the Eurasian starling is an adaptable opportunist that can use its sharp, strong bill to find food almost anywhere. It feeds mainly on open ground, foraging in groups that probe the earth for small animals, but it may also catch airborne insects in flight. In winter it gathers in vast flocks to roost for the night in trees, or on buildings.

BIRDS

EURASIAN STARLING

Sturnus vulgaris

Location: Europe, western Asia, introduced elsewhere

Length: Up to 22 cm (8¾ in)

Diet: Insects, worms, seeds, berries

Changing plumage
In winter, a starling's dark plumage is peppered with buff spots. These are the pale tips of its feathers, which wear off by spring to reveal a breeding plumage of glossy black with an iridescent green and purple sheen. The birds then moult after the breeding season and return to their winter plumage.

An estimated 150 million Eurasian starlings live in North America, all descended from just 60 birds released in New York in 1890.

Noisy song
Many perching birds have musical songs, but the starling is not one of them. Its song is a throaty medley of whistles, gurgles, clicks, and creaking noises, which often includes mimicry of other bird calls. Each bird has its own repertoire, and they can even be trained to mimic human sounds.

Hole nesters
Starlings nest in any holes they can find – in trees, rocky crevices, or in the roofs of buildings. Each pair line their nest hole with dry grass, moss, feathers, and other soft materials to form a cushion for a clutch of pale blue eggs. Both parents incubate the eggs and feed the young when they hatch.

Probing the ground
When a starling is searching for food on soft ground, it uses an unusual foraging technique. As it walks forwards, it thrusts its strong, sharp bill into the ground and then opens it to enlarge the hole. It does this time after time until it locates an insect grub or worm that it can pull out and swallow.

TEST PROBE

SUCCESS!

Sky dance
As the summer breeding season ends, starlings abandon their nests and start spending the night in mass communal roosts. Before settling down for the night these flocks perform spectacular manoeuvres known as murmurations, which involve thousands of birds swooping through the sky in coordinated waves that resemble clouds of black smoke.

VERMILION FLYCATCHER

Pyrocephalus rubinus

Location: North, Central, and South America

Length: Up to 15 cm (6 in)

Flycatchers feed by flying up from a perch and snatching insects out of the air. The male of this species has a vivid red body and black wings; females are grey and white, for camouflage when incubating eggs.

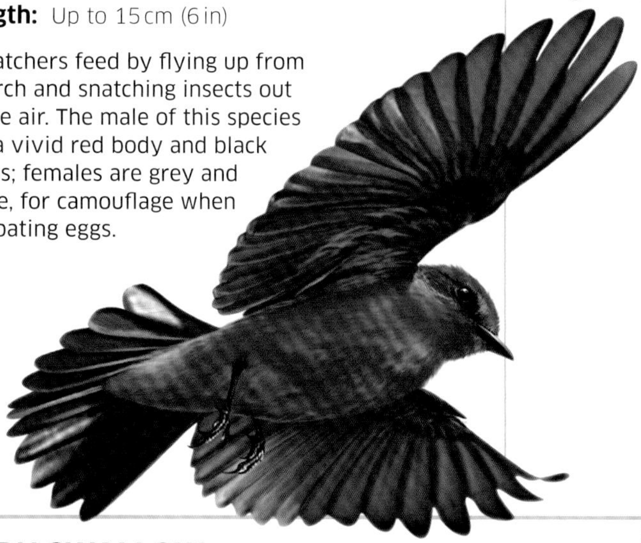

SUPERB LYREBIRD

Menura novaehollandiae

Location: Southeastern Australia

Length: Up to 96 cm (37¾ in)

Lyrebirds spend their days on the forest floor and roost in trees at night. Males have spectacular tail plumes, which they use in elaborate courtship displays, designed to attract as many females as possible.

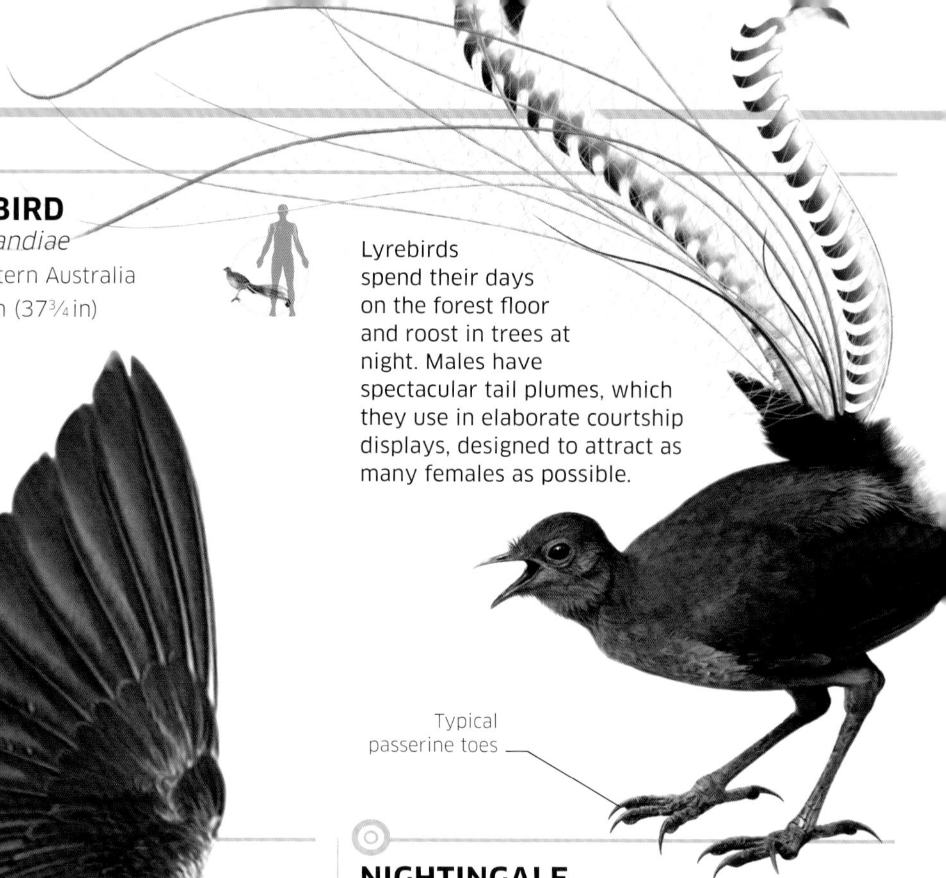

BARN SWALLOW

Hirundo rustica

Location: Worldwide except Antarctica

Length: Up to 18 cm (7 in)

Like many passerines, this bird is an excellent flier – a graceful, aerial hunter that catches insects in flight and makes long migrations to and from the tropics each year. It often nests in buildings so, unlike many bird species, it has benefitted from the worldwide growth of the human population.

NIGHTINGALE

Luscinia megarhynchos

Location: Europe, western Asia, Africa

Length: Up to 16.5 cm (6½ in)

Many passerines are described as songbirds, with males that sing to claim territory and attract females. The song of the male nightingale is one of the most tuneful and inventive of all. The bird's brown plumage hides it from hungry predators.

SUPERB FAIRY-WREN

Malurus cyaneus

Location: Southeastern Australia

Length: Up to 14 cm (5½ in)

Most perching birds raise their young in pairs, but this species has devised a way of spreading the workload – the vividly coloured breeding male and his mate recruit their relatives to help. These are usually younger, less colourful males, which help gather food for the young.

EURASIAN NUTHATCH

Sitta europea

Location: Europe, Asia

Length: Up to 14 cm (5½ in)

The perching birds' specialized, gripping feet allow many of them to be highly acrobatic when foraging for food. The Eurasian nuthatch is one of the most agile; it can run head-first up and down tree trunks, and even search tree bark for insects while hanging upside down.

18 The approximate **number of days** it takes for a **male baya weaver** to **build his nest**.

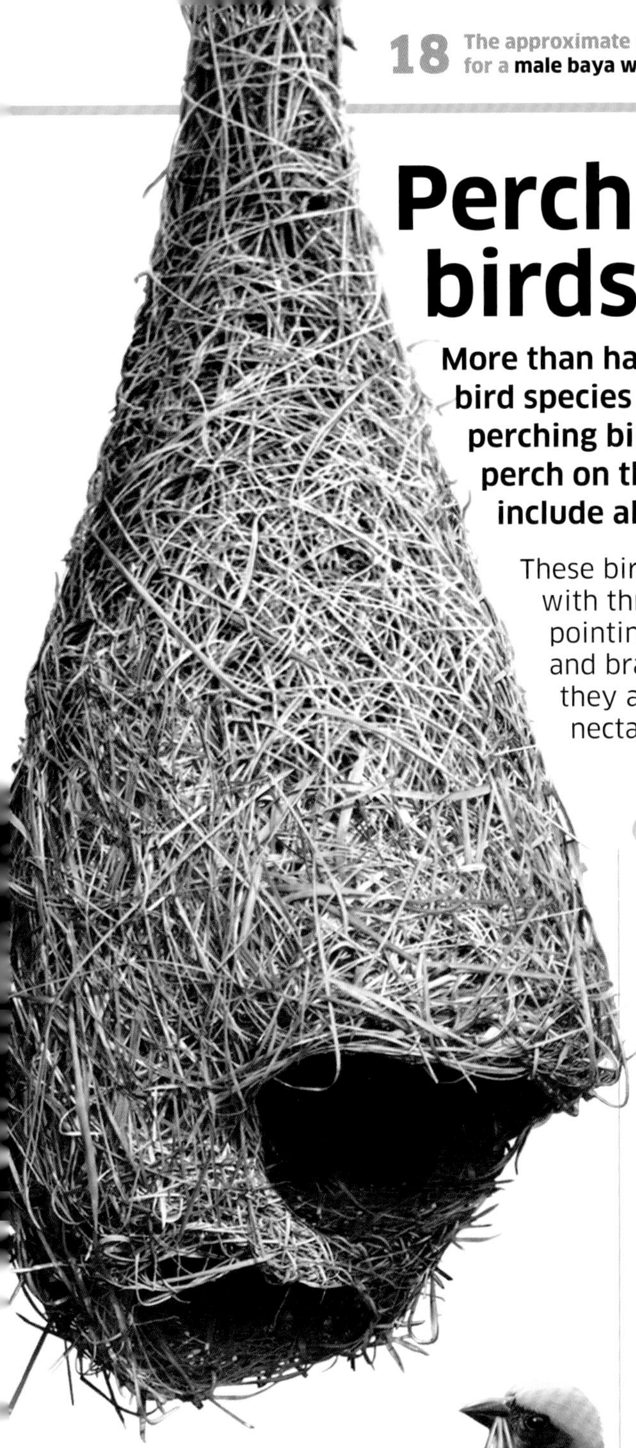

Perching birds

More than half of the world's bird species are passerines, or perching birds. They share an ability to perch on the most slender twigs, and include all the most musical songbirds.

These birds all have the same foot structure, with three toes pointing forwards and one toe pointing back. This allows them to grip twigs and branches securely. Apart from their feet, they are very diverse, ranging from delicate nectar-feeders to powerful scavengers.

SOUTHERN DOUBLE-COLLARED SUNBIRD

Cinnyris chalybeus

Location: Southern Africa

Length: Up to 12 cm (4¾ in)

Sunbirds are the African equivalents of hummingbirds – nectar-feeders with males that have dazzling, iridescent plumage. The long bill of this species gives easy access to flowers.

RED-BACKED SHRIKE

Lanius collurio

Location: Europe, western Asia, Africa

Length: Up to 18 cm (7 in)

Shrikes are hunters that behave like hawks, seizing lizards, mice, and large insects and tearing them apart with their hooked bills. The red-backed shrike has a habit of impaling its prey on thorns, for eating later.

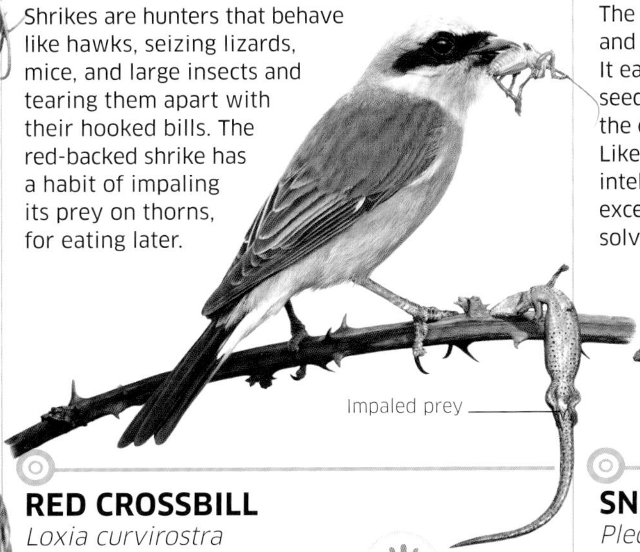

RAVEN

Corvus corax

Location: North America, Europe, Asia

Length: Up to 69 cm (27¼ in)

The raven is the biggest of the crows, and the most powerful perching bird. It eats a wide variety of foods, from seeds to meat scavenged from the carcasses of animals. Like most crows, it is very intelligent, possessing excellent problem-solving skills.

BAYA WEAVER

Ploceus philippinus

Location: India to Southeast Asia

Length: Up to 15 cm (6 in)

Many perching birds lay their eggs in carefully made nests. The bottle-shaped nest of the baya weaver is one of the most elaborate, woven by the male from grass blades and strips of palm leaf. Many pairs of birds may nest together, with up to 30 nests hanging from branches of the same tree.

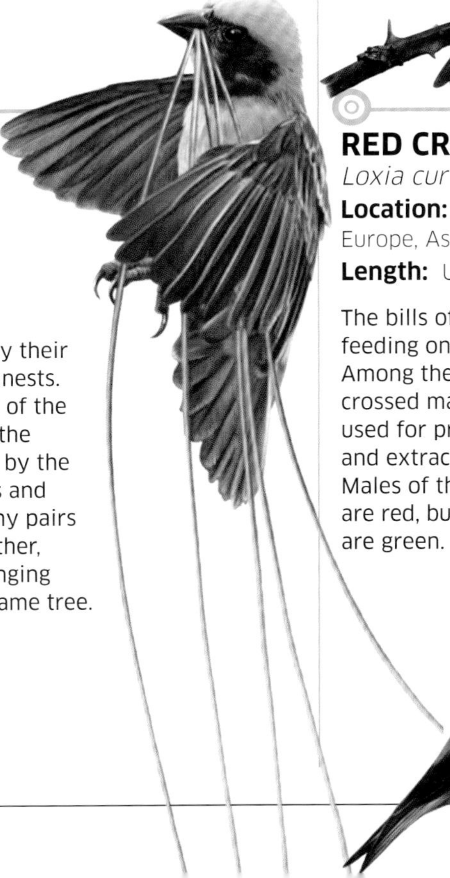

RED CROSSBILL

Loxia curvirostra

Location: North America, Europe, Asia

Length: Up to 16.5 cm (6½ in)

The bills of passerines are adapted for feeding on a variety of different foods. Among the most specialized are the crossed mandibles of the crossbills, used for prizing open pine cones and extracting the seeds. Males of this species are red, but females are green.

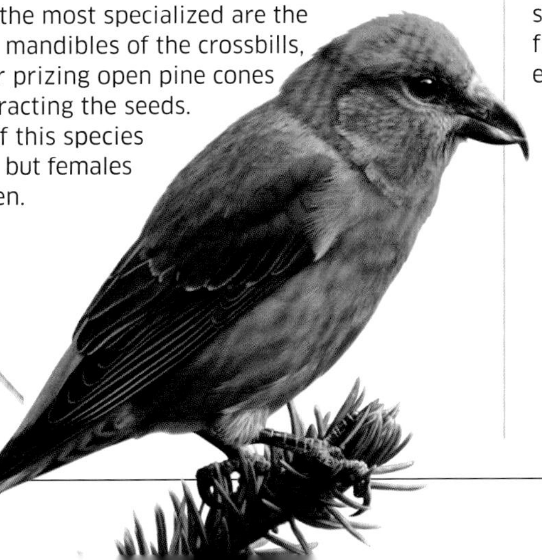

SNOW BUNTING

Plectrophenax nivalis

Location: North America, Europe, Asia

Length: Up to 16.5 cm (6½ in)

Although many perching birds are small, they are surprisingly tough. The sparrow-sized snow bunting, for example, breeds further north than any other land bird, even nesting on the northern tip of Greenland. Its mainly black and white plumage provides good camouflage on the icy Arctic tundra.

MAMMALS

Furry mammals are the most familiar animals to us because we are also mammals, with most of the same features and needs. Mammals include an amazing diversity of creatures with very different lifestyles, ranging from delicate bats to giant whales, adapted to thrive in every habitat on Earth.

WHAT IS A MAMMAL?

Mammals first appeared about 220 million years ago, at about the same time as the first big dinosaurs. These early mammals were very small, but when the giant dinosaurs were wiped out at the end of the Mesozoic Era, 66 million years ago, mammals started evolving into bigger forms that took their place. Mammals' warm-blooded, furry bodies have enabled them to live almost anywhere and spread all over the world, from tropical forests to icy polar oceans.

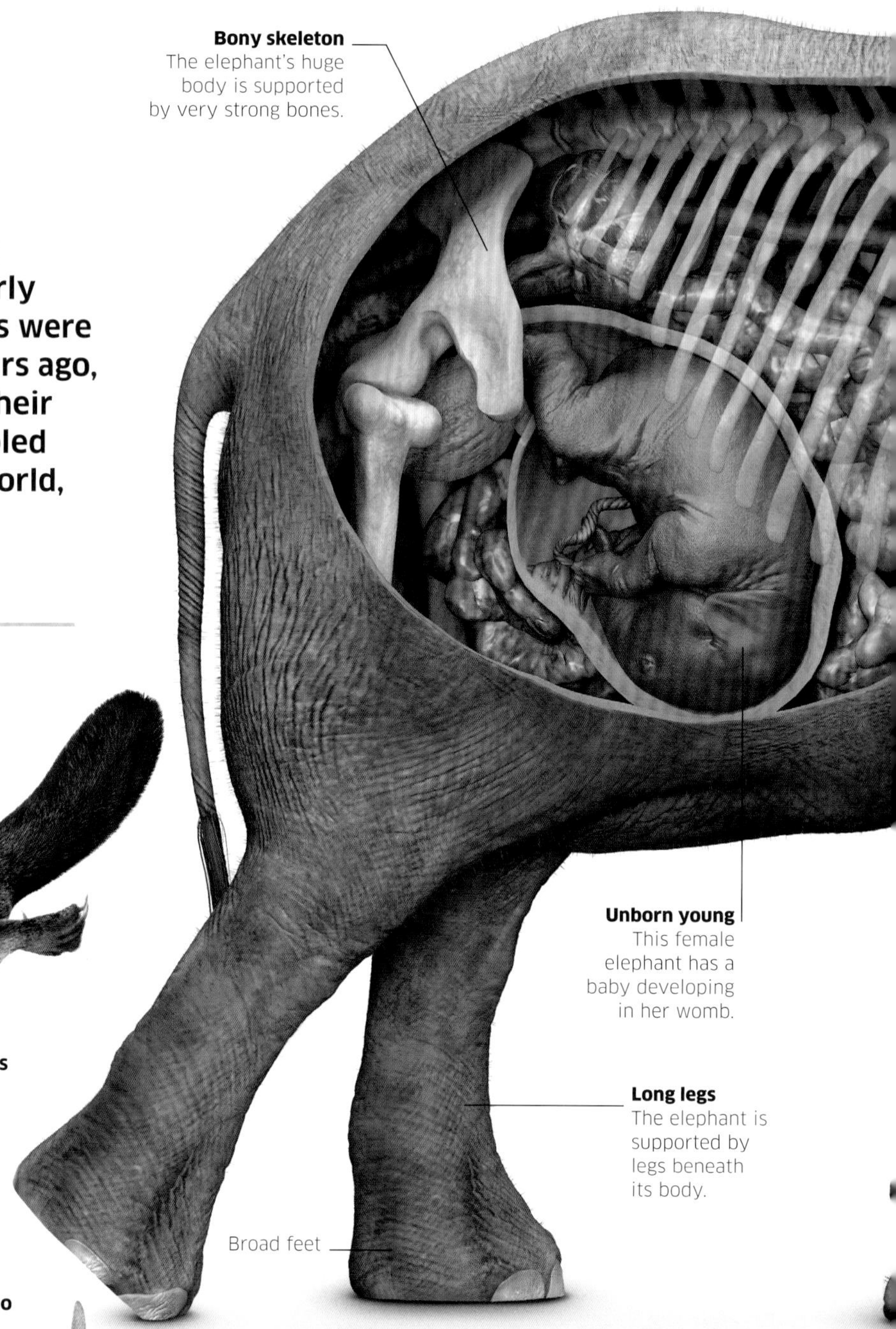

TYPES OF MAMMAL

Mammals occur in various shapes and sizes, with bodies specialized for life in many habitats. Despite this they all share the same basic biology apart from a fundamental difference in the way they reproduce.

Monotremes
Many of the earliest mammals laid eggs, and a few still do. Known as monotremes, they include the platypus and four species of spiny echidnas, which all live in Australia and nearby New Guinea. The babies that hatch from the eggs feed on their mothers' milk, just like other mammals.

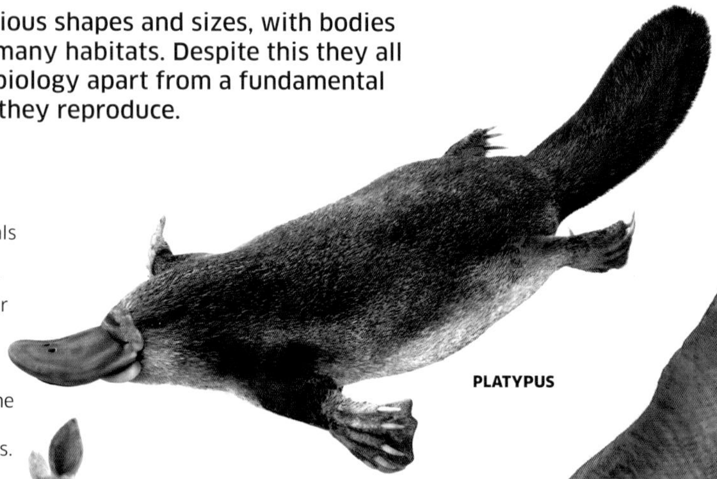
PLATYPUS

Marsupials
A female marsupial, such as a kangaroo, gives birth to very small, barely formed young that crawl into a pouch on her belly. There the young drink milk enriched with all the nutrients they need to develop into fully-formed babies. Most marsupials live in Australia, New Guinea, and South America.

RED KANGAROO

Placentals
The vast majority of mammals give birth to well-formed young that have developed for a long time inside the mother's body. The unborn young are nourished by fluids passing through an umbilical cord attached to the mother by an organ called the placenta, so they are known as placental mammals.

BACTRIAN CAMEL

KEY FEATURES

Whether they are monotremes, marsupials, or placentals, all mammals share a number of key features. They are warm-blooded vertebrates, which feed their infant young on milk until their digestive systems can cope with solid food. Most mammals have hair, although some have spines or even scales. Finally, all mammals except monotremes give birth to live young.

Vertebrates
All mammals have internal skeletons made of bone.

Warm-blooded
A mammal turns food energy into heat to keep warm.

Most bear live young
They give birth to young instead of laying eggs.

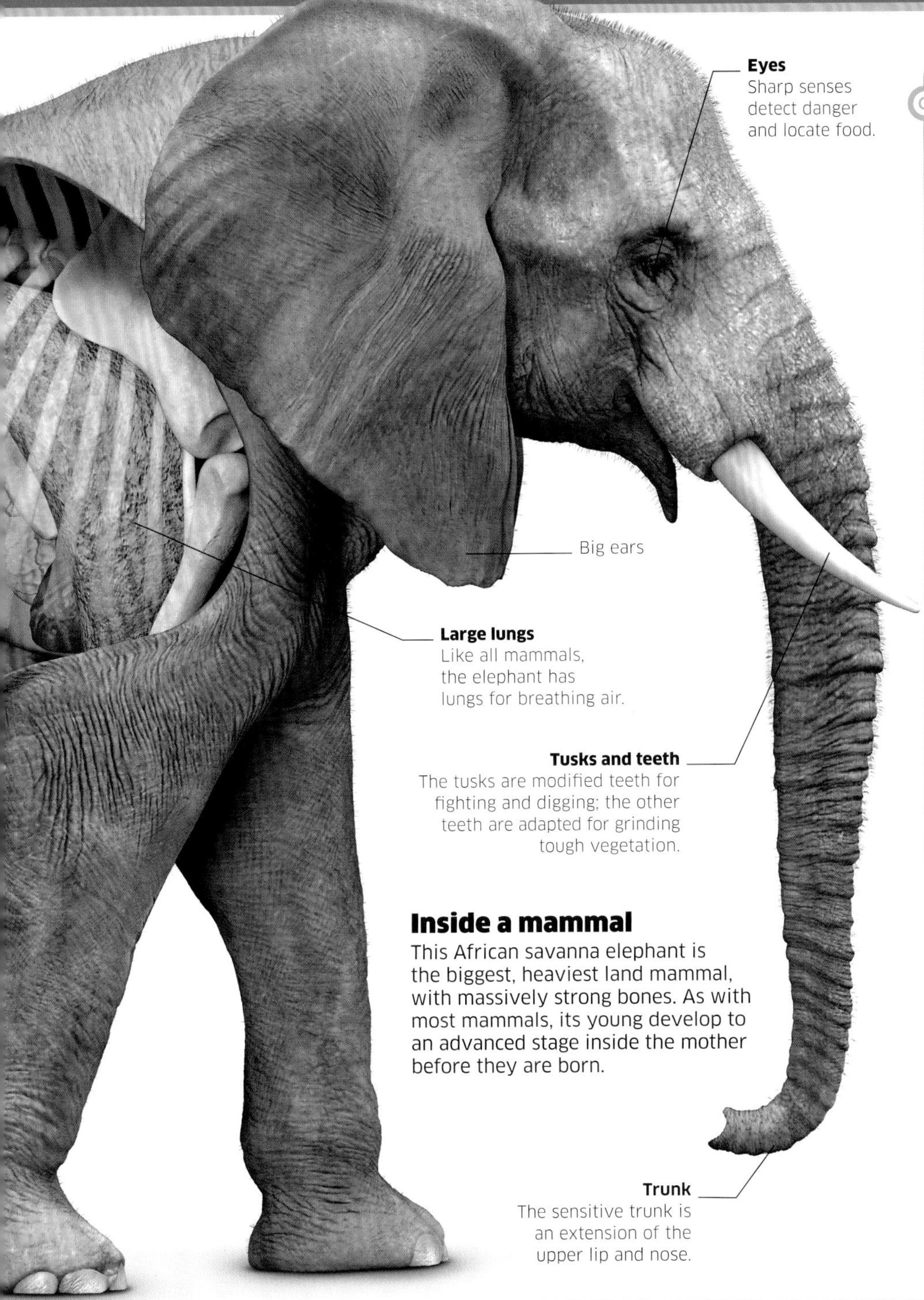

Inside a mammal

This African savanna elephant is the biggest, heaviest land mammal, with massively strong bones. As with most mammals, its young develop to an advanced stage inside the mother before they are born.

WARM AND SAFE

Most of the energy that a mammal gets from its food is used to generate body heat. This allows mammals to live in cold climates, but also means they need to eat a lot. Good insulation reduces heat loss and saves energy, which is why many mammals have coats of dense, warm fur. The tough keratin that forms hair and fur may also form defensive spines or scales.

Blubber
Nothing saps body heat faster than cold water, so marine mammals need a lot of insulation. Dolphins have thick layers of insulating fat, known as blubber, beneath their skin.

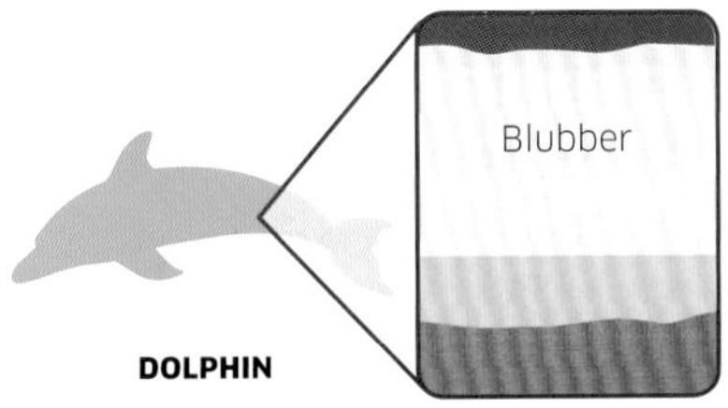

Fur
A bear has an outer coat of long, tough guard hair that protects an inner coat of dense, woolly underfur. The guard hair sheds water, keeping the underfur dry so it retains an insulating layer of air.

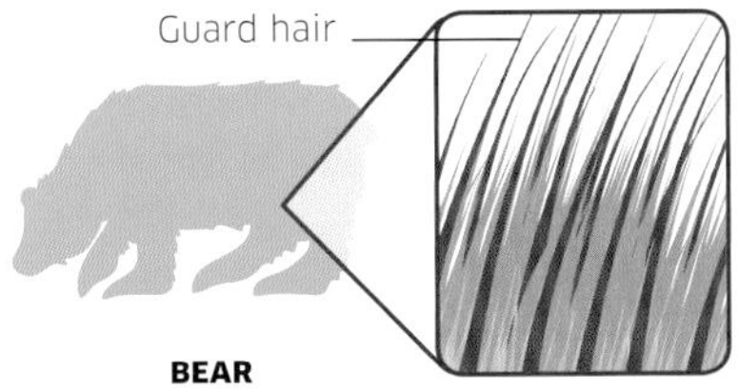

Spines
The spines of a porcupine are modified hair, made of the same material but much thicker, stiffer, and very sharp, to protect the animal from its enemies. Hedgehogs and echidnas have the same adaptation.

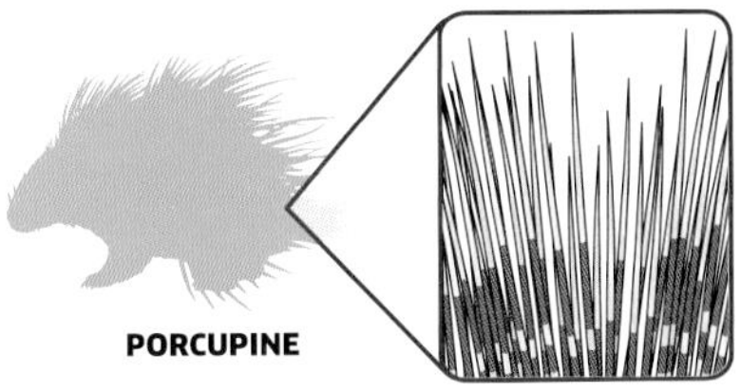

Scales
A pangolin's overlapping scales are modified hairs, made of keratin and fused together. An armadillo also has scaly armour, but it is reinforced by large bony plates.

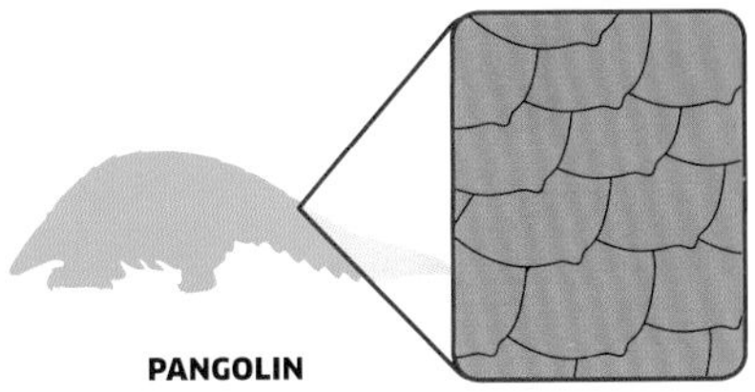

TO MAKE ENOUGH ENERGY TO KEEP WARM, SOME SMALL MAMMALS MUST EAT MORE THAN TWICE THEIR WEIGHT IN FOOD EVERY DAY.

Young fed on milk
The milk contains nutrients vital to young mammals.

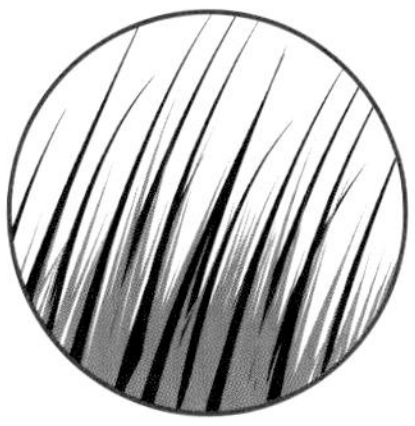

Most have hair or fur
Hair or fur traps air to help retain vital body heat.

MOTHER'S MILK

All young mammals feed on milk during their early lives. The nutrient-rich liquid is produced in the mother's body and secreted through mammary glands. This timber wolf is nursing a litter of several cubs, but many mammals give birth to just one or two infants at a time. A baby orangutan, for example, stays with its mother for up to eight years, and is nourished by her milk for its first two to three years of life.

When the first **stuffed platypus** was seen in Europe **in the 1700s** people thought it **so strange it must be a hoax**, stitched together from **bits of different animals**.

Monotremes

The monotremes are an extraordinary group of mammals that lay eggs like those of reptiles, instead of giving birth to live young. There are just five living species, all found in Australia and New Guinea.

Monotremes were once more widespread, at least in the southern continents – in 1991 fossil remains were found in South America. But the only surviving monotremes are the spiny echidnas and the platypus. With its rubbery bill and broad tail, the platypus looks very different from the echidnas, and they probably started evolving in different ways more than 20 million years ago.

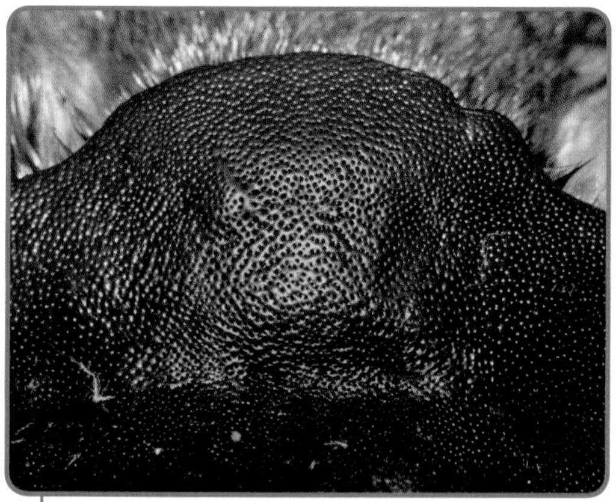

Sensitive surface
The rubbery, pliable bill is dotted with electroreceptors. These detect the faint electrical nerve activity of animals such as worms and insect larvae hidden in the mud at the bottom of streams. The bill is also highly sensitive to touch.

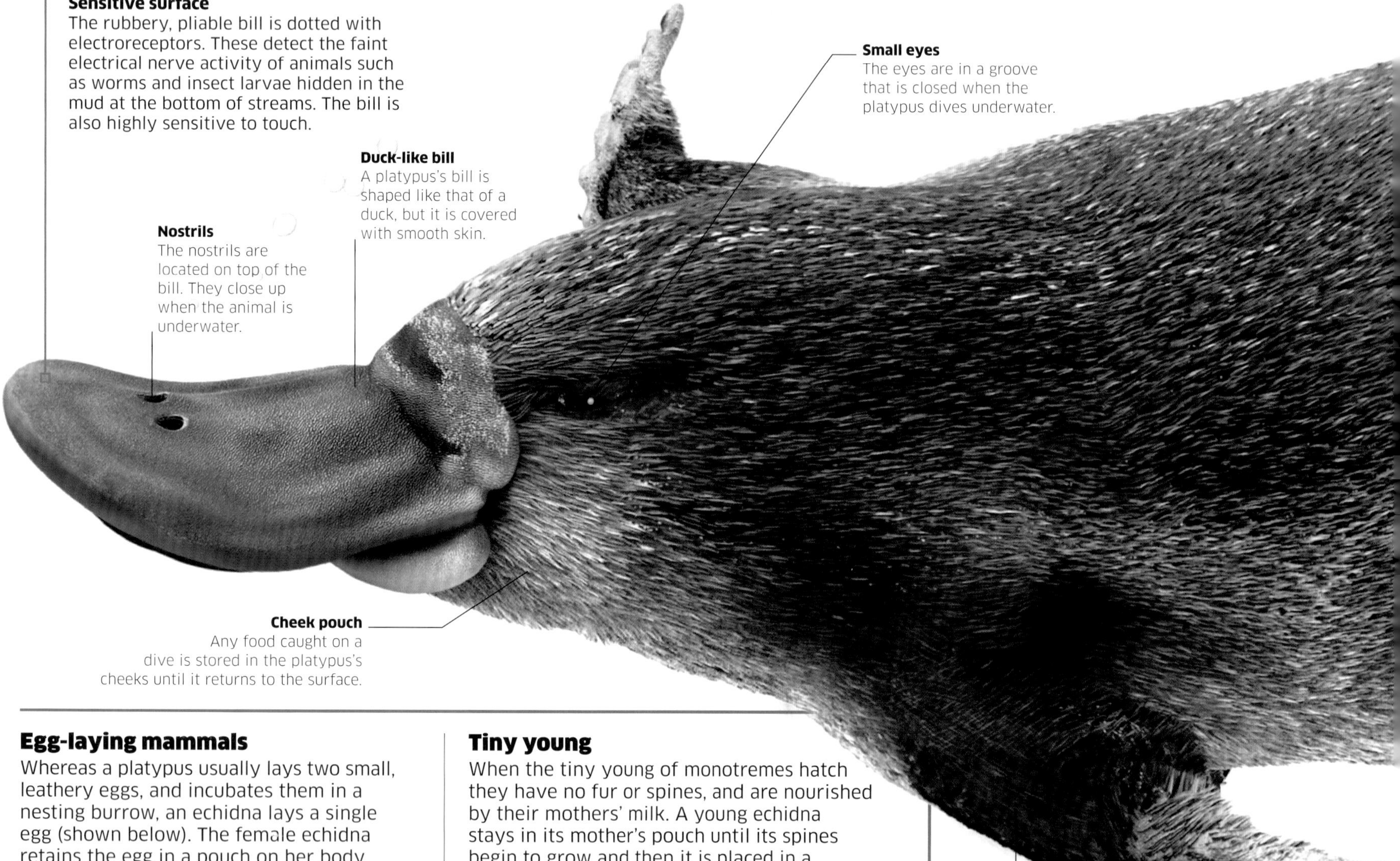

Small eyes
The eyes are in a groove that is closed when the platypus dives underwater.

Duck-like bill
A platypus's bill is shaped like that of a duck, but it is covered with smooth skin.

Nostrils
The nostrils are located on top of the bill. They close up when the animal is underwater.

Cheek pouch
Any food caught on a dive is stored in the platypus's cheeks until it returns to the surface.

Short legs
The legs extend sideways from the body, more like those of a reptile than a mammal.

Egg-laying mammals

Whereas a platypus usually lays two small, leathery eggs, and incubates them in a nesting burrow, an echidna lays a single egg (shown below). The female echidna retains the egg in a pouch on her body for 10 days until it hatches.

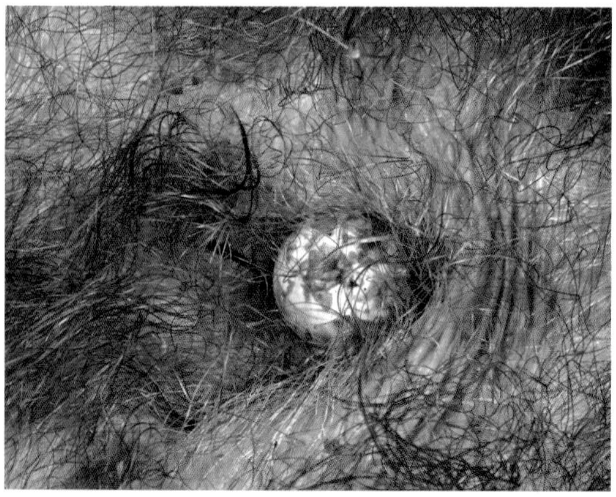

Tiny young

When the tiny young of monotremes hatch they have no fur or spines, and are nourished by their mothers' milk. A young echidna stays in its mother's pouch until its spines begin to grow and then it is placed in a nursery burrow.

MAMMALS

PLATYPUS

Ornithorhynchus anatinus

Location: Eastern Australia and Tasmania

Length: Up to 60 cm (23¾ in)

Diet: Aquatic invertebrates

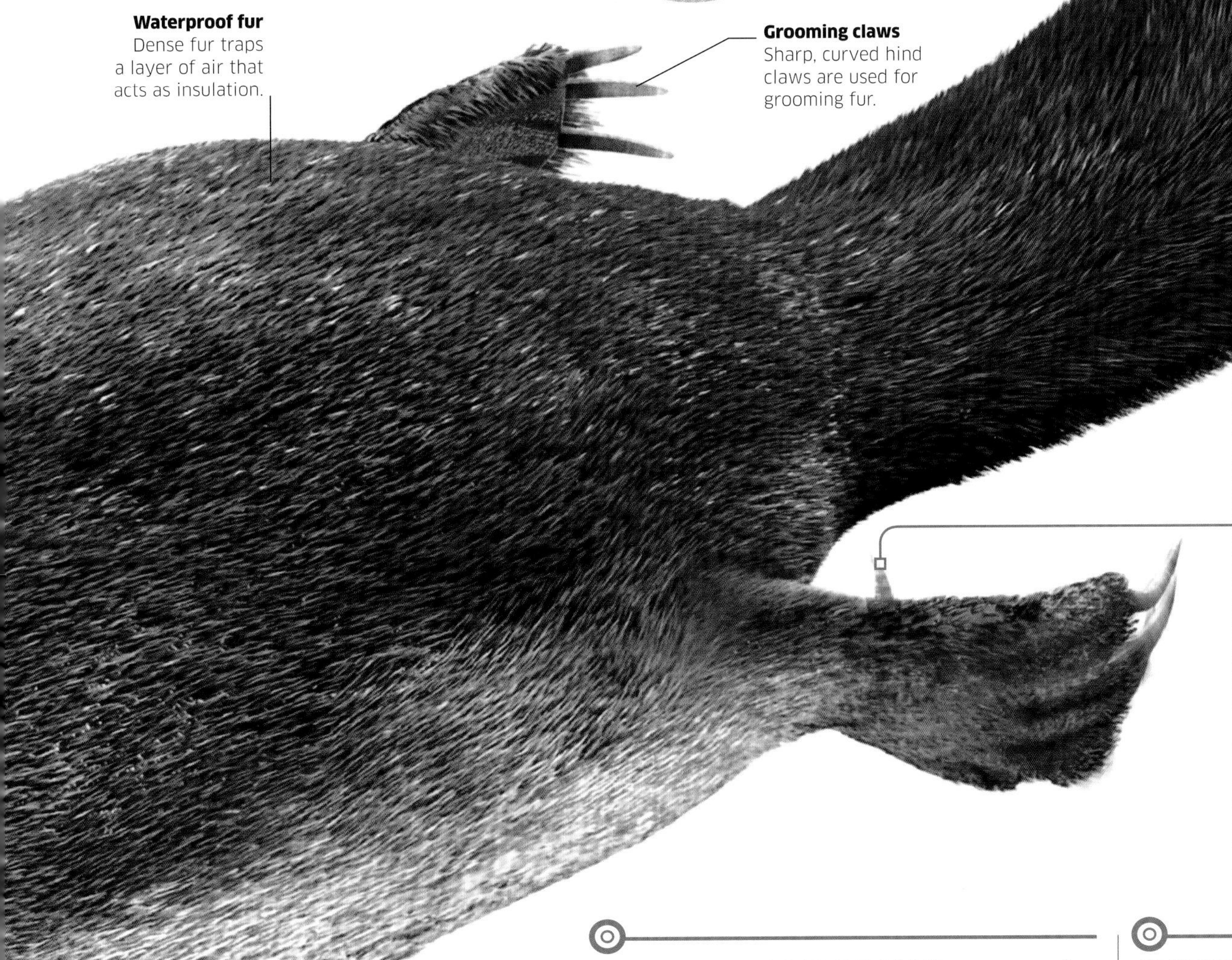

Flat tail
The broad tail is used for steering underwater, and stores energy-rich fat.

Waterproof fur
Dense fur traps a layer of air that acts as insulation.

Grooming claws
Sharp, curved hind claws are used for grooming fur.

Venomous spur
A male platypus has a horny spur on each ankle, connected to a venom gland in the animal's thigh. The venom is mostly for defence, but males also use their spurs in fights with rival males.

Platypus
With its broad, webbed feet and large tail, the platypus is well-equipped for its semi-aquatic way of life. By day it remains inside its burrow, dug into an earth bank, emerging at night to search the muddy bottom of shallow pools for food.

Webbed feet
The platypus drives itself though the water with its big, webbed forefeet.

WESTERN LONG-BEAKED ECHIDNA

Zaglossus bruijnii

Location: New Guinea

Length: Up to 77 cm (30¼ in)

There are three species of long-beaked echidna, all very rare. This one lives in the tropical mountain forests of New Guinea, where it uses its long snout to feed on earthworms, hooking them from their burrows with a long, mobile, spiny tongue.

SHORT-BEAKED ECHIDNA

Tachyglossus aculeatus

Location: Australia and New Guinea

Length: Up to 45 cm (17¾ in)

This is the most widespread species of echidna. It is covered with stout spines, and curls into a ball for defence. It is sometimes called the spiny anteater because it feeds mainly on ants and termites, but it also eats other insects and spiders.

Red kangaroos sometimes gather in huge groups of up to 1,500 animals.

Red kangaroo

The biggest Australian mammal, and the largest of all marsupials, the red kangaroo is a spectacularly agile creature adapted for life on dry grassland. Its powerful hind legs enable it to bound across the open landscape at speed with minimal effort.

Kangaroos have evolved one of the most efficient ways of moving at speed. Instead of running, they hop, and every time a kangaroo lands, its long hind feet flex at the ankle and stretch the strong elastic tendon at the back of each leg. The tendon then recoils, hurling the animal back into the air. It works so well that a red kangaroo can cover up to 9 m ($29\frac{1}{2}$ ft) in a single bound, easily outdistancing any enemy.

Boxing males
Mature males are not territorial, but they do fight over females. These fights usually take the form of ritual boxing matches, as each male jabs at his rival with strong arms, trying to knock him over. If this does not work they may wrestle, or kick with both legs while supporting their weight with their tails.

MAMMALS

RED KANGAROO

Osphranter rufus

Location: Australia

Height: Up to 1.4 m ($4\frac{1}{2}$ ft)

Diet: Mostly grass

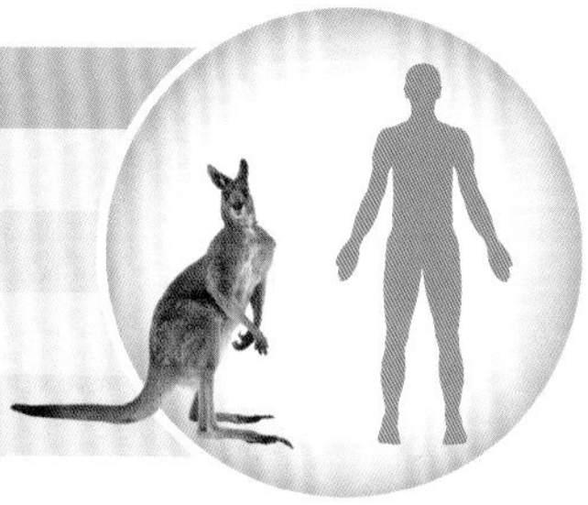

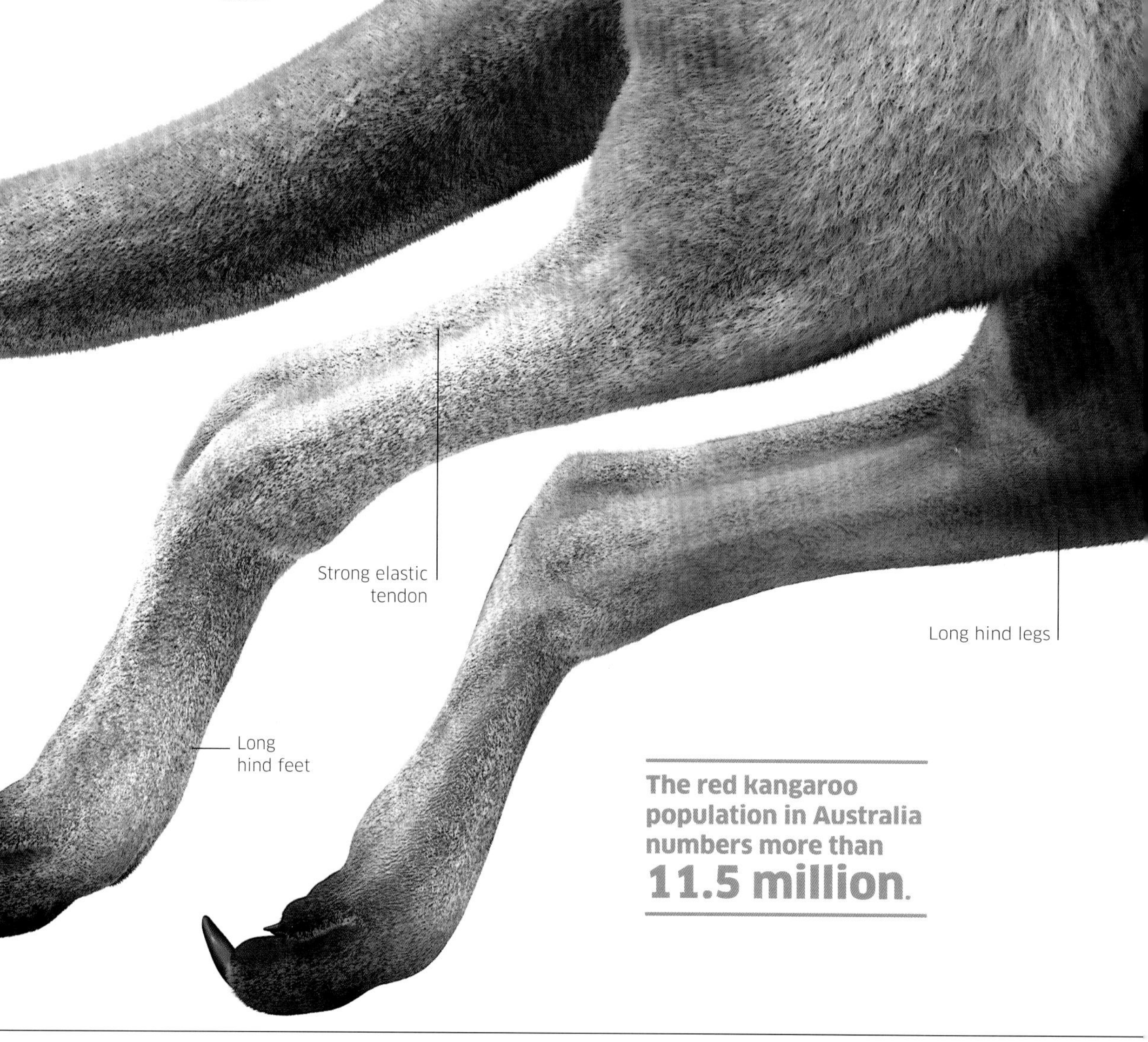

Tripod tail
The red kangaroo's long, heavy tail balances its head and body as it hops on its hind legs. But when the kangaroo is standing still it uses the tail as a prop, sitting back on it so it forms a stable tripod with its feet. This extra support helps the kangaroo to conserve energy.

The red kangaroo population in Australia numbers more than 11.5 million.

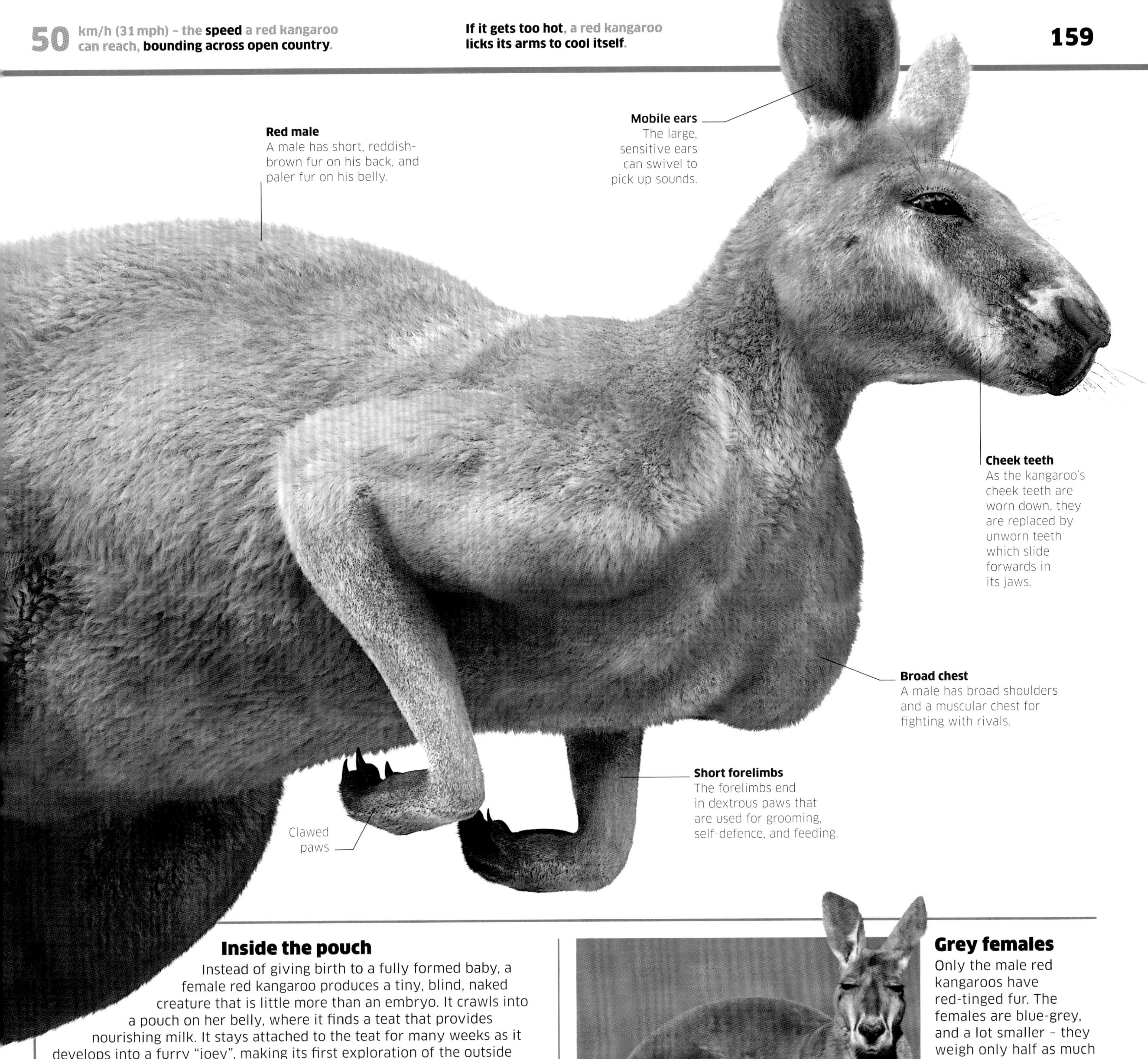

Inside the pouch

Instead of giving birth to a fully formed baby, a female red kangaroo produces a tiny, blind, naked creature that is little more than an embryo. It crawls into a pouch on her belly, where it finds a teat that provides nourishing milk. It stays attached to the teat for many weeks as it develops into a furry "joey", making its first exploration of the outside world six months later.

Grey females

Only the male red kangaroos have red-tinged fur. The females are blue-grey, and a lot smaller – they weigh only half as much as males. However, a female may also carry the extra burden of a young "joey" in her pouch until it is at least seven months old.

The sugar glider **can glide** 50 m (164 ft) or more on its **flight membrane** of stretched skin.

VIRGINIA OPOSSUM
Didelphis virginiana
Location: North and Central America
Length: Up to 50 cm ($19\frac{3}{4}$ in)

A highly adaptable opportunist eater that can thrive on a diet of scraps scavenged from bins, the Virginia opossum is common in many US cities. It is well known for its defence tactic of playing dead, lying with its mouth open and its tongue hanging out.

SOUTHERN MARSUPIAL MOLE
Notoryctes typhlops
Location: Australian deserts
Length: Up to 14 cm ($5\frac{1}{2}$ in)

This burrower has enormous claws on its front feet for digging, a cylindrical body with short fur, and a horny protective shield on its nose. It is quite blind, relying on scent to locate the insect larvae and earthworms that it eats.

NUMBAT
Myrmecobius fasciatus
Location: Southwestern and southern Australia
Length: Up to 29 cm ($11\frac{1}{2}$ in)

The stripy numbat is a specialist termite eater, finding the insects mainly by scent and scooping them up with its long, sticky tongue. Once widespread, it is now endangered and restricted to a few protected areas.

TASMANIAN DEVIL
Sarcophilus harrisii
Location: Tasmania
Length: Up to 65 cm ($25\frac{1}{2}$ in)

The biggest carnivorous marsupial, the Tasmanian devil is a hunter and scavenger with massively powerful jaws for killing prey and crushing bones. It hunts alone, and can take prey up to the size of a small kangaroo.

YELLOW-FOOTED ANTECHINUS
Antechinus flavipes
Location: Eastern and southwestern Australia
Length: Up to 13 cm (5 in)

With a diet of insects, spiders, worms, and similar animals, this small marsupial is remarkable for the way the male has just one breeding season throughout his whole life. He has multiple partners but uses up so many of his body's resources that he soon dies.

GREATER BILBY
Macrotis lagotis
Location: Australian deserts
Length: Up to 55 cm ($21\frac{3}{4}$ in)

With its long ears and burrowing habit, the greater bilby is like a rabbit, but has a much broader diet and is adapted for survival in the desert. Active only at night, it gets all the moisture its body needs from its food, and never has to drink.

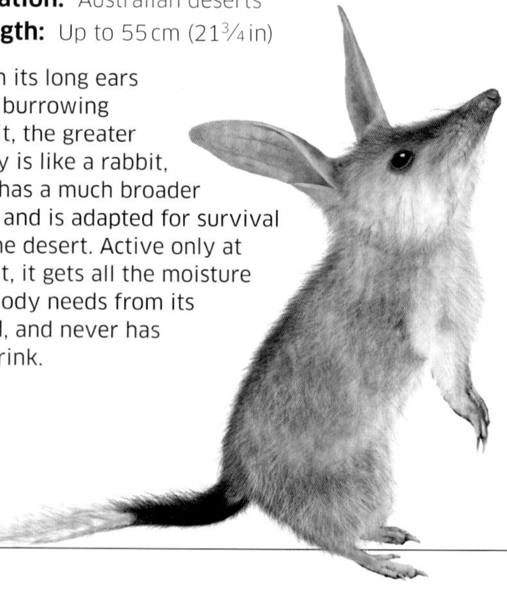

KOALA
Phascolarctos cinereus
Location: Eastern Australia
Length: Up to 82 cm ($32\frac{1}{4}$ in)

One of the most familiar marsupials, the koala feeds exclusively on the leaves of certain eucalyptus trees – a very poor diet that is hard to digest and has little food value. Koalas cope with this by using very little energy, spending most of their lives asleep.

Tree climber
Strong, sharp claws give a secure grip on tree bark.

20,000 The **number of termites** a numbat **can eat in a day.**

A Tasmanian devil's **jaws and teeth are so strong** that it can **bite through thick steel wire.**

COMMON WOMBAT

Vombatus ursinus

Location: Eastern Australia, Tasmania

Length: Up to 1.15 m (3¾ ft)

A ground-dwelling relative of the koala, with a similar sturdy, bear-like build, the wombat eats grass and can sometimes be seen grazing in fields alongside sheep. It has long claws that it uses to dig an extensive tunnel system. It usually spends the day underground, emerging at night to feed.

COMMON BRUSHTAIL POSSUM

Trichosurus vulpecula

Location: Australia, New Zealand

Length: Up to 55 cm (21½ in)

One of the most widespread Australian marsupials, this nocturnal climber has adapted well to life in cities. Although mainly a leaf-eater, it also preys on small animals and eats kitchen scraps.

SUGAR GLIDER

Petaurus breviceps

Location: Australia, New Guinea

Length: Up to 21 cm (8¼ in)

As its name suggests, this small nocturnal marsupial can glide from tree to tree on a furry membrane of skin stretched between its limbs. The "sugar" part of its name refers to its taste for sugary tree sap and flower nectar, but during the summer it feeds mainly on insects.

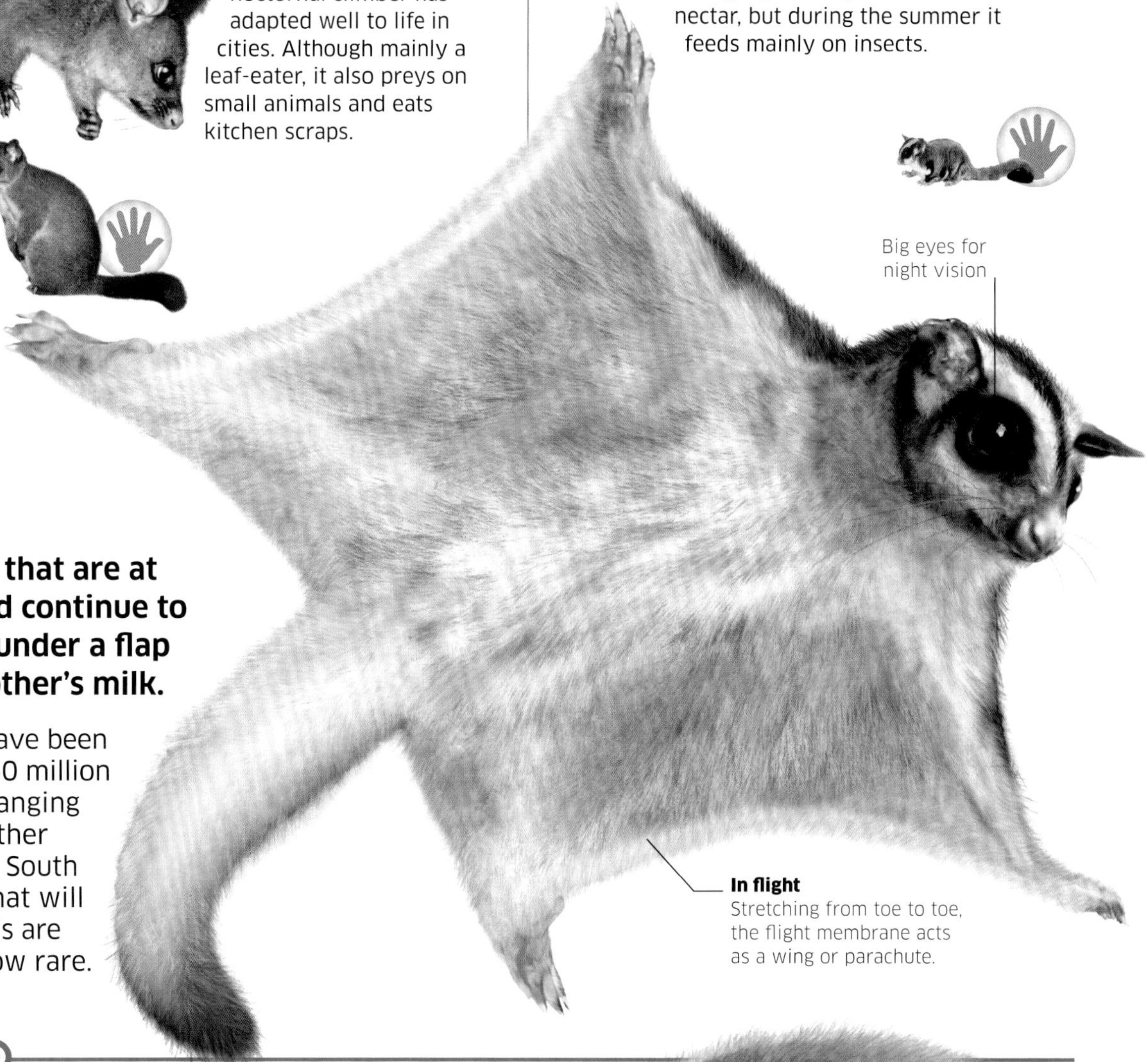

Marsupials

All marsupials give birth to young that are at an early stage of development, and continue to grow inside a protective pouch or under a flap of skin where they feed on their mother's milk.

Most marsupials live in Australia, where they have been isolated from other land mammals for at least 50 million years. They have a wide variety of lifestyles ranging from sleepy leaf-eaters to fierce carnivores. Other marsupials – the opossums – live in North and South America, where most species are omnivores that will eat almost anything. These American marsupials are flourishing, but many Australian species are now rare.

HONEY POSSUM

Tarsipes rostratus

Location: Southwestern Australia

Length: Up to 9 cm (3½ in)

The tiny honey possum feeds almost exclusively on flower nectar and pollen, gathering them with a very long tongue that has a brush-like tip. This means that it can live only in places where flowers open all year round.

GOODFELLOW'S TREE-KANGAROO

Dendrolagus goodfellowi

Location: New Guinea

Length: Up to 84 cm (33 in)

This is one of 10 kangaroo species that are adapted for life in trees. It has shorter back legs than a typical kangaroo, and strong front legs with hooked claws for gripping branches. It feeds at night on leaves and fruit.

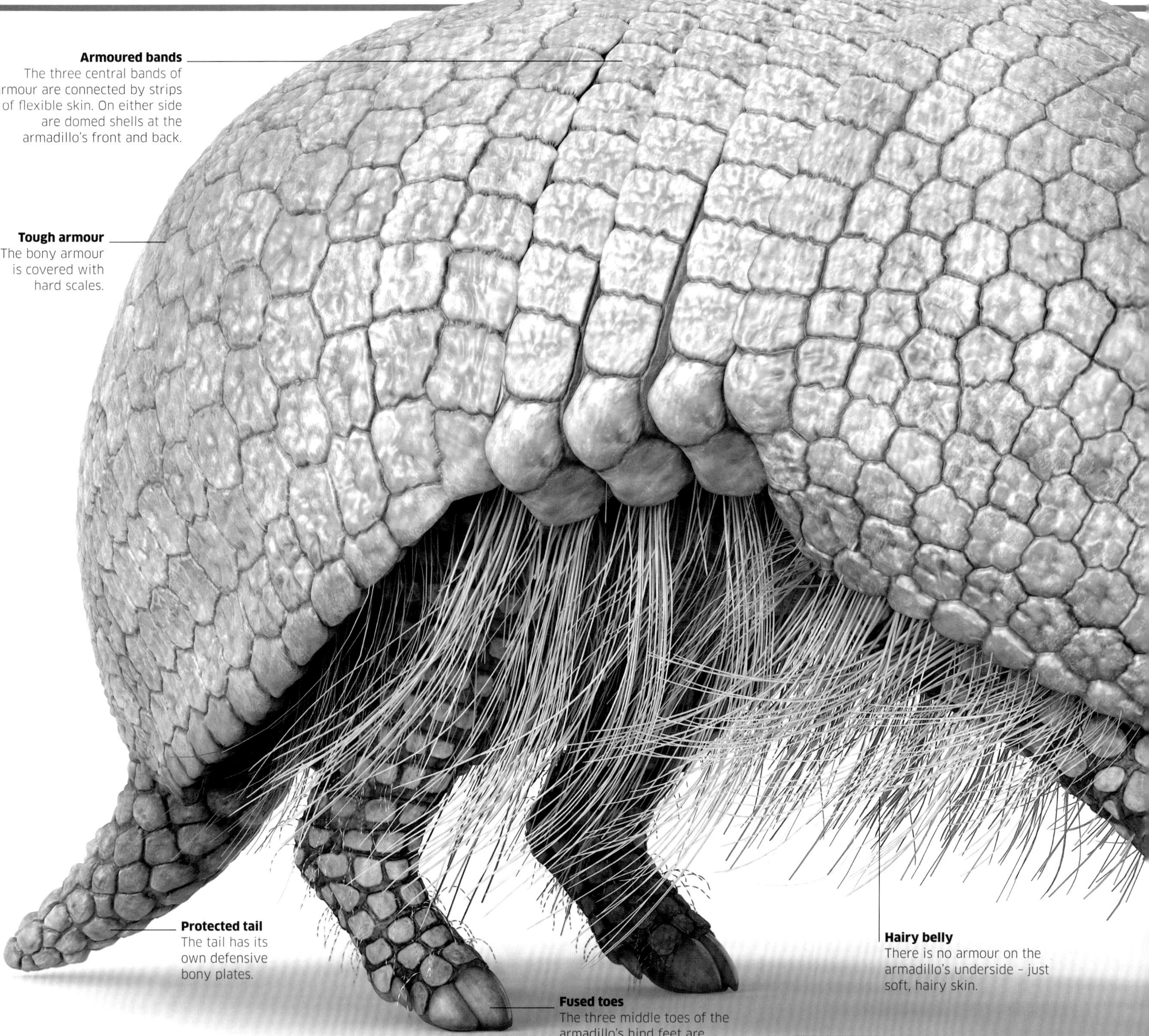

Three-banded armadillo

The armadillos are a family of 21 species, yet the Brazilian three-banded armadillo is one of just two species that can roll themselves into an armoured ball. The strong, bony carapace protects the armadillo from most of its predators.

Armadillos are unique among mammals in having bony armour. Other mammals have spines or scales, but only armadillos have defensive plates of bone, linked by narrow, bony bands that allow movement. This species feeds on ants and termites using its long, sticky tongue.

A layer of air under its armour
acts as insulation, keeping the armadillo cool in hot desert climates.

MAMMALS

THREE-BANDED ARMADILLO

Tolypeutes tricinctus

Location: Brazil

Length: Up to 28 cm (11 in)

Diet: Insects

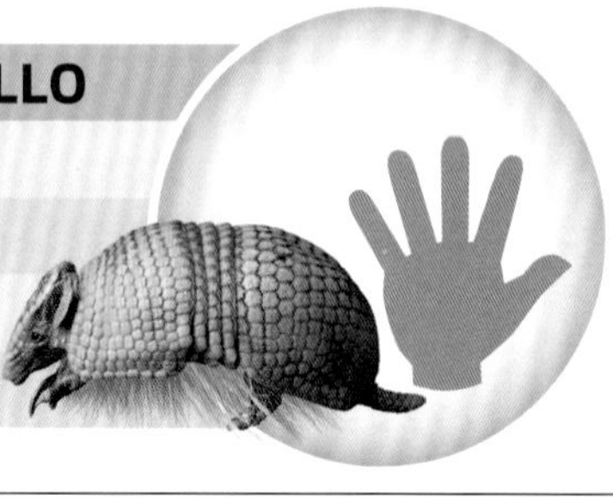

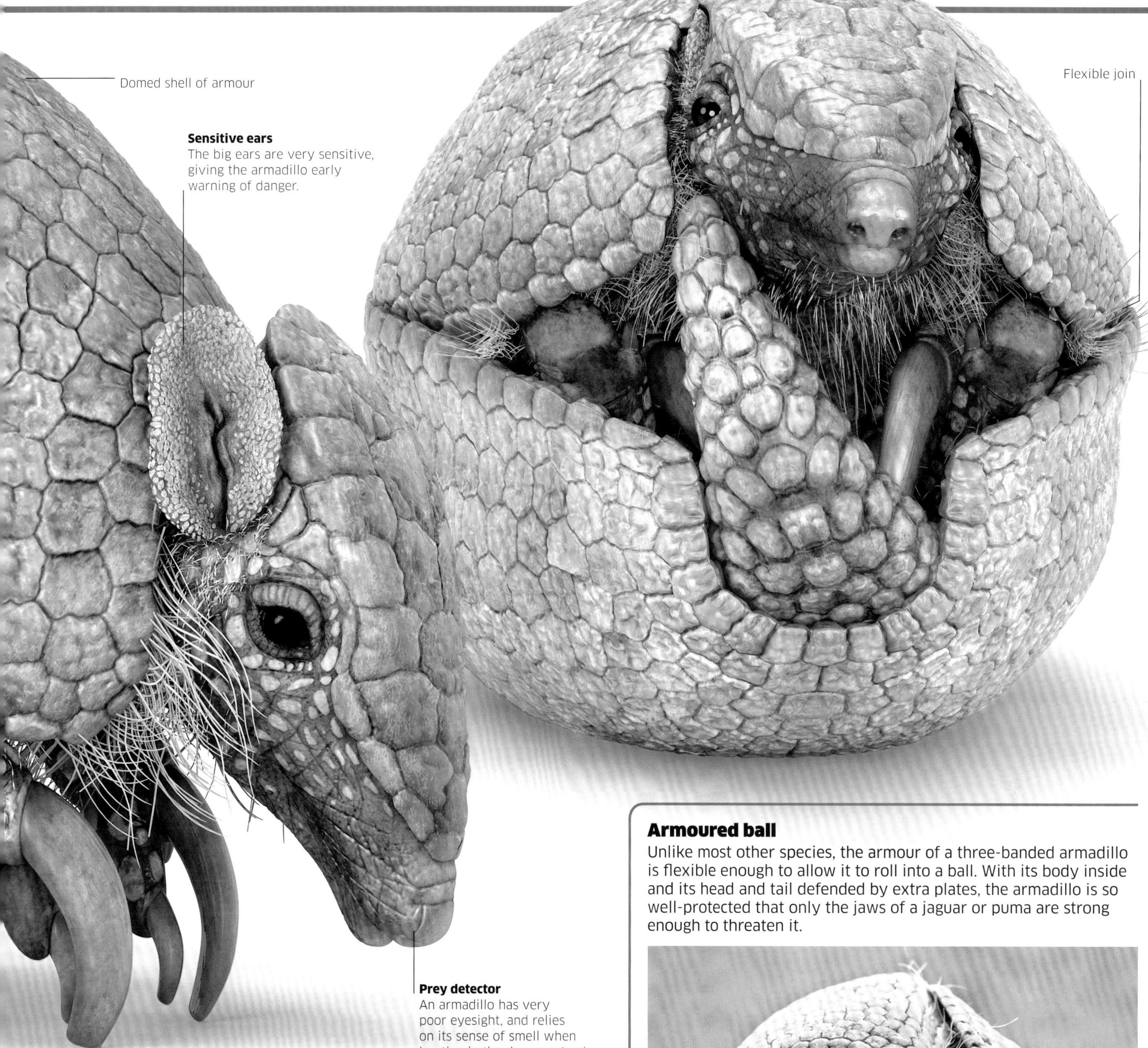

Armoured ball

Unlike most other species, the armour of a three-banded armadillo is flexible enough to allow it to roll into a ball. With its body inside and its head and tail defended by extra plates, the armadillo is so well-protected that only the jaws of a jaguar or puma are strong enough to threaten it.

Digging claws
Foraging with its nose close to the ground, the armadillo hunts ants and termites by scent. When it detects its insect prey, it starts digging with the massive claws on its front feet. The armadillo works fast to make a hole, then pushes its head in and starts scooping up the insects with its tongue. It may eat hundreds of them in just a few minutes.

A giant anteater's **tongue** is up to **60 cm (2 ft) long.**

MAMMALS
GIANT ANTEATER
Myrmecophaga tridactyla
Location: Central and South America
Length: Up to 1.2 m (4 ft)
Diet: Ants, termites

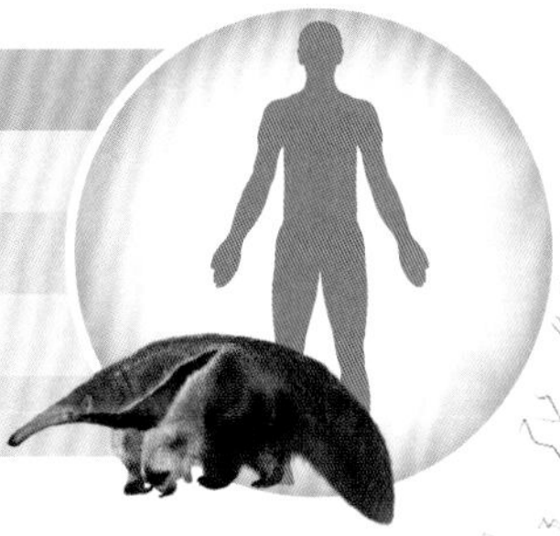

Giant anteater

Highly specialized for its insect-eating way of life, the giant anteater is one of the most distinctive of all mammals. Its huge front claws, elongated snout, and extra-long tongue enable it to rip into the nests of its ant and termite prey, and devour them by the thousand.

Widespread across tropical America, the anteater is a relative of the tree-living sloths, which feed exclusively on leaves. But the anteater is an insectivore, adapted for gathering large numbers of small prey. It occasionally raids the nests of wild bees, but usually targets ants' nests and termite mounds. Unlike other American anteaters, this species hunts and sleeps on the ground, relying on camouflage and powerful claws for defence against predators.

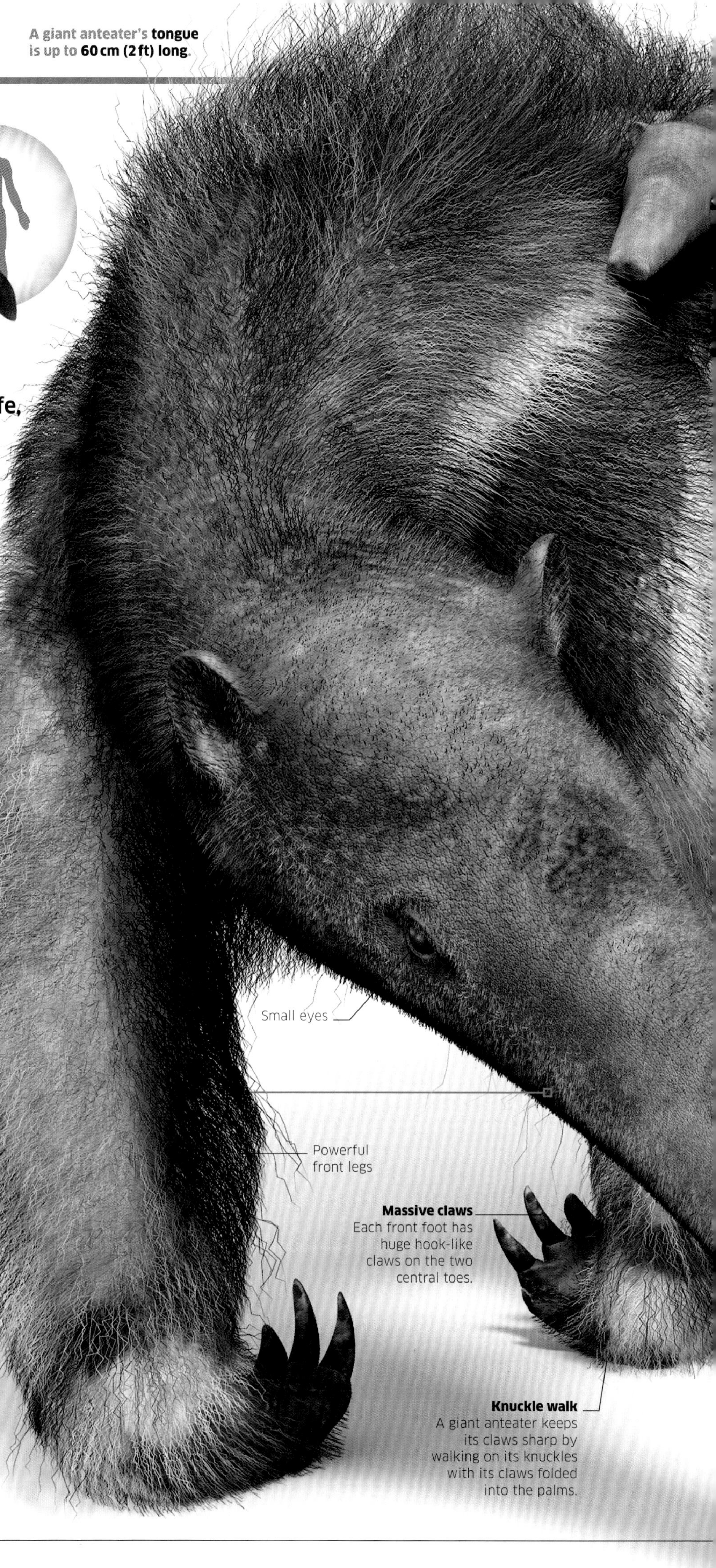

Bulk-feeder
A hunting anteater breaks into an ants' nest with its claws, inserts its long snout, and starts feeding. It can flick its long tongue in and out at an astonishing rate – nearly three times a second – and each time the tongue's sticky surface traps numerous ants and drags them into the anteater's mouth.

Precious burden
A female carries her single baby on her back until it can fend for itself.

Short legs
The hind legs are shorter than the front legs.

Clawed feet
The hind feet have short, strong claws on each of the five toes.

Tubular snout
The anteater's snout is extended to form a long tube, with a tiny mouth at the end.

Bushy tail
In hot weather a giant anteater spends most of the day asleep, curled up beneath its enormous bushy tail. The tail helps camouflage it, especially when it is sleeping in the shade of bushes. It also keeps the anteater warm in cold weather, and at night.

Lethal defence

If a giant anteater senses danger it will do its best to run away, or even swim for safety. But if it is cornered, it will rear up on its hind legs and threaten its attacker with its big, sharp front claws. The threat is no bluff – a slash from the claws can inflict serious injury. Giant anteaters have been known to kill people and even jaguars, their most formidable enemies.

A mole can **shift 540 times its own body weight** of earth **every day**.

European mole

Rarely seen above ground, the mole is well known for the molehills it creates all over grassland – the results of its constant tunnelling in search of prey.

Moles are dedicated tunnellers, with bodies specially adapted for the job. The European mole is typical, with a cylinder-shaped body and short, velvety fur. It has tiny eyes and very small ear flaps, but huge, spade-like front feet for digging through soil. It preys mainly on earthworms, which it catches in its tunnels.

MAMMALS

EUROPEAN MOLE

Talpa europaea

Location: Europe

Length: Up to 16 cm ($6^{1}/_{4}$ in)

Diet: Earthworms, insect larvae

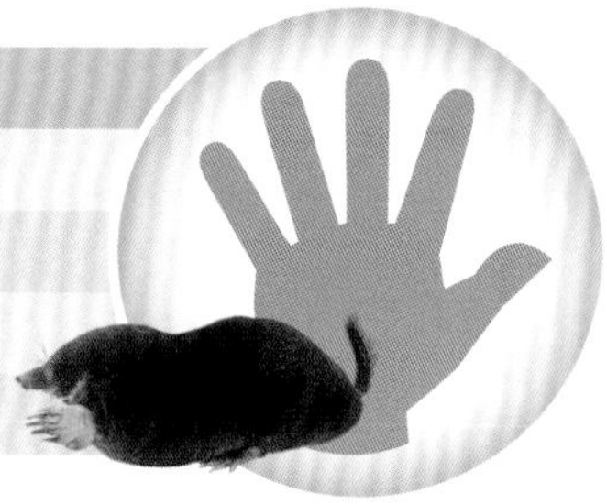

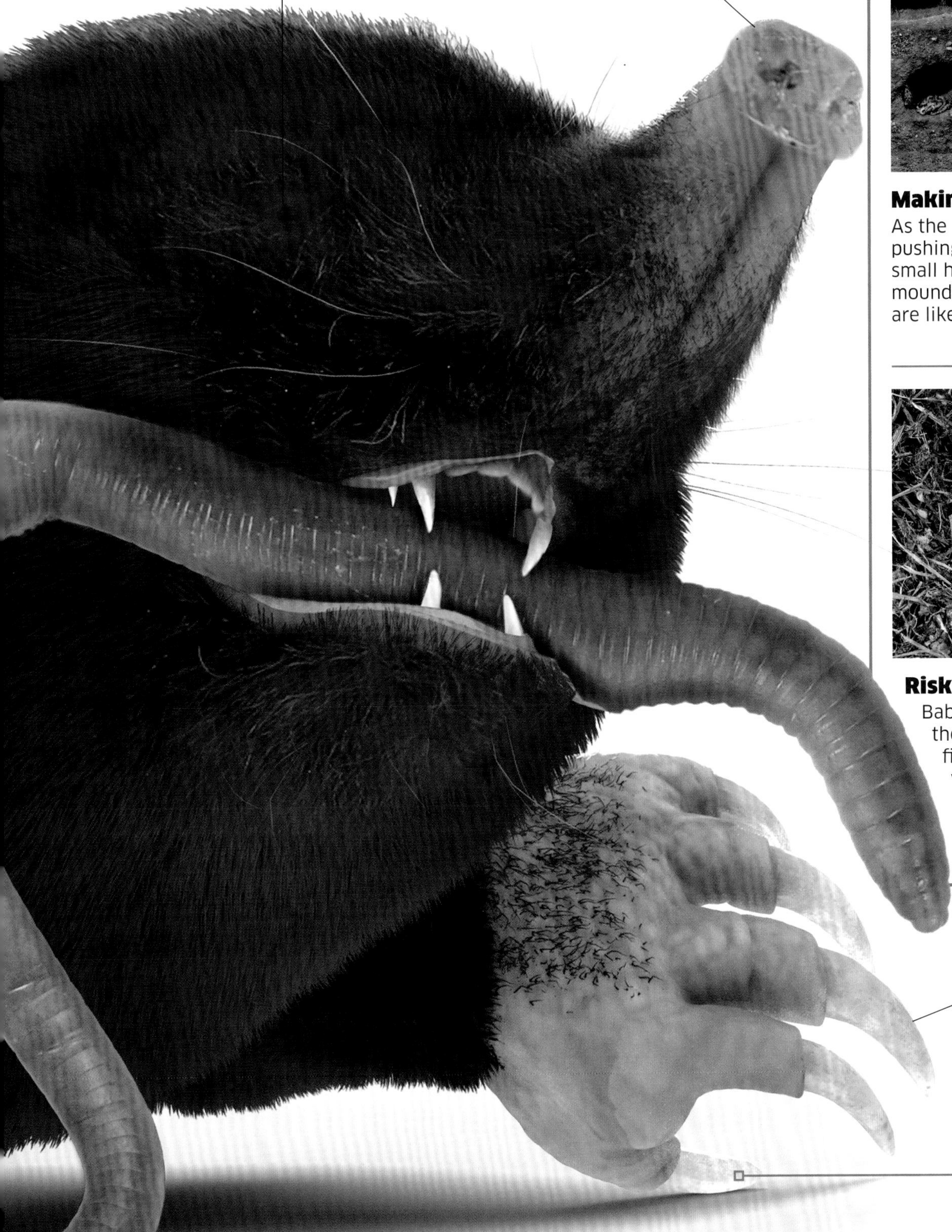

Tiny eyes are hidden by fur

Super senses
A mole relies on its sensitive nose and whiskers to locate prey in the dark.

Digging claws
The powerful, clawed forefeet turn outwards for efficient earth-moving.

Making molehills

As the mole burrows, it gets rid of waste soil by pushing it up above ground. Mostly the mole leaves small heaps of soil, but sometimes it creates a large mound that it uses as a nest – especially if its tunnels are likely to get flooded during heavy rain.

Risky journey

Baby moles are born in spring and stay with their mother, feeding on her milk, for four to five weeks. The young moles are at their most vulnerable to predators as they emerge above ground from their mother's tunnel system to find new places to live.

The mole's saliva is toxic to earthworms, allowing it to paralyze the worms and store them to eat later.

Extra digging power
The excavator-like action of the mole's forefeet is boosted by an extension to its wristbone. This supports a pad next to the mole's thumb, and acts like an extra thumb. It cannot bend, but it helps with digging. The only other mammal with a similar adaptation is the giant panda.

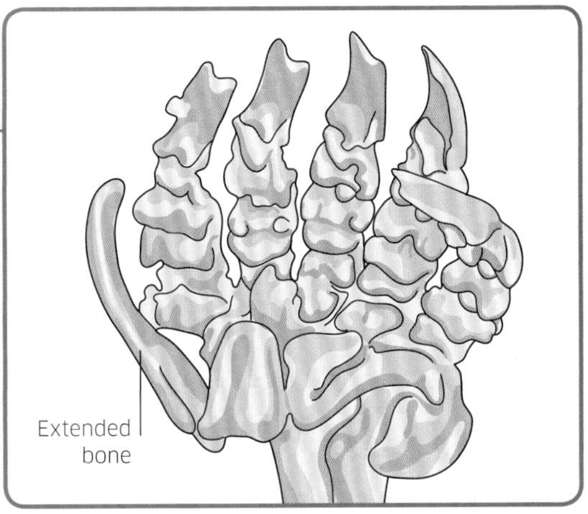

100 kg (220 lb) – the **weight** of a **newborn African elephant calf** – as much as a **heavyweight boxer**.

Multi-purpose tool
The elephant's trunk is formed from its nose and upper lip. Highly mobile and strong, yet very sensitive, the trunk makes an ideal tool for investigating and gathering food, drawing in water, signalling to other elephants, and generating loud, trumpeting calls.

Elephants

Instantly recognizable by their long, mobile trunks and colossal size, elephants are the biggest and heaviest land animals. They are renowned for their intelligence and long memories, but also seriously endangered by hunting for their meat and ivory tusks.

Elephants are adapted for eating large quantities of coarse grass, leaves, and bark. They have massive teeth for grinding their tough food to a pulp, and extensive digestive systems for processing it. They spend at least three-quarters of their time feeding or looking for food, travelling in closely bonded social groups led by mature females.

MAMMALS

AFRICAN SAVANNA ELEPHANT

Loxodonta africana

Location: Sub-Saharan Africa

Length: Up to 7.5 m (24½ ft)

Diet: Grass, leaves, bark

African savanna elephant

The biggest elephant, with long, curved tusks in both sexes, the African savanna elephant lives mainly on open grasslands with scattered trees. Its huge ears radiate heat, stopping the elephant overheating under the tropical sun.

AFRICAN FOREST ELEPHANT

Loxodonta cyclotis

Location: Central Africa

Length: Up to 4 m (13 ft)

As its name indicates, this elephant lives in the dense lowland rainforests of tropical Africa. Smaller than the savanna elephant, with straighter tusks, it eats a lot more leaves and less grass. Like all elephants, it communicates in the dense forest with very deep calls, inaudible to humans.

ASIAN ELEPHANT

Elephas maximus

Location: Southern and Southeast Asia

Length: Up to 6.4 m (21 ft)

An Asian elephant has smaller ears than an African elephant, and a high-domed head. Typically, only the males have tusks. It lives in a variety of habitats from dense forests to grasslands, and there are three local subspecies – the Indian, Sri Lankan, and Sumatran elephants.

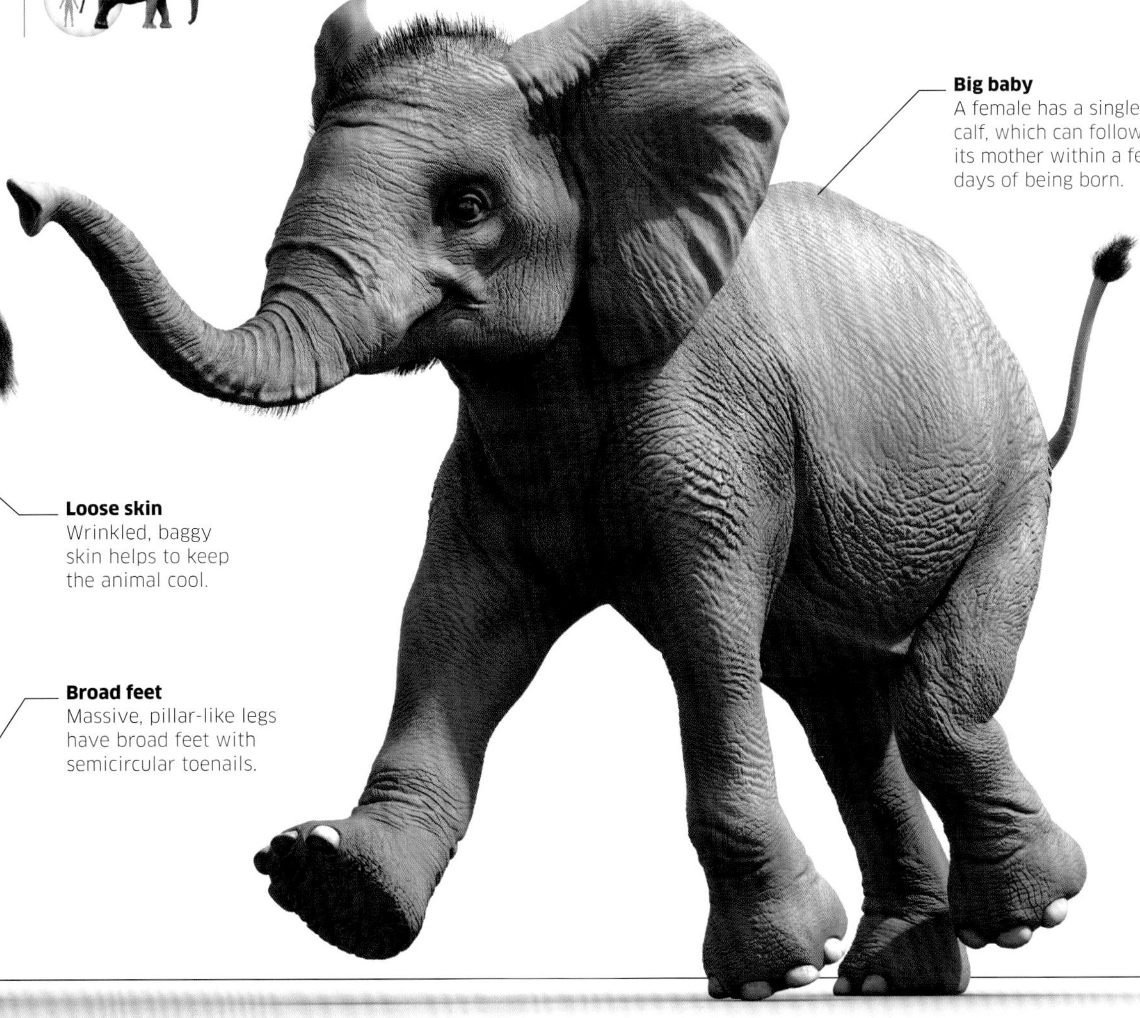

North American beaver

One of nature's busiest architects, the beaver uses its tree-felling skills to transform the landscape of its native forests – creating dams, lakes, and impregnable fortresses where it is safe from its enemies.

A beaver is a giant nocturnal rodent – an aquatic relative of squirrels and mice. Like them, it has big, chisel-bladed front teeth for gnawing its food, but the beaver also uses them to cut down trees. It needs trees to build its lodge, which it surrounds with a defensive moat of deep water by using more timber and mud to dam a forest stream. When the water freezes over in winter the beavers stay active beneath the ice, feeding on the leaves and buds of branches stored underwater.

Webbed feet
When swimming fast, the beaver drives itself through the water with its large webbed rear feet and using its paddle-shaped tail like a rudder. It can swim slowly using its tail alone.

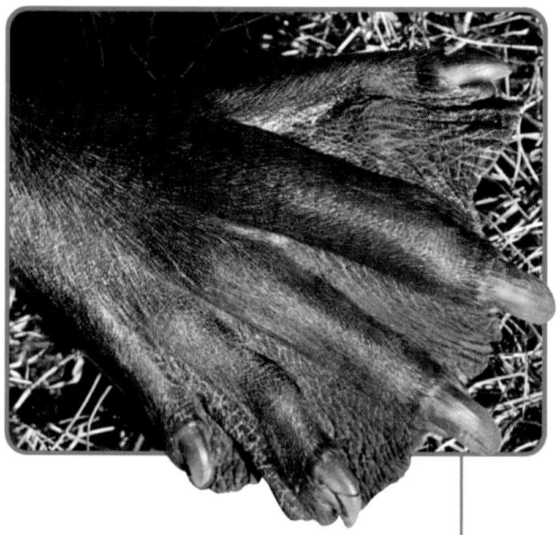

Flat tail
Highly adapted for swimming, the tail is scaly, hairless, and flattened like a paddle. The beaver slaps it on the water to warn other beavers of danger.

MAMMALS

NORTH AMERICAN BEAVER

Castor canadensis

Location: North America, Mexico

Length: Up to 88 cm (34½ in)

Diet: Tree bark, leaves, twigs

The longest-known beaver dam extended for 850 m (2,790 ft).

Fortified lodge

The beaver's dam can be well over 1.8 m (6 ft) high, and creates a pond that is about 0.9 m (3 ft) deep. The water floods the entrance to the lodge, which is built from a pile of sticks hollowed out to create a living space. Mud plastered over the sticks freezes in winter, so no predator can get in. Occasionally, muskrats will cohabit with beavers.

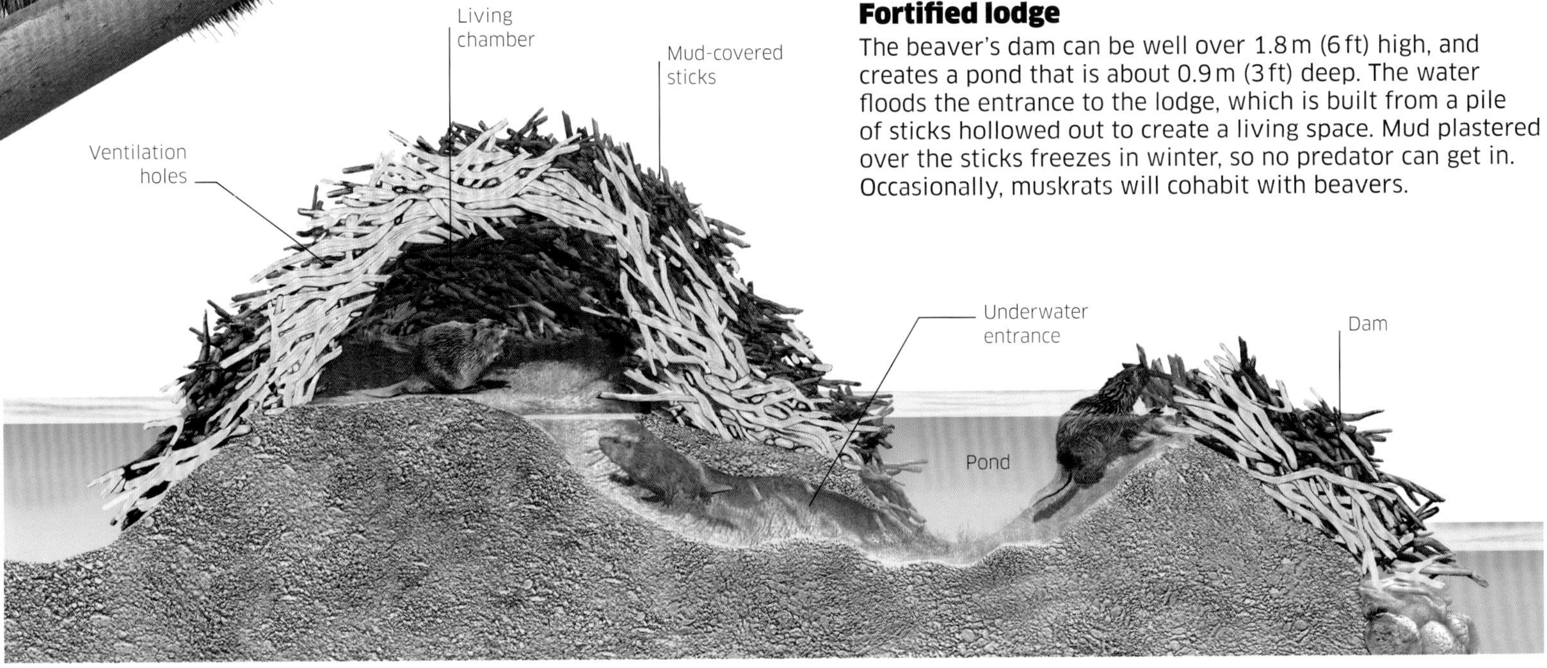

The biggest **prairie dog town** ever found was home to some **400 million prairie dogs**.

EURASIAN RED SQUIRREL

Sciurus vulgaris

Location: Eurasia

Length: Up to 22 cm (8¾ in)

The agile red squirrel lives mainly in the trees, favouring conifer forests with a plentiful supply of seed-bearing cones. It uses its gnawing teeth to strip the cones to get at the seeds inside. It is now rare in some parts of Europe owing to competition with grey squirrels introduced from America.

BLACK-TAILED PRAIRIE DOG

Cynomys ludovicianus

Location: North America

Length: Up to 38 cm (15 in)

This ground squirrel lives on the virtually treeless American prairie grasslands, in burrow systems known as prairie dog towns. In the past some of these were colossal, covering huge areas and occupied by millions of animals.

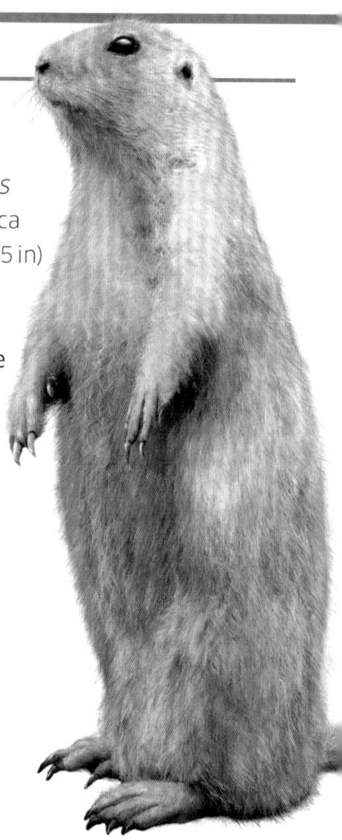

HAZEL DORMOUSE

Muscardinus avellanarius

Location: Europe

Length: Up to 9 cm (3½ in)

Resembling a miniature squirrel, this small woodland animal spends more than half its life asleep, hibernating from November to May. When awake it feeds mainly in the trees, gathering berries, nuts, flowers, and sometimes insects.

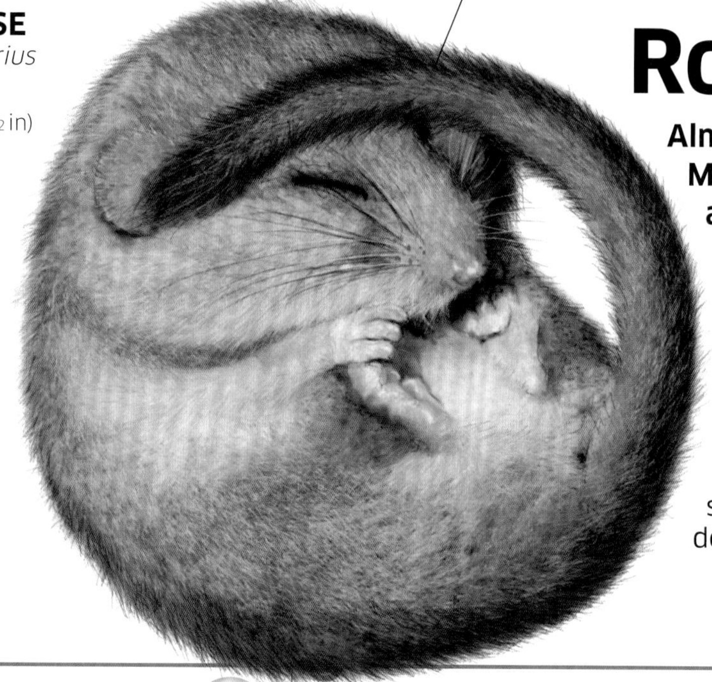

Rodents

Almost half of all mammal species are rodents. Mostly small, plant-eating animals such as mice and squirrels, they are all equipped with big, self-sharpening front teeth for gnawing tough foods.

Rodents live in virtually every habitat from tropical rainforests to the Arctic tundra and scorchingly hot, dry deserts. Most live on seeds, nuts, fruit, and juicy roots, but a few are hunters of small animals, or omnivores that will devour almost anything.

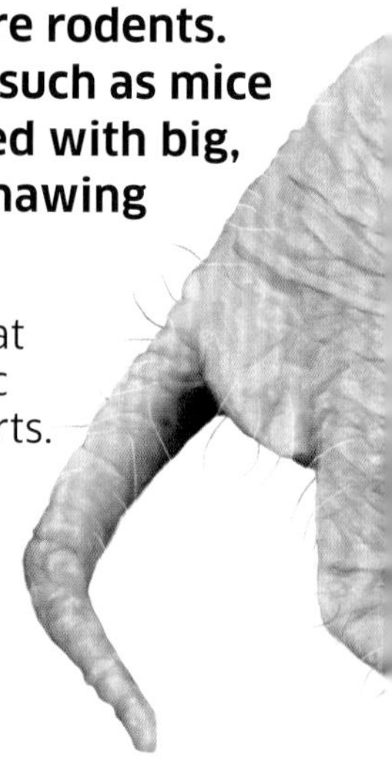

LONG-EARED JERBOA

Euchoreutes naso

Location: Eastern central Asia

Length: Up to 9 cm (3½ in)

This is one of many desert jerboas and is adapted for hopping, with long feet and a lengthy tail for balance. This enables it to range widely in search of scarce food, and to escape its enemies.

NORWAY LEMMING

Lemmus lemmus

Location: Northern Scandinavia

Length: Up to 13.5 cm (5¼ in)

This Arctic species is a prolific breeder and may produce so many young in a good year that food shortages can occur. This forces the lemming to make mass migrations to find new habitats. It is the staple prey of Arctic foxes and snowy owls.

A **springhare** can cover **2 m (6½ ft)** or more in **one bound**.

Lions have been known to **die of wounds inflicted** by the **quills of porcupines** they have attacked.

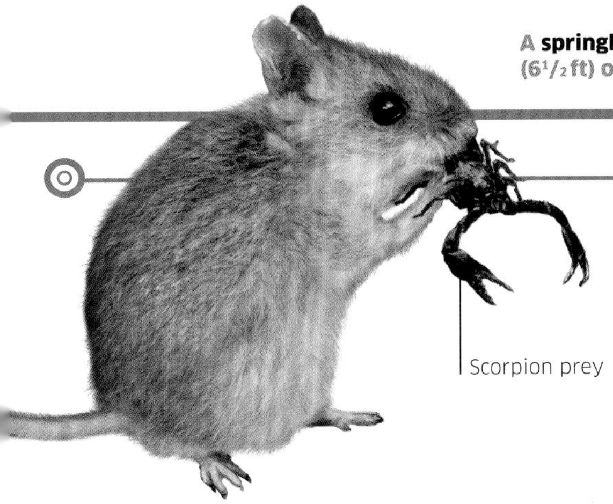

NORTHERN GRASSHOPPER MOUSE

Onychomys leucogaster

Location: North America

Length: Up to 13 cm (5 in)

Most rodents are dedicated vegetarians, but this one is a hunter. It mainly preys on insects, but has been known to kill and eat smaller mice and even small snakes and lizards. It is also known for its remarkably loud, shrill calls.

BLACK RAT

Rattus rattus

Location: Eurasia, Africa, Australasia, North America

Length: Up to 22.5 cm (8¾ in)

Along with some other species, the black rat has been accidentally spread around the world by travelling on human ships. It is famous as a carrier of bubonic plague, the disease that killed half the human population of Europe in the 14th century.

SOUTH AFRICAN SPRINGHARE

Pedetes capensis

Location: Southern Africa

Length: Up to 43 cm (17 in)

Despite its name this is not a hare, but a rodent. However, it can certainly spring, leaping like a kangaroo on its long hind legs, balanced by its long, bushy tail. It lives in deserts, hiding in a burrow by day and only feeding at night.

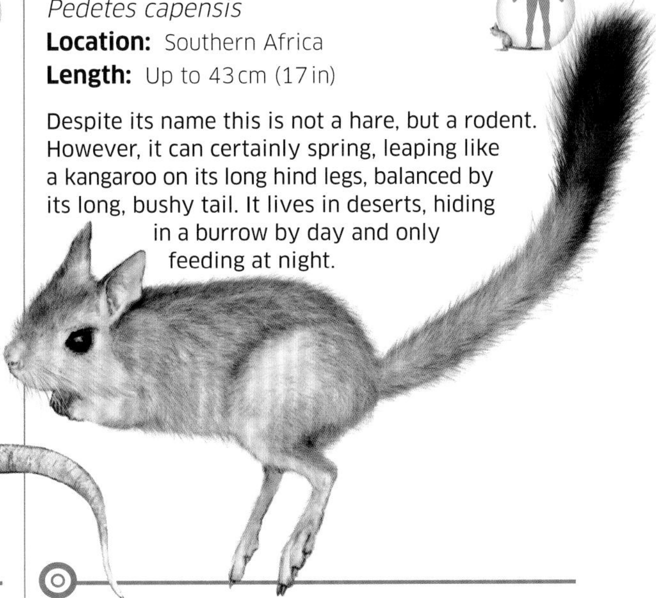

NAKED MOLE RAT

Heterocephalus glaber

Location: Eastern Africa

Length: Up to 9.2 cm (3½ in)

This extraordinary rodent lives in colonies that are each controlled by a single breeding queen, rather like colonies of honeybees. The colonies occupy burrows that the mole-rats dig with their teeth, kicking the loose earth out of the burrow entrance.

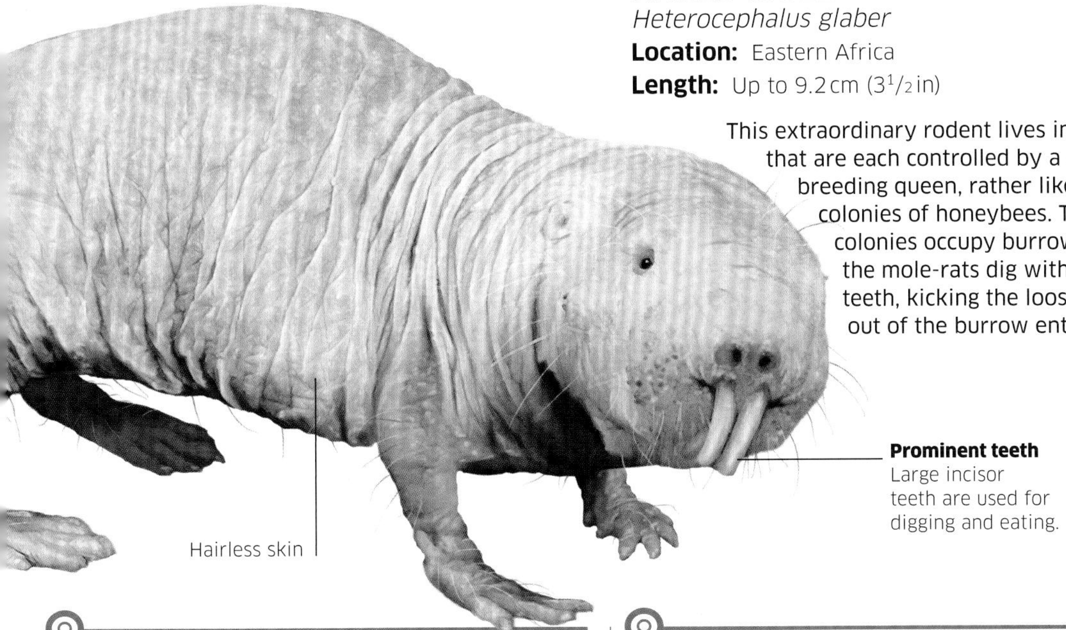

LONG-TAILED CHINCHILLA

Chinchilla lanigera

Location: Chile and South America

Length: Up to 23 cm (9 in)

The chinchilla lives in the Andes mountains, where it survives the harsh climate thanks to a dense coat of fur. It emerges at night when temperatures are at their lowest to feed on seeds and grasses, and other small animals.

CRESTED PORCUPINE

Hystrix cristata

Location: Africa, Italy

Length: Up to 1 m (3¼ ft)

If attacked, this porcupine raises up its spectacularly long quills and shakes its tail, which is equipped with special broad, hollow quills that produce a hiss-like rattle. If its enemy takes no notice, the porcupine may charge it tail-first, to embed the sharp quills in its attacker's skin.

CAPYBARA

Hydrochoerus hydrochaeris

Location: Tropical South America

Length: Up to 1.3 m (4¼ ft)

The biggest of all rodents, the pig-sized capybara lives in swamps and flooded grasslands where it has a semi-aquatic way of life, feeding mainly on grasses and aquatic plants. It has a scent gland on top of its snout, which is much bigger in mature males.

Rabbits and hares

With their long ears and bounding gait, rabbits and hares are instantly recognizable. They live almost worldwide, from the tropics to the High Arctic, and some occur in vast numbers.

Together with the rodent-like pikas, they form a group called the lagomorphs, which means "hare-shaped". They are closely related to rodents such as squirrels and mice, but have slightly different teeth and are more strictly vegetarian. Rabbits are typically burrowers that bolt underground for safety when threatened, but most hares are long-legged athletes that live in open country and rely on fast getaways to escape their enemies.

Wide field of view
Big, bulging eyes high on the sides of the head give virtually all-round vision.

Big ears
Very long ears catch the slightest sound that could betray a predator.

Strong legs
The hare's very long hind legs allow it to run at high speeds.

Able to hit 70 km/h (43 mph), the brown hare can run as fast as a greyhound.

Brown hare
Renowned for its agility, the brown hare can easily outrun most of its enemies, often changing direction rapidly to evade pursuers. During the spring breeding season, reluctant females drive off over-eager males by sparring with their paws like boxers.

Brown fur sometimes turns reddish

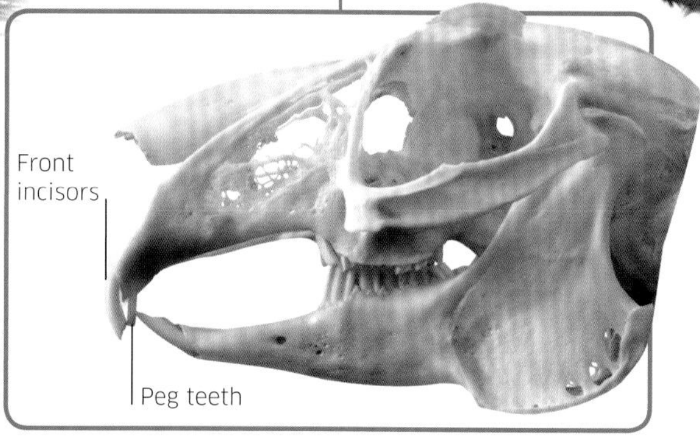

Peg teeth
A hare has big, rodent-like incisor teeth that grow constantly to compensate for wear, with a big gap behind them that allows it to hold a lot of food in its mouth. However, unlike a rodent, a hare also has a pair of small peg teeth that have almost no function.

MAMMALS

BROWN HARE

Lepus europaeus

Location: Eurasia; introduced elsewhere

Length: Up to 70 cm (27½ in)

Diet: Grass, herbs, bark

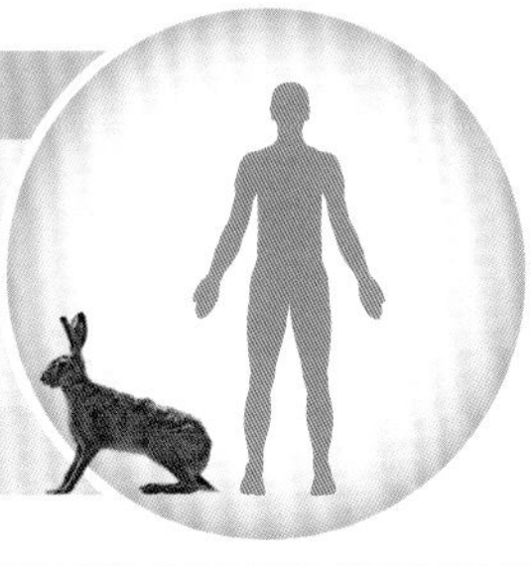

BLACK-TAILED JACKRABBIT

Lepus californicus

Location: Mexico, Western USA

Length: Up to 60.5 cm (23¾ in)

The enormous ears of the jackrabbit are vital to its survival in hot, dry deserts and grasslands, since they act as radiators that give off excess heat to the air and help the animal keep cool. Despite its name the jackrabbit is a hare, with long legs that give it the speed to escape a coyote.

ARCTIC HARE

Lepus arcticus

Location: Arctic Canada, Greenland

Length: Up to 67 cm (26½ in)

This incredibly hardy hare lives in large groups and is adapted for the freezing climate with a very thick coat of white fur. It has shorter ears than is usual for a hare, reducing heat loss.

AMAMI RABBIT

Pentalagus furnessi

Location: Amami islands, Japan

Length: Up to 51 cm (20 in)

An elusive, nocturnal inhabitant of dense forest, the Japanese Amami rabbit is a survivor of a type of rabbit that was once widespread in Asia, but is now almost extinct. It lives in burrows that it digs with its long claws.

EUROPEAN RABBIT

Oryctolagus cuniculus

Location: Western Europe; introduced elsewhere

Length: Up to 55 cm (21¾ in)

Once restricted to Spain, France, and North Africa, the European rabbit has been spread to many other parts of the world, and in Australia it has become a pest. It digs extensive burrow systems, emerging mainly at night to nibble on grasses and leaves.

VOLCANO RABBIT

Romerolagus diazi

Location: Mexico

Length: Up to 36 cm (14¾ in)

With a stumpy body and short ears, this is one of the smallest and rarest rabbits. It lives only on the forested slopes of four volcanoes to the south of Mexico City, where its habitat and future are threatened by farming and road building.

EASTERN COTTONTAIL

Sylvilagus floridanus

Location: North and Central America

Length: Up to 48.5 cm (19 in)

The most common of many similar species known as cottontails, this is the American equivalent of the European rabbit. But instead of digging its own burrows, it occupies holes dug by other animals such as ground squirrels.

Lemurs use their **keen sense of smell** to pick up **scents** left by other lemurs.

RING-TAILED LEMUR

Lemur catta

Location: Madagascar

Length: Up to 46 cm (18 in)

Its distinctive tail makes this the most recognizable of the lemurs. It lives in large, noisy groups, searching for fruit, leaves, and small animals in the forest trees, but unusually it also spends a lot of time on the ground.

WHITE-FOOTED SPORTIVE LEMUR

Lepilemur leucopus

Location: Madagascar

Length: Up to 26 cm (10¼ in)

The sportive lemurs were given their name because they look like boxers when they are defending themselves. This species is probably the smallest of the family – a dedicated leaf-eater that, because of the very low food value of its leafy diet, devotes most of its time to either eating or resting.

Lemurs

Found only in Madagascar, the lemurs are a diverse group of primates related to the ancestors of monkeys and apes. Highly adapted for life in the forest trees, many are superbly acrobatic climbers.

Arriving in Madagascar at least 40 million years ago, the lemurs evolved into up to 120 species ranging from tiny mouse lemurs to gorilla-sized giants. Each species was adapted to a particular way of life on an island with a wide variety of habitats – some were adaptable omnivores, while others were specialists. But 17 species (including the giant lemurs) are now extinct, and many more are endangered by destruction of their wild habitats.

BLUE-EYED BLACK LEMUR

Eulemur flavifrons

Location: Madagascar

Length: Up to 45 cm (17¾ in)

The males and females of most lemurs look the same, but in this critically endangered species only the males are black. Females are reddish-brown, with paler fur on their underside. Apart from many humans, this is the only primate with blue eyes. It feeds mainly on fruit and flowers.

MADAME BERTHE'S MOUSE LEMUR

Microcebus berthae

Location: Madagascar

Length: Up to 9.5 cm (3¾ in)

This huge-eyed, nocturnal animal is the smallest of the tiny mouse lemurs, and the smallest of all primates. It is very agile, climbing through trees and shrubs in search of fruit, flowers, nectar, insects, and small vertebrates such as geckos and chameleons.

During the dry season, the **mouse lemur eats sugary honeydew** produced by sap-sucking flower bugs.

Verreaux's sifaka
Highly specialized for climbing, this big lemur cannot walk or run in the usual way. Instead, it skips sideways over the ground on its hind legs, with its arms held out for balance, like a dancer.

Long hands
Verreaux's sifaka spends most of its life in the treetops, foraging for leaves and fruit. Both its hands and feet are adapted for gripping branches with long thumbs and opposable, thumb-like big toes.

Powerful hind legs
This lemur can make impressive leaps from branch to branch.

MAMMALS

VERREAUX'S SIFAKA

Propithecus verreauxi

Location: Madagascar

Length: Up to 48 cm (19 in)

Diet: Leaves, fruit, bark

INDRI

Indri indri

Location: Madagascar

Length: Up to 72 cm (28¼ in)

The biggest lemur, this strikingly patterned near relative of Verreaux's sifaka is unique in having only a very short tail. Like other lemurs it holds its body vertically while leaping through the trees, and clings to branches with its large hands.

AYE-AYE

Daubentonia madagascariensis

Location: Madagascar

Length: Up to 37 cm (14½ in)

This extraordinary animal has a very slender middle finger that it uses to extract timber-boring insect grubs from their burrows – almost like the mammal equivalent of a woodpecker. It also uses its finger to scoop out the pulp of ripe fruit.

A howler monkey **can smell ripe fruit** up to 2 km (1¼ miles) away.

77 per cent of a **howler monkey's day** is **spent resting**.

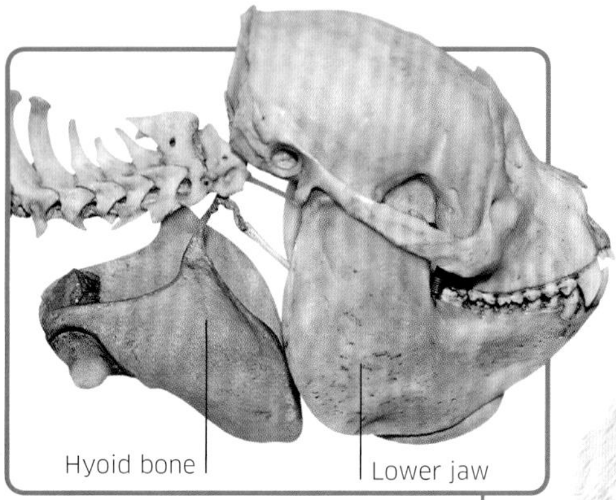

Voice box
A howler monkey has an enlarged larynx (voice box) for producing deep, resonant calls. It is supported by a huge, hollow hyoid bone behind the massive lower jaw. The jaw and hyoid of a male howler (shown above) are bigger than those of a female.

Tight hold
Baby howlers are born with a golden coat. They cling to the fur on their mother's back to be transported around.

Keeping track
Groups of howlers start and end each day by whooping at each other. This tells them where their competitors are.

Shared mothering
Mother howler monkeys care for and carry each others' babies in a practice called "allomothering".

Long tail
The tail measures up to 65 cm (25½ in) long, matching the length of the body.

Mobile toes
Long toes give the monkey a secure grip on branches high above the ground.

Sensitive underside
The underneath of the tail lacks hair. It is extra sensitive and able to identify things by touch.

Paraguayan howler

The booming calls of tropical American howler monkeys are the loudest noises made by any land animal on Earth. The monkeys howl to defend their feeding territory and their females, with each troop calling in unison to warn neighbouring troops not to trespass on their patch.

The males howl loudest, filling the rainforest with sound at dawn and during the day as each troop responds to its neighbours, but females howl too. Unusually the females are a different colour from the males, being olive-buff while the males are black. Howler monkeys usually live in small troops in the tropical forests of central South America. They spend most of their time high in the tree canopy feeding on fruit and leaves.

The guttural, roaring territorial calls of Paraguayan howlers can be heard 5 km (3 miles) away.

22 The **highest number** of howlers in a troop. Usually there are **between 5 and 8**.

A Paraguayan howler monkey can **live for up to 20 years**.

MAMMALS

PARAGUAYAN HOWLER

Alouatta caraya

Location: Central South America

Length: Up to 65 cm (25½ in)

Diet: Leaves, fruit

Leafy diet

Unusually for a monkey, the Paraguayan howler eats a lot of leaves as well as fruit. Leaves are easier to find, but are far less nutritious. The monkeys select the youngest leaves, but they have to eat a lot of them. They save energy by spending much of the day asleep and not moving far.

Japanese macaques **live in regions** where the **winter temperature** can fall as low as **-15°C (5°F)**.

Monkeys

From big, powerful, dog-faced baboons to miniature, silky-coated marmosets, monkeys are the most varied of all primates, famous for their agility, sociable natures, and intelligence.

Most monkeys are tropical tree-dwellers that feed mainly on fruit. In tropical forests, trees are in fruit all year round, but fruiting trees can be scattered and hard to find. So typical monkeys have become very skilled at moving through trees, and have good colour vision for spotting ripe fruit among the leaves. Their excellent memories also help them remember where to find good food sources. Monkeys are divided into two categories: Old World monkeys from Africa and Asia, and New World monkeys from tropical America.

JAPANESE MACAQUE

Macaca fuscata

Location: Japan

Length: Up to 65 cm (25½ in)

Sometimes called the snow monkey because of its chilly mountain habitat, this monkey is unusual because it does not live in the tropics. It eats fruit, plus green plants, juicy roots, and seeds when fruit is scarce. It is most famous for bathing in hot volcanic springs to keep warm in winter.

DE BRAZZA'S MONKEY

Cercopithecus neglectus

Location: Central Africa

Length: Up to 54 cm (21¼ in)

This is one of the most colourful and widespread species of guenon, a type of long-tailed African monkey, mainly found in tropical forests. It prefers swampy forests, where small groups forage for food.

MANDRILL

Mandrillus sphinx

Location: Central Africa

Length: Up to 1.1 m (43¼ in)

The mandrill is the largest monkey and closely related to the baboon. Males have bright red-and-blue faces, with the colouring most vivid in dominant males. Mandrills spend most of their time on the ground and eat a wide variety of foods, from fruit, eggs, and leaves to small mammals.

ANGOLAN COLOBUS

Colobus angolensis

Location: Central and East Africa

Length: Up to 66 cm (26 in)

Also called the black-and-white colobus, this slender rainforest monkey is one of the most striking Old World species, with a white ruff around its face and a silky, white mantle over its shoulders. An agile climber, it lives high in the trees in large troops, feeding mainly on leaves.

GEOFFROY'S TUFTED-EAR MARMOSET

Callithrix geoffroyi

Location: Eastern tropical Brazil

Length: Up to 23 cm (9 in)

Squirrel-sized marmosets are the smallest monkeys. Like other species, this marmoset gouges holes in tree bark with its teeth so it can eat the sugary gum that oozes out.

GOLDEN LION TAMARIN

Leontopithecus rosalia

Location: Eastern tropical Brazil

Length: Up to 33 cm (13 in)

Once widespread, this small, sleek tamarin is now very rare. An agile climber, it uses its long, clawed fingers to search among dense foliage for fruit and insects.

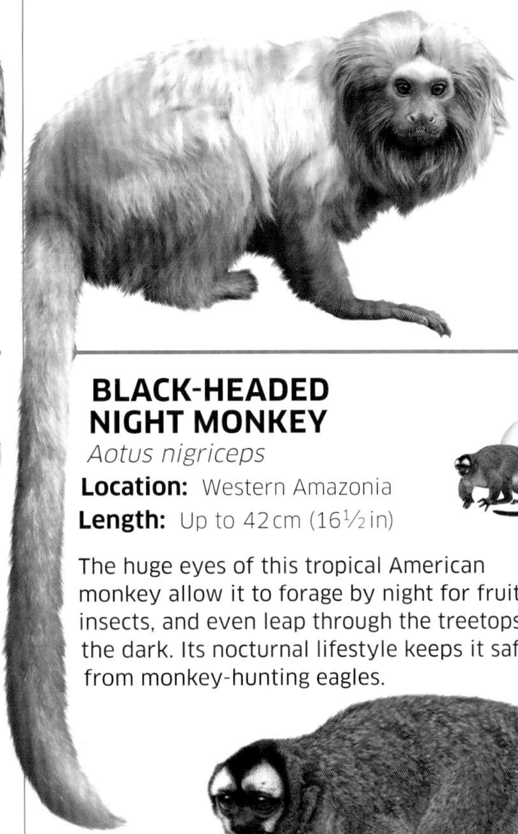

GUIANAN BROWN CAPUCHIN

Sapajus apella

Location: South America

Length: Up to 46 cm (18¼ in)

Widespread in South America, the capuchins include a wide variety of sociable, mainly tree-living species. The Guianan brown capuchin is one of the most common – an adaptable omnivore that can thrive in many different types of forest.

PROBOSCIS MONKEY

Nasalis larvatus

Location: Borneo

Length: Up to 76 cm (30 in)

Named for its large, fleshy nose, this Old World monkey lives in tall forest trees where it eats fruit and leaves. Always found close to water, it is an excellent swimmer.

Fleshy nose The nose is much longer in adult males.

BLACK-HEADED NIGHT MONKEY

Aotus nigriceps

Location: Western Amazonia

Length: Up to 42 cm (16½ in)

The huge eyes of this tropical American monkey allow it to forage by night for fruit and insects, and even leap through the treetops in the dark. Its nocturnal lifestyle keeps it safe from monkey-hunting eagles.

Long, thin digits with straight nails

CENTRAL AMERICAN SPIDER MONKEY

Ateles geoffroyi

Location: Central America

Length: Up to 63 cm (24¾ in)

This spider monkey gets its name from its extremely long, spidery limbs, and even longer, prehensile (grasping) tail. These equip the monkey perfectly for its acrobatic way of life, searching for fruit high in the rainforest canopy. It uses its almost thumbless hands as hooks to swing from tree branches.

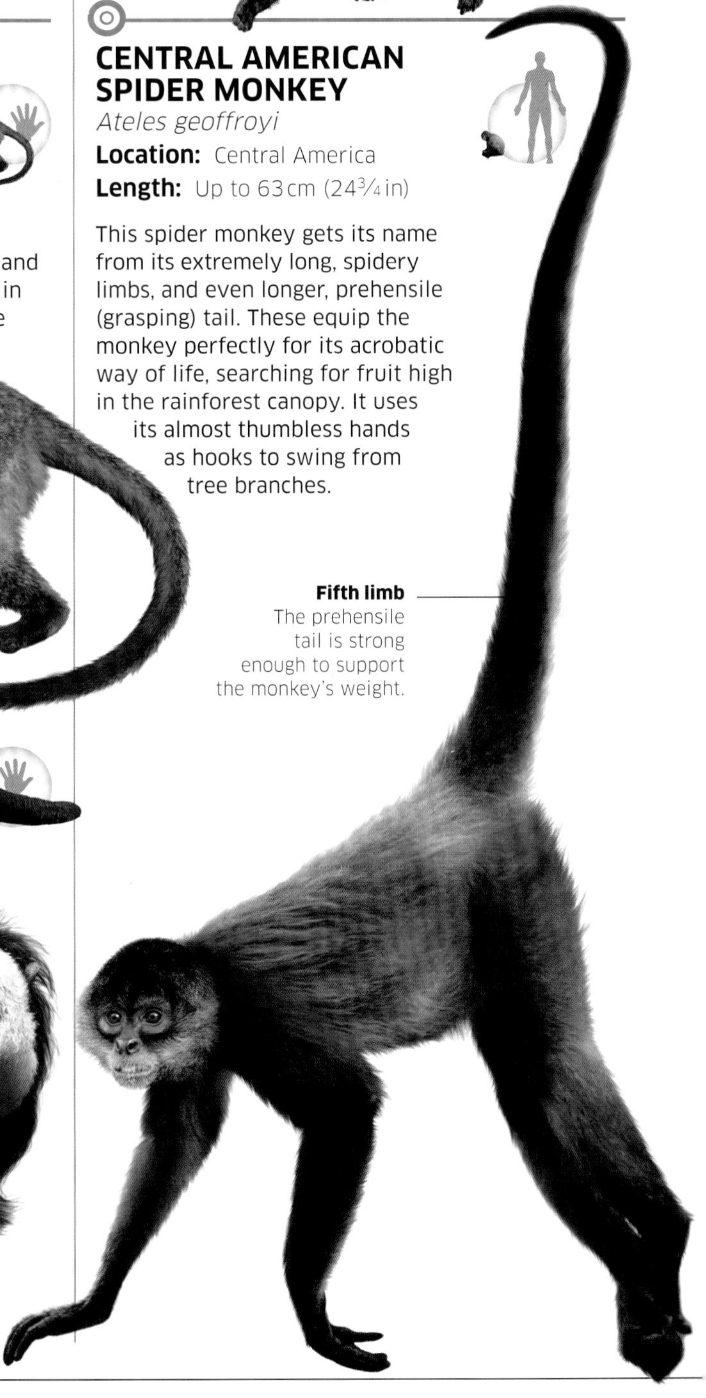

Fifth limb The prehensile tail is strong enough to support the monkey's weight.

BALD UAKARI

Cacajao calvus

Location: Western Amazonia

Length: Up to 57 cm (22½ in)

The vivid red face of this monkey is a sign of its good health – weaker individuals have paler faces, and are not as successful at finding mates. It lives mainly in the seasonally flooded forests of the upper Amazon, foraging in the treetops for seeds and fruit.

WHITE-FACED SAKI

Pithecia pithecia

Location: Northern South America

Length: Up to 41.5 cm (16½ in)

Only the male of this species has the distinctive white face, which contrasts with his black fur; females are browner. Pairs often remain together for life.

The birth rate for orangutans is very low. On average a female orangutan has
one baby every 9.3 years.

FLANGED MALE

UNFLANGED MALE

Late developers

A dominant male has broad, fleshy flanges on his cheeks, a big throat pouch for amplifying his calls, and a cape of long hair. He uses these features to impress females and rivals, including unflanged males. Unflanged males exhibit a kind of arrested development and may never develop flanges, though they can still reproduce.

Nesting in the trees

Every day an orangutan builds two types of nests high in the trees – a day nest and a night nest. These are woven from branches and foliage. Orangutans learn how to make these from each other, so the first nest this baby builds will be an attempt to copy the one she is sharing with her mother.

Sumatran orangutan

Superbly adapted for swinging through the canopy of their native forests, orangutans move slowly, always testing first that branches can hold their weight. They spend their lives high in the branches, rarely visiting the ground.

MAMMALS

SUMATRAN ORANGUTAN

Pongo abelii

Location: Sumatra

Height: Up to 99 cm (39 in)

Diet: Fruit, leaves, and insects

Orangutans live on the South East Asian islands of Borneo and Sumatra. Although they look similar, the two populations are now considered separate species. They feed mainly on fruit gathered from high in the rainforest trees, as well as tree-living termites and birds' eggs. Orangutans are highly intelligent but less sociable than other apes, often preferring to forage and sleep alone. Sumatran orangutans are longer and slimmer than Bornean orangutans, and more endangered due to rainforest destruction.

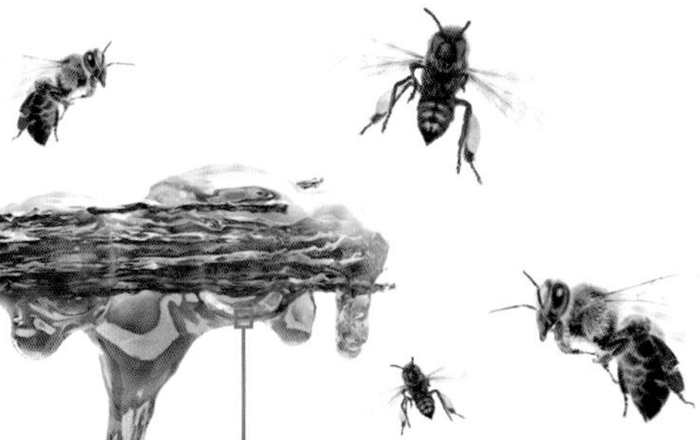

Using tools
Orangutans use sticks as tools to dig for termites or collect honey from beehives.

Thumb and fingers
Four long fingers and an opposable thumb, like on a human hand, give a strong grip.

Long arms
An orangutan's armspan can measure up to 2.25 m (7½ ft) from fingertip to fingertip.

Quick learners
Each local group of orangutans has its own ways of finding food, building nests, and even communicating with its neighbours. Baby orangutans learn skills from their mother, such as how to use tools to dig insects out of their timber burrows. A baby lives with its mother until it is at least 7 years old.

209 kg (460 lb) – the **weight of a male gorilla**; twice as much as a female.

Mountain gorilla

The mighty gorilla is the biggest of the apes – a forest giant that is one of our closest living relatives. Highly intelligent, it lives in family groups defended by a single mature "silverback" male, who uses his prodigious strength to keep rival males at bay.

There are two species of gorilla, western and eastern. Mountain gorillas are a subspecies of the eastern. They live in the upland forests of eastern central Africa, where most of their food consists of leaves and stems gathered near the ground. Since these items have poor nutritional value, the gorillas must spend most of their time eating, chewing each mouthful thoroughly with their massive cheek teeth to extract as much nutrition as possible.

Silverback
The short, silver-grey hair on a mature male's back begins to grow when he reaches 14 years old.

Shaggy coat
Mountain gorillas have longer coats than other gorillas.

Fighting stance
Gorillas get around by "knuckle walking" on all fours; they only stand to fight or to beat their chests.

Rival males may fight to the death, but first they try to scare each other away by roaring and beating their chests.

Family structure
A typical mountain gorilla family group is made up of three or four adult females, with four or five young of different ages, fathered by one mature male. The male defends the family from predators and any rival males who might try to drive him out and kill his young. As long as this does not happen, the family group will stay together.

A wild gorilla may live for 40 years or more.

The mountain gorilla is the rarest gorilla species, with fewer than 1,000 left in the wild.

Skull crest
A ridge of bone anchors massive jaw muscles.

Unique prints
Each gorilla has its own individual fingerprints.

Sharp weapons
Males have long, sharp canine teeth for fighting.

Big build
The arms are longer and the chest is broader than those of chimps.

Hairy hands
A gorilla's hands are very like human hands but stronger and a lot hairier.

On the defence
The defending silverback first barks and stares at his attacker, then he starts hooting and stands upright, throwing vegetation at him. If the attacker still doesn't back down, he will charge.

Toe grip
All apes have very mobile toes. Their big toes are opposable, like their thumbs, so they can grip branches with their feet. Mountain gorillas spend most of their time on the ground because they eat pith, stems, leaves, bark, and occasionally ants and don't need to climb to find food. Despite their weight, adult west African gorillas regularly climb trees to gather fruit.

Seeing in colour

Gorillas and other apes have excellent colour vision. In particular, and unlike many mammals, they are sensitive to red and orange. This enables them to pick out ripe fruit, which is a valuable part of their diet.

MAMMALS

MOUNTAIN GORILLA

Gorilla beringei beringei

Location: Eastern Central Africa

Height: Up to 1.96 m (6½ ft)

Diet: Leaves, pith, bark, stems, fruit

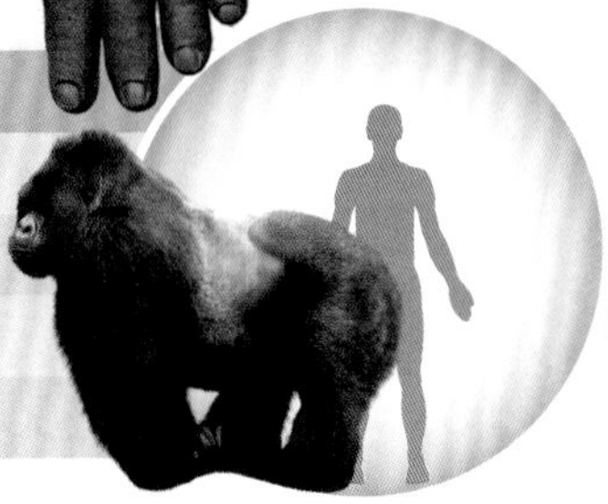

Apes

There are two main groups of apes. The first consists of the long-armed gibbons, adapted for life high in the trees. The other is the great apes, which includes the chimpanzee and its two close relatives, bonobos and humans. Orangutans and gorillas (see pp.182–185) also belong to this group.

The apes include the most spectacularly agile primates. The 19 species of gibbons use their long arms to swing gracefully through the treetops. The great apes are the largest of the apes and are considered the most intelligent primates.

WESTERN HOOLOCK GIBBON

Hoolock hoolock

Location: South Asia

Length: Up to 81 cm (32 in)

Like all gibbons, the hoolock has very long arms and powerful shoulders adapted for swinging from branch to branch. The male has white eyebrows that contrast dramatically with his black fur; the female is a grey-brown colour.

LAR GIBBON

Hylobates lar

Location: S. E. Asia

Length: Up to 42 cm ($16\frac{1}{2}$ in)

The lar gibbon varies from black to sandy brown, but always has a ring of white hair surrounding its black face. It lives in family groups high in the trees of tropical rainforests, where it feeds mainly on fruit. It rarely, if ever, comes down to the forest floor.

NORTHERN WHITE-CHEEKED CRESTED GIBBON

Nomascus leucogenys

Location: S. E. Asia

Length: Up to 53 cm ($20\frac{3}{4}$ in)

Only the black-furred male of this species has white cheeks; the female is pale brown with a dark face. Like other gibbons, they form long-lasting pairs. They mainly eat fruit, supplemented by young, tender leaves and small animals.

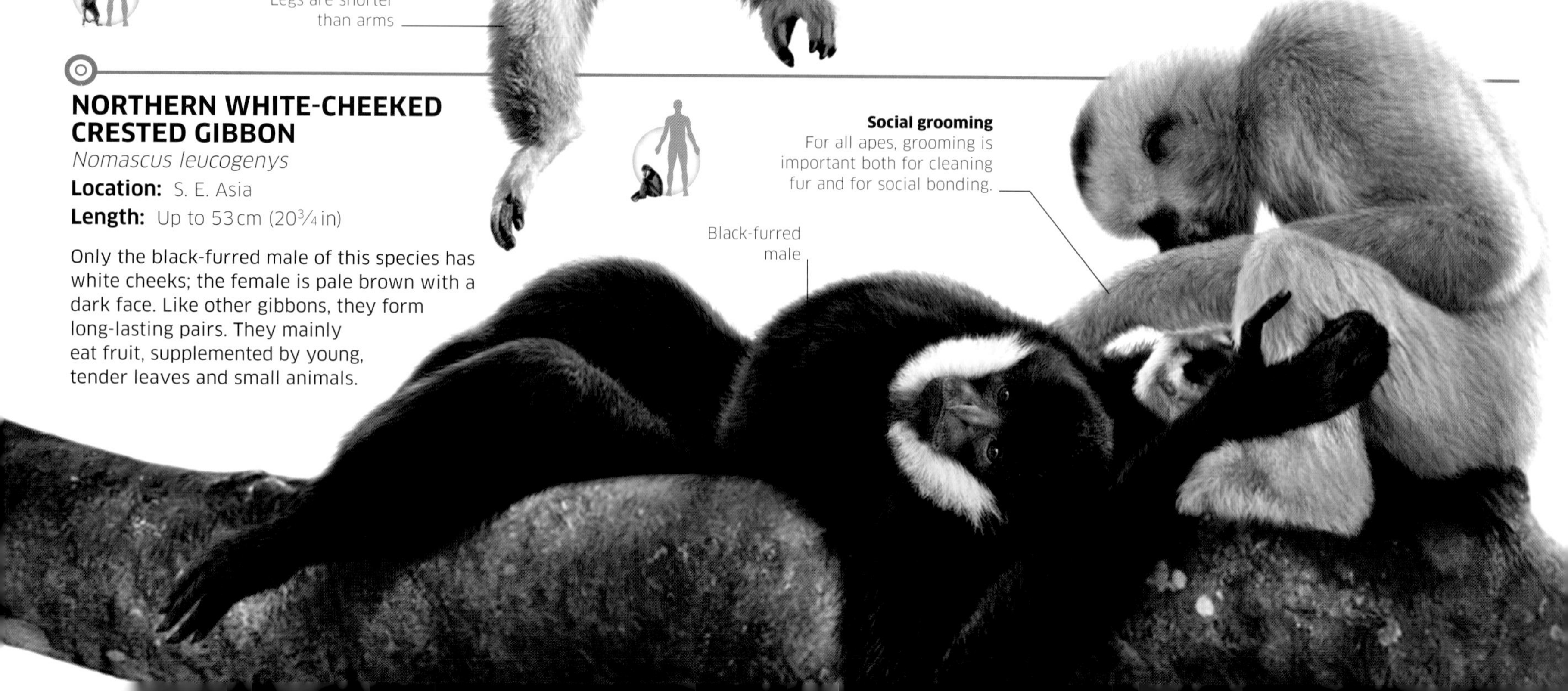

The calls of the siamang can be heard through the forest up to 2 km (1¼ miles) away.

Chimpanzees live in societies of up to 150 members, but split up into smaller groups to find food.

SIAMANG

Symphalangus syndactylus

Location: S. E. Asia

Length: Up to 90 cm (35½ in)

All gibbons defend their territories with loud calls, but the siamang has the loudest – a resonant hooting amplified by an inflatable throat sac. Pairs often call in duet for 15 minutes or more, especially in the early morning, and are answered by neighbouring siamangs.

BONOBO

Pan paniscus

Location: Central Africa

Length: Up to 83 cm (32¾ in)

This is the rarer of the two species of chimpanzee, with longer legs and a lighter build. It lives both in the trees and on the ground in tropical rainforests, travelling over the forest floor by "knuckle walking" on all fours. It eats mainly fruit supplemented by leaves, eggs, insects, and small vertebrates.

COMMON CHIMPANZEE

Pan troglodytes

Location: Central and west Africa

Length: Up to 96 cm (37¾ in)

With a stockier build than the bonobo, the common chimpanzee lives in male-dominated territorial groups in a variety of habitats. It eats a lot of fruit, but uses tools to forage for insects and also kills larger animals, including monkeys.

Chimpanzees have been known to sharpen sticks to spear bushbabies hiding in tree holes.

Using echolocation, a bat can **detect a flying moth** from up to 6 m (19½ ft) away.

INDIAN FLYING FOX
Pteropus giganteus
Location: India, S.E. Asia
Length: Up to 25 cm (10 in)

This big, tropical fruit bat is one of many that range through the forest at night looking for fruit to eat. During the day it roosts in trees, hanging upside down from branches by its feet. Several hundred flying foxes can live in the same tree.

GREATER HORSESHOE BAT
Rhinolophus ferrumequinum
Location: Europe, Asia
Length: Up to 7 cm (2¾ in)

Like most small bats, this species catches insects whilst flying. It detects airborne moths and beetles by echolocation – emitting a stream of high-pitched clicks and listening for echoes. A horseshoe-shaped structure on its nose focuses the clicks.

GHOST BAT
Macroderma gigas
Location: N. Australia
Length: Up to 14 cm (5½ in)

This big, tropical bat owes its name to its very thin, almost transparent wings and its ghostly pale grey fur. It is a powerful hunter with very large teeth, able to seize, kill, and eat lizards, mice, small birds, and even other bats.

LESSER LONG-NOSED BAT
Leptonycteris yerbabuenae
Location: North and Central America
Length: Up to 9 cm (3½ in)

This unusual bat is a nectar-feeder, which targets the flowers of cacti and agaves in the deserts. The plants bloom at night to attract the bat, which has an extra-long, brush-tipped tongue for lapping up nectar. It can also can hover to drink from the flowers.

GREATER BULLDOG BAT
Noctilio leporinus
Location: Central and South America
Length: Up to 13.2 cm (5¼ in)

Big bats can hunt large prey, and the greater bulldog bat specializes in catching fish. Able to detect ripples in the water made by fish as they surface, it scoops them up with its tail membrane and claws. Many males have bright orange fur.

Bats

A quarter of all mammal species are bats – the only living vertebrates apart from birds that are capable of powered flight. Other mammals, reptiles, and even frogs can glide, but bats can fly, with such agility and precision that most of them live by catching insect prey in mid-air.

A bat's wings consist of sheets of stretchy skin supported by hugely elongated finger bones. The skin membranes extend to the bat's legs, and often to its tail. Some bats have long, narrow wings for speed; others have shorter, broader wings for agility. Unlike typical birds they fly at night, and most use echolocation to navigate in the dark.

MAMMALS
BROWN LONG-EARED BAT
Plecotus auritus
Location: Europe and Central Asia
Length: Up to 5.5 cm (2¼ in)
Diet: Insects, spiders

1,240 The **number of species** of **bat** worldwide.

A brown long-eared bat **may live** for up to **22 years**.

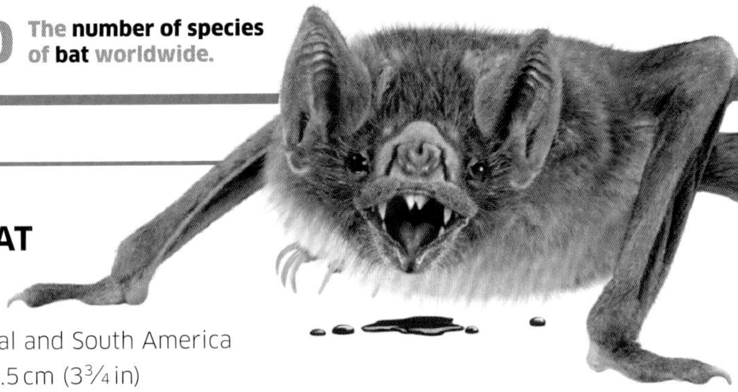

COMMON VAMPIRE BAT

Desmodus rotundus

Location: Central and South America

Length: Up to 9.5 cm (3¾ in)

The vampire bats of tropical America feed on blood. They use their razor-sharp front teeth to make small slits in the skin of large animals, then lap up the blood with their long tongues. Vampire bats can also run and jump over the ground, using their folded wings as legs.

Folding ears
The bat tucks its enormous ears away under its wings when it is roosting by day.

Wing fingers
Elongated finger bones stretch the wing membrane and support it in flight.

Echolocation

All insect-eating bats are equipped with a sophisticated echolocation system. As a bat flies, it produces a stream of high-frequency clicks. These are reflected from obstacles and prey as echoes, which the bat's ears pick up and translate into a "sound picture" of its surroundings. This allows it to navigate and hunt in total darkness.

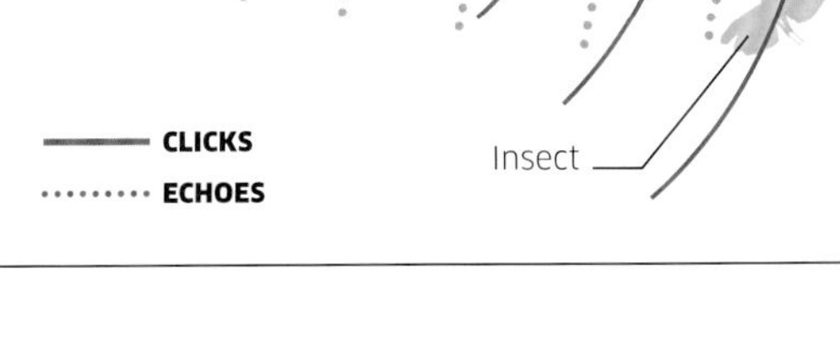

Brown long-eared bat

The enormous ears of this European bat enable it to hear the faintest sounds made by insects or spiders in the dark. They also allow the bat to use unusually quiet echolocation calls for finding its way through the trees, and targeting insect prey in flight.

A long-eared bat has excellent eyesight, and often uses it to hunt prey on moonlit nights.

70 km/h (43 mph) – the **top speed** a grey wolf **can run.**

Meat-slicing teeth
Like nearly all the carnivores (mammals of the order Carnivora), a wolf has special cheek teeth known as carnassials. They are modified chewing teeth that work together like scissor blades to slice meat from bone. Wolves also have long, pointed canine teeth for seizing prey.

Grey wolf

The ancestor of all domestic dogs, the grey wolf was once familiar across all northern continents. Now, its eerie howl is rarely heard outside the remote regions of the far north and a few mountain refuges.

The wolf is a member of the order Carnivora – a group of mammals that take their name from the fact that many are specialized carnivores, or meat-eaters. Wolves prey mainly on other mammals, ranging from mice to full-grown bison, but are rarely strong enough to tackle large prey alone. Instead an extended family works together as a hunting pack. Using their intelligence and communication skills, the wolves mount a joint attack, then share the spoils between them.

MAMMALS

GREY WOLF

Canis lupus

Location: Europe, Central Asia

Length: Up to 1.6 m (5¼ ft)

Diet: Mainly large mammals

Apart from human hunters, the grey wolf's main enemies are Siberian tigers.

Long snout
The wolf's long snout contains extended nasal passages that help give it an acute sense of smell. Wolves rely heavily on detecting scents for both tracking their prey and communicating with each other. They can also assess the health of an individual from its smell.

Night sight
A wolf has poor colour vision but can see well at night, when it is often active.

Variable colour
The coat ranges from very dark to almost white, depending on local race.

Long legs
Slender, long legs allow the wolf to sustain a prolonged chase without tiring.

Running spikes
Stout claws grip the ground as the wolf pursues its quarry.

Body language

Wolves are highly social animals that use gestures and body language to communicate. Each pack is led by a breeding pair. Here a female shows submission to the "alpha male" by crouching with her ears lowered while he raises his tail in a gesture of dominance.

Early learning

Although only the alpha female breeds, the whole pack helps to raise and feed her pups. By degrees they learn to fend for themselves, playfighting and competing for food around the den, then eventually accompanying the adults on hunting expeditions.

African wild dogs can **run at speeds** of more than **50 km/h (31 mph)**.

Only around **3,000–5,500** African wild dogs **remain in the wild**.

Family values
Each dog pack is led by an alpha pair made up of a breeding female and male. There are usually more males than females in a pack and they help the alpha pair raise their young. When the pups reach maturity many of the males stay on to help, but the young females leave to start new packs.

Cryptic colours
This is the most flamboyantly patterned of all dogs, with blotches of black, tan, yellow, and white splashed all over its body. The random pattern provides perfect camouflage in forests, scrub, and tall grass, allowing the dogs to get close to their prey before being seen.

African wild dog

Lean, lightweight, and long-legged, the African wild dog is one of the world's most effective hunters – a tireless runner that pursues its prey to the point of exhaustion, then relies on the mutual strength of the pack to pull it to the ground.

The wild dog is one of the most social carnivores, and cannot survive on its own. Its whole life revolves around the pack – an extended family of up to 30 adults and young that live and hunt together in the woodlands and broad, grassy plains of tropical Africa. Each pack roams over a vast area in search of prey such as gazelles, antelopes, and even full-grown zebras.

MAMMALS
AFRICAN WILD DOG
Lycaon pictus
Location: Sub-Saharan Africa
Length: Up to 1.4 m (4½ ft)
Diet: Mainly large mammals

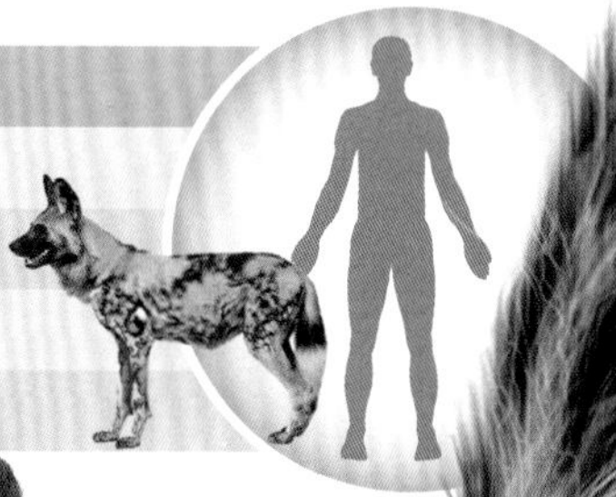

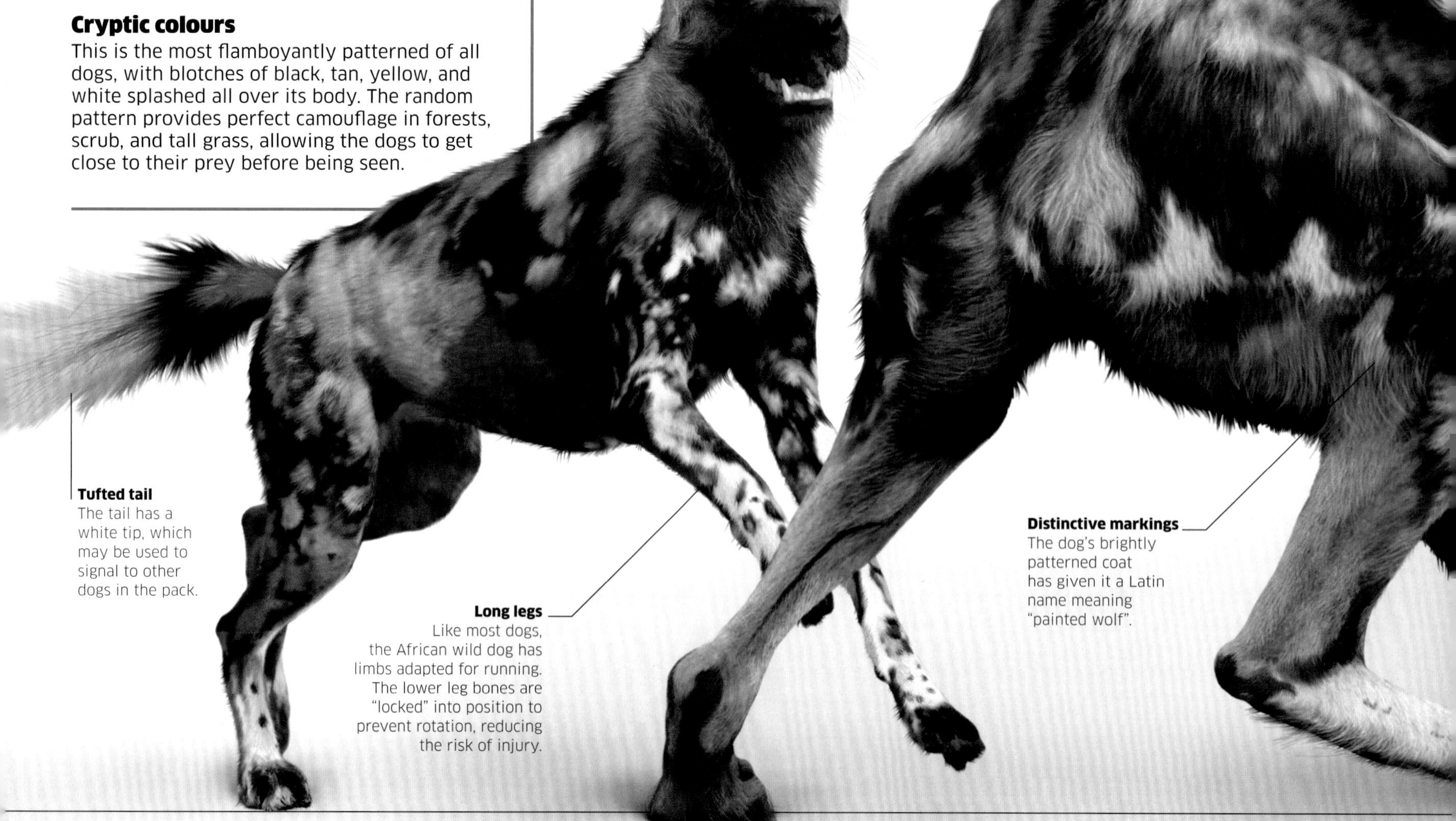

80 per cent of all wild dog hunts **end in a kill**.

Wild dogs produce **litters** of between **6 and 16 pups**, more than any other wild canid.

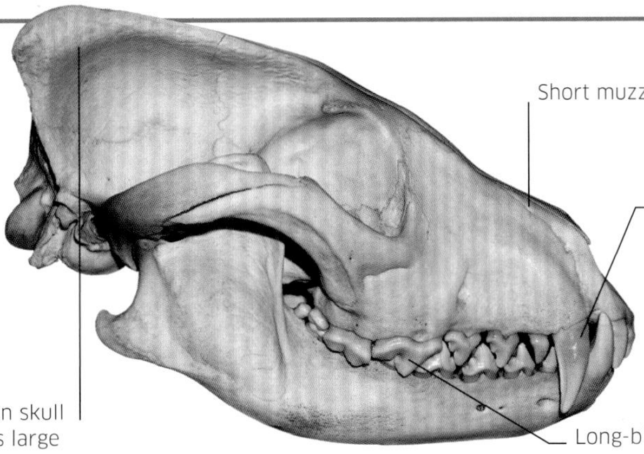

Strong weapons
The massively built jaws are shorter than those of most dogs, giving the jaw muscles extra leverage to grip struggling prey. The meat-slicing carnassial teeth have longer blades than usual, for scissoring through the tough hide and flesh of big animals.

The raccoon dog is the **only canid** that **hibernates in winter**.

The **hairy soles** of the **fennec fox's feet** offer **protection** from **hot desert sand**.

Canids

Wolves, wild dogs, and foxes all belong to the Canidae family – the canids. They are among the most successful carnivores, although most of them also eat other foods.

With their long legs and lithe bodies, many canids are built for running after prey in open country. However, it is because they are so adaptable and eat a variety of foods that they are successful. Most foxes hunt in wooded terrain where there is plenty of cover for stalking prey, while the bat-eared fox is a specialized insect-eater. Many canids hunt alone, but nearly all of them live in groups based on close family ties and social interaction.

ETHIOPIAN WOLF

Canis simensis

Location: E. Africa

Length: Up to 1 m (3¼ ft)

This elegant, tawny red relative of the grey wolf lives in the high, cold mountains of central Ethiopia, where it hunts grass rats and other small mammals. Habitat destruction and human activity have made it the rarest, most threatened canid.

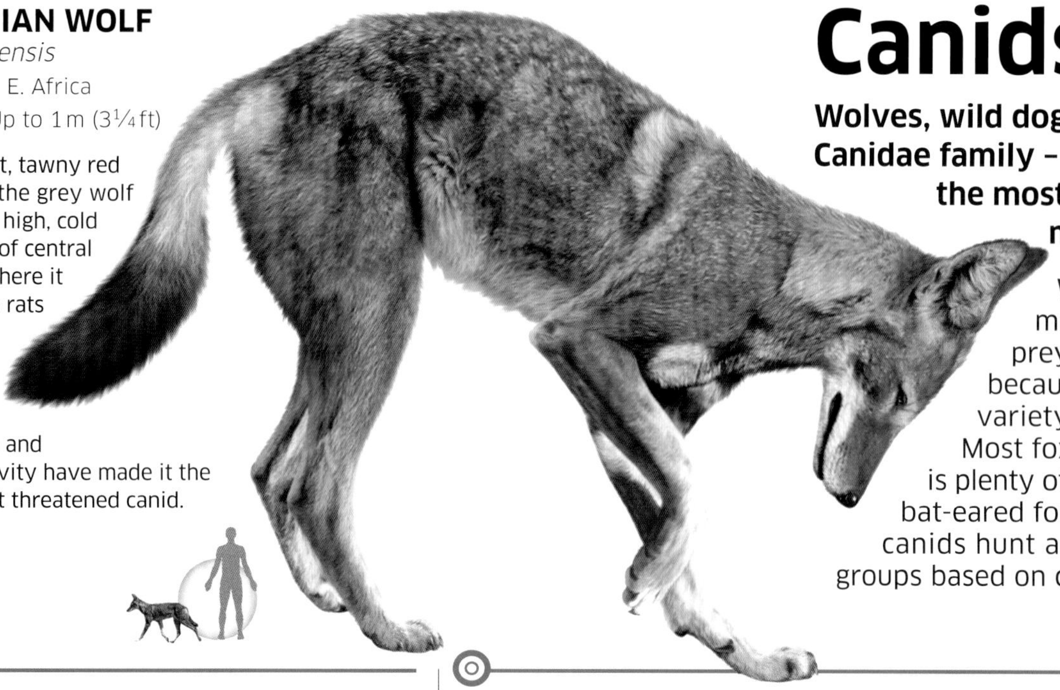

CRAB-EATING FOX

Cerdocyon thous

Location: South America

Length: Up to 77.5 cm (30½ in)

Like most canids, this South American fox is an opportunist that will eat all kinds of foods, from fruit to small mammals. But it gets its name from its habit of hunting crabs on muddy riverbanks.

DHOLE

Cuon alpinus

Location: Asia

Length: Up to 1.35 m (4½ ft)

The south Asian equivalent of the African wild dog, the almost wholly meat-eating dhole hunts in packs for large prey such as deer and young water buffalo. It has a complex social life, living in large clans that may include several breeding females.

MANED WOLF

Chrysocyon brachyurus

Location: South America

Length: Up to 1.15 m (3 ft)

Although it looks like a big, very long-legged red fox, the South American maned wolf is neither a wolf nor a fox but belongs to a group of its own. It hunts alone on the grassland for small prey, using its big ears to locate victims in the long grass. This canid also eats a lot of fruit, especially a type of wild tomato known as the wolf-apple.

CULPEO

Lycalopex culpaeus

Location: South America

Length: Up to 92 cm (36¼ in)

One of several closely related South American foxes known locally as "zorros", this adaptable hunter ranges high into the Andes mountains in search of prey.

RACCOON DOG

Nyctereutes procyonoides

Location: Europe, Asia

Length: Up to 70 cm (27½ in)

Well described by its name, this east Asian canid has a dark raccoon-like mask and very long, thick winter fur. Unusually, it is well able to climb trees to reach fruit – part of a broad diet that includes insects, mice, toads, and even fish.

BAT-EARED FOX

Otocyon megalotis

Location: E. and southern Africa

Length: Up to 60 cm (23½ in)

Uniquely for a canid, this fox is a specialist. It uses its huge ears to locate termites and beetles on the African grasslands, crunching them up with its many small chewing teeth.

BUSH DOG

Speothos venaticus

Location: Central and South America

Length: Up to 75 cm (29½ in)

Typical dogs and foxes are lean, long-legged animals, but the South American bush dog is the exception. Built like a terrier, with short legs and a compact head, it is a dedicated predator, hunting in packs for large rodents and pig-like peccaries.

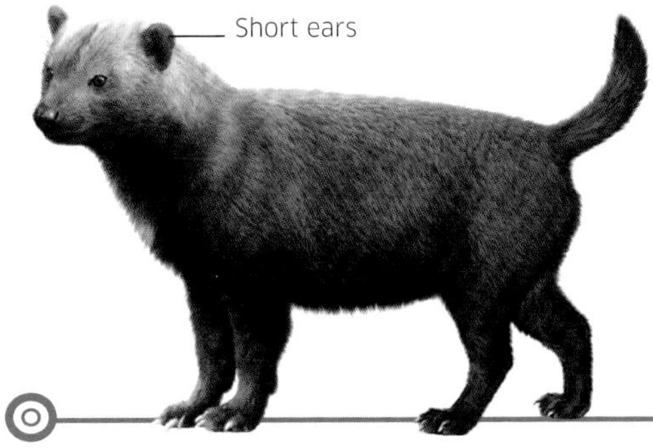

NORTHERN GREY FOX

Urocyon cinereoargenteus

Location: S. Canada to South America

Length: Up to 66 cm (26 in)

Found throughout much of the United States and Central America, this fox is closely related to the ancestors of all other canids. It has several primitive features, including an ability to climb trees and jump from branch to branch to find food.

FENNEC FOX

Vulpes zerda

Location: N. Africa

Length: Up to 41 cm (16 in)

The smallest of the canids, this North African desert fox has huge ears that it uses to locate mice, lizards, and other prey in the dark. Its ears also radiate heat, helping the fox to keep cool.

RED FOX

Vulpes vulpes

Location: Arctic, North America, Europe, Asia, N. Africa, Australia

Length: Up to 90 cm (35½ in)

Widespread in all the northern continents, and introduced to Australia, the red fox can live almost anywhere, from Arctic tundra to big cities. It hunts small mammals, but also eats insects, worms, fruit, and carrion.

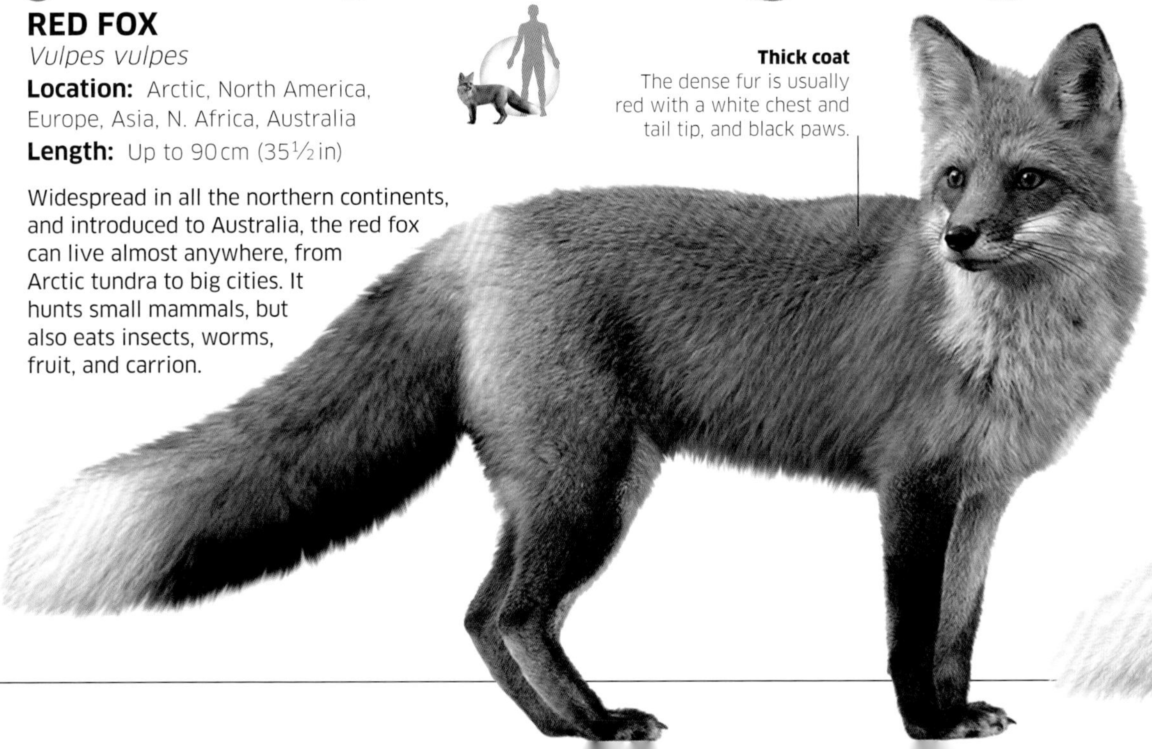

ARCTIC FOX

Vulpes lagopus

Location: N. Canada, Alaska, Greenland, N. Europe, N. Asia

Length: Up to 39.5 cm (15½ in)

Specialized for life in the bitter chill of the far north, the Arctic fox has an amazing resistance to cold thanks to its extremely thick fur. This is typically pure white in winter, but far darker in summer.

A grizzly bear will **eat** almost **anything it can find or catch**, from mushrooms to adult bull bison.

Grizzly bear

Bulky and powerful, the grizzly bear and its close relatives are the biggest American carnivores living south of the Arctic.

The grizzly bear is a North American subspecies of the brown bear, which also lives in Europe and Asia. The grizzly is named for its "grizzled" or silvered fur, not its grisly habits, although it is certainly capable of killing and eating large animals. Usually it feeds on smaller animals, plants, berries, and nuts in late summer, and Alaskan bears eat salmon caught during their annual spawning migration.

MAMMALS

GRIZZLY BEAR

Ursus arctos horribilis

Location: North America

Length: Up to 2.8 m (9 ft)

Diet: Fruit, plants, meat, fish

Winter sleep
In winter, food is scarce. The bears cope by fattening up in late summer, then spending the winter asleep in a snug den. Their body temperature drops by just a few degrees while they sleep so that they can become active again relatively quickly.

Grizzled fur
The fur of a grizzly bear has pale silvery or golden tips, giving it a pale-flecked or "grizzled" appearance. The fur of other subspecies such as the Alaskan Kodiak bear is a deeper, richer brown.

A grizzly bear can **sleep for more than six months** without eating or drinking.

Flat-footed
A bear walks on the soles of its feet and not on its toes like most other carnivores.

An adult male grizzly bear can **weigh up to 360 kg (793 lb)**.

A bear **preparing for its winter sleep eats so much** that it **doubles its weight**.

Scavenging grizzly bears are **powerful enough to drive wolves away** from their kills.

Small eyes
Grizzlies have reasonable eyesight, though their sense of smell is better.

All-purpose teeth
Although the bear has long canines, its other teeth are not specialized for eating meat because it is an omnivore (eats many foods).

Massive claws
The bear has long, strong but blunt claws that it uses for digging and hooking fish. Young bears may use them to climb trees, but the adults weigh too much.

Salmon fishing

In coastal Alaska, grizzly bears satisfy more than half of their annual food needs by catching salmon that swim upriver from the sea in summer to spawn. The bears gather in large numbers at some sites, with the biggest males claiming the best fishing spots.

Watching and waiting
A bear wades into the water and waits. The fish will have to leap this waterfall to swim upstream.

Leaping prey
Intent on making its way upriver to its spawning site, the salmon does not notice the bear waiting in ambush.

Success!
With a snap of its jaws, the bear seizes the salmon in mid-leap. It will carry its prize on shore to eat it.

A giant panda must eat up to 14 kg (31 lb) of bamboo a day to get the nutrients it needs.

1,600 The estimated number of giant pandas in the wild.

Rearing young
Females usually give birth only once every two years. Although twins are common, the mother rarely raises more than one cub. A newborn panda is tiny, blind, and helpless. For its first few months, the cub is cared for by its mother in a special den, only beginning to walk at around three months old. It remains dependent on its mother until it is two years old.

MAMMALS

GIANT PANDA

Ailuropoda melanoleuca

Location: East Asia

Length: Up to 1.8 m (6 ft)

Diet: Bamboo

Giant panda

A familiar symbol of the world's endangered wildlife, the giant panda is under threat of extinction. It is a type of bear that feeds almost exclusively on bamboo – a giant grass that grows abundantly in the upland forests of the panda's native central China.

All bears, except the polar bear, eat a lot of plant material. But the giant panda is a specialist that eats meat only very rarely. It is equipped for its bamboo diet with big chewing teeth and a unique adaptation of its forepaws, which allows it to grip its food. However, bamboo is so low in nutrition that the panda has to spend most of its day picking and eating the juiciest shoots it can find.

A giant panda spends 16 hours eating every day.

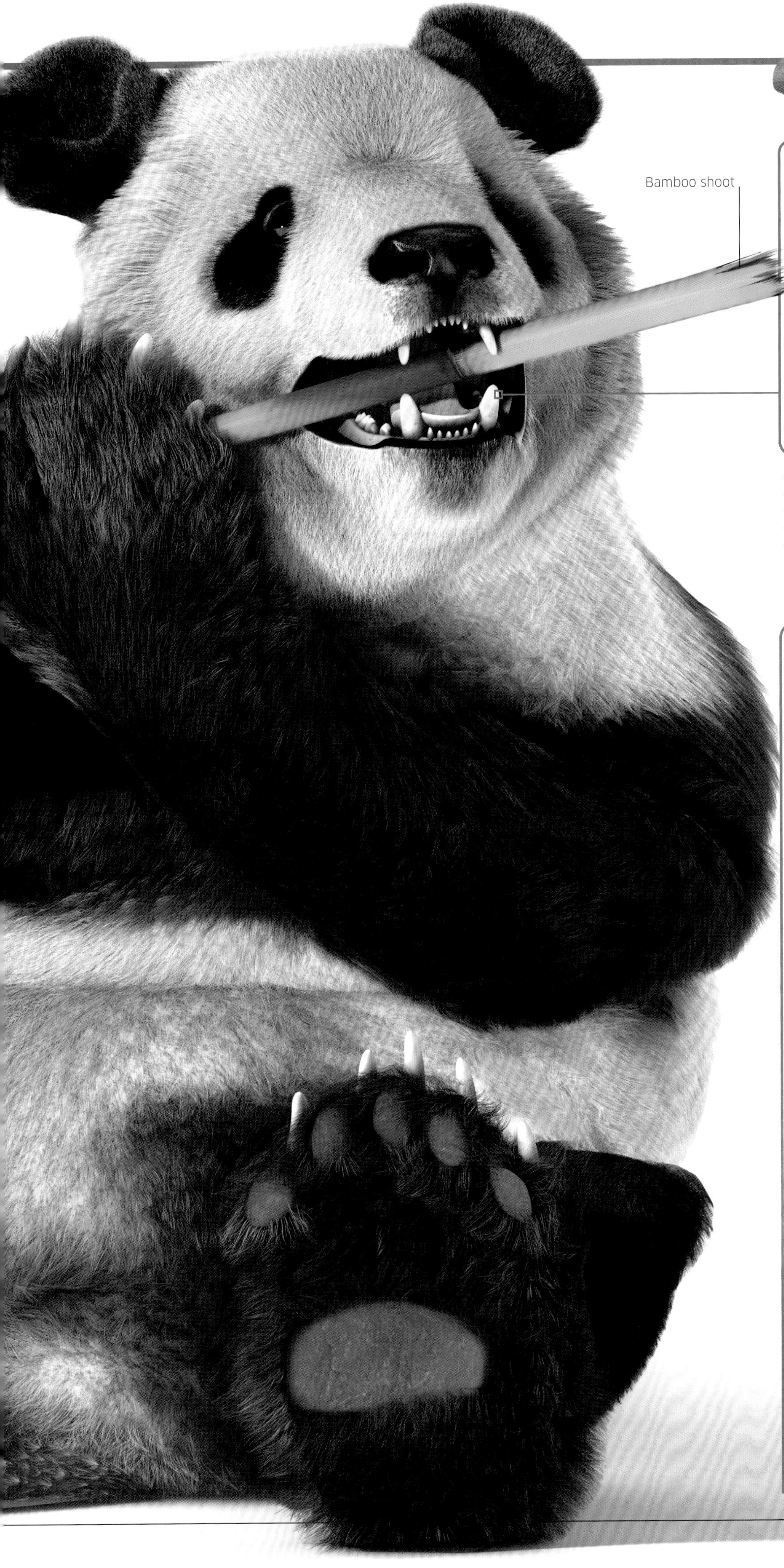

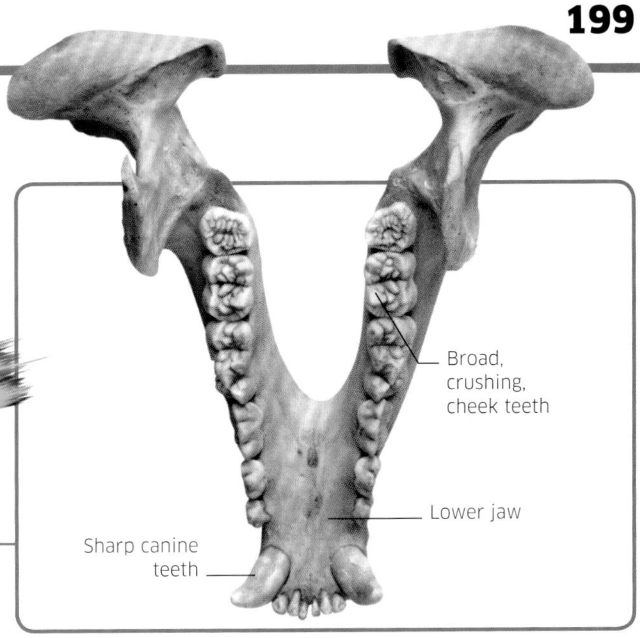

Grinding teeth
Compared to other bears, the panda has massive cheek teeth to crush and grind its food and release the juices inside the fibrous plant cells. Its large, muscular stomach helps reduce the bamboo to a pulp. However, its digestive system is more like that of a carnivore than a typical grazing animal, and it cannot digest much of the tough plant fibre it eats.

Surrounded by food

The giant panda is a bamboo-eating specialist because bamboo is so plentiful in its native forests. But much of the bamboo it eats passes through its body without being digested, so the panda must eat a huge amount. When it is not feeding, it saves energy by sleeping.

Conservation

For thousands of years the giant panda flourished. But much of its forest habitat has been cleared for farming, and the panda is now threatened with extinction. It survives in the wild thanks to special panda reserves, and it is also being bred in captivity.

800 kg (1,764 lb) – the **weight** of an **adult male polar bear**.

SUN BEAR
Helarctos malayanus
Location: Southeast Asia
Length: Up to 1.5 m (5 ft)

The smallest bear, with short fur well suited to its tropical habitat, the sun bear is a good climber and spends much of its life in the trees. It feeds mainly on fruit, but also breaks into bee nests so it can use its very long tongue to lap up honey.

Long tongue
The tongue can protrude up to 25 cm ($9^3/_4$ in) to reach for honey.

SPECTACLED BEAR
Tremarctos ornatus
Location: South America
Length: Up to 1.9 m ($6^1/_4$ ft)

Also known as the Andean bear, this is the only South American bear. Restricted to the northern Andes mountains, it can be found in scrubby desert and grassland, but favours mountain forests where it climbs trees in search of nuts, fruit, and bark. It consumes very little meat, but does eat insects, snails, and small mammals.

Long, narrow snout

Sharp teeth
The teeth of a polar bear are sharper than those of other bears, and are used for killing prey and tearing it apart. But its teeth are not as well adapted for meat-slicing as those of other predators, since it evolved from omnivorous brown bears that started hunting seals in the far north.

Bears

The bears are the biggest of the carnivores – the order of mammals that includes hunters such as wild dogs and tigers. But while at least one bear can rival the tiger in ferocity, most are omnivores that feed mainly on fruit, nuts, and even insects.

The ancestors of bears were dog-like hunters, but over time most bears became adapted for eating a variety of nutritious foods. Their teeth became less specialized than those of typical carnivores, and the sharp meat-slicing blades gave way to broader cheek teeth for crushing and grinding vegetable foods. But many bears still kill and eat animals, and the polar bear is a full-time meat-eater.

MAMMALS
POLAR BEAR
Ursus maritimus
Location: Arctic seas and coasts
Length: Up to 2.8 m (9 ft)
Diet: Seals, small whales, seabirds

SLOTH BEAR

Melursus ursinus

Location: India

Length: Up to 1.9 m (6¼ ft)

The sloth bear is a specialized insect-eater that preys largely on ants and termites. Its upper and lower lips can be protruded to form a tube for sucking up swarming insects, and it has large, powerful claws for breaking into termite nests.

ASIATIC BLACK BEAR

Ursus thibetanus

Location: Himalayas and eastern Asia

Length: Up to 1.9 m (6¼ ft)

This forest bear spends up to half its time in the trees, searching for a wide variety of foods including insects, honey, fruit, nuts, and fungi. But it also attacks and eats larger animals such as mountain goats and even water buffalo.

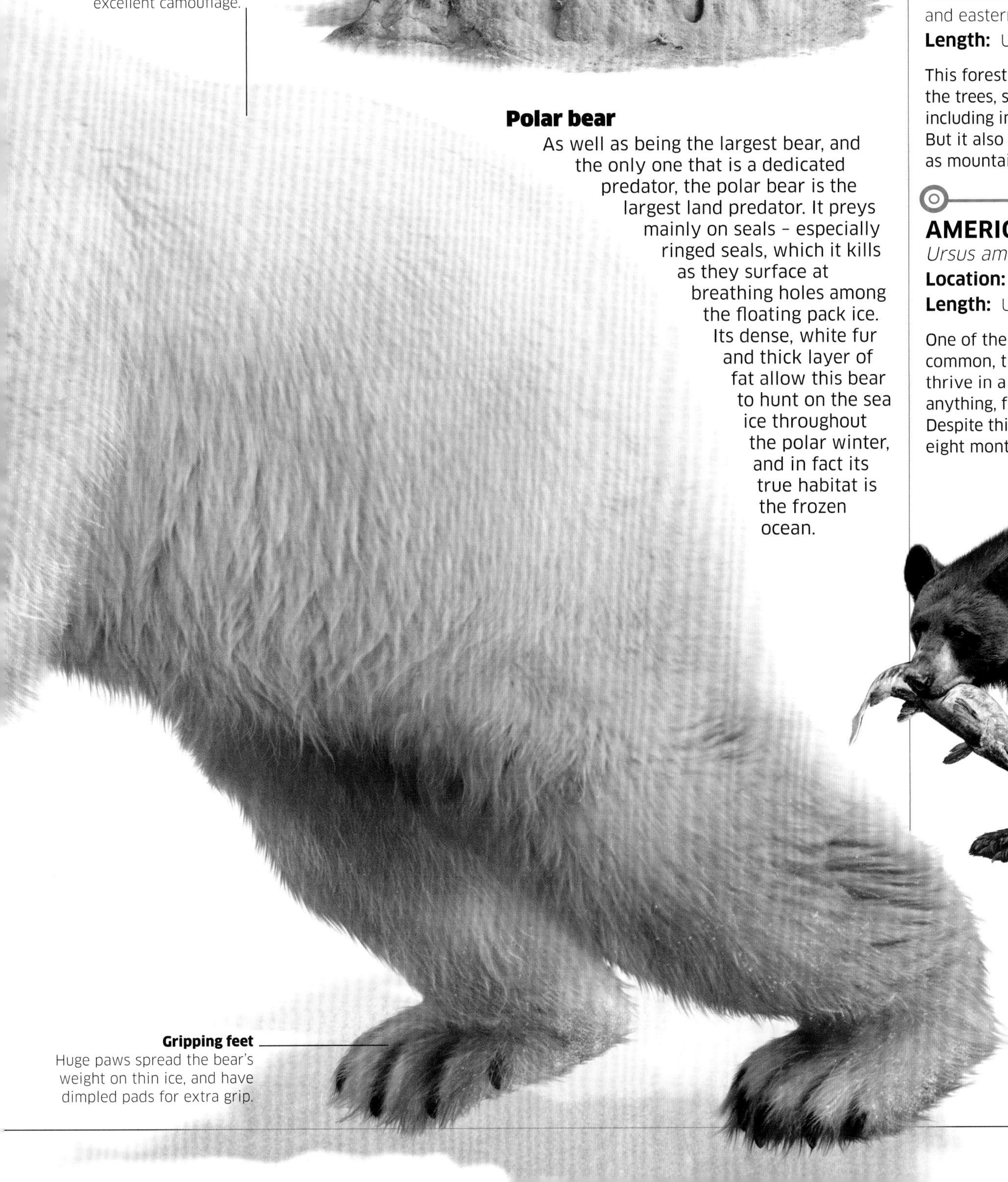

Polar bear

As well as being the largest bear, and the only one that is a dedicated predator, the polar bear is the largest land predator. It preys mainly on seals – especially ringed seals, which it kills as they surface at breathing holes among the floating pack ice. Its dense, white fur and thick layer of fat allow this bear to hunt on the sea ice throughout the polar winter, and in fact its true habitat is the frozen ocean.

AMERICAN BLACK BEAR

Ursus americanus

Location: North America

Length: Up to 1.9 m (6¼ ft)

One of the best-known bears, and the most common, this is an adaptable opportunist that can thrive in a wide variety of habitats and eat almost anything, from tender leaves to fish and young deer. Despite this, it sleeps through the winter, for up to eight months in the far north.

A polar bear can smell a seal on the ice from more than 1 km (½ mile) away.

A mother stays with a newborn pup for about seven days, then leaves it for three days to go hunting.

California sea lion

California sea lions are sociable and live in noisy, crowded groups called colonies, near rocky ocean shores. They are also intelligent, highly efficient hunters of fast-swimming fish and squid. They can dive to depths of 30 m (100 ft) or more, holding their breath for up to ten minutes.

Sea lions and fur seals are known as "eared seals" because they have visible ear flaps, unlike true seals such as the harp seal. They also have much longer front flippers, which they use both for moving on land and driving themselves through the water. While the females are sleek and graceful, the males are burly, aggressive heavyweights.

Taking the air
When a sea lion wants to take a breath, it has to contract its cheek muscles to open its nostrils. When it relaxes, its nostrils automatically close to keep the water out as it dives. Unlike a human, the sea lion breathes out before diving, reducing its buoyancy.

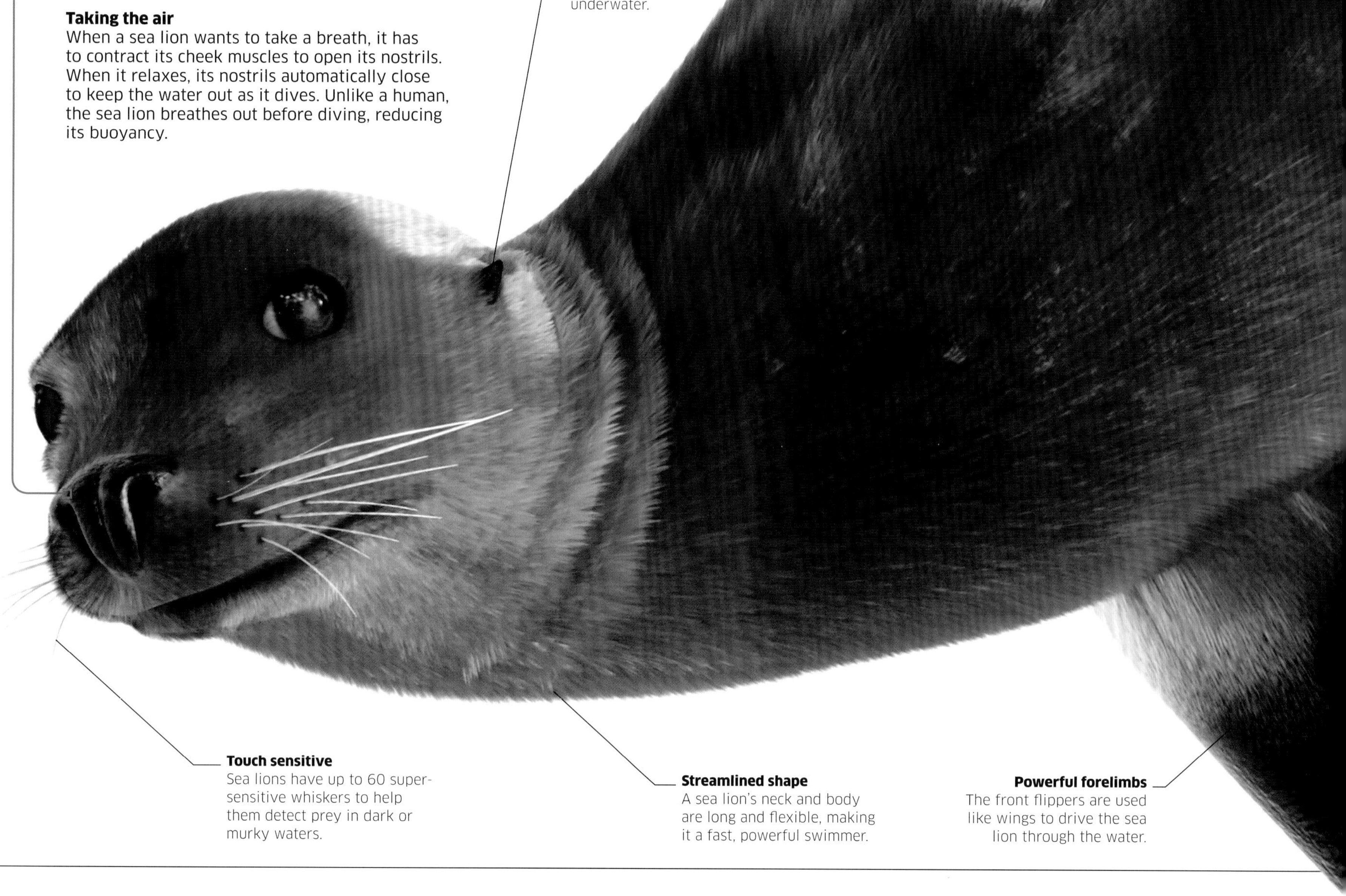

Temperature control
To raise or lower its body temperature, the sea lion raises one flipper out of the water as it swims. This exposes blood vessels, which either absorb warmth from the sun or release excess heat into the atmosphere.

Ear flaps
The sea lion's ears look small, but it has good hearing, especially underwater.

Touch sensitive
Sea lions have up to 60 super-sensitive whiskers to help them detect prey in dark or murky waters.

Streamlined shape
A sea lion's neck and body are long and flexible, making it a fast, powerful swimmer.

Powerful forelimbs
The front flippers are used like wings to drive the sea lion through the water.

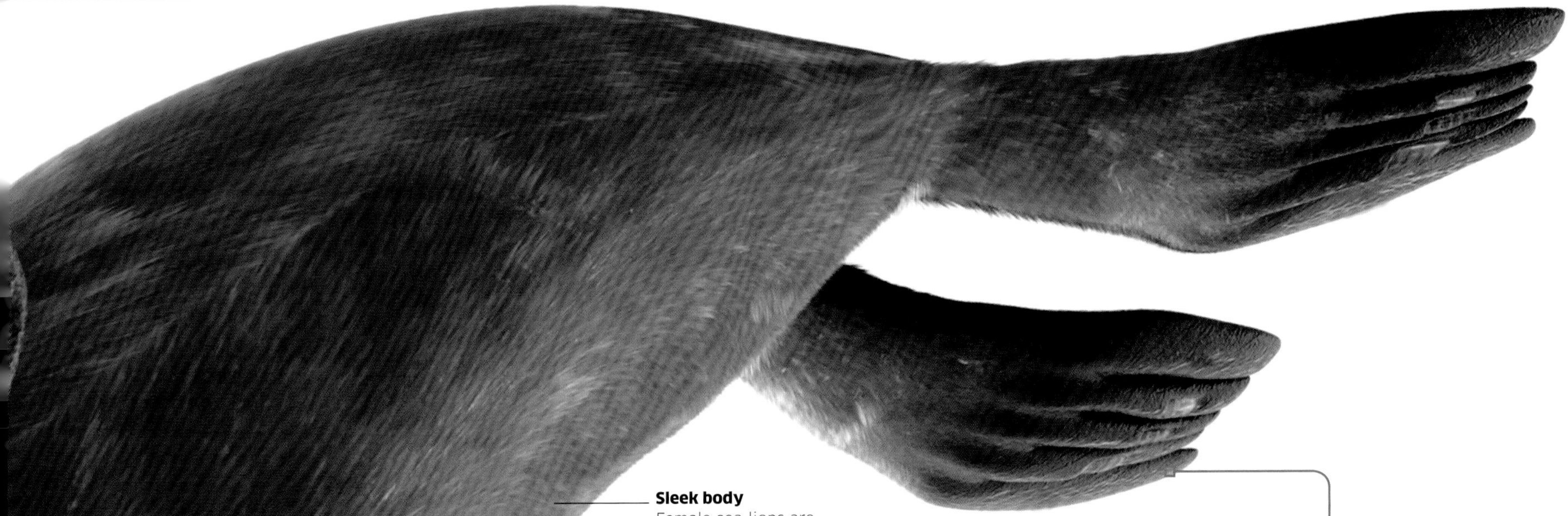

Sleek body
Female sea lions are smaller and sleeker than the males and have a paler, tan colouring.

Insulating layer
A thick layer of fat (blubber) under its skin keeps the sea lion warm in cold waters. Blubber also stores energy – especially important for males, because they stop eating during the breeding season.

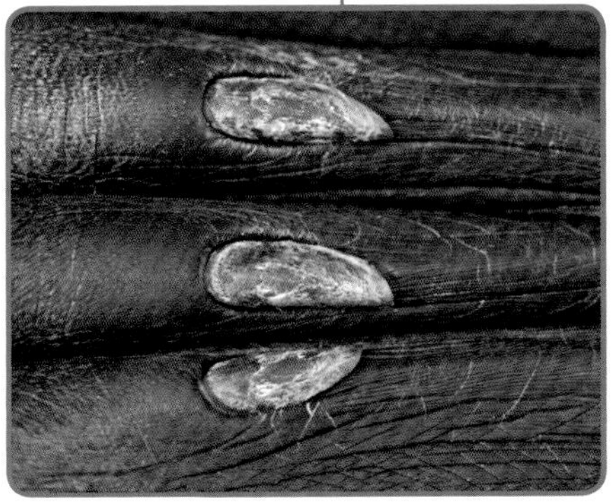

Multi-purpose flippers
The sea lion's hind limbs extend into long flippers, which are used mainly for steering in the water, but which can also be rotated forwards for moving on land. The bones do not reach the end of each flipper, and end in small toenails.

MAMMALS

CALIFORNIA SEA LION

Zalophus californianus

Location: Western USA

Length: Up to 2.4 m (8 ft)

Diet: Fish, squid

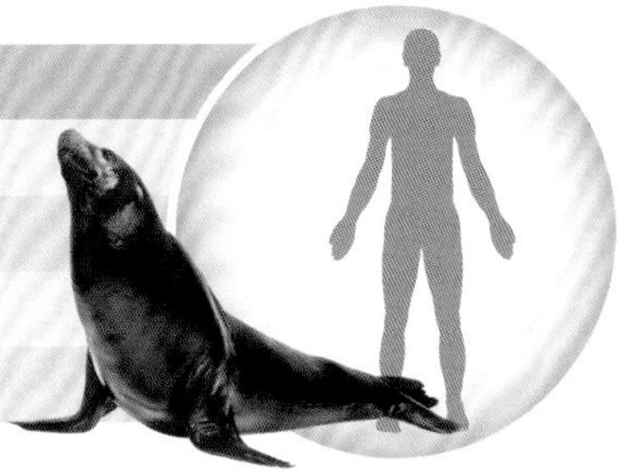

The main predators of California sea lions are **orcas and great white sharks,** which ambush the sea lions while they are swimming at the surface.

On all fours

To move on land, a sea lion supports most of its weight on its front flippers, turning its hind flippers forwards so it stands on all fours. Then, by arching its back, it moves both its hind limbs forwards, and raises its front end to do the same with its front flippers. It can move surprisingly fast in this manner.

Heavyweight males

In the breeding season, male sea lions fight each other fiercely for females, which they gather together in harems. The winners defend their harems, barking aggressively to discourage rivals. The largest males are the most successful in these conflicts, so they get to breed with the most females and pass on their genes to the next generation. An adult male sea lion can be three times as heavy as a female.

Female hooded seals **feed milk to their young** for less than **12 days** – the **shortest nursing period** of any mammal.

The **crabeater seal** is probably the **most numerous large mammal on Earth**, apart from humans.

NORTHERN FUR SEAL

Callorhinus ursinus

Location: North Pacific

Length: Up to 2.1 m (6¾ ft)

Similar to sea lions, the fur seals are eared seals with extra-thick fur that helps them survive colder waters. This species is the biggest, with massively built males that compete to mate with the sleeker, lighter females.

WALRUS

Odobenus rosmarus

Location: Arctic waters

Length: Up to 3.5 m (11½ ft)

Instantly recognizable by its long tusks, the walrus uses its sensitive whiskers to locate clams buried in soft, shallow sea beds. Both sexes have tusks, but a male's are bigger. The walrus's thick, wrinkled skin turns pink as it warms up after emerging from the sea.

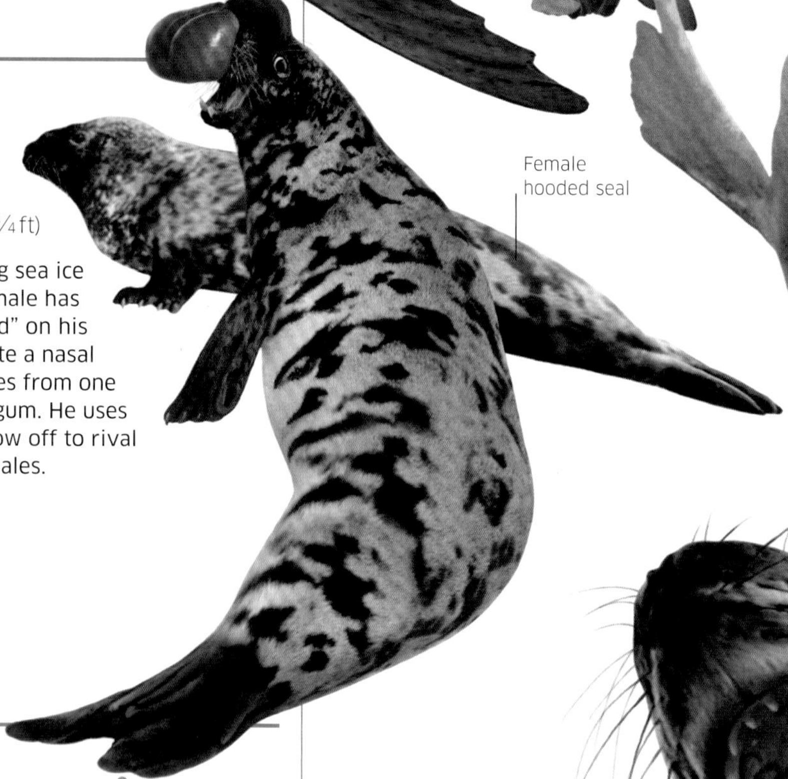

Female hooded seal

HOODED SEAL

Cystophora cristata

Location: North Atlantic to Arctic Ocean

Length: Up to 2.7 m (8¾ ft)

This seal lives on drifting sea ice around Greenland. The male has an inflatable black "hood" on his snout, and can also inflate a nasal membrane so it protrudes from one nostril like pink bubble gum. He uses these adornments to show off to rival males and to attract females.

BEARDED SEAL

Erignathus barbatus

Location: Arctic waters

Length: Up to 2.5 m (8¼ ft)

The bearded seal is a bulky animal that uses its luxuriant whiskers to search the sea bed for clams and similar prey. It breeds on drifting sea ice.

Efficient flippers
As with all true seals, the leopard seal's hind flippers point backwards, enabling it to propel itself easily through the water.

LEOPARD SEAL

Hydrurga leptonyx

Location: Antarctic waters

Length: Up to 3.4 m (11 ft)

Named for its ferocity as much as for the black spots on its hide, the leopard seal is a powerful predator that hunts other seals and penguins. It often lurks close to floating ice, where it can ambush prey that dives into the water. It also eats a lot of shrimp-like krill and fish when this is available.

Up to 78 per cent of crabeater seals have scars and injuries from failed leopard seal attacks.

CRABEATER SEAL

Lobodon carcinophaga

Location: Antarctic waters

Length: Up to 2.4 m (7¾ ft)

Millions of crabeater seals live on sea ice in the cold Southern Ocean. They feed almost exclusively on shrimp-like krill – straining them from the water with elaborate multi-lobed teeth that interlock to form a very efficient sieve.

SOUTHERN ELEPHANT SEAL

Mirounga leonina

Location: Antarctic waters

Length: Up to 5 m (16½ ft)

Male elephant seals are hulking giants, up to five times heavier than the relatively slim females. They fight each other for control of females on the breeding beaches of cold Southern Ocean islands, roaring loudly through their enlarged noses.

HARP SEAL

Pagophilus groenlandicus

Location: North Atlantic to Arctic Ocean

Length: Up to 1.7 m (5½ ft)

Harp seals breed in colonies on sea ice. They favour sites where the ice is too thin and unstable to carry the weight of a polar bear, hoping to keep their white-coated pups safe. But this does not protect them from human hunters, who kill many harp seals every year.

RIBBON SEAL

Histriophoca fasciata

Location: North Pacific, southern Arctic Ocean

Length: Up to 1.5 m (5 ft)

Most seals have drab coloration, but this one has a striking pattern of black with broad white bands. It breeds on drifting sea ice and each female ribbon seal raises her pup alone.

Seals

Specialized for hunting at sea, seals are marine carnivores. But unlike some ocean mammals, they cannot spend their entire lives at sea – they must return to land to breed.

Seals form a group known as the pinnipeds. There are three types – the eared seals, the walrus, and the true seals. Eared seals include the sea lions and fur seals. As well as the external ear flaps for which they are named, they have long front flippers and can move quite well on land. The walrus is similar but with long tusks. True seals have hind limbs specialized for swimming and move on land with difficulty.

A skunk's spray can be **smelt** by a human up to **1 km (½ mile) away**.

Striped skunk

Many animals are armed with defensive weapons to keep predators away, but few of these are as effective as a skunk's. Any predator that tries to attack it risks being drenched in a blast of foul-smelling chemicals.

Skunks are nocturnal, solitary carnivores that are similar to the badgers and weasels. But despite being technically a carnivore, the striped skunk eats a variety of foods – mostly insects, but also small mammals, carrion, and some fruit and other plant material. It can live in a variety of habitats, including woodlands, forests, agricultural land, and even towns. During the winter, the striped skunk spends most of its time in an underground den and can lose up to half its body weight.

Alarm signal
If the skunk is disburbed, its fur will stand on end.

Facing the enemy
When cornered, and while still facing the threat, a skunk can bend its rear around and direct the spray.

Narrow jaw
The jaws and teeth are adapted for eating insects and other small animals.

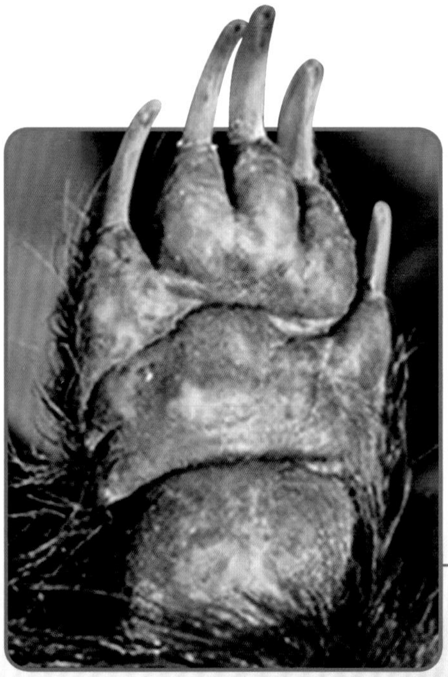

Digging claws
The skunk's front feet are equipped with five long, stout claws, which it uses to dig in the soil for food. A lot of its prey consists of juicy insect grubs that it digs out of the ground. It may also excavate its own den, although it often uses a ready-made burrow dug by another animal.

Flat feet
A skunk walks on the soles of its feet, like bears do.

MAMMALS

STRIPED SKUNK

Mephitis mephitis

Location: North America

Length: Up to 40 cm (15¾ in)

Diet: Small animals, fruit

Danger sign
The long, bushy tail is raised like a flag as a warning, and to keep it out of the way of the chemical spray.

Stinky spray
The skunk's secret weapon is concocted by a pair of musk glands beneath its tail. Many mammals have these, which they use to scent-mark their territory. But the skunk's glands produce a peculiarly noxious mixture of acrid, sulphurous chemicals.

Warning stripes
The skunk's bold black-and-white stripes are unique to each individual. The distinctive markings act as a warning to potential enemies. Any animal that has been sprayed by a skunk will keep well clear in future.

Fair warning

When faced by a predator such as this red fox, a skunk tries to warn it off by raising its tail, hissing menacingly, and stamping its feet. But if this has no effect, the skunk turns its back and aims its noxious spray at its enemy's face. This not only smells disgusting but is so intensely irritating if it gets in an attacker's eyes that it can cause temporary blindness.

When feeding, a honey badger **devours every scrap of its prey**, including its **bones, skin, and hair or feathers**.

Honey badger

Renowned for its ferocity when backed into a tight corner, the honey badger is a powerful mustelid – a relative of the weasels – that is prepared to eat almost any animal it can catch, including highly venomous snakes.

Although mainly a carnivore, the honey badger owes its name to its taste for the honeycomb of wild bees, which it rips from their nests without regard for their stings. It is possible that it does not feel them, for it has a very thick skin that makes it fearless in both attack and defence. An adaptable opportunist, it flourishes in a wide range of habitats from semi-deserts to dense rainforest.

Long front claws
The honey badger's front feet are armed with five long, extremely strong claws, which it uses to excavate its own burrows and dig prey animals out of theirs. The claws also enable it to climb trees in search of bees' nests, and tear the timber apart to expose the honeycomb.

Venomous prey

Few predators dare tackle a highly venomous cobra, but the honey badger is not deterred. Its thick skin may be too tough for the cobra's fangs to penetrate, but some think that the badger has some immunity to the nerve poison in the snake's venom. This allows it to attack and eat a cobra – or similar snake – without risking a fatal bite.

Face-off

A honey badger is astonishingly bold when faced with powerful enemies. If escape is impossible it turns and fights, and honey badgers have even been known to attack and drive away lions. Its thick, loose skin makes it hard to get a secure grip on, and even more difficult to kill, so most big hunters leave it well alone.

MAMMALS

HONEY BADGER

Mellivora capensis

Location: Africa and southern Asia

Length Up to 96 cm (38 in)

Diet: Animals, fruit, honey

The jaws and teeth of a wolverine are strong enough to crack the thigh bone of a moose.

Mustelids

Typical mustelids are sleek, sinuous, fiercely predatory land animals that often hunt and kill animals bigger than themselves. But some mustelids hunt in the water, and others are stocky omnivores.

The predators are the weasels, mink, and polecats – short-legged, low-slung hunters that are built for pursuing prey in underground burrows. Martens have a similar build, but are adapted for leaping through the trees, while otters are equipped for swimming and diving. The badgers, by contrast, are specialized for digging in search of small prey, and eat a very wide range of foods.

SEA OTTER

Enhydra lutris

Location: North Pacific shores

Length: Up to 1.2 m (4 ft)

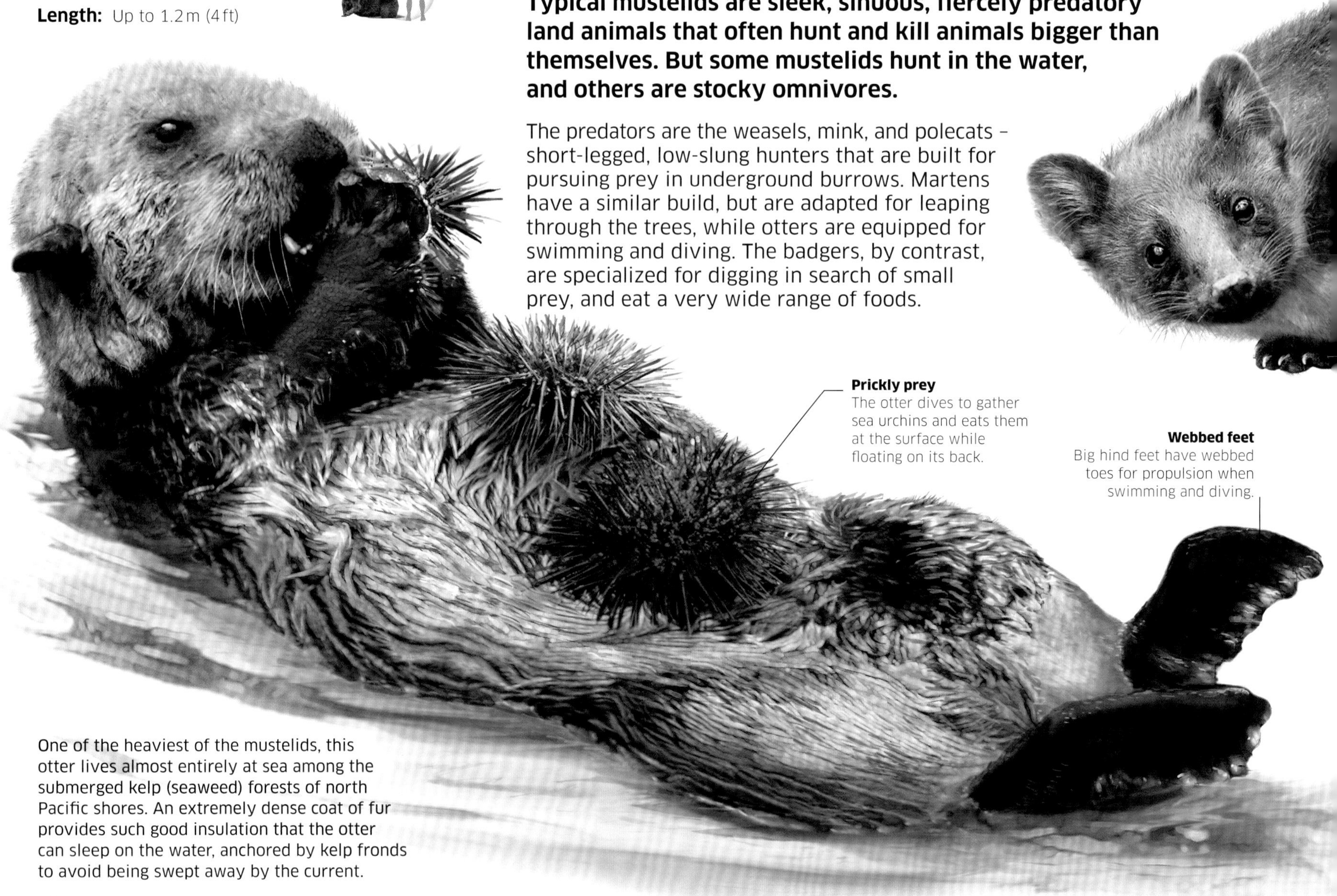

One of the heaviest of the mustelids, this otter lives almost entirely at sea among the submerged kelp (seaweed) forests of north Pacific shores. An extremely dense coat of fur provides such good insulation that the otter can sleep on the water, anchored by kelp fronds to avoid being swept away by the current.

EURASIAN OTTER

Lutra lutra

Location: Eurasia, northwest Africa

Length: Up to 82 cm (32¼ in)

This elegant aquatic hunter has a tapering tail and dense, short fur that give it perfect streamlining underwater. It mainly hunts fish in rivers, lakes, and shallow coastal seas, locating them in cloudy water with its long, sensitive whiskers.

WOLVERINE

Gulo gulo

Location: Northern Eurasia, North America

Length: Up to 1.5 m (5 ft)

One of the biggest mustelids, the wolverine lives in the northern forests and Arctic tundra, where it hunts and scavenges for prey as large as reindeer. It has hugely powerful jaws for gnawing at frozen meat and crushing bones.

EUROPEAN PINE MARTEN

Martes martes

Location: Europe, western Asia

Length: Up to 58 cm (23 in)

Unlike other mustelids, martens regularly hunt in trees, and have sharp semi-retractable claws for climbing. The European pine marten is one of the best known; active mainly at night, it leaps from branch to branch with effortless grace to pursue squirrels. It also hunts on the ground for other small animals.

Furry tail The marten's long, furry tail helps it keep its balance.

EUROPEAN BADGER

Meles meles

Location: Europe, western Asia

Length: Up to 90 cm (35½ in)

The European badger uses its sturdy clawed feet to create extensive burrow systems, and to dig up juicy roots, insect grubs, and other small animals, including entire wasps' nests. It feeds mainly on earthworms, but it may take ground-nesting birds, moles, hedgehogs, and similar prey. It also eats a lot of fruit and nuts.

LEAST WEASEL

Mustela nivalis

Location: Northern Eurasia, North America

Length: Up to 26 cm (10¼ in)

Although this is the smallest mustelid, it is a formidable hunter. Its slender, flexible body is primarily adapted for chasing mice and voles through their runs and burrows, but it can kill much larger prey. In the far north its fur turns pure white in winter.

White underside

A tiger's **night vision** is at least **six times better** than a human's.

4,000 The **number of tigers** remaining **in the wild**.

Tiger

The largest of the big cats, the tiger is one of the most powerful predators on Earth. Relying on its enormous strength, it is specialized for hunting big prey.

Few predators regularly hunt alone for animals larger than themselves, but a tiger may take on a buffalo six times its own weight. Stealthily it creeps as close as possible, then charges and leaps on its victim from behind. Smaller animals may be killed with a bite to the top of the neck while larger animals are seized by the throat and throttled.

White flashes
Seen from the back, each ear is black with a central patch of pure white. During an aggressive encounter, the tiger flattens and twists its ears so that the spots are visible from the front. This suggests the flashes are mainly used as a warning.

Camouflage

Whereas most big cats have plain or spotted coats, the tiger has unusual dark stripes. They act as very effective camouflage, especially among long grass where they mimic the vertical pattern of light and shade. The stripes break up the tiger's outline, allowing it to get very close to its target without being detected, as it stalks prey before launching an attack.

Retractable claws

The claws are adapted for seizing prey, rather than traction when running. Normally they are retracted into sheaths, which keeps their tips needle-sharp. But when the tiger leaps on a victim, its front legs straighten and the claws extend automatically to seize hold of its quarry.

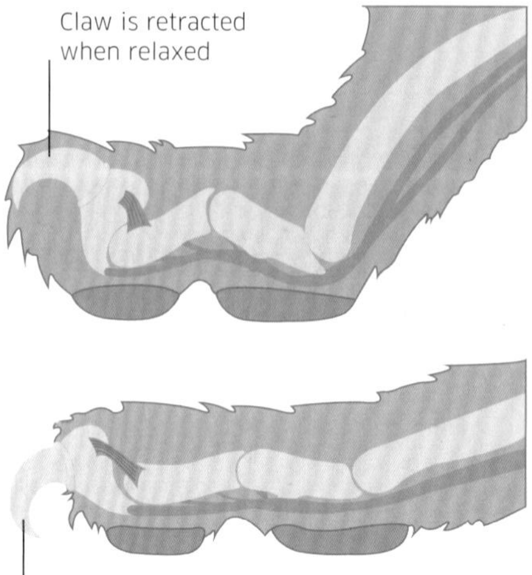

Touch sensitive
Long whiskers help the tiger feel its way in the dark.

Rounded ears
Although its ears are small, a tiger has excellent hearing.

Furry ruff
Males have a large ruff of fur around their necks.

Canine tooth
Carnassial teeth

Killing power
Like all cats, the tiger has big, meat-slicing carnassial teeth but no chewing teeth. This gives it a short jaw, which maximizes the pressure that its powerful jaw muscles exert on the huge, prey-killing canine teeth.

MAMMALS

TIGER

Panthera tigris

Location: S. and E. Asia

Length: Up to 2.9 m (9½ ft)

Diet: Mainly large hoofed mammals

A cheetah can **accelerate** to its **top speed** from a **standing start** in **less than 3 seconds**.

7 m (23 ft) – the **distance a cheetah can cover** with **a single stride**.

Cheetah

No animal can run faster than a cheetah. This highly specialized cat is uniquely adapted for accelerating faster than most sports cars, and pursuing its prey over short distances at blistering speed. Only the swiftest, most agile of its quarry can hope to escape.

The cheetah is different from other cats, which rely on stealth, strength, and sharp claws for hunting. By contrast the cheetah is a sprinter, like a greyhound, with the same slender build, flexible spine, and long legs. But it must creep as close as possible before launching its attack, because it cannot keep up its speed for very long.

MAMMALS

CHEETAH

Acinonyx jubatus

Location: Africa, W. Asia

Length: Up to 1.4 m (4½ ft)

Diet: Small grazing animals

Vital tail
The long tail helps the cheetah balance when turning at speed.

Curved claw
Each foreleg has a sharp, curved dew claw on the inner side, just above the foot. The cheetah uses the claw to trip prey up when it is within range. Once it has its victim on the ground, the cat kills it with a suffocating throat bite.

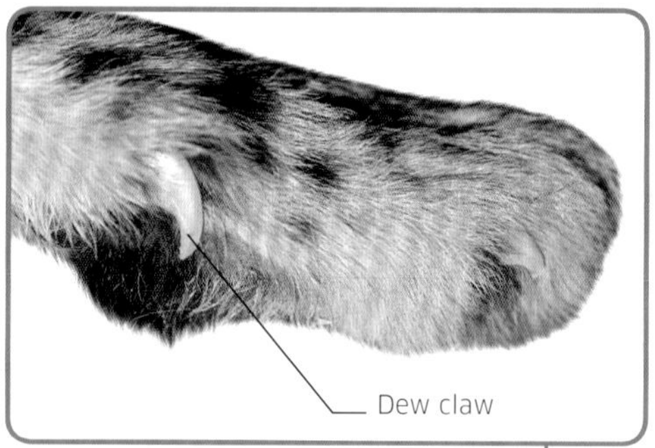

In for the kill
Cheetahs usually hunt small, fast gazelles, which are often agile enough to elude them by quicky changing direction. The cheetah's quick bursts of speed can cause it to overheat, and once it catches its prey and kills it, the cat may have to recover for up to 20 minutes before it is able to start eating.

Running claws
The main claws lack fleshy sheaths, so are always exposed. They provide grip like the spikes on running shoes.

A cheetah can reach speeds of up to
93 km/h (58 mph).

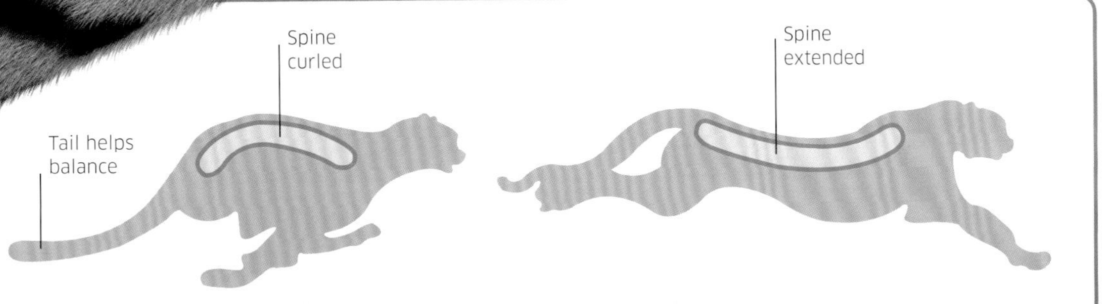

Flexible spine

The cheetah owes its astonishing speed to its extremely long stride, which allows it to cover a lot of ground with each step. It has very long legs, and their effective length is increased by a flexible spine. When the cheetah is moving at full speed the spine curls up to allow the hind legs to reach forward, then straightens and extends in the opposite direction to allow them to push back further than usual.

Small teeth
Compared with typical big cats, the cheetah has small canine teeth. This is because it has extra-large nostrils to take in all the air it needs for a high-speed chase. The nostrils take up a lot of space in its skull, leaving no room for broad upper-canine tooth roots.

Until about **12,000 years ago**, lions **roamed a larger area** of Earth than any other mammal, **except humans**.

Family life
A lion pride varies in size according to location and the availability of prey. It consists of up to eight adult females, their young, and between one and three adult males, who defend the territory and protect the pride from rival males.

Hunting tactics
Lionesses are the main hunters for the pride. They stalk prey to within 30 m (98½ ft) before launching an attack, and often work together to surround an animal and cut off its escape.

Lion

Almost as big as tigers, and with the same body adaptations for killing large prey, lions are the only big cats that live in groups, called prides. Males and females look different, reflecting their separate roles within the pride.

Female lions, or lionesses, are sleek, fast, and agile. They are effective hunters, either alone or in pairs and groups. Males are much bigger and more muscular. When they fight for control of prides, the biggest males nearly always win, so they get to mate with the most females and the cubs inherit their strength. Male lions are strong enough to kill large prey, but they usually leave hunting to the more athletic females.

Magnificent mane
Male lions' manes range in colour from golden to very dark, and tend to darken with age. The darker and thicker the mane, the more attractive the male is to females.

An adult male lion's roar
is so loud it can be heard up to 8 km (5 miles) away.

Tufty tail
Among cats, the tuft at the tip of the tail is unique to lions.

MAMMALS

LION

Panthera leo

Location: Africa, India

Length: Up to 2.5 m (8 ¼ ft)

Diet: Mainly hoofed mammals

A snow leopard **kills** an average of **one large animal every two weeks**.

Snow leopards can hunt at **altitudes of 3,000–4,500 m** (9,840–14,760 ft).

Snow leopard

The most elusive of the big cats, the snow leopard is rarely seen due to its solitary nature and extreme habitat. It lives in some of the highest, coldest, most hostile mountain terrain on Earth and is uniquely adapted to survive in this harsh environment.

Native to the mountain ranges of Asia, including the Himalayas and the vast Tibetan plateau, the snow leopard is a solitary hunter that preys on a variety of animals ranging from ground squirrels to camels. Its main prey are ibex and wild sheep, which it pursues over steep, rocky slopes with astounding agility. Its large lungs ensure that it gathers enough oxygen from the thin mountain air, while its very thick fur keeps it warm.

MAMMALS

SNOW LEOPARD

Panthera uncia

Location: Central Asia

Length: Up to 1.25 m (4 ft)

Diet: Mammals and ground birds

Long fur
The snow leopard's long, thick fur gives it a stocky appearance. It can grow up to 12 cm (5 in) long in winter.

Furry feet
The soles of a snow leopard's feet are unusually furry. This helps to prevent the cat losing heat through its feet, and may improve its grip on bare rock. The feet are also broader than those of most cats; they spread its weight across deep snow, helping to stop the animal from sinking in.

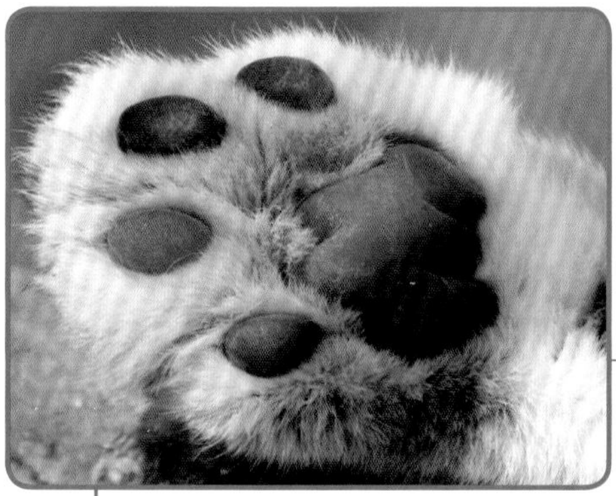

Deep breather
Big nasal cavities allow the snow leopard to inhale large amounts of air at a time.

Coat markings
Dark-grey and black spots provide camouflage

6,500 The maximum number of **snow leopards thought to be left in the wild**. There may be **as few as 4,000**.

A snow leopard uses its **thick, very furry tail** like a duvet, **to keep warm** while it is asleep.

A snow leopard can kill prey **up to three times its own weight.**

Short legs
The legs are relatively short, adapted for agility rather than speed.

Lean, muscular body

Balancing tail
The snow leopard's extra-long, bushy tail helps the animal to keep its balance when leaping from rock to rock in pursuit of prey. Snow leopards often chase fast-moving animals such as ibex down very steep slopes, gaining speed as they race downhill, but rarely missing their footing on the rocky terrain.

Hidden in plain view

A snow leopard prefers to ambush prey from above in the dim light of dawn or dusk. Using rocks and shrubs for cover, it relies on its superb camouflage to stay concealed from potential prey. Even in broad daylight it can be very difficult to pick out when crouching quietly on a boulder, the mottled pattern of its coat blending seamlessly with the patchwork of lichen and bare rock.

Rocky nursery

Typically solitary, male and female snow leopards meet to mate in late winter. Between one and five cubs are born just over three months later, in a rocky den. Initially blind and helpless, the cubs stay with their mother for at least 18 months before leaving to find their own hunting territories.

Purebred **European wildcats** are **becoming rare** because of **interbreeding with wild-living** (feral) **domestic cats**.

Wild cats

Dedicated predators, cats are adapted for eating meat and nothing else. They cannot chew, and their short jaws and big, stabbing canine teeth are specialized weapons for grabbing and killing prey.

The cat family is divided into two groups. The pantherines, most of which can roar, include most of the big cats. Non-pantherines cannot roar, and are usually smaller – although this group does include the cheetah and puma. Cats are almost all solitary hunters that rely on stealth to get close enough to prey to launch an attack.

CARACAL

Caracal caracal

Location: Africa, Arabia, Southwest Asia

Length: Up to 1.1 m (3½ ft)

Also known as the desert lynx, this cat's most obvious feature is its long, lynx-like, black-tufted ears. The caracal is a nocturnal hunter, mainly of small mammals, birds, and reptiles, but it will also take on larger, faster animals, such as antelope.

SERVAL

Leptailurus serval

Location: Sub-Saharan Africa

Length: Up to 92 cm (36¼ in)

This tall African cat is adapted for stalking through long grass, listening for small prey with its huge, mobile ears. Compared to its overall body size, it has the longest legs of any cat species.

EUROPEAN WILDCAT

Felis silvestris silvestris

Location: Europe

Length: Up to 66 cm (26 in)

Related to the ancestor of the domestic cat, the European wildcat looks similar to a pet tabby, but with a bushier tail. Rare and very shy, it is a ferocious hunter of small mammals. Other subspecies of the wildcat live in Africa and Asia.

OCELOT

Leopardus pardalis

Location: Central and South America

Length: Up to 1 m (3¼ ft)

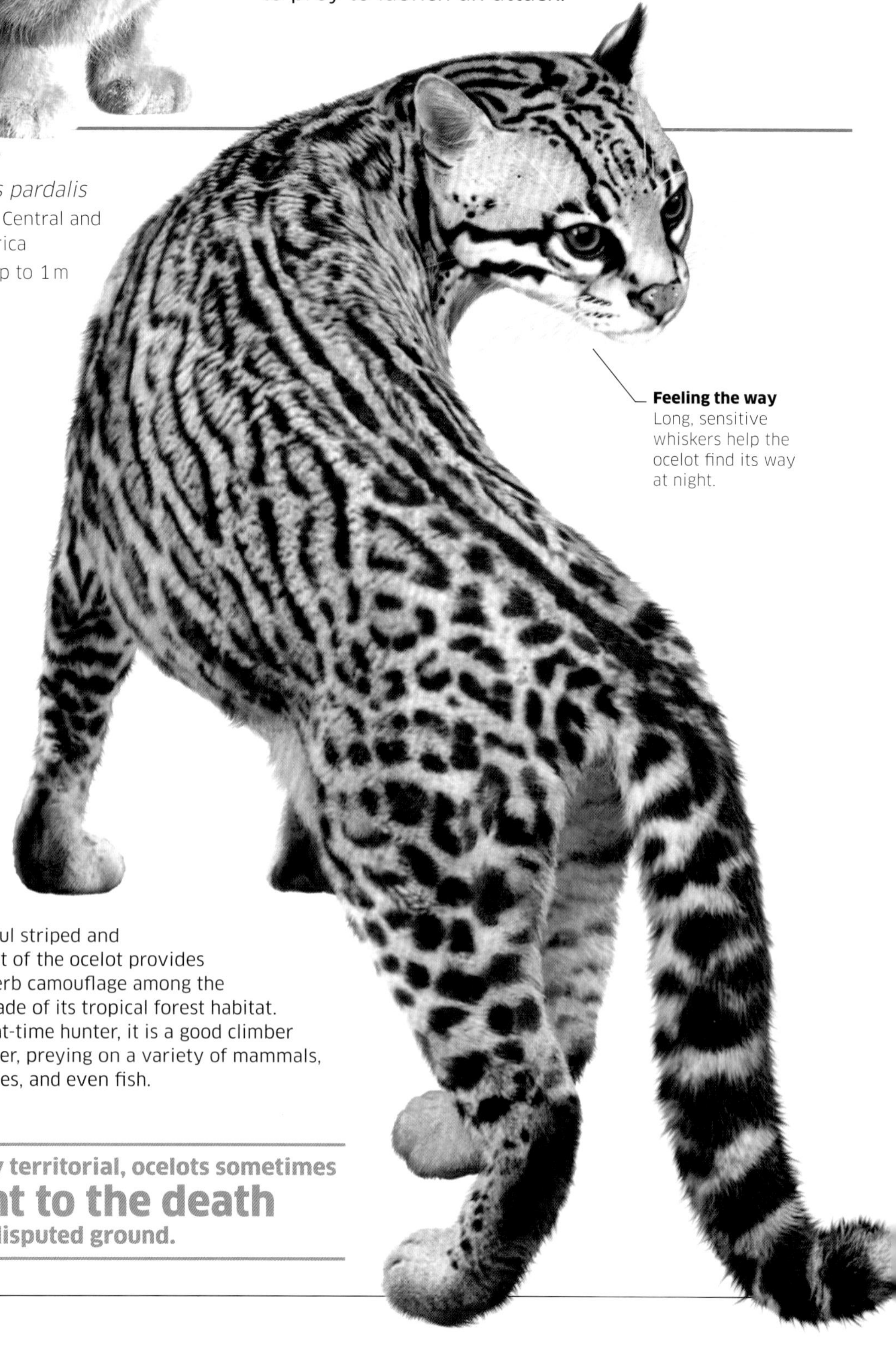

The beautiful striped and spotted coat of the ocelot provides it with superb camouflage among the dappled shade of its tropical forest habitat. A lone, night-time hunter, it is a good climber and swimmer, preying on a variety of mammals, birds, reptiles, and even fish.

Highly territorial, ocelots sometimes
fight to the death
over disputed ground.

EURASIAN LYNX

Lynx lynx

Location: Eastern Europe, Asia

Length: Up to 1.1 m (3½ ft)

Like all lynxes, this species has black-tufted ears and a short tail. It hunts mainly in cold, northern forests where its large, furry paws stop it from sinking into deep snow. It can kill animals up to four times its size, such as reindeer.

MARBLED CAT

Pardofelis marmorata

Location: Southeast Asia

Length: Up to 62 cm (24½ in)

Like many cats, this beautifully marked small cat is an excellent climber, but is unusual in that it spends much of its time in trees. High in the tropical forest canopy, it hunts birds, squirrels, lizards, and similar small prey, mostly at night.

PUMA

Puma concolor

Location: Americas

Length: Up to 1.6 m (5¼ ft)

Also known as the cougar, or mountain lion, the puma is one of the biggest non-pantherine cats, and is strong enough to kill a moose. Adaptable to different habitats, it has a vast range across the Americas, living in deserts, prairies, forests, and mountains.

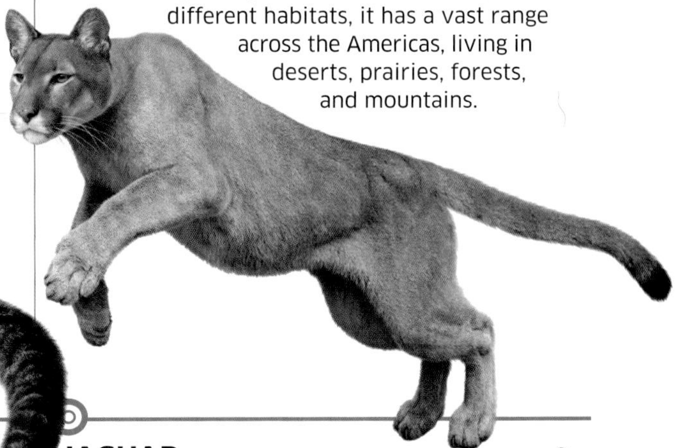

PALLAS'S CAT

Otocolobus manul

Location: Central Asia

Length: Up to 65 cm (25½ in)

Its short legs and very thick fur give this cat an unusually stocky, bulky appearance. Its fur provides insulation against the bitter chill of the Himalayas and the Tibetan plateau.

FISHING CAT

Prionailurus viverrinus

Location: Southern Asia

Length: Up to 1.1 m (3½ ft)

This is the only cat that feeds mainly on fish. It usually scoops them out of the shallows along the banks of rivers, but it will also dive underwater and swim after particularly tempting prey.

JAGUAR

Panthera onca

Location: Central and South America

Length: Up to 1.7 m (5½ ft)

The biggest American cat, and the only New World pantherine, the jaguar is found in a variety of forest habitats and swampy grasslands. It preys on anything it can catch, from mice to crocodilians.

INDOCHINESE CLOUDED LEOPARD

Neofelis nebulosa

Location: Eastern Asia

Length: Up to 1.1 m (3½ ft)

A dramatically marked species, the clouded leopard has exceptionally long canine teeth that enable it to kill prey much larger than itself, such as deer and wild pigs. It is a very good climber, and has been seen running head-first down tree trunks and hanging upside-down from branches.

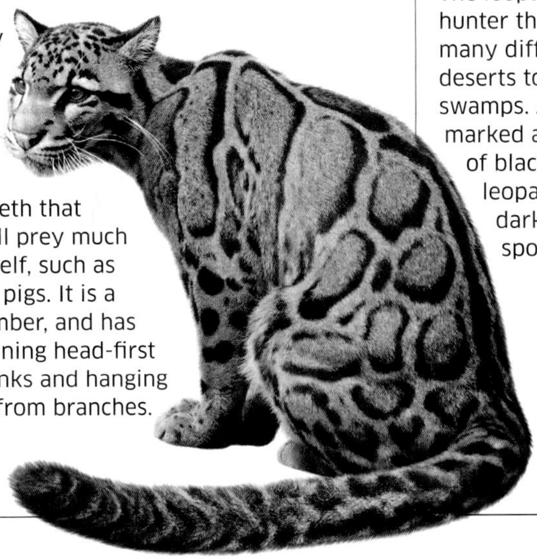

LEOPARD

Panthera pardus

Location: Africa, southern Asia

Length: Up to 1.9 m (6¼ ft)

The leopard is a stealthy hunter that can survive in many different habitats, from deserts to jungles and swamps. All leopards are marked all over with clusters of black spots – even black leopards, whose very dark fur masks their spotted pattern.

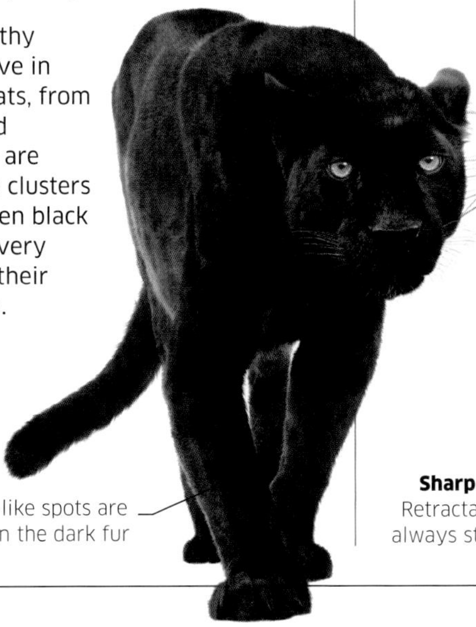

In Tanzania's **Ngorongoro Crater**, spotted hyenas obtain **90 per cent** of their food by **hunting**.

15 minutes – the time it can take a **group of hyenas** to **eat a zebra**.

Scavenging lions often **steal the kills** of less powerful hyenas.

MAMMALS

SPOTTED HYENA

Crocuta crocuta

Location: Sub-Saharan Africa

Length: Up to 1.6 m (5¼ ft)

Diet: Other mammals, carrion

60 km/h (37 mph) – the **speed** at which a **spotted hyena** can **chase its prey**.

14 kg (31 lb) – the amount of **meat** a spotted hyena can **eat at a sitting**.

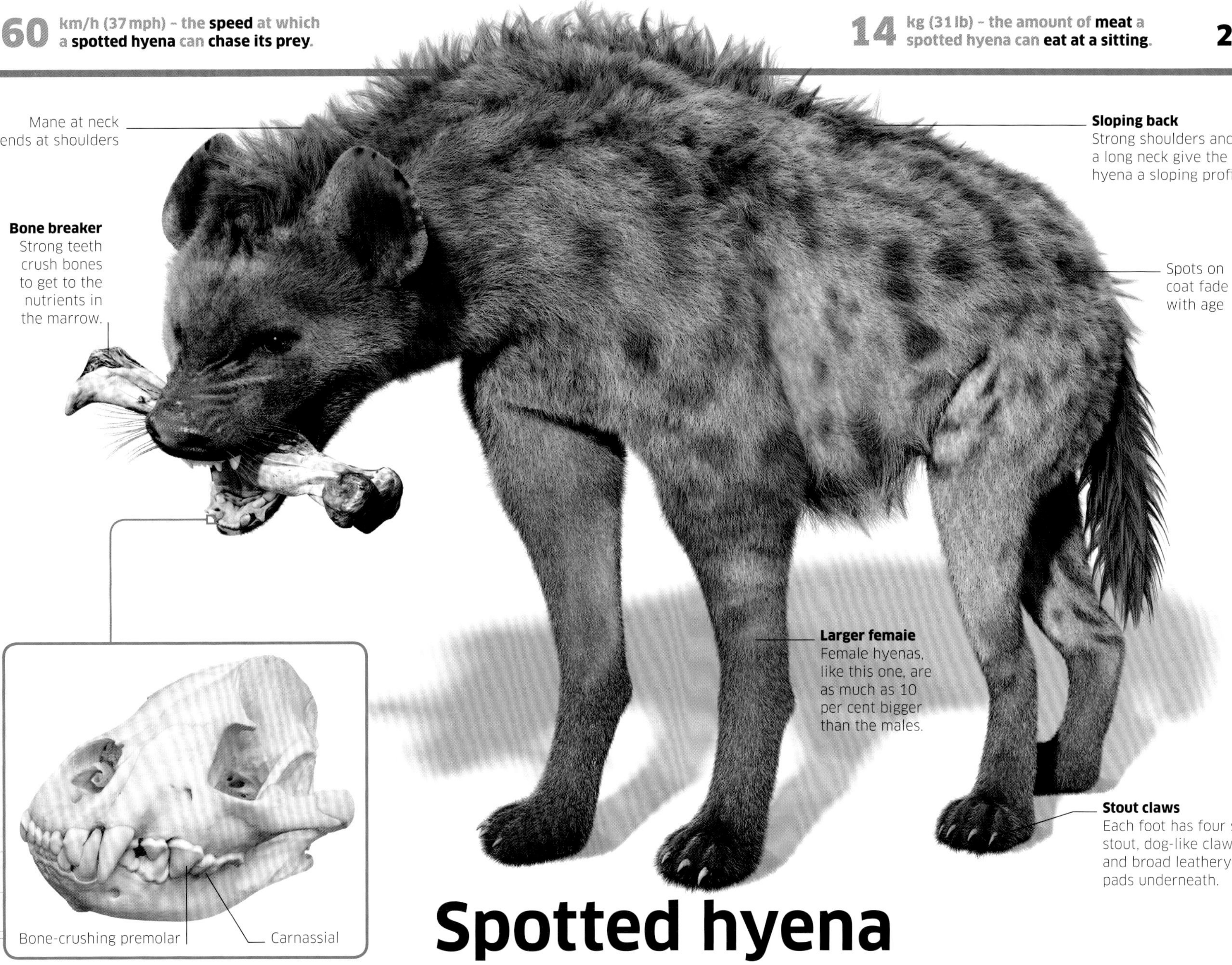

Bone-crushing teeth
The hyena's massively muscled jaws are armed with huge, conical premolar teeth that are strong enough to shatter the leg bones of a giraffe. These lie in front of sharp, blade-like carnassial teeth, similar to those of cats and dogs, for scissoring through tough hide, meat, and sinew.

Spotted hyena

Sometimes known as the laughing hyena because of its eerie cackling calls, this scavenger is also one of the most lethally effective predators on the African plains.

The spotted hyena is adapted for scavenging the remains of the dead, with hugely powerful jaws and teeth for cracking the bones that other carnivores discard, and a digestive system that can process every part of a carcass. Despite this it mainly kills live prey, often hunting in packs. Its combined talents have made it the most successful big carnivore in Africa.

Hyena society
Spotted hyenas live in female-dominated clans of up to 80 animals, although most clans are smaller. Young females stay in the clan, while young males leave to join neighbouring clans.

Hunting
Other hyena species are primarily scavengers, but in most parts of its range (the area where it lives) the spotted hyena is mainly a hunter. It tackles small prey alone, but hunts in packs for big prey such as zebras or even African buffalo. The hyenas wear down their victim by a long chase that can cover up to 5 km (3 miles), then launch a joint attack.

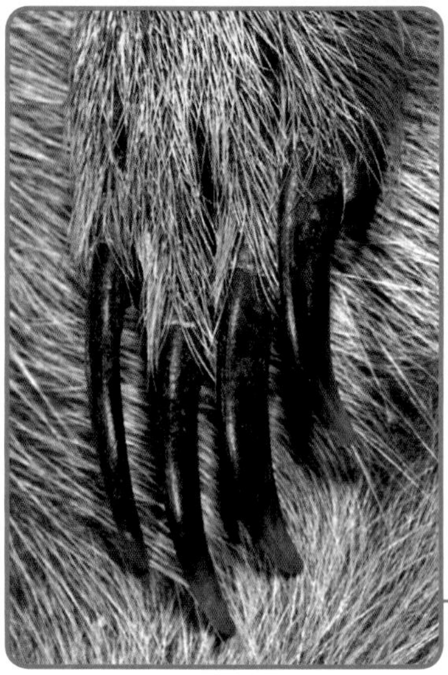

Digging claws
The very long claws on the meerkat's front paws are adapted for digging – both to make burrows and to dig for insects and small mammals. A meerkat can dig very quickly, shifting its own weight in sand in just a few seconds.

Closeable ears
The meerkat can close its small ears tightly to keep out sand and dust whilst digging.

High viewpoint
Standing upright on a rock, mound, or bush helps the meerkat spot potential danger as early as possible.

Slender feet
The hind legs have powerful thighs but small, slender feet.

Balancing tail
The dark-tipped tail helps the meerkat balance when standing upright.

Meerkat

Its habit of standing up on its hind legs, either to watch for predators or bask in the morning sun, has made this slender desert mongoose one of the most instantly recognizable of African mammals.

The various species of mongoose are small, ground-dwelling carnivores. The meerkat is one of the most sociable, living in clans of around 20 in large networks of underground burrows, dug in the sandy soil of southern African deserts. These clans hunt insects and other small animals by daylight, while one meerkat stands guard. When it spots danger, it gives a warning bark or whistle. The other meerkats then run for safety to the nearest burrow entrance.

Venomous prey

Meerkats often eat scorpions, and may have some immunity to the powerful venom. But the meerkat usually avoids being stung by grabbing the scorpion and biting off its tail, which carries the sting. The scorpion is then defenceless and makes an easy prey. A meerkat pup, such as the one pictured left, is taught to do this by adults in its clan.

Group sunbathing

Each meerkat clan is dominated by one breeding pair that produces most of the young. Other male and female adults in the clan help to care for the breeding pair's pups. Each morning, the whole clan may gather outside the burrow to warm up after the cold desert night. They either lie on their backs or stand upright, soaking up as much sunlight as possible.

MAMMALS

MEERKAT

Suricata suricatta

Location: Southern Africa

Length: Up to 29 cm (11½ in)

Diet: Insects and other small animals

Sensitive snout
The meerkat uses its excellent sense of smell to sniff out prey, and to identify other meerkats, either as clan members or enemies.

Anti-glare patches
Dark markings around the eyes improve the meerkat's vision by reducing glare from the sun.

A meerkat can make **different alarm calls** depending on whether it spots predators on the ground or in the air.

Heat-absorber
Dark skin beneath the fur warms up fast when the meerkat stands upright to soak in the sun.

Hunter's view
The eyes face forwards, giving binocular (two-eyed) vision, which enables the meerkat to see in 3D and judge distances accurately.

Desert camouflage
Grey-brown fur provides good camouflage in the scrubby, sandy deserts of southern Africa.

All the Przewalski's horses alive today are descended from 12 wild horses captured in the early 20th century.

AFRICAN WILD ASS
Equus africanus
Location: Northeast Africa
Length: Up to 2 m (6½ ft)

The wild ancestor of the domestic donkey, this is the smallest of the horse family. It lives in the dry grasslands and deserts of Somalia and nearby regions, where it survives on a diet of tough desert plants and can go without water for up to three days.

ONAGER
Equus hemionus
Location: Western and central Asia
Length: Up to 2.5 m (8¼ ft)

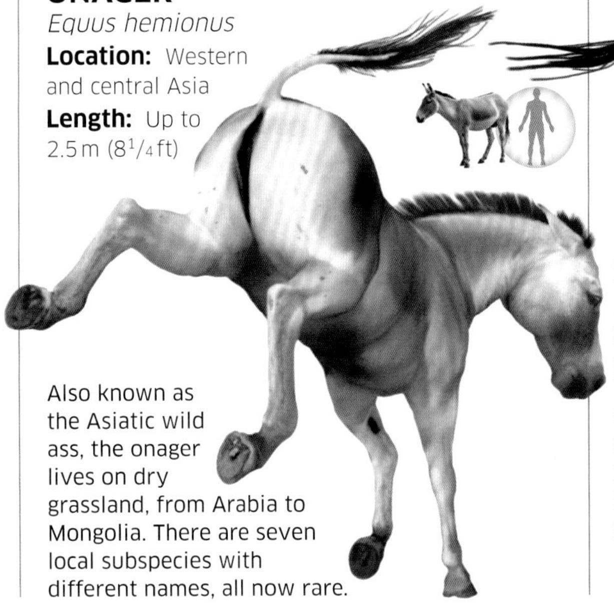

Also known as the Asiatic wild ass, the onager lives on dry grassland, from Arabia to Mongolia. There are seven local subspecies with different names, all now rare.

KIANG
Equus kiang
Location: Central Asia
Length: Up to 2.1 m (6¾ ft)

Closely related to the onager, but with a darker coat, the kiang lives on the high Tibetan plateau to the north of the Himalayas. It is the least threatened of the wild asses, and sometimes gathers in large herds of 100 or more.

PRZEWALSKI'S HORSE
Equus przewalskii
Location: Central Asia
Length: Up to 2.8 m (9¼ ft)

This is the only surviving truly wild horse that is related to the ancestors of domestic horses. Discovered in Mongolia in the 1870s but almost wiped out in the 20th century, it has been reintroduced to its native range and appears to be slowly increasing in numbers.

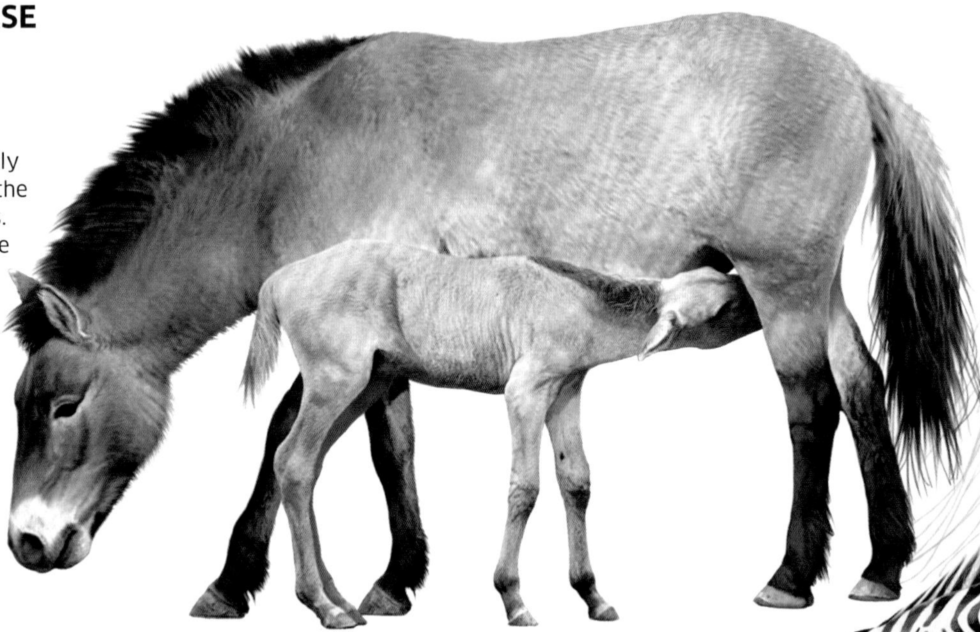

Fly whisk
Mobile tail has a tuft of long hair for brushing away biting flies.

MOUNTAIN ZEBRA
Equus zebra
Location: Southwest Africa
Length: Up to 2.6 m (8½ ft)

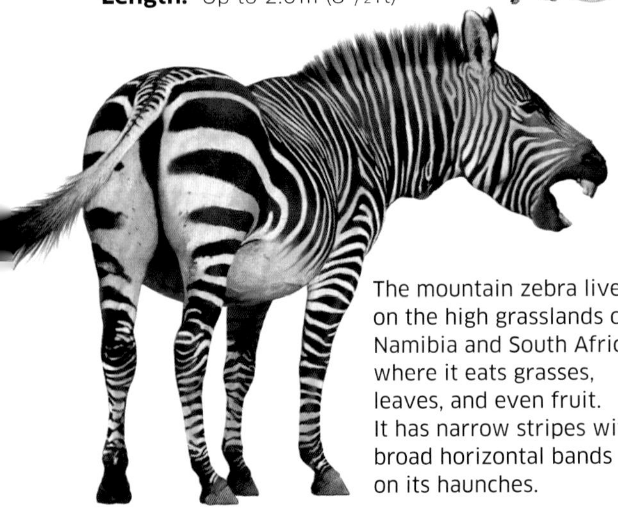

The mountain zebra lives on the high grasslands of Namibia and South Africa, where it eats grasses, leaves, and even fruit. It has narrow stripes with broad horizontal bands on its haunches.

GRÉVY'S ZEBRA
Equus grevyi
Location: East Africa
Length: Up to 2.7 m (8¾ ft)

The biggest and rarest of the zebras, Grévy's zebra has narrow stripes and a slender head. Restricted to a few dry grasslands in east Africa, it wanders nomadically in search of food and water. When breeding, males form groups which occupy and defend large territories.

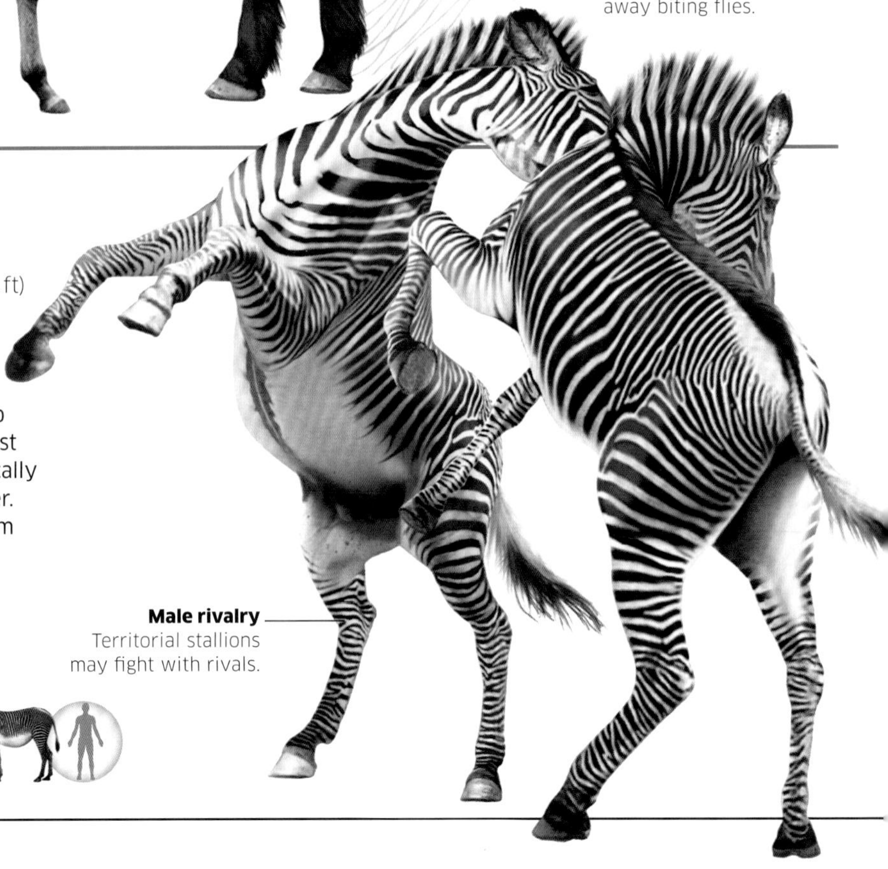

Male rivalry
Territorial stallions may fight with rivals.

A **newborn Grévy's zebra** can stand after just six minutes, and **run away from predators within 45 minutes**.

Onagers are **among the fastest hoofed mammals**, able to **run at 70 km/h (43 mph)**.

Horses

Domestic horses are familiar worldwide, but most of their wild relatives are now very rare. Only the kiang and the plains zebra roam the grasslands in large herds, like the domestic horse's ancestors.

Horses are adapted for life on open plains, where there is no cover and the only defence against powerful predators is to outrun them. Long legs and specialized hooves give horses the speed they need, while their big teeth enable them to feed on coarse, abrasive grass.

Bristly mane
The striped mane is coarse and bristly, and stands upright.

Plains zebra
Beneath its stripes, the plains zebra has all the familiar features of horses – a long muzzle so it can graze while keeping watch for danger, big chewing teeth, long legs, and a single large hoof on each foot. The reason for its bold stripes is unknown, but theories include helping the herd to blend in as one, keeping the animal cool, and even warding off insect bites.

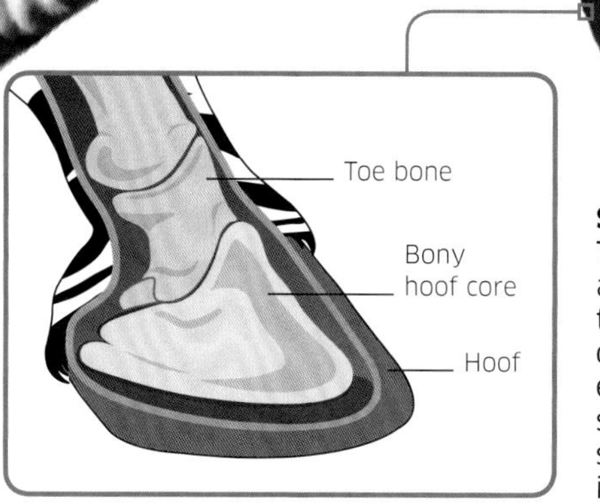

Single hoof
The ancestors of zebras, horses, and asses had three or more toes. But after millions of years of evolution, now just one toe on each foot remains, capped by a strong hoof. The result is a strong, shock-absorbing foot ideal for running at speed.

MAMMALS

PLAINS ZEBRA

Equus quagga burchellii

Location: Eastern and southern Africa

Length: Up to 2.5 m ($8^1/_4$ ft)

Diet: Grass, leaves, buds

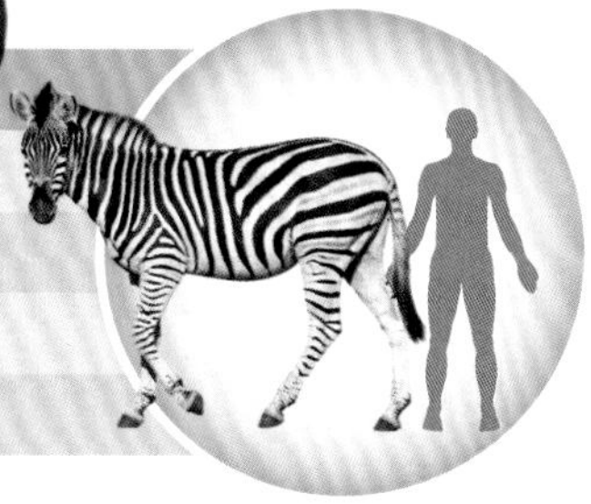

Black rhinoceros

With its huge horned head and thick hide, the black rhinoceros is a survivor from a prehistoric age of giant herbivores. Now critically endangered by illegal hunting, it is restricted to a few wildlife reserves in eastern and southern Africa.

The black rhinoceros is a heavyweight browser – an animal that feeds by gathering the leaves and tender shoots of bushes and trees. These do not contain a lot of nutrients, but the rhino's great size enables it to eat them in bulk to get the nutrition it needs. Its horns can kill enemies such as lions, and are also used in fights between rivals, often inflicting lethal wounds.

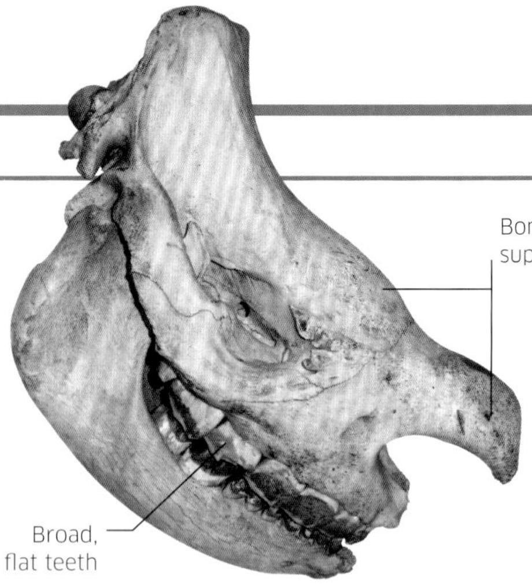

Massive skull
The black rhinoceros has a heavy skull and jaw, with large cheek teeth but no front teeth. Its horns rest on bony supports, with an extension of the skull supporting the larger front horn.

Armed protection

In the late 20th century, the black rhinoceros was almost wiped out by poachers, who today still sell its horn for use in traditional Chinese medicine or for dagger handles. It is now strictly protected within fenced reserves, often by armed guards, but numbers are still low. This blind baby rhino is one of many that face continued threats to their survival.

BLACK RHINO

WHITE RHINO

Pointed or square?

While the foliage-browsing black rhino has a pointed, prehensile upper lip for grasping leaves, the African white rhino is a grazer, with a square lip for cropping grass at ground level.

1.3 m (4¼ ft) – the **length** of the **largest-known black rhino horn**.

There are only about **5,000** black rhinos **alive today**.

55 km/h (34 mph) – the **top speed** of a **black rhino**.

MAMMALS

BLACK RHINOCEROS

Diceros bicornis

Location: Africa

Length: Up to 3.8 m (12½ ft)

Diet: Leaves, twigs

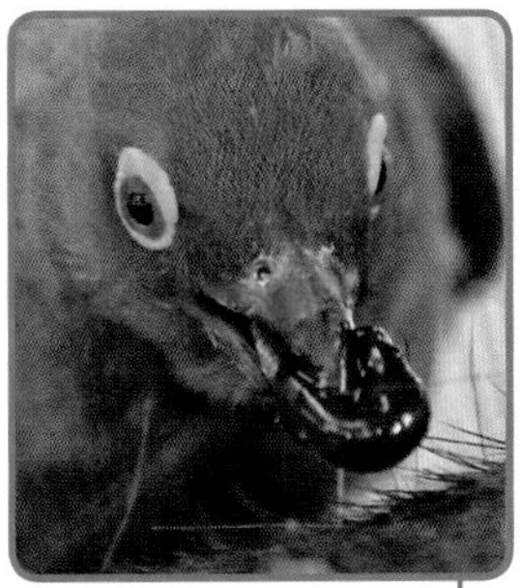

Friend or foe?
The rhino is often attended by red-billed oxpeckers, which remove skin parasites such as bloodsucking ticks. But oxpeckers also pick at wounds to make them bleed, so they can drink the rhino's blood.

Horn structure
The horn is an outgrowth of the skin and is made of hair-like keratin fibres fused into a solid mass.

Wrinkled skin
To protect it from the sun's glare, rhinos coat their thick, rough skin in layers of mud.

Prehensile lip
The rhino uses its pointed, mobile upper lip to pluck stems and leaves.

Up to half of all male black rhinos die of injuries caused **by the horns of rival males.**

The wild **Bactrian camel** is so rare that it is **critically endangered** in its natural habitat.

MAMMALS

DROMEDARY

Camelus dromedarius

Location: North Africa, Arabia, introduced to Australia

Length: Up to 3.4 m (11 ft)

Diet: Leaves, grasses

Camelids

Specialized for life in deserts and high mountains, camelids can survive some of the most hostile climates on Earth. Their toughness has made them vital assets to humans.

As well as two types of camels, camelids consist of the South American guanaco and vicuña, and the domestic animals derived from them. The guanaco is the ancestor of the llama, selectively bred for centuries as a beast of burden, while the vicuña is the ancestor of the alpaca, bred for its luxuriant wool. The Arabian dromedary was domesticated at least 4,000 years ago, and is now considered extinct in the wild throughout its native range.

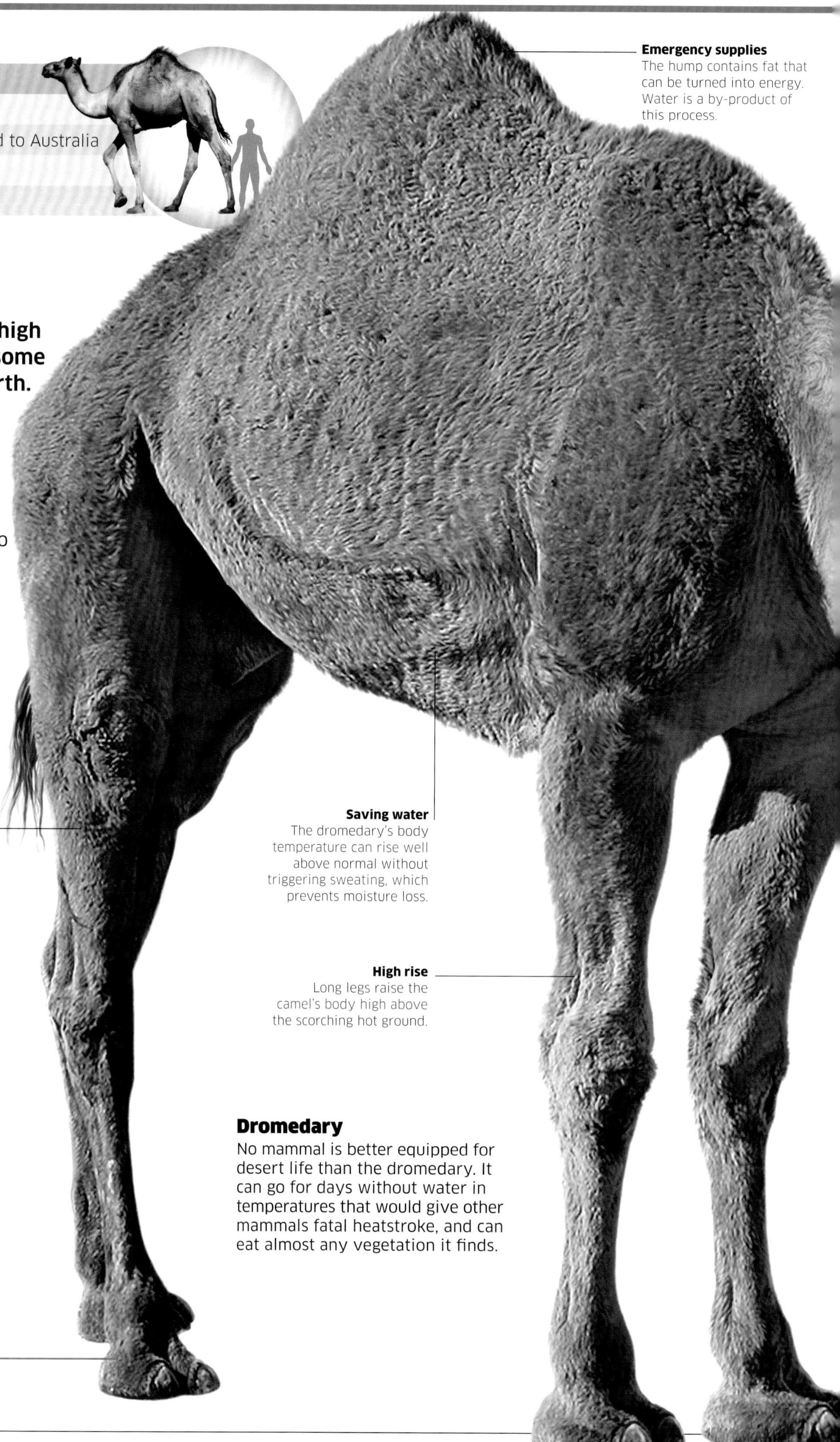

Emergency supplies
The hump contains fat that can be turned into energy. Water is a by-product of this process.

Sun screen
A thick coat of fur keeps the dromedary's skin relatively cool.

Saving water
The dromedary's body temperature can rise well above normal without triggering sweating, which prevents moisture loss.

High rise
Long legs raise the camel's body high above the scorching hot ground.

Desert feet
The broad, two-toed feet of the dromedary are well-adapted to walking across wind-blown dunes, spreading under the dromedary's weight to stop the animal sinking into the soft, dry sand. However, their soles can be injured by walking over sharp stones.

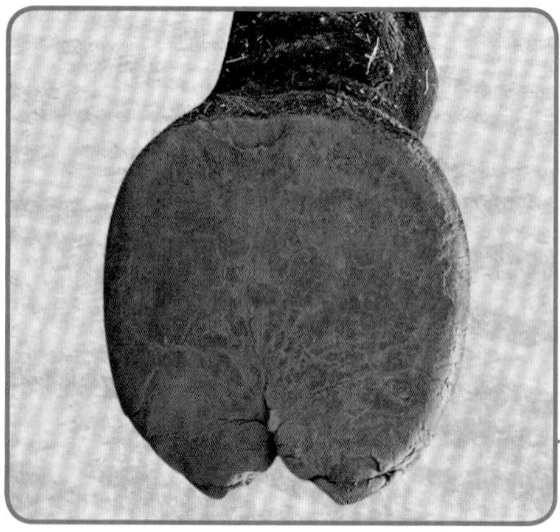

Dromedary

No mammal is better equipped for desert life than the dromedary. It can go for days without water in temperatures that would give other mammals fatal heatstroke, and can eat almost any vegetation it finds.

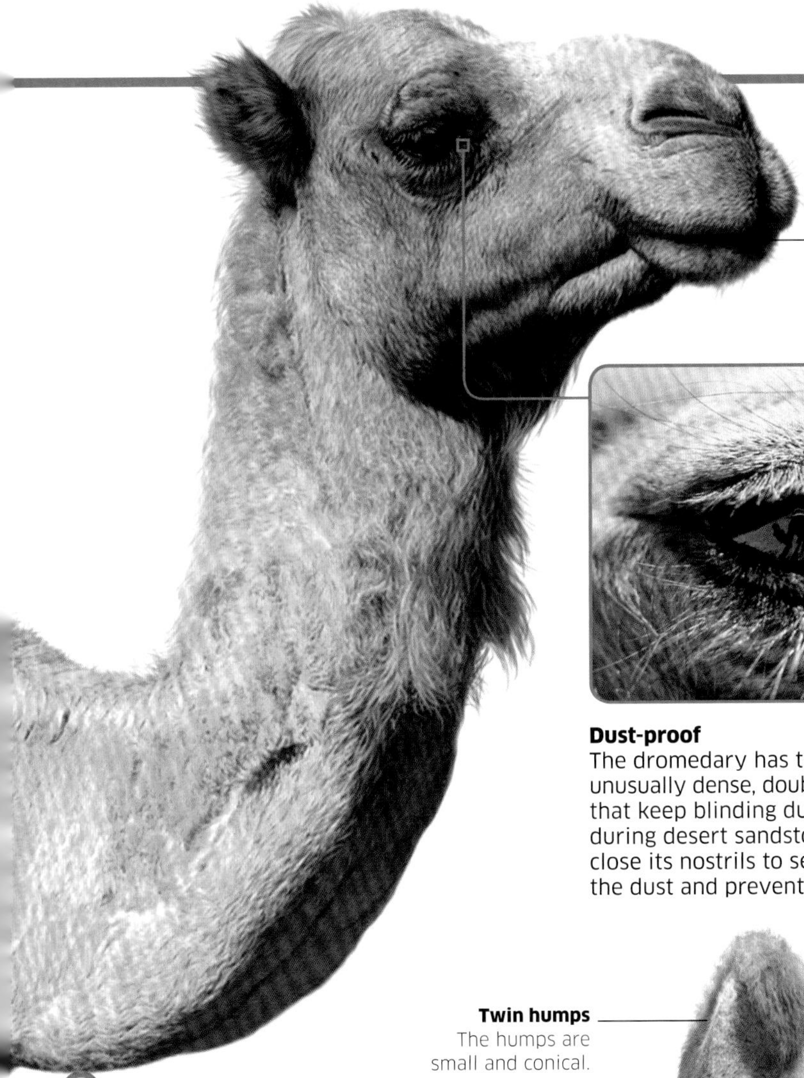

Thornproof lips
Tough skin on its lips enables the dromedary to eat thorny desert shrubs.

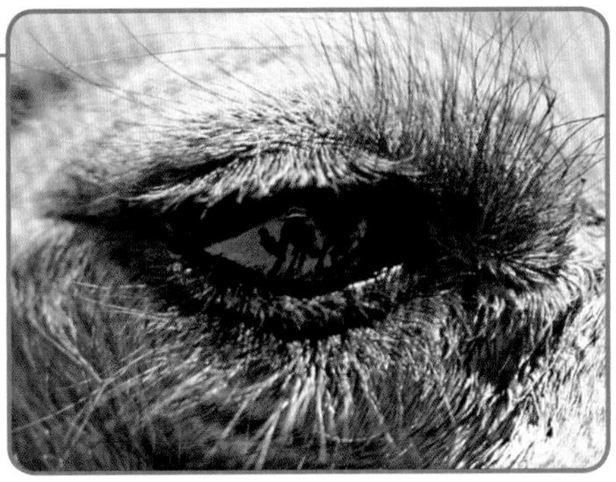

Dust-proof
The dromedary has thick eyebrows and unusually dense, double-layered eyelashes that keep blinding dust out of its eyes during desert sandstorms. It can also close its nostrils to seal them against the dust and prevent choking.

VICUÑA

Vicugna vicugna

Location: Andes, South America

Length: Up to 1.9 m (6¼ ft)

The graceful, lightly built vicuña lives in the rugged central Andes mountains, on high grassy plains, and in the Atacama Desert, where temperatures plunge to below freezing at night. It is kept warm by a dense coat of soft, fine wool that led to its domestication and the evolution of the thick-woolled alpaca.

Twin humps
The humps are small and conical.

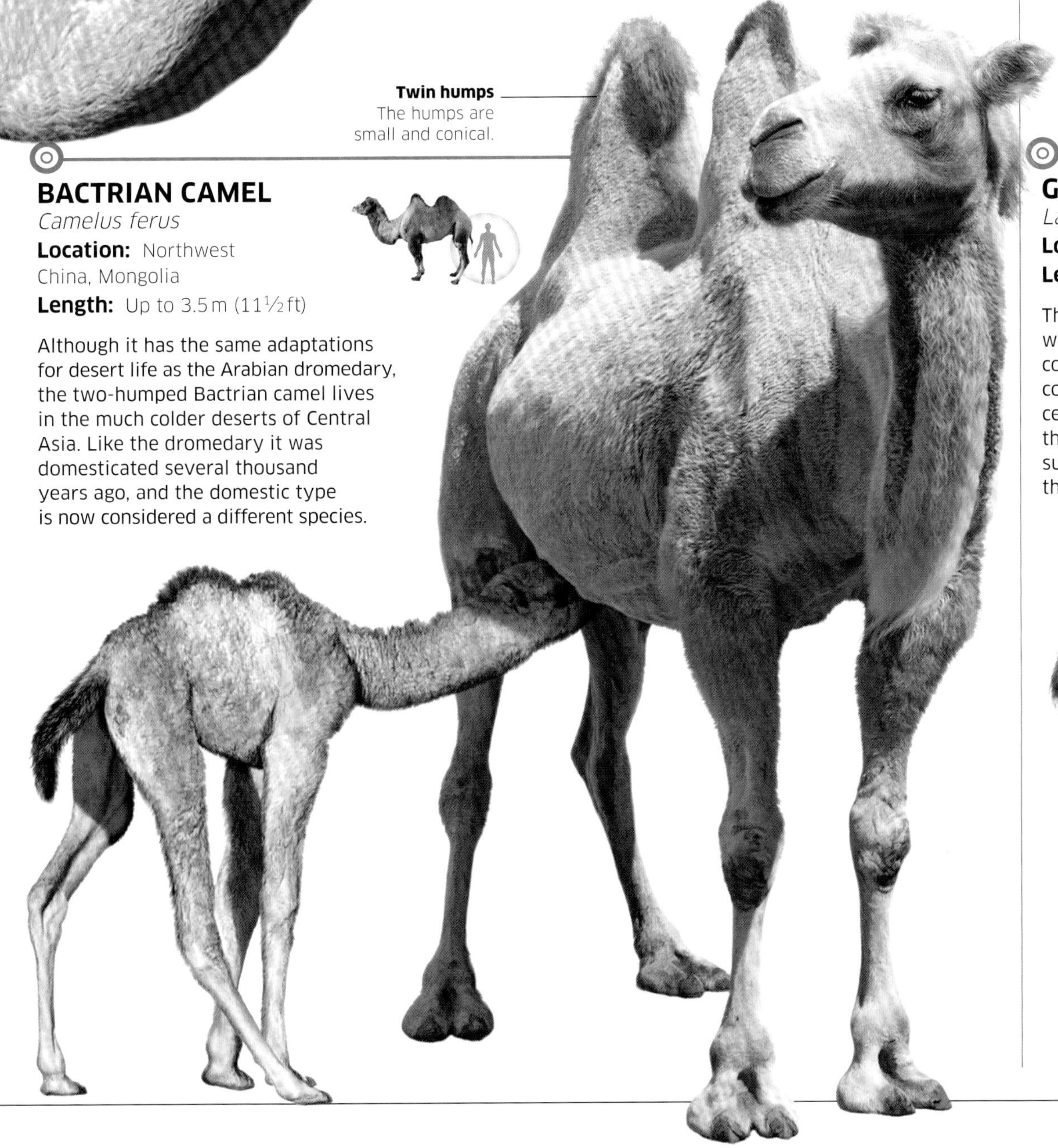

BACTRIAN CAMEL

Camelus ferus

Location: Northwest China, Mongolia

Length: Up to 3.5 m (11½ ft)

Although it has the same adaptations for desert life as the Arabian dromedary, the two-humped Bactrian camel lives in the much colder deserts of Central Asia. Like the dromedary it was domesticated several thousand years ago, and the domestic type is now considered a different species.

GUANACO

Lama guanicoe

Location: South America

Length: Up to 2.1 m (7 ft)

The guanaco lives across South America, where it is well-adapted for cold, dry conditions. Its blood has a very high concentration of oxygen-carrying red cells which enable it to live in the thin, high-altitude air. It can even survive in the Atacama Desert – the driest hot desert on Earth.

Unlike most pigs, warthogs spend the night in underground burrows.

The upper tusks of a male warthog are up to 30 cm (11¾ in) long.

Sparse hair
The body is thinly covered with bristly hair.

Cooling mud
Like most pigs, the warthog enjoys wallowing in liquid mud. It does this partly to cool down in the tropical African climate, because its skin does not have sweat glands. But the coating of mud also helps protect the skin from sunburn, and from biting flies that could carry disease.

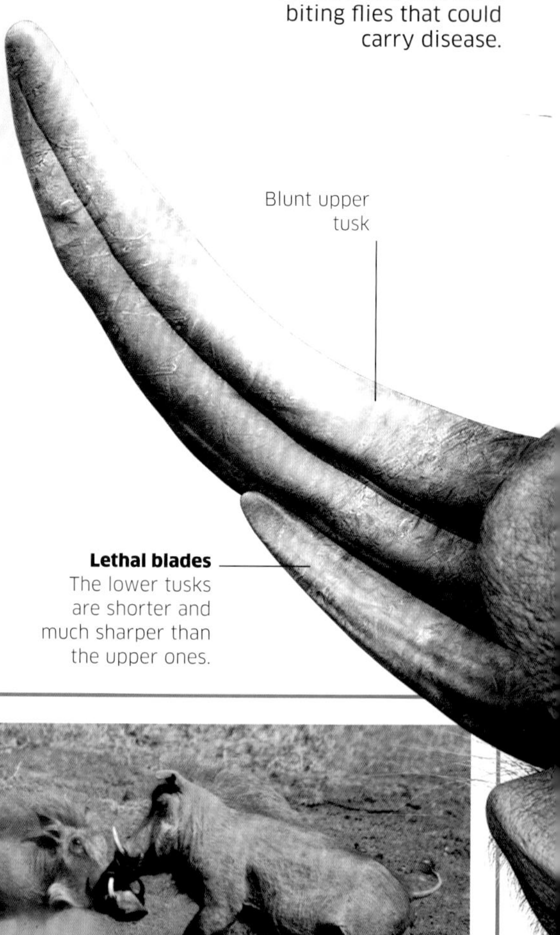

Blunt upper tusk

Lethal blades
The lower tusks are shorter and much sharper than the upper ones.

Common warthog

Despite its huge tusks and strange, warty face, the warthog is a type of wild pig. It is one of only two pig species that lives on grasslands instead of in woodlands and forests, and it is adapted for eating the most abundant food available in its habitat – grass.

The warthog's spectacular upper tusks are used mainly for defence against powerful predators such as lions and leopards. The lower pair is honed to a sharp edge by grinding against the upper pair every time the animal closes its mouth. These lower tusks can inflict serious injuries, but they are mostly used for unearthing juicy roots to supplement the warthog's grassy diet.

On bended knee

The warthog's ability to eat grass is vital to its survival on the African savanna. Its short neck and relatively long legs make grazing tricky, so it goes down on its "knees", which are actually modified wrist joints. Thick skin pads on the joints prevent injury as the warthog grazes, shuffling along in its kneeling position.

Head to head

Mature males defend their territories from other males, ramming each other with their blunt upper tusks. The warts on their faces prevent serious injury and the fights are more like ritual combats than bloody struggles.

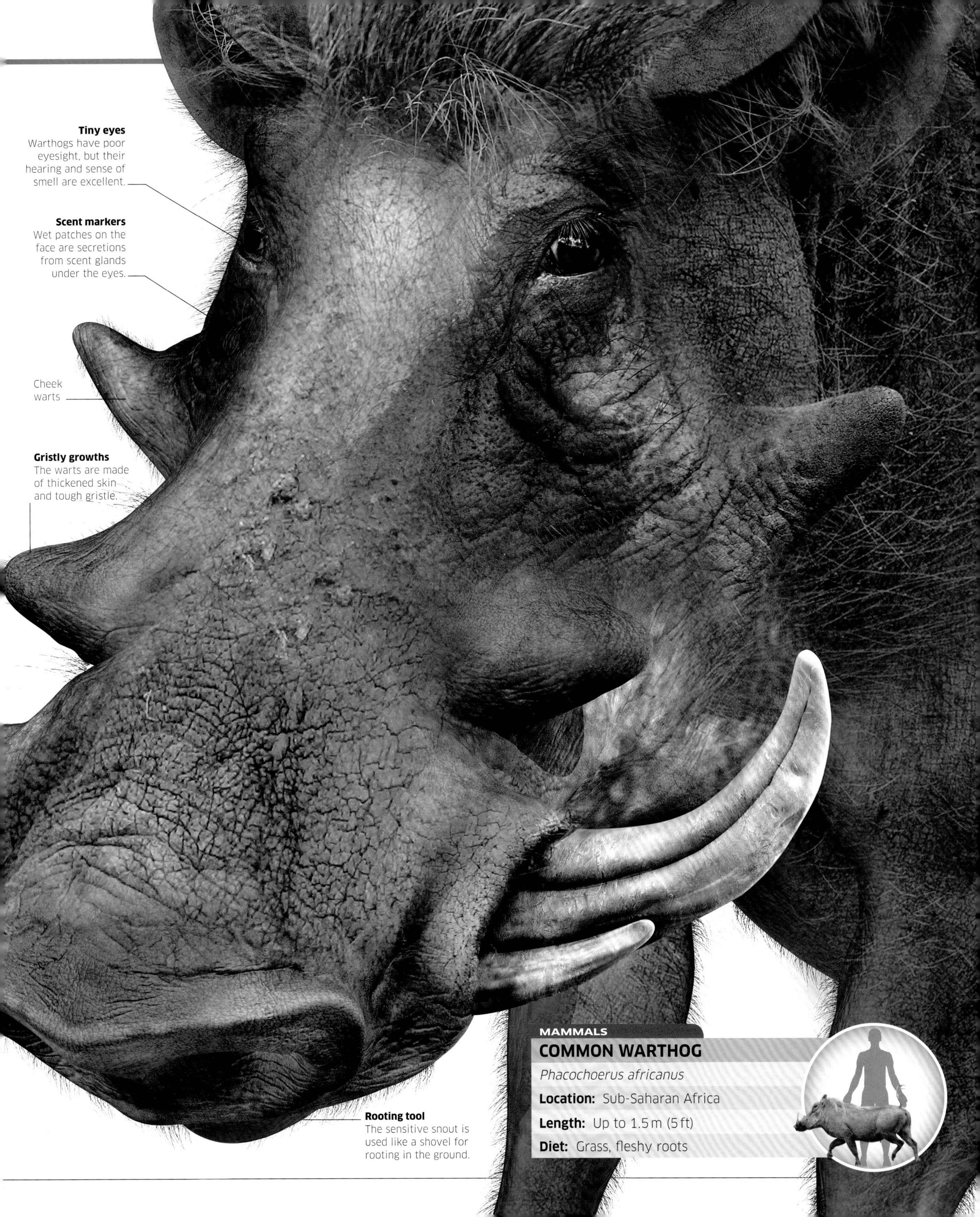

MAMMALS

COMMON WARTHOG

Phacochoerus africanus

Location: Sub-Saharan Africa

Length: Up to 1.5 m (5 ft)

Diet: Grass, fleshy roots

Western red deer

The spectacular antlers of the red deer stag are weapons, status symbols, and proof of his strength. Only the stags with the biggest antlers stand a good chance of seeing off their rivals and impressing breeding females.

The red deer is one of the biggest deer species and, as with most deer, only the male has antlers. These are shed and regrown each year, reaching full size in time for autumn when the strutting, roaring stags compete to control a harem of females to mate with. They only fight as a last resort, locking antlers and trying to push each other backwards until one gives way.

MAMMALS

WESTERN RED DEER

Cervus elaphus

Location: Europe to E. Asia

Length: Up to 2.05 m (6¾ ft)

Diet: Leaves, grass

Spotted young

Red deer are born with spotted coats that improve their camouflage in grass. They can stand within a few hours of birth, and are able to follow the adults by the time they are 3 or 4 weeks old. They must quickly learn to rely on speed to escape predators.

Male and female

Female red deer are smaller than the males, and have no antlers. This shows that the antlers are purely for impressing and fighting with other red deer. If they were needed for survival, females would have them too. In deer species that must compete for food, the females are more likely to have them.

Fighting is dangerous, and every year many stags are **injured or killed** by stronger rivals.

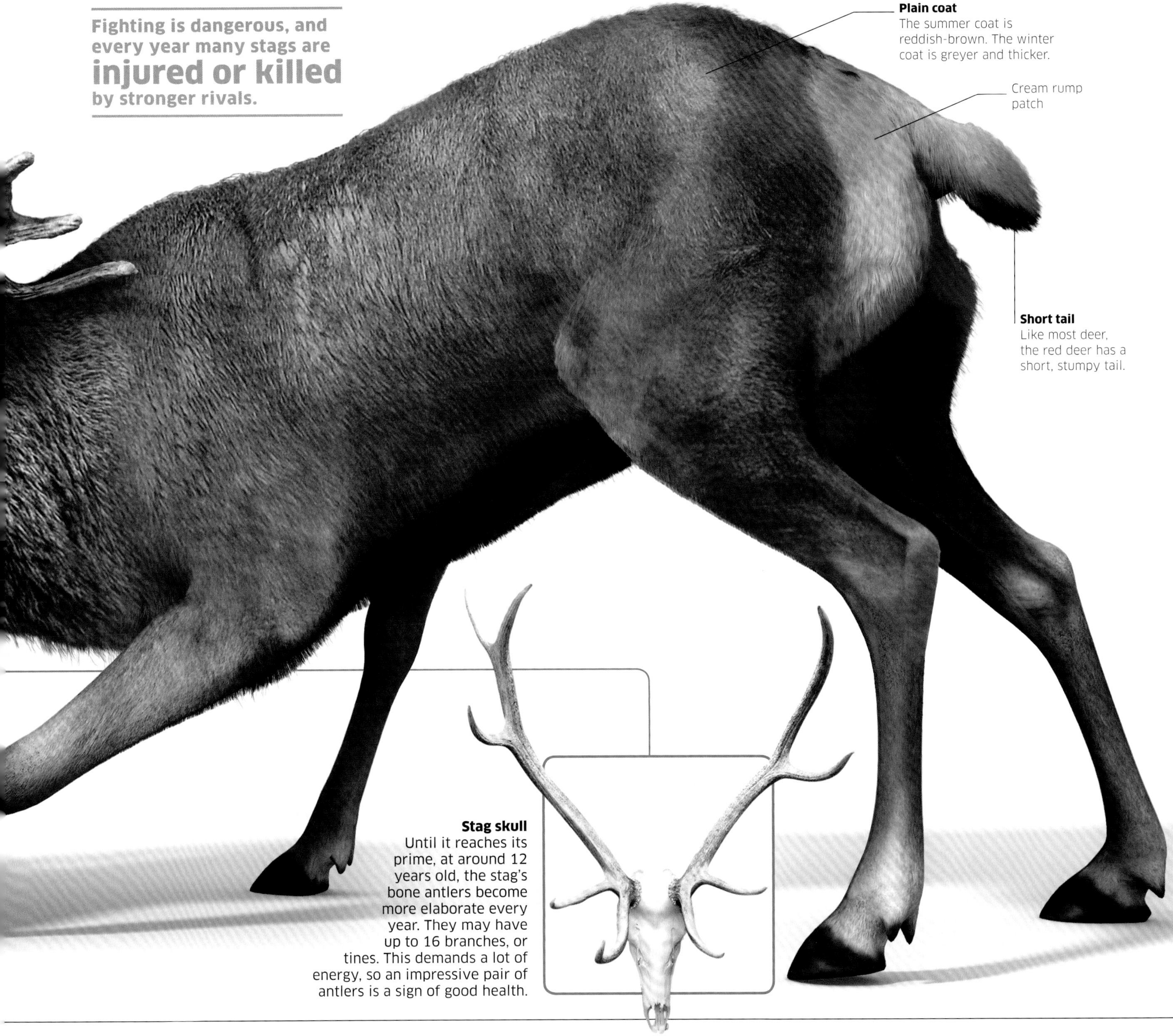

1 m (3 ft) – the **length** of the **horns** of an **Alpine ibex**.

Dorsal crest
When a springbok is alarmed or excited, two folds of skin along its lower back open up to reveal a crest of white fur. The reason for this is unclear, but it certainly draws attention, alerting other springboks and warning them of possible danger.

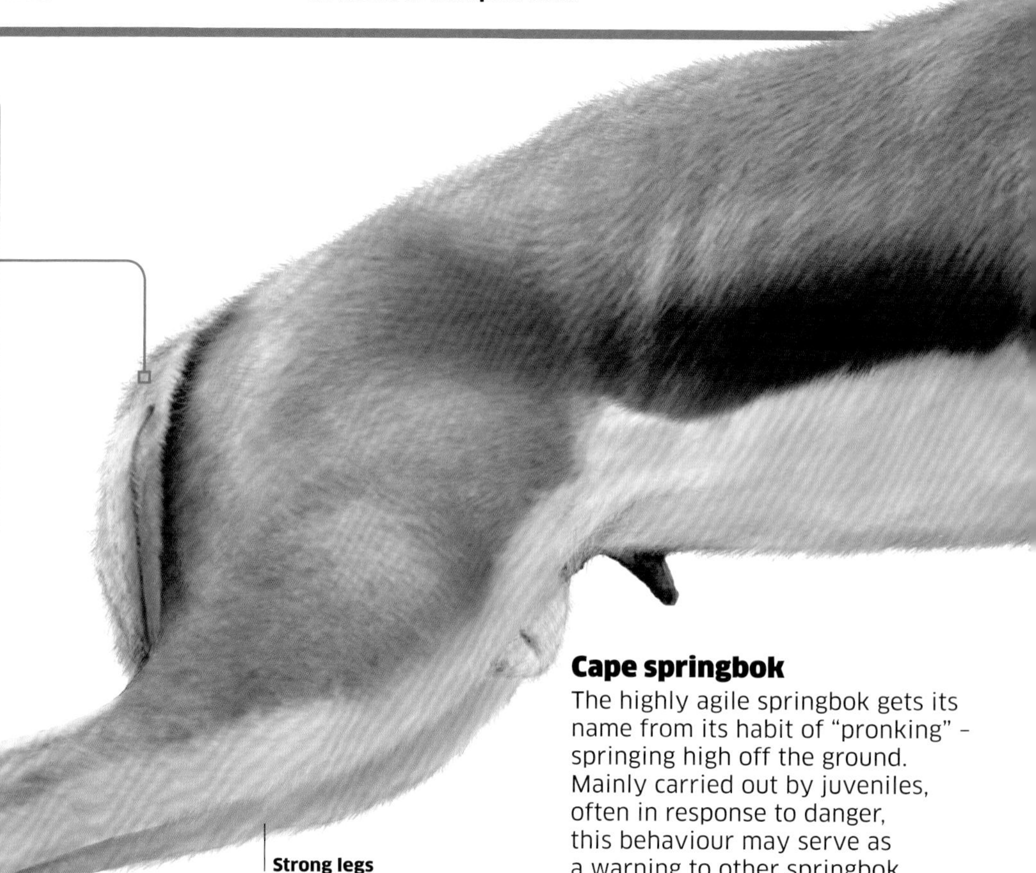

Bovids

Ranging from elegant gazelles to hulking, heavyweight bison, the bovids are the most diverse of the hoofed animals. Many of them are distinguished by their spectacular horns.

The bovids are two-toed, hoofed animals similar to deer. Like deer they are adapted for eating leaves and grass, with complex, four-chambered stomachs for processing their bulky, fibrous food. Some are territorial animals that live in pairs or small family groups, but many more roam widely in large herds.

Strong legs
Powerful muscles enable the springbok to leap high.

Cape springbok
The highly agile springbok gets its name from its habit of “pronking” – springing high off the ground. Mainly carried out by juveniles, often in response to danger, this behaviour may serve as a warning to other springbok, and to demonstrate fitness, encouraging any enemies to pick on a weaker victim.

MAMMALS
CAPE SPRINGBOK
Antidorcas marsupialis
Location: Southwestern Africa
Length: Up to 1.1 m (3½ ft)
Diet: Grass, leaves

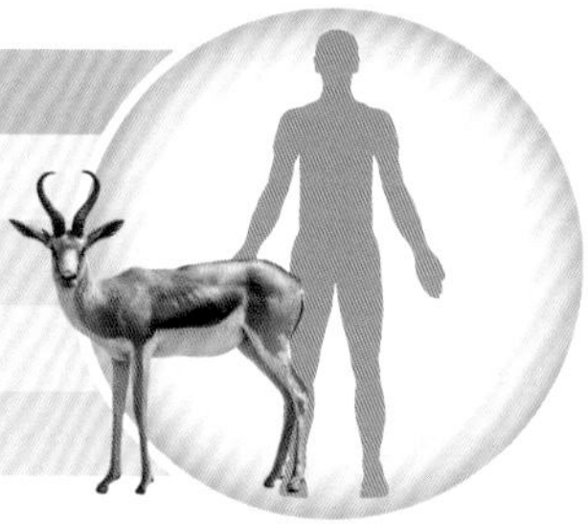

SERENGETI WHITE-BEARDED WILDEBEEST
Connochaetes mearnsi
Location: Eastern and southern Africa
Length: Up to 2.4 m (8 ft)

This chunky, heavy-headed antelope lives in big herds on the African savannas. It makes regular mass migrations around the grassy Serengeti plains, during which it risks falling prey to lions, wild dogs, spotted hyenas, and Nile crocodiles.

SOUTHERN GERENUK
Litocranius walleri
Location: Eastern Africa
Length: Up to 1.4 m (4½ ft)

Also called the giraffe-necked antelope, the gerenuk is an extremely slender, long-legged, agile animal that regularly stands on its hind legs to reach low tree foliage. It rarely drinks, because its food provides all the moisture it needs.

Standing tall
By balancing on its hind legs, the gerenuk can reach the juicy leaves of acacia trees.

AMERICAN BISON

Bison bison

Location: North America

Length: Up to 3.8 m ($12\frac{1}{2}$ ft)

The bison, or buffalo, once roamed the American prairies in vast herds, but was hunted to near-extinction in the 1800s. Bulls are colossal, with massive forequarters for fighting with rivals.

ALPINE IBEX

Capra ibex

Location: Southern Europe

Length: Up to 1.35 m ($4\frac{1}{2}$ ft)

The ibex is a wild goat, famous for its agility and sure-footedness in the steep, rocky terrain of its native mountains. Both sexes have horns though the male's are particularly spectacular. He uses them to spar with other males.

MUSK OX

Ovibos moschatus

Location: N. America, Greenland

Length: Up to 2.3 m ($7\frac{1}{2}$ ft)

A relative of sheep and goats, the musk ox is adapted for life on polar tundra, where it scrapes away snow to feed on grass, leaves, and lichens. It is often preyed upon by Arctic wolves.

ARABIAN ORYX

Oryx leucoryx

Location: Middle East

Length: Up to 2.3 m ($7\frac{1}{2}$ ft)

The striking-looking Arabian oryx was hunted to near-extinction by the 1970s, but has been saved by captive breeding and reintroduction. Specialized for desert life, it roams widely in search of grass that has grown in the wake of recent rainfall.

When **galloping** the giraffe can reach a **top speed** of **60 km/h (37 mph)**.

No two giraffes have exactly the **same coat pattern**.

Giraffe

The majestic giraffe is the tallest of all living animals. Its astonishing height enables it to browse high in the the treetops, where it has the pick of tender young leaves that shorter animals have no hope of reaching.

Being so tall creates problems. The giraffe has to have an unusually big heart to pump blood up to its brain, and a system for preventing fainting when it raises its head after lowering it to drink. The giraffe must also breathe fast to get enough air into its lungs. But its uniquely long neck and legs allow it to spot danger from a distance, and males use their necks to wrestle with rivals.

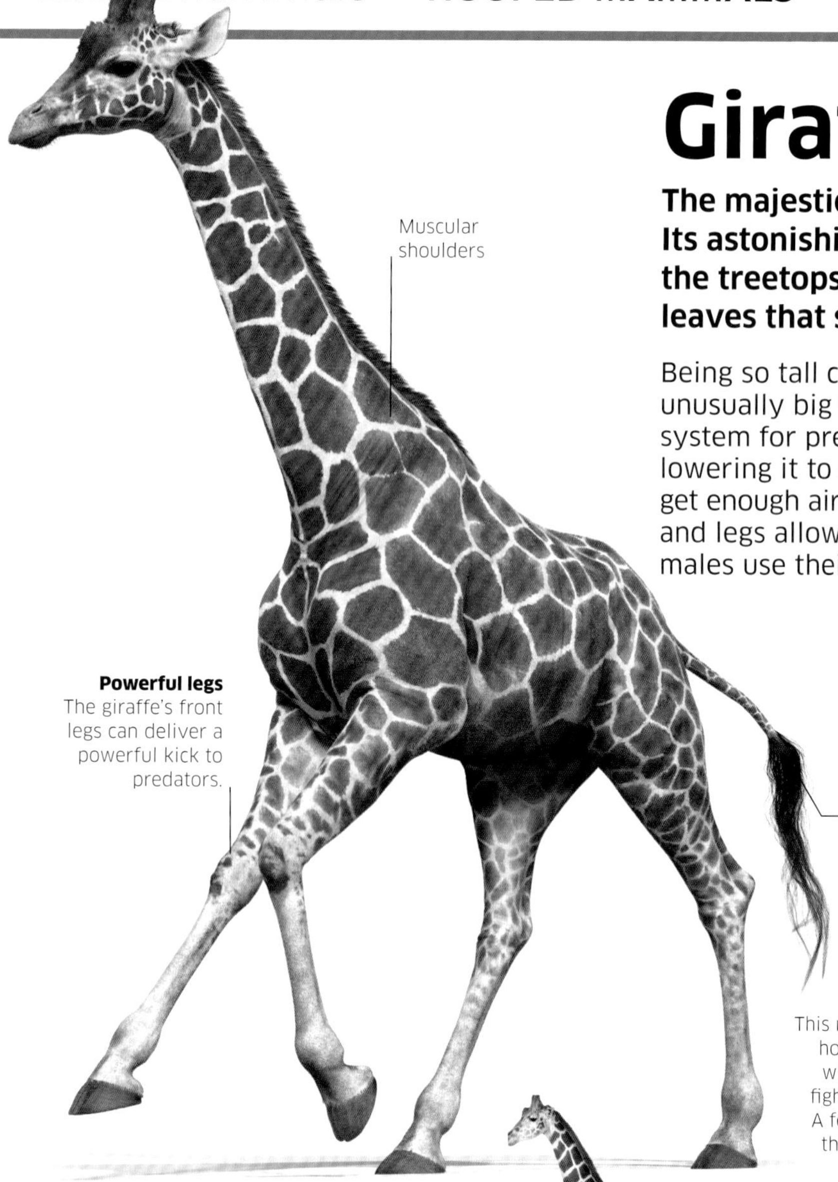

MAMMALS

GIRAFFE

Giraffa camelopardalis

Location: Africa

Height: Up to 6 m (19¾ ft)

Diet: Leaves

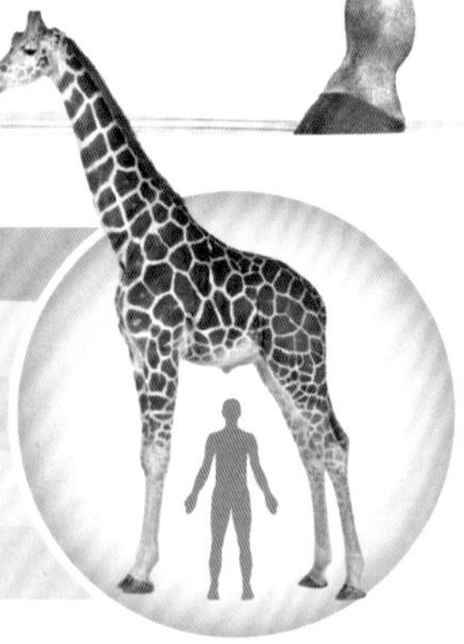

Flexible tongue
The giraffe often feeds on the tall acacia trees that dot the African savanna grasslands. But acacia twigs are very thorny, so it uses its long, mobile tongue to probe between the thorns and pull leaves into its mouth. It then uses its teeth to strip the leaves. The skin of the giraffe's tongue and lips is unusually thick, to stop the thorns piercing them.

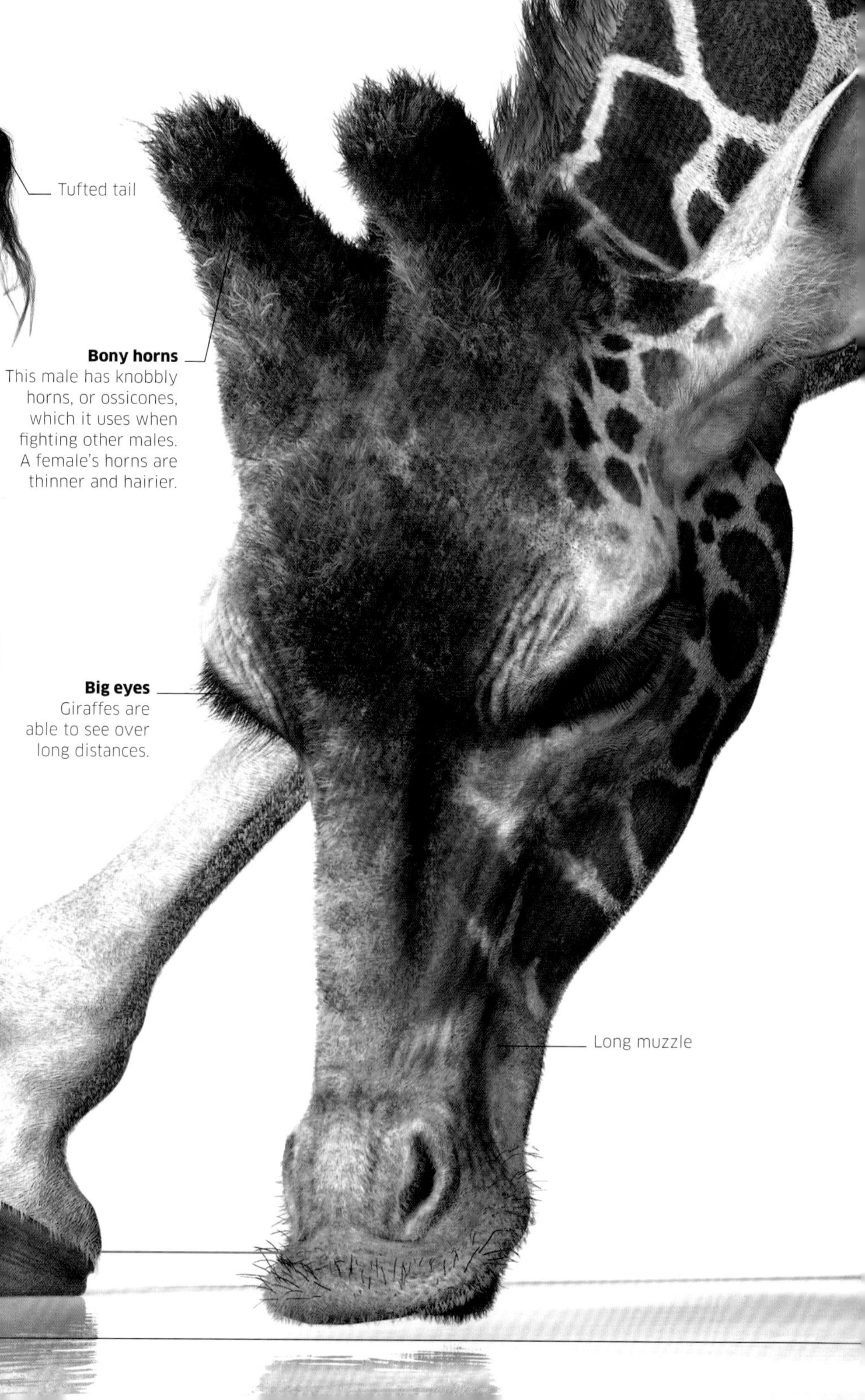

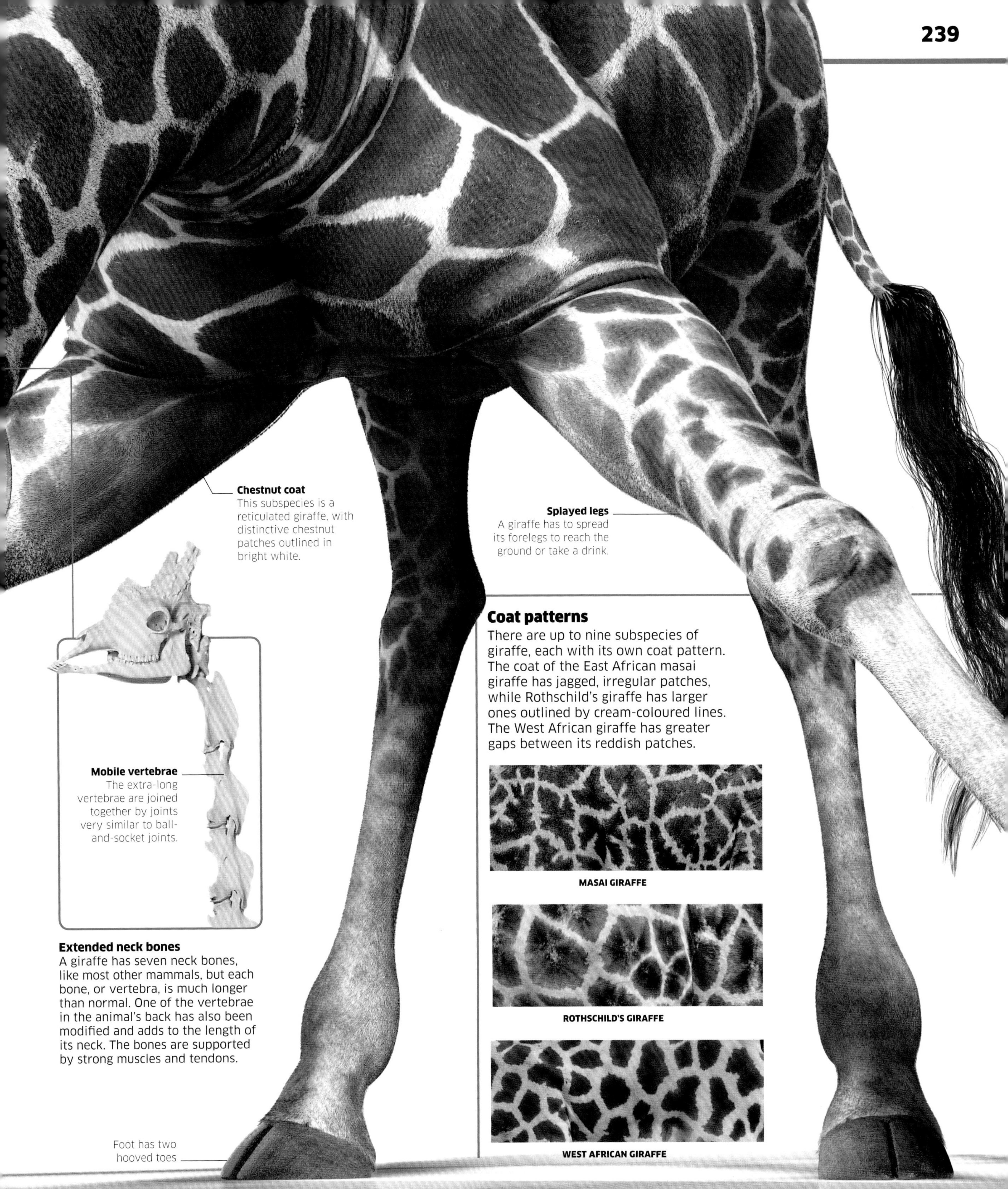

Chestnut coat
This subspecies is a reticulated giraffe, with distinctive chestnut patches outlined in bright white.

Splayed legs
A giraffe has to spread its forelegs to reach the ground or take a drink.

Mobile vertebrae
The extra-long vertebrae are joined together by joints very similar to ball-and-socket joints.

Extended neck bones
A giraffe has seven neck bones, like most other mammals, but each bone, or vertebra, is much longer than normal. One of the vertebrae in the animal's back has also been modified and adds to the length of its neck. The bones are supported by strong muscles and tendons.

Foot has two hooved toes

Coat patterns

There are up to nine subspecies of giraffe, each with its own coat pattern. The coat of the East African masai giraffe has jagged, irregular patches, while Rothschild's giraffe has larger ones outlined by cream-coloured lines. The West African giraffe has greater gaps between its reddish patches.

MASAI GIRAFFE

ROTHSCHILD'S GIRAFFE

WEST AFRICAN GIRAFFE

A hippo can weigh more than 2,000 kg (4,400 lb), as much as 25 heavyweight boxers.

Hippopotamus

Despite its seemingly lazy lifestyle, the hippopotamus's unpredictable, aggressive nature makes it one of the most dangerous of African mammals.

There are only two kinds of hippo, and it has no other land-living relatives. In fact, DNA evidence shows that the hippo's closest relatives are whales, which is appropriate, as water plays a key role in a hippo's survival. By day, the hippo must escape the fierce African sun by submerging itself in water. At night, it emerges to graze on land for up to five hours, often travelling far from its daytime habitat.

Daily wallow
The hippo's skin is thick, but it dries out much faster than the skin of most mammals, so it spends much of its day wallowing in rivers or lakes. If a hippo stays out of the water for too long, its skin will be damaged by the sun and could even crack.

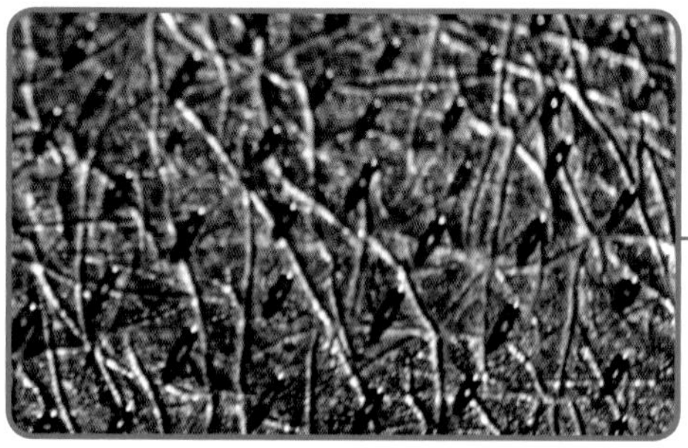

Natural sunblock
Glands within the hippo's skin secrete an oily fluid that turns reddish orange when exposed to the air. Pigments in the fluid act as a sunblock, absorbing the rays from the sun that cause sunburn. They also fight bacteria, helping wounds heal quickly.

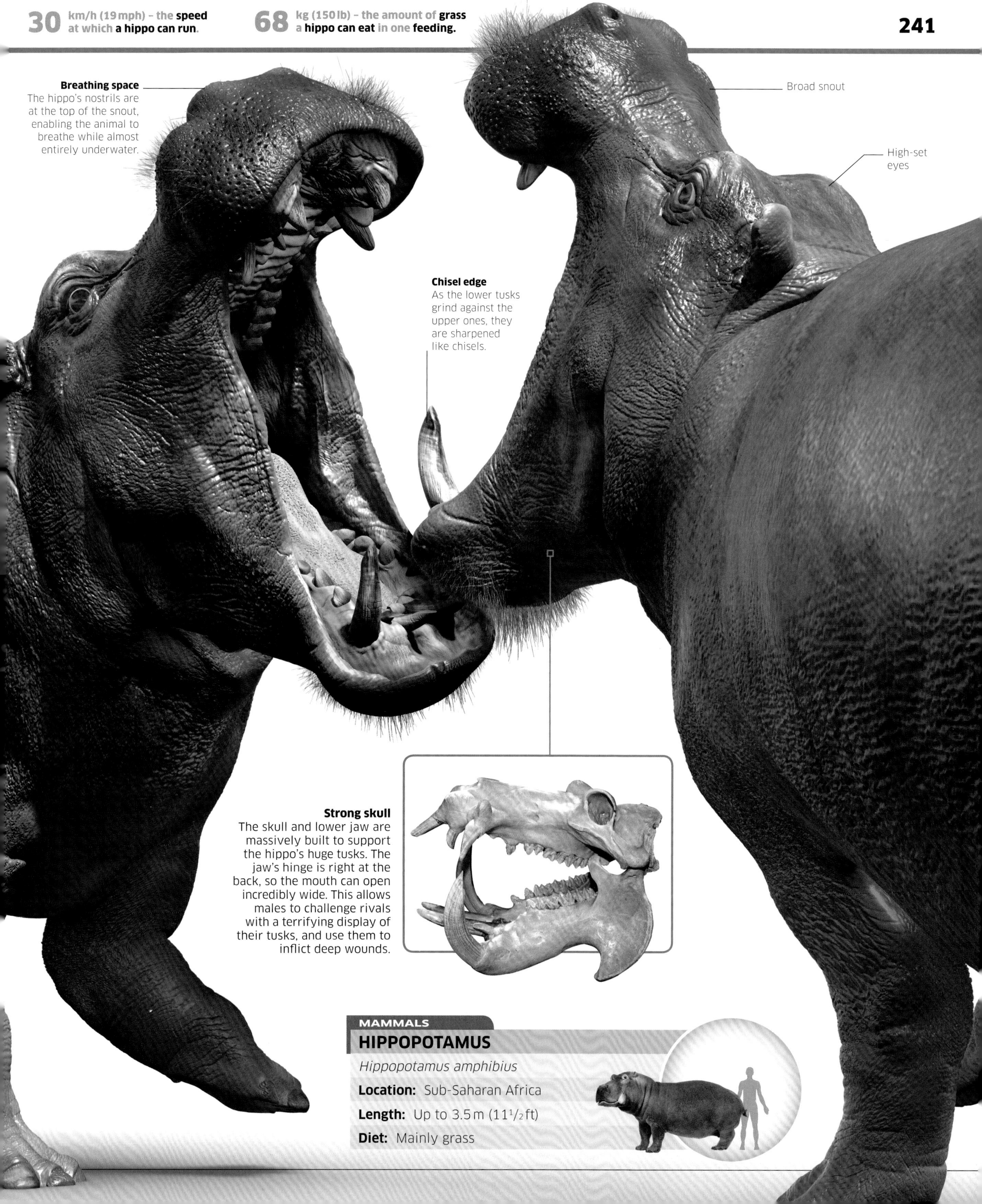

Breathing space
The hippo's nostrils are at the top of the snout, enabling the animal to breathe while almost entirely underwater.

Broad snout

High-set eyes

Chisel edge
As the lower tusks grind against the upper ones, they are sharpened like chisels.

Strong skull
The skull and lower jaw are massively built to support the hippo's huge tusks. The jaw's hinge is right at the back, so the mouth can open incredibly wide. This allows males to challenge rivals with a terrifying display of their tusks, and use them to inflict deep wounds.

MAMMALS

HIPPOPOTAMUS

Hippopotamus amphibius

Location: Sub-Saharan Africa

Length: Up to 3.5 m (11½ ft)

Diet: Mainly grass

Female orcas can live to be more than **90 years** old.

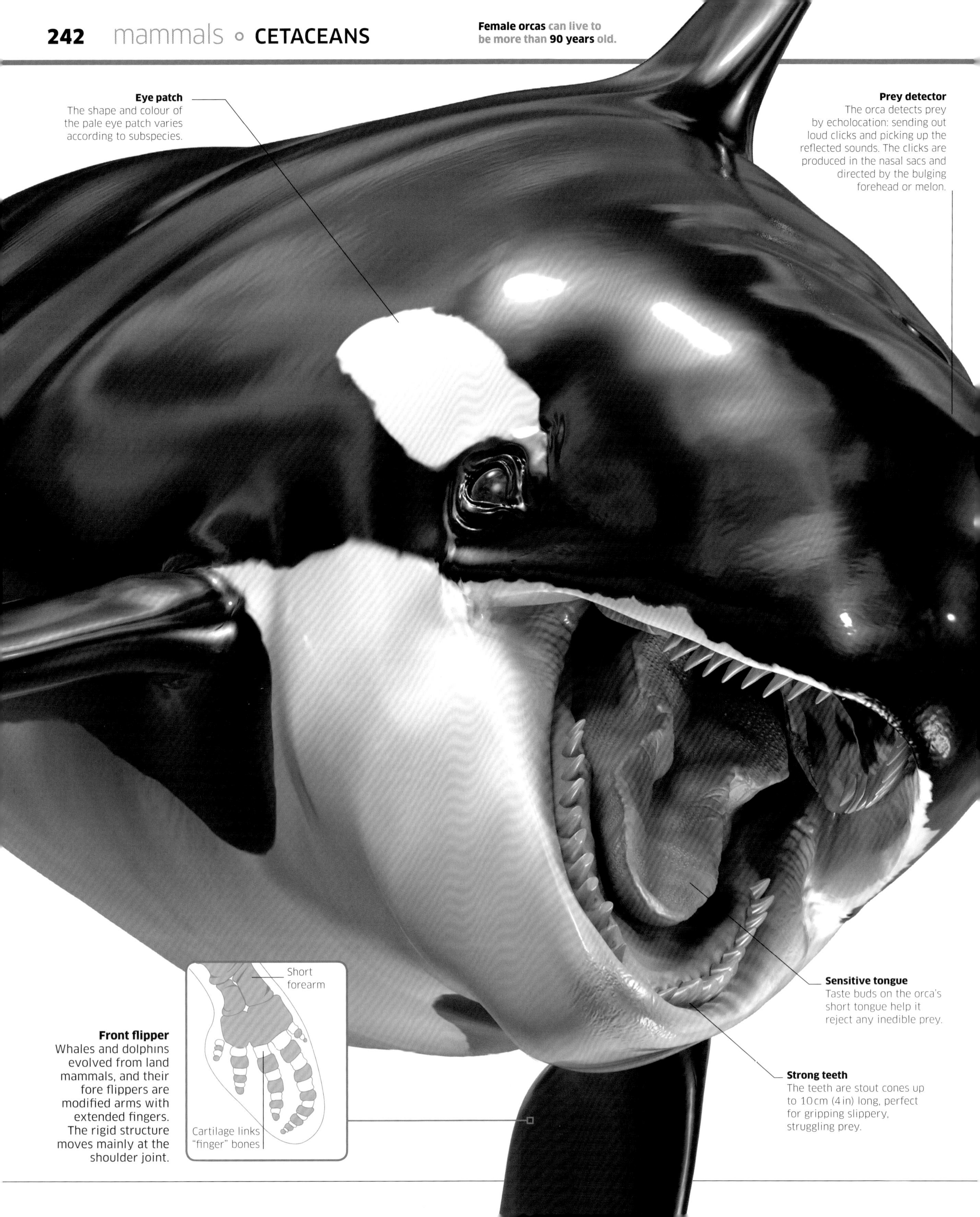

Eye patch
The shape and colour of the pale eye patch varies according to subspecies.

Prey detector
The orca detects prey by echolocation: sending out loud clicks and picking up the reflected sounds. The clicks are produced in the nasal sacs and directed by the bulging forehead or melon.

Sensitive tongue
Taste buds on the orca's short tongue help it reject any inedible prey.

Strong teeth
The teeth are stout cones up to 10 cm (4 in) long, perfect for gripping slippery, struggling prey.

Front flipper
Whales and dolphins evolved from land mammals, and their fore flippers are modified arms with extended fingers. The rigid structure moves mainly at the shoulder joint.

Dorsal fin
A female orca has a tall triangular dorsal fin, but this is only half the height of a male's. The shape of the fin varies, and can be used to identify individual orcas.

Blowhole
Like all mammals the orca breathes air. Its nostril is a hole in the top of its head, which remains closed while the orca is underwater.

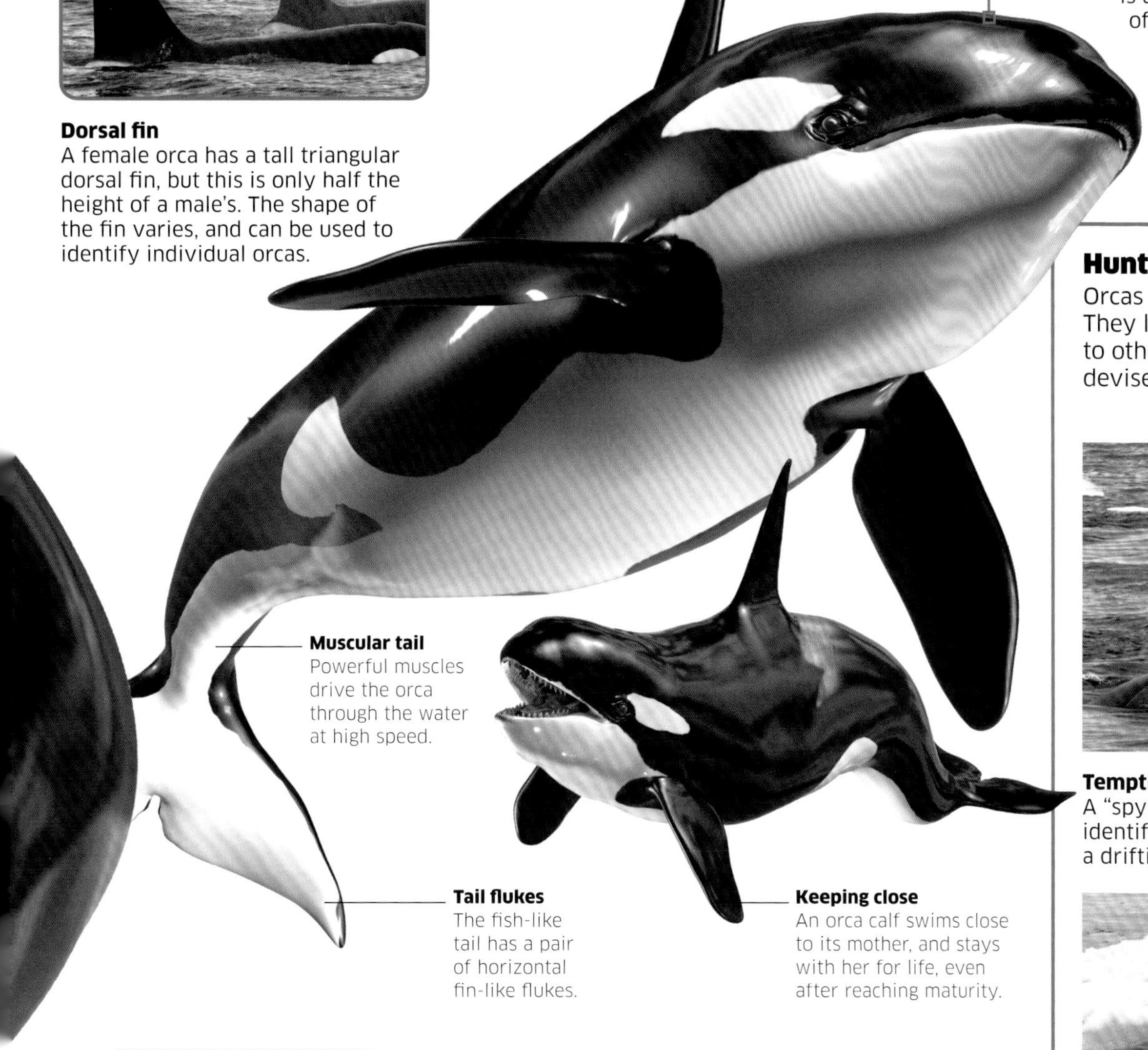

Muscular tail
Powerful muscles drive the orca through the water at high speed.

Tail flukes
The fish-like tail has a pair of horizontal fin-like flukes.

Keeping close
An orca calf swims close to its mother, and stays with her for life, even after reaching maturity.

MAMMALS

ORCA

Orcinus orca

Location: Worldwide

Length: Up to 9.8 m (32 ft)

Diet: Various marine animals

Orca

Also known as the killer whale, the orca is actually a giant dolphin that uses its intelligence and power to stalk and seize prey ranging from small fish to sharks, seals, and even whales.

One of the most powerful predators on the planet, the orca prowls the world's oceans in family groups that specialize in hunting particular types of prey. Some are experts at rounding up shoals of fish, using a complex repertoire of sounds to coordinate their group tactics, while others team up to outwit and ambush other marine mammals.

Hunting together

Orcas are among the most intelligent of all animals. They learn fast and can also pass on their knowledge to others. This allows family groups to work together to devise new, often ingenious ways of catching prey.

Tempting target
A "spyhopping" orca lifts its head from the water to identify prey. Here, one has spotted a Weddell seal on a drifting ice floe near Antarctica.

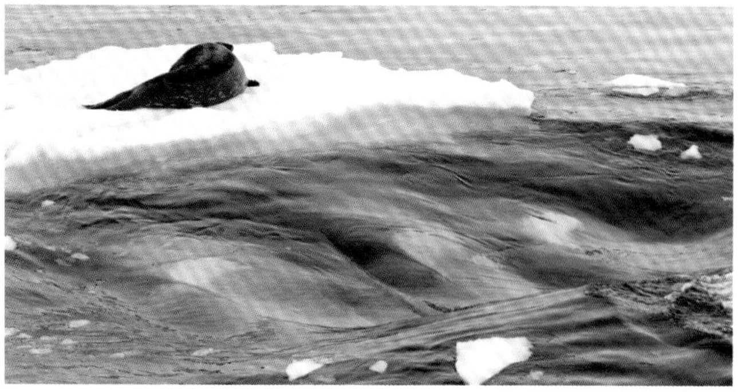

Joint action
Swimming in perfect formation, the orcas surge towards the ice floe and dive beneath it. This pushes up a wave that bears down on the floating ice.

Mission accomplished
The wave strikes the ice and washes over it in a wall of water. The helpless seal is swept off the floe and into the jaws of the waiting orcas.

Every year, most humpbacks **migrate to breed** in warmer waters, covering more than **8,300 km (5,157 miles) each way**.

Humpback whale

Renowned for its spectacular leaps right out of the water, the humpback is one of the baleen whales – ocean giants that feed by filtering seawater for small animals. It is one of the largest and heaviest living things on the planet.

The humpback is a type of whale known as a rorqual, which has a series of pleats extending beneath its body from its chin to its belly. When the whale is feeding, the pleats allow the throat to expand like a balloon and hold a huge volume of water. The whale uses its colossal tongue to force the water out of its mouth, through a mesh of bristly plates called baleen. The whale then swallows the fish and other small animals trapped by the baleen, before gulping another giant mouthful of water.

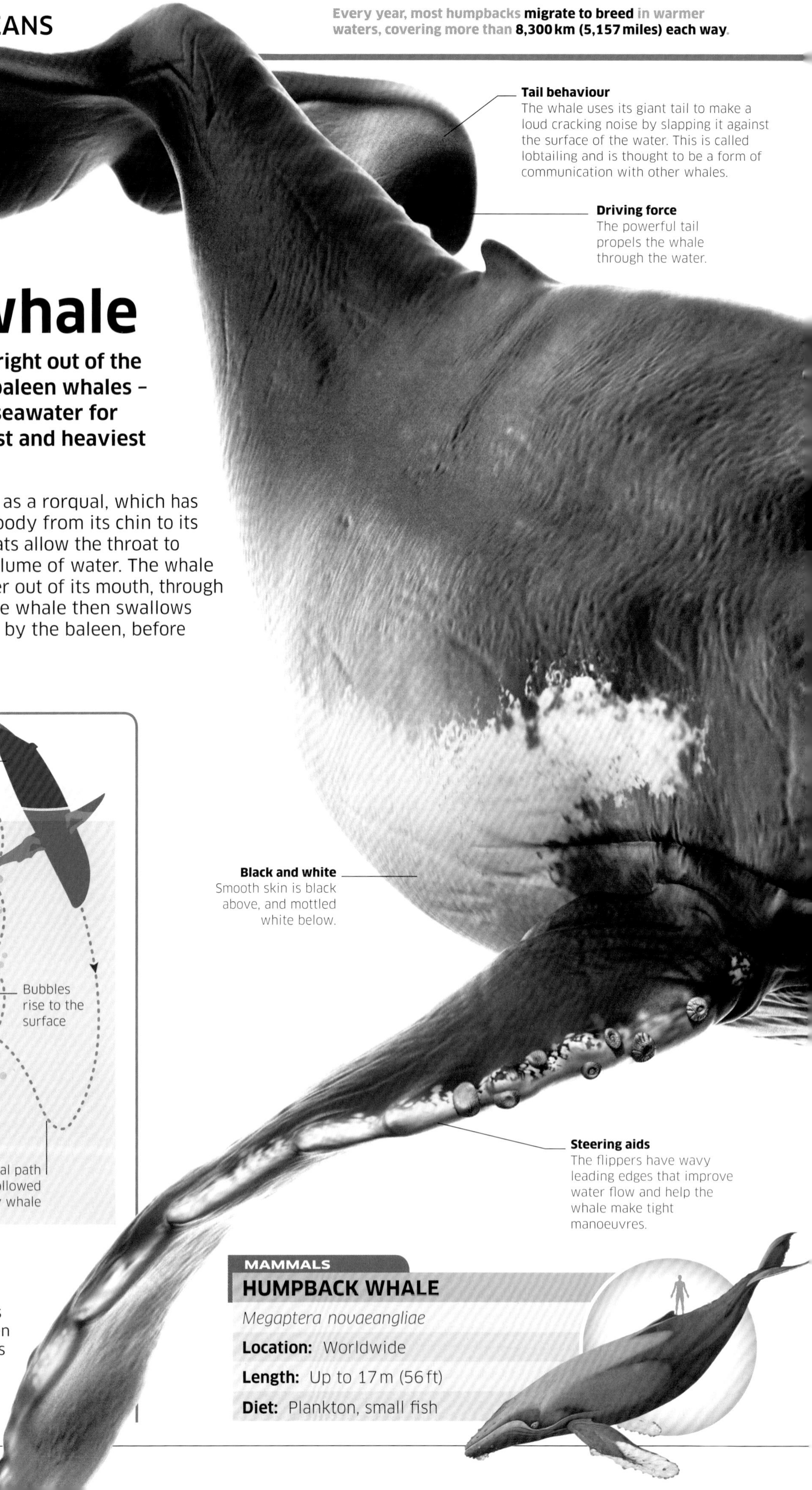

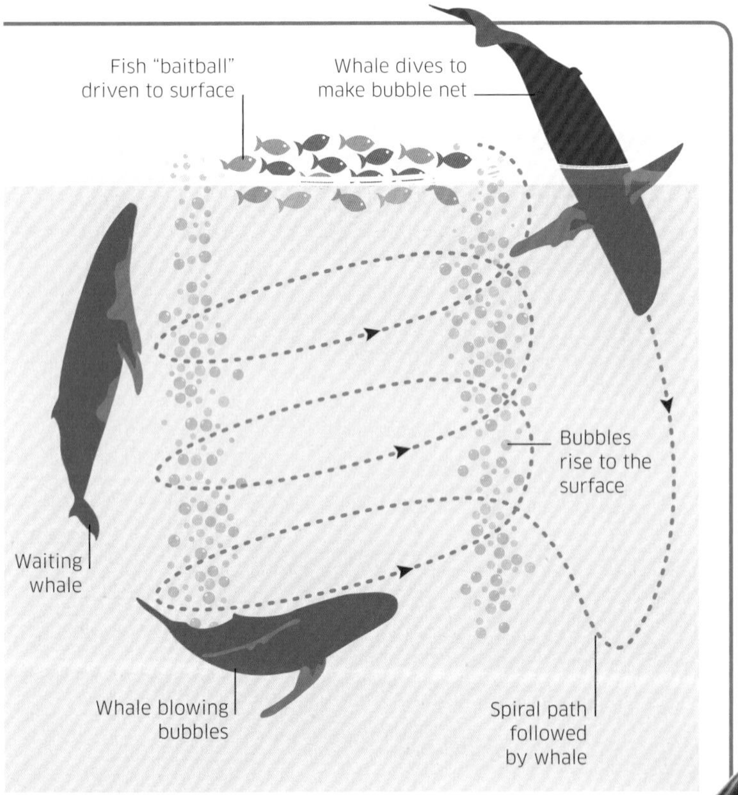

Bubble-net feeding

In northern oceans humpback whales often prey on small fish. They herd the shoals by circling around them while one whale breathes out to make a cylindrical "net" of bubbles. When the fish are tightly packed together, the whales surge up from below with their huge mouths open to swallow hundreds in a single gulp.

MAMMALS

HUMPBACK WHALE

Megaptera novaeangliae

Location: Worldwide

Length: Up to 17 m (56 ft)

Diet: Plankton, small fish

34 tonnes – the **weight of a humpback whale**, more than **three times** that of an adult **African savanna elephant**.

An **adult humpback** can eat **more than 1,000 kg (2,200 lb)** of **small fish and krill** every day.

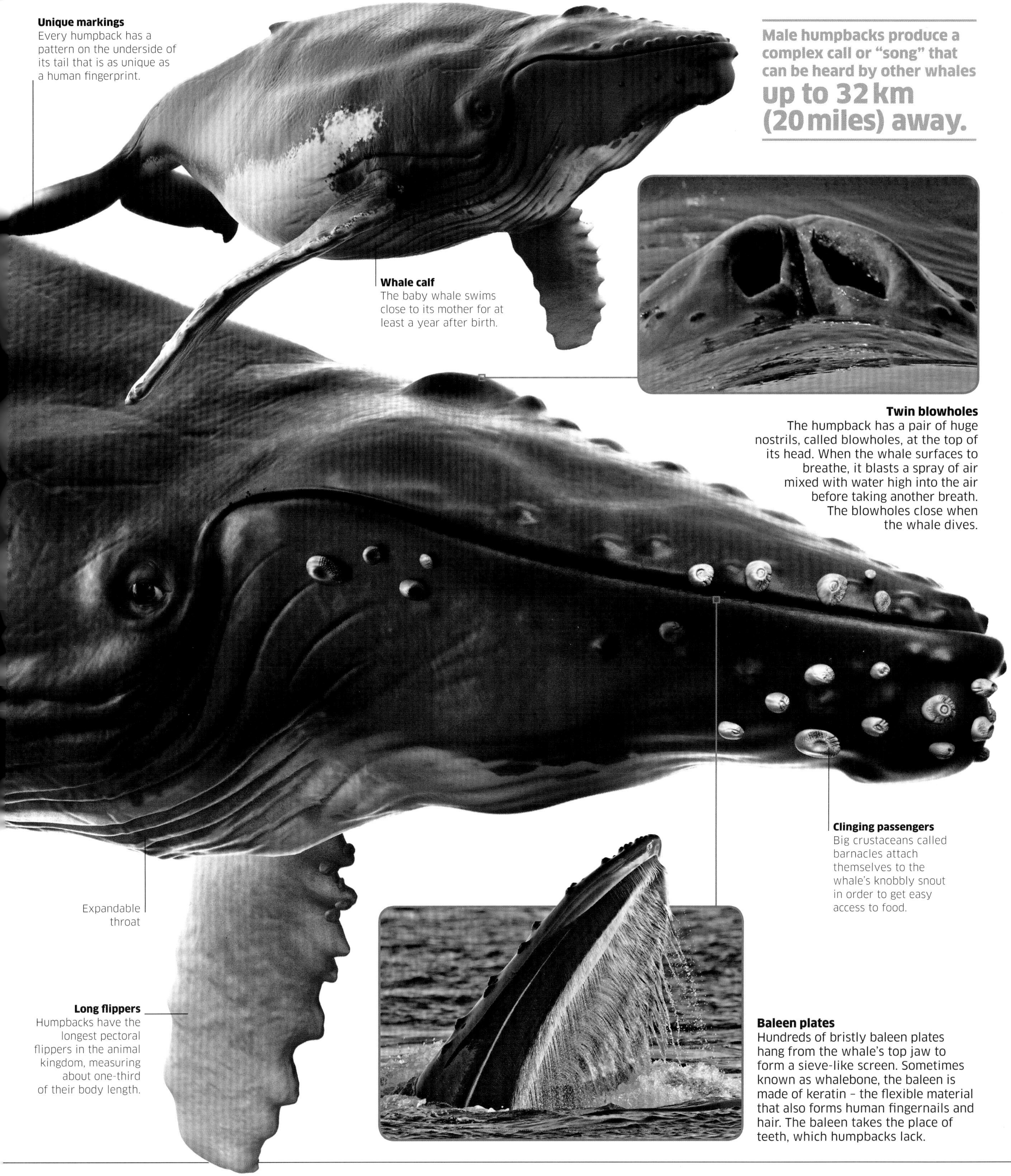

Unique markings
Every humpback has a pattern on the underside of its tail that is as unique as a human fingerprint.

Whale calf
The baby whale swims close to its mother for at least a year after birth.

Male humpbacks produce a complex call or "song" that can be heard by other whales up to 32 km (20 miles) away.

Twin blowholes
The humpback has a pair of huge nostrils, called blowholes, at the top of its head. When the whale surfaces to breathe, it blasts a spray of air mixed with water high into the air before taking another breath. The blowholes close when the whale dives.

Clinging passengers
Big crustaceans called barnacles attach themselves to the whale's knobbly snout in order to get easy access to food.

Expandable throat

Long flippers
Humpbacks have the longest pectoral flippers in the animal kingdom, measuring about one-third of their body length.

Baleen plates
Hundreds of bristly baleen plates hang from the whale's top jaw to form a sieve-like screen. Sometimes known as whalebone, the baleen is made of keratin – the flexible material that also forms human fingernails and hair. The baleen takes the place of teeth, which humpbacks lack.

145 tonnes – **the estimated weight of the largest blue whale.**

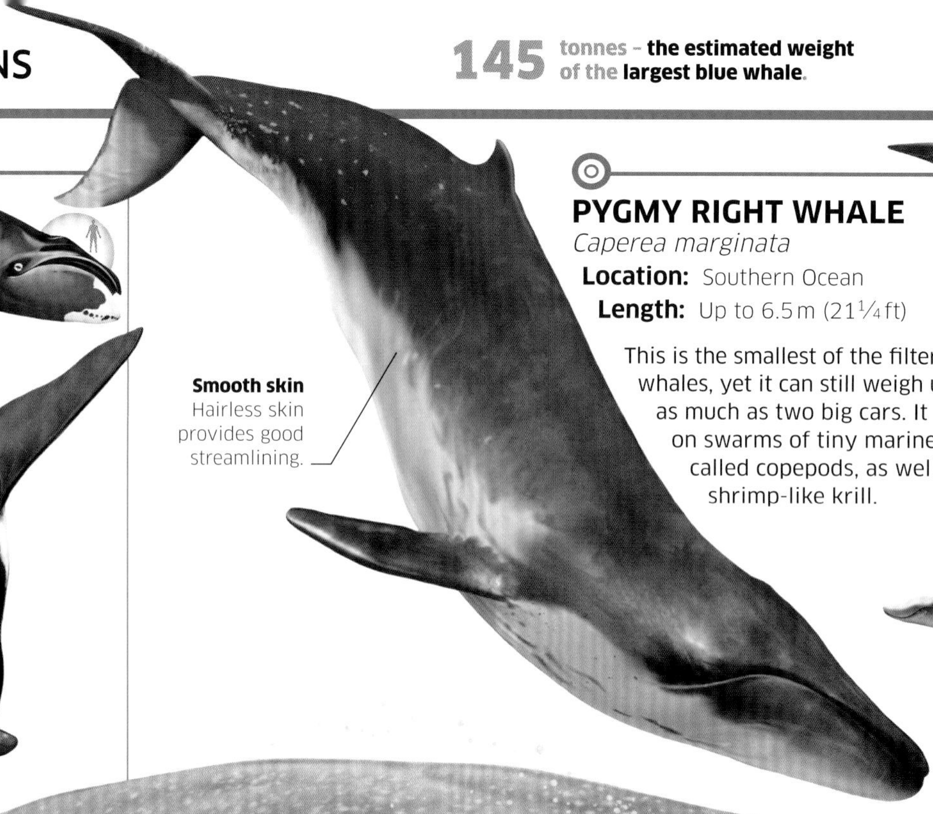

BOWHEAD WHALE

Balaena mysticetus

Location: Arctic seas

Length: Up to 20 m (66 ft)

The high-arched jaw of the bowhead whale is adapted for straining prey from the water as the whale swims forwards. Water is forced through a deep slot at the front of its jaws, and out through the filtering baleen plates at the side.

PYGMY RIGHT WHALE

Caperea marginata

Location: Southern Ocean

Length: Up to 6.5 m (21¼ ft)

This is the smallest of the filter-feeding baleen whales, yet it can still weigh up to 3.5 tonnes – as much as two big cars. It feeds mainly on swarms of tiny marine crustaceans called copepods, as well as larger, shrimp-like krill.

BLUE WHALE

Balaenoptera musculus

Location: All oceans

Length: Up to 32.6 m (107 ft)

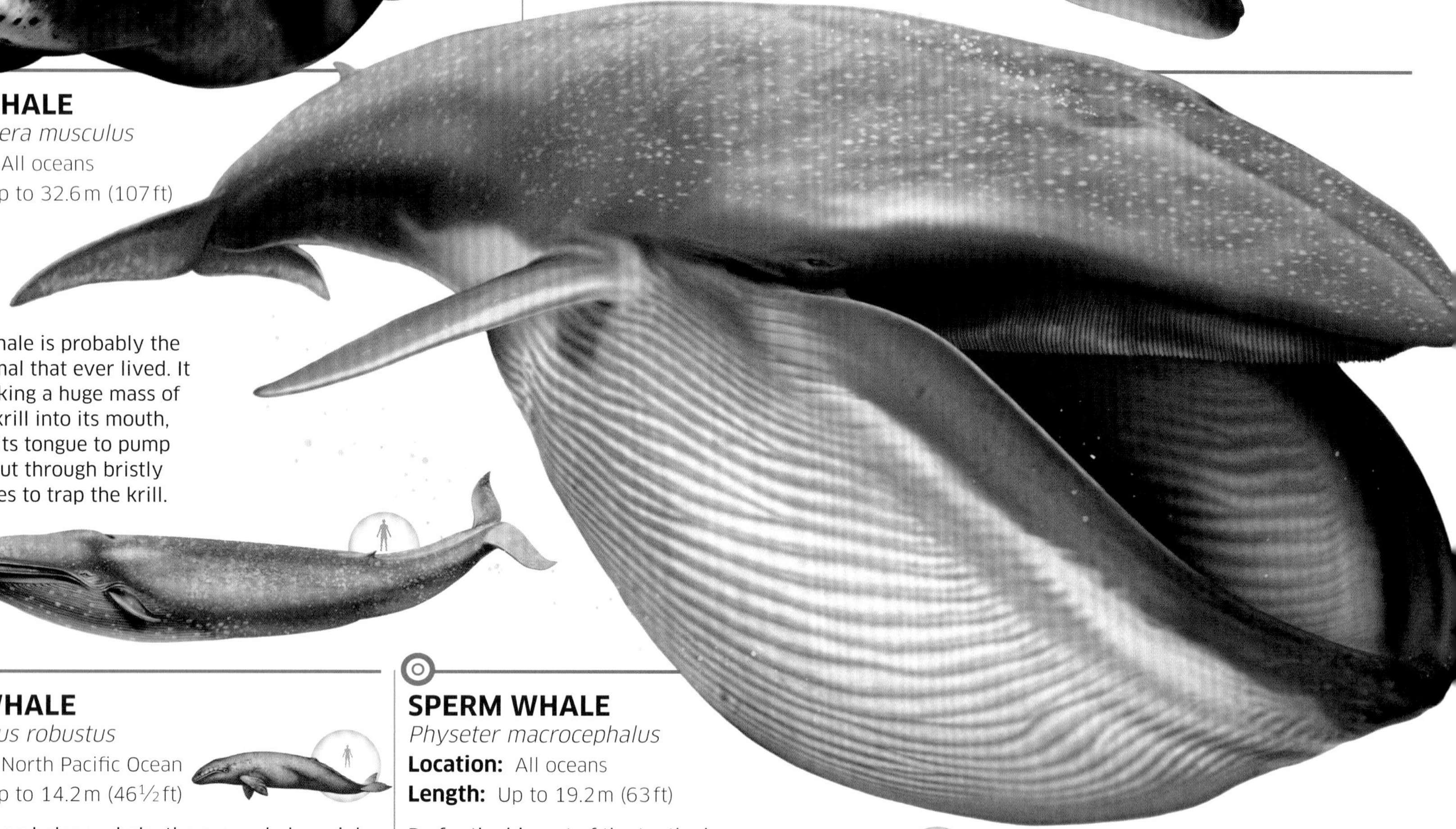

The blue whale is probably the largest animal that ever lived. It feeds by taking a huge mass of water and krill into its mouth, then using its tongue to pump the water out through bristly baleen plates to trap the krill.

GRAY WHALE

Eschrichtius robustus

Location: North Pacific Ocean

Length: Up to 14.2 m (46½ ft)

Uniquely for a baleen whale, the gray whale mainly feeds on animals such as clams, worms, and crab-like crustaceans gathered from the sea bed. It does this by swimming along the bottom on its side to plough up soft mud and filter it for prey.

SPERM WHALE

Physeter macrocephalus

Location: All oceans

Length: Up to 19.2 m (63 ft)

By far the biggest of the toothed whales, the sperm whale has an enormous box-shaped head containing a waxy oil that helps it adjust its buoyancy. This is vital to its way of life, because it dives to immense depths to prey on deep-water squid.

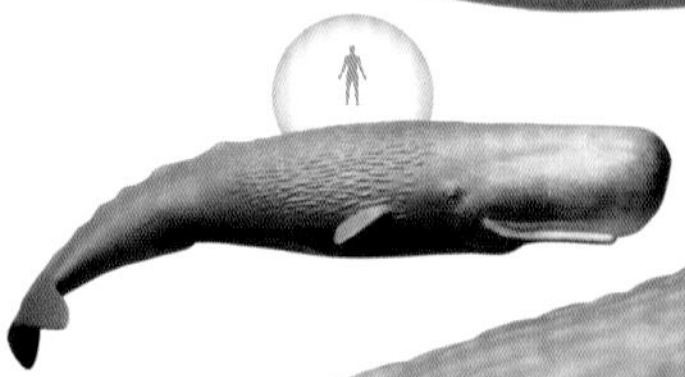

The spiral tusk of a **narwhal** can grow to **3 m (10 ft) long**.

In 2011, a **Cuvier's beaked whale** dived to a **depth of 2,992 m (9,816 ft)** – the **deepest recorded dive** by any mammal.

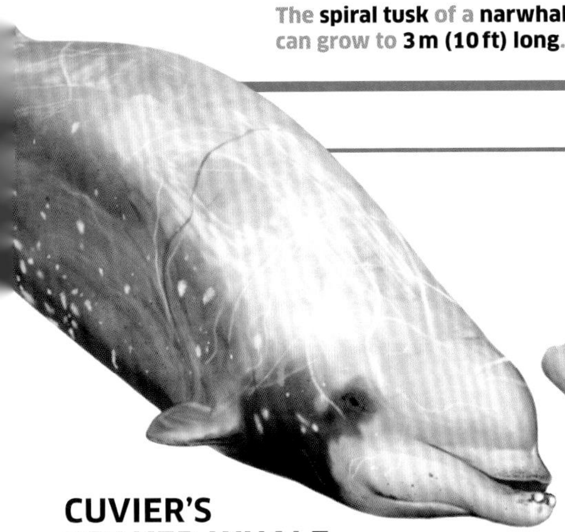

CUVIER'S BEAKED WHALE

Ziphius cavirostris

Location: All oceans except Arctic

Length: Up to 7 m (23 ft)

Named for their beak-like snouts, the mysterious beaked whales are rarely seen because they live in the open ocean. This is the most widespread of 22 species, and has a protruding lower jaw, which in mature males is adorned with large peg-like teeth.

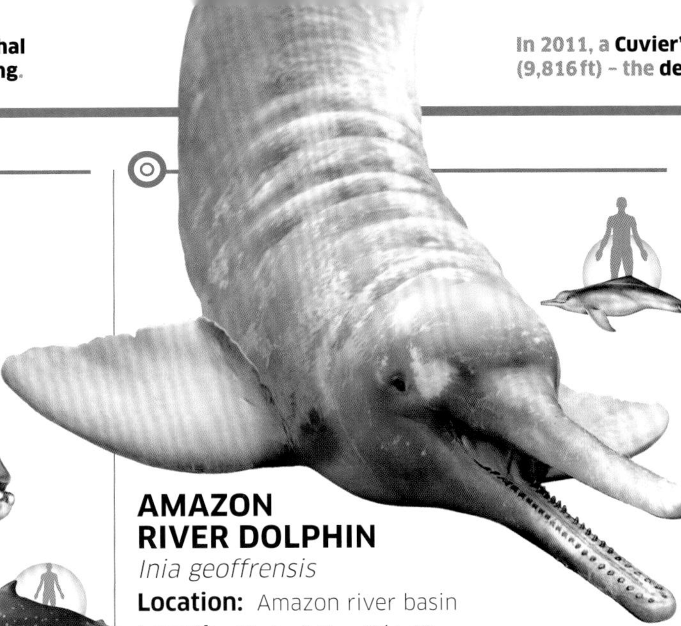

AMAZON RIVER DOLPHIN

Inia geoffrensis

Location: Amazon river basin

Length: Up to 2.5 m ($8^1/_4$ ft)

One of a small number of freshwater dolphins, this lives in muddy waters, where it hunts largely by underwater echolocation. Its long snout is lined with two types of teeth for dealing with different types of prey, including fish, crabs, and turtles.

NARWHAL

Monodon monoceros

Location: Arctic seas

Length: Up to 5 m ($16^1/_2$ ft)

The narwhal is remarkable for the spiral tusk that projects from the male's upper jaw. This is now thought to be a sensory organ, able to pick up changes in the narwhal's environment, but it is also used for fighting and attracting a mate.

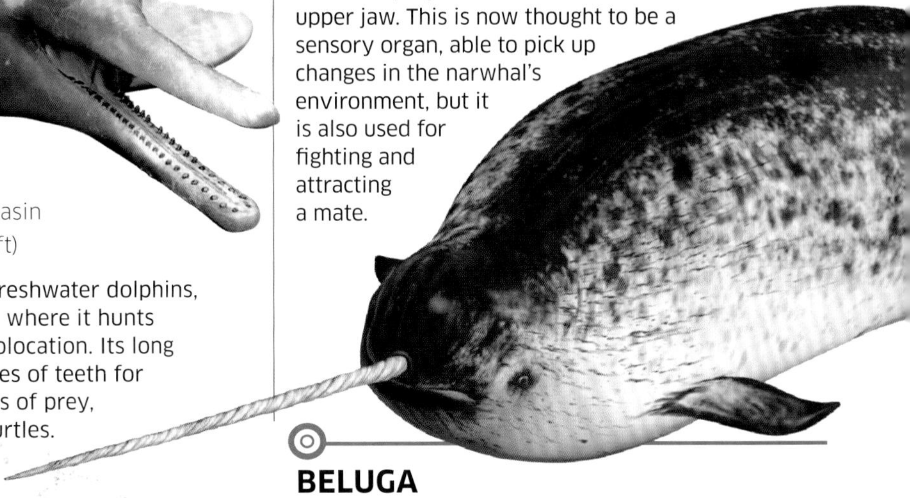

Cetaceans

This group – the whales, dolphins, and porpoises – includes the biggest animals on the planet. The largest and most powerful marine predator, the orca **(see pp.242–243)****, belongs to this group, as well as some of the most intelligent of all animals.**

Cetaceans are the most highly specialized of all marine mammals, feeding and breeding at sea. There are two types – the giant baleen whales that filter small animals from the water, and the group of generally smaller toothed whales, including dolphins and porpoises, which prey on larger fish and squid.

BELUGA

Delphinapterus leucas

Location: Arctic seas

Length: Up to 4.5 m ($14^3/_4$ ft)

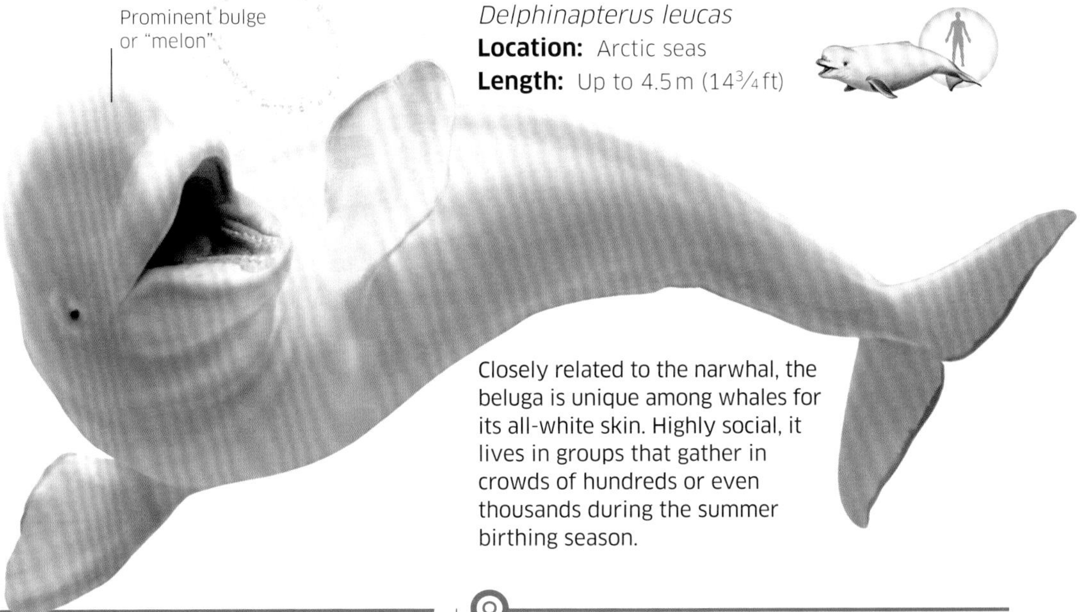

Closely related to the narwhal, the beluga is unique among whales for its all-white skin. Highly social, it lives in groups that gather in crowds of hundreds or even thousands during the summer birthing season.

VAQUITA

Phocoena sinus

Location: Gulf of California

Length: Up to 1.5 m (5 ft)

The smallest and rarest porpoise, the vaquita is found in very shallow waters and feeds on fish and squid. Because of its limited range it is the most seriously endangered of all marine mammals.

COMMON BOTTLENOSED DOLPHIN

Tursiops truncatus

Location: All warm oceans

Length: Up to 3.8 m ($12^1/_2$ ft)

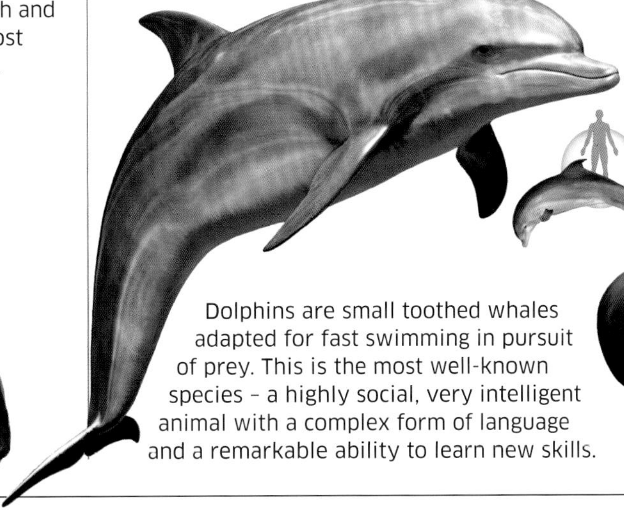

Dolphins are small toothed whales adapted for fast swimming in pursuit of prey. This is the most well-known species – a highly social, very intelligent animal with a complex form of language and a remarkable ability to learn new skills.

LONG-FINNED PILOT WHALE

Globicephala melas

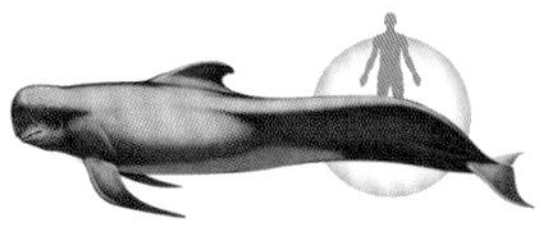

Location: North Atlantic and Southern Oceans

Length: Up to 6.7 m (22 ft)

This is a large dolphin, but with an unusually bulbous forehead. This forehead swelling, or melon, contains a structure that – as with all toothed whales – focuses the animal's echolocation clicks, enabling it to detect prey in dark water.

ANIMAL SCIENCE

Everything about an animal – its appearance, behaviour, and the way its body functions – is the result of natural selection. Over millions of years of evolution, animals have adapted to their environment in countless different ways. The result is the astonishing diversity of the animal kingdom today.

Body shapes

There are an estimated 7.8 million species of animals on Earth, of which scientists have so far identified and listed about 1.4 million. Every one of these animals has a body shape that is perfectly adapted to its environment and lifestyle. Animals need to be able to move (at least a little), find and eat food, and take in oxygen. The bodies of species as unalike as a coyote, a coral, and a cockroach can do all these things equally well, although their shapes and internal systems are very different.

BODY SYMMETRY

Animals can be grouped according to their body symmetry – the way their bodies are planned. Most have bilateral symmetry, in which one side of the body is a mirror image of the other. A few animals have a radial or circular shape, with body parts arranged round a central area. Very simple animals have no symmetry at all.

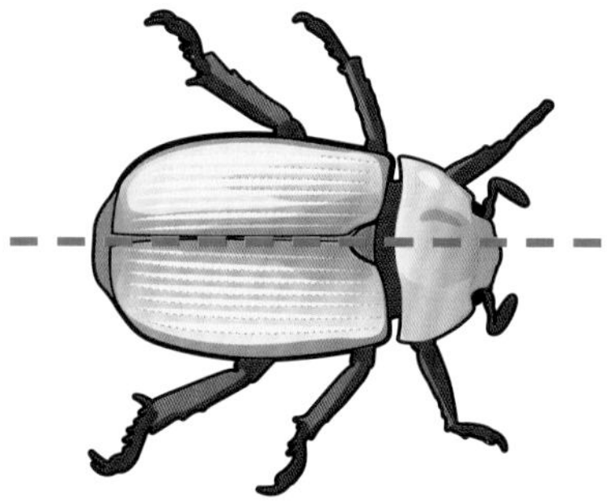

GOLD BEETLE

Bilateral

A body shape with bilateral symmetry has a head at one end, equipped with a mouth and the main sense organs. Legs and other appendages always develop in pairs, with an equal number on either side of the body. Bilaterally symmetrical animals include all vertebrates, arthropods, molluscs, and worms.

SEA ANEMONE

Radial

Jellyfish, corals, and their relatives have radial symmetry. There is no head, and the mouth is in the centre of the body. Such animals usually have no separate waste outlet, or anus – everything enters or exits the body through one opening. Adult starfish, sea urchins, and similar animals also have a radial symmetry but develop from larvae with bilateral symmetry.

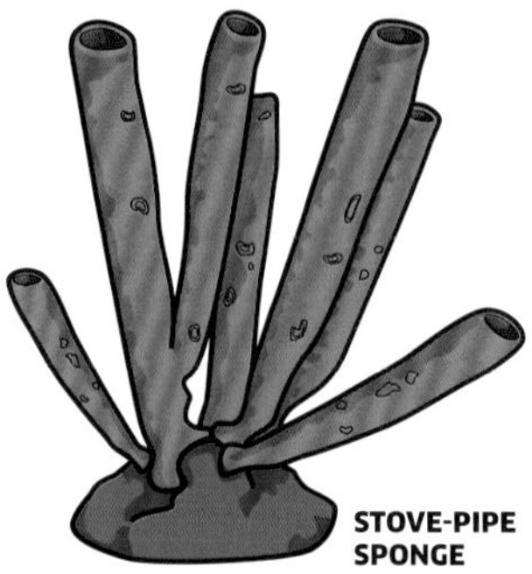

STOVE-PIPE SPONGE

Asymmetrical

The simplest and most primitive body plans are those of the sponges and placozoa, which are marine animals with no symmetry at all. Sponge bodies grow as tubes and channels, while placozoa are tiny flattened bodies made of just two cell layers. These animals absorb oxygen and small food particles through their body surface.

BODY FORMS

More than 99 per cent of animals have a bilaterally symmetrical body shape – at least for a part of their life cycle. However, there is still a huge amount of variety. Evolution has adapted the bilateral animal body to suit different habitats and ways of life.

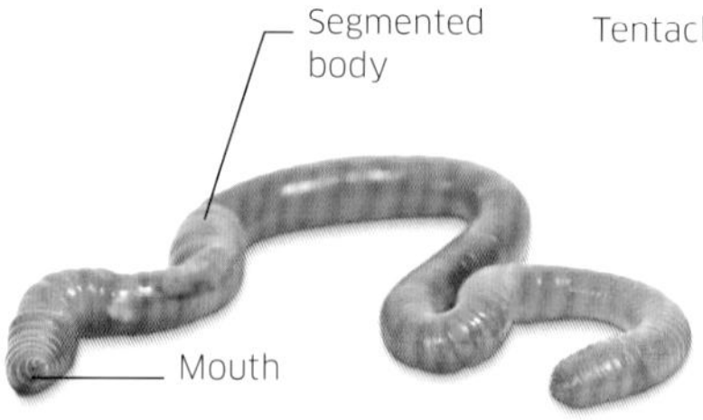

Earthworm
The earthworm, a species of annelid worm, has a burrowing body with no legs or other appendages. Its body is made up of repeated segments.

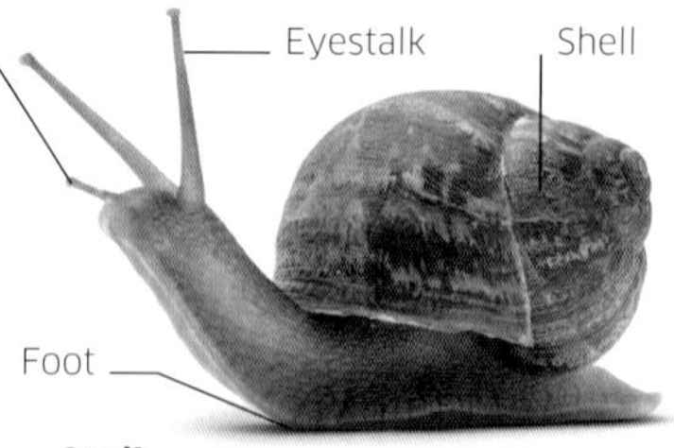

Snail
Belonging to the mollusc phylum, the snail moves around on a fleshy foot. Its main body, or mantle, is protected by a waterproof shell.

Lizard
Like all vertebrates, this lizard has a body arranged around an internal skeleton with a supporting spine. This lizard is an example of a reptile. At one end is the head (and brain) and, in most vertebrates, the body ends in a tail.

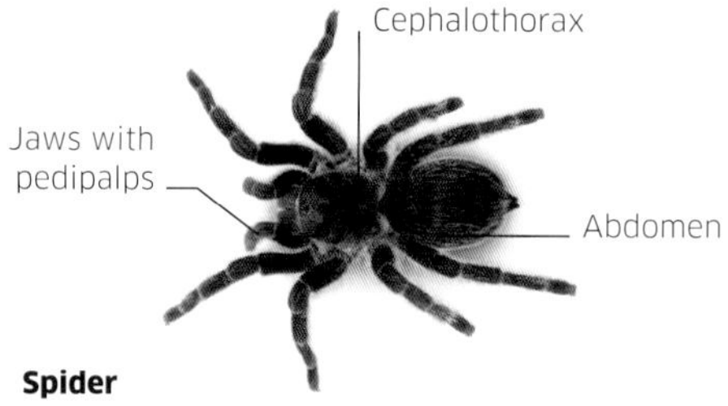

Spider
An example of an arachnid, the spider has two body sections: the cephalothorax, which comprises the head and thorax, and the abdomen. Its eight legs and its arm-like pedipalps are connected to the cephalothorax.

Pigeon
Birds have four limbs like most land vertebrates, but the first pair are modified into wings. A covering of feathers increases the wing and tail areas, while adding hardly any extra weight.

Crab
A crustacean and, along with insects and spiders, a member of the arthropod phylum, this crab gets its body shape from a hard outer covering, or exoskeleton.

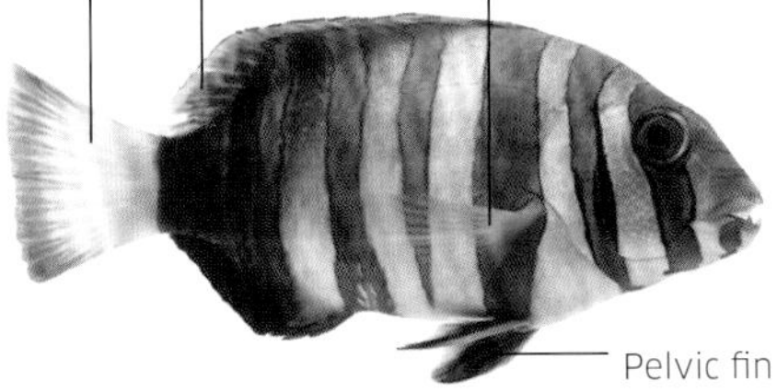

Fish
A fish body is smooth and streamlined. The tail, or caudal fin, provides swimming power. Other fins on the body provide stability and are used for steering.

Dragonfly
Insects such as this were the first organisms to evolve flight. Most insects have two pairs of functioning wings, which develop separately from their three pairs of legs.

Orangutan
Mammals, such as this ape, are generally four-limbed vertebrates. As an ape, this orangutan has no tail, a feature that is shared with the human body shape.

Long arms
Apes have longer forelimbs than hind limbs.

BODY SYSTEMS

Most animals have body organs that work together in sets, called systems, with special tasks. Each system must coordinate with all the others to allow the body to function properly. The main systems include: skeletal, muscular, nervous, circulatory, digestive, excretory, reproductive, and respiratory. These systems are arranged in various ways to suit different types of animal.

Simple invertebrates

A flatworm is one of the simplest animals, but its internal anatomy is still organized into organs and body systems. However, it has a nervous system without a brain, and no heart or circulatory system. The digestive system is highly branched.

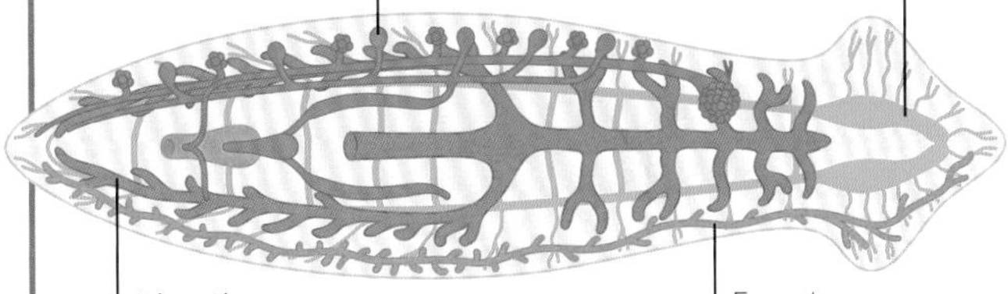

FLATWORM

Vertebrates

Land vertebrates, from frogs and birds to mammals, share the same body systems, although these are often modified to suit size, lifestyle, and habitat. For example, very fast-moving hunting animals, such as a dog or a cheetah, have bigger lungs compared to other, slower animals of the same size.

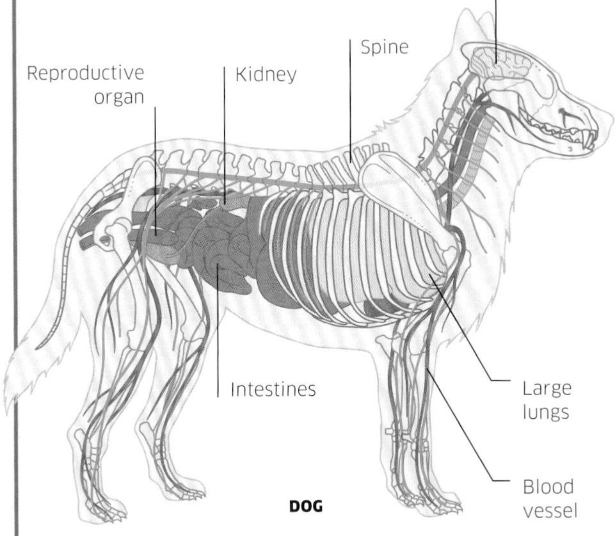

DOG

Key

- Circulatory system
- Digestive system
- Respiratory system
- Excretory system
- Nervous system
- Reproductive system

Life cycles

An animal's life cycle is its progress from birth or hatching through a period of development to adulthood, when it can produce its own young. A life cycle may last a few weeks only, or take years to complete. Many young animals are just small versions of their parents. Others are quite different from the adults in their early stages, both in appearance and the way they live. To transform into adults, such animals undergo a change known as metamorphosis. This is what happens when caterpillars turn into butterflies or tadpoles become frogs.

DIRECT DEVELOPMENT

Birds, reptiles, and mammals – which include these foxes – grow by direct development. When they are born or hatch from an egg, the young have the same body systems and anatomical features as the adult, although they are not capable of reproducing. At first, many are fed and cared for by their parents until they are able to look after themselves. Most rapidly develop the feeding habits and behaviour of the adults.

INCOMPLETE METAMORPHOSIS

Many insects, such as grasshoppers, have a life cycle known as incomplete metamorphosis. The immature (young) insect, or nymph, grows in stages as it moults (sheds) its outer skeleton several times with no dramatic changes. It looks like a small adult and eats the same foods.

1 NYMPH After hatching from an egg, the tiny nymph begins to feed. It has no wings, just buds where they will develop. As it grows, the nymph moults its outer skeleton over five stages.

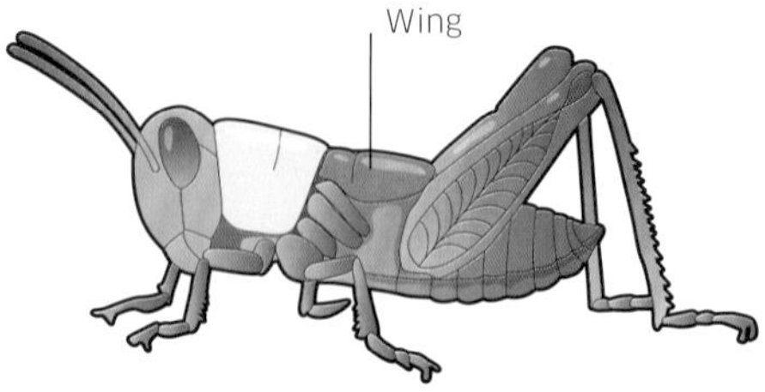

2 HOPPER The final immature stage of the life cycle is called the hopper. The wings are beginning to grow but the animal cannot fly. It hops with its long hind legs.

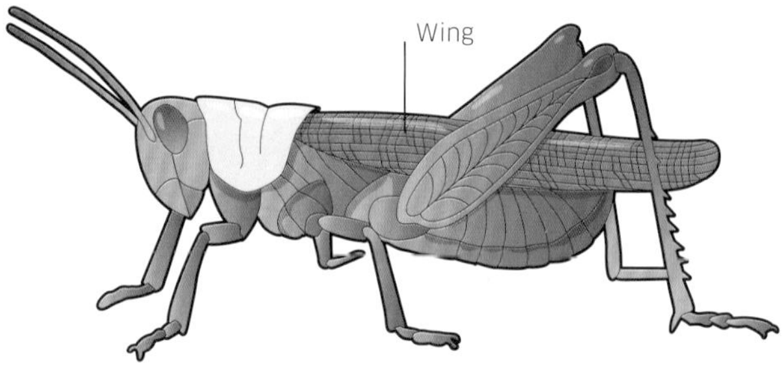

3 ADULT After the final moult, the grasshopper has become an adult with long wings capable of flight. It will now mate and lay eggs of its own. This entire life cycle takes about six weeks to complete.

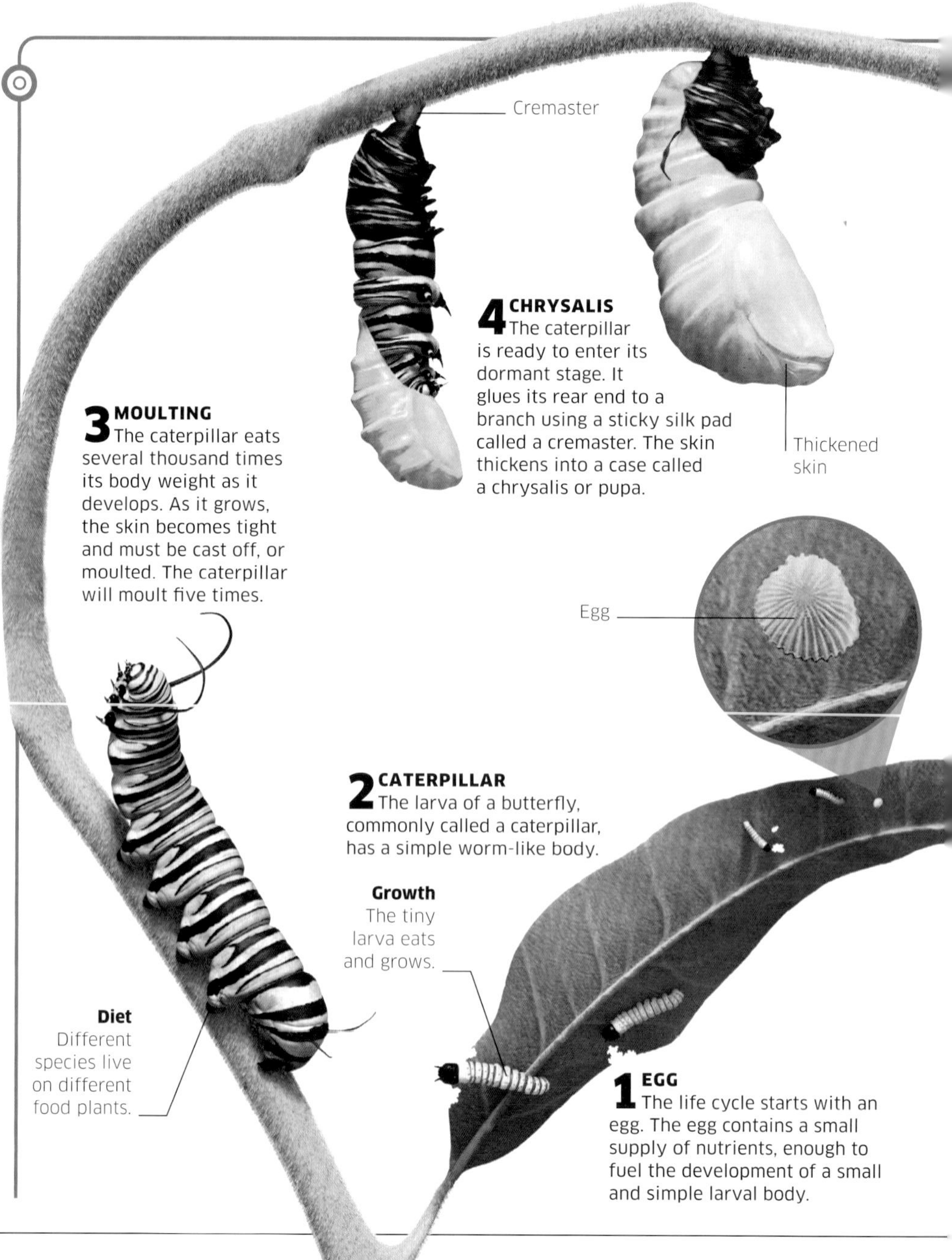

1 EGG The life cycle starts with an egg. The egg contains a small supply of nutrients, enough to fuel the development of a small and simple larval body.

2 CATERPILLAR The larva of a butterfly, commonly called a caterpillar, has a simple worm-like body.

3 MOULTING The caterpillar eats several thousand times its body weight as it develops. As it grows, the skin becomes tight and must be cast off, or moulted. The caterpillar will moult five times.

4 CHRYSALIS The caterpillar is ready to enter its dormant stage. It glues its rear end to a branch using a sticky silk pad called a cremaster. The skin thickens into a case called a chrysalis or pupa.

MOULTING

As some animals grow, their outer layer does not grow with them. In a process called moulting – similar to incomplete metamorphosis in young insects – they cast off the too-tight layer to allow further growth. Animals that moult include crustaceans such as lobsters and crabs, which shed their outer shells. A new soft shell beneath soon hardens. Snakes moult by shedding their top layer of skin, often in one piece.

DIVISION OF GENERATIONS

When animals produce large numbers of offspring at a time, the adults can find themselves competing with the younger generation for food and space. Some species get round the problem by having a life cycle in which the young start off as larvae, living and feeding quite differently from their parents.

Tadpole
The eggs (spawn) of a frog hatch into a form of larvae called tadpoles. A tadpole lives entirely in water, eating plants or smaller animals. It grows legs as it develops into an adult.

Frog
Unlike its tadpole offspring, an adult frog is able to survive and feed on land as well as in water. Most species of frogs prey on insects and small land animals.

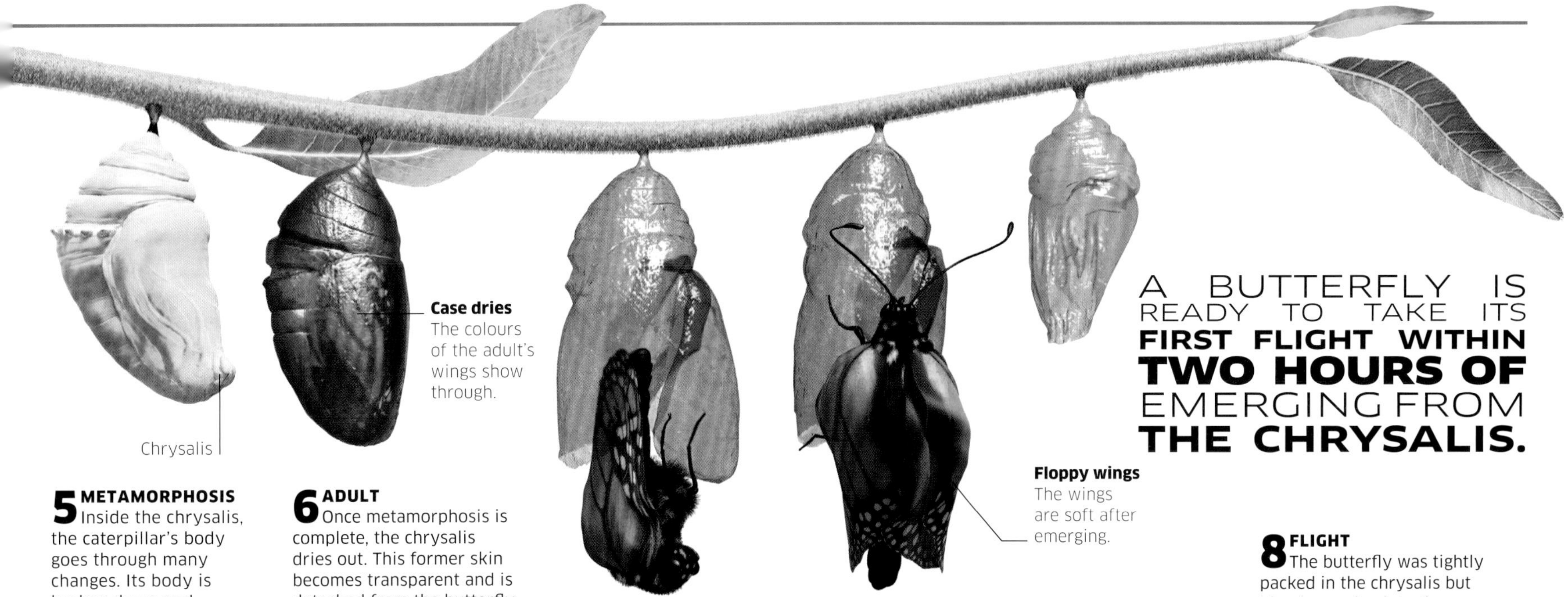

Case dries
The colours of the adult's wings show through.

Chrysalis

Floppy wings
The wings are soft after emerging.

A BUTTERFLY IS READY TO TAKE ITS **FIRST FLIGHT WITHIN TWO HOURS OF** EMERGING FROM **THE CHRYSALIS.**

5 METAMORPHOSIS
Inside the chrysalis, the caterpillar's body goes through many changes. Its body is broken down and rebuilt into adult form.

6 ADULT
Once metamorphosis is complete, the chrysalis dries out. This former skin becomes transparent and is detached from the butterfly waiting inside.

7 EMERGENCE
The transformation, fuelled by food stored in the caterpillar's body, has taken about two weeks. Now the chrysalis splits open from the head end, and the adult hauls itself out.

8 FLIGHT
The butterfly was tightly packed in the chrysalis but blood pumping into the creased wings soon opens them. Once the outer skeleton dries and hardens, the insect will fly off.

Ready to fly
The crumpled wings rapidly expand and stiffen.

COMPLETE METAMORPHOSIS

The most elaborate life cycles are seen in insects such as butterflies, beetles, and flies. These animals develop by complete metamorphosis. They begin life as a larva, hatched from an egg. The larva, which is very different from the adult, grows fast before taking a dormant form called a pupa or, in butterflies and moths, a chrysalis. During this stage, the larva's body is completely reorganized into the adult form.

Movement

All animals, even the simplest, need to be able to move at some stage in their life cycle. Animals move to find food, to seek shelter, to escape from danger, or to find a mate to breed with. Animals can move over land or underground, in water, or through the air – some can move effectively in more than one environment. The size and shape of an animal's body reflect the type of skeleton it possesses and the ways in which it can move.

MOVING THROUGH THE AIR

Several kinds of animal, including squirrels, snakes, and frogs, are able to glide through the air. But only three groups are able to fly: birds, bats, and insects. They all have wings, which they flap to produce an upward force that lifts them into the air. Some birds, such as this kestrel, can hover in one spot while they scan the ground for prey.

TYPES OF SKELETON

Animal movement is powered by muscles – fibres that contract (shorten) to pull on the body. Muscles cannot work by themselves – they need a skeleton of some kind to pull against. There are three main kinds of skeleton.

Hydrostatic skeleton
An earthworm's body contains fluid, and can change shape. The worm has two layers of muscle, which work in different directions. One squeezes around the body, stretching it out lengthways. The other squashes the body up, making it short and fat. By alternating these two actions, the worm moves forwards.

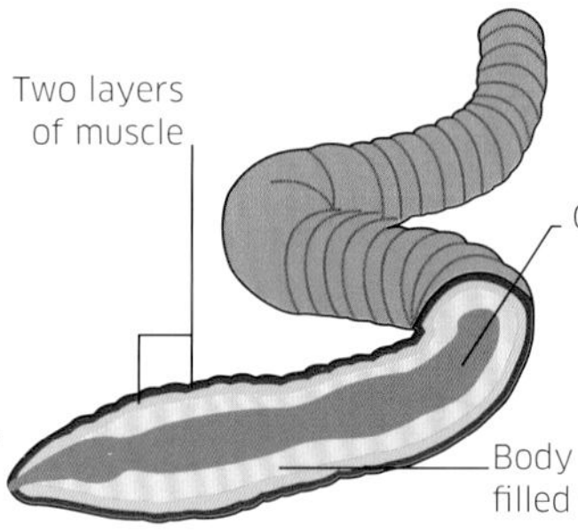

EARTHWORM BODY

Exoskeleton
Arthropods, such as insects, have a hard but flexible external skeleton. The muscles pull on the inside of the skeleton to make it move. Muscles can only pull, not push, so they work in opposing pairs.

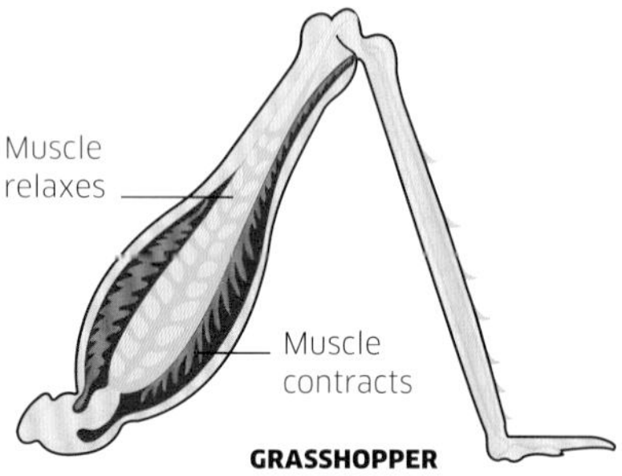

GRASSHOPPER LEG

Endoskeleton
Vertebrates, such as gorillas, have a skeleton inside their body, made from dozens of connected bones. Muscle pairs are attached to the bones by strong cords, called tendons. When one muscle contracts the opposing muscle relaxes.

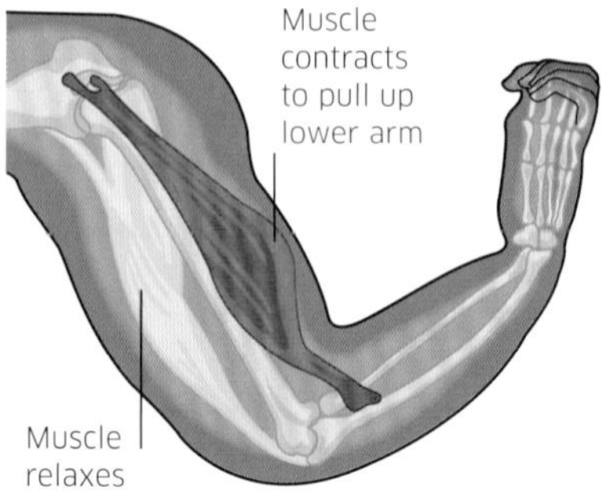

GORILLA ARM

Running
Fast-running animals often have long legs. In hoofed animals, such as zebras, only the very tips of the toes make contact with the ground. The tips of the toes are protected by a hard hoof.

MOVING IN WATER

Animals can move through water by crawling along the sea bed, by floating wherever the currents take them, or by swimming. A streamlined shape helps swimming animals move more efficiently in the water.

How a fish swims
Most fish use their caudal fin (tail) to propel them. This fin is usually moved by a wave motion of the whole body.

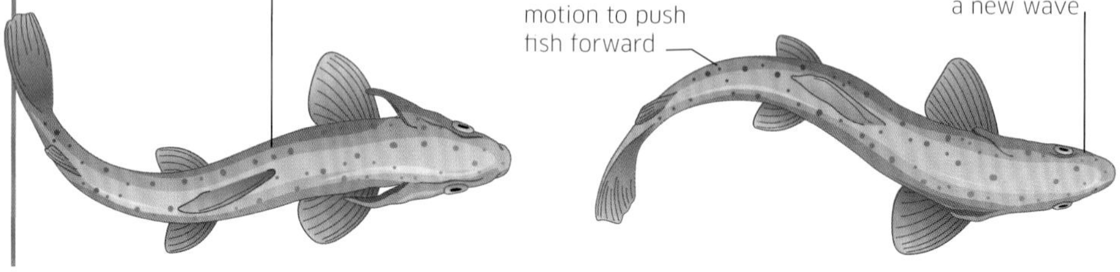

Flying
A bird flies by flapping its wings; the downstroke pushes the air down and back, moving the bird's body up and forwards. This is followed by an upstroke, where the bird lifts its wing ready for another downstroke.

Smaller feathers
These create a smooth outline for better airflow over the wing.

Insect wings

Bird and bat wings are forelimbs that are modified for flight. Insects, on the other hand, have two or four thin, stiff wings, which are attached to the thorax (body).

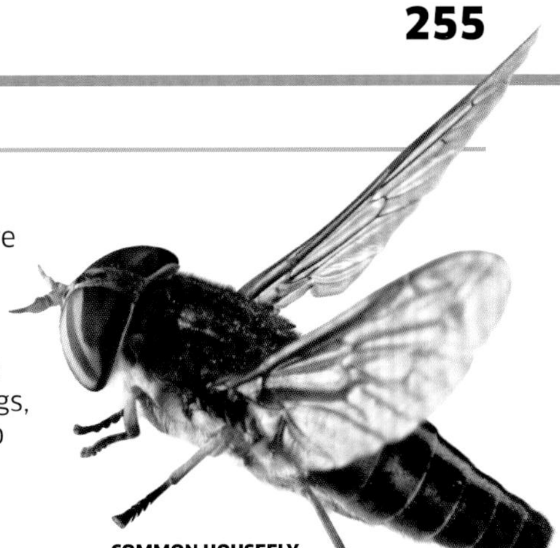

COMMON HOUSEFLY TAKES FLIGHT

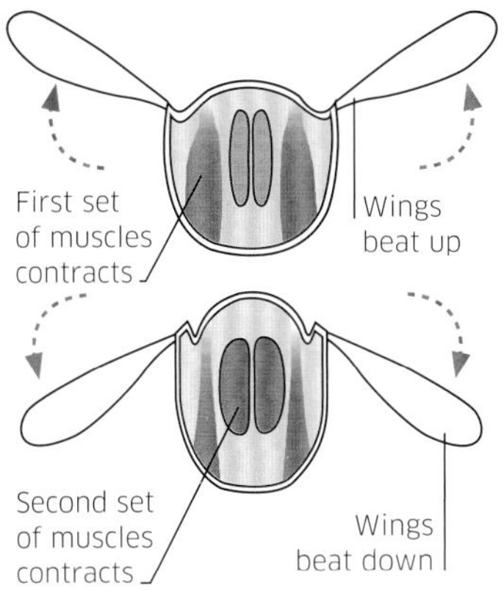

Insect flight
Some insects beat their wings by changing the shape of their thorax. One set of muscles pulls the thorax down, making the wings stroke up. Then another set contracts, pulling the sides of the thorax in, and pushing the top up, making the wings beat down.

MOVING ON LAND

Land animals move in a huge variety of different ways, with some species adapted to running very fast, others to burrowing, climbing, or hopping on the ground. Most land animals move on legs. This involves shifting the body's weight from one limb (or set of limbs) to another in a controlled way to move along.

Jungle swingers
All apes, such as these chimpanzees, have very flexible shoulder joints. This allows them to move quickly through trees by swinging from branch to branch.

Snake movement
Legless animals, such as snakes, move in different ways, using their muscles and ribs. The concertina movement shown here is useful for moving in a narrow space.

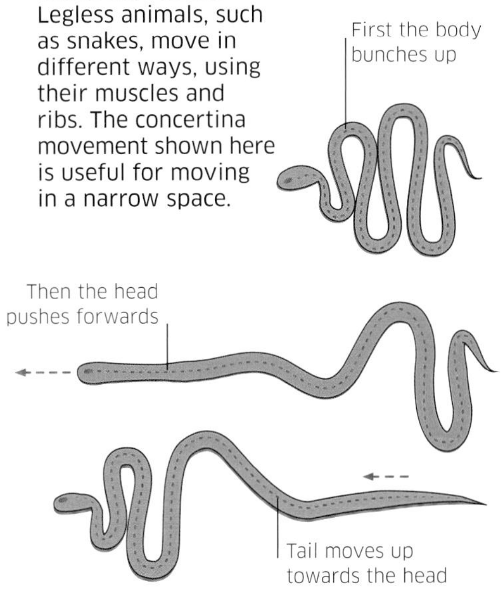

Jet propulsion
Some marine animals, such as cuttlefish (left), squid, and octopuses, use jet propulsion to shoot away from danger. The cuttlefish blasts water out of its body cavity at high pressure through its siphon tube, thrusting its body backwards at great speed.

SESSILE FEEDERS

Many aquatic animals are sessile, meaning that they spend their adult lives anchored in one place on the sea bed. They can move parts of their body to collect food but they cannot change their location once they have settled. This sea pen looks like a seaweed but it is actually a sessile relative of the jellyfish.

Feeding

All living things need food, which they convert into energy to move, grow, or repair their bodies. Plants can make their own food by using the Sun's energy, but in order to survive, all animals have to consume other living things or their remains – from grasses, seaweeds, and plants to insects, fish, or mammals. Some animals can feed on a variety of different foods, but others are adapted to finding and eating one particular type.

FUEL FOR LIFE

Animals obtain energy from food by a process called respiration. First, the food is digested and converted into glucose. The glucose mixes with oxygen breathed in and carried in the blood to the cells. This process produces energy for the animal to use, plus carbon dioxide and water as waste products.

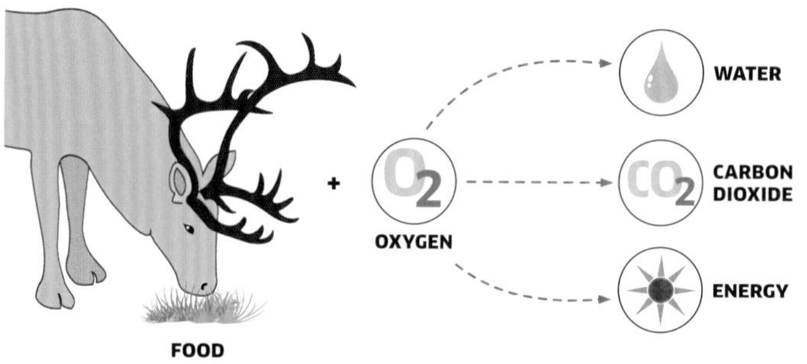

DIFFERENT DIETS

Some simple animals, such as sponges, are anchored to one spot and filter food from the water in which they live. Herbivores eat only plants, while carnivores eat other animals. Some animals, including humans, are omnivores – they eat both animals and plants.

THE RACCOON'S ABILITY TO EAT JUST ABOUT ANYTHING HAS MADE IT **A SUPER-SURVIVOR,** ABLE TO LIVE IN MANY DIFFERENT **HABITATS, INCLUDING CITIES, DESERTS, AND MOUNTAINS.**

Unfussy omnivores
A raccoon will eat whatever food it can find, from plants, insects, or fish to leftover human meals. Its small paws have flexible fingers, enabling it to grasp and handle all kinds of different foods.

Liquid diet
This hummingbird's diet consists only of the liquid nectar produced by flowers. Its fast-beating wings allow it to hover in the air, while its long bill probes deep into the flower and sips the sweet, sugary nectar.

Plant-eaters
Animals that eat plants are herbivores. These deer eat grass, leaves, bark, and other plant parts. Plant matter is hard to digest, so herbivores often spend long periods eating to obtain the nutrients they need.

Filter-feeders
The whale shark feeds by sucking big gulps of water into its huge, gaping mouth. Filter pads in the shark's mouth trap small fish and other marine creatures, which the shark then swallows.

Waste-recyclers
The dung of grazing animals contains undigested plant matter, which is a useful source of food for the dung beetle. It forms the dung into a ball and rolls it to its nest to feed to newly hatched grubs.

DIET AND TEETH

The arrangement of teeth in an animal reveals a lot about the food it eats. Venomous snakes use sharp fangs to poison prey before they swallow it. Mammals' teeth are specialized for different jobs such as biting, crushing, slicing, chewing, and grinding. Most mammals have several types of teeth, and their form varies depending on their diet.

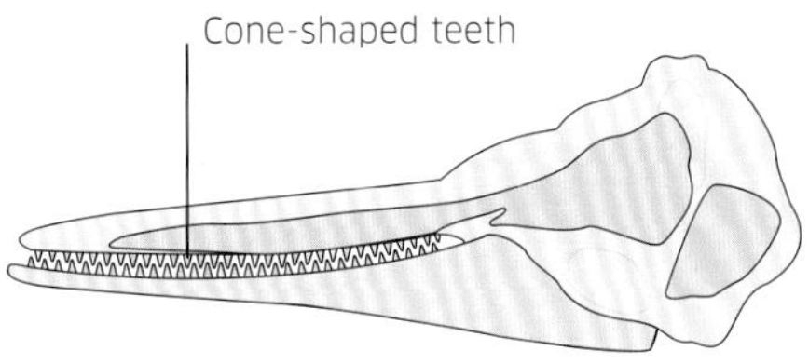

Dolphin
A dolphin's teeth are perfect for seizing and holding on to slippery fish. Unusually for a mammal, all the teeth are the same shape and size.

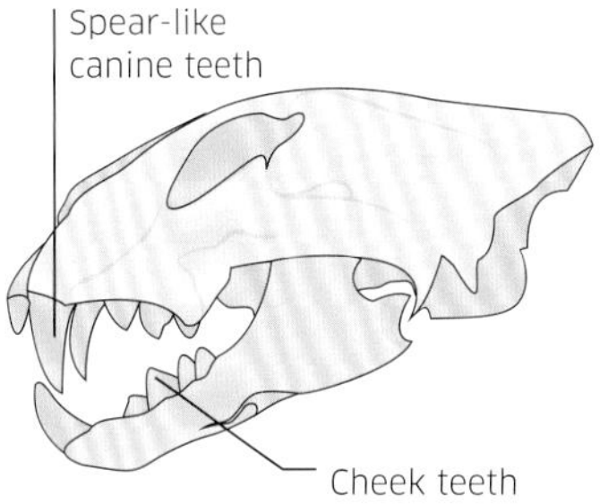

Lion
A lion has long, pointed canine teeth for seizing and stabbing prey, and scissor-like cheek teeth (molars) for slicing it into small enough chunks to swallow.

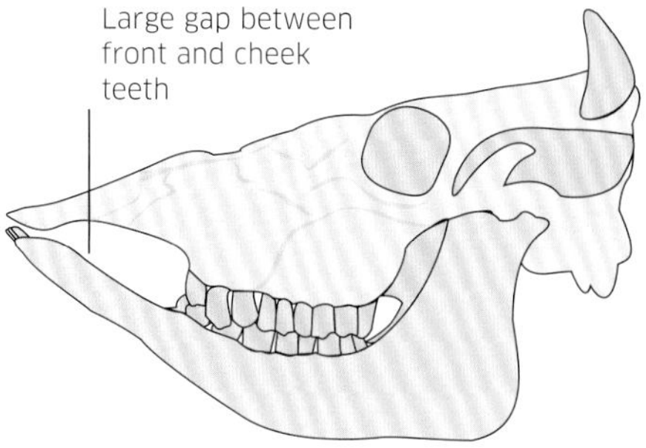

Cow
Grazing animals, such as cows, eat grass, which is difficult to digest so they have big, flattened cheek teeth for grinding it to a digestible pulp.

High-energy hunting
Predatory animals are carnivores that kill and eat other animals. Meat is very nutritious, but predators often have to spend a lot of precious energy stalking, chasing, and killing their prey.

Predator meets prey
A black-backed jackal stalks and pounces on a sand grouse that has come to drink at a water hole.

VISION

Sight is important for nearly all animals, both predators and prey, although a few that live in total darkness, such as moles, do not need good vision. Various kinds of eyes occur in different animal groups. Arthropods, such as insects and spiders, usually have two types of eye: ocelli, which are simple light detectors; and compound eyes for all-round vision. In vertebrates, including humans, eyes may be placed facing forwards or set on the sides of the head.

Ocelli
Spiders and other arthropods often have simple eyes called ocelli alongside more complex eyes. Ocelli detect light changes and, in some species, judge distance. They have a single lens. Usually, ocelli are paired and cluster on top of the head.

Compound eye
Arthropods have compound eyes, which are divided into sometimes thousands of separate compartments, each with a tiny lens. Compound eyes detect movement but not great detail. They are most developed in flying insects, such as this robber fly.

Vertebrate eye
Mammals, reptiles, birds, fish, and some invertebrates such as the octopus, all have two eyes. These eyes work like a camera, with a lens that focuses light on sensitive cells at the back of the eye. They detect light, motion, and colour.

SMELL AND TASTE

These two closely linked senses use special cells called chemoreceptors. In mammals, chemoreceptors are found in the nose, where they detect smells, and in the mouth, where they identify tastes. These cells pass information to the brain, which sorts everything into known or unknown, pleasant or unpleasant. Other animals taste and smell with chemoreceptors located in other parts of the body. Many insects trace smells with their antennae and have taste buds on their feet. Snakes pick up scent molecules in the air with their tongue.

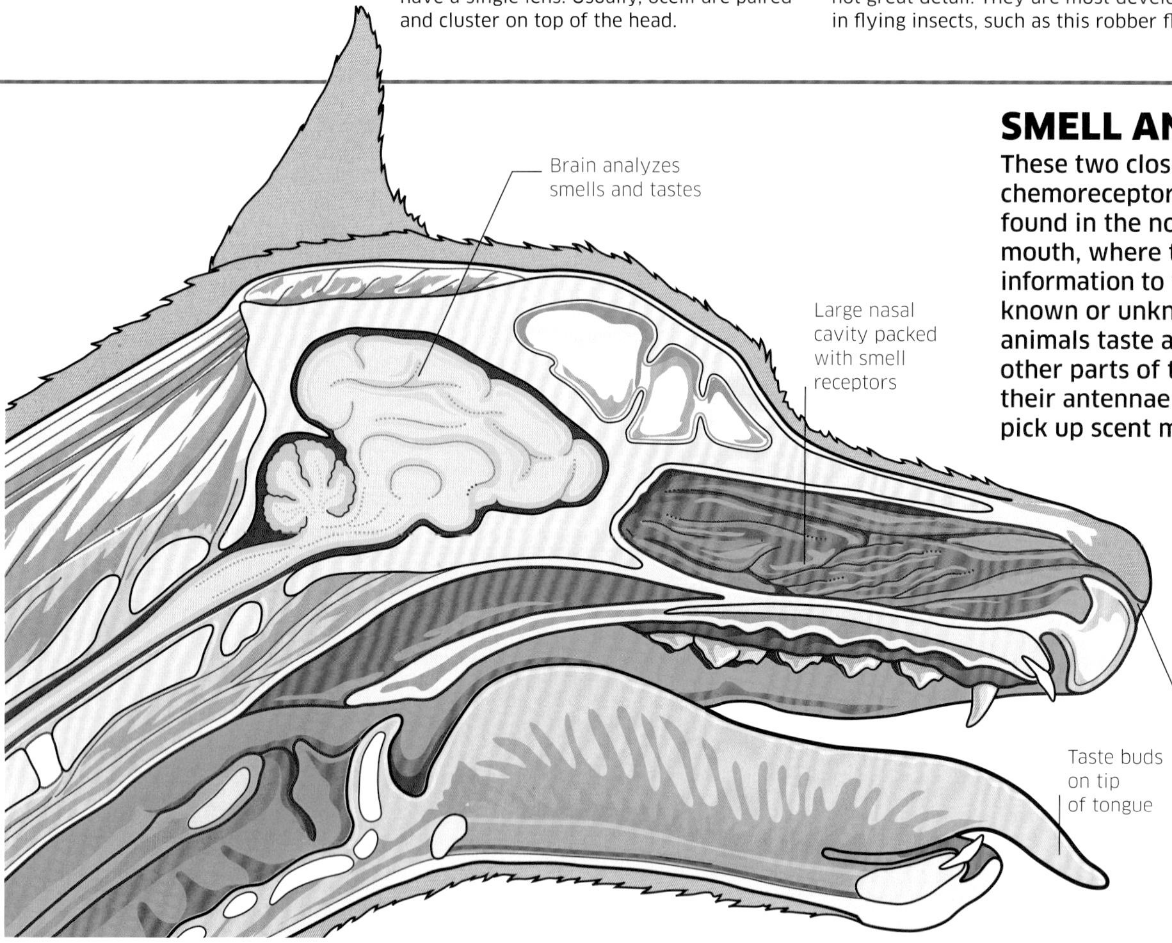

THE PART OF A DOG'S BRAIN THAT ANALYZES SMELLS IS PROPORTIONATELY 40 TIMES LARGER THAN IN A HUMAN.

Super-sensitive nose
A dog's nose has more than 125–300 million smell receptors, compared to six million in humans. Dogs can move each nostril independently, which enables them to work out the precise direction from which a scent is coming.

Fine-tuned antennae
This male emperor moth has chemoreceptors in its two feathery antennae. These are so sensitive they can detect chemicals called pheromones, given off by a female moth, 5 km (3 miles) away.

Picky tastes
Dolphins have no sense of smell, but they do have taste buds, which are located at the base of their tongue. If they have plenty around them to eat, they show a preference for some food fish over others.

Tasting with the feet
Butterflies and many other insects have chemoreceptors in their feet. These function in much the same way as taste buds on other animals' tongues, telling the insect which flowers provide the right food.

Senses

Animals need senses to find food, mates, and shelter, stay in touch with their social group, and avoid predators. In many animals, the five senses of sight, sound, smell, taste, and touch are much more efficient than they are in humans. Not only that, some animals possess extra senses to meet their particular needs. There are nocturnal snakes that hunt in complete darkness by detecting infrared radiation from the warm bodies of prey. Birds can "read" Earth's magnetic field – important for navigating on migration. And sharks can pick up electric signals given off by other animals.

TOUCH

A keen sense of touch is vital for animals that move in the dark. Cats, both big and small, have sensitive whiskers that they use as navigation aids at night. In a similar way, catfish, which live in murky waters, use whisker-like barbels around their mouth to feel their way towards food. The best sense of touch could belong to the almost blind star-nosed mole. Its bizarre tentacled snout has 25,000 touch receptors.

HEARING

Animals use their sense of hearing to listen for prey, or approaching predators, and to pick up mating calls and other sound messages. Whales and elephants talk to each other over long distances with sounds that are below the lowest range of human hearing. Bats hunting insects in the dark send out very high-frequency soundwaves that echo back when they meet something. The bat hears the echo and uses it to locate its source.

SOME BATS CAN HEAR SOUNDS PITCHED AT **100 KHZ OR MORE,** FIVE TIMES HIGHER PITCHED **THAN A HUMAN EAR CAN DETECT.**

Listening for underground sounds
The bat-eared fox has acute hearing to help it locate the small animals, such as insects, that it hunts for food on the African savanna. The huge ears pick up the tiniest soundwaves from underground prey.

External eardrum
The eardrums of a frog are just below the surface of the body. In some species, the eardrum, known as the tympanum, can be seen as a thin membrane next to the frog's eye, visible in the photograph above.

Ears in surprising places
Long-horned grasshoppers have ears on their knee joints, while the short-horned species have their eardrums on their abdomen. Grasshoppers can recognize the songs of their own species.

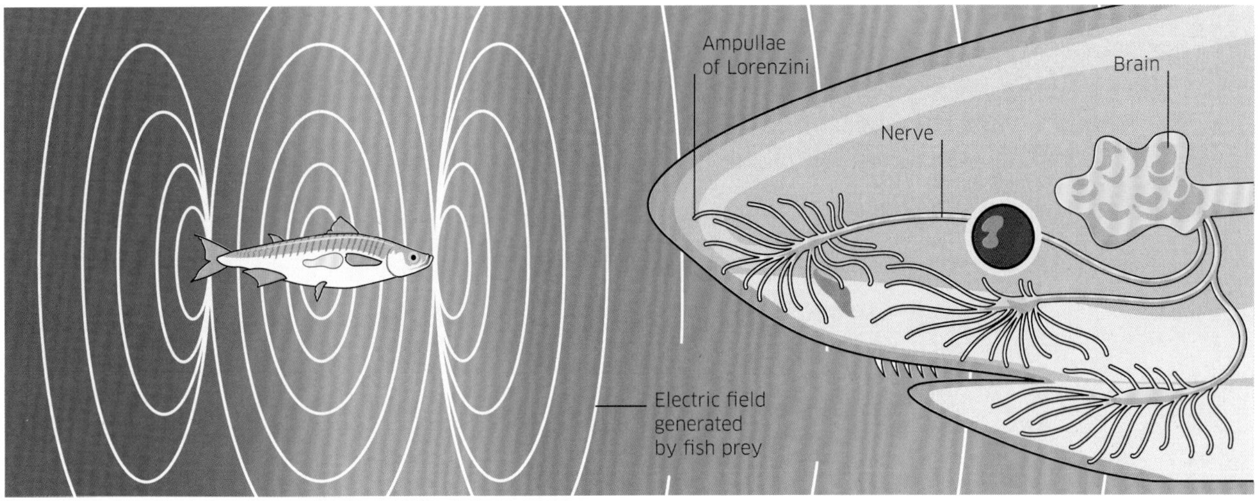

SUPER SENSE

Sharks have a special ability. They can detect the slightest of the electric signals that all animals produce. Known as electroreception, this sense allows them to locate prey. A shark's electric sensors, called the ampullae of Lorenzini, consist of electroreceptor cells found in pores on the shark's snout. The cells pick up the electric signals that travel by water and send messages by nerve pathways to the shark's brain.

Communication

Even animals that lead mostly solitary lives sometimes need to get in touch with others. They may want to advertise their presence, stake a territorial claim, or, most often, attract a mate. Some animals communicate by sending out sounds or smells recognizable to those nearby. Many use visual signals such as body language or colour changes. Good communication is particularly important among a group, as it helps to keep everyone safe and prevent fighting.

VISUAL SIGNALS

Animals can communicate without making a sound. They do this with visual signals – body language that has a clear meaning to others of the same species. From scaring off rivals to raising the alarm or attracting a mate, a lot can be said with tails, teeth, and flashy colours.

Submissive behaviour
This African wild dog is anxious to avoid trouble. It is lowering its head to show that it does not pose a threat to the leading dog in the pack.

CALLS AND SONGS

Animals are most vocal in the mating season, when species of many types call to attract a mate. But some calls are used year round, because many animals use sounds as commands or warnings. The vervet monkey, for example, has a whole range of alarm calls that spell out exactly what danger threatens.

Vervet monkey
Highly social vervet monkeys use a range of sounds to warn other members of their troop about specific threats. A grunting call warns of attack from above. A squeaky honking call tells the group to climb into trees to avoid big cats. A rattling call alerts other monkeys that a snake is close by.

Birdsong
A strong song shows a male bird is healthy and would make a good mate. This European robin is singing to mark its breeding territory.

Croaking frog
Many frogs call to attract a mate, making deep croaks or high-pitched chirps. This red-eyed tree frog is inflating its vocal sac to amplify its call.

Noisy grasshopper
Insects can make noises with their bodies using a technique called stridulation. Grasshoppers stridulate by rubbing their hind legs over their forewings.

Tail flash
When it is frightened by something, a white-tailed deer bounds away with its tail held up, revealing a white fluffy warning signal to other deer nearby.

Courtship display
A male bird of paradise shows off its bright plumage. The extravagance and colours of its feathers show females that it will make a healthy mate.

Colour changes
Chameleons change the colour of their skins depending on mood. Brighter colours may mean fear or anger. Wild patterns mean the lizard wants a mate.

Open wide
This hippo is not yawning. It is showing off its large jaw and massive tusks as a warning to others that they should not pick a fight with it.

HONEYBEE DANCE

Foraging honeybees tell the rest of the hive where they have found a supply of nectar and pollen by performing a "waggle" dance. The direction and speed of the dance spells out the distance, location, and quality of the food.

MAKING SIGNS

Territorial animals leave signs to show they are in charge of the area. These can include piles of dung, claw marks, and scraps of fur, often scented with urine. Any animal ignoring such signs risks being challenged to a fight by the territory's owner.

Bear scrape
These claw marks were made by a brown bear. The height of the scratches up the trunk shows others how big the bear is.

USING SMELLS

Scent is the most common form of animal communication, with many animals having a keen sense of smell. Every animal has a unique scent that identifies it. To members of the same species, changes in body scent can communicate information such as mood, health, or breeding status.

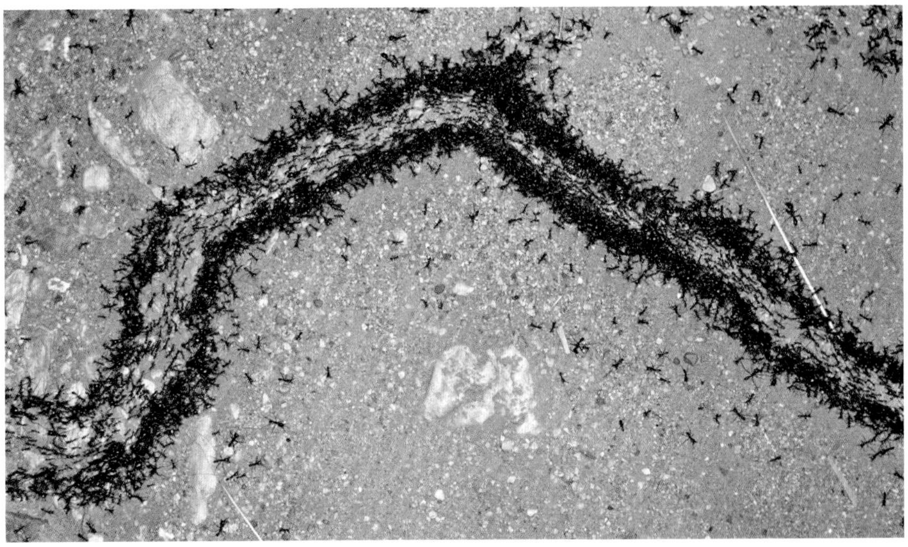

Using pheromones
Pheromones are chemical messages that influence an animal's behaviour. These army ants are releasing pheromones as they swarm over the ground, leaving a trail for ants coming behind to follow.

Scent marking
Most mammals have glands on the face, bottom, or belly that secrete scented oils. An animal rubs the glands on objects around its habitat to leave a scent as a sign to other animals. This ring-tailed lemur, a species found only on the island of Madagascar, is balancing on its front limbs to mark a small tree with the scent glands beneath its tail. Male lemurs also have scent glands on their wrists and chest.

MALE RING-TAILED LEMURS HAVE **STINK FIGHTS** IN MATING SEASON. THEY RUB THEIR TAILS OVER **THEIR SCENT GLANDS** THEN WAVE THE SMELLS AT RIVALS.

Finding a mate

Looking for a mate is a serious business in the animal kingdom. The success of a species depends on males and females pairing up to breed. This may mean the straightforward selection of a partner, or partners, of the opposite sex, but many male animals use elaborate courtship displays to attract an admiring audience of potential mates. Some males resort to violent trials of strength, fighting with one another for the right to claim females. Timing is everything. Most animals have only a short breeding season in which to find a mate.

THE RIGHT CHOICE

Animals instinctively know what makes one mate a better choice than another. For example, the stag with the loftiest antlers or the peacock with the most splendid tail are likely to have the most success attracting females. Their appearance suggests superior health and survival skills – qualities that some of their offspring have a good chance of inheriting.

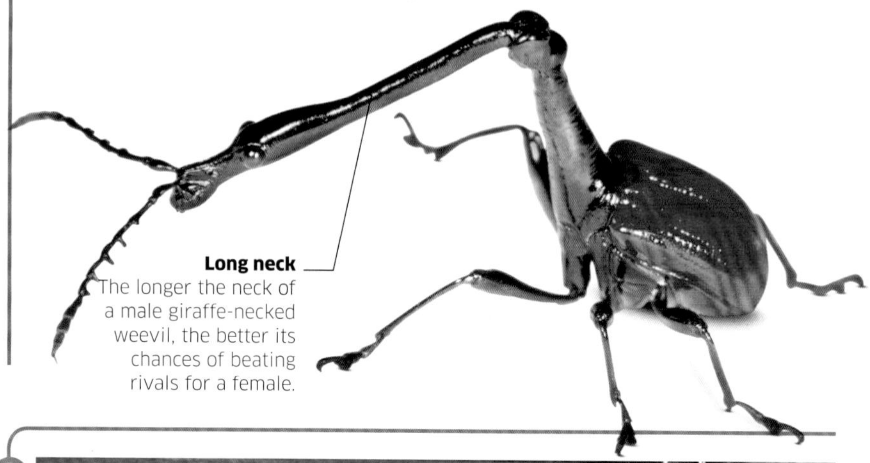

Long neck
The longer the neck of a male giraffe-necked weevil, the better its chances of beating rivals for a female.

DESIGNED FOR PURPOSE

In many species, the sexes are very different in colour, size, and shape. Known as sexual dimorphism, such differences develop when characteristics useful to a species pass from one generation to the next. These could be, for example, extra large size in males or protective colouring in females.

Colour variation
Male and female hairy blennies, a small species of warm-water fish, show different colours and patterns. The male, on the left, also develops a red flush during courtship to attract females.

BREEDING COLONY

Many birds, especially seabirds such as these puffins, gather in large groups, or colonies, to find a mate and breed. The hundreds of birds in the colony also provide greater protection from predators while the females sit on eggs or look after young chicks.

GOING COURTING

Courtship means impressing a possible partner, or even several partners. Many male animals show off in front of the females by putting on courting displays. Birds sing and some, including grouse and cranes, dance. Whales and frogs call and sing too. Courting monkeys and doves preen each other. Some spiders and insects bring gifts. Wrens build nests to display their construction skills. Other animals show off by fighting.

Lekking
In spring, male sage grouse strut around a display area called a "lek", in front of watching females. The females tend to choose the most impressive males.

Calling
By inflating their throat sac, male frogs call to attract females. If a female comes close, the male calls louder, faster, or at a different pitch to show he wants to mate.

Dancing
The most elaborate courtship displays are performed by male birds of paradise. They spread and shake their brightly coloured feathers, and dance on branches or on the ground.

PAIR BONDING

Most birds, and a few mammals, pair up with a single mate for at least part of the breeding season. Such a partnership, called pair bonding, often lasts only until a family has been reared and becomes independent. Some species renew their pair bond in following years, or even stay together for life.

Sealing the deal
Male and female great crested grebes show their willingness to pair up by exchanging gifts of water weed. They perform an elaborate ceremony called the "weed dance" to confirm their bond.

Fighting
Bull elephant seals deliberately crash into each other on the beach in a battle for supremacy. The winner gains access to a harem of female seals.

Bower building
Male satin bowerbirds build stick structures, or bowers, on the ground, adding flowers, berries, and other bright decorations. Females pick the male whose bower they prefer.

POLYGAMY

When animals mate with several different partners during a single breeding season, this is called polygamy. Baboons, like the male and his group of females shown below, are polygamous. So, too, are deer and some antelope, reptiles, and some birds. A partnership of one male and one female is called monogamy.

Reproduction

All animals need to reproduce: unless they create new generations of their own kind, their species would quickly die out. Most animals produce offspring by sexual reproduction, where an adult male and female pair up to create young. This method means that the offspring inherit features from both parents, making the species more varied and resilient. But some animals can reproduce on their own, producing offspring that are exact copies of their parent.

External fertilization
In most fish and water-dwelling animals, fertilization takes place outside the female's body. Males and females release sperm and eggs directly into the water, where they mingle so that fertilization occurs. In this picture, a male salmon is releasing his sperm over a clutch of eggs.

IT TAKES TWO

Sexual reproduction involves a male and a female. They each produce sex cells – the male's are called sperm, and the female's are called eggs. In a process known as fertilization, the sperm and egg cells join together to form a new cell, which grows into the offspring of the two parents. Fertilization can take place inside or outside the mother's body.

Tight hold
The male grips the female's abdomen with his own.

Waiting game
The butterflies may stay locked together in this position for up to an hour.

Internal fertilization
In most land animals, males and females mate and fertilization takes place inside the female's body. Butterflies mate tail-to-tail, with the male butterfly depositing his sperm into a pouch inside the female's abdomen. She keeps the sperm there until she is ready to lay her eggs, using it to fertilize the eggs just before depositing them on a plant.

LIVE YOUNG

After fertilization, the new cell divides many times until it becomes an embryo. In some animals, most commonly mammals, the embryo will stay inside the mother's body until it is ready to be born. The embryo grows inside an organ called the womb, receiving nutrients from the mother's body and continuing to develop until birth.

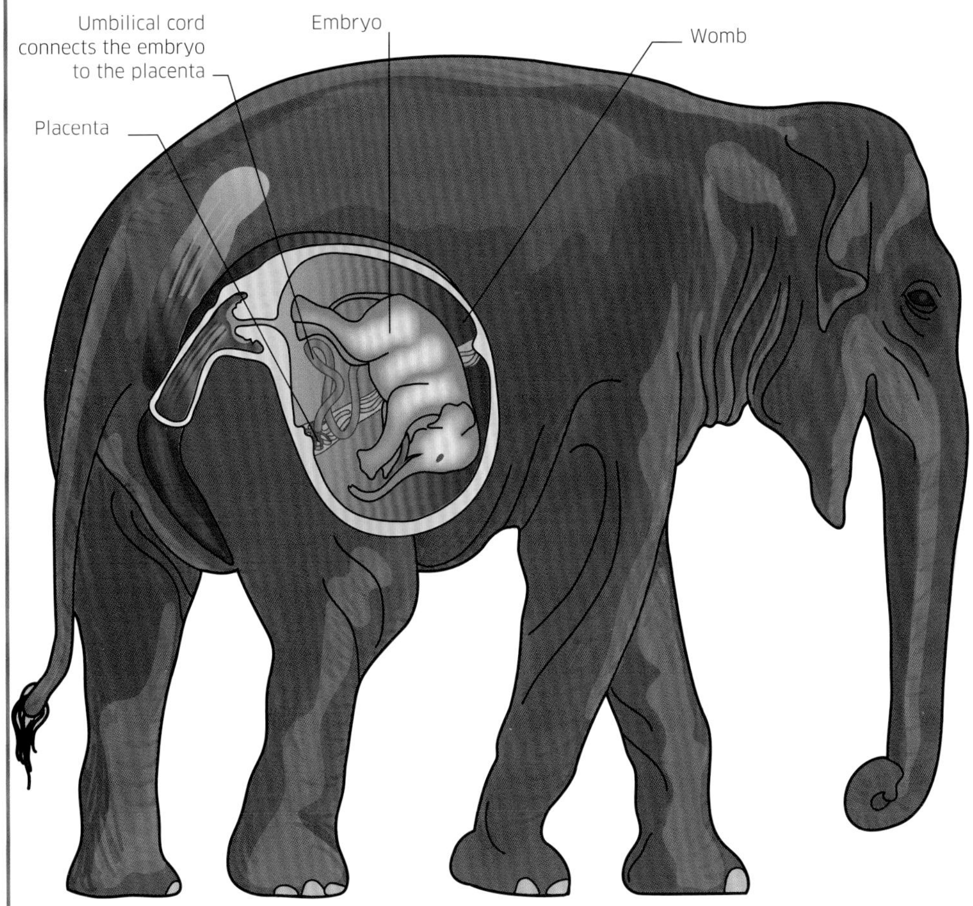

A safe place to grow
In placental mammals, such as elephants, the developing embryo receives nutrients from the mother and gets rid of waste through a temporary organ called the placenta, which grows in the womb.

A BABY ELEPHANT GROWS **INSIDE ITS MOTHER'S** WOMB FOR 22 MONTHS. **THE ELEPHANT'S IS THE LONGEST PREGNANCY OF ANY MAMMAL.**

LAYING EGGS

Most animals lay eggs in which the embryo develops outside the mother's body until it is ready to hatch. Some eggs have protective shells, but many, such as frogs' eggs, do not. Some species look after their eggs until the young hatch; others leave their eggs immediately after laying them.

Life-support system
A bird's egg (right) contains everything the embryo needs to develop. The hard, outer shell provides protection, while letting air in and out. The yolk provides nourishment for the growing embryo.

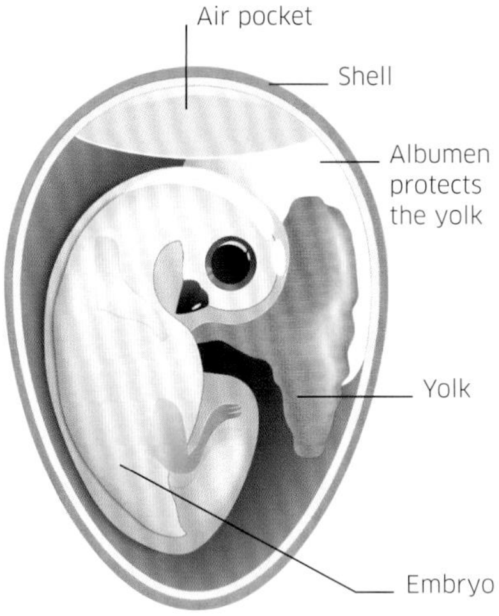

Slimy slug
Slug eggs are soft and jelly-like.

Emerging caterpillar
Butterfly eggs have a thin, brittle casing.

Breaking out
Crocodiles use a special tooth to break out of their leathery shells.

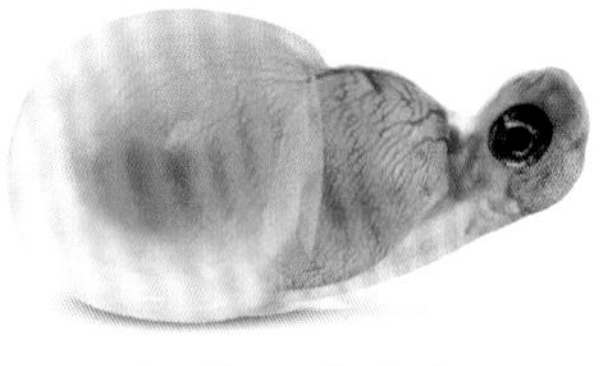

See-through shell
Fish eggs are soft and almost transparent.

WHEN MATES ARE SCARCE

Some snails, slugs, and worms are able to produce both eggs and sperm, so they can reproduce without a mate if none is available. Other animals can start life as one sex and change into the other as they mature.

Changing sex
The bluehead wrasse is an example of a fish that can change sex. Most are born female, but they will often change colour and become male later in life if there are not enough males for reproduction to take place.

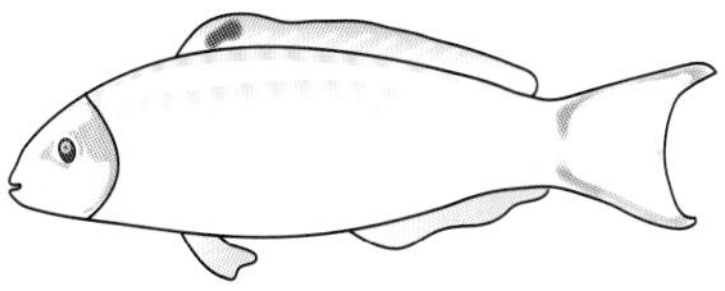

FEMALE BLUEHEAD WRASSE

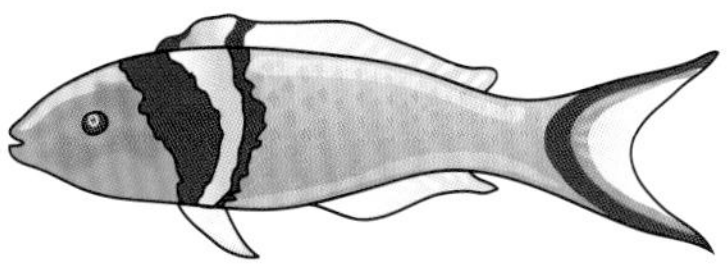

MALE BLUEHEAD WRASSE

GOING IT ALONE

Asexual reproduction is where one animal produces an offspring that is an exact copy of itself. Some animals are able to do this under certain circumstances, as a way of rapidly increasing their numbers, but most of these animals will reproduce sexually as well.

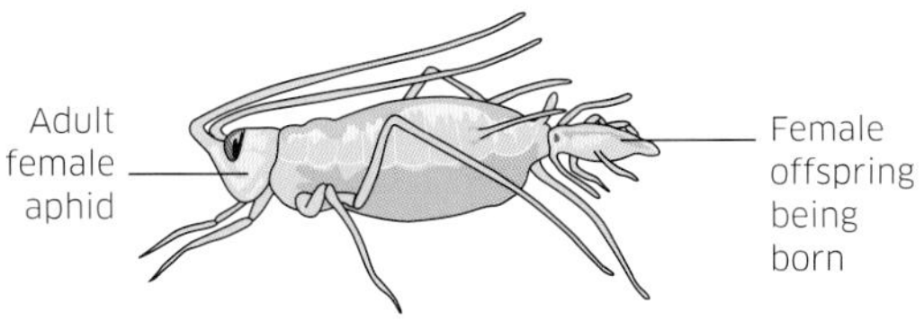

Mass cloning
Female green aphids are able to produce offspring without using sperm. A female can produce up to 40 generations of young – all female clones of herself – in one season.

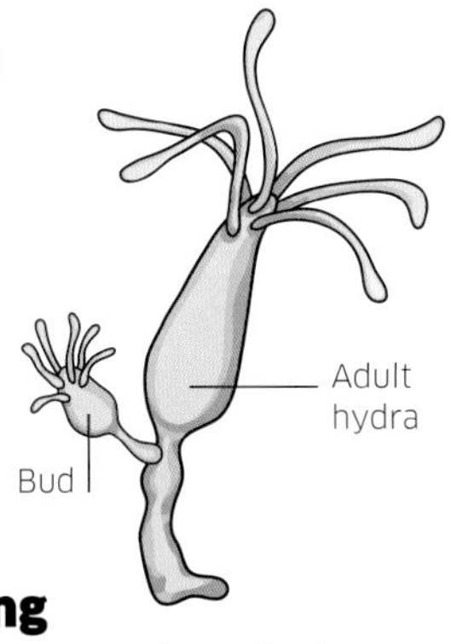

Budding
Some animals, such the hydra (a small water creature), can reproduce by growing buds on their body. The buds then break off to form a new, identical individual.

Parenting

For an animal species to survive, its members must successfully complete their life cycles, producing young that in their turn go on to reproduce. Different species have different approaches to the all-important task of raising the next generation. Many animals put a lot of time and energy into feeding and protecting their families when they are very young and teaching them life skills as they grow up. Others concentrate their energies on producing offspring in enormous numbers. When the job of breeding is over, such species do not provide parental care. They depend on a few of their many young surviving all perils to become adults and parents themselves.

BREEDING STRATEGIES

Animal species have various ways of keeping their numbers stable. Some produce huge, low-maintenance broods to guarantee one or two survivors. Others with single offspring make long-term efforts to keep their young safe into adulthood.

Strength in numbers
By laying thousands of eggs, a frog ensures that some of her young will survive, even though she does nothing to care for them. Most of the eggs, or the tadpoles that hatch, are eaten by predators, but maybe a tiny number of new frogs will develop.

One at a time
Koalas usually give birth to only one baby at a time, every year or two. Each infant will be carefully protected. With so few young animals coming along to replace the previous generation, koala populations grow slowly and are vulnerable to threats to survival.

CARE-PROVIDERS

Parenting duties can be very hard work. Birds are often tireless carers, burning up a lot of energy raising a brood. Both the parent birds may take on the task together. However, in most animal species the female alone is the caregiver. Many mothers stay with their young long enough to teach them survival skills. In just a few species – mostly fish – the fathers raise the offspring without assistance from a mate.

Sibling rivalry
These chicks must compete with each other to survive, begging their parent for food by squawking constantly. The parent will feed the loudest chick first, because its noises endanger the nest. It often happens that a weaker and quieter chick is ignored by the parent, and so dies from starvation.

Dedicated dad
This male jawfish stores its eggs in its mouth to keep them safe as they develop. After laying her eggs, the female leaves while the male is still fertilizing them. He remains the sole carer, unable to eat until the eggs hatch out.

Offering protection
Crocodiles lay their eggs high on riverbanks, inside nests dug into the ground. The mother guards the nest fiercely until the eggs hatch, then gently uses her massive jaws to help the baby crocs emerge and to carry them down to the water.

BABY-MINDERS

In some social groups, animals share the parenting of all the young, a phenomenon called allomothering. For example, a female silvered leaf monkey will carry and feed any baby in the group, regardless of whether or not she has children of her own. The young of this species have golden fur, so adults can see them easily.

POUCH-CARRIERS

Marsupial mammals, such as kangaroos and possums, carry their young in a pouch (marsupium) on the mother's belly. Babies, called joeys, are tiny and helpless at birth. They spend many weeks in the pouch, attached to the mother's nipple and drinking her milk, before they are strong enough to go outside.

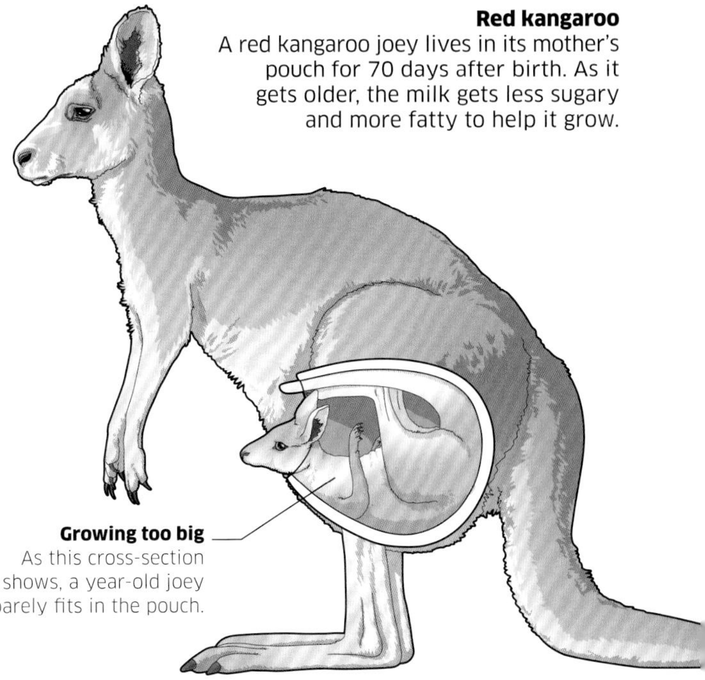

Red kangaroo
A red kangaroo joey lives in its mother's pouch for 70 days after birth. As it gets older, the milk gets less sugary and more fatty to help it grow.

Growing too big
As this cross-section shows, a year-old joey barely fits in the pouch.

Teaching lifeskills
These cheetah cubs are chasing a baby gazelle as their mother watches. When they are old enough, they will follow their mother on hunts and see how she stalks prey before chasing and killing it. The young cheetahs will practise this technique and by the time they are a year old, they will be able to catch their own food.

Habitats and ecosystems

A habitat is the environment in which an animal lives. Animals have adapted to survive in all kinds of habitats and everything about an animal – its anatomy, behaviour, and life cycle – is closely linked to its living conditions. In every habitat many different factors influence an animal's lifestyle. These factors include temperature, rainfall, and the amount of sunlight. The survival of one kind of animal is also affected by what other organisms are living in the habitat. Within habitats, living things interact with each other and their environment to form communities called ecosystems.

BIOMES

The study of habitats is called ecology. Ecologists divide the planet into different regions, called biomes, according to their climate (weather conditions and temperature). A biome's animals and plants are similar, but there are a great number of different ecosystems within each biome.

Polar regions
These are the coldest places on Earth – dark for much of the winter, and despite being so icy, there is very little rainfall. Conditions are so extreme that few animals can spend all year here.

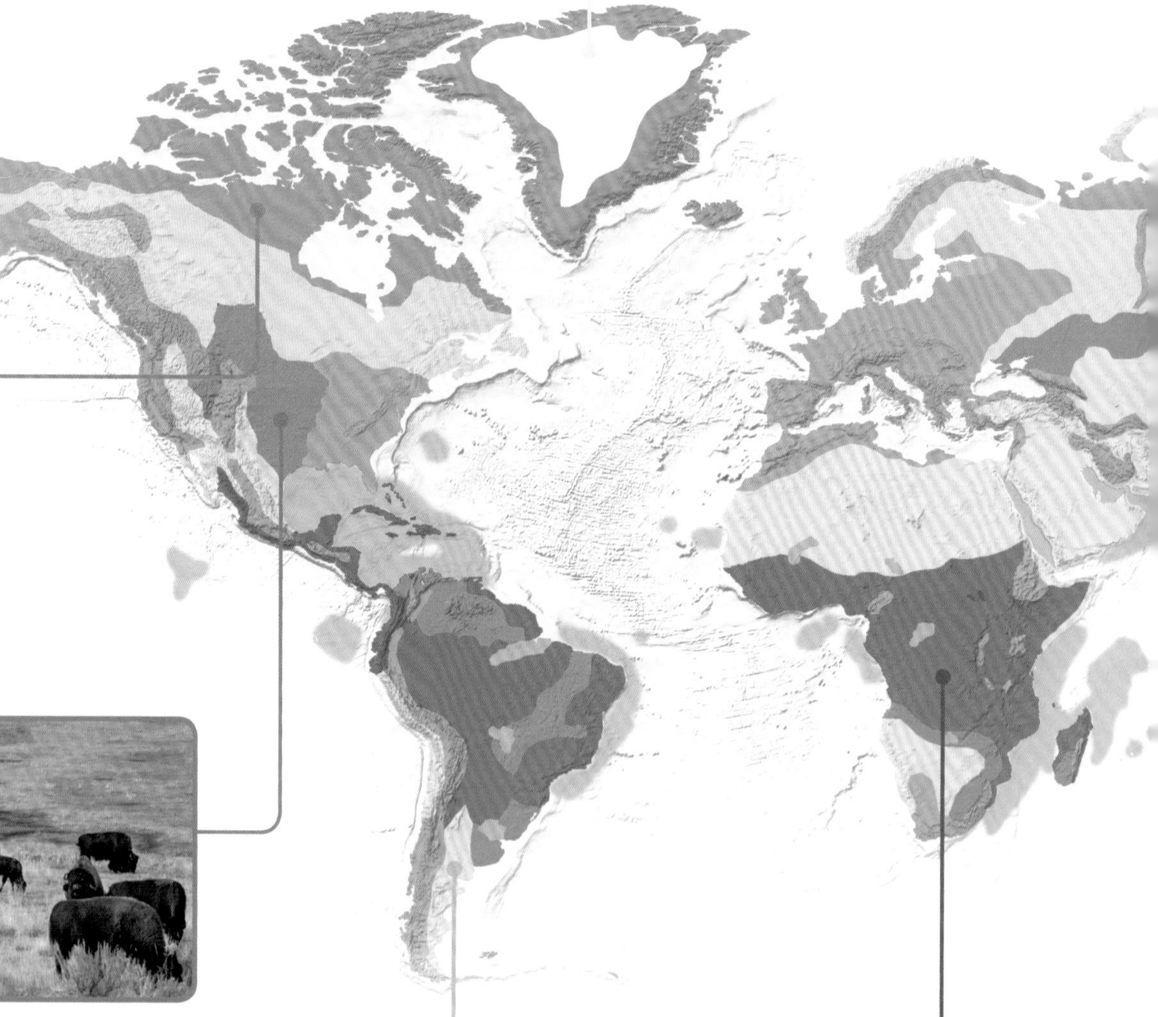

Tundra
In areas bordering the polar regions, the winter is long and the soil is frozen, so trees cannot grow. In the short summer, predators such as lynx arrive to prey on the many different animals who come to feed on the fast-growing plants that spring up.

Grassland
Fast-growing grasses fill the vast regions where the rainfall is too low for many trees to grow. Grasslands are home both to herds of large, grazing animals, and to small, burrowing mammals.

Desert
Land with less than 25 cm (10 in) of rainfall per year is desert. Very few plants grow here. A few animals, such as snakes, are adapted to the extreme temperatures and can survive long periods without eating or drinking.

Rainforest
Most rainforests are in tropical regions, where high rainfall and hot temperatures are perfect for plants to grow. Rainforests support more animal life than any other land habitat – including monkeys, snakes, birds, and insects.

Mountains
A mountain can include different habitats – the greater the height, the colder and harsher the conditions. Only the hardiest animals, such as goats and birds of prey, can live at very high altitudes.

HALF OF ALL KNOWN PLANT AND ANIMAL SPECIES LIVE IN RAINFORESTS.

Coniferous forest
These evergreen forests, also known as taiga, grow in regions with long, cold winters. The trees' strong, needle-like leaves allow snow to slide off. Bears, birds of prey, and wolves all live in the cold forests of the far north.

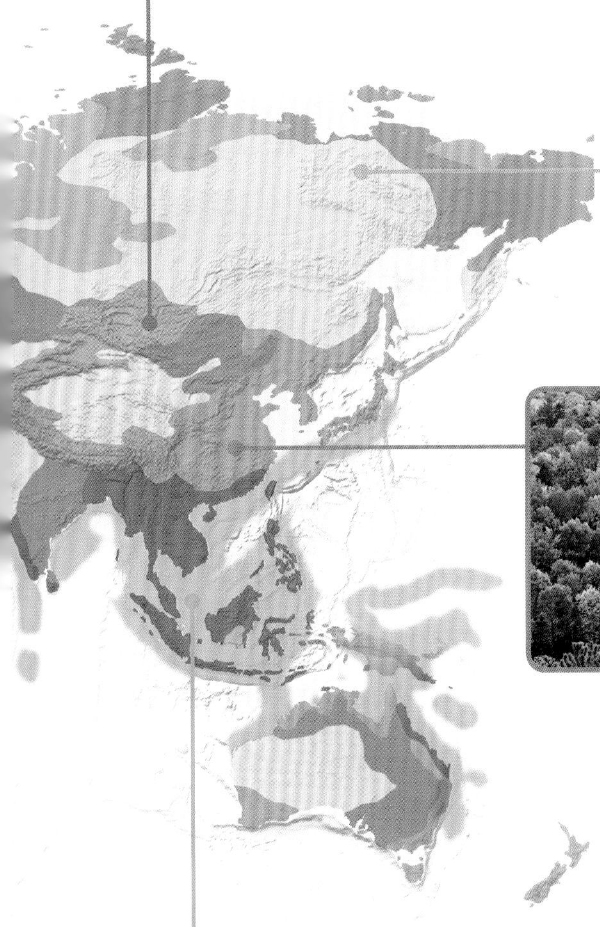

Temperate forest
These forests grow in areas where summers are warm, winters are cool, and there is rain all year round. Trees are deciduous, meaning that they save energy by dropping their leaves in winter. The trees provide a variety of berries, nuts, leaves, and seeds for animals such as squirrels, birds, and deer to feed on.

Coral reef
Shallow, sunlit seas in warm regions are often filled with colonies of simple animals called corals. These coral reefs are the richest habitats in the oceans, home to a dazzling variety of crustaceans, sharks, and other fish.

OCEANIC ZONES

The oceans cover 70 per cent of Earth's surface, but their depth – on average 3.7 km (2 1/4 miles) – means they make up more than 99 per cent of Earth's habitat. Conditions for life change with increasing depth, so the oceans contain different habitat zones.

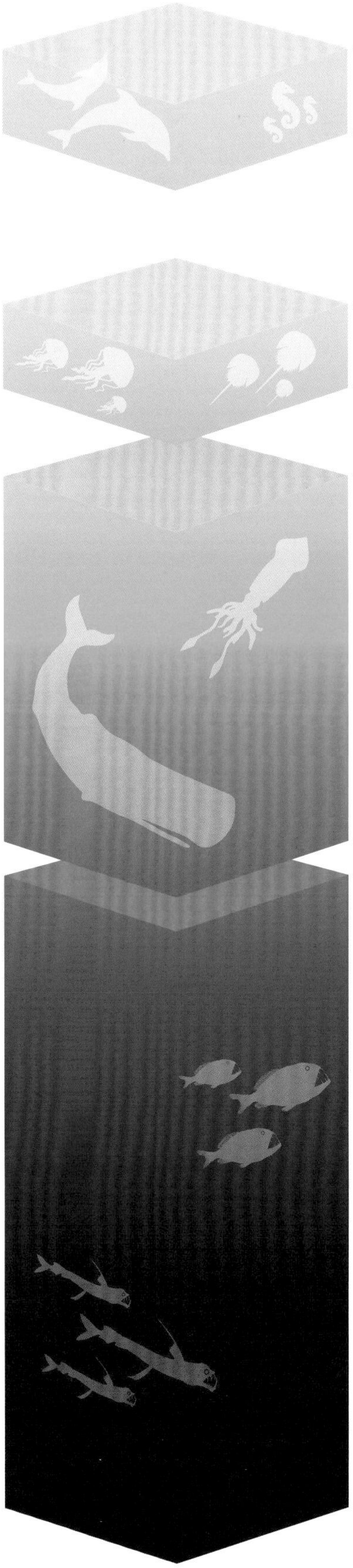

Sunlit zone
The first 200 m (656 ft) of the ocean are filled with sunlight during the day. This zone is by far the richest in marine life.

Twilight zone
Small amounts of light reach down as far as 1,000 m (3,280 ft), but not enough for algae to grow. Animals in this zone either eat dead organisms sinking from the sunlit zone or they migrate upwards to feed.

Dark zone
Below 1,000 m (3,280 ft), it is dark 24 hours a day. The only light is bioluminescence – a type of light produced by some animals or by the bacteria living inside them.

Abyssal zone
The area below 2,000 m (6,560 ft) is the largest ocean habitat. But it contains the fewest animals – those adapted to survive total darkness, crushing water pressure, scarce food, and near-freezing temperatures.

Food webs

All animals need food to give them energy to move around, grow, repair their bodies, and reproduce. Different animals have different diets: some eat plants, some eat other animals. The way living things are linked together according to what they eat is called a food chain, and interlinked food chains form networks called food webs. Energy passes from one organism to another in a food web. The original source is usually the sun, whose energy is harnessed by photosynthesizing plants.

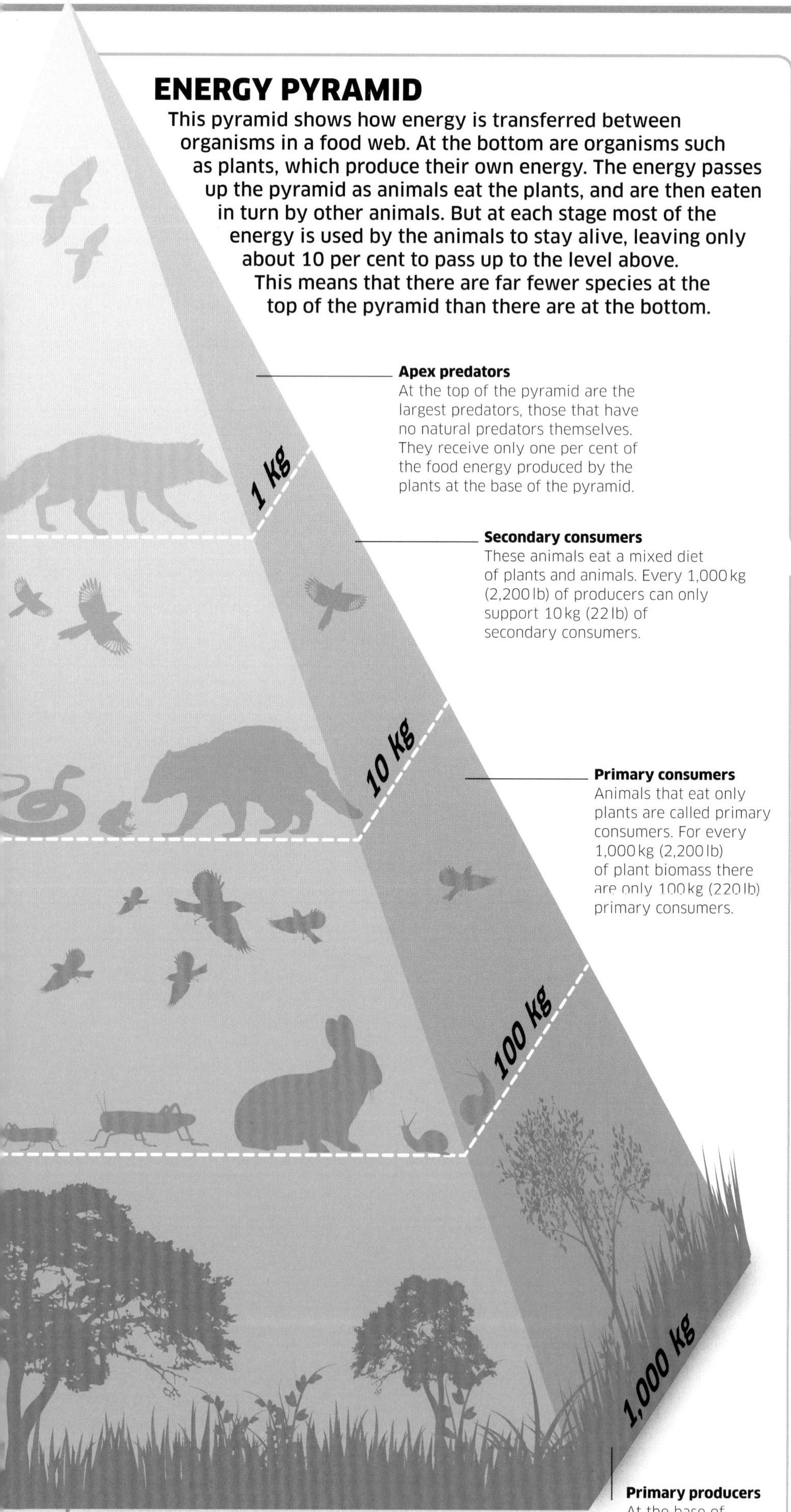

ENERGY PYRAMID

This pyramid shows how energy is transferred between organisms in a food web. At the bottom are organisms such as plants, which produce their own energy. The energy passes up the pyramid as animals eat the plants, and are then eaten in turn by other animals. But at each stage most of the energy is used by the animals to stay alive, leaving only about 10 per cent to pass up to the level above. This means that there are far fewer species at the top of the pyramid than there are at the bottom.

Apex predators
At the top of the pyramid are the largest predators, those that have no natural predators themselves. They receive only one per cent of the food energy produced by the plants at the base of the pyramid.

Secondary consumers
These animals eat a mixed diet of plants and animals. Every 1,000 kg (2,200 lb) of producers can only support 10 kg (22 lb) of secondary consumers.

Primary consumers
Animals that eat only plants are called primary consumers. For every 1,000 kg (2,200 lb) of plant biomass there are only 100 kg (220 lb) primary consumers.

Primary producers
At the base of the pyramid is 1,000 kg (2,200 lb) of plant biomass.

Biomass

This pyramid uses biomass – the total quantity of organisms in a given area – to show how energy passes up a food web. It gives the combined weight of the organisms, rather than counting the number of organisms themselves.

Producers and consumers

An animal can be defined by what it eats and where it fits within a food web. All animals are consumers, which means they are organisms that get energy by consuming food. Plants are producers; they do not eat (consume) but produce the energy they need from sunlight using the process of photosynthesis.

Carnivore
A meat-eating animal is called a carnivore. The carnivores tend to be concentrated at the top of the pyramid, where there is less energy to go around. The limited energy supply is one reason why wolves are much less common than rabbits.

Omnivore
Animals with a mixed diet of plant and animal foods are called omnivores. Omnivores are often the secondary consumers in a food pyramid – feeding on both the producers and on the primary consumers.

Herbivore
Primary consumers, such as rabbits, eat only plants. They are herbivores. They usually have easy access to plant food but need to eat a lot of it to get all the nutrients they need.

Plants
The primary producers at the bottom of many food pyramids are plants. Plants convert the energy in sunlight into sugars using photosynthesis. This sugar is the source of all the food energy that flows through the food web.

ARCTIC FOOD WEB

A food web shows what the animals in a particular habitat eat. Often webs are complex, with some animals eating more than one type of food. In this Arctic food web, the primary producers are plant-like organisms called phytoplankton, and the primary consumer, zooplankton, has the largest biomass.

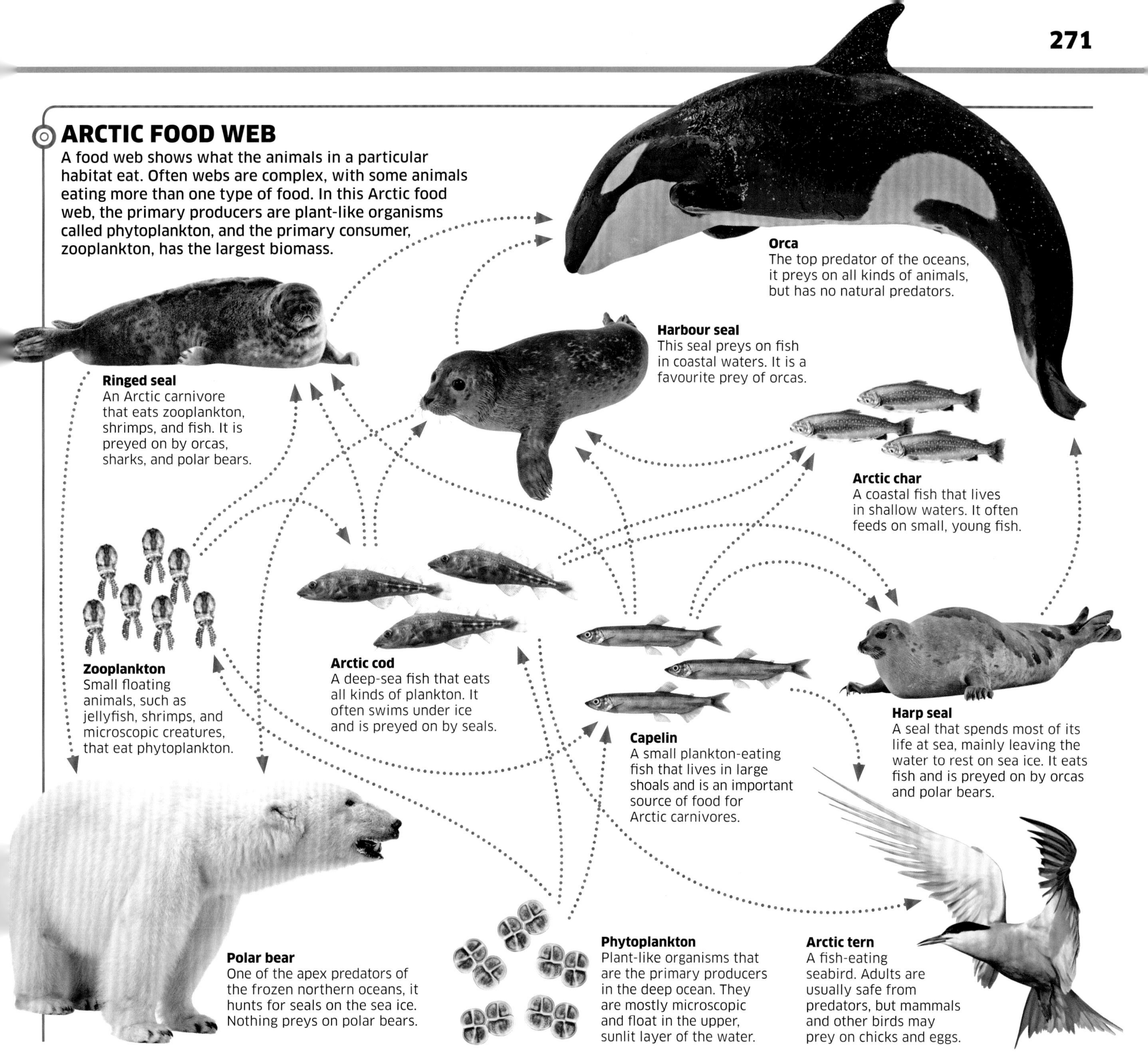

Orca
The top predator of the oceans, it preys on all kinds of animals, but has no natural predators.

Harbour seal
This seal preys on fish in coastal waters. It is a favourite prey of orcas.

Ringed seal
An Arctic carnivore that eats zooplankton, shrimps, and fish. It is preyed on by orcas, sharks, and polar bears.

Arctic char
A coastal fish that lives in shallow waters. It often feeds on small, young fish.

Zooplankton
Small floating animals, such as jellyfish, shrimps, and microscopic creatures, that eat phytoplankton.

Arctic cod
A deep-sea fish that eats all kinds of plankton. It often swims under ice and is preyed on by seals.

Capelin
A small plankton-eating fish that lives in large shoals and is an important source of food for Arctic carnivores.

Harp seal
A seal that spends most of its life at sea, mainly leaving the water to rest on sea ice. It eats fish and is preyed on by orcas and polar bears.

Polar bear
One of the apex predators of the frozen northern oceans, it hunts for seals on the sea ice. Nothing preys on polar bears.

Phytoplankton
Plant-like organisms that are the primary producers in the deep ocean. They are mostly microscopic and float in the upper, sunlit layer of the water.

Arctic tern
A fish-eating seabird. Adults are usually safe from predators, but mammals and other birds may prey on chicks and eggs.

DEEP-SEA FOOD WEB

In the deep sea, where there is no sunlight, the primary producers are not plant-like organisms, but bacteria. These bacteria live around hydrothermal vents – where undersea volcanoes heat the water – and extract nutrients from the water. Zooplankton consume these bacteria, and are in turn fed on by larger animals living around the vent.

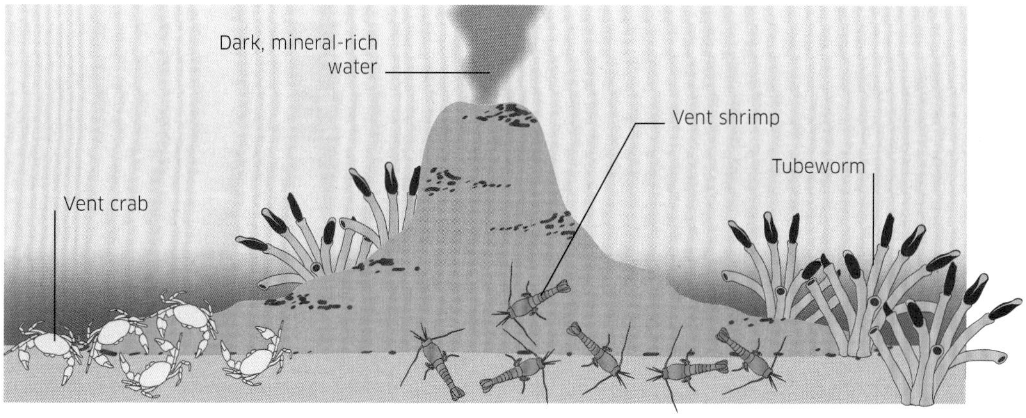

Black smoker
A hydrothermal vent that gushes out dark, mineral-rich water is called a black smoker. The bacteria that live around black smokers get their energy from this water, and not from sunlight as other primary producers do.

Attack and defence

A predator hunts and attacks other creatures – its prey – in order to eat. To get the better of their prey, predators usually have keen senses, quick reactions, strong and agile bodies, and hunting weapons such as sharp teeth or beaks and long claws. Some predators use their superior speed to catch their prey. Others lurk hidden among leaves or in long grass – perhaps disguised by camouflage – before ambushing their victims. But prey animals have evolved defences that help them survive. This may be the ability to run away fast or to fight back hard.

WELL ARMED

Animals have evolved a wide range of weapons to take down and dismember prey, from the crushing claws of a lobster to a bird of prey's sharp, hooked beak. Many animals have weapons they use to defend themselves, such as an elephant's tusks or a buffalo's huge horns. The bristly hairs of some caterpillars attach themselves to a predator and cause irritation, while bombardier beetles can squirt toxic chemicals to fend off attackers.

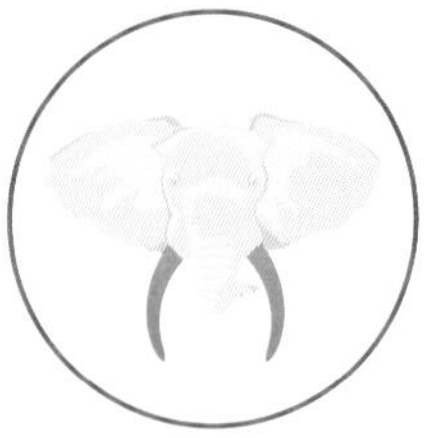

TUSKS

HORNS

ON THE ATTACK

Many animals hunt alone, using their superior speed to catch prey, or hiding, perfectly still, ready to ambush unsuspecting prey. Other predators build traps or use trickery to catch their victims. Animals of some species work as a team, pitting their wits against larger or more difficult prey than they could manage by themselves.

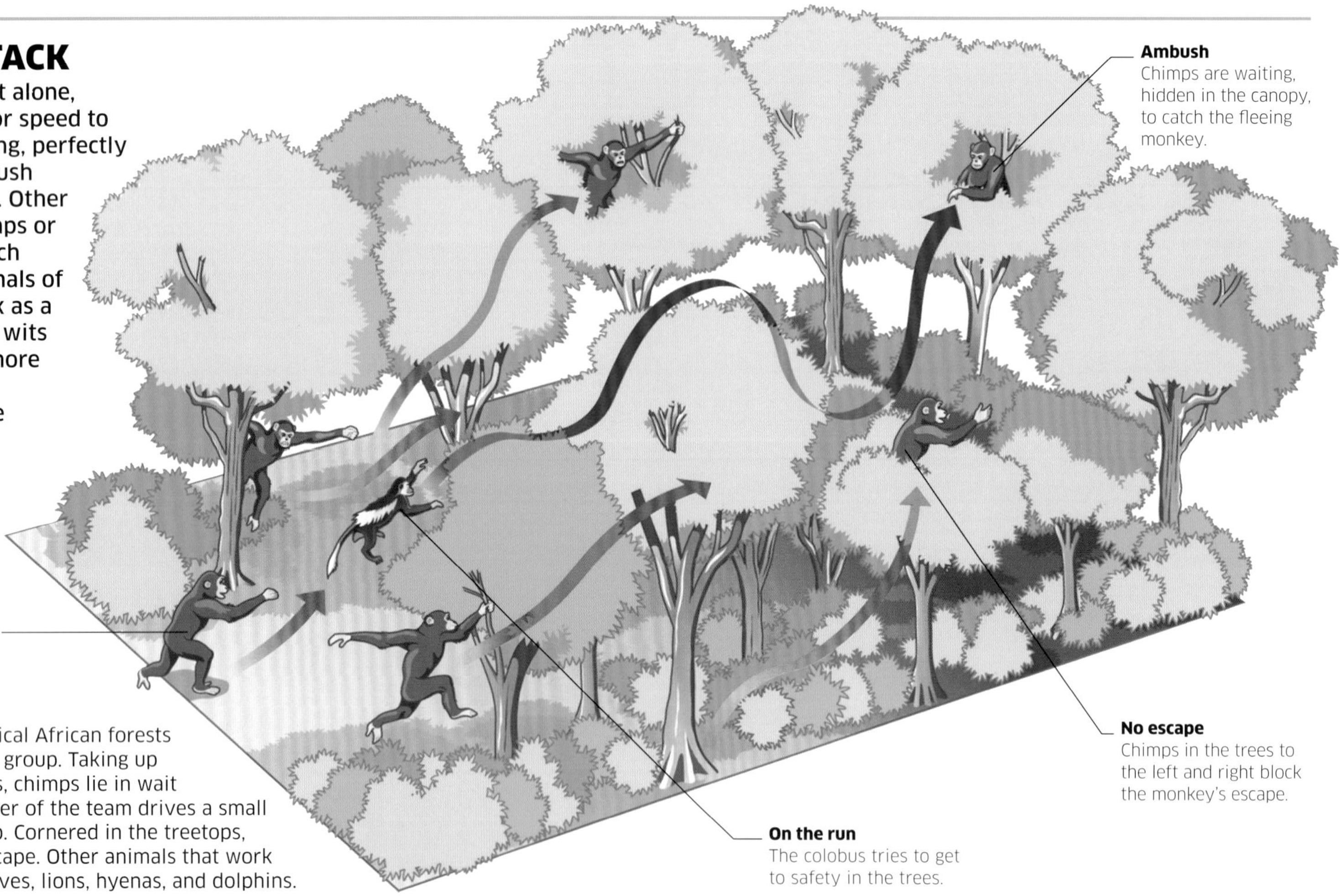

Group attack

Chimpanzees in tropical African forests sometimes hunt as a group. Taking up positions in the trees, chimps lie in wait while another member of the team drives a small monkey into the trap. Cornered in the treetops, the monkey can't escape. Other animals that work together include wolves, lions, hyenas, and dolphins.

Fast reactions
A chameleon sits in wait, then quickly shoots out its sticky tongue to catch a passing insect.

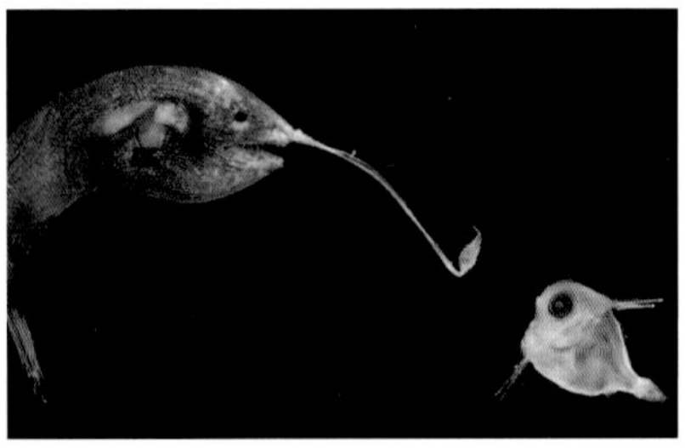

Tempting trick
The anglerfish has a luminous lure to attract smaller fish. When the fish gets close enough the anglerfish grabs it.

Caught in a trap
A spider's sticky web traps a passing insect. The spider then spins more silk around its victim to ensnare it totally.

Stealth and speed
A leopard slinks, unseen, until it is almost in reach of its prey. Then, with a lightning dash, it pounces to kill.

PINCERS

CLAWS

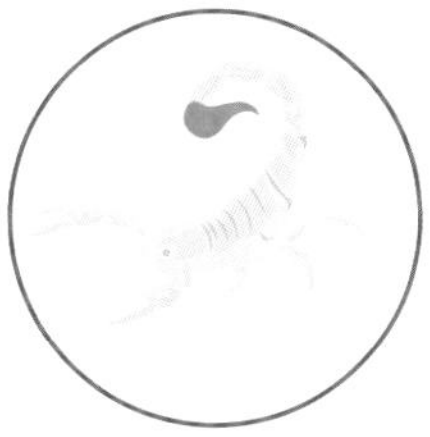

STINGER

BILL

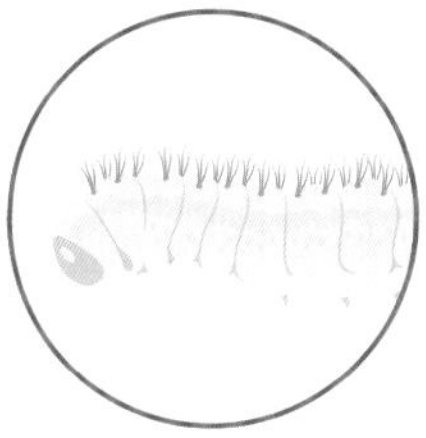

BRISTLY HAIRS

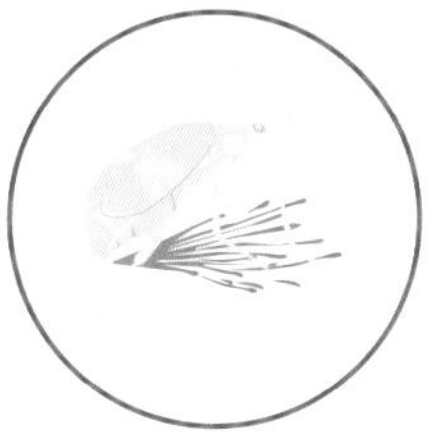

TOXIC SPRAY

CHEMICAL WEAPONS

Many animals use chemical weapons for attack or defence. Scorpions and wasps have venomous stings, and some spiders and snakes have venomous bites. These may be used to paralyze prey, allowing a predator to kill and eat the victim. Animals can also use venom to defend themselves, though they may give a warning first. A rattlesnake, shown here, shakes its tail, for example, because its supply of venom is limited and it will avoid using it unless it has to.

SELF DEFENCE

When animals come under attack from predators they have various means of defending themselves. Those with horns, antlers, tusks, or venom will fight back. But there are lots of other methods. Some animals blend with their surroundings or seek safety in a group; others deliberately stand out from the crowd.

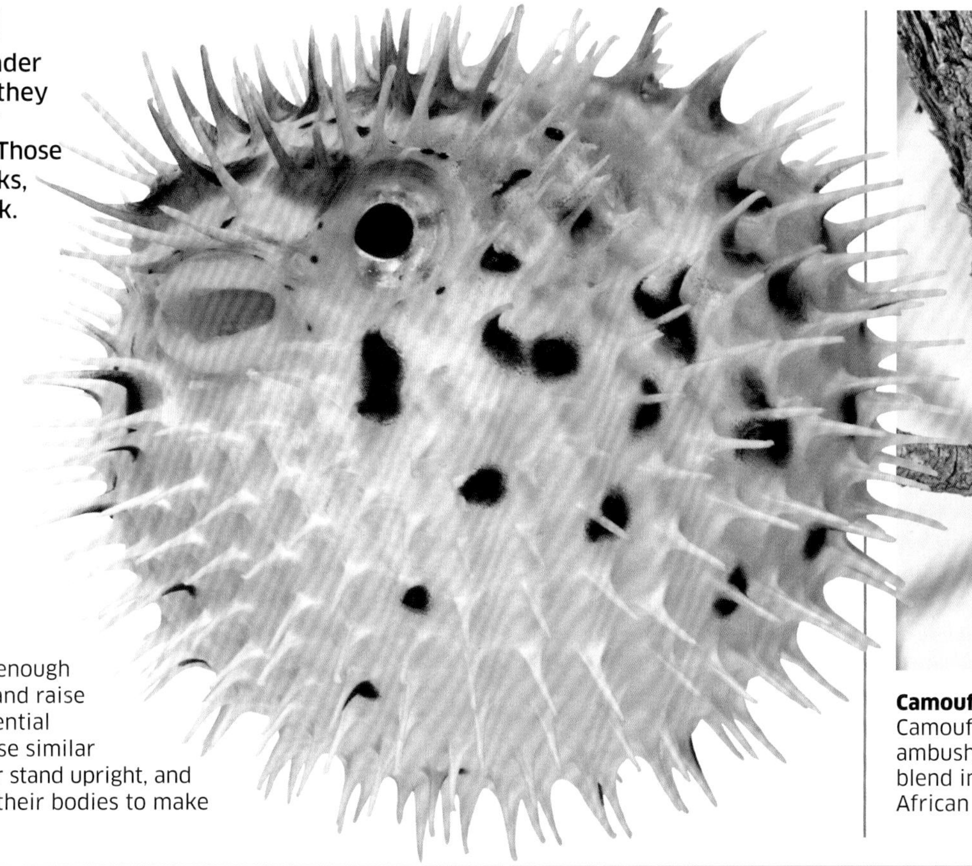

All puffed up

A pufferfish can swallow enough water to increase in size and raise its spines to put off a potential predator. Other animals use similar tactics. Cats make their fur stand upright, and toads and lizards puff up their bodies to make themselves look bigger.

Camouflage
Camouflage is used both by hiding prey and ambushing predators. An animal whose colours blend in with its surroundings – such as this African scops owl – is less likely to be seen.

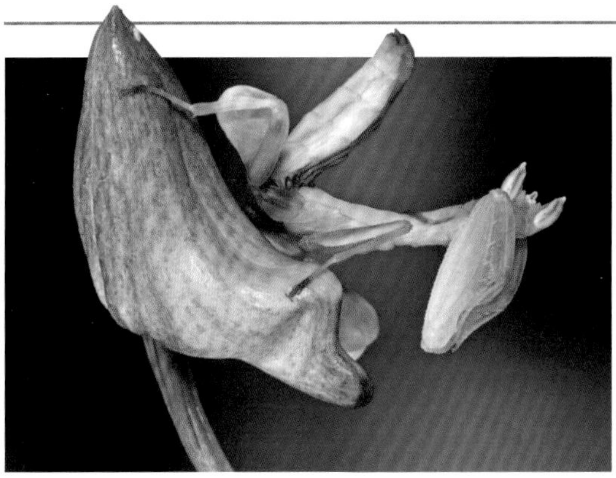

Mimicry
A Malaysian orchid mantis is very well concealed on this orchid. Its shape and colour mimic those of the flower to camouflage it from passing prey.

Warning and poison
Some tree frogs have foul-tasting or poisonous flesh. They advertise this with bright colours that predators recognize as a warning to stay away.

Sticking together
There are lots of pairs of eyes and ears in this wildebeest herd to sense danger. Staying in a tight group, the animals are less likely to be attacked.

Living together

Animals often live in groups or close to other animals of the same species. Some animal groups are social, with members cooperating with each other to survive. Other groups are much looser: members do not work together but gain from living near to each other. Some animals live closely alongside others of a different species, in symbiotic relationships that may be beneficial or neutral. But a relationship can also be harmful, when one animal lives as a parasite on another.

ANIMAL GROUPS

Large animal groupings are most common in habitats such as oceans and grasslands, where food is evenly or widely distributed. In other habitats animals may prefer to hunt alone. Animals often form large groups for migration, for greater efficiency, or for safety.

School
A school of fish provides safety. With every fish moving in exactly the same direction, the school looks like one large animal.

Skein
Some migratory birds move in V-shaped formations or "skeins" to reduce the drag forces from headwinds during long flights.

Solitary animal
Forest animals often live alone because the trees that they feed on may be widely spread, and the food source limited.

TEAM WORK

Ant, wasp, termite, and honeybee colonies are the most organized animal groups of all. They use a system called eusociality, where every member works to help one female (or male and female pair) to reproduce. The majority of the group, the workers, give up their own chance to reproduce in order to help the queen produce young.

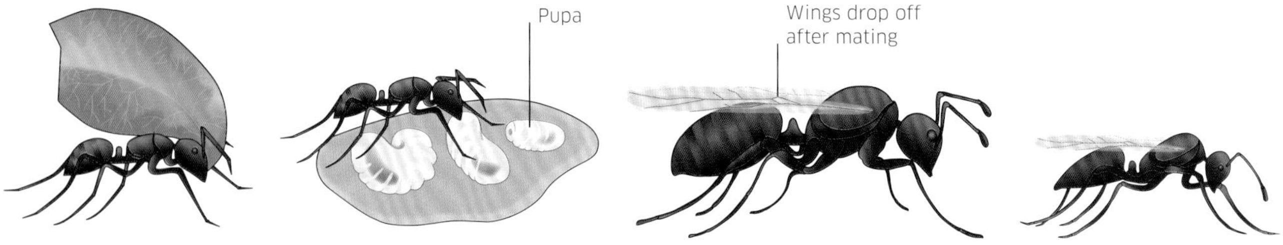

Forager
An older worker collects leaves to grow fungi to feed the colony.

Worker
A smaller worker tends to the young in the nest.

Queen
The queen is the mother of all workers in the colony.

Male
Winged males mate with young queens but do not join the colony.

TYPES OF ROLES IN A LEAFCUTTER ANT COLONY

SOCIAL GROUPS

Truly social groupings involve members cooperating with each other to find food, raise young, and defend themselves. Mammals are the most social animals: lions form groups called prides, whales live in pods, a chimpanzee group is a troop, and wild dogs live in a pack. It is common for many members of these groups to be related. Individuals will help other group members to make sure their offspring thrive.

Elephant family
Social groups often have a hierarchy, with some members more dominant than others. Elephants live in family groups led by an older female. Male elephants leave the family when they reach adulthood, then they live mostly alone.

SYMBIOSIS

When animals live closely alongside those of another species, it is called symbiosis, which means "living together". Sometimes both animal partners gain from this relationship, but in other cases only one side gets a benefit.

CLEANER WRASSES MAINTAIN **"CLEANER STATIONS"** WHERE OTHER REEF FISH **COME FOR GROOMING.**

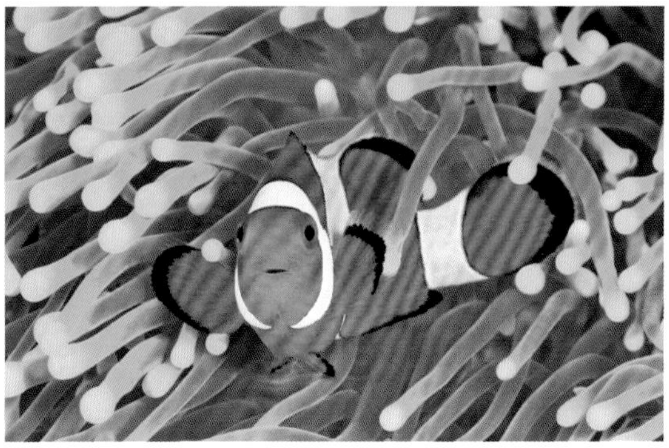

Anemone and clownfish
Clownfish live among the stinging tentacles of an anemone. The stings keep the fish's predators away and in return, the fish cleans dirt and parasites from the anemone's tentacles.

Impala and oxpecker
The oxpecker is a small bird that feeds on the ticks and lice hosted by impala. The impala tolerates the oxpecker because it keeps its fur and skin clean, but the bird may also open wounds to lap up the blood.

Cleaner wrasse
The small blue-and-yellow cleaner wrasse lives in a coral reef. It receives regular visits from larger, often predatory, fish, which allow it to nibble away irritating dead skin and parasites.

PARASITES

Another type of symbiosis is parasitism. Parasitic animals have a one-sided relationship with their hosts, where only the parasite gains, while the host is weakened, or occasionally killed. Parasitoids lay their eggs in or on a host animal, who will become a food source for their young.

Endoparasite
A tapeworm is an endoparasite, meaning it lives inside its host's body. It hooks itself to the lining of the intestines and absorbs the host's supply of digested food straight through its skin.

Ectoparasite
A hard tick is an ectoparasite, meaning it lives on the outside of the host. The tiny tick sucks its host's blood before falling off to digest its meal. Its bites can transmit diseases.

Parasitoid
This caterpillar is covered in the eggs of a parasitoid wasp. When the eggs hatch, the wasp larvae will eat their way into the caterpillar. Such wasps use a specific host species as a source of food during their larval stage, killing it in the process.

BROOD PARASITE

Some parasites exploit a host species to raise their young for them. This is called brood parasitism. The host invests time and energy in raising young that are not its own, and may lose its real young in the process. The most famous brood parasite is the common cuckoo.

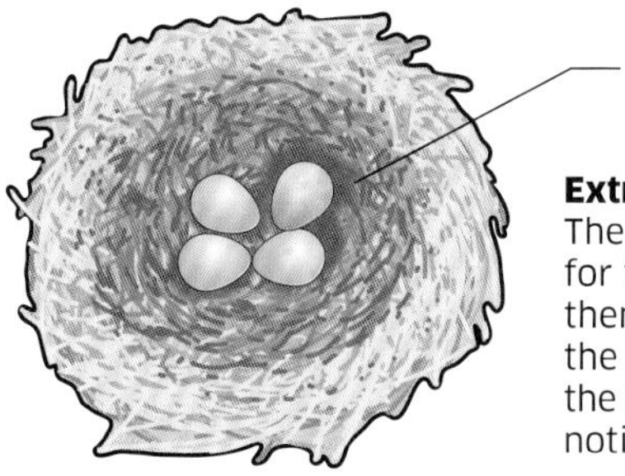

Extra egg
The female cuckoo waits for the host to lay eggs, and then lays one of her own when the nest is unattended. When the host returns she does not notice the extra egg.

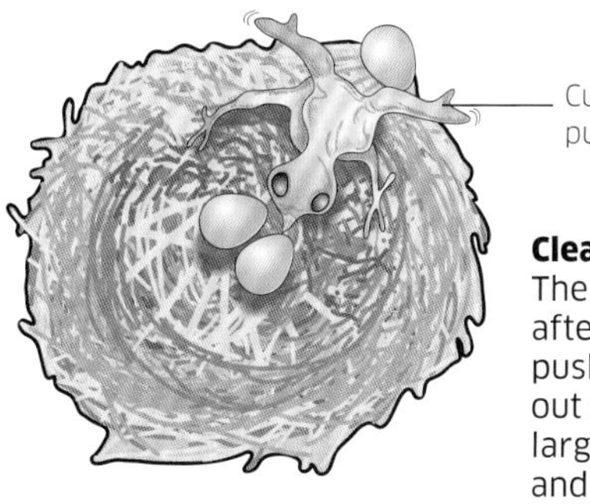

Clear out
The cuckoo chick hatches after about 12 days. It will push any unhatched eggs out of the nest. It is always larger than the host chicks and will steal their food.

Cuckoo in the nest
The cuckoo chick copies the begging call of the host chicks, and is fed more often than they are. They soon die of starvation.

Migration

A migration is a journey made by an animal on a regular basis to and from different areas. It is usually undertaken every year, though it may be made every day, and usually follows the same route. Most animals set off in large groups and travel together. Migrations can be hazardous journeys over land or sea, crossing mountain ranges, predator-filled rivers, or deserts where food is scarce. Some species may stop off to rest or to breed along the way. This can mean that some of the animals that start out do not complete the journey, and it is their offspring who go on to reach the destination.

WHY ANIMALS MIGRATE

Although migration can involve many dangers, the benefits outweigh the risks. These include a more plentiful food supply, better breeding conditions, and less extreme weather conditions.

For food
A migration route will always lead to a location where there is a plentiful food supply. The trigger may be an abundance of food in one area, or a lack in another.

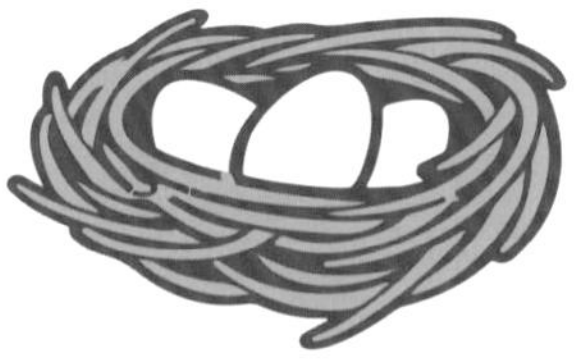

Reproduction
Solitary animals often migrate each year to a mass breeding area, which is suitable for raising young and where they can find a mate.

MIGRATION ROUTES

In general, migratory animals follow the same route each year. Many have learned it by following their parents on their first migration, though animals such as the salmon and the monarch butterfly make the journey only once in their lives. This map and the accompanying photographs show some major migration routes and the animals that follow them.

Caribou
These large deer, also called reindeer, spend the summer in herds on the cold, treeless plains of North America. As winter approaches the herds fragment, and the deer head south into the forests where they shelter from the extreme winter weather. They migrate north again to breed.

Monarch butterfly
From their summer breeding grounds in North America and southern Canada, a mass migration of monarch butterflies travels south in autumn to spend winter in California and Mexico. Winds carry them along the 4,800-km (3,000-mile) journey at speeds of up to 130 km/h (80 mph).

Humpback whale
These whales spend the summer feeding in polar waters. In winter, they head to warmer breeding grounds in tropical waters where they give birth to calves and find a new mate. Then the whales, along with their calves, swim back to the poles to fatten up.

Climatic conditions
Migrations are often connected to the seasons. A change in the weather from poor to good, or from wet to dry, may trigger animal journeys.

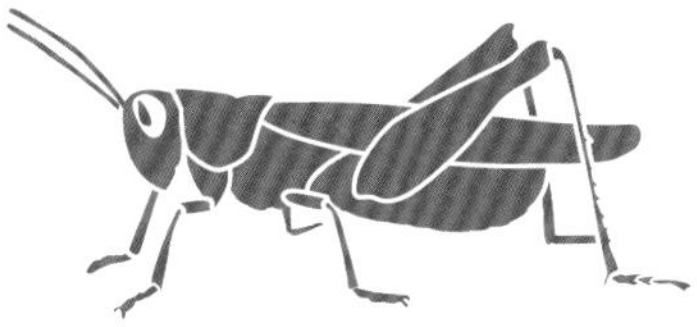

Overcrowding
Animals such as locusts migrate from overcrowded food sources. Their swarming behaviour is stimulated by bodily contact as they crush against each other.

MASS MOVEMENTS

Following a cool summer, seeds and berries can be scarce by winter. Feeding areas become overcrowded, triggering birds, such as these waxwings, to fly much further south than usual to find food. This is called an irruption and may mean that the birds travel as far as 1,500 km (930 miles) outside their normal range. The swarming of locusts is another example of irruption.

Atlantic salmon
Salmon make a single lifelong migration. They hatch in rivers and spend a year or two there before heading out to sea, where they grow to full adult size. The fish then return to the same river, swim upstream to the breeding ground, mate, lay eggs, and then die.

Arctic tern
This seabird makes the longest migration of any animal, moving from the Arctic to the Antarctic and back again each year. It breeds in the Arctic summer and then heads to the Antarctic to feed during the summer there. The round trip is about 75,000 km (46,600 miles).

White-bearded wildebeest
Every year 1.5 million wildebeest migrate through the Serengeti grasslands of East Africa. Wildebeest are adapted to feed on short grass, and need plenty of water, so the herds follow the rains, which cause fresh grass to grow in different areas of the grasslands throughout the year.

Barn swallow
Swallows are a common sight in Europe, North America, and Asia in early summer as they migrate from wintering grounds in Africa and South America to spend the warmer season in the northern hemisphere. They make nests and breed before flying south again in autumn.

VERTICAL MIGRATION

Many marine organisms make a migration every 24 hours, travelling from the surface to the depths of the oceans. During the day, the surface waters are brightly lit, and animals such as jellyfish swim to the darker depths to avoid predators. As night falls, these animals move up to the now-dark surface to feed – but dive down again at dawn.

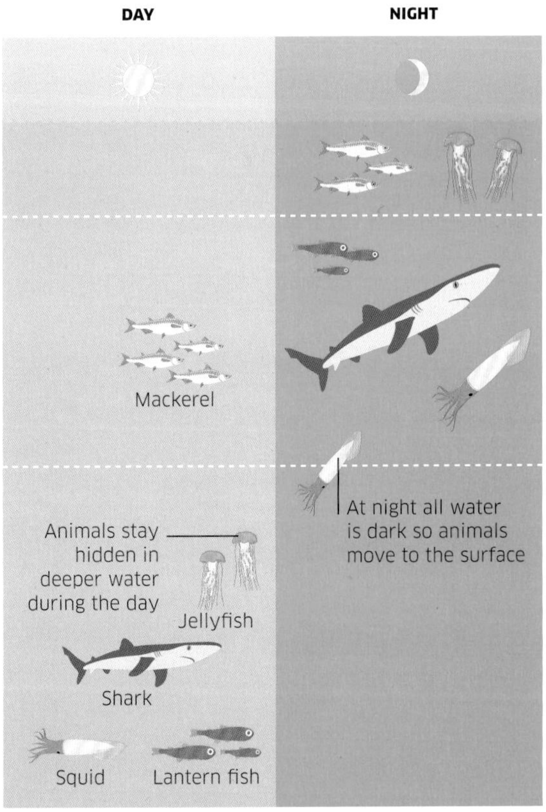

DAILY MIGRATION IN THE OCEANS

KRILL MIGRATE TO DEPTHS OF MORE THAN **900 M (3,000 FT) DAILY** TO ESCAPE BEING EATEN.

Animals in danger

It is natural for animals in the wild to kill or be killed, or be affected by natural disasters, such as earthquakes or forest fires. But animals today are facing a new and urgent threat – from humans. As natural habitats disappear to make room for expanding towns and cities, or are polluted by chemicals and rubbish, thousands of animal species are disappearing every year.

UNDER THREAT

Many animals are in urgent danger – every year, up to 30,000 species are at risk of extinction. The IUCN (International Union for Conservation of Nature) publishes an annual "Red List" of animals that are vulnerable or in danger of extinction, but many species, particularly amphibians and reptiles, have not yet been evaluated.

Key

Approximate percentage of species evaluated by the IUCN that have been classified as "threatened".

FISH
19% of evaluated species

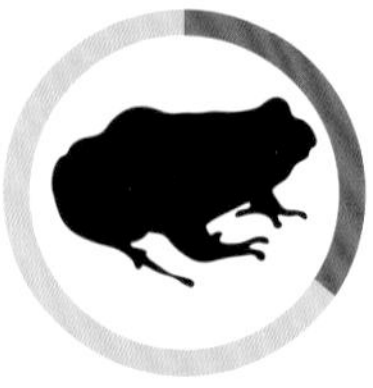

AMPHIBIANS
37% of evaluated species

REPTILES
27% of evaluated species

BIRDS
23% of evaluated species

MAMMALS
28% of evaluated species

DIFFERENT THREATS

The biggest problem for many species is the loss of their habitat. If animals can no longer find territory that provides shelter, enough food, and the possibility of finding a mate, they will soon die out.

VERTEBRATE ANIMALS ARE BECOMING EXTINCT AT THE FASTEST RATE FOR 65 MILLION YEARS.

Pollution
The planet's land, waterways, and air can be contaminated in many different ways: for instance, by industrial and farming chemicals, by sewage and other waste, or by gases emitted by cars and vehicles. Oil spills, which occur either in tanker accidents or when oil tanks are cleaned at sea, kill birds and marine life (right), and can damage coastal habitats for decades.

Deforestation
When forests are felled for fuel, or to make room for farms, cities, or roads, many animals lose their homes. This disrupts the complex food web, which threatens all animals in the degraded area.

Changing climate
Earth's climate is getting hotter, a process speeded up by factors such as air pollution and deforestation. As polar icecaps melt, sea levels rise, and deserts spread, habitats are disappearing fast.

Alien invaders
Animals, such as the grey squirrel (above), that humans introduce to habitats where they do not belong can be harmful to native species – preying on them or competing for food or nest sites.

HOPE FOR THE FUTURE

Protecting wildlife is crucial for the future of the planet. Good biodiversity (the range of animals and plants in a habitat) not only benefits threatened animals, but also humans. We rely on healthy ecosystems to provide us with essentials, such as food, water, shelter, and medicines. To maintain Earth's biodiversity, we urgently need to find ways to protect threatened species and their habitats.

Captive breeding
Animals facing extinction are sometimes taken from the wild to be bred in captivity. Their offspring are released back into the wild. A worldwide programme involving captive breeding has successfully increased the population of golden lion tamarin (above), giving the species a greater chance of survival.

Protected areas
National parks and nature reserves are areas set aside for animals to live in naturally, protected from human interference. The Ngorongoro Crater Conservation Area in Tanzania (above) is home to around 25,000 large animals.

Fighting poaching
Some animals are at risk from illegal hunting because their skins and body parts are used for clothes, jewellery, or to make medicine. In Kenya (above), tonnes of elephant tusks are seized and destroyed every year, in an effort to deter the criminals who poach and trade in ivory.

KEEPING TRACK

In order to help conserve animal populations, we need to learn more about how they live. Animals, such as this elephant seal, can be fitted with transmitters or cameras to track their movements as they feed, breed, or migrate. Knowing about animals' habits and behaviour helps conservationists to make decisions about how best to help protect them.

GONE FOREVER

The animal kingdom is constantly changing, with new species emerging and other ones dying out, but extinctions caused by humans are more and more common. We have wiped out hundreds of species in the past two centuries, from the dodo, a flightless bird from the island of Mauritius, to the Atlas bear, Africa's only native bear.

Thylacine
The thylacine, or Tasmanian wolf, was a marsupial that lived on the Australian island of Tasmania. It was hunted by farmers because they believed it attacked sheep, and it also suffered from competition with wild dogs. The last known thylacine (left) died in a Tasmanian zoo in 1936.

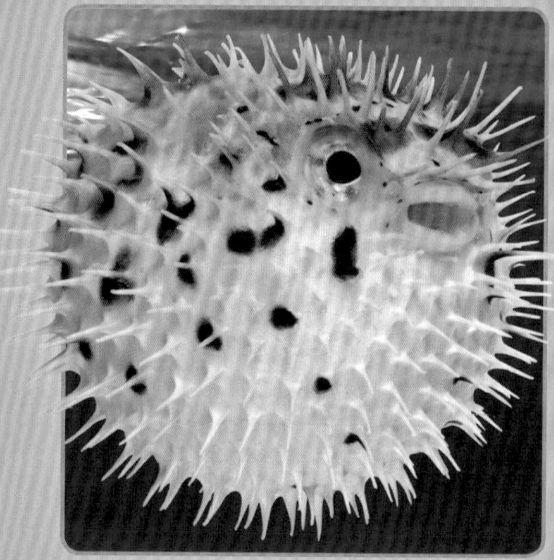

GLOSSARY AND INDEX

Glossary

ABDOMEN
In vertebrates, such as mammals, the part of the body containing the digestive and reproductive organs; in arthropods, the rear part of the body.

ALGAE
Plant-like organisms that can make food using energy from the sun.

AMPHIBIAN
A vertebrate that usually lives in water when young, turning into an air-breathing adult that can live on land. Many return to the water to breed.

ANAL
Near or associated with the animal's anus, as in the anal fin of a fish.

ANTENNAE
A pair of sense organs that detect movement and chemicals in the air.

AQUATIC
Describes organisms that live in water.

ARACHNID
One of a group of invertebrates that includes spiders and scorpions.

ARTHROPOD
An invertebrate animal with an external skeleton and jointed legs.

BACTERIA
Microscopic organisms with a simple, single-celled form.

BILATERAL SYMMETRY
A body that can be divided into two parts that mirror each other has bilateral symmetry.

BINOCULAR VISION
Seeing the same thing with two eyes at the same time. It enables animals to see in 3D and judge distance.

BIVALVE
A mollusc such as a clam, with two half-shells joined by a hinge.

BUOYANCY
The ability to float.

CAMOUFLAGE
Colours and patterns that make an animal hard to see.

CANINE TEETH
In meat-eating mammals, long, pointed teeth, used for seizing prey.

CANNIBAL
An animal that eats its own kind.

CARAPACE
Bony plates forming the upper part of animals such as crustaceans.

CARBOHYDRATE
An energy-rich, sugary substance, made from carbon dioxide and water.

CARBON DIOXIDE
A gas that forms a small part of the atmosphere. Some living things, such as plants, can use it to make food.

CARCASS
The body of a dead animal.

CARNASSIAL TEETH
Specialized cheek teeth of carnivorous mammals, used for slicing meat.

CARNIVORE
A meat-eating animal, or any member of the order Carnivora, such as a cat.

CARTILAGINOUS
Made of the tough, flexible material called cartilage.

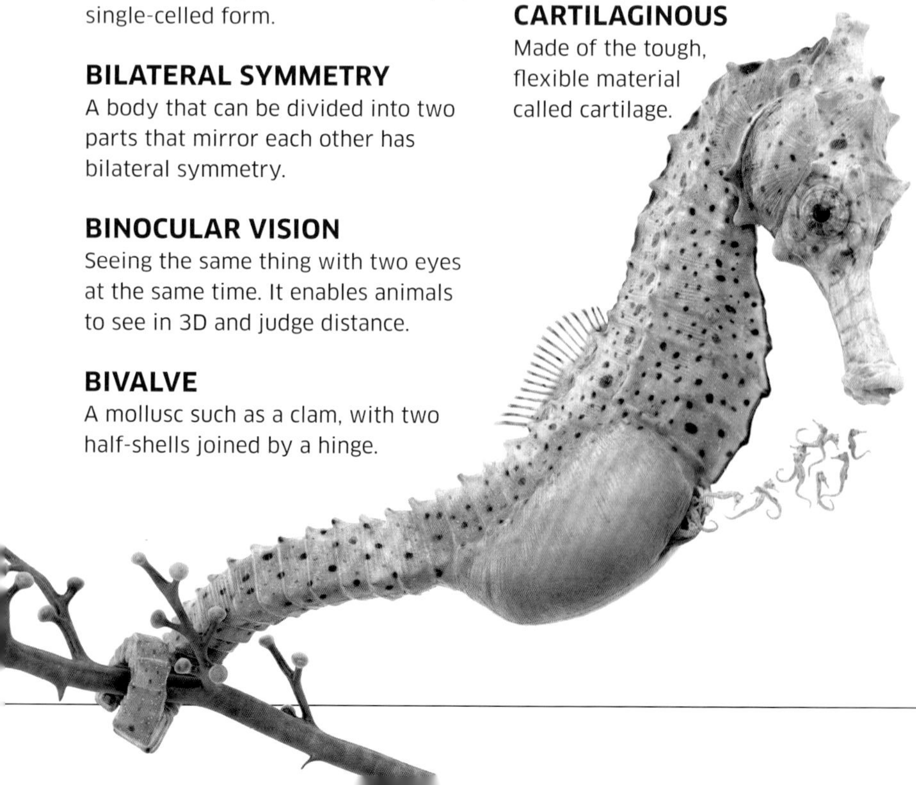

CAUDAL
Near or related to an animal's tail, as in the caudal fin of a fish.

CELL
The smallest unit of life. It can exist as a single cell, or form part of a more complex organism.

CEPHALOPOD
One of a group of molluscs that includes octopuses and squid.

CETACEAN
A whale, dolphin, or porpoise.

CHORDATE
A large phylum (group) of animals that includes all vertebrates.

CNIDARIAN
A phylum of animals that includes jellyfish, corals, and sea anemones.

COLONY
A group of animals or other organisms that live together.

COMPOUND EYES
In insects and crustaceans, eyes made up of hundreds of elements, each with its own tiny lens.

CRUSTACEAN
An animal with a hard external skeleton and paired, jointed legs, such as a crab or shrimp.

DNA
The abbreviation for deoxyribonucleic acid, a material found in the cells of animals and plants that carries instructions for how a living thing will look and function.

DORSAL
Describes something near or related to an animal's back, such as a fin.

ECHINODERM
One of a phylum that includes spiny-skinned marine animals such as starfish and sea urchins.

ECHOLOCATION
A way of locating objects in air or water by transmitting sound pulses and detecting the echoes.

EVOLUTION
The process of change over time, brought about by natural selection.

EXOSKELETON
The tough external skeleton of an animal such as an insect.

EXTINCT
Having died out completely.

FANG
Sharp, hollow, tooth-like structure that injects venom.

FERTILIZATION
The joining of male and female cells so they develop into seeds or a new organism.

FLUORESCENT
Describes something that absorbs energy and turns it into light, so it glows.

GASTROPOD
A type of mollusc that crawls on its belly, such as a snail.

GILLS
Organs used for breathing underwater.

HABITAT
A place where wildlife lives.

HERBIVORE
An animal that feeds on plants.

HYDRAULIC
Powered by liquid pressure.

IMMATURE
Not yet adult or able to breed.

IMMUNE
Unaffected by something dangerous, such as venom or a disease.

INCISOR
A chisel-shaped biting tooth at the front of a mammal's mouth.

INCUBATE
To keep eggs warm so they can develop and hatch.

INSECT
An arthropod with six legs and three body parts. Many also have wings.

INSULATION
A substance, such as fat, fur, or feathers, that stops heat escaping from an animal's body.

INVERTEBRATE
An animal that lacks a backbone.

IRIDESCENCE
Glittering colours created by the way light reflects from a textured surface.

KERATIN
A tough structural protein found in hair, feathers, scales, and claws.

LARVA
The immature stage of animals that hatch from eggs and undergo metamorphosis (complete change) to become adults.

MAMMAL
One of a group of warm-blooded, often hairy vertebrates with females that feed their young with milk.

MARSUPIAL
A mammal that gives birth to young at an early stage of development and carries them inside a pouch.

MATURE
Old enough to breed.

MOLLUSC
One of a group of invertebrates that includes snails, clams, and squid.

MONOGAMOUS
Having one breeding partner.

MONOTREME
A small group of mammals that lay eggs, such as the duck-billed platypus.

MUTATION
A permanent change in the DNA of an organism.

MYRIAPOD
An animal, such as a centipede, with many more than four pairs of legs.

NECTAR
A sugar solution produced by flowers to attract pollinating animals.

NOCTURNAL
When an animal is active at night.

NUTRIENT
A substance essential for life to exist and grow.

OMNIVORE
An animal that eats plants and meat.

OPPOSABLE
Opposite to, as in the fingers and thumb of the human hand.

ORGANISM
A living thing.

OXYGEN
The gas vital for most forms of life, taken in during respiration and used to convert food into energy.

PALPS
Short, paired structures near the mouth of many invertebrates, usually for handling food.

PARASITE
An organism that lives in or on another (its host), and has a negative effect on it.

PHOTOSYNTHESIS
The process by which green plants use the sun's energy to make carbohydrates from carbon dioxide and water.

PIGMENT
A substance that gives something colour.

PLACENTAL
Describes mammals in which pregnant females grow a temporary organ (the placenta) that nourishes the developing young inside the mother.

PLANKTON
Small organisms that drift in the water.

POLLEN
Tiny grains produced by flowers, which contain the male cells needed to fertilize seeds.

POLYGAMOUS
Having more than one breeding partner.

POLYP
A cnidarian animal that is attached to a hard surface and may be part of an interconnected colony.

PREDATOR
An animal that kills other animals for food.

PREHENSILE
Able to coil round an object and grip it. A monkey's tail is prehensile.

PREY
An animal eaten by another animal.

PROBOSCIS
A long snout, or similar organ.

PROTEIN
A substance that a living thing makes and uses to form its tissues.

RADIAL SYMMETRY
An organism has radial symmetry if any dividing line through its centre produces two mirror-image halves.

REGENERATE
To re-grow part of the body.

REPTILE
One of the animal group that includes turtles, lizards, crocodiles, and snakes.

ROOST
To settle for the night, or a place where birds or bats do this.

SALIVA
Fluid produced from the mouth that starts the process of digestion.

SCAVENGER
An animal that lives on dead animals' remains and other organic waste.

SCHOOL
A large number of fish that swim in a co-ordinated way. Also the name for a group of porpoises or dolphins.

SCUTE
A tough, horny or bony plate.

SIPHON
A tube used by aquatic molluscs to draw water into the body or pump it out. Used for different purposes, including respiration and movement.

SPAWNING
Releasing eggs and sperm into water so they come together and fertilization can take place.

SPECIES
A group of similar organisms that can interbreed and produce fertile offspring like themselves.

SPERM
Male cells of animals that fertilize female eggs, enabling them to develop.

STERILE
Not able to breed.

SUBSPECIES
A variant of a species, usually only found in a particular area.

TALONS
The powerful claws of a bird of prey or an owl.

TENDON
A strong, slightly stretchy cord that attaches muscles to bones.

TENTACLE
Seen mainly in invertebrates, a mobile extension of an animal's body, sometimes armed with stinging cells.

THORAX
The middle part of an insect's body or the part of a mammal between the neck and abdomen.

TUBE FEET
Water-filled mobile projections in echinoderms, used for movement, feeding, and respiration.

VASCULAR
Describes something related to a network of veins.

VENOM
Poison that a biting or stinging animal uses for hunting or defence.

VERTEBRAE
The bones that form the backbone of an animal such as a bird or mammal.

VERTEBRATE
An animal with a backbone.

VESTIGIAL
An anatomical feature that has become reduced to the point where it has little or no function.

Index

Page numbers in **bold** type refer to main entries

Acknowledgments

The publisher would like to thank the following people for their assistance in the preparation of this book: Sheila Collins, Kshitiz Dhobhal, Mik Gates, Pooja Pipil, Heena Sharma, and Jemma Westing for design assistance; Ann Baggaley, Carron Brown, Stella Caldwell, Agnibesh Das, Charlie Galbraith, and Deeksha Saikia for editorial assistance; Nishwan Rasool for additional picture research; Kealy Wilson and Ellen Nanney from the Smithsonian Institution; Hazel Beynon for proofreading; and Jackie Brind for the index.

Smithsonian Enterprises:
Kealy E. Gordon, Product Development Manager
Ellen Nanney, Licensing Manager
Brigid Ferraro, Vice President, Education and Consumer Products
Carol LeBlanc, Senior Vice President, Education and Consumer Products
Chris Liedel, President

Curator for the Smithsonian:
Dr. Don E. Wilson, Curator Emeritus of the Department of Vertebrate Zoology, National Museum of Natural History, Smithsonian

The publisher would like to thank the following for their kind permission to reproduce photographs:

(Key: a-above; b-below/bottom; c-centre; f-far; l-left; r-right; t-top)

123RF.com: tudor antonel adrian 25tc, Andreas Altenburger 160cl, Ivanov Arkady 108crb, belizar 229tl, bennymarty 236cr, Vladimir Blinov 237bl, Oxana Brigadirova 261tc (Chameleon), Steve Byland 145cla, 150tc, cla78 269ca, James Anak Anthony Collin 258tl, Berangere Duforets 188cla, Абаджева Марина 103cb, 108clb, dirk ercken 90tc, Iakov Filimonov 117crb, 194clb (DHOLE), Teresa Gueck 16cb, 46tl, Ruth Hallam 126crb, Irina Iglina 201ca, Eric Isselee 45crb, 109clb, 134tl, 150cl, 160bc, 172tc, 173tr, 181tl, 207tr, 220tc, 221tr, 238c, Michal Kadleček 197bc (hunting salmon), Anan Kaewkhammul 221cr, kajornyot 138tr, Naveen Kalwa 62cr, Olga Khoroshunova 127crb, Micha Klootwijk 103c, Michael Lane 87crb, 145tc, 145crb, 210bl, Sommai Larkjit 161cra, Keith Levit 127tc, Peter Llewellyn 179br, Tracie Louise 150bl, Bruce MacQueen 129cra, Maurizio Giovanni Bersanelli 236bc, Andreas Meyer 65bc, moori 221c, Christian Musat 237cb, NewAge 139tl, Wannee Nimcharoen 151bl, Duncan Noakes 216c, 233br, coroiu octavian 151c, Alexander Ogurtsov 255br, Alexandr Pakhnyushchyy 183crb, 208cb, Heiti Paves 143tr, photoroad 186clb, Alex Popov 191tc, Dmytro Pylypenko 126clb, Eduardo Rivero 145clb, Ron Rowan 175bc, Andrei Samkov 190tc, shsphotography 269cb, Alexey Sokolov 145cra, Hagen Ueberfuhr 258tc, Sergei Uriadnikov 187tr, Pavlo Vakhrushev 19cr, Vasiliy Vishnevskiy 180cla, Allan Wallberg 150bc, wirojsid 187tc, wrangel 133cla, 134tc, 220clb, Teerayut Yukuntapornpong 26c, Michael Zysman 110ca; **Alamy Stock Photo:** David A. Northcott / Corbis 102clb, The Africa Image Library 232bc, AfriPics.com 273br, age fotostock 27clb, Andrew Trevor-Jones 262bc, Arco Images GmbH 197br, Arctic Images 200c, Matthew Banks 67cr, RIEGER Bertrand / hemis.fr 117bc, Juniors Bildarchiv / F260 83bc, Juniors Bildarchiv / F304 255c, Juniors Bildarchiv / F349 223br, Ger Bosma 34tc, 34cl, Arco / C. Hütter 117clb, J & C Sohns / imageBROKER 103tl, David Chapman 260br, Chris Godfrey Wildlife Photography 218cl, Hugh Clark / Nature Photographers Ltd 188br, JAMES D WATT / Stephen Frink Collection 245cra, Ethan Daniels 71br, 255bl, Sarah Darnell / RGB Ventures / SuperStock 235tr, David R. Frazier Photolibrary, Inc. 183tl, David Tipling Photo Library 262cr, Reinhard Dirscherl 275tl, Keith Douglas 197cr, dpa picture alliance archive 103tc, Arnold Drapkin / ZUMAPRESS.com 243tl, Mark Duffy 173cla, Val Duncan / Kenebec Images 219cr, Stuart Dyer 105cr, Jason Edwards / National Geographic Creative 156tl, Richard Ellis 276bc, Dirk Ercken 7tr, Roger Eritja 38cl, FLPA 66bc, 140bl, 158clb, 191cr, 191crb, 266tc, Fve Media 116cla, Eric Gevaert 279tl, John Gibbens / Design Pics Inc 204cla, André Gilden 212tc, GM Photo Images 9tr, Paul Gordon 230bl, Bill Gorum 112tr, Peter Haygarth 272br, Jonathan Hewitt 183br, Martha Holmes / Nature Picture Library 240cla, Christian Hütter 34bc, Alex Hyde / Steve Bloom Images 262tr, imageBROKER 214bl, Arco Images / Wegner, P. 263br, Niebrugge Images 278crb, Jason O. Watson 99crb, Sarah Cheriton-Jones 259tr, Juniors Bildarchiv GmbH 274b, David Keith Jones / Images of Africa Photobank 239c, blickwinkel / Koenig 115c, 174crb, Tim Laman / National Geographic Creative 261tc, Volker Lautenbach / imageBROKER 263t, Don Johnston_MA 219bl, William Manning 279tr, Thomas Marent / Rolf Nussbaumer Photography 181clb, Doug McCutcheon 277c, Michael Patrick O'Neill 61br, 262cl, MichaelGrantWildlife 85crb, Mint Images Limited 116bl, Zeeshan Mirza / ephotocorp 115tl, MShieldsPhotos 171tc, William Mullins 148clb, Juan Muñoz / age fotostock 86tl, National Geographic Creative 185cr, Natural History Museum, London 133cra, Naturepix 45cl, Michael Nolan / robertharding 136br, Norman Owen Tomalin / Bruce Coleman Inc. 159bc, Photoshot License Ltd 254-255tc, Pink Sun Media 181cb, Sergio Pitamitz / Corbis 168cl, Premaphotos 248cl, 260crb, Radius Images 155br, robertharding 240tr, Willi Rolfes / Premium Stock Photography GmbH 235tc, Andreas Rose / imageBROKER 186cb, blickwinkel / S Gerth 277tc, blickwinkel / Sailer 266tr, Joel Sartore / National Geographic Creative 162br, 202cl, Kevin Sawford 87cb, Malcolm Schuyl 142cb, 264b, Aditya "Dicky" Singh 186tr, Uwe Skrzypczak 254c, Tom Soucek / Design Pics Inc 198tl, inga spence 199cr, 203bl, Walt Stearns / Stephen Frink Collection 75cr, Steve Bloom Images 136tr, tbkmedia.de 232br, McPHOTO / vario images GmbH & Co.KG 9cla, Dave Watts 239bc, Terry Whittaker 221tc, WILDLIFE GmbH 42bl, 43tr, 204clb, Wildscotphotos 205cla, blickwinkel / Woike 148c, blickwinkel / Wothe 136tl, Bernd Zoller / imageBROKER 140bc; **Ardea:** Steve Downer 25cr, Jean-Paul Ferrero 276br, Adrian Warren 104tr, M. Watson 124clb, 165crb; **Australian Antarctic Division:** Tony Bojkovski 125tr; **Biosphoto:** Régis Cavignaux 167cr, Fabrice Chanson 177c; **Barrie Britton:** 146tc; **Caters News Agency:** 209crb; **Corbis:** 132cla, 277bc, Alaska Stock 252tr, Theo Allofs 192tl, Theo Allofs / Minden Pictures 150tr, Annie Griffiths Belt 9clb, Ingo Arndt / Minden Pictures 84tr, 196bl, 272bc (Monarch), FLPA / Bernd Rohrschneider 161ca, Jürgen & Christine Sohns / imageBROKER 194cl, Clouds Hill Imaging Ltd. 64br, Sylvain Cordier / Copyright : www.biosphoto.com / Biosphoto 234tr, Daniel J. Cox 131br, 205c, Stephen Dalton / Minden Pictures 49bc, 115cr, 115bl, 188ca, J. David Andrews / Masterfile 136cl, Reinhard Dirscherl 16cb (Jellyfish), Reinhard Dirscherl / / age fotostock Spain S.L. 256bc, DLILLC 77tl, Suzi Eszterhas / Minden Pictures 177tr, Warren Faidley 118cr (SKY), Katherine Feng / Minden Pictures 199br, Dave Fleetham / Design Pics 261tl, 266bl, Gallo Images 216cl, Sergey Gorshkov / Minden Pictures 210crb, 243tr, Darrell Gulin 175tc, Heidi & Hans-Juergen Koch / Minden Pictures 253cla, Martin Harvey 238bl, Huetter, C 183tc, Imaginechina 172cb, Mitsuhiko Imamori / Minden Pictures 30bl, Jonathan Irish / National Geographic 192cl, Stephen J. Krasemann / All Canada Photos 170clb, Adam Jones / Visuals Unlimited 50clb, Wolfgang Kaehler 143clb, Frans Lanting 160tr, 239cb, Boden / Ledingham / Masterfile 207cr, Albert Lleal / Minden Pictures 42cb, 113c, 141cr, Thomas Marent / Minden Pictures 185br, 273bl, ZSSD / Minden Pictures 50cla, Momatiuk - Eastcott 205ca, Alan Murphy / BIA / Minden Pictures 143cr, Nature Connect 53cl, Andrey Nekrasov / imageBROKER 24ca, Flip Nicklin / Minden Pictures 70c, Richard T. Nowitz 268bc, Pete Oxford / Minden Pictures 107crb, 135tr, 177bc, D. Parer & E. Parer-Cook / Minden Pictures 22bl, 156bl, Norbert Probst / imagebroker 72tc, Fritz Rauschenbach 43cr, Mary Robbins / National Geographic My Shot / National Geographic Creative 228br, Sciepro / Science Photo Library 275cl, Zack Seckler 135cr, Roland Seitre / Minden Pictures 157cr, 160clb, 180cl, 188tr, 226clb (Kiang), Anup Shah / Minden Pictures 183tr, Paul Souders 204cb, 268cl, 272bl, Visuals Unlimited 271cb, Kennan Ward 276bl, 277cl, 277bl, 278bl, Fotofeeling / Westend61 98cl, Terry Whittaker / FLPA 219br, Steve Winter / National Geographic Creative 216tl, David Wrobel / Visuals Unlimited 18br, Norbert Wu / Minden Pictures 272bc, Michael S. Yamashita 147br, Christian Ziegler / Minden Pictures 188c; **Dorling Kindersley:** Thomas Marent 259c, Hanne and Jens Eriksen 126tr, Andy and Gill Swash 194cla, Blackpool Zoo 231tr, Blackpool Zoo, Lancashire, UK 173cb, 176tl, 226clb, British Wildlife Centre, Surrey, UK 211tr, 234bc, Cotswold Wildlife Park 127ca, 143bl, 172cra, Cotswold Wildlife Park & Gardens, Oxfordshire, UK 164tc, Peter Janzen 88crb, Forrest L. Mitchell / James Laswel 251ca, Twan Leenders 82cb, 89tc, 96clb, 100tr, 101tl, Liberty's Owl, Raptor and Reptile Centre, Hampshire, UK 51crb, 132cr, 133br, 141br, 142tr, 142cr, 142clb, 143ca, The National Birds of Prey Centre, Gloucestershire 132tc, Natural History Museum, London 8bl, 8bc, 27crb, 40tr, 40clb, 40cb, 41cla, 45clb, 64clb, 99cr, 199tr, 246crb, 247cla, Dr. Paddy Ryan 127cb, Dr. Peter M Forster 69cr, Linda Pitkin 69tc, John White 89cl, Wildlife Heritage Foundation, Kent, UK 214ca, 218tr, Jerry Young 89tl, 89clb, 117tr, 157crb, 189ca, 190bc, 192ca, 271clb; **Dr Don Hodgers:** 35bl; **Dreamstime.com:** 3quarks 271cl, 197bc, Aaskolnick 45cr, Guido Amrein 204br, John Anderson 269bl, Andreanita 256br, Kushnirov Avraham 183cr, Mikhail Blajenov 117cr, 138cl, 201cla, Lukas Blazek 181cr, Stephen Bonk 275bl, Canvaschameleons 102br, Neal Cooper 151cra, Daexto 12bc, Kim Deadman 99tr, Jelle Dekker 17cr, Olga Demchishina / Olgysha 30c, Demerzel21 268br, Designua 265cra, Divehive 58cr, Maria Dryfhout 273tr, Morten Elm 107tr, Christopher Elwell 256bl, Dirk Ercken 273bc, Geza Farkas 40crb, Simone Gatterwe 243cb, Goruppa 271c, Krzysztof Grabiec 268cra, Hakoar 138ca, Jeffrey Holcombe 268cb, Hotshotsworldwide 179bc, Hungchungchih 198tr, Isselee 109br, 129clb, Junkii 129bc, Kajornyot 259cl, Denise Kappa 196tr, Karin59 133cl, Ivan Kmit 269cla, Brian Kushner 132ca, Lucasdm 215br, Ludek Lukac 172clb, Vladimir Melnik / Zanskar 271cr, Mgkuijpers 103crb, Mikelane45 131tc, 138tl, 227bc, Maurizio Milanesio 28clb, Mychadre77 12ca, 16cl, Perseomedusa 127c, PeterWaters 52tr, Photooasis 40tc, Pnwnature 26tl, Michael Price 271tr, Konstantin Pukhov 237cr, Rafael Ben-ari 133cb, Paulo Resende 100tc, Jason P Ross 93cb, 99bc, Rqs 44tc, Scattoselvaggio 174br, Science Pics 12bl, Shijianying 45cb, Brandon Smith 201cr, Andrey Sukhachev 7tl, Tbel 258br, Teo1000 170bc, Pavel Trankov 250tc, Trubavin 181cl, Woravit Vijitpanya 108cra, Vincentstthomas 181tr, Vladvitek 138cb, Marion Wear 160tl, Jinfeng Zhang 259cr; **Edith Smith / Shady Oak Butterfly Farm:** 41tr; **FLPA:** Samuel Blanc / Biosphoto 205crb, Bill Coster 124tr, Berndt Fischer / Biosphoto 208bl, Robin Hausmann / Imagebroker 230tc, Jurgen & Christine Sohns 164bl, 232tr, Donald M. Jones / Minden Pictures 262bl, Michael & Patricia Fogden 108cb, Minden Pictures 223bl, Philip Perry 228bc, Photo Researchers 73tr, 92tl, Chris & Tilde Stuart 193tl, 228tr; **Fotolia:** Chrispo 139clb, Eric Isselee 241br, Strezhnev Pavel 152cr, 248c (water), 282cr (water), Stefan Zeitz / Lux 139bc; **Getty Images:** Anadolu Agency 279cr, Adek Berry / Afp 76tl, Jonathan Bird 69tr, Ger Bosma 256c, Mark Carwardine 77cra, David Cayless 214cb, Peter Chadwick 257, David Courtenay 203br, Stephen Dalton 32tr, Daniel.Candal 123tl David W. Macdonald 224bl, Thomas Dressler 273cr, Michael Durham 255tr, Mark Garlick / Science Photo Library 9ca, Martin Harvey 224tl, Richard Herrmann 25tr, Jared Hobbs 149cra, Don Johnston 245bc, Larry Keller 256cr, Rene Krekels / NiS / Minden Pictures 90br, Kenny Lee 128tr, Wayne Lynch 263bl, John E Marriott 271tl, Mint Images - Frans Lanting 147cr, Paul Nicklen 125cr, Daniele Occhiato / Buiten-beeld 260cra, Pal Teravagimov Photography 149c, 260cl, Panoramic Images 185bl, Doug Perrine 74bl, Rob Reijnen / Minden Pictures 8tc, Richard Du Toit 267b, Manoj Shah 278br, Stocktrek Images 7tc, Suhaimi Sulaiman / EyeEm 267tl, David Tipling / Digital Vision 118c (snow), Iwan Tirtha 266cb, Visuals Unlimited, Inc. / Adam Jones 275tc, Visuals Unlimited, Inc. / Marty Snyderman 275tr, v_ac_md 210tl, Mark Webster 54cl, Steve Winter 212bc; **Hans Hillewaert:** 29br; **imagequestmarine.com:** 55tr; **Jeroen Kooijman:** 51bl; **Jocelyn Rastel Lafond:** 207bc; **National Geographic Creative:** Des & Jen Bartlett 209cr; **naturepl.com:** Eric Baccega 130tc, Dave Bevan 149crb, 149br, Bristol City Museum 8c, Jane Burton 71tl, 166tr, Brandon Cole 258bc, Georgette Douwma 23tl, Suzi Eszterhas 203cr, Laurent Geslin 260tr, Tony Heald 236tc, Kathryn Jeffs 243crb, 243br, Klein & Hubert 224bc, Steve Knell 149bl, Tim Laman 262br, Grzegorz Lesniewski 261bc, Mark MacEwen 169tr, Luiz Claudio Marigo 163bl, Mark Payne-Gill 163br, George McCarthy 87cr, Michael D. Kern 49bl, Owen Newman 158tc, David Noton 278cr, Fred Olivier 125br, Constantinos Petrinos 70tl, Michael Pitts 104c, Michel Poinsignon 7tc (Fly agaric fungi), Richard Du Toit 261tr, Gabriel Rojo 279bl, Jeff Rotman 24clb, Roland Seitre 156bc, 175clb, Anup Shah 261br, 266bc, Martin Camm (WAC) 246cra, 247clb, Dave Watts 279br, Bert Willaert 86br; **Dick Newell:** 206bl; **Michael S. Nolan:** 107br; **Oceanwidelmages.com:** Gary Bell 64tc; **Photoshot:** Gerald Cubitt / NHPA 176cb, Paulo de Oliveira / NHPA 62tl, 63tr, Nigel Downer 54bl, D. Robert Franz 129cr, Martin Harvey / NHPA 228bl, Daniel Heuclin 157cb, Gerhard Koertner / NHPA 263bc, Mel Longhurst / Bruce Coleman 241cb, Thorsten Negro / Imagebroker 109cra, Oceans Image 68cl, Kjell Sandved 231ca, David Slater / NHPA 90bc, Layer, W. / Picture Alliance 195cr; **Press Association Images:** Themba Hadebe / AP 229tc; **Professor John R. Hutchinson,The Royal Veterinary College, United Kingdom:** 178tl; **Reuters:** 33br, Usa-Religion / Eagles Reuters / Rick Wilking 130br; **Lindsay Richards:** 106bl; **Chris Schuster:** 36cla; **Science Photo Library:** 39bl, Eye Of Science 6tr, Andy Harmer 35crb, Edward Kinsman 113cra, Dr Morley Read 275c, Sinclair Stammers 261cr; **SeaPics.com:** C & M Fallows 75tr, Chris Huss 264tc; **www.skullsunlimited.com:** 223cl, 239cl; **stevebloom.com:** Jany Sauvanet / Biosphoto 111tr; **SuperStock:** Animals Animals 196cl, Biosphoto 243cr, Minden Pictures 184br, 258bl, Roland Seitre / Minden Pictures 159bl; **Jean-Christophe Theil:** 110bc; **Tom M. Fayle:** 32cl; **Skulls Unlimited International, inc./ ww.SkullsUnlimited.com:** 235bc; **Karen Warkentin:** 85bl